THE MODERN LAW OF MARINE INSURANCE

VOLUME TWO

THE MODERN LAW OF MARINE INSURANCE

Volume Two

EDITED
BY

D. RHIDIAN THOMAS
M.A., LL.B., A.C.I.Arb.
Professor of Maritime Law and Director of the Institute of International Shipping and Trade Law at the Department of Law, University of Wales Swansea

LLP

LONDON NEW YORK HONG KONG
2002

Informa Professional
(a division of
Informa UK Ltd)
Informa House
30–32 Mortimer Street
London W1W 7RE
Great Britain
professional.enquiries@informa.com

EAST ASIA
Informa Asia Publishing
Sixth Floor, Hollywood Centre
233 Hollywood Road
Hong Kong
informa.asia@informa.com

British Library Cataloguing in Publication Data
A catalogue record for this book
is available from the
British Library

ISBN 1 84311 120 9

Text set in 10/12pt Plantin by
Mendip Communications Ltd, Frome, Somerset
Printed by CPI, UK

TABLE OF CONTENTS

CHAPTER 2 INCORPORATION OF TERMS INTO REINSURANCE AGREEMENTS *Professor Robert Merkin*

CHAPTER 3 VALUED POLICIES *Professor Howard N. Bennett*

CHAPTER 9 JURISDICTION IN CONTRACTUAL DISPUTES ON MARINE INSURANCE AND REINSURANCE CONTRACTS TO WHICH THE EC JURISDICTION CONVENTION APPLIES *Yvonne Baatz*

CHAPTER 10 MARINE INSURANCE LAW: A SAN ANDREAS FAULT BETWEEN THE COMMON LAW AND CIVIL LAW *Professor Marc A. Huybrechts*

FOREWORD

In his foreword to the first volume published in 1996, Lord Mustill highlighted the apparent deceptiveness of the law of marine insurance. It might seem no more than the offspring of the market, but it was an area of law of great intellectual depth. That first volume was, as Lord Mustill stated, an impressive contribution to the recent development of the law. This second volume is again an impressive and timely contribution to that development.

It is nearly one hundred years since the codification of marine insurance law in the UK in the Marine Insurance Act 1906; there is scant prospect of any substantial revision to that code, despite the fundamental changes in commerce and the insurance and financial markets which have occurred since then. Thus, the development of English law which has had widespread international influence in this field must rest upon the practices and standard forms of those markets, the decisions of the courts and upon the work of the scholar.

This volume continues the contribution of the scholar to that development by a timely examination of topics of considerable contemporary importance, beginning with a masterly guide to the task that lies ahead. Some topics are of obvious contemporary relevance such as the chapters on the incorporation of terms and jurisdiction. At first sight one might, however, wonder why it is necessary to examine the elements of insurable interest resting as they do on wagering policies and Acts of 1745 and 1906 or the legal principles in relation to valued policies where so much of the important case law extends back into the nineteenth century. Both these subjects have, however, been the subject of very recent litigation; the detailed scholarship contained in this volume is essential to any real understanding of these subjects and hence the need for change and development.

The development of the English law of marine insurance must also take account of developments in the other great common law jurisdictions and in the civil law. Two common law jurisdictions, namely Australia and the USA, are covered in this volume, and also included is a comparative survey of the relevant common law and civil law systems. Collectively these contributions provide a wealth of material that is not easily accessible.

Although the primary scope of the volume is marine insurance, its relevance is not confined to that field of law. Not only do the principles that have their origin in marine insurance continue to influence other fields of insurance and reinsurance law, but the chapters of this volume have a scope that extends beyond marine insurance. No one who has to deal with a topic in any field of insurance or reinsurance law that is covered by this volume could fail to benefit from its close study; the person who does so may in that way make a real contribution to the much needed development of the law.

Mr. Justice John Thomas
Judge in charge of the Commercial Court
Royal Courts of Justice
London

EDITOR'S NOTE

Anthologies, whether or not in the essay form, are best allowed to stand in the historical context from which they emerge. This is the outlook which prevails with regard to the present publication. With a single exception, the object has not been to update and refine the contributions which appeared in Volume 1 of *The Modern Law of Marine Insurance*, published in 1996, but to publish a new anthology of contributions which reflect points of interest, developments and debates in marine insurance law and practice at the commencement of the twenty-first century.

Volume 2, therefore, is a very distinct publication which expands the range of subjects covered and reflects a new contemporariness. But apart from its content the broad philosophy remains the same, namely to address the dynamic of the modern law and practice of marine insurance and to subject to close analysis those topics which have been identified by the contributors as being of significant contemporary importance and relevance.

The two volumes are complementary, for together they construct a comprehensive and systematic picture of the relevant law and practice. The appendices to Volume 1 are of continuing relevance to the present contributions but, save for the Marine Insurance Act 1906, are not reproduced in the appendices to Volume 2, which are restricted to recording certain pertinent developments which have taken place subsequent to the publication of Volume 1.

It is hoped that all with an interest in English marine insurance law and practice will regard the publication of this second volume as timely. It appears at the same time as the London market is engaged on a major appraisal of its organisation, processes and forms, and when serious questions are being raised about the appropriateness of the Marine Insurance Act 1906, in particular its ability to provide a legal framework for contemporary market practice and the future electronic market which cannot be too far away. Talk of reform is gathering pace and part of the essential armoury of the reformer is a good command of apposite comparative law. This second volume provides assistance in that regard by including three comparative contributions tracing developments on the continent, in Australia and the USA.

THE EDITOR

PROFESSOR D. RHIDIAN THOMAS is Professor of Maritime Law and Director of the Institute of International Shipping and Trade Law at the Department of Law, University of Wales Swansea. He is author of *Maritime Liens* (British Shipping Laws Series) published by Stevens & Sons; *The Law and Practice Relating to Appeals from Arbitration Awards* and *The Default Powers of Arbitrators*, both published by LLP, and has contributed extensively to the journal literature in his fields of interest. He is consultant editor of *International Maritime Law*, co-editor of *Arbitration International* and assistant general editor of the *Journal of International Commercial Law*. He is a member of the British Maritime Law Association and chairman of the Sub-Committee on Mortgages and Ship Arrest, of the Chartered Institute of Arbitrators and the British Insurance Law Association.

THE CONTRIBUTORS

YVONNE BAATZ qualified as a solicitor in 1981. She practised with two leading firms of solicitors in the City of London, specialising in shipping litigation. She is a senior lecturer in the Law Faculty at the University of Southampton and a member of the Institute of Maritime Law. She is a contributor to Gaskell, Asariotis and Baatz, *Bills of Lading: Law and Contracts* (2000); Yates, *Contracts for the Carriage of Goods* (Looseleaf), both published by LLP; and to *Marine Insurance at the turn of the Millennium*, ed by Huybrechts, (1999), Intersentia. She is also a joint contributor to *Interests in Goods*, 2nd edition, ed by Palmer and McKendrick, (2000), LLP.

HOWARD N. BENNETT is Hind Professor of Commercial Law at the University of Nottingham, where he was previously a Lecturer and Senior Lecturer. His main interests lie in the law of international trade and maritime law, secured finance and general contract law. He holds a record of published research in insurance contract law, the financial aspects of international trade law and secured lending. He is the author of *Law of Marine Insurance* (1996, Oxford University Press).

SARAH C. DERRINGTON is a Senior Lecturer in law and Director of the Centre for Maritime Law at the University of Queensland. She maintains a practice at the private Bar, exclusively in shipping law. Her main area of research is marine insurance law and her PhD thesis was a comparative study of non-disclosure, misrepresentation and breach of warranty in contracts of marine insurance. She is the author of a number of articles on marine insurance law and various aspects of admiralty jurisdiction and practice.

ROBERT P. GRIME has recently retired from the post of Professor of Maritime Law at Southampton University. He taught for many years at Southampton and has also been a visiting professor in a number of overseas universities in the United States, New Zealand and China. He was instrumental in establishing, in 1982, the Institute of Maritime Law at Southampton and served as its Director for six years. He is the author of *Shipping Law* (Sweet and Maxwell) and regularly produces the Shipping Law section in the annual *All England Law Reports Review*, as well as publishing articles and papers on aspects of maritime law and marine insurance.

JULIAN HILL is a solicitor and was a partner at the leading firm of shipping and insurance lawyers, Ince & Co., from 1974 until May 2001, specialising in insurance, reinsurance and shipping matters. He acted as an adviser to the London marine insurance market on the Institute Clauses and at the UNCTAD sessions on marine insurance. He has been a visiting lecturer at the City University Business School, teaching marine insurance and shipping law. He is the editor and co-author of *O'May on Marine Insurance* and a contributor to *Halsbury's Laws of England on Admiralty* and the *Encyclopaedia of Forms and Precedents on Shipping*. He currently acts as a consultant and arbitrator.

SUSAN L. H. HODGES is a Senior Lecturer in the Cardiff Business School at Cardiff University. She is the author of *Law of Marine Insurance* and *Cases and Materials on Marine Insurance Law* (both published by Cavendish Publishing), and co-author of *Principles of Maritime Law* (published by LLP). She has also published articles addressing issues on various aspects of shipping law. Her main areas of interests are in admiralty law, the law of marine insurance and the law relating to the carriage of goods by sea.

MARC A. HUYBRECHTS is Professor of Maritime and Transport Law and teaches at the University of Leuven, Antwerp and ITMMA. He has lectured at the Universities of Xi'an, Beijing and Dalian in the PRC; Kanzai University, Osaka, Japan; UCT, South Africa; and is a visiting professor at the University of Maritime Law, Dalian, PRC. He is a member of the Antwerp and Brussels Bar; a titulary member of the CMI, and a former Vice-President of the Belgian Committee of Norske Veritas. He is editor of the Transport Law section of *International Encyclopaedia of Laws* and the Maritime and Transport Law section with Larcier Publishers. His journal publications are many and extend over the fields of maritime and marine insurance law. He is a member of the editorial board of *Tijdschrift voor Vervoer en Recht* (SDU).

NICHOLAS LEGH-JONES QC has been in practice at the Commercial Bar in London for over thirty years. His chambers are at 20 Essex Street. He specialises in insurance law and has contributed to the last four editions of *MacGillivray on Insurance Law*, of which he is now the general editor. In 1998 he became a visiting professor at King's College, London, and teaches insurance law and the law of carriage of goods by sea to graduate students taking the LL.M degree in the University of London.

ROBERT MERKIN is Lloyd's Law Reports Professor of Commercial Law at Southampton University and a consultant to Barlow Lyde & Gilbert. He is author of a number of texts on insurance, reinsurance and arbitration law, and contributed to the first volume of *Modern Law of Marine Insurance*. He edits *Lloyd's Law Reports: Insurance and Reinsurance, Insurance Law Monthly, Arbitration Law Monthly* and *Commercial Conflict of Laws*, all published by LLP.

BARIŞ SOYER is a Lecturer in law at the University of Wales Swansea, where he is also a member of the Institute of International Shipping and Trade Law. He was previously a Lecturer at the University of Exeter. His postgraduate education was in the University of Southampton from where he obtained his PhD degree in 2000. He is the author of *Warranties in Marine Insurance* (2001, Cavendish Publishing). This book was the joint winner of the Cavendish Book Prize 2001. His principal research interest is in the field of marine insurance, but his interests extend broadly throughout maritime and contract law. He is the author of a growing list of journal articles in these areas. He is also the liaison editor of the *Journal of International Commercial Law*.

MICHAEL F. STURLEY is the Stanley D. and Sandra J. Rosenberg Centennial Professor at the University of Texas Law School, where his primary interests are in maritime and commercial law. He is active in the work of the Maritime Law Association of the United States (where he co-chairs the Marine Insurance Study Group and was the Reporter for the Cargo Liability Rules Study Group) and the Comité Maritime International (where he is a Titulary Member and the Issues of Transport Law Rapporteur). He also serves as the book review editor for *The Journal of Maritime Law and Commerce*.

TABLE OF CASES

TABLE OF LEGISLATION

All references are to paragraph numbers or to Appendices. Appendix numbers in italic type indicate where the material is set out in full.

TABLE OF E.C. LEGISLATION

TABLE OF CONVENTIONS

INTRODUCTION

MARINE INSURANCE LAW IN CONTEXT

THE RIGHT HONOURABLE LORD MUSTILL
Lord of Appeal in Ordinary 1992–1997

The law of marine insurance, like all other types of commercial law, is a child of the markets; both of the contemporary market which it serves, and of the former markets which in the past engendered, shaped and abraded the rules constituting the law of today. The demands of the markets generate practices which successively solidify into tacit understandings, informal principles, explicit rules of the trade, and common forms of contract. These are the foundations of the legal norms which are thereafter the framework of the market, and lend it stability. In turn, however, the bedrock of the law is constantly subjected to abrasion and accretion by fresh demands, to which through the same process as before the law responds by creating new norms. The speed of the response varies according to the capacity of the legal order at any given time to refresh itself, and by the current perception of the priority to which the satisfaction of the particular demand is entitled in the use of limited opportunities for legal innovation.

The fact that commercial law exists in a state of mutual dependency with a market, and with the economic order which lies behind the market, does not mean that it is somehow lower class, that its origins in activities aimed at making money automatically deprive it of intellectual rigour and conceptual elegance. Happily, the sort of snobbery which for centuries ruled out commercial law as a worthy object of study in mainstream academic life has largely, if not quite completely, disappeared – as witness the fact that the present volume comprises materials of notable value to both the practitioner and the student of law, in the widest sense of the term. For a historical illustration of how economics and markets can engender a self-contained system of legal norms possessing both conceptual rigour and practical value, one need look no further than the law concerning bills of exchange. This inspired invention of the mediaeval Lombards, which enabled funds to be transferred without the physical movement of specie, creating a transferable obligation which in the hands of a bona fide transferee for value was protected against disputes stemming from the underlying transaction and also from defences based on intermediate fraud, want of consideration and the like, led to a body of law which both sprang from a market and greatly increased the practical serviceability of the market from which it sprang. This intimate link with a homogeneous and efficient international market gave the law on commercial paper a unique internal consistency, so much so that when it became the subject of the Sir Mackenzie Chalmers' most successful codification the law had in a sense already codified itself. The rather daunting terminology tended to discourage the casual reader which is probably why it was so little taught, yet a little persistence disclosed a topic so perfectly articulated that it almost seemed to have aesthetic as well as practical virtues.

There is, however, another lesson to be learned from this branch of commercial law. The more tightly a body of law is bound into the structure and practice of a market, the more vulnerable it is to radical shifts in the needs and methods of that market. It would be mistaken to say that the commercial bill has disappeared as an instrument of trade, but within a working lifetime its use has been largely overtaken by electronic and other devices. How many specialist advisers today have actually handled an original bill of exchange, or even consulted the Bills of Exchange Act, 1882? The law is just as good as it was, but it is no longer so useful, or so worthy of continuous refurbishment. The commercial world has left it behind.

I do not, of course, suggest that the law of marine insurance is undergoing a similar decline. At least for the foreseeable future the economic order will require large volumes of bulky or weighty goods, and large quantities of individual packages unsuitable or uneconomical for carriage by air, to be moved round the world; and, *faute de mieux*, they will have to be carried by ships. Maritime commerce seems likely to persist, bringing with it the risks of marine adventures; and these risks will, in the main, continue to be insured. ("In the main", for there are certain types of marine risk of such magnitude or character which are possibly becoming incapable of insurance, at least in full, or by conventional methods). This insurance will continue to require the support of a workmanlike body of marine insurance law. Such a law already exists, though many believe it to be flawed. Moreover, although it has not the smooth precision of the law of bills, it possesses an undeniable intellectual charm, which has attracted and continues to attract the very best legal minds. Pothier, Emerigon, Marshall, Park, Phillips, Parsons, Mansfield, Abbott, Arnould, Maclachlan, Cohen: the list could be greatly enlarged. (I omit notable contemporaries and near contemporaries to avoid invidious selection.) This law will continue to exist, and so will the law of insurance at large. Market changes will not sweep it away.

All the same, we must recognise that insurance law has been, and will be in the future, at the mercy of changes not only in market practices and priorities, but in deeper economic and social imperatives. Instances are easy to find. Devastating fires created the need for a new kind of insurance, and the exposure to huge losses made sharing of risks through reinsurance imperative. So also with third part liability cover. Until the emergence of a recognisable law of tort there was little need for liability insurance. The accelerating development of industrial methods in the late eighteenth and early nineteenth centuries led to a desperate increase in accidents and disease among workers. For much of the nineteenth century employers were largely immune from liability for these abuses, first because the employee had to prove "negligence" (and let us not forget that we had to wait until the lifetimes of at least some of us for the emergence of a generalised English law of responsibility for lack of care), and then because employers could require the claimant to surmount defences of contributory negligence, voluntary acceptance of risk, and co-worker responsibility. At that stage, the risk of injury and disease rested largely with the employee – and also with those who lived nearby, also exposed to risks which it has taken decades for the law to acknowledge. Society accepted this distribution of risk, and would not have accepted the transfer of risk to an insured employer, with the inevitable increase in the cost of factory-made products.

The great humanitarian movements of the nineteenth century eventually bore fruit in legislation which fundamentally changed the insurance market. Fault-free employers' liability may have been inadequate, but it imposed on employers not only an incentive to reduce the risks by better practice, but also the need to redistribute the risks by insurance and, as the volume of claims soared, by reinsurance. Later, the arrival of motor transport created a vast new reservoir of potential claims which had to be protected, in due course by compulsory insurance. Two world wars and various less extensive episodes of international violence bred a greatly enhanced demand for war risk cover. These and similar enlarged categories of risk increased the opportunities for profitable insurance, without creating (except when premiums were depressed) any large new demand for dispute resolution and for hard-edged rules on which dispute resolution could be based. Legal uncertainties remained, but the need to have them removed was not pressing, and the development of insurance law, and in particular of marine insurance law, was at best adventitious and narrow in scope. It is, therefore, not surprising that well into the twentieth century the law remained much the same as it had been in the days of Lord Justice Scrutton, and indeed to a great extent as it had been more than a century before when Lord Mansfield marked out its crucial features. For the time being the textbook law marked time, whilst the world and its market moved on.

This apparent stability and practicality was however an illusion, for the 1970s saw the beginnings of fundamental changes in the market, which imposed on the law of insurance as practised in the London market stresses which it was unable to meet, leaving scars which will not be healed for many years, if ever.

The market

The immediate context of marine insurance law is, of course, the marine insurance market, and until recently there was no reason to look beyond it. The law of non-marine insurance did not wash across to the marine field on any large scale, and reinsurance was not a source at all, being conducted out of sight under a regime designed to exclude contentious dispute resolution mechanism, applying explicitly extra-legal norms. Reinsurance was a world apart, and litigation concerning it was virtually unknown until the pathological features of the London market during and after the 1970s started to bring it before the courts.

The position is now entirely changed. Marine underwriting was by tradition a tightly run ship, conducted from one generation to the next without marked changes either in method or in the broad character of the business: namely that it was short-tail business covering a narrow range of homogeneous risks whose overall incidence tended to vary, if at all, only slowly with time. In general, the underwriting was conservative, and although it was naturally aimed at profitability the margins were comparatively small. By the 1980s the picture had become entirely different. It is true that the marine market, viewed as a separate entity, which it was in formal terms, may not have diverged from its former practices. But in practical terms this view was misleading. The place of classical marine insurance in the universe of insurance as a whole became greatly diminished, and the role of marine disputes as a source of principles applying across the board became greatly diminished. This trend was the outcome of a transformation in the economics, size, aspirations, methods and spirit of the London insurance market as a whole. These changes had already become detectable a considerable time before. There was a perception that Lloyd's was becoming less competitive than in the past; that an important cause was the narrowness of its capital base; and that more money should be attracted into the market. The strategy succeeded to the extent that the capacity of the market expanded sharply, creating both the opportunity and the need to put the capacity to use.

These opportunities were found in a burgeoning American market. After the second world war there developed a culture which took for granted a right to be protected against misfortune, manifesting itself through the welfare state in the United Kingdom and other European countries, and across the Atlantic in a growth of consumerism (and, later, environmentalism) which, allied with a native instinct for litigation, created a massive new exposure to claims, against which potential defendants sought protection through liability cover in innumerable shapes and forms. Certain British insurers, notably including certain of those in Lloyd's, tapped this market, with a gratifying surge of revenue. The trouble was, that those who sought and obtained the new business had in many cases insufficient idea of what they were doing, and were tempted to leave the mundane and well-trodden paths of an experienced market with relatively stable loss-ratios, for the trackless wilderness of long-tail American liability insurance – and got lost in it, to the ruin or near ruin of their syndicate members. Whether the continuing emergence in the legal arena of ancient wrongs coupled with fantastical verdicts from juries in certain American states is something which could and should have been predicted is not for discussion here. It is enough to say that whatever the future of the traditional London market, it will never be the same again.

There was a different aspect of the context, more purely economic in nature, which is easily forgotten today. Two features converged. First, there were stratospheric interest rates which made it especially valuable for underwriters to have the use of the premium income. Prime rate almost touched 22 per cent at the beginning of the 1980s, which made the cash flow from income a valuable asset in its own right. At the same time there were equally stratospheric rates of tax (83 per cent for the top tranche) in respect of which Lloyd's underwriters had a uniquely favourable treatment – to such an extent that they were in a real sense loss-sharing with the Revenue, becoming metaphorically co-insurers with the tax-payers at large. These factors made it possible to write a losing book and still turn a profit. For a time the conditions for risk-bearers were uniquely favourable: but only for a time. There is a tendency among market people – not of course limited to them – to take it for granted that existing conditions, particularly if favourable, will go on for ever. In this particular market, the transient economic context distracted attention from the fact that what always matters with insurance is the quality of risk. Ventures into new fields demanded particular care in the examination of unfamiliar risks. In the prevailing atmosphere of euphoria that care was, at least in some conspicuous instances, totally neglected, with results which those with time to spare can find rehearsed in chilling detail in the specialist law reports.

These results were exacerbated by the emergence of specialist types of reinsurance on a scale and with methods which were largely new. To accommodate the size of the exposures, successive layers of retrocession would be stacked on top of the more direct coverage. The further a layer was from the individual primary risk the harder it was to form a perception of that risk on which it could be rated. Indeed, when there were successive layers of whole-account insurance those individual risks disappeared entirely from view, so that rating assessments had to be made on quite different bases, or indeed, as it now appears in retrospect, on no basis at all.[1]

There was one additional feature, not peculiar to the London market, but nevertheless with a special impact upon it, namely the emergence of reinsurance on a scale and with a prominence and influence entirely new. Although by comparison with the ancient practice of marine insurance it is comparatively recent, reinsurance has a sufficient history to detect successive expansions of coverage in kind and extent in response to successive socio-economic trends. Thee is no space to enter into this here, but there was never anything specially conservative about the reinsurance industry from the 1930s onwards. All the same, from about the mid-1970s the picture changed in a way which has left a lasting imprint on the traditional markets. In earlier days "follow the fortunes" meant just that, but as the layers were stacked ever higher, to accommodate ever larger exposures, the opportunities for disputes about the placing of the cover and the aggregation of risks became much more extensive. Moreover, whilst the reinsurer of primary cover had the possibility of looking behind the reinsured at the risk itself this became progressively less likely as the layer progressed, so that the judgment related at least as much to the cedant as to the ceded risk. This was most particularly the case with the reinsurance of a whole account. If this happened successively a very few times the retrocessionaire became totally cut off from any appreciation of what cover was actually granted to the individual primary insured, with his own particular exposure to risk. Other considerations came into play, and it is not an extravagant metaphor to say that much of what happened during this period was not reinsurance underwriting at all, in the traditional sense, but the arbitraging of premiums.

The result of all this has been to destroy for ever the traditional equilibrium of the

[1] The bizarre story of the "LMX Spiral" illustrates in breathtaking detail the extent to which the rational appreciation of risks of the kind which made Lloyd's great could be abandoned in favour of what seemed like simpler ways of making money.

London insurance market in a peaceful corner of which the law of marine insurance had been evolved for very many years. Apocalyptic language would be out of place, particularly since at the moment of writing it is impossible even to tell whether current proposals for the restructuring of Lloyd's will be favourably received, and if so with what consequences. It is however obvious that although marine insurance will continue to exist, where and in what form and in what circumstances it will be undertaken are bound to be different from before; and this means that the role of the English common law in the shaping of a response to new economic challenges cannot be the same as it has been in the past.

The sources

Before considering the nature and effects of these challenges it is convenient to say something about the sources of marine insurance law. These are, as with other forms of law, threefold: codes; precedents; and doctrine. In addition, there is an important source of practical rule-making, in the shape of common contractual forms.

There are by now several aspects of commercial law which are the subject either of international conventions, committing the participants to a unified body of substantive law, or harmonising initiatives seeking similar ends by non-mandatory bodies of rules. Marine insurance law has not been one of these. A set of international rules was created by the International Law Association at the very end of the nineteenth century when that body was more concerned with private law than it is today, but it was soon overtaken by the English Marine Insurance Act, 1906, and seems to have led nowhere. The Act itself, although a purely domestic statute, acted in practice as a kind of informal international harmonisation, since the great bulk of marine business was written in London on English forms, and even where entered into abroad was heavily dominated by rating perceptions founded, intuitively or otherwise, on English concepts. Later in the century important initiatives were taken in Scandinavia, which continue to be brought forward whenever international codification is considered; but notwithstanding the considerable merits of the Norwegian Plan and similar formulations these have not flourished greatly outside their native soil. Latterly, more concerted efforts were made to promote harmonisation, at least in the areas thought to be most problematical. The United Nations Commission on International Trade Law produced some standard rules, but they have not been widely used. With some difficulty the Comité Maritime International (CMI), which had previously abjured any venture into this field was persuaded to take it up, and a study group was formed for that purpose. Good work was done, particularly on the comparative law aspects,[2] and there was some optimism that the project could be carried forward at full speed, although the President of CMI warned that the subject would "continue in the CMI work programme for some years to to come".[3] In the event, the idea was tepidly received by the biennial conference of the CMI in 2001, and authority was given to do no more than keep the study group in being. There the matter rests for the foreseeable future.

---

[2] See the materials on the websites of the CMI and the British Maritime Law Association www.comitemaritime.org and www.bmla.org.uk

[3] www.comitemaritime.org/singapore/report/report.html

The prospects for a less ambitious codification limited to English law do not seem much brighter. Even the general desirability of codification as a method of advancing the law is far from universally accepted.[4] An outstanding report on insurance law reform published by the Law Commission, under the Chairmanship of Lord Justice Kerr, had no offspring. The most recent large-scale recension of English commercial law, the Arbitration Act 1996, has had a following wind in the shape of the current wave of political and professional support for the reform of civil litigation, and was almost certainly found a place in the Parliamentary timetable only because widespread prior consultation with almost unanimously favourable results had guaranteed a virtually unopposed passage. Nothing of this kind could be hoped for in relation to marine insurance. Perhaps if all the interests could make common cause – a novelty in this field – it might be possible to slip through Parliament some minimalist reforms on individual topics, but the prospect of anything approaching a full legislative code seem for the present to be remote.

We are thus left with the Act of 1906. On many topics this provides a sufficient basis for decision, but on others it does not, as recent litigation has shown, and the reported cases remain, as they have always been, the primary resource for the practitioner, both lay and professional. Here there is a paradox. One of the principal virtues claimed for the common law method is its flexibility, its ability to address within a continuous course of development new changes in circumstances and new angles on old problems. Yet it has become plain in recent years that in the field of marine insurance the law has failed to provide even clear solutions for old problems, and still less a solid intellectual base for the development of the law into new territory. Why is this so? I suggest two principal reasons, although there may be others. The first is the paucity of reported authority, the raw materials of a developing law. A rough count of entries in the law reports tends to confirm my own recollection that until the last decade the flow of such materials has been modest indeed. I say "tends to" confirm, because the common law system is vulnerable as before an age when electronics permits the dissemination of all the materials on a particular subject, regardless of legal significance or worth, and at the same time enables the texts to be searched for apparent relevance, the corpus of legal authority was exposed both to vagaries in the selection of cases to reprint and also to idiosyncrasies of indexing which could cause important *dicta*, and indeed sometimes decisions, to fall completely out of sight.[5] Quite apart from these erratic features the corpus was in crude terms simply too small. Reliable statistical information does not exist, but it does seem that if the numbers reported are even a rough indicator of the volume of disputes large or important enough to be thought worth fighting to a finish (and it must be remembered that cases turning on legal issues of practical importance may be settled simply to avoid the public determination of those issues) it is possible to determine an ebb and flow of numbers roughly coupled to prevailing economic and market conditions.

[4] Amongst several authoritative expositions of why codification may hinder rather than help the process the observations of Lord Goff of Chievely call for particular mention: (1983) Proc Brit Acad 169.

[5] Even in the days of Mr. R P Colinvaux, a notable editor of law reports, and an equally notable scholar of the law of insurance.

Thus, obviously, in the aftermath of a conflict one would expect to find a temporary upturn attributable to disputes under war-risk cover, and on the delineation between marine and war risks; and this is what one does find (allowing for the time-lag between claim and judgment, and between judgment and law report) after each of the worlds wars, and in the aftermath of (for example) the successive upheavals in the Middle East. Spasmodic outbursts of terrorism also leave their marks on the reports, often years after the event. For a time, points of law become fashionable, and then subside. Equally, more general economic trends leave perceptible traces. For example, when times are bad in the world of international trade, when freights are weak, and newly built ships are coming onto the market in numbers which create an over-supply of older vessels, there is a temptation for a small minority of shipowners to combine economy with profit by sinking their ships for the insurance moneys. Clumps of law reports show from time to time that the temptation has not always been resisted.[6] Less conspicuous are the influences which diminish the flow of reported cases. For example, there may be periods of stability in the market, or in the political world at large, where predictions of loss ratios are not greatly falsified by unexpected increases in the incidence of casualties, and where novel eventualities call for novel perspectives on established risks. Again, there may be times when, for one reason or another, disputants tend to settle rather than fight.[7]

Once these statistical anomalies are smoothed out, the law reports show that the supply of marine insurance cases to the corpus of authority has been too meagre to do more than support a relatively stable market, with a fairly low level of dispute. When in the last two decades of the twentieth century, fundamental changes in size, scope, method and spirit transformed the London market into something entirely new, there was no choice but to press into service such authorities as there were, but the results have not been uniformly satisfactory. The principles established by Lord Mansfield and his great successors were a practical response to the commercial context of their times, but the context is scarcely recognisable today.

Nor does the future offer the hope of a fresh infusion of reported cases. To be reported, disputes have to reach the courts and to result in judgments. This seems even less likely under recent procedural innovations than it has been in the past. In the first place, the trickle of cases reaching the Court on appeal from arbitrations is likely to dry up completely, or nearly so, given the obstacles placed in the way by the Arbitration Act 1996 . As for litigation, it would be out of place here to raise questions about the quality of judgments in an atmosphere where hearing time is sharply curtailed in the interests of speed and economy. For the moment at least, the standard seems to be as high as before. But the emphasis now being officially placed on the

[6] Equally, the temptation to report these cases has not been resisted. Acres of space are devoted to narratives which often make good reading, but which are entirely without significance for the development of the law.

[7] In the early years of the present writer's practice the sole commercial judge sat only intermittently. For one reason or another, litigation was not in fashion. Reports of marine insurance cases appeared at the rate of roughly one per annum.

imperative to settle rather than fight must inevitably (unless the initiative fails in its aims) mean that the flow of judgments from which the law evolves will be even more limited than it was before the explosion of reinsurance and negligence litigation. It would, of course, be quite absurd to say that anybody, except perhaps those professionally concerned, would want to see a repetition of the endless and bottomless litigation which followed, years after the event, the events which brought the London market nearly to its knees, and it would be even more absurd to maintain that settlements were to be deprecated because they inhibit (in this field as well as others) the development of commercial law through traditional means. The fact is, though, that they do have this effect. Reinsurance litigation there has certainly been – such a flood of it that a specialist series of reports has been inaugurated to catch the tide. But when decisions on complex facts, and on individual forms of wording, are set aside, it must be doubted whether the principles of insurance law have been greatly extended or clarified.

Turning to the third source, namely *la Doctrine*, the corpus of generally accepted theory based on the works of authoritative writers, whilst this is an important source of law in civilian countries, it has had a disappointingly small impact on English marine insurance law. The masterpieces of the past are available[8] but in an adversarial system the courts depend on the materials found for them by counsel; and although when deciding commercial cases the judges are admirably served by the thoroughness of the arguments, the Bar's culture of research does not usually extend to old textbooks, even in fields where the current law is itself old; and the new general treatises, some of which are excellent, do not always have the depth of focus to provide the court with a sufficient basis for moving the law forward on individual topics. Again, although some practitioners in the market have produced thoughtful studies, they are few. In general, the market itself does not possess or want the contacts with "academic" law which could make it a force in the evolution of doctrine.[9]

Finally, there are the standard forms around which marine insurance law has traditionally been built. Whether such forms are themselves to be regarded as sources of law is a jurisprudential issue which we need not debate, for there is no doubt that in one way or another they have been the foundation of marine insurance law not only in England but also (for many years) elsewhere. Their inadequacy for this purpose, seen

[8] In the basement of the Middle Temple Library there stood ready at hand a copy of Boulay Patay's commentary on Emerigon, from which it was possible to deduce without difficulty the origins of the peril "takings at sea", the subject of the erroneous decision in *Nishima Trading Co. v. Chyoda Fire and Marine etc* subsequently corrected, without reference to this source, in *Shell International Petroleum Co. v Gibbs (The Salem)* [1983] 1 All E.R. 745.

[9] What a contrast with the situation when, in the 1970s a series of multi-disciplinary seminars on aspects of commercial law were promoted in Scandinavia. It was only with difficulty that two or three English lawyers were persuaded to attend—although, naturally, the proceedings were in English. The seminar on marine cargo insurance was so impressive that attempts were made to import a similar venture into England, with support from the market. Underwriters were simply not interested. It is not simply *schadenfreude* which prompts the thought that if the market leaders had paid even a little attention to what they were being told in the run-up to the LMX disaster the underwriters would have saved themselves money, and their names in some cases from ruin.

from an intellectual standpoint, has long been a reproach. Generations of commentators, and many judges, have entertained themselves by making fun of a law which consists essentially of a commentary on one particular form of words which has changed little for six hundred years,[10] whose meaning after all those years is still not precisely ascertained, and whose practical effect has had to be bolstered either by the physical adhesion to the contractual documents of standard clauses (often including those designed for quite other purposes), or by cross references to equally inappropriate formulae. All of this is fair game. It is quite right to complain, from a lawyer's point of view, that even late into the 1980s the central cover of "perils of the seas" was still not fully understood.[11] Equally, the concept of covering maritime war risks by reference, not to a definition of those risks but to the body of risks excluded from the standard marine policy by the standard war risks exceptions, could not on any intellectual basis be defended.[12] The task of making sense of contracts comprising a patchwork of "boilerplate" clauses, drawn apparently at random from files of handy wordings, and therefore lacking any clear internal logic has wearied and irritated so many of those called upon to perform it.

All this is fair game, but perhaps the lawyers do not think enough about how the market actually works. Even if an underwriter sitting in his box with a queue of brokers calling for immediate decisions on the acceptance of risks had been temperamentally inclined to apply himself to the precise definition of the risks, refining one form of wording after another, he would very soon be out of business if he spent much time on it. For simple economic reasons the translation of risk into words was for subordinates, who would have no incentive to innovate and no direct access to the subjective intentions of those who had actually devised the cover. The risk of discontinuity between the intentions and the expression of them was one which the market tacitly accepted for economic reasons, and not necessarily through indolence or lack of intellectual capacity. Again, and this is an important point often overlooked by commentators, the use of standard forms provided a stable basis for rating, enabling the underwriter to weigh up the proffered line without the need to assess every risk by reference to the implications of its own individual wording. However inadequate they might be linguistically, however lacking in cohesion the collection of perils which they enumerated, the SG Policy and its satellites established a cover

---

[10] I do not apologise for recalling, once again, the description of a marine policy given in *The Merchant of Prato*, the masterly epitome by Iris Origo of the working papers of a merchant conducting international trade from mediaeval Italy. The words are largely familiar, and the relative importance of the perils has waxed and waned in a way which may be thought to illustrate the link between the market and the law. In Datini's time, voyages were short, or performed in short stages, and the "taking" perils were more predominant than in later times, when the maritime perils were of much greater importance. Latterly, perhaps, conditions may be giving the "taking" perils a greater importance than in more orderly times. Space does not permit an examination of how the relative importance of different aspects of marine insurance may ebb and flow in accordance with large scale shifts in economic and political circumstances.

[11] *Miss Jay Jay* [1987] 1 Lloyd's Rep. 32.

[12] The result was that a casualty which fell within the standard war risk exclusions was not covered under the war risk policy if it would not have been covered under the standard marine policy without the exclusions. The overlapping rings of inclusion and exclusion became in practice indecipherable without recourse to diagrams. The exasperated complaint of Mocatta J in *Panamanian Oriental v. Wright* [1971] 1 Lloyd's Rep. 487 fell on deaf ears.

whose general extent could be taken for granted by the underwriter, in the light of his experience, as the starting point for his commercial judgment. For this purpose it did not matter that the form was expressed to cover a risk, "letters of mart and countermart", which had ceased to exist when privateering was abolished (except for the United States) by the Declaration of Paris in 1860, or that the meaning of the cover in respect of "rovers" has been lost in the mists of time. There were practical reasons, beyond conservatism and obtuseness, why these old wordings lasted for so long. "Better the Devil . . . ."

Be that as it may, it could scarcely be claimed that marine insurance law and perhaps even more conspicuously reinsurance law (the two being for lawmaking purposes now inextricably linked) is drawn from sources which enable it to respond without strain and uncertainty to the challenges of the twenty first century. It is not right that two fundamental aspects of the good faith doctrine should require consideration by the House of Lords within the space of a few years, and even then should still be clouded by controversy after the appeals had been decided. It is perhaps too easy to blame the judges. They have a duty to apply and develop the law, not to tear it up and start again. It can be convincingly argued that this is the only way forward; that in a context so fundamentally changed from that existing in the days of Lord Mansfield and his great coevals and successors that their artifact has simply become obsolete and ought to be scrapped. and (if only a way can be found) replaced by something fitted to the demands of the present and the foreseeable future.

Easy enough to say, and plenty are saying it. But how is it to be done?

Cohesion or fragmentation?

If marine insurance law is a reflection of the economic order, at a few removes, what kind of order will it reflect? Some of those still in practice can recall how, in the aftermath of atrocious events, it had been hoped that even under the threat of global destruction there could emerge a world society which, salving its wounds under the firm but kindly authority of the United Nations, would put behind it the dreadful past and stride forward into a free, just and harmonious future. Stability would be restored, and world trade would continue as before, although facilitated by steady technological advances. In such a world, the law of international trade would continue to evolve in the traditional way, in the direction of a practically based and intellectually coherent global legal order. Half a century later, it is quite clear that this optimistic vision has not only failed to materialise, but that its fulfilment is not even in sight on the distant horizon. What we have seen, during the intervening years, is not a steady progress but a series of violent discontinuities. Technical innovation there has certainly been, but on a scale and in directions quite unpredictable. Moreover the innovations have been not only rapid but accelerating. The breathless rate of change has put a more measured progress out of reach.

For a time it seemed that the internationalisation of international trade law might come about in a different way. Information technology revolution would cause national boundaries to be dissolved by infinite communicability. There might not be harmony, but there would better understanding. In the language of the early idealists of radio broadcasting, Nation would speak truth unto Nation, but not through official media. Rather, individuals would speak frankly to individuals, creating a *de facto* cohesive force at the level of politics, ethics and economics. From this, there might spring new cohesion of world trade, carrying with it a new cohesion of international trade law.

Unfortunately, this rosy picture has very soon been revealed, if not as a false dawn, at least as a new dawn of excessive optimism. At the moment of writing, the prospect seems bleak for the spontaneous emergence of a unified world trade, such as was starting to happen in the days of Francesco Datini, and thereby for the spontanous development of a unified law of marine insurance. Perhaps before long things will reverse; perhaps the numerous non-governmental organisations, the numerous bilateral trade agreements, and so on, will glue the fragments of the world economic order together again; but for the moment we must work on the assumption that there will not emerge within any useful time-span a world situation stable enough to breed a unified economic regime, bringing in its train a unified economic law. If the small corner of economic law represented by our present subject is to move forward, or even survive, we should perhaps lower our sights and think in terms of "micro", not "macro", having regard to ignore the wider horizons only to the extent of being on the alert for major shifts, and working on the basis (without caring to say so publicly) that marine insurance is a modest cottage industry, best left alone to produce its own local artifacts in its own local ways.

Before reconciling ourselves to this humbler vision we should take conscious note of certain forces which are currently shaping the insurance law whose interests the present branch of the law exists to serve. The first is the environmental movement, now so deeply embedded in the contemporary psyche that it is easy to forget how modern it is. The significance of this movement is not only that it has created enormous and novel demands on the financial structures of world trade, but that it has brought into the close world of commerce, and hence into the still more closed world of those who insure commerce, a wholly fresh cast of players. These are not just new faces. The liability insurance market, which includes to a very significant extent the market for maritime liability cover, groups of people who are not interested in the things which have traditionally interested those in the markets: for example weighing potential profit against the risk of loss; measuring cost against benefit in monetary terms; and so on. It is not that they are uninterested in money, but they do not think primarily in terms of it. Moreover traditional methods of analysis have little appeal. Those concerned are zealots, not moderates; in the main they are not easy to do business with. Their influence on the insurance market has been destabilising.

Equally disruptive has been an influence already touched upon: the culture of support and blame. The assumption that if something goes wrong someone or some agency will intervene to put it right, or (if this does not happen) that somebody will pay for a remedy – and indeed will be forced to pay, in the guise of punitive damages, what really amounts to an interpersonal fine. No doubt the underwriting disasters of some years ago can to a significant extent be put down to bad practice, but those in the market say thirty years ago cannot be blamed for a failure to foresee the full extent to which by the turn of the century the traditional precepts of self-reliance, candour and moderation will have not only lost their influence over the size and character of disputes, but also the spirit in which business as a whole is carried on. In a world where the idea that someone's word is his bond seems an anachronism, the creation of a serviceable law of international trade may call for some of its most basic assumptions to be taken out and dusted down.

Other market forces are at work: the appearance of vertical integration amongst hitherto insulated operators; horizontal mergers and acquisitions amongst the principal players; the attenuation and possible disappearance of the subscription market. Those involved will be fewer, but with more individual clout. Some hold that this integration will breed a more homogeneous practice, permitting the growth of new standardised wordings, round which a self-harmonised law can once again coalesce. Others argue for a contrary tendency. The newer and larger want to express their individual bargains in their own individual ways, having the time and incentive to be less slapdash than their predecessors. Each forecast is persuasive, and it is hard for the moment to see which will prove correct. But what does seem clear is that the days when the market predominance of London enabled it automatically to lead the world on practice, and hence to lead the world on the law associated with the practice, have now gone and will not come back. This is not defeatist. No better law than English marine insurance law having any semblance of universal acceptance has yet emerged, and the opportunities for the theoreticians and practice to align it with the needs of the global market are there for the taking.

The Scholar's response

It might be thought that in the light of the trends which I have identified the research in depth of classical marine insurance problems is fruitless, and that it would be better to wait until the dust settles and the shape of a new insurance regime has emerged when a new law can be forged, more suited to the realities of the contemporary scene.

To a degree, this would be right. There are areas which time is passing by. For example, the law which governs accounting between assured, broker and insurer. The law of disclosure, derived from primary insurances on single hulls for short periods on adventures about which little was known, and that little was mostly within the knowledge of the assured, has little to do, so it might be complained, with life in the upper atmospheres of excess reinsurance. And so on. Perhaps scholarly attention should be shifted to the new problems of the new economic order, anticipating where it might be be heading, and leaving the old problems to moulder peacefully in the books.

I do not think so, provided we approach insurance law with rather different methods. There will always be a place for the majestic encyclopaedic tomes, and for the drafts of worldwide codes, but a concentration of intellectual resources on individual areas will I believe yield greater practical benefits. The continuing exploration and consolidation of the existing law is at least as important as more ambitious ventures aimed at tomorrow, for the world of maritime commerce is a world which is continuous with the past. Yet the new features of the economic world make new demands, so that the scholars who establish the bedrock must have an eye to them. It may be that third party liabilities and reinsurance, whose quite sudden emergence in practical prominence has brought their underpinnings of law into the twentieth century breathless and rather dishevelled, now call for closer scholarly attention. From these and similar endeavours there might emerge a series of minimalist epitomes of individual topic, terse propositions with commentary and authority in support, similar to those of the more old fashioned textbooks. The outcome would be a jigsaw, not a "through-composed" code, but the pieces, once there are enough of them, will make up a picture whose elements can be modernised and repainted in response to current market demands. In short, they could be the elements of a "Restatement", consisting neither of the "wilderness of single instances" nor of a date-stamped code, obsolescent almost before it is printed.

This does not mean that the enterprise should be anglo-centric. The English market, the English forms and the English practitioners no longer dominate the world. The start which gave England dominance may not yet be wholly dissipated, in spite of the recent mishaps. But those who seek an effective marine insurance law or, indeed, any law of international commerce, should be constantly looking around, constantly on the alert for ideas from elsewhere. Not just Europe and Scandinavia but nowadays Australasia. ... Tomorrow Asia and South America ... the day after ... Where? It should not matter where, if alertness prevails. We do not need a feeble compromise, milking the various systems for the uncontroversial parts of each. Rather, where the circumstances are as volatile as they are today, there are opportunities for scholars and practitioners to come forward with enterprising ideas. But the more the context is novel and unstable, the greater the need for sound traditional scholarship. The law and market move forward together. Both look backwards whilst advancing to the future. Volumes such as the present adopt realistic methods to yield reliable solutions. I hope they will continue to do so.

CHAPTER 1

HELD COVERED CLAUSES IN MARINE INSURANCE

PROFESSOR RHIDIAN THOMAS

1A INTRODUCTION

Held covered clauses are a familiar feature of the contractual terrain of marine insurance policies, though by no means restricted to marine insurance.[1] Evidence of their existence dates back to the late nineteenth century[2] and in contemporary practice the Institute Clauses[3] are positively peppered with such clauses, and others may exist as special or brokers' clauses. In practice they are alluded to as h/c clauses and this mode of abbreviation is adopted in this contribution. In general terms the purpose of a h/c clause is to offer protection to an assured, within the limits and subject to the conditions of the clause, by giving the assured the option of obtaining cover beyond that agreed in the policy. The underwriter is under an obligation to *1.1*

1. See, *American Airlines Inc. v. Hope* [1974] 2 Lloyd's Rep. 301 (aviation insurance); *Kirby v. Consindit Societa Per Azioni* [1969] 1 Lloyd's Rep. 75 (builders' risks, third party liability and contract liability).

2. *Simon Israel & Co. v. Sedgwick* [1893] 1 Q.B. 303; *Hyderabad (Deccan) Co. v. Willoughby* [1899] 2 Q.B. 530.

3. Produced by The Institute of London Underwriters (International Underwriting Association) and conveniently published annually in *Reference Book of Marine Insurance Clauses* (Witherby Publishing, London).

provide the extended cover but subject, customarily, to the discretionary right to demand an additional premium and/or amended terms of cover.[4]

1.2 Extended cover, as is made available under a h/c clause, may be understood in two general senses. First, in a literal sense, with the invocation of a h/c clause increasing the range of the cover beyond that agreed in the policy. And, second, in a protective sense, with invocation preserving the negotiated cover from the threat of being lost. It will be a matter of drafting and construction whether any particular h/c clause embraces both or only one of these senses. Donaldson J (as he then was) in *Liberian Insurance Agency Inc. v. Mosse*[5] recognised both senses when he said of the h/c clause there under consideration,[6] "the whole object of the clause is to keep the underwriter on risk, notwithstanding that, in the absence of the clause, he would be discharged from liability or the risk would fall outside the policy". But however the extended cover comes about, in each case the underwriter is assuming additional risk, either because the range of the cover is enlarged or because the existing cover is being accepted on changed terms and conditions. It is the assumption of additional risk which justifies the existence of the customary concomitant right to demand additional premium.

1.3 Held covered clauses are quite widely used in marine insurance and they represent a convenient and flexible way for an insured to manage his insurance requirements. Where they exist it is possible to analyse the cover as divided into two general parts. There is the risk defined in the policy from its inception and for which a premium has been agreed and paid,[7] customarily referred to as the policy premium. There is also the additional risk which the insured may elect to bring into existence under the terms of a h/c clause, which is optional and conditional, and in respect of which an additional premium is customarily payable. In relation to a marine policy it is, therefore, possible to speak of policy premium cover and additional premium cover. In every case, the held covered events will be identified by the h/c clause and the fact that the underwriter is prepared to accept the obligation to provide the additional cover indicates that it is a risk which the underwriter would have been prepared to include in the original cover, subject to any necessary adjustment to the premium and/or terms.

1.4 Held covered clauses are a question of contract and, therefore, the drafting may vary, though a material measure of standardisation has been built up over the years, assisted by the widespread use of the Institute Clauses. They are adopted in a great range of different situations and, therefore, as a generic group they cover a wide variety of held covered events.[8] But in matters of procedure and specified conditions precedent they are very uniform. The requirement that the assured give notice of his intention to invoke the h/c clause is universal, and the same may be said of the

4. For textbook commentaries, see Arnould, *Law of Marine Insurance and Average*, Vol. III, Gilman (1997, Sweet & Maxwell, London), paras 46–53; Bennett, *The Law of Marine Insurance* (1996, OUP, Oxford) pp.308–316. Most textbooks do not attempt to isolate the subject of held covered clauses, but address them sporadically in the context of the discussion of held covered events.

5. [1977] 2 Lloyd's Rep. 560, 567.

6. The clause is considered *infra* in the text, under the title "Voidable Risks", para. 1.56 *et seq.*

7. Sometimes on a deferred basis, as when the premium is paid by instalments.

8. *The Litsion Pride* [1985] 1 Lloyd's Rep. 437, 465, where Hirst J recounts the submission of counsel (Mr Gordon Pollock QC) and the use of the phrase "family of clauses".

underwriter's right to demand additional premium. The further right to demand amended terms of cover enjoys prominence but is far from being universal. The precise drafting of a h/c clause is important, for in order to claim the additional cover, an assured must comply precisely with the terms and conditions of the clause.

The Marine Insurance Act 1906 virtually ignores the subject of h/c clauses. They are not directly defined or recognised by the legislation, yet their existence in market practice is acknowledged by s.31(2), which makes a material contribution to ensuring the legal validity of h/c clauses as binding contracts.[9] 1.5

Once it is recognised that the object of a h/c clause is to provide protection to an assured in circumstances when the policy cover is inadequate, unavailable or subject to termination or repudiation, it is possible to recognise the kinds of circumstance when a h/c clause may be utilised in practice. These appear to be when: 1.6

(a) A risk arises outside the scope of the cover defined in the policy.[10] This is necessarily a very broad proposition. The definition of insurance cover is a contractual concept governed by the terms and conditions of the marine insurance contract and their proper construction. At the core of the contractual definition will be stipulations indicating the subject-matter of the insurance, insured and excluded losses, duration of the cover and other circumstances relevant to the application of the cover, and the conditions on which the risk has been underwritten. Where a condition is characterised as suspensory, the effect of breach is to suspend the cover for as long as the breach persists.[11] The underwriter's obligation to indemnify the assured is restricted to the contractually defined cover. There is no legal obligation to indemnify for loss falling outside the ambit of the contract.

(b) The underwriter has the right to elect to avoid a marine policy for breach by the assured of the general duty of good faith, or for failure to disclose material facts, or for misrepresentation of material facts.[12] In these circumstances the remedy of avoidance operates retrospectively and nullifies the contract *ab initio*. The remedy is remarkably powerful for not only does it enable the underwriter to resist a claim for indemnity, it also places at risk any preceding settlement under the policy, which may be revisited and unravelled. The remedy of avoidance is not always available, it is possible for a breach of the duty of utmost good faith to occur after the termination of the contractual period of cover.[13]

(c) The underwriter has a particular statutory right to elect to avoid the marine insurance contract, beyond the general rights considered in the preceding paragraph. The only example of such a right is found in the Marine Insurance Act 1906, s.42(1). In relation to a voyage policy[14] the section establishes an implied condition that the adventure shall be commenced

9. The sub-section is considered *infra* under the title "Additional Premium", para. 1.103 *et seq.*

10. Considered *infra* under the title, "Risks outside the policy cover", para. 1.25 *et seq.*

11. *Farr v. Motor Traders Mutual Insurance Society* [1920] 3 K.B. 669; *De Maurier (Jewels) Ltd v. Bastion Insurance Co.* [1967] 2 Lloyd's Rep 550.

12. Considered *infra* under the title "Voidable Risks", para. 1.56 *et seq.*

13. Considered *infra* under the title "Application of the Doctrine of Utmost Good Faith", para. 1.121 *et seq.*

14. Considered *infra* under the title "Voyage based risks", para. 1.34 *et seq.*

within a reasonable time.[15] and in the event of breach of the condition, the underwriter may avoid the contract.[16] If it were not for the statutory provision, the necessity of commencing a maritime adventure to which a voyage policy attached within a reasonable time would probably be viewed as a matter touching on the definition of the risk insured, which was probably the position under the preceding common law.[17]

(d) The contractual cover is lost for breach of warranty.[18] When the assured is in breach of warranty the liability of the underwriter under the policy is discharged automatically from the moment of the breach, unless the underwriter waives the breach. No election on the part of the underwriter is required. The liability of the underwriter is expunged prospectively, antecedent liabilities arising prior to the breach are unaffected. Beyond the liability of the underwriter a breach of warranty does not terminate the contract of insurance, so even following a breach it remains open to the underwriter to take the aid of the contract and enforce contractual rights, such as a right to claim a premium payment.[19] In English law a breach of warranty has particularly harsh consequences.

(e) The contractual cover is lost for breach of a term of the marine insurance contract other than a warranty.[20] The terms of a marine insurance contract may be as various as those associated with contracts generally. In all instances breach could lead to a claim for damages, but of greater relevance in the context of an insurance contract breach of a particular term could result in the assured's claim for indemnity being justifiably rejected. Such a consequence might flow when it is shown that the assured is in breach of a condition precedent to the making of a claim or to the insurer's liability with regard to a claim; or of a condition in the traditional contractual sense of the word, the breach of which could be accepted as repudiatory; or of an intermediate term, the breach of which was sufficiently grave in its nature or as to its consequences to justify the breach being treated as equivalent to a breach of a contractual condition.

The above categories are not necessarily exclusive but collectively they do provide an effective account of the sources of potential risk to negotiated marine cover, and, therefore, also the reasons for the adoption of h/c clauses in contemporary practice. Within each category there are identifiable legal principles which are a potential source of prejudice to the assured, but where a h/c clause is available and invoked the prejudice is countered, with cover either maintained or obtained.

1.7 There is, of course, no obligation on an assured to invoke a h/c clause; the clause merely gives the assured the right of election. But if the assured exercises the right,

15. Subject to the qualification in s.42(2) that no implied condition exists if the delay was caused by circumstances known to the insurer before the contract was concluded.

16. Provided the right has not been waived: see s.42(2) and *Bah Lias Tobacco and Rubber Estates v. Volga Insurance Co.* (1920) 3 Ll. L. R. 155.

17. *De Wolf v. Archangel Maritime Bank and Insurance Co. Ltd* (1874) L.R. 9 Q.B. 451; *Maritime Insurance Co. v. Stearns* [1901] 2 K.B. 912.

18. Considered *infra* under the title, "Breach of Warranties", para. 1.65 *et seq.*

19. *Bank of Nova Scotia v. Hellenic Mutual War Risks Association (Bermuda) Ltd (The Good Luck)* [1992] 1 A.C. 233.

20. Considered *infra* under the title "Breach of policy terms not being warranties", para. 1.75 *et seq.*

which is done by giving notice, the underwriter is obliged to hold the assured covered, subject usually to the right to the payment of additional premium and/or amended conditions of cover. The rights of the underwriter are embodied in the clause and as with contractual rights generally may or may not be asserted. It is always open to the underwriter to waive a contractual right, though the right to notice is probably such a central mechanism to the operation and analysis of h/c clauses that it is indispensable.[21]

Although h/c clauses are a question of contract, and, therefore, formulated by the agreement of the parties and consequently capable of displaying range and variety, they are in keeping with general principle subject to the constraints of legality and public policy. It is unimaginable that a h/c clause could make it possible to obtain insurance on an unlawful marine adventure[22] or provide the means of circumventing the requirement of insurable interest.[23] It is equally improbable that a h/c clause could oblige an underwriter to indemnify a fraudulent claim. *1.8*

1B THE PROBLEM OF CHARACTERISATION

In subjecting to scrutiny the topic of h/c clauses there arises the unavoidable and, in this instance, troublesome question of definition. How precisely is the subject-matter of the present inquiry to be defined and thereby identified and distinguished from other similar policy terms. In the preceding prolegomenon nothing was attempted beyond a description of the characteristics common to many, possibly most, h/c clauses, and further to admit the possibility of contractual variation. But otherwise the question of definition was ignored as if it were self evident, which it is not. *1.9*

In the practice of insurance the phrase "held covered" is used widely and in a range of different circumstances. This flexible usage will come as no surprise to those familiar with the marine insurance markets, for the markets are concerned with the placement of risks and not with concepts, categories and language, but it is a further cause of the prevailing uncertainty and adds momentum to the quest for an acceptable and helpful definition. It is doubtful, therefore, whether market practice can provide a sound foundation for the establishment of a definition which is both explanatory and discriminatory; nor is the Marine Insurance Act 1906 of any assistance. It also has to be made clear that in seeking a definition, the object is not to draw a line between what is valid and invalid, but to elicit meaning and understanding. A clause which serves a purpose analagous to that associated with h/c clauses as will be defined below may be unambiguously valid and provide for the mutual interests of the parties, and yet in strictness not be a h/c clause. The object is to bring order and comprehension to a hitherto diverse and fragmented subject by identifying the conceptual framework of h/c clauses, and thereby providing the means of identification and distinguishing. *1.10*

For the purpose of this contribution a h/c clause is perceived as a clause which on its *1.11*

21. For further comment see *infra* under the title, "The Operation of H/C Clauses", para 1.86 *et seq.*

22. *Cf.* Marine Insurance Act 1906, s.3(1). Hereafter all future references to the Act will be by the abbreviated format MIA 1906.

23. MIA 1906, s.4. See, further, Chapter 4.

proper construction, irrespective of the precise words used, gives to the assured an optional facility for obtaining extended cover beyond that given in the policy, the extended cover being continuously available from the moment of the held covered event or otherwise (and much more rarely) in the nature of a reattachment of cover, and obtainable as of right provided the assured gives notice (customarily required to be prompt) of the held covered event. On receipt of a valid notice, the underwriter is obliged to provide the extended cover subject to such contractual rights as the underwriter may enjoy under the terms of the h/c clause. The usual position is for the underwriter to have the right to demand additional premium and/or amended policy conditions, but these contractual rights are not seen as essential pre-conditions to the characterisation of a h/c clause. Even if absent, which would be very rare in practice, the clause may continue to be characterised as a h/c clause. There would seem to be nothing to preclude a h/c clause being drafted on terms which defined the underwriter's obligation in unqualified terms, thereby implying that the additional cover was to be on policy terms.

1.12 The question of definition is a matter of substance and not form. The precise language of the clause is not conclusive: nor should h/c clauses be understood restrictively and in terms of predetermined categories. What is crucial is the intent of the parties as communicated by the language used.[24] Simply because the parties have used the phrase "held covered" this is not of itself conclusive that they intend the consequence considered in the preceding paragraph: and, on the other hand, the absence of the phrase does not preclude a clause being construed as a h/c clause. It is true that most h/c clauses as herein defined contain the words "held covered", but it is equally possible for the words to be used when the parties do not intend to indicate any special and particular notion, and are doing no more than defining cover or the duration of cover or the concluding of a temporary agreement as to cover. A clear illustration of a clause being a h/c clause and yet not containing the words "held covered" is provided by Clause 5.1.(the Transit Clause) of the Institute War Clauses (Cargo)1.1.82. Further examples are provided by Clause 1.3 of Institute Fishing Vessel Clauses 20.7.87 and Clause 1.4. of Institute Time Clauses (Hulls) 1.11.95. Clause 9 of Institute Cargo Clauses (A),(B), and (C) 1.1.82, describes itself as a "shall remain in force" type of clause, but it is quite clearly a "held covered" clause as defined in this contribution.

The same principles prevail when a clause incorporates ideas which are closely associated with h/c clauses. The concept of additional premium offers a clear illustration. The fact that a clause imposes an obligation on an assured to pay additional premium is far from being conclusive evidence that the clause is a h/c clause. The reference to additional premium may indicate no more than that cover beyond that specified in the standard terms is being provided and for that the assured must pay additional premium.[25]

1.13 It is clear that the proposed definition of a h/c clause does not necessarily correspond with market practice, where the words "held covered" may be more

24. *Cf. The Litsion Pride* [1985] 1 Lloyd's Rep. 437, 467–471, *per* Hirst J.

25. For example, Institute Malicious Damage Clause 1.8.82; and Institute FOSFA Supplementary Clauses (3): Ship Navigation and Management 1.7.85 (For use in conjunction with Institute FOSFA Trade Clauses (B) and (C)).

widely, variously and capriciously used. This is not to criticise market practice, it is merely a factual observation, but the practice contributes to the prevailing uncertainty and underlines the need for a clear characterisation.

In practice the words "held covered" tend to be used whenever there arises in prescribed circumstances an obligation to pay additional premium, as in the practice relating to the insurance of war risks.[26] The same tendency exists when an underwriter is happy to accept a risk notwithstanding that premium and/or terms are yet to be agreed. In particular there are two examples to note. An underwriter in accepting a brokered risk may agree to hold covered pending ratification by the proposer. And on a renewal the underwriter may agree to hold covered, so allowing the renewal slip to be presented subsequently and after the renewal date. Both are London market practices which provide temporary cover and are strictly limited in duration to a specified number of days. Whatever be the nature of these temporary covers, whether binding in law or honour only, they are very different phenomena from a h/c clause as a source of optional additional cover, but they are similar in that they are practices which protect the interests of assureds.

A h/c agreement also connotes a particular contractual relationship between assured and underwriter.[27] So far as the assured is concerned there is no obligation to claim the additional cover. What is conferred is the right to elect to extend cover. It is for the assured to decide whether or not to take the initiative and activate the facility. If the assured decides not to invoke the clause there can be no allegation of breach of contract, nor does the assured come under any additional obligation. As is the case with an arbitration agreement, a h/c clause which is not invoked exists passively. Only when triggered does the clause assume an active existence and defines the legal relationship between assured and underwriter. An assured who decides not to invoke the h/c clause accepts his insurance cover as originally defined in the policy. 1.14

In contrast, the position of the underwriter is very different, for the underwriter is under an immediate contingent obligation to provide the additional cover as defined in the h/c clause. The contingency is the election of the assured. When the assured elects to invoke the h/c clause, providing the invocation is in strict accordance with the terms of the clause, the underwriter has no option but to agree to provide the additional cover. Failure to do so amounts to breach of contract, and given the nature of the underwriter's promise and the circumstances in which the underwriter is likely to be called upon to perform the promise, it is arguable that performance of the promise may be enforced by an order of specific performance. The position of the underwriter is usually safeguarded by the contractual right to demand an additional premium and/or amended policy conditions, which are analysed as conditions precedent to the additional cover.[28]

Central to the concept of a h/c clause is the requirement of notice. The assured makes his election by giving notice of the held covered event to the underwriter. 1.15

26. See the later discussion, in para. 1.18, of the War Risk Trading Warranties clause considered in *The Litsion Pride* [1985] 1 Lloyd's Rep. 437.

27. This particular question is returned to and analysed later in the text, under the title "A Final Question of Legal Analysis", para. 1.141 *et seq.*

28. For further consideration of the contractual rights of underwriters see *infra* under the title "The Operation of H/C Clauses", para. 1.86 *et seq.*

Notice is a contractual concept and how it is to be given may be governed by the terms of the h/c clause. In contemporary practice it is almost a universal requirement that the notice be prompt, but otherwise little, if anything, is stipulated as to the form of the notice.[29] The requirement of notice emphasises the optional and elective nature of a h/c clause, when viewed from the perspective of the assured, and therefore it is a fundamental and indispensable element in the definition. The requirement of prompt notice also serves to keep the assured honest, for it precludes the assured holding back and giving notice and paying the additional premium only if loss occurs.

Where the requirement of notice is absent, the clause, it is suggested, cannot be regarded as a h/c clause, even though it is otherwise definitive of cover. So clauses which protect the policy cover or give automatic extension of cover without the requirement of notice, such as genuine "shall remain in force" clauses[30] and "deferred termination" clauses,[31] or those which give a commitment to negotiate a reinstatement agreement,[32] are for the purpose of this contribution not regarded as h/c clauses. What such clauses do is to define the original cover, albeit obliquely, or commit to an extension of cover through re-negotiation.

1.16 The additional cover obtained by invoking a h/c clause would appear to come into existence not from the date of the notice but from the occurrence of the held covered event. The notice may ante- or post-date the held covered event and even the insured loss, and when it is the latter it seems clear that the cover is established retrospectively.[33] This is the way most h/c clauses work, but not necessarily all. Sometimes the effect of h/c clauses is to achieve "re-attachment of cover", as in Clauses 5.1. and 5.3. of Institute War Clauses (Cargo) (1.1.1982). These clauses make provision only for the re-establishment of cover which has terminated, and with invocation, therefore, having no retrospective effect. With regard to such clauses there is no continuity of cover from the held covered event, but nonetheless there appears to exist no reason to deny them recognition as h/c clauses.

1.17 The problem of characterisation is particularly well illustrated by the contractual provisions which came forward for consideration in *The Good Luck*.[34] The precise contractual terms are set out in a footnote to the text,[35] but their effect was as follows. Under the Rules of the Hellenic Mutual War Risks Association (1982 edn.) the

29. The notice obligation is analysed further *infra* under the title "The Operation of H/C Clauses", para. 1.87 *et seq.*

30. For example, Institute Cargo Clauses, (A), (B) and (C), 1.1.82, Clause 8.3; Institute War Clauses (Cargo) 1.1.82, Clause 5.5.

31. For example, Institute Time Clauses (Hulls), 1.11.95, Clauses 4.2, 5.1 and 5.2.

32. For example, Institute War and Strikes Clauses (Hulls)—Time 1.11.95, Clause 6.1; LL.L.Rep. (2001), Vol. 1, 389.

33. For further comment on this issue see *infra* under the titles "Notice" and "A Final Question of Legal Analysis", at paras 1.87 *et seq.* and 1.141 *et seq.* respectively.

34. [1992] 1 A.C. 233.

35. Rule 20 provided:

"A. The Directors have power under Rule 26 to specify any ports, places, countries, zones or areas (whether on land or sea) as Additional Premium Areas and to specify any special terms, conditions, exceptions, or limitations of or to the Association's cover which shall apply while an entered ship shall be or remain in any such area.

B. If an entered ship shall proceed to or be or remain in any Additional Premium Area, then (subject to paragraphs C and D of this rule):

(i) The owner shall continue to be insured while the ship proceeds to or is or remains within such area.

directors of the Association had the power to designate additional premium areas and also the terms which were to apply when an entered ship was present in any such area. The Rules set out a scheme under which the cover was provided automatically subject to prompt notice, the pre-determined terms, and agreement on additional premium. If prompt notice was not given the directors had a discretion to reject any claim arising from the presence of the entered ship in an additional premium area. An owner who did not want the additional cover could obtain suspension of cover whilst the entered ship was in the additional premium area by giving an appropriate written notice.

At first instance, Hobhouse J (as he then was) considered the rule to be "essentially" a held covered provision and, in the House of Lords, Lord Goff appears to have agreed with this analysis.[36] Quite clearly many of the elements of a h/c clause, as considered earlier, were present, namely the obligation of the Association to provide the cover, the requirement of prompt notice and the obligation to agree additional premium and new terms. Nevertheless, the drafting and slant of the various elements of the contractual rules were very different from h/c clauses found in market marine policies and possibly reflected the distinctive ethos of a mutual association. The difference probably also accounted for the guarded use of the adverb "essentially" by the judiciary when characterising the clause.

The crucial question is whether the particular form of the Rules also embodies a difference of substance from a h/c clause as characterised in this contribution, and it probably does. The general effect of the Association rule was to give continuous cover subject to conditions and an obligation to pay additional premium. The

---

PROVIDED ALWAYS that:
It is a condition of the insurance given by the Association that the Owner shall give prompt notice to the Association of the fact that the entered ship will enter, has entered or is in the Additional Premium Area as soon as the Owner knows of such fact. If any Owner shall fail to give prompt notice to the Association shall be entitled, if the Directors in their discretion so determine, to reject any and all claims arising out of events occurring while the ship is in the Additional Premium Area but in such event the Association shall return to the Owner any additional premium which may have been paid pursuant to (iii) below.

(ii) The terms of the insurance of the entered ship during such period shall be those which have been agreed between the Owner and the Association. . . .

(iii) The Owner shall pay to the Association an additional premium to be arranged.

C. An Owner shall be entitled to give written notice to the Association at any time before the entered ship enters an Additional Premium Area stating that he desires the cover of the entered ship to be suspended while the ship is within the said area. If notice in writing is given as aforesaid then:

(i) The cover given by the Association in respect of the ship so specified shall be suspended and the Owner shall remain uninsured in respect of such ship during the period while the ship is and remains in the Additional Premium Area.

(ii) The Owner shall be under no liability to pay any additional premium in accordance with paragraph B(iii) of this rule but shall not be entitled to any return of contributions paid or payable in respect of the entered ship unless the directors in their absolute discretion otherwise determine.

Unless a notice shall have been given pursuant to this paragraph before the ship enters the designated Additional Premium Area, the provisions of paragraph B of this Rule shall be applicable. . . .

E. Where the entered ship is mortgaged the owner shall not be entitled to give notice under paragraph C of this rule or to negotiate under paragraph D of this rule any deduction and the maximum cover available from the Association unless he shall have obtained and produced to the Association the consent of his mortgages to the suspension or reduction of the cover. . . ."

36. *Ibid.*, at p.250.

obligation to give prompt notice was not necessary to invoke the additional cover, which is the traditional purpose of notice, but to affirm the operation of a cover already in place and to ensure the payment of additional premium. And even if prompt notice was not given, the cover appeared to survive, but subject to the discretion of the directors to reject any claim made under the extended cover. The continuity of the cover was particularly emphasised by the position of a member who did not want the additional cover. To occupy this position the member had to give written notice to the Association, whereas under a traditional h/c clause the assured occupies this position by not giving notice.

When the Association rules are construed in their entirety they emerge more as a conditional continuation of cover provision than a h/c clause as herein defined, but so far as their practical effect is concerned they are closely allied to such a h/c clause and the judicial description of them as being "effectively" a h/c clause probably strikes the right kind of chord.

1.18 The question which arose in *The Litsion Pride*[37] was capable of being given a much more decisive answer. Hirst J (as he then was) had to decide whether the War Risk Trading Warranties clause (11.5.82.) incorporated into a S.G. policy was in the nature of a held covered or continuation of cover clause. The substance of the clause, to the extent relevant for present purposes, was as follows:

> "This coverage shall extend worldwide, but in the event of a vessel or craft insured hereunder sailing for, deviating towards, or being within the Territorial Waters of any of the Countries or places described in the Current Exclusions as set out below (including any port area that at the date of this notice constitutes part of such a country or place however it may hereafter be described) additional premium shall be paid at the discretion of insurers hereon.
>
> Information of such voyage or deviation shall be given to insurers as soon as practicable, and the absence of prior advice shall not affect the cover hereon. In the event of the insured not requiring continuation of coverage for a vessel proceeding into or remaining within an excluded area, he shall so advise insurers hereon before the commencement of such voyage, deviation or period, and it shall be at the insurer's discretion whether and on what terms the insurance shall be reinstated."

The trading clause in the slip provided:

> "World-wide trading subject to current war risk exclusions 11.5.82 or held covered."

Hirst J refused just to presume that the clause belonged to the held covered category of clauses.[38] The precise language of the clause had to be addressed and construed. Adopting this approach Hirst J reasoned that the clause could not be regarded as a simple h/c clause with no express provision as to notice. It was an extensive and elaborate clause with detailed provisions as to notices for various purposes. It left no gaps to be filled. When the express language was examined there was no mention of condition or condition precedent, and no indication whatsoever that failure to give the necessary information as soon as practicable would result in loss of cover. On the contrary, cover continued even in the absence of punctual information of a relevant event being given to the underwriters, and additional premium was payable unless the assured had terminated cover by advising the underwriters in the way provided by the clause. On a proper construction of the clause

37. [1985] 1 Lloyd's Rep. 437.

38. *Ibid.*, pp.467–471. Contrast the comments of Lord Hobhouse on the case in *Manifest Shipping Company v. Uni-Polaris Shipping Company Ltd and Others, The Star Sea* [2001] 2 W.L.R. 170, 195, para. 71.

the requirement that the information specified should be given to the underwriters as soon as practicable could not be understood as a condition precedent and this was a very material consideration in coming to the conclusion that the clause could not be considered an ordinary held covered clause. The information obligations under the clause were contractual and any default on the part of the assured amounted to a breach of contract, with the remedies of the underwriters also contractual.

A final illustration is provided by the Australian case *Australia & New Zealand Banking Group Ltd v. Compagnie D'Assurances Maritimes Aeriennes et Terrestres*.[39] A fishing vessel was insured in the Paris market on the basis of a contract which incorporated Institute Fishing Vessel Clauses 20.7.87. The basic contract included a trading limits clause and a clause which provided "continuation and breach of warranty clauses held covered with or without notice". Clause 3 of Institute Fishing Vessel Clauses provided: 1.19

> "Held covered in case of any breach of warranty as to locality . . . provided notice be given to the Underwriters immediately after receipt of advices and any amended terms of cover and any additional premium required by them be agreed."

The conflict between the clauses is immediately visible.

A casualty took place outside the specified trading limits and prior to that event the assured had not given any notice that the vessel was operating outside policy limits. The underwriters rejected the assured's claim under the policy.

In giving judgment for the assured the reasoning of the court appears to have taken the following path. The trading limits clause in the contract was construed to be a warranty as to locality and, therefore, it fell within the held covered clauses in the contract and Institute Clauses. The conflict between the notice requirements in these two clauses was resolved by giving priority to the clause in the basic contract. In the result the assured was held covered notwithstanding the absence of notice, with the underwriters taking the risk of the dangers associated with the absence of a notice requirement, though the court considered the assured to owe a duty of good faith.

Clause 3 of the Institute Fishing Vessel Clauses is unambiguously a h/c clause as defined in this contribution. What was described as a held covered provision in the contract is with equal clarity not such a clause. It amounts to an additional premium provision which operates automatically and independently of notice. Once the vessel went outside policy limits the cover continued and the assured was obliged to pay additional premium.

The concept of a h/c clause which has been developed in the preceding discussion is what many might describe as a conventional or customary h/c clause. The clauses to be found in the Institute Clauses and which expressly declare themselves to be h/c clauses predominantly fall readily into this characterisation. But form is not the determining factor and cautious scrutiny must be the governing frame of mind. Ultimately, it will be a question of construction whether or not a particular clause falls within the concept of a h/c clause as here defined. 1.20

39. [1995] Lloyd's Rep. I.R. 464.

1C COMMERCIAL FUNCTION

1.21 In embarking on a legal analysis of h/c clauses it is important not to overlook their potential commercial function. They obviously give assureds the benefit of an optional, flexible and secure additional cover, but more particularly they are also capable of providing a device by which assureds may regulate premium costs.

1.22 Premiums on marine risks are rarely negligible, and on occasions may be relatively highly rated, with the relationship between premium and risk an obvious element in the rating process. An assured who has negotiated both policy and additional premium cover is in a position to protect himself from the premium costs of additional cover until a h/c risk actually materialises or is certain to arise or is likely to occur. The policy cover is subject to the terms agreed and premium is payable whether or not an insured risk materialises. Additional premium cover is of a very different character, with premium payable only if the held covered risk occurs or is imminent. Held covered risks are often of a kind less likely to occur, but if they do the consequences can be very grave. Consequently, they can be highly rated risks, and, therefore, they are the kind of risk the assured is quite happy to divorce from premium cover because of the cost implications and also the improbability of obtaining any benefit from the enhanced premium paid. A h/c clause enables the assured to avoid the risk of a wasted premium payment and yet retain an insurance commitment from the underwriter. The assured is only obliged to pay the additional premium in the event of the contingency of the h/c risk actually or being virtually certain to occur.

1.23 An example of the process is provided when a h/c clause is associated with a territorial warranty.[40] The object of the warranty is to manage the risk by regulating the places the insured vessel may be sent to by the assured, with the particular purpose of keeping the vessel away from high risk places and regions. The warranty by its nature also serves to moderate premium rates, which the assured no doubt is happy to take advantage of, and provided the ship keeps within warranty limits only the policy premium is payable. The existence of the associated h/c provision means that the warrant limits may be broken and extra-warranty trading engaged upon, subject to whatever limits the clause itself may impose, in return for the payment of additional premium. By definition, extra-warranty trading involves additional risks and will attract a higher premium rating, but the assured is not obliged to bear this cost for as long as the insured vessel trades within warranty limits. Only when the vessel enters waters outside the warranty limits or when it is known that this is the future intention of the vessel is the assured required to address the question whether to trigger the h/c provision and pay the additional premium commensurate with the additional risk. But if the ship stays throughout within the warranted territorial limits no additional premium becomes payable.

40. For example, Institute Time Clauses (Hulls) 1.11.95, Clause 3 (Breach of Warranty).

1D "HELD COVERED" CLAUSES IN CONTEMPORARY PRACTICE

It is now proposed to identify and categorise h/c clauses that appear in contemporary practice by reference to the "held covered" events which they target, though the discussion which follows makes no pretence to be comprehensive. This is a fertile method of categorisation, for the wide scope and variety of h/c clauses is primarily accounted for by the range of held covered events that they identify. But otherwise the method has no formal or legislative significance, nor does it have any direct legal significance, for the legal analysis of h/c clauses would seem to be uninfluenced by the nature of the held covered event. 1.24

1D.1 Risks outside the policy cover

An underwriter agrees to indemnify the assured not generally, but only to the extent specified in the policy. Even an "all risks" policy is not what it appears to be on its face.[41] The limits of the cover may be ascertained from the subject-matter insured; the insured risks and exclusions; time, voyage, territorial and employment considerations; and the terms and conditions upon which the risk is assumed. A risk which falls outside the ambit of the contractual cover is borne by the assured and to this extent the assured is his own insurer. It follows that all insurance entails an element of co-insurance between assured and underwriter. The risk of a loss suffered by the assured falling outside the ambit of the policy cover and being borne by the assured may be countered or at least minimised by a h/c agreement. 1.25

1D.1(i) Subject-matter insured

The risk assumed by the underwriter is restricted to the subject-matter of the insurance, whether ship, cargo, freight or some other interest, and consequently the statutory rule that the subject-matter insured must be designated in a marine policy with reasonable certainty is readily appreciated.[42] Subject to the satisfaction of this requirement it is for the parties to determine how the subject-matter is to be designated. It may be done with precision or generally and in an imprecise way.[43] The greater the imprecision the greater the possibility of uncertainty arising as to what has been insured, and any conflict concerning this question is determined having regard to the proper construction of the words used. In construing general words notice may be taken of any relevant provisions of the Marine Insurance Act 1906,[44] trade and market usages[45] and understandings, with the overriding object of the exercise being to determine the intention of the parties.[46] 1.26

Quite clearly, the more widely the subject-matter of an insurance is designated the less likely the possibility that a loss to a particular subject-matter will fall outside the 1.27

41. *Cf. British and Foreign Marine Insurance Co. v. Gaunt* [1921] 2 A.C. 41.
42. Section 26(1).
43. As appears to be acknowledged in s.26(3).
44. See, in particular, First Schedule, Rules for Construction of Policy, Rules 15–17.
45. Section 26(4).
46. Section 26(3).

ambit of the policy. There are several ways an assured can obtain breadth of designation. First, as already observed, by defining the subject-matter in a broad and general manner. Second, by a contractual provision which defines the subject-matter in a way which allows for accretions and subtractions, as may be provided for under builders' risks[47] and fleet insurances. Third, by negotiating a variation of the original cover, with the variation endorsed on the original policy. And fourth, by agreeing an appropriately drafted h/c clause, though in contemporary practice this is rarely done.

1.28 In principle there is nothing to preclude a h/c clause being drafted so as to enable an assured to extend the policy cover to a subject-matter not designated in the original policy. The analogy can be made with a fleet policy where it is customary for the parties to enter into a "new and/or acquired" agreement, the effect of which is that the underwriter agrees to hold covered any new or second-hand tonnage acquired by the assured during the currency of the policy, subject to the payment of additional premium and subject to any stipulated conditions.

1.29 A clause found in earlier editions of the Institute Clauses, but which in contemporary practice appears to have lost its appeal, was to the following effect, "Held covered at a premium to be arranged in case . . . of any omission or error in the description of the interest . . .". The word "interest" has been held to be a reference to the subject-matter of the insurance[48] and, therefore, the question arises whether the clause could have a relevance to the current discussion. The answer is probably in the negative, for the clause appears to apply only to an erroneous description of the designated subject-matter and does not provide an avenue by which a non-designated subject-matter can be brought within the ambit of cover.

1.30 In *Overseas Commodities Ltd v. Style*[49] a h/c clause of the kind here under discussion was incorporated into two cargo policies issued with regard to a consignment of French pork butts marked LNMS 8/9 and LNMS 26. The markings were considered to be descriptive of the subject matter of the insurance. Practically all the tins actually shipped bore a range of other markings, which rendered them goods outside the subject-matter of the insurance. The assured failed in the attempt to take the aid of the h/c clause, though the reasons for this are far from clear. The judge was clearly influenced by the fact that the assured could not correct the misdescription and considered this a sufficiently valid reason for not applying the clause. Another way of explaining the decision is that goods were shipped which were not intended to be covered by the policies, as distinct from wrongly described shipped goods which were intended to be covered.[50]

1D.1(ii) Insured risks

1.31 With regard to the subject-matter of the insurance, the underwriter undertakes to indemnify the assured only for insured risks. An insured risk may be defined in terms

47. See, Institute Clauses for Builders' Risks, 1.6.88.

48. *Hewitt Bros v. Wilson* [1915] 2 K.B. 739, 744, *per* Lord Reading CJ (CA); *Liberian Insurance Agency v. Mosse* [1977] 2 Lloyd's Rep. 560, 567, *per* Donaldson J. See the further discussion of the case *infra* under the title "Voidable Risks", para. 1.56 *et seq.*

49. [1958] 1 Lloyd's Rep. 546.

50. *Cf. Hood v. West End Motor Car Parking Co.* [1916] 2 K.B. 395 (CA).

of losses, perils and causation, which are all contractual concepts. To claim under the policy the assured must show that a loss of a kind defined in the policy has been suffered and that that loss has been caused by a peril specified in the policy, with it open for the policy to also specify the appropriate test of causation.[51] The position is a little different under an all risks policy,[52] and it may also be further varied by express agreement.[53]

It follows that if the assured suffers a loss with regard to the subject-matter of an insurance, but cannot establish the loss to be an insured loss, there is no right of recovery under the policy.[54] But again the limitations of the policy may be overcome by an appropriately drafted h/c clause, though such clauses are uncommon. 1.32

In *Greenock Steamship Co. Ltd v. Maritime Insurance Co. Ltd*[55] the h/c clause in the policy before the court, to the extent to which it is relevant, provided, "held covered in case of . . . unprovided incidental risk . . . at a premium to be hereafter arranged". The clause itself was not in issue but the effect of the clause would seem to be that it enabled the assured to negotiate additional cover with regard to any "incidental risk" not expressly specified in the policy. The obvious difficulty which arises concerns the meaning of the word "incidental", which raises a question of construction. Quite clearly it is a word of restricted meaning and appears to allude to risks which are incidental to the designated risks. The clause would not permit the assured to hold covered additional and wholly independent risks. 1.33

1D.1(iii) Voyage-based risk

Marine risks may be underwritten on a voyage or time basis, or a combination of both.[56] In contemporary practice voyage policies predominate in cargo insurance,[57] but with regard to hull and machinery insurance they are usually only adopted in particular circumstances.[58] This is in contrast to the historical position when voyage policies predominated, a fact evidenced by the attention voyage policies receive in the Marine Insurance Act 1906. An entire section of the legislation, titled "The Voyage" and spanning ss.42 to 49, is devoted to them but, so far as contemporary practice is concerned, the section probably represents the least relevant part of the legislation.[59] 1.34

The broad effect of the statutory provisions is to define the risk assumed by an underwriter when cover is given on a voyage basis. A voyage risk is perceived, expressing matters in a very general way, as one that runs from, or from and at, the 1.35

51. *Cf.* s.55(1); *The Popi M* [1985] 2 Lloyd's Rep. 1.
52. *Cf. British and Foreign Marine Insurance Co. v. Gaunt* [1921] 2 A.C. 41.
53. As evidenced by the Institute Clauses, particularly the Cargo Clauses.
54. Section 55(1).
55. [1903] 1 K.B. 367.
56. Section 25(1).
57. See, for example, Institute Cargo Clauses A, B and C 1.1.82 and the various Special Trades Clauses.
58. Examples of which are the delivery voyage of a new or second-hand ship; and the final voyage of a ship sold for scrap.
59. For general commentaries on this part of the 1906 Act see Arnould, *Law of Marine Insurance and Average*, Vol. 1, 16th edn., Mustill and Gilman (1981, Stevens & Sons), Chapter 14; Bennett, *The Law of Marine Insurance* (1996, OUP), Chapters 14 and 15; Hodges, *Law of Marine Insurance* (1996, Cavendish Publishing Ltd), Chapter 4.

specified place of departure to the specified place of destination,[60] with the connecting voyage commenced within a reasonable time from concluding the contract of marine insurance,[61] and thereafter prosecuted with reasonable despatch throughout[62] and without deviation,[63] unless the delay or deviation is excused.[64]

1.36 Subject to the terms of the policy, if the actual voyage is not performed in accordance with this concept of a voyage risk, it is not one that the underwriter has agreed to insure and consequently any losses that occur are outside the scope of cover. The statutory provisions achieve this result by various analytical techniques. If the place of departure or destination is not that specified in the policy, the risk does not attach.[65] If there is a change of voyage, which occurs when after the commencement of the voyage the destination of the ship is changed, the underwriter is discharged from liability as from the time the determination to change the voyage is manifested.[66] Without lawful excuse, to deviate from the contemplated voyage or to prosecute the voyage without reasonable despatch discharges the underwriter from liability as from the time of the deviation or the delay becoming unreasonable.[67] And finally, if the voyage is not commenced within a reasonable time, the underwriter may avoid the contract.[68]

1.37 A perennial problem relating to the voyage provisions is the question of whether they are applicable to the warehouse to warehouse cover provided in contemporary cargo insurance under the terms of the various Institute Cargo Clauses.[69] The legislative drafting is erratic and often bewildering and does not provide a clear answer.[70] Nonetheless, the general effect of the statutory provisions, when examined collectively, suggests that what is contemplated is a sea voyage between ports and/or places. This would be consistent with early cargo insurance policies[71] but out of step with contemporary practice.[72] It is of course clear that the statutory restrictions can be overcome by express contract and also it is not wholly impossible that analogous provisions might be implied at common law. The modern Institute Cargo Clauses appear to recognise that by one legal route or another the statutory provisions apply to the extended cover given. Clause 8.3 seems to offer evidence of this, but without ever expressly making the point, by providing that cover "shall remain in force . . . during delay beyond the control of the Assured, any deviation . . . and during any variation of

60. Sections 25(1), 43, 44 and 45. And also the First Schedule, Rules for Construction of Policy, Rules 2 and 3.

61. Section 42(1). The implied condition may be displaced by evidence that the delay was caused by circumstances known to the insurer before the contract was concluded or by proof of waiver; see s.42(2).

62. Section 48.

63. Sections 46 and 47.

64. Section 49.

65. Sections 43 and 44.

66. Section 45. The section was recently considered in *Fraser Shipping Ltd v. Colton and Others* [1997] 1 Lloyd's Rep. 586 (CA).

67. Sections 46 and 48.

68. Section 42(1). See also para. 1.6(c) *supra*.

69. Specifically the Transit Clause, which appears as Clause 8 in the various Institute Cargo Clauses.

70. In s.25(1) and ss.42–49 there are to be found words and phrases capable of supporting both sides of the debate.

71. Which were restricted to voyage risks.

72. Where multimodal transport contracts are dominant, except in relation to bulk commodities.

the adventure arising from the exercise of a liberty granted to shipowners or charterers under the contract of affreightment".

The preceding discussion reveals that there is considerable technicality about the legal perception of a voyage risk and an assured may readily run foul of them with prejudicial consequences. There are various ways of protecting against these dangers. One way is to define the voyage in a very flexible manner. Another is to counter the statutory provisions by overriding express contractual provisions. Yet a further way is to agree h/c terms, which is frequently done in modern voyage policies. *1.38*

A prime example is provided by Clause 2 of Institute Voyage Clauses Hull, 1.11.95. The clause appears under the sub-title "Change of Voyage" and provides: *1.39*

> "Held covered in the case of deviation or change of voyage ... provided notice given to the Underwriters immediately after receipt of advices and any amended terms of cover and any additional premium required by them be agreed."

The clause aligns closely with ss.45 and 46 of the Marine Insurance Act 1906, which address change of voyage and deviation respectively, and it is probable that the clause is to be construed in the context of the legal matrix established by the Act. Thus the contractual meaning of change of voyage and deviation are likely to echo their statutory meanings, and with the statutory concept of excused deviation also likely to be incorporated into the contractual construction.

The clause is a contractual device by which the assured can avoid the consequences of termination of cover which would otherwise result in the event of deviation and change of voyage, but it also recognises that with a deviation or change of voyage there arises a change in the nature of the voyage risk assumed by the underwriter and that this justifies the imposition of additional premium and new terms to the extent appropriate.

Another significant example is provided by Clause 10 of Institute Cargo Clauses (A) 1.1.82, which provides: *1.40*

> "Where after attachment of this insurance, the destination is changed by the Assured, 'held covered' at a premium and on conditions to be arranged subject to prompt notice being given to the Underwriters."

Again the clause aligns with s.45 of the Marine Insurance Act, but without there being a precise parallel, for destination within the meaning of the clause may involve an inland place. Nonetheless, the clause appears to presume that the principle embodied in s.45 applies both to marine and land destinations. However, the clause only applies when the destination is changed by the assured, which would be an exceptional circumstance, whereas s.45 applies to any circumstance when the destination of the ship is changed. Where, as is much more likely, the destination is changed by the carrier, it is probable that cover is retained under Clause 8.3 of Institute Cargo Clauses, which protects cover, as already observed, in the face of "any deviation ... and ... any variation of the adventure arising from the exercise of a liberty granted to shipowners or charterers under the contract of affreightment".

Whereas ordinary cargo insurance is provided on a warehouse to warehouse basis, the same is not true of war risks cargo insurance, which is restricted to the period of sea transit. The restriction dates from the War Risks Waterborne Agreement and the current position is set out in Clause 5.1 of Institute War Clauses (Cargo) 1.1.82. *1.41*

Under the clause, cover extends from the loading of the cargo to its unloading at the final port or place of discharge, or on the expiry of 15 days after arrival at the final port or place of discharge, whichever occurs first. There is a h/c provision if the vessel is forced to leave the final port or place of destination without unloading the cargo, and with the additional cover extending to the further voyage made by the vessel, whether it terminates at the original or a substitute port or place of destination, and with cover following rearrival or arrival extending for a maximum of 15 days.

This particular h/c clause attracts two observations. First, it is a rare example of a h/c clause appearing in the Institute Clauses without it expressly declaring itself to be a "held covered" clause. But, having regard to the definition previously promulgated in this contribution, it is unambiguously a h/c clause. Second, the effect of the h/c provision is to "reattach" cover. This indicates that the original policy cover has ceased and suggests that not only has the vessel failed to unload the cargo but that she has been in the final port or place of discharge for more than 15 days. The additional cover attaches from the time the vessel sails on the new voyage. When there exists a gap in time between the expiration of the 15-day period and the commencement of the second voyage, in the absence of some other special arrangement, the assured is without cover, for the h/c arrangement does not date back to the expiration of the original policy cover but to the moment the vessel sets sail on the additional voyage.

1.42 The relationship between voyage conditions and h/c clauses came very clearly to the surface in *Mentz, Decker & Co. v. Maritime Insurance Co.*[73] The voyage policy in question had been issued "for a voyage to a port of loading in Costa Rica and thence to a port of discharge in the United Kingdom". The insured perils included barratry of the master, and the policy contained a h/c clause in the following terms:

> "In the event of the vessel making any deviation or change of voyage it is mutually agreed that such deviation or change shall be 'held covered' at a premium to be arranged, provided due notice is given by the assured on receipt of advice of such deviation or change of voyage."

In July 1907, the ship received orders to load at Cocos Bay, in Costa Rica. The master, in breach of the orders, did not proceed directly but first took the ship to Cocos Island, which was several hundred miles out of his course, and which trip he made for his personal benefit. Thereafter, he went to Cocos Bay and loaded a homeward cargo. On leaving Cocos Bay the master again did not proceed directly, and in breach of his directions and for his personal benefit he again took the ship to Cocos Island, where the ship stranded and became a total loss.

On the facts of the case it was held that there had been no deviation and, therefore, the primary cover under the policy survived. The reason for this determination was that the physical deviation amounted to barratry by the master, which was an insured peril, and, therefore, the deviation was excused in pursuance of s.49(1)(g) of the Marine Insurance Act 1906. But even if the physical deviation had not been barratrous, the court was of the clear opinion that the assured would have been able to take advantage of the h/c clause. The clause was directly pertinent to the issue which had arisen on the facts of the case. With regard to the applicability of the clause the only real question which arose was whether the assured could have satisfied the obligation to give "due notice", having regard to the fact that any notice would follow

73. [1910] 1 K.B. 132.

the actual loss of the vessel. This particular question is returned to later in this contribution when the question of "notice" is examined.

1D.1(iv) Time-based risk

When insurance is given on a time basis, the underwriter is on risk for the period of time specified in the policy. A time policy is defined by the 1906 Act as a "contract... to insure the subject-matter for a definite period of time".[74] It follows that in a time policy the precise moment cover commences and terminates can be crucial issues, with the answer turning on the proper construction of the relevant policy terms. The general rule is that a loss is covered only if it occurs within the contractual period of cover, but whether it is necessary for both the peril and loss to occur within the policy period, or whether it is sufficient that only one should so occur, is again a question of construction.[75] *1.43*

Apart from cargo insurance, in contemporary practice most marine insurance is done on a time basis. This is particularly true of hull and machinery insurance and also of the mutual cover provided by P and I Clubs.[76] It used to be the case that a marine time policy could not extend beyond 12 months, but this rule has long been abandoned[77] and in contemporary practice the question of duration is one of contract. *1.44*

With regard to time policies, losses which pre- or post-date the insured period are *prima facie* not covered. It follows that insurances on ships require prudent management. The commencement date probably offers less difficulty, and special circumstances sometimes can be countered by ante-dating the cover, subject to the assured's discharge of the duty of utmost good faith.[78] Termination of cover potentially offers greater difficulty for there is often the real prospect of the insured ship still being at sea at the time the cover ceases. The danger of being off cover may be avoided if there is an option to extend cover in the policy, or by the prudent management of the renewal, or by negotiating an extension of the existing cover until the ship arrives at her destination. But in the circumstances prevailing, these options may not be available to an assured, and it is this kind of situation which appears to be targeted by the Continuation Clause which is a standard component of the various Institute Time Clauses (Hulls), though it falls well short of giving full assurance. *1.45*

Clause 2 of Institute Time Clauses (Hulls), 1.11.95, provides: *1.46*

> "Should the Vessel at the expiration of this insurance be at sea and in distress or missing, she shall, provided notice be given to the Underwriters prior to the expiration of this insurance, be 'held covered' until arrival at the next port in good safety, or if in port and in distress until the Vessel is made safe, at a pro rata monthly premium."

It is quite clear that this is not a straightforward continuation provision. At the time

74. Section 25(1). The sub-section also recognises that a time element may be introduced into a voyage policy. For the interpretation of the phrase "definite period of time" see *The Eurysthenes* [1976] 2 Lloyd's Rep. 171.

75. *Cf. Kelly v. Norwich Union Fire Insurance Society Ltd* [1989] 2 Lloyd's Rep. 333; *Lockyer v. Offley* (1786) 1 T.R. 252.

76. With respect to which it is well understood that cover runs for 12 months from noon Greenwich mean time on 20 February.

77. Section 25(2) was repealed by the Finance Act 1959.

78. The duty is discussed *infra* under the title "Application of the Doctrine of Utmost Good Faith", para. 1.121 *et seq.*

of the expiration of the policy one of two possible circumstances must prevail. Either the insured vessel must be at sea and in distress or missing, simply being at sea is not sufficient; or the insured vessel must be in port and in distress. Again, simply being in port is not sufficient. In either case the additional cover is dependent on notice being given prior to the expiration of the original cover and the payment of a pro rata monthly premium.

When at the termination of cover the vessel is at sea, the vessel is held covered until she arrives at the next port (not necessarily her port of destination) in good safety. The reference to good safety suggests that the additional cover continues after the vessel's arrival at her next port until such time she can lie safely in that port. When, at the termination of cover, the vessel is in port, the vessel is held covered until she is made safe. Apart from premium, the additional cover is on the same terms and conditions as the policy cover.

The clause offers no protection to neglectful or absent-minded assureds. On the contrary, it only provides protection to assureds who because of the circumstances prevailing at the termination of the cover are unlikely, or at least will find it difficult, to renew the insurance.

1D.1(v) Territorial limitations

1.47 In marine insurance, cover is often limited by reference to territorial considerations. By definition the sea is a hazardous environment, but some marine areas may be more hazardous than others and the degree of hazard may vary with the seasons and the occurrence of geological events. In turn the natural dangers of the marine environment may be compounded by external factors such as belligerency, civil unrest, political hostility and the like. These various factors are considerations which are likely to be taken into account in assessing and rating a risk and often result in insurance being given subject to territorial prohibitions or additional premium zones.

1.48 But it must not be assumed that territorial limits are always associated with endeavours to manage the potential variations in the marine risk. Sometimes they are used to emphasise what may be described as the natural territorial limitation of a risk, as in the case of Port Risks[79] and Builders' Risks[80] insurance. In other instances, the limitation may be associated with the nature of the insured subject-matter, as with the insurance of yachts, though in this case the limits are described as navigational and not territorial, but nothing of substance appears to turn on the change of language.[81]

1.49 The predominant effect of Institute Warranties 1.7.76 is to impose territorial limitations on the navigation of insured vessels. The signal characteristic of the clause is that it achieves this not through the definition of the risk but by the alternative route of extracting obligations in the nature of warranties from assureds. An assured who is in breach of Institute Warranties is consequently just not simply off cover but is in danger of losing the prospective part of his insurance cover.

1.50 Territorial limits may be absolute or qualified in nature. The former are often described as prohibited areas. Where they are of the latter kind it is customary to

79. See, for example, Institute Time Clauses—Hulls Port Risks 20.7.87.
80. See, for example, Institute Clauses for Builders' Risks 1.6.88.
81. See, for example, Institute Yacht Clauses 1.11.85.

provide that the insured vessel is allowed to enter an extra-territorial zone subject to giving notice and paying additional premium, thus the description additional premium area. One mechanism by which the additional cover may be obtained is a h/c clause, though other and closely related contractual provisions are also used, albeit not strictly h/c clauses.[82] The process is well illustrated by the contemporary practice with regard to the insurance of war risks, a particular example of which is provided by *The Good Luck* which was considered earlier in this contribution.[83]

There are ample examples of h/c clauses being adopted when cover is subject to territorial limitations. In Institute War and Strikes Clauses—Cargo Stored Afloat in Mechanically Self-propelled Vessels, 1.6.82, Clause 6, which appears under the title Change of Location, provides: 1.51

> "Held covered, subject to prompt notice and a premium to be arranged, in the event of the named storage vessel proceeding outside the limits of the area specified in this insurance."

This somewhat special cover is customarily provided subject to the named storage vessel remaining within the sea and territorial limits specified in the policy. The storage vessel is off cover if she proceeds outside the prescribed limits, but the existence of the h/c clause enables the assured to arrange additional cover should it be necessary to breach the limitations, but subject to the conditions specified.

Another example is provided by Institute Container Clauses—Time, 1.1.87, 1.52
Clause 9, styled Limits Clause in the margin, which provides:

> "Each container is covered, including whilst on deck, within the sea and territorial limits specified in the Schedule below. Breach of these limits 'held covered' at a premium to be agreed, subject to prompt notice being given to the Underwriters."

The import of the clause is reasonably clear and requires little elaboration. The insured containers are covered only when operated within the sea and territorial limits specified. The h/c clause puts in place an additional cover facility for an assured who wishes to use insured containers outside the prescribed limits, subject to giving prompt notice and the payment of additional premium.

1D.1(vi) Employment limitations

The insured risk may be restricted not only to a specific subject-matter, but also to 1.53
situations when the subject-matter is being employed in specific ways. The positive and negative aspects of this proposition may be defined in the policy. When the subject-matter is being employed otherwise than in a specified way there is no cover, but the limitation may again be overcome by an appropriately drafted h/c clause.

With regard to hull and machinery insurance on time and voyage terms the purpose 1.54
of the Navigation clause, which appears as Clause 1 in the relevant Institute Clauses—Hulls, is to indicate generally circumstances relating to the use and employment of the insured ship when cover does and does not prevail. For the purpose of the present discussion Clause 1.4 is particularly illuminating. It provides:

> "In the event of the Vessel being employed in trading operations which entail cargo loading or discharging at sea from or into another vessel (not being harbour or inshore craft) no claim shall be recoverable under this insurance for loss or damage to the Vessel or liability to any other

82. As on the facts in *The Litsion Pride* [1985] 1 Lloyd's Rep. 437, considered *supra* under the title "The Problem of Characterisation", para. 1.18.

83. *Supra* fn.34.

> vessel arising from such loading or discharging operations, including whilst approaching, lying alongside and leaving, unless previous notice that the Vessel is to be employed in such operations has been given to the Underwriters and any amended terms of cover and any additional premium required by them have been agreed."

The gist of the clause is to make it clear that the insured vessel is not covered with regard to loss, damage and third party liability when engaged in transhipment of cargo at sea in the course of the vessel's trading operations. Transhipment of cargo not in the course of trade, and lightering operations are not within the clause. The vessel is off cover not only during the transhipment operation but also whilst approaching, lying alongside and leaving the transhipment place.

The limitation on the policy cover is not absolute, for the clause also makes provision for additional cover to embrace transhipment operations of the kind contemplated by the clause, subject to giving previous notice and agreeing to amended terms and additional premium, if demanded. The clause does not expressly declare itself to be a h/c clause, but again it is undoubtedly such a clause.

1.55 Another technique for the regulation of the use of the subject-matter of insurance is to incorporate appropriately drafted warranties into the policy.[84]

1D.2 Voidable risks

1.56 Simply because an insurer agrees to underwrite a risk it does not follow that the insurer's commitment is thereafter inescapable. There are many forms of conduct which may render marine insurance contracts voidable and, therefore, also the risk underwritten. The principal causes are where an assured is in breach of the general duty of utmost good faith, or of the particular duty of pre-contract disclosure, or of the pre-contact duty not to misrepresent material facts and circumstances.[85]

1.57 In the face of a voidable risk, the underwriter has an election whether to affirm or avoid the risk. Once made the election is irrevocable. An affirmation, which may be express or implied, erases the preceding breach of duty and the contract stands valid, whereas avoidance operates retroactively and expunges the contract of marine insurance. The contract is totally aborted and everything done under the assumption that a valid contract existed is at least liable to be unravelled.[86]

1.58 The legitimate avoidance of a risk represents an effective defence to an underwriter, though, in the absence of fraud, there is an obligation to return the premium.[87] For assureds and their brokers this area of the law represents dangerous ground for the remedy is not tied to fraudulent or negligent conduct. An assured may be honest and blameless, and yet be in breach of a duty which renders the risk voidable.[88] Where an assured is in breach of the duty of utmost good faith and the policy is avoided, then not

84. See, for example, Institute Yacht Clauses 1.11.85, Clause 3.2.

85. The doctrine of utmost good faith is examined in more detail *infra* under the title "Application of the Doctrine of Utmost Good Faith", para. 1.121 *et seq.*

86. For recent judicial analysis of the points made in this paragraph see *Manifest Shipping Company Ltd v. Uni-Polaris Shipping Company Ltd and Others, The Star Sea* [2001] 2 W.L.R. 170; *K/S Merc-Scandia XXXXII v. Certain Lloyd's Underwriters* [2000] E.W.C.A. Civ. 1275; [2001] 2 Lloyd's Rep. 563.

87. Section 84(3)(a).

88. *Carter v. Boehm* (1766) 3 Burr. 1905; *Ionides v. Pacific Fire & Marine Insurance Co.* (1871) LR 6 Q.B. 674. *Container Transport International Inc. v. Oceanus Mutual Indemnity Association (Bermuda) Ltd* [1984] 1 Lloyd's Rep. 476; *Pan Atlantic Insurance Co. Ltd v. Pine Top Insurance Co. Ltd* [1995] A.C. 501.

only may the immediate claim be justifiably rejected by the underwriters, but there is also the risk that payments made under any earlier settlements will have to be returned.[89]

The question of the voidablity of a marine risk is not so touched by considerations of public policy as to be incapable of subjugation to the will or agreement of the parties. It has already been seen that it is open to the underwriter to overlook conduct which renders the policy voidable and affirm the contract. So also by express contract the remedy of avoidance may be re-fashioned or even excluded.[90] It follows that in principle there can be no objection to a circumstance which renders a marine risk voidable being designated by the parties a held covered event, but there is little or no evidence of such clauses playing a significant part in contemporary practice. *1.59*

Under former editions of the Institute Cargo Clauses, a clause was adopted which is of potential relevance to the current discussion, and which has already been noted earlier in this contribution,[91] the surviving equivalent of which is Clause 10 of the Institute Cargo Clauses (A), (B) and (C). An example of the clause is provided by Institute Cargo Clauses (FPA) 1.1.63, Clause 4, known as the Change of Voyage clause. It provides: *1.60*

> "Held covered at a premium to be arranged in case . . . of any omission or error in the description of the interest vessel or voyage."

The clause, in the first place, relates to "interest (meaning subject-matter of the insurance)[92] vessel or voyage" which are all individual criteria relevant to the definition of the risk which the underwriter has assumed.[93] And second to any "omission or error in the description" thereof. The word "description" is ambiguous. It must embrace words defining the "interest" insured. But more broadly it could also include words describing the attributes and qualities of the "interest" insured. The distinction between words of identification and words describing the identified subject-matter may represent a very fine line, yet it is the kind of distinction which the law is accustomed to having to draw. It is, however, uncertain on the basis of the authorities, such as they are, whether the distinction is of significance. The trend in the cases appears to have been to take a broad view of the concept of words of description and effectively to merge the bifurcation suggested above, but subject to the limitation that words describing attributes and qualities are only relevant if they also serve to identify the subject-matter of the insurance. But even when subject to this limitation, any "omission or error" relating to the "description" of the "interest" is capable of being a material non-disclosure or misrepresentation.

In *Hewitt Bros v. Wilson*[94] the clause in issue was not in the precise same terms as Clause 4 above and provided: *1.61*

> "In the event of . . . any incorrect definition of the interest insured it is agreed to hold the assured covered at a premium (if any) to be arranged."

89. *Manifest Shipping Company Ltd v. Uni-Polaris Shipping Company Ltd and Others, The Star Sea* [2001] 2 W.L.R. 170, 187, *per* Lord Hobhouse.

90. *Toomey and Others v. Eagle Star Insurance Co. Ltd (No. 2)* [1995] 2 Lloyd's Rep. 88; *HIH Casualty and General Insurance Ltd v. New Hampshire Insurance Co. and Others* [2001] 2 Lloyd's Rep. 161.

91. *Supra* under the title "Subject-matter insured", para. 1.26 *et seq.*

92. *Supra* fn.48.

93. *Supra* under the title "Risks outside the policy cover", para. 1.25 *et seq.*

94. [1915] 2 K.B. 739.

On the facts of the case the interest of the insurance was defined simply as "Machinery" and insured against all risks. The assured failed to disclose that some of the machinery shipped was second-hand. It was accepted that this amounted to a material non-disclosure which rendered the policy voidable subject to the h/c clause. It was held that the h/c clause was available to the assured who could, notwithstanding the non-disclosure, maintain cover subject to the terms of the h/c clause.

The reasoning of Bailhache J, which was affirmed by the Court of Appeal, is instructive. The h/c clause, on its proper construction, did not apply to every non-disclosure of material fact, but only those that affected the definition of the subject-matter of the insurance and rendered it incorrect. Moreover, and again as a matter of construction, the h/c clause did not apply to dishonest conduct such as intentional misdescription or concealment. It was confined to circumstances where the assured had made a mistake or acted under a misapprehension.

On the facts of the case there had been a mistake or misapprehension, for although the assured had intentionally described the interest insured as "Machinery", while being perfectly aware that at least part of the machinery was second-hand, nonetheless the assured had acted in the belief that this represented a sufficiently correct definition of the interest insured and, therefore, had acted honestly throughout. In the result, the assured could rely on the h/c clause.

1.62 This approach was followed by Donaldson J in *Liberian Insurance Agency Inc. v. Mosse.*[95] The precise issue in the case was whether Liberian brokers who had discharged by payment a judgment made in Liberia in respect of cargo damage, as they were obliged to do under Liberian law, could claim an indemnity against London underwriters. A central question in the litigation was whether the underwriters would have been obliged to indemnify the assured if a claim had been made directly against the underwriters, so that it could be said that the Liberian brokers, in making payment under the Liberian judgment, were discharging a liability of the underwriters. In the context of the contemporary law, the brokers were attempting to establish a restitutionary entitlement.

On the facts of the case, a miscellaneous parcel of enamelware was insured in respect of a voyage from Hong Kong to Monrovia. The parcel included plates, mugs, basins, ladles, dishes, bowls and spittoons. The items were packed in 3,545 wooden cases and 823 cartons. The risk was offered to the market under the description "Enamelware (cups and plates) in wooden cases" and valued at $168,956, which represented the CIF price plus 10 per cent. As required by the documentary credit the parcel was insured under Institute Cargo Clauses (All Risks), 1.5.55, Clause 4 of which provided, "'Held covered' at a premium to be arranged in case of change of voyage or any omission or error in the description of the interest vessel or voyage".

Donaldson J was satisfied that there had been misrepresentation and/or non-disclosure in placing the risk. There had been a failure to disclose that the cargo was in part packed in cartons; that a significant portion of the enamelware had been touched up by overpainting and that the parcel was an end stock or job lot and had been purchased at a cheap price. All these considerations were judged to be material to the writing of the risk, and the court was satisfied that if any one had been disclosed a

95. [1977] 2 Lloyd's Rep. 560.

prudent underwriter would have refused to write the risk on "all risks" terms or would have imposed FPA conditions. Consequently the underwriters would have been entitled to avoid the policy unless the assured was entitled to invoke the h/c clause.

As for the h/c clause, Donaldson J was satisfied, following authority, that the reference to "interest" was an allusion to the subject matter of the insurance and not the assured's insurable interest in the subject-matter; and further that the clause only applied to misdescriptions or non-disclosures relating to the subject-matter. But it had no application when an intent to deceive could be established, which on the facts was not the case.

It was held that the h/c clause was *prima facie* applicable, but nonetheless on the special facts of the case it could not avail the assured for it would not have been possible in other regards to satisfy the terms of the clause. In particular, it would not have been possible to fix a new premium at a reasonable commercial rate. This aspect of the subject is returned to later in this contribution. In the upshot, the London underwriters would not have been directly liable under the cargo policy and consequently the Liberian brokers could not establish the essential precondition necessary to succeed under their claim to be indemnified by the London underwriters.

A reflection on this case suggests that Donaldson J appears to have taken a very broad view of words descriptive of the subject matter of the insurance and went some way beyond recognising words that were descriptive solely for the purposes of identification.

Although Clause 4 of the former Institute Cargo Clauses has virtually disappeared from contemporary practice, similar clauses are on occasions found in special covers. An example is provided by Institute FOSFA Supplementary Clause (4) Grade Clause, which is intended for use in conjunction with Institute FOSFA Trades Clauses, and which provides: 1.63

> "Held covered at a premium to be arranged in event of omission or error in description of grade, quality and/or other technical characteristics of the insured commodity, as named in the relevant FOSFA contract."

In the final analysis it will be a question of construction whether the language of a particular h/c clause recognises non-disclosure and misrepresentation as held covered events, and the clauses and cases which have been considered illustrate the difficulties imprecise words can cause. Somewhat analogous issues have arisen about the province of errors and omissions clauses in reinsurance contracts, which have been construed as not embracing non-disclosure and misrepresentation.[96] 1.64

1D.3 Breach of warranties

Of all the terms found in contracts of marine insurance none is more threatening and harsh than the warranty. A warranty, which may be express or implied,[97] is a promise given by the assured by which the assured "undertakes that some particular thing shall or shall not be done, or that some condition shall be fulfilled, or whereby he 1.65

96. *Highlands Insurance Co. v. Continental Insurance Co.* [1987] 1 Lloyd's Rep. 109; *Pan Atlantic Insurance Co. v. Pine Top Insurance Co.* [1995] 1 A.C. 501; *Toomey and Others v. Eagle Star Insurance Co. Ltd (No. 2)* [1995] 2 Lloyd's Rep. 88.

97. Section 33(2).

affirms or negatives the existence of a particular state of facts".[98] Whether a particular term is a warranty is a question of intention which is to be deduced from the proper construction of the words agreed by the parties.[99] There is no requirement that any precise form of words be adopted, but an express warranty must be included in or endorsed on the policy, or included in a document incorporated by reference into the policy.[100]

1.66 There is no requirement that a warranty must be material to the risk and the terms of a warranty must be exactly complied with.[101] The consequences of breach are particularly grave, for from the moment of the breach, the insurer is discharged from liability under the policy.[102] The discharge is automatic and requires no election by the underwriter.[103] The policy is not avoided, with the consequence that it remains valid for the period up to the breach. Even after the breach, the policy remains intact. What is expunged is any prospective liability of the underwriter thereunder. The rights of the underwriter survive.[104] These consequences flow even if the breach of warranty is remedied and complied with before loss is suffered.[105]

1.67 A warranty is perceived in legal analysis as a condition precedent to the underwriter's liability under a policy.[106] It represents the basis on which the cover is given, and, in turn, this perception serves to explain the prejudicial consequences to an assured of breach of warranty.[107]

1.68 A breach of warranty may be waived by the underwriter,[108] and it is also possible for the parties to determine by contract what are to be consequences of a breach of warranty.[109] To this extent the severity of the law may be assuaged.

1.69 Another way of allaying the severity of the law is by making breach of warranty a held covered event, and this practice is frequently followed. A broad variety of warranties are to be found in the Institute Clauses and others may be introduced on the placement slip. Without a special provision to hold covered in the face of breach of warranty, the assured is almost entirely at the mercy of his underwriters.

1.70 A clear and significant example is provided by clause 3 of the Institute Time Clauses—Hulls, 1.11.95. The clause appears under the sub-title "Breach of Warranty" and provides:

---

98. Section 33(1). See, further, Chapters 5 and 6.

99. Section 35(1). In *Thomson v. Weems* (1884) 9 App. Cas. 671, at p.684, Lord Blackburn indicated, "In policies of marine insurance I think it is settled by authority that any statement of a fact bearing upon the risk introduced into the written policy is, by whatever words and in whatever place, to be construed as a warranty . . .".

100. Section 35(2).

101. Section 33(3).

102. Section 33(3).

103. *Bank of Nova Scotia v. Hellenic Mutual War Risks Association (Bermuda) Ltd, The Good Luck* [1992] A.C. 233. See also *State Trading Corporation of India Ltd v. M. Goledetz Ltd* [1989] 2 Lloyd's Rep. 277, 287, *per* Kerr LJ.

104. *Bank of Nova Scotia v. Hellenic Mutual War Risks Association (Bermuda) Ltd, The Good Luck, ibid.* at pp.202–203 *per* Lord Goff.

105. Section 34(2).

106. *Bank of Nova Scotia v. Hellenic Mutual War Risk Association (Bermuda) Ltd, The Good Luck, ibid.*, at p.202, *per* Lord Goff.

107. *HIH Casualty and General Insurance Ltd v. New Hampshire Insurance Co. and Others* [2001] 2 Lloyd's Rep. 161, 185, *per* Rix LJ.

108. Section 34(3).

109. Section 33(3) declares the consequence of a breach of warranty to be "subject to any express provision in the policy".

> "'Held Covered' in case of any breach of warranty as to cargo, trade, locality, towage, salvage services or date of sailing, provided notice be given to the Underwriters immediately after receipt of advices and any amended terms of cover and any additional premium required by them be agreed."

This clause is widely adopted in the Institute Clauses and its drafting attracts several observations. It does not apply to all warranties but only those specified, whether express or arising by implication, and then only to the extent they are embodied in the marine policy. In Institute Time Clause—Hulls, 1.11.95, express warranties with regard to towage and salvage are to be found in Clause 1.1, but others may be introduced by special agreement or by implication from the provisions of the Marine Insurance Act 1906. Some of the undertakings given by the assured in Clause 4 relating to the classification of the insured ship are probably warranties, but they are not included: nor is the warranty relating to additional insurances set out in Clause 22.2. But otherwise the procedural and substantive provisions of the clause are quite standard.

A similar but less comprehensive h/c clause is found in Institute War and Strikes Clauses Hulls—Time, 1.11.95. Clause 2 provides: *1.71*

> "'Held Covered' in case of breach of warranty as to towage or salvage service provided notice be given to the Underwriters immediately after receipt of advices and any additional premium required by them be agreed."

The clause is more restrictive, for it is confined to breaches of warranty relating to towage and salvage services. The conditions capable of being attached are also less demanding. The underwriter may only demand additional premium; the conditions of the policy cover cannot be amended.

Held covered clauses of the kind here under consideration are not confined to time policies but also appear in voyage policies. Clause 2 of the Institute Voyage Clauses (Hulls), 1.11.95, provides: *1.72*

> "Held covered in case of . . . any breach of warranty as to towage or salvage services, provided notice be given to Underwriters immediately after receipt of advices and any amended terms of cover and any additional premium required by them agreed."

Again the clause is restrictive for it is confined to breach of warranties relating to towage and salvage, but otherwise the demandable amended cover relates to both premium and conditions.

Beyond the examples offered by the Institute Clauses, the case of *Greenock Steamship Co. Ltd v. Maritime Insurance Co. Ltd*[110] provides a particularly useful illustration of the interaction between a h/c clause and breach of warranty. A h/c clause in a voyage policy provided, "'held covered' in case of any breach of warranty . . . at a premium to be hereafter arranged". The insured ship sailed on one stage of her voyage, from Montevideo to St Vincent, insufficiently coaled and consequently she was in breach of the implied warranty of seaworthiness. In the result the underwriters ceased to be on risk once the vessel sailed from Montevideo subject to the applicability of the h/c clause. The clause applied generally to "any breach of warranty" and Bigham J held that these general words included the implied warranty *1.73*

110. [1903] 1 K.B. 367.

of seaworthiness. Once the breach was discovered it was open to the assured to demand the additional cover offered under the clause subject to any additional premium commensurate with the new risk that might be exacted by the underwriters. Significantly, Bigham J held that the h/c clause continued to be available to the assured even if the breach of warranty was not discovered until after the loss occurred. The decision of Bigham J was affirmed on appeal, although the Court of Appeal confined itself to the question of seaworthiness and did not address the proper construction of the h/c clause.

1.74 There may be a doubt whether a h/c clause is capable of applying to a breach of warranty which the assured, at the time the risk is accepted, knows is certain to occur. This is to be distinguished from the situation where the assured appreciates that a breach of warranty may occur as a deliberate result of the way the insured ship is managed (or navigated) and which does not represent a position of any difficulty. The doubt arises, it would seem, by analogy with the way h/c clauses are construed in relation to voyage deviations.[111] If a limitation does exist it is suggested that it is one of construction and not law. It would seem that there is nothing in principle to prevent an appropriately drafted h/c clause from applying to breach of warranties which the assured knows are certain to occur.

1D.4 Breach of policy terms not being warranties

1.75 In marine insurance, and probably in insurance generally, there has been something resembling a historical fixation with warranties, with the consequence that alternative characterisations were little developed. Over the last two decades the position has begun to change radically, with it being recognised increasingly that the terms of insurance contracts may mirror those found in contracts generally.[112] In contemporary law, therefore, it is quite plainly recognised that the characterisation of the terms of an insurance contract is a question of construction, with the court concerned to divine objectively the intention of the parties from the words they have agreed in their contract.[113]

Beyond traditional insurance warranties and terms defining the risk and exclusions, a term of a contract of marine insurance may be characterised in various ways.

1.76 It may be a condition precedent to the liability of the underwriter on a claim under the policy.[114] This is to be contrasted with a term which is a condition precedent the policy or the continuation of the policy[115] or the liability of the underwriter under the policy.[116] If the condition is not satisfied, the underwriter may reject the claim, but otherwise the policy remains in place, as also does the liability of the underwriter

111. For a general survey, see, Arnould's *Law of Marine Insurance and Average* (Vol. 1) (16th edn.), Mustill and Gilman (1981, Stevens & Son), Chapter 14.

112. *K/S Merc-Scandia XXXXII v. Certain Lloyd's Underwriters and Others* [2001] E.W.C.A. Civ. 1275, para. 13 *per* Longmore LJ, [2001] 2 Lloyd's Rep. 563.

113. *Virk v. Gan Life Holdings plc* [2000] Ll. I.R. Rep. 159, 162 *per* Potter LJ. See also *Hiddle v. National Fire and Mutual Insurance Co. of New Zealand* [1896] A.C. 372.

114. See Clarke, *The Law of Insurance Contracts* (3rd edn. LLP Ltd), p.521, n.9.

115. *Cf. The Zeus V. Zeus Tradition Marine Ltd v. Bell* [2000] 2 Lloyd's Rep. 587.

116. Which will probably be analysed as a warranty; see, *supra*, para. 1.65 *et seq.*

under the policy. Procedural stipulations and conditions relating to the making of a claim under the policy are often construed as being condition precedents of this kind.[117]

It may alternatively be a condition, intermediate term or warranty[118] in the traditional contractual senses of those terms. In respect of a breach of any of these terms damages is available if loss can be established. But the same is not true of the right to accept the breach as repudiatory and so terminate the contract, with the consequence that the contract is expunged prospectively. This consequence only arises if the term breached is a condition; or in the case of a serious breach of an intermediate term, the seriousness of the breach being judged by reference to the nature of the breach or the consequences of the breach. In these two instances the innocent contractor has the right to elect either to accept the breach as repudiatory or affirm the contract, but in each case the right to damages remains. When this analysis is applied to insurance contracts it provides ways by which it is open to an underwriter to terminate cover by accepting a breach of a policy term as repudiatory. The significant contrast with breach of warranty, is that the cover is terminated prospectively only; there is no retrospective avoidance.[119] 1.77

In one further regard it may be that a term in an insurance contract may be characterised in a way that has no application in general contract law. A term may exist, the breach of which, when seriously prejudicial to the interests of the underwriter, entitles the underwriter to reject the resulting claim but without it being repudiatory of the contract as a whole.[120] 1.78

In *The Litsion Pride*[121] the obligation of the assured to give information to the underwriters under a War Risks Trading Warranties clause was construed not as being a condition precedent to the additional cover but as a contractual obligation, which Hirst J appears to have been prepared to characterise as an intermediate term. In *K/S Merc-Scandia XXXXII v. Certain Lloyds Underwriters and Others*[122] an obligation in a liability policy to keep underwriters fully advised in the event of an occurrence that might result in a claim was accepted as being a clause the serious breach of which entitled the underwriters to reject the claim, but without it otherwise being repudiatory of the whole contract. In the Court of Appeal there appears to have existed an inclination towards the acceptance of the possibility that the clause might have been an intermediate term. 1.79

It is clear that it is open to an assured to protect himself against the adverse effect of the breach of any category of contractual term considered above by obtaining the agreement of the underwriter to treat the breach as a held covered event. In practice 1.80

117. *Cf. Pioneer Concrete (UK) Ltd v. National Employer's Mutual General Insurance Assn Ltd* [1985] 2 All E.R. 395; *Virk v. Gan Life Holdings plc* [2000] Ll.I.R. Rep. 159.

118. In relation to an insurance contract, a warranty is often described as a mere condition, but whatever the language used, breach of such a term sounds in damages only: see, *Re Bradley and Essex and Suffolk Indemnity Society* [1912] 1 K.B. 415; and the argument in *Svenska Handelsbanken v. Sun Alliance and London Insurance plc* [1996] 1 Lloyd's Rep. 519.

119. For a review of the law, see *K/S Merc-Scandia XXXXII v. Certain Lloyd's Underwriters and Others* [2001] E.W.C.A. Civ. 1275, para. 13, *per* Longmore LJ, [2001] 2 Lloyd's Rep. 563.

120. *Alfred McAlpine plc v. BAI (Run-Off) Ltd* [2000] 1 Lloyd's Rep. 437; *K/S Merc-Scandia XXXXII v. Certain Lloyd's Underwriters and Others, ibid.*

121. [1985] 1 Lloyd's Rep. 437.

122. [2001] E.W.C.A. Civ. 1275, [2001] 2 Lloyd's Rep. 563.

this does not appear to be done. The Institute Clauses do not appear to go this far, but it is not possible to comment on the contemporary practice of brokers. The reason may be the fairly recent development of this area of the law and, therefore, the possibility that the impact of the breach of policy terms other than warranties has yet to be keenly felt in the market.

1E CONSTRUCTION OF H/C CLAUSES

1.81 The issue of whether a h/c clause is applicable, and also the respective rights and obligations of assured and underwriter under the clause will depend on the language adopted by the parties and its proper construction. The drafting of h/c clauses does vary and this is true also of those found in the Institute Clauses; and, of course, brokers' h/c clauses may be wholly ad hoc.[123] It follows that the first step to be taken when considering the applicability of a h/c clause is to have regard to the precise words used, and the second is to determine the proper construction of the adopted words.[124]

1.82 A h/c clause in a marine policy is part of a contractual agreement entered into by commercial parties. The parties are invariably mature commercial people or entities with access to expert advice and who act through experienced and professional brokers. There is, therefore, no reason why h/c clauses should attract any special consideration when it comes to the question of their proper construction. There is every reason for thinking that they are to be construed in the same way as commercial contractual provisions generally.

1.83 When addressing a question of construction the function of the court is to ascertain the intention of the parties from the words used, taking into account the factual matrix and purpose of the contract under consideration.[125] Contracts do not exist in a void; they must be examined in the context in which they were entered into.[126] The factual matrix is a very broad concept and includes anything that may influence the way contractual words are to be understood,[127] but it does not include the previous negotiations of the parties,[128] their subjective declaration of intention,[129] and post-contract conduct.[130] The process is objective, the test being what meaning a reasonable person with access to the agreed words of the parties and to the facts relating to the wider context of the agreement would give to the agreement.[131] There is a weighty presumption that contracting parties intend that the agreed words should bear their "natural and ordinary meaning",[132] but the presumption may be displaced by the wider context or when it is recognised that the parties have fallen into error in

123. *Cf. Thames and Mersey Marine Insurance Co. Ltd v. HT Van Laun & Co.* [1917] 2 K.B. 48.

124. *Liberian Insurance Agency Inc. v. Mosse* [1977] 2 Lloyd's Rep. 560, 566, *per* Donaldson J; *The Litsion Pride* [1985] 1 Lloyd's Rep. 437, 467–471, *per* Hirst J.

125. *Abuthnott v. Fagan, Deeny, Goodawalker (No. 2)* [1994] 3 Re LR 168, 171–172; *Reardon Smith Line Ltd v. Yngvar Hansen-Tangen* [1976] 1 W.L.R. 989; [1976] 2 Lloyd's Rep. 621.

126. *Prenn v. Simmonds* [1971] 1 W.L.R. 1381, 1385, *per* Lord Wilberforce.

127. *Kingscroft Insurance Co. Ltd and Others v. Nissan Fire & Marine Insurance Co. Ltd (No. 2)* [1999] Ll. I.R. Rep. 603, 613, *per* Moore-Bick J; *Investors Compensation Scheme Ltd v. West Bromwich Building Society etc* [1998] 1 W.L.R. 896, 912, *per* Lord Hoffmann.

128. *Wickman Machine Tool Sales Ltd v. Schuler* [1974] A.C. 235.

129. *The Aragon* [1975] 2 Lloyd's Rep. 216, 221, *per* Donaldson J (as he then was).

130. *Whitworth Street Estates Ltd v. James Miller and Partners Ltd* [1970] A.C. 583.

131. *Investors Compensation Scheme Ltd v. West Bromwich Building Society etc* [1998] 1 W.L.R. 896, 912, *per* Lord Hoffmann; *BCCI v. Ali* [2001] 2 W.L.R. 735, 749, *per* Lord Hoffmann.

132. *National Bank of Shajah v. Dellborg* (Court of Appeal, unreported, 9 July, 1997). *Charter Reinsurance Co. Ltd v. Fagan* [1997] A.C. 313, 384, *per* Lord Mustill.

their choice of words or grammatical syntax.[133] But the process has its limitations and, in the guise of construction, it is not open to a court to improve or re-write the contract of the parties.[134] Where the parties have failed to use words to indicate their true contractual intention, the remedy is an order of rectification and not judicial creativity.[135]

The modern approach to the construction of commercial contracts is mature, commercially sensitive and built on a strong foundation of common sense. The early authorities did not always display these qualities and such authorities must now probably be viewed with caution. *Hewitt Bros v. Wilson*,[136] decided in 1915, is an early case which anticipates, but yet falls short of, the modern approach. The precise h/c clause before the court has been considered previously[137] and when it came to construing the clause Lord Reading CJ expressed the opinion:[138] 1.84

> "We must ... construe the language of this clause according to the recognised canons of construction, even if we think that the meaning thereby obtained is unreasonable."

No objection can be taken to the reference to the recognised canons of construction, though their nature has probably changed in the intervening years. But the willingness to apply these canons even if they result in an unreasonable conclusion is a position a contemporary commercial judge would be reluctant to accept. In contemporary law, the acknowledged canons would not be elevated to such a dominant position. They exist to assist the process of ascertaining the intention of the parties, not to usurp it. Ultimately, every recognised canon of construction may yield to the fundamental goal of determining the intention of the parties from the words used and the context in which they have been used. In the words of Aiken J,[139] "although 'rules' of construction are a guide to the intention of the parties, they are not the masters of the parties' intention".

A contemporary commercial judge would also be reluctant to accept a construction which leads to an unreasonable conclusion as representing the true intention of the parties, unless the words were incapable of an alternative construction. The prevailing judicial approach is to be found in the much relied on dictum of Lord Reid in *Wickman Machine Tool Sales Ltd v. Schuler*.[140] He said:[141] 1.85

> "The fact that a particular construction leads to a very unreasonable result must be a relevant consideration. The more unreasonable the result the more unlikely it is that the parties can have intended it, and if they do intend it the more necessary it is that they shall make that intention abundantly clear."

The *dictum* exudes common sense but it also emphasises that there is no rule against unreasonableness; only a rule that an unreasonable construction will be accepted only if compelled by the words used by the parties.

---

133. *Kingscroft Insurance Co. Ltd and Others v. Nissan Fire and Marine Insurance Co. Ltd (No. 2)* [1999] Ll. I.R. Rep. 603, 613–614, *per* Moore-Bick J.
134. *Charter Reinsurance Co. Ltd v. Fagan, supra.*
135. *Kingscroft Insurance Co. Ltd and Others and Nissan Fire & Marine Insurance Co. Ltd (No. 2), supra.*
136. [1915] 2 K.B. 739.
137. *Supra*, fn.94.
138. *Ibid.*, at pp.743–744.
139. *HIH Casualty and General Insurance Ltd v. Chase Manhattan Bank* [2001] 1 All E.R. (Comm.) 719, 743.
140. [1974] A.C. 235.
141. *Ibid.*, at p.251.

1F THE OPERATION OF H/C CLAUSES

1F.1 Introduction

1.86 The additional cover provided by h/c clauses is not a matter of invocation *simpliciter*. The clauses stipulate conditions which must be satisfied by the invoking assured, and these conditions are in the nature of conditions precedent to the underwriter's obligation to provide additional cover.[142] If the conditions are not satisfied, the underwriter is not obliged to provide the additional cover. Beyond this, there is no notion of breach of contract giving the underwriter a remedy in damages. The condition precedents are in their nature absolute obligations. Either they are satisfied or they are not; questions of degree do not arise.

The requirement of notice is universal and in this contribution notice has been identified as an essential prerequisite if a clause is to be properly characterised as a h/c clause.[143] Notice represents the trigger by which a h/c clause is activated. The further conditions which may be prescribed are a matter of contract, but in practice the parties never go beyond vesting in the underwriter the right to demand additional premium and/or amended terms of cover. The former right is invariably present, but the latter less so.

The invocation of h/c clauses may give rise to difficulties where there are co-insurers. A common and effective method of avoiding potential difficulties is by agreeing a "leading underwriter agreement", whereby the leading underwriter(s) receives notice and agrees the level of additional premium and/or new terms of cover on behalf of the following co-insurers.[144]

It is now proposed to consider in greater depth each of the identified conditions precedent.

1F.2 Notice

1.87 The assured claims his right to additional cover by giving valid notice in compliance with the stipulations set out in the h/c clause. In the absence of an express provision the requirement of notice will be implied.[145] The reasons served by giving notice have been considered earlier.[146]

1.88 The requirement of notice raises four associated issues, namely: the question of the substance of the notice; the question of the communication of the notice; the question of the form of the notice; and the question of the time within which notice must be given. The answers to all of these questions will derive from the proper construction of the express or implied provisions of the h/c clause in question.

---

142. *The Litsion Pride* [1985] 1 Lloyd's Rep. 437, 463 *et seq per* Hirst J. See also *Mentz, Decker and Co. v. Maritime Insurance Co.* [1910] 1 K.B. 132.

143. See *supra* under the title, "The Problem of Characterisation", para. 1.9 *et seq.*

144. Though how precisely a "leading underwriter clause" is to be legally analysed remains a question of some discussion, see, *Roadworks (1952) Ltd v. Charman* [1994] 2 Lloyd's Rep. 99; *Mander v. Commercial Union Assurance Co. plc* [1998] Lloyd's Rep. 1R9; *Unum Life v. Ege Sigorta CA*, July 2001, unreported.

145. *Greenock Steamship Co. v. Maritime Insurance Co.* [1903] 1 K.B. 367; *Hood v. West End Motor Car Parking Co.* [1917] 2 K.B. 38(CA); *Thames and Mersey Marine Insurance Co. Ltd v. HT Van Laun & Co.* [1917] 2 K.B. 48 (HL).

146. See *supra* under the title "The Problem of Characterisation", para. 1.9 *et seq.*

With regard to the matter of substance, the wider context dictates that the notice must indicate to the underwriters that the assured is claiming the right to be held covered. On occasions this is an express requirement.[147] No precise form of words is required; it is sufficient if on their proper construction the words used by the assured are sufficient to make it clear to the underwriters that the assured is claiming the additional cover provided for under the h/c clause. In the words of Donaldson J[148] (as he then was), to take advantage of a h/c clause the assured "must give notice to underwriters expressly or impliedly seeking cover in accordance with the clause". Although unlikely to be this curt in practice, a bare notice, provided it is understood to be a held covered notice, appears to carry the implied representation that the assured is seeking the additional cover available under the clause. 1.89

As this dictum also indicates, the notice must be given to the underwriters. What amounts to an effective communication between parties standing in a contractual relationship is a question with many dimensions, with the answer very often depending on the facts and circumstances of individual cases. 1.90

It is unnecessary to pursue all the possibilities in the present context, for in practice this aspect of the operation of h/c clauses appears to be unproblematical. It is likely that an assured would satisfy his obligation if it can be shown that notice has been delivered or communicated to the underwriters' usual place of business. A notice communicated to an agent authorised to receive notice on behalf of the underwriters would quite clearly be sufficient. But if the agent is acting in fraud of his principal and the matter of which he has notice is relevant to the fraud, that knowledge is not to be imputed to the principal.[149] Questions of agency could arise when notice is given to a broker or to one co-insurer, though the agency question is likely to have been expressly or impliedly addressed when a "leading underwriter agreement" has been entered into. When the underwriter is a corporate entity, which is likely to be the case predominantly, the question may arise how notice may effectively be given to such an entity. This again may raise a question of agency, or the need to identify a person who can be recognised as representing the company, so that notice given to that person may be regarded as notice given to the company. In this context, however, it may be unnecessary to identify anyone occupying an elevated position in the company, or who can be regarded as representing the directing mind and will of the company. It may well be sufficient if notice is given to an employee employed in the business of providing and managing insurance.[150]

Unless there is an express stipulation in the h/c clause regulating the matter, there is no requirement as to form. The notice may be communicated in any form whatsoever, and also through intermediaries, provided it amounts to an effective communication. 1.91

In practice most attention is given to the time within which notice is to be given, with contemporary h/c clauses containing a number of differently worded express provisions. In the event of a h/c clause being silent on the point, as were many of the 1.92

---

147. For example, Institute Cargo Clauses (A), (B) and (C), Clause 9.
148. *Liberian Insurance Agency Inc. v. Mosse* [1977] 2 Lloyd's Rep. 560, 566.
149. *Belmont Finance Corp. Ltd v. Williams Furniture Ltd* [1979] Ch. 250, 261–262, *per* Buckley LJ.
150. *Cf. P & W Syndicates v. P & W Reinsurers* [1996] 1 Lloyd's Rep. 241, where the interpretation of s.18(1) was in issue.

older clauses, the implication is read into the clause that notice has to be given within a reasonable time of learning of the held covered event.[151] What is a reasonable time is a question of fact to be decided on the facts and circumstances of each case.[152] The appropriate approach has been enunciated in the following terms by Donaldson J:[153]

> "What time is reasonable will depend on all the circumstances. Thus, if the assured learns the true facts while the risk is still current, a reasonable time will usually be a shorter period than if this occurs when the adventure has already ended. If the assured learns the true facts when the insured property is in the grip of a peril, which is likely to cause loss or damage, a reasonable time will be very short indeed."

1.93 In contemporary practice h/c clauses usually make express provision for the time within which notice must be given. The standard obligation is to require notice to be given "promptly"[154] or "immediately"[155] after receipt of advices, and less frequently it is required that notice be given "prior"[156] or "previous"[157] to a specified event. Words such as "promptly" and "immediately" convey the clear indication that once an assured is aware that a held covered event has occurred or will or may occur, notice must be communicated at once and without delay, at the first practicable moment, to the underwriters if additional cover is required.[158] The use of such words also suggests that the toleration shown in some of the older cases when considering the obligation to give notice within a reasonable time is no longer possible under the express language of the contemporary law.[159]

1.94 There would seem to be a clear distinction between an obligation to give "prompt" or "immediate" notice and an obligation to give notice within a reasonable period of time. The latter appears capable of being sensitive to the prevailing circumstances of the assured and consequently of accommodating a degree of delay that would not be entertained when the obligation is defined in terms of the former words. Nonetheless, in *Liberian Insurance Agency Inc. v. Mosse*,[160] Donaldson J appears to suggest that there is no difference between the two formulations. His observations were addressed to the Note which appeared in the former Institute Cargo Clauses, requiring notice under a h/c clause to be given promptly. At the time h/c clauses were frequently silent on the question of notice and, therefore, the requirement of reasonable notice was implied. This produced an ostensible conflict between a substantive h/c provision in the

151. See cases cited in fn.145.

152. Section 88. *Thames and Mersey Marine Insurance Co. Ltd v. H T Van Laun & Co.* [1917] 2 K.B. 48, 51, *per* Lord Halsbury LC, "Reasonableness in such a matter as to the time of giving notice depends of course upon the particular circumstances of the case".

153. *Liberian Insurance Agency Inc. v. Mosse* [1977] 2 Lloyd's Rep. 560, 566.

154. For example, Institute Cargo Clauses (A), (B) and (C), Clauses 9 and 10.

155. For example, Institute War and Strikes Clauses Hulls—Time (1.11.95), Clause 2; Institute Time Clauses Hulls, Port Risks incl. Limited Navigation (20.7.87), Clause 1.2.

156. For example, Institute Time Clauses (Hulls) (1.11.95), Clause 2.

157. For example, Institute Time Clauses (Hulls) (1.11.95), Clause 1.5.

158. For the construction of the word "immediately" in an insurance warranty, see, *Berns & Koppstern Inc. v. Orion Insurance Co. Ltd* [1960] 1 Lloyd's Rep. 276; 1960 AMC 1379 (US Dist. CT).

159. *Mentz, Decker and Co. v. Maritime Insurance Co.* [1910] 1 K.B. 367, where notice was given many months after the ship had been lost. Held to be within time because nothing could have been done by the underwriter following the receipt of the notice. *Thames and Mersey Marine Insurance Co. Ltd v. Van Laun* [1917] 2 K.B. 48n, where a 14-day delay was considered condonable. See also *Greenock Steamship Co. v. Maritime Insurance Co.* [1903] 1 K.B. 367.

160. [1977] 2 Lloyd's Rep. 560.

Clauses and the Note, which in turn brought into issue the legal status of the Note, a question which will be considered later. Donaldson J endeavoured to resolve the conflict by reasoning that prompt notice really meant reasonable notice, and that a notice not promptly given would almost inevitably equally amount to a notice not given within a reasonable time. He said:[161]

"It may be objected that it is unfortunate to use the words 'prompt notice' when what is meant is notice within a reasonable time. However, in the context of a clause which may impose on underwriters, and indirectly upon reinsuring underwriters, risks which they have never specifically accepted, I do not think that notice which is other than prompt could ever be said to be given within a reasonable time. In my judgment, the use of the word 'prompt' is not only justifiable but also desirable in explanation of the obligation which is implicit in the clause itself."

Although the precise issue Donaldson J was addressing has ceased to be one that survives in the contemporary law, nonetheless, even when viewed retrospectively the approach taken is a little curious. The draftsman is scolded for using the word "prompt" when what he intended, or should have intended, was that notice was to be given within a reasonable time. Whatever may be made of this speculation, the word "prompt" was used in the Note and, therefore, that was the word which fell to be construed. The idea of reasonableness is a prominent idea in the law and it is sufficiently understood to suggest that it cannot be confused with the idea of promptness. Promptness conveys an urgency which introduces a demand on personal conduct which goes beyond the requirement of acting reasonably in the context of the prevailing circumstances.

It is necessarily the case that the requirement of notice, whatever the degree of 1.95
expedition with which the notice is to be given, cannot be divorced from knowledge of the "held covered" event. This point is strongly recognised when the phrase "after receipt of advices"[162] or a similar phrase is adopted in the drafting of a h/c clause. In *Liberian Insurance Agency Inc. v. Mosse*, Donaldson J[163] in construing the h/c clause there in issue drew together the elements of knowledge and expedition and observed,

"The assured seeking the benefit of the clause must give prompt notice to the underwriters of his claim to be 'held covered' as soon as he learns of the facts which render it necessary for him to rely upon the clause".

The question next arises, what precisely is meant by knowledge? Obviously, there is 1.96
no difficulty when actual knowledge can be established: but does knowledge extend to include categories of constructive knowledge, such as the knowledge an assured has denied to himself by turning a blind eye, or the knowledge the assured would have acquired had he acted with reasonable competence in the management of his affairs? These wider questions seem to be unanswered by authority, but it is doubtful if the courts would reject out of hand the notion of constructive knowledge, albeit entertaining it very cautiously. It is hard to believe that blind eye or Nelsonian knowledge would not be recognised, for this is knowledge which the assured has

161. At pp.566–567.
162. For example, Institute Time Clauses (Hulls) 1.11.95, Clause 3; Institute Voyage Clauses (Hulls) 1.11.95, Clause 2.
163. *Supra* at p.568.

deliberately denied himself.[164] But great caution is necessary if the attempt is made to relate knowledge to the negligence of the assured, with the argument advanced that an assured is deemed to know that which would have been discovered by making reasonable inquiries, and probably the temptation is to be resisted.[165] The circumstances an assured may find himself in when invoking a h/c clause must not be lost sight of, and it may be that this wider notion of constructive knowledge is also excluded on the proper contruction of such phrases as "on receipt of advices". Where the assured is a corporate entity, as will predominantly be the case, the question will again arise as to whether the knowledge of corporate officers and employees is capable of being regarded as the knowledge of the company itself.

1.97 There does not seem to exist any inherent limitation on the giving of notice unless such a limitation is introduced by the express terms of the h/c clause. The tendency has been to construe h/c clauses unrestrictively, though ultimately all turns on the express terms. Thus, and of great significance, the right to be held covered is not restricted by reference to the occurrence of the loss. In *Greenock Steamship Co. Ltd v. Maritime Insurance Co. Ltd*,[166] Bigham J, at first instance, held that the h/c clause in question held good even though the held covered event was not discovered until a loss had occurred. By implication this also makes it clear that in the absence of an express term to the contrary, notice may be given even though it is not open to the underwriter to protect himself by re-insurance.[167]

1.98 Further, the right to be held covered is not restricted in its exercise to the period of cover. In *Overseas Commodities Ltd v. Style*,[168] McNair J considered it plain on the authorities that a h/c clause could be invoked not only after the occurrence of loss, but also after the period of the policy had expired. But, quite obviously, in all regards the assured must comply with the other requirements relating to the giving of notice which may be stipulated in the h/c clause.

1.99 These principles of construction may of course be displaced or modified by express terms, but there is little evidence of this in contemporary practice. But even when adopted it seems that such an express term will only have this effect if the intent is irresistibly clear. In *Mentz, Decker & Co. v. Maritime Insurance Co.*[169] Hamilton J rejected argument that the use of the phrase "due notice" prevented the assured giving notice after loss had occurred. The phrase could not be read as meaning "that no notice is to be considered 'due' unless it is given at a time when the underwriter can still protect himself by reinsurance".[170]

1.100 Held covered clauses are drafted in a way that at least suggests that they are intended to operate retroactively rather that proactively, in other words the intention appears to be that notice is to be given following and not before the occurrence of a held covered event. When used, the phrase "after receipt of advices" has an element

164. *Cf. The Eurysthenes* [1977] Q.B. 49, 68, *per* Lord Denning, "If a man, suspicious of the truth, turns a blind eye to it, and refrains from inquiry—so that he should not know it for certain—then he is to be regarded as knowing the truth".

165. *Ibid.*, "Negligence in not knowing the truth is not equivalent to knowledge of it".

166. [1903] 1 KB 367, 376. See also *Hewett v. London General Insurance Co.* (1925) 23 LL. L. Rep. 243.

167. *Mentz, Decker & Co. v. Maritime Insurance Co.* [1910] 1 K.B. 132, 135.

168. [1958] 1 Lloyd's Rep. 546,

169. *Supra* fn.167.

170. *Supra*, p.135.

of such a connotation, but it is far from conclusive. Nonetheless, unless the express words suggest the contrary, there would seem to be no justification for construing a typical h/c clause restrictively and confined to the giving of retroactive notice. An owner or manager may become aware in advance of a likely held covered occurrence, and may even consciously take a managerial decision which is certain to result in the occurrence of a held covered event. In these circumstances it will amount to good management to ensure that the additional cover available under the h/c clause is in place in advance, and this would appear to be possible under a typical contemporary h/c clauses. Beyond being possible, it may also be the obligation of the assured. The requirement to give prompt notice may be assessed not only by reference to the knowledge of an assured of a held covered event, but also by reference to the knowledge possessed of an event which it is known will happen.

To return finally to the Note which is a standard feature of the various Institute Cargo Clauses. It declares: 1.101

> "It is necessary for the Assured when they become aware of an event which is 'held covered' under this insurance to give prompt notice to the Underwriters and the right of such cover is dependent upon compliance with this obligation."

The Note reinforces the fact that notice must be promptly given and that prompt notice is a condition precedent to the obligation of the underwriters to provide the additional cover. Although it may be the case that the Note serves a useful function in publicising these important features of a h/c clause, as a matter of law the Note in contemporary practice appears to serve little, if any, purpose. It essentially reproduces what is expressly stipulated in the great majority of h/c clauses found in the Institute Cargo Clauses, and also the legal analysis of such clauses. There is, therefore, harmony between the substantive h/c provisions and the Note. The problem that confronted Donaldson J in *Liberian Insurance Agency Inc. v. Mosse*,[171] which has been considered earlier, does not survive. But, nonetheless, the Note survives and the question of its precise legal significance, therefore, continues to enjoy a currency.

The essential question is whether the Note is part of the contract of marine insurance when the parties have contracted on the basis of one of the Institute Cargo Clauses which incorporates the Note. The Note is quite clearly not one of the numbered clauses, yet it is virtually a standard printed provision which alludes to and is intended to explain the h/c provisions embodied in the numbered clauses which constitute the main substance of the contract. The content of the Note is of material importance to assureds and its appearance cannot be dismissed as incidental or administrative.

In *Liberian Insurance Agency Inc. v. Mosse*,[172] Donaldson J doubted, but without deciding, whether the Note was part of the contract. Donaldson J was greatly influenced by the fact that the Note was not one of the numbered clauses. However, there is no reason for thinking that the precise form in which a provision appears in a commercial contract is conclusive as to the intention of the contracting parties. A provision which appears as a Note may be as much a part of a substantive commercial 1.102

171. [1977] 2 Lloyd's Rep. 560.
172. *Ibid.*, at p.566.

contract as, for example, a marginal statement. Ultimately, it is a question of construction, taking into account the contract as whole. It would appear that a strong argument could be put forward in support of the contractual status of the Note. Nonetheless, the doubt expressed by Donaldson J is probably more justified today than when uttered, for the Note in the contemporary Institute Cargo Clauses is purely declaratory of the terms and effect of h/c clauses embodied in the contract. The absence of conflict renders academic the question of the contractual status of the Note.[173] But even if not contractual, the Note would seem to be part of the wider factual matrix of the contract and, therefore, regard could be had to it when construing the h/c clauses.

1F.3 Additional premium

1.103 A customary feature of a h/c clause is the obligation of the assured to agree additional premium, if demanded by the underwriter, as a condition of the additional cover. The justification for the additional premium derives from the fact that the underwriter is obliged to assume additional risk, beyond that initially agreed in the policy. The same fact establishes the basis for the distinction between additional and policy premium.

1.104 In establishing the obligation to pay additional premium the drafting of h/c clauses may vary. Some make clear the conditional obligation of the assured, with additional premium only payable if demanded by the underwriters, as where the phrase "if required" is used.[174] Others are drafted in a way that appears to suggest that additional premium will be demanded, thereby suggesting that assureds are under an obligation to pay additional premium.[175] Of course, all will depend on the proper construction of the words used, but it may be anticipated that the courts would require very compelling language before accepting that underwriters had lost the right of election. In the case of contemporary h/c clauses, as a general proposition it is probable that underwriters retain a choice whether or not to demand additional premium even if the clause does not make this expressly clear.

1.105 In giving notice to be held covered the assured will, therefore, be aware of the potential obligation to agree additional premium. But beyond establishing an obligation to pay additional premium, the vast preponderance of h/c clauses make no express provision relating to the quantum of the additional premium or the method by which it is to be computed. A small minority of clauses specify an obligation to pay a reasonable premium,[176] but, as will be seen later in the text, this makes little, if any, contribution to an understanding of the obligation. Others may specify for the payment of a pro rata premium,[177] which is a much more precise formula.

1.106 Following the invocation of a h/c clause, in most instances the additional premium payable will be settled by negotiation. Complications may arise when there are

173. See also the Special Note incorporated into the Institute Frozen Foods and Institute Clauses 1.1.86, and the Note incorporated into the Institute Standard Conditions for Cargo Contracts 1.4.82.

174. See, for example, Institute Cargo Clauses (A), (B) and (C), Clause 9.

175. See, for example, Institute Cargo Clauses (A), (B) and (C), Clause 10.

176. See, for example, Average Disbursement Clauses (A) and (B), Clause 3.

177. See, for example, Institute Time Clauses (Hulls) 1.11.95, Clause 2.

co-insurers, but these may be circumvented by agreeing a leading underwriter clause. In the event of dispute or failure to agree, the question may be referred to arbitration or the courts. Until the additional premium is fixed by agreement or otherwise, it would seem that no right of action exists against the assured for any premium amount.[178] The reason for this preclusion, it would seem, is the absence of any sum which can be defined and described as indisputably due.[179] But it would, probably, be possible to assess a minimum premium sum due, which, together with the subsequent development of a more liberal civil jurisdiction to make interim payment orders,[180] may suggest that the legal principle is open to reconsideration. Nonetheless, even if the additional premium cannot be pursued by action until quantum is settled, the underwriter, quite clearly, is on risk from the moment notice is given.

There is also what appears to be the surprising suggestion to be found in authority that an underwriter may demand the payment of additional premium when a held covered event occurs but without any loss subsequently being suffered, even though the assured has not elected to invoke the clause by giving notice. This opinion is expounded by Hamilton J in *Mentz Decker & Co. v. Maritime Insurance Co.*,[181] and where the h/c clause in question, which has been considered earlier in the text, is quite clearly within the characterisation of a h/c clause adopted in this contribution The opinion, however, has subsequently been queried judicially[182] and it is impossible to reconcile the opinion with the analysis of a h/c clause developed in this contribution.[183] In principle it would seem that an assured is not under any obligation to pay additional premium until notice is given and the held covered provision is thereby invoked. Of course, the position may be different where the clause requiring the giving of notice or information to the underwriter is not strictly a h/c clause.[184] 1.107

Where the parties are in dispute or fail to agree an additional premium there is no risk of the h/c agreement being nullified on the ground that it represents an agreement to agree, which in English law does not amount to a valid contractual agreement.[185] This possible argument is anticipated and countered by section 31(2) of the Marine Insurance Act 1906, which provides: 1.108

> "Where an insurance is effected on the terms that an additional premium is to be arranged in any given event, and that event happens but no arrangement is made, then a reasonable additional premium is payable."

The sub-section appears to have been drafted with h/c clauses directly in mind, though its application is not restricted to such clauses.[186] The phrase "additional premium" is to be understood in the sense developed in the text, namely premium

178. *Kirby v. Cosindit S.P.A.* [1969] 1 Lloyd's Rep. 75.
179. *Ibid.*, p.79 *per* Megaw J.
180. See, CPR, r. 25.7 and Practice Direction—Interim Payments.
181. [1910] 1 K.B. 132 at p.135 where Hamilton J observes: "it is impossible to construe the clause as giving the assured an option to be covered or not as he chooses, but I think that in the event of the ship arriving safely the assured would be bound to give the notice and the underwriter would be entitled to his premium".
182. *The Litsion Pride* [1985] 1 Lloyd's Rep. 437, 470, *per* Hirst J.
183. See *infra* under the title "A Final Question of Legal Analysis", para. 1.141 *et seq.*
184. See *supra* under the title, "The Problem of Characterisation", para. 1.9 *et seq.*
185. *May and Butcher v. R* [1934] 2 K.B. 17.
186. *The Litsion Pride* [1985] 1 Lloyd's Rep. 437, 468 *per* Hirst J.

payable over and above the policy premium, including any loaded rating payable when a certain state of affairs exists. With regard to the word "arrangement", Donaldson J[187] has indicated that it means "agreed or, in default of agreement, fixed by an arbitrator or by the Court".

The impact of s.31(2) is to introduce into every h/c clause a conditional implied statutory term to the effect that where the parties fail to agree an additional premium, the assured is under an obligation to pay a reasonable additional premium. It would seem that this obligation arises once the assured gives notice according to the terms of the clause. As with contractual implications generally, the implication which derives from the sub-section is capable of being displaced by an express contractual term, and this in all probability continues to be the case even if the sub-section is interpreted not as establishing an implied term but a distinct statutory rule. As observed previously, the substance of s.31(2) is on occasions made an express term of a h/c clause,[188] and it is always open to the parties as a question of contract to agree on the additional premium payable or the means by which it is to be calculated.

The existence of the implied term offers protection to assureds for it indicates the most an assured may be compelled to pay by way of premium for the additional cover. It probably also indicates that an assured who refuses to negotiate or negotiates in bad faith cannot be said to be in breach of contract.

1.109 What is a reasonable premium raises a question of fact[189] to be answered primarily by reference to market practice at the relevant point in time. The concept of a reasonable premium is to be assessed by reference to the current market rating of the additional risk. It is possible for the additional premium to be agreed in advance, as where a pro rata premium is agreed; or it may be assessed by reference to a fixed scale accepted in the market. But otherwise a market rate must be determined, and for this purpose evidence may be given by witnesses experienced in the workings of the market and the placement of the kind of risk in question. The overriding objective is to determine the market rate current at the time of the held covered event. This is the test implicitly suggested by s.31(2). It follows that any previous agreement between the parties as to premium rating is not relevant.[190]

1.110 In addressing the question of the appropriate market rate commensurate to the additional and new risk assumed by the underwriter, knowledge of the "held covered" event is attributed to the parties, and particularly to the underwriter. The decision in *Greenock Steamship Co. Ltd v. Maritime Insurance Co. Ltd*[191] is instructive both as to the test to be applied in determining a reasonable additional premium and also as to how the test is to be applied in individual circumstances, including occasions when notice is given after loss. The case has previously been considered in the context of the relationship between h/c clauses and breach of warranty.[192] It will be recalled that an insured vessel embarked on a voyage stage inadequately coaled and therefore in an unseaworthy condition. This amounted to breach of warranty with cover terminated,

187. In *Liberian Insurance Agency Inc. v. Mosse* [1977] 2 Lloyd's Rep. 560, at p.568.
188. *Supra* n.176.
189. Section 88.
190. *Cf. The Litsion Pride* [1985] 1 Lloyd's Rep. 437, 468 *per* Hirst J. See also *American Airlines Inc. v. Hope* [1973] 1 Lloyd's Rep. 233, 241 *per* Lord Denning MR.
191. [1903] 1 K.B. 367.
192. *Supra*, under the title "Breach of Warranties", para. 1.65 *et seq.*

save that there was also a h/c clause which stipulated breach of warranty to be a "held covered" event. The parties failed to agree an additional premium and the question was referred to the court for determination. In the abstract, Bigham J[193] considered the question before the court to be: "what is a reasonable premium for the added risk?" Applying the question to the factual context of the case, Bigham J formulated the question, "What might an underwriter fairly require as a premium for insuring a steamer which starts on a voyage short of coal?"

Responding to the question, Bigham J considered that an underwriter confronted by such a risk would be justified in taking into account two material considerations. First, the probable losses that would occur. Because the insured vessel was inadequately coaled, alternative sources of fuel would be required, which of necessity must come from the ship's fittings or spars, and from the cargo. These losses, in turn, would be general average losses for which the underwriter would be responsible to the insured owner. Bigham J considered that the underwriter would be entitled to take into account these probable losses in assessing a reasonable premium. Second, and additionally, Bigham J considered that the underwriter could take into account the increased risk of the total loss of the ship as a result of her being sent on a voyage inadequately bunkered.

Applying these two principles to the facts of the case, Bigham J concluded that the underwriter was entitled to charge an additional premium at least equal to the average loss claimed by the assured owner for ship's fittings and spars burnt, and the sum paid for cargo needed as fuel. In the event the claim under the policy was equalled by the entitlement of the underwriter to additional premium, and the claim of the assured, therefore, failed.

In *Mentz, Decker & Co. v. Maritime Insurance Co.*[194] Hamilton J followed the approach of Bigham J. On the facts of the case the insured vessel was lost following a deviation, which was a held covered event in the voyage policy. The assured gave notice to be held covered following the loss.[195] One question which came forward for consideration related to the basis on which the additional premium was to be assessed where the assessment did not take place until after the insured vessel was lost. Hamilton J answered the question by indicating, "the premium is to be calculated as it would have been calculated by the parties if they had known of the deviation at the time that it happened".[196] But, obviously, knowledge of the subsequent loss was not to be taken into account. 1.111

In addressing the question of the assessment of the additional premium it is clear that the courts have eschewed abstraction and resolved that the question must be confronted as a live market issue. The approach has also had implications for the proper construction of h/c clauses. 1.112

The additional risk contemplated by a h/c clause must be marketable, in the sense that it must be capable of being placed in the market at a reasonable commercial premium. If it is not so marketable, a h/c clause in customary form has no application. Under such a clause the underwriter is not giving an unqualified undertaking to 1.113

193. *Ibid.*, p.375.
194. [1910] 1 K.B. 132.
195. See fn.73.
196. *Ibid.*, pp.134, 135.

maintain cover, whatever the circumstances. His undertaking is of a commercial nature: the assured will be held covered providing the additional risk is of a kind that is acceptable to the marine insurance market.

1.114 In determining the marketability of a risk, regard must also be had to the terms and conditions which may be attached to the additional cover,[197] for these will indicate the wider framework within which the market assessment of the additional risk will take place. This shows that particular importance will be attached to the question whether the additional premium is to be assessed on the basis of the original policy terms, or whether amended terms of cover can be demanded. The response of the market to a presented risk may well depend on the terms that may be attached as a condition of the acceptance of the risk. A risk which is unacceptable in one form may nonetheless be marketable if protective terms can be attached to the cover. Many h/c clauses entitle underwriters to insist on amended terms of cover;[198] many are silent on the question. In the latter case the marketability of an additional risk must be assessed on the basis of the agreed policy terms. But where amended terms of cover may be insisted on, the question of the marketability of the additional risk is assessed in the context of the power to insist on amended terms.[199]

1.115 However, the marketability of a risk is not determined solely by reference to the ability to achieve a market placement. There is also the question of the reasonableness of the additional premium. Most risks would be capable of being placed against a premium rating equal to or in excess of 100 per cent of the sum insured, but it would be hopelessly unrealistic to accept this approach to the determination of the marketability of a risk for the purpose of h/c clauses. Predominantly, the market operates at the other extreme, with premiums rated at a very low percentage of the sum insured. The issue, therefore, is how great a rise in the premium rating from these low levels is permissible for the additional risk to continue to be perceived as marketable and, therefore, within the h/c clause? There is no precise answer to this question. Most certainly the answer cannot be contemplated in terms of fixed percentages or other rigid notions of scale.

1.116 The courts have developed a broad and flexible approach, which unsurprisingly revolves about the concept of a reasonable commercial premium. In *Liberian Insurance Agency Inc. v. Mosse*[200] Donaldson J set out the approach in the following terms:

> "the clause only applies if the assured on the basis of an accurate declaration of all the facts affecting the risk but excluding knowledge of what was to happen in the event, could have obtained a quotation in the market at a premium which could properly be described as 'a reasonable commercial rate'".

The approach brings into issue a question of fact, and with the answer depending on the facts and circumstances of each individual case. It is essentially a market question to be answered by those from within the market with the appropriate knowledge, expertise and experience.

---

197. Considered *infra* under the title "Amended Terms", para. 1.117 *et seq.*
198. *Ibid.*
199. *Ibid.*
200. [1977] 2 Lloyd's Rep. 560, at p.568.

1F.4 Amended terms

In holding an assured "held covered", by the terms of the h/c clause the underwriter may be entitled to demand amended terms of cover.[201] The power is invariably in the nature of an option and customarily exists in addition to the entitlement to demand additional premium; rarely, if ever, does it exist as an independent right. Where the entitlement exists and it is exercised, the agreement by the assured to the amended terms of cover is a condition precedent to the additional cover which the underwriter is obliged to provide. Where the entitlement does not exist, the underwriter cannot insist on a change to the policy terms as a condition of the additional cover.[202] 1.117

On the face of a customary h/c clause the right to insist on amended terms of cover is unqualified, but it is highly improbable that it will be construed in an unrestricted way, so allowing underwriters to insist on any terms they please. There appears to be no judicial authority on the point, but nonetheless there would seem to be good reason for thinking that the construction of the right will follow by analogy that relating to the right to demand additional premium, notwithstanding that s.31 of the Marine Insurance Act 1906 has no application to additional terms.[203] In other words, it is suggested that the right to demand that the assured agree amended terms of cover is restricted to a power to demand reasonable commercial terms.[204] Not only is this a practical and commercial way forward, but it also provides protection to assureds. Since s.31 has no application, the suggested position can only be achieved by reference to the proper construction of the clause or by importing an implied term. 1.118

If this is a correct approach to the construction of h/c clauses the question next arises, what is meant by reasonable commercial terms? The answer in all probability can be anticipated again by analogy with the more developed law relating to the concept of a reasonable additional premium. It is of course open to the parties to agree in the h/c clause the amended terms of cover to apply if the provision is invoked but this is never done in practice. Where the subsequent agreement of the parties is also not possible the matter can be referred to a court or arbitrator. In resolving this matter it seems inevitable that an objective test be adopted, namely, what terms and conditions would customarily be demanded by a prudent underwriter as a condition of agreeing to underwrite the particular additional risk? The application of the test raises a question of fact[205] and, as with the question of a reasonable additional premium, it is primarily a market question. 1.119

If the additional risk cannot be rendered acceptable to the market with the imposition of reasonable amended terms of cover, then again by analogy and as a question of construction, it is probable that the h/c clause does not come into effect and the underwriter is not under any obligation to provide the additional cover. But it will be virtually impossible to sustain this line of argument where it has been possible initially to assess an additional premium by reference to a "reasonable commercial rate". Such a determination equally suggests the existence of a market view of the 1.120

201. For example, Institute Time Clauses (Hulls) 1.11.95, Clause 1.4.

202. *Liberian Insurance Agency v. Mosse* [1977] 2 Lloyd's Rep. 560, 567 *per* Donaldson J.

203. Considered *supra* under the title "Additional Premium", para. 1.103 *et seq.*

204. See, Bennett, *The Law of Marine Insurance* (1996), p.312, where a similar opinion is expressed.

205. Section 88 is not directly applicable but nonetheless is indicative of the proper approach to the question.

terms, if any, on which the cover should be accepted. The relationship between the acceptance and rating of a risk and the power to attach terms of cover has already been commented on.[206]

1G APPLICATION OF THE DOCTRINE OF UTMOST GOOD FAITH

1.121 It has been judicially confirmed on several occasions that an assured who seeks to invoke a h/c clause must conduct himself with the utmost good faith in his dealings with the underwriters. The judicial comments can be traced to the judgment of McNair J in *Overseas Commodities Ltd v. Style*,[207] where he observed:

> "To obtain the protection of the 'held covered' clause, the assured must act with the utmost good faith towards the underwriters, this being an obligation which rests upon them throughout the currency of the policy."

The principle was endorsed by Donaldson J in *Liberian Insurance Agency Inc. v. Mosse*,[208] where, in summarising the impact of h/c clauses generally, he commented:

> "The assured cannot take advantage of the clause if he has not acted in the utmost good faith."

Elsewhere in his judgment Donaldson J spoke of utmost good faith as "a condition precedent to the application of the clause";[209] and of the obligation of the assured to make "an accurate declaration of all the facts affecting the risk but excluding knowledge of what was to happen in the event . . .".[210]

1.122 These early authorities have been approved in the subsequent and very substantial judicial consideration which has take place of the doctrine of utmost good faith, and in particular of the application of the doctrine after the contract of marine insurance has been entered into. In *The Star Sea*[211] Lord Hobhouse appears to endorse the dictum of McNair J in *Overseas Commodities v. Style* and otherwise says nothing to cast doubt on the correctness of the case. In *K/S Merc-Scandia XXXXII v. Certain Lloyd's Underwriters*[212] Longmore LJ, in giving the judgment of the Court of Appeal, identified "held covered" cases as a category which has been held to require "the exercise of good faith by the insured".

1.123 The only occasion to date when the existence of the duty has come close to assuming a relevance is in *Overseas Commodities Ltd v. Style*,[213] though ultimately the case was decided on other grounds. The facts of the case have been considered previously,[214] but they bear repeating to the extent necessary for the present

---

206. *Supra*, under the title "Additional Premium", para. 1.103 *et seq.*
207. [1958] 1 Lloyd's Rep. 546, 559.
208. [1977] 2 Lloyd's Rep. 560, 568.
209. *Ibid.*, p.567.
210. *Ibid.*, p.568.
211. *Manifest Shipping Company Ltd v. Uni-Polaris Shipping Company Ltd and Others, The Star Sea* [2001] 2 W.L.R. 170, 186. See also, *The Litsion Pride* [1985] 1 Lloyd's Rep. 437, 512, *per* Hirst J.
212. [2001] E.W.C.A. Civ. 1275, para. 22.
213. *Supra*, fn.207.
214. *Supra*, fn.49.

discussion. It will be recalled that two marine policies on tins of French butts bearing specified code marks had been taken out by consignees. The tins actually shipped predominantly bore different code marks. The underwriters were held not to be liable for the losses which had occurred, ostensibly because the code markings went to the description of the subject matter insured and consequently the tins actually shipped were not within the policy.

The assured attempted to save cover by arguing the applicability of a h/c clause in each policy, the precise terms of which have previously been considered.[215] McNair J considered there to be a difficulty facing the assured in developing this argument emanating from the conduct of the assured. When the discrepancy in the code markings surfaced the underwriters pressed the assured for an explanation. In response the assured instructed its buying agent to make inquiries of the manufacturer seller, which was duly done. The buying agents passed on to the assured two letters it had received from the seller. Each letter bore the same date, but otherwise set out different and inconsistent explanations for the discrepancy. Subsequently, only the letter containing the explanation more favourable to the assured's position was forwarded to the underwriters.

McNair J was of the view that had the underwriters been aware of the full position they would have been reluctant to consider favourably the assured's argument that the policies should be corrected as a matter of mere formality. The failure on the part of the assured to make full disclosure was considered by McNair J to be a breach of the assured's on-going duty of utmost good faith. Consequently, if the h/c had been applicable to the facts, which it was considered not to be, the conduct of the assured would have represented a ground for denying the assured the right to take the benefit if the h/c clause.

In these early authorities the effect of breach of the duty of good faith was not expressly to the fore, but the understanding appears to have been that what the assured lost was the additional cover. It was never argued, or even contemplated, that a lack of good faith could result in the avoidance of the original contract of marine insurance.[216] 1.124

There is the suggestion that an analogous position exists with regard to the implementation of additional premium provisions in marine policies, which are not strictly h/c clauses.[217] It is probable, however, that this view must now be responded to cautiously and re-examined in the light of the judicial development of the post-contractual application of the duty of utmost good faith which is currently in progress. 1.125

There was little examination of the general duty of utmost good faith in the early authorities just considered. Beyond the acceptance of the applicability of the duty to h/c clauses there was no wider discussion of issues of legal principle, nor of the implications and questions of remedy. At most, the cases amount to a tacit recognition that in invoking a h/c provision by giving notice, the assured is under a duty to disclose material information of which he had knowledge and not to 1.126

215. *Supra*, fn.48.
216. *Cf. K/S Merc-Scandia XXXXII v. Certain Lloyd's Underwriters* [2001] E.W.C.A. Civ. 1275, para. 22 *per* Longmore LJ, [2001] 2 Lloyd's Rep. 563.
217. *The Litsion Pride* [1985] 1 Lloyd's Rep. 437. See fn.37 *supra*.

misrepresent material information. In the subsequent years the judicial analysis of the doctrine of utmost good faith has progressed at a significant pace, as has academic writing,[218] and it is now a much more elaborate and sophisticated doctrine, though still a doctrine in a state of active development and flux, which confers on it an elusive quality which it is hoped will disappear as the doctrine achieves maturity. These subsequent developments are of great significance not only because comprehension is the better because of them, but also because they signal the path that future developments in the law may take. It follows that any contemporary analysis of the impact of the doctrine of utmost good faith on the implementation of h/c clauses must take them into account.

1.127 It is readily appreciated that the doctrine of utmost good faith has its source in s.17 of the Marine Insurance Act 1906, and that the particular duties established by ss.18–20 amount to specific applications of the doctrine and not to a definition of the province of the general doctrine. Sir Mackenzie Chalmers, the renowned draftsman of the 1906 Act, in a commentary on the legislation expressly denied that the special sections were exhaustive of the general duty defined in s.17,[219] and subsequently the same view has been adopted in the case law.[220]

1.128 Section 17 is drafted in very wide terms.[221] Beyond making it clear that the general duty of utmost good faith arises as a matter of law and is mutual in its application, and that the remedy for breach of the duty is restricted to avoidance of the contract of marine insurance, all is presented in a very general vein.[222] In contrast, the specific duties recognised in ss.18–20 are defined with particularity and it is plain that they are restricted to the negotiating and pre-contractual phase.[223] In relation to their

218. See Bennett, "Mapping the Doctrine of Utmost Good Faith in Insurance Contract Law" [1999] LMCLQ 165, 204, Baatz, "Utmost Good Faith in Marine Insurance Contracts", in Huybrechts (ed.), *Marine Insurance at the turn of the Millenium* (Vol. 1), pp.15–33; Soyer, *The Star Sea – A Lode Star?* [2001] LMCLQ 438.

219. Chalmers & Owen, *The Marine Insurance Act 1906* (1907, Butterworths), note to s.17.

220. See the *dicta* of the Court of Appeal in *Container Transport International Inc. v. Oceanus Mutual Indemnity Assoc. (Bermuda) Ltd* [1984] 1 Lloyd's Rep. 476, which have not on this wider question been overruled by the decision of the House of Lords in *Pan Atlantic Insurance Co. Ltd v. Pine Top Insurance Co. Ltd* [1995] 1 A.C. 501.

221. The section provides: "A contract of marine insurance is a contract based upon the utmost good faith, and, if the utmost good faith be not observed by either party, the contract may be avoided by the other party".

222. See, generally, *Container Transport International Inc. v. Oceanus Mutual Indemnity Assoc. (Bermuda) Ltd* [1984] 1 Lloyd's Rep. 476; *Banque Financiere de la Cite SA v. Westgate Insurance Co. Ltd* [1991] 2 A.C. 249; *Pan Atlantic Insurance Co. Ltd v. Pine Top Insurance Co. Ltd* [1995] 1 A.C. 501.

223. Sections 18–20 provide:

"*Disclosure by assured*

18.(1) Subject to the provisions of this section, the assured must disclose to the insurer, before the contract is concluded, every material circumstance which is known to the assured, and the assured is deemed to know every circumstance which, in the ordinary course of business, ought to be known by him. If the assured fails to make such disclosure, the insurer may avoid the contact.

(2) Every circumstance is material which would influence the judgment of a prudent insurer in fixing the premium, or determining whether he will take the risk.

respective province of application each specific duty is exhaustive.[224] No similar limitation applies to s.17. It is a general duty capable of touching upon any aspect of the insurance relationship, extending to both the pre-contractual and post-contractual phases, save for the areas covered by the specific duties.[225]

The focus of the recent judicial and academic debates about the doctrine of utmost good faith has been concerned with its application during the post-contractual phase. The issues are many and often complex. As an initial step, it is essential to recognise that once a contract of marine insurance is concluded, the relationship between the parties changes significantly.[226] The fact of the contract means that there are in existence contractual rights and obligations, and consequently also the possibility of contractual remedies. It also impacts on the effect of the remedy of avoidance, which when effected after a contract has been concluded may result not only in the contract 1.129

(3) In the absence of inquiry the following circumstances need not be disclosed, namely:
   (a) Any circumstance which diminishes the risk;
   (b) Any circumstance which is known or presumed to be known to the insurer. The insurer is presumed to know matters of common notoriety or knowledge, and matters which an insurer in the ordinary course of his business, as such, ought to know;
   (c) Any circumstance as to which information is waived by the insurer;
   (d) Any circumstance which it is superfluous to disclose by reason of any express or implied warranty.

(4) Whether any particular circumstance, which is not disclosed, be material or not is, in each case, a question of fact.

(5) The term "circumstance" includes any communication made to or information received by the assured.

Disclosure by agent effecting insurance

19. Subject to the provisions of the preceding section as to circumstances which need not be disclosed, where an insurance is effected for the assured by an agent, the agent must disclose to the insurer:
   (a) Every material circumstance which is known to himself, and an agent to insure is deemed to know every circumstance which in the ordinary course of business ought to be known by, or to have been communicated to, him; and
   (b) Every material circumstance which the assured is bound to disclose, unless it come to his knowledge too late to communicate it to the agent.

Representations pending negotiation of contract

20.(1) Every material representation made by the assured or his agent to the insurer during the negotiations for the contract, and before the contract is concluded, must be true. If it be untrue the insurer may avoid the contract.

(2) A representation is material which would influence the judgment of a prudent insurer in fixing the premium, or determining whether he will take the risk.

(3) A representation may be either a representation as to a matter of fact, or as to a matter of expectation or belief.

(4) A representation as to a matter of fact is true, if it be substantially correct, that is to say, if the difference between what is represented and what is actually correct would not be considered material by a prudent insurer.

(5) A representation as to a matter of expectation or belief is true if it be made in good faith.

(6) A representation may be withdrawn or corrected before the contract is concluded.

(7) Whether a particular representation be material or not is, in each case, a question of fact."

224. But with regard to circumstances that don't fall precisely within the provisions of ss.18–20, the general duty under s.17 may apply to the pre-contractual period: see *Container Transport International Inc. v. Oceanus Mutual Indemnity Association (Bermuda) Ltd* [1984] 1 Lloyd's Rep. 476, 512, *per* Parker LJ.

225. See cases cited *infra*.

226. See the discussion in *Manifest Shipping Co. Ltd v. Uni-Polaris Shipping Co. Ltd and Others, The Star Sea* [2001] 2 W.L.R. 170.

being vacated but also in the undoing of previous contractual dealings which at the time of their doing were perfectly valid. The coming into existence of a contract of marine insurance does not exclude the duty of utmost good faith, but it does bring into question the relationship between the duty and the contract.[227]

1.130 The questions that may arise are many. Does the general duty of utmost good faith apply to all aspects of the insurance relationship between the parties or is its application selective? Is the general duty confined to the contractual period of the insurance or is it capable of continuing thereafter, and, if so, when precisely does the duty terminate? Is the duty founded on s.17 in all cases, or is it possible for the duty in its application to the post-contractual period to derive from the express or implied terms of the contract of marine insurance? And what precisely are the consequences of breach of duty during this phase? Is avoidance the universal remedy or are there alternative remedies? Does avoidance always allude to the original contract of insurance or can it relate to a severable part of the original contract, or, possibly, some other identifiable contractual relationship which in some way impacts on or renews the original contract of insurance? If the duty is founded on contract, does breach of the duty result in the traditional contractual remedies being available, and possibly to the exclusion of avoidance? And what of the case where an assured's conduct amounts both to breach of the duty of utmost good faith and of contract? What are the remedies available to the underwriter and in this regard what is the relationship between the two categories of remedy?

1.131 The judicial answers so far given to these questions, stated at their most general, reveal the recognition of an on-going general duty of utmost good faith, extending through the post-contractual period, and continuing until a claim form in litigation is issued.[228] That during the period of the contract the general duty applies when the parties negotiate a variation[229] or renewal[230] of the cover; when a fraudulent claim is made;[231] when invoking a h/c clause[232] and possibly also an additional premium provision;[233] when giving information to an insurer pursuant to an express or implied contractual obligation;[234] and when an insurer under a liability policy takes over the assured's defence to a claim.[235] It is, however, clear that these categories which have so far been recognised in the developing law do not define the scope and application of the general doctrine.[236] The doctrine has the potential to develop further and embrace

227. See, *K/S Merc-Scandia XXXXII v. Certain Lloyd's Underwriters* [2001] E.W.C.A. Civ. 1275; [2001] 2 Lloyd's Rep. 563.

228. *Manifest Shipping Company Ltd v. Uni-Polaris Shipping Company Ltd and Others, The Star Sea* [2001] 2 W.L.R. 170.

229. *Lishman v. Northern Maritime Insurance Co.* (1875) LR 10 CP 179; *Iron Trades Mutual v. Cie de Seguros* [1991] 1 Re L.R. 213, 224; *The Star Sea* [2001] 2 W.L.R. 170.

230. *K/S Merc-Scandia XXXXII v. Certain Lloyd's Underwriters* [2001] E.W.C.A. Civ. 1275; [2001] 2 Lloyd's Rep. 563, 571.

231. *Manifest Shipping Company Ltd v. Uni-Polaris Shipping Company Ltd and Others, The Star Sea* [2001] 2 W.L.R. 170.

232. See cases considered *supra*.

233. *The Litsion Pride* [1985] 1 Lloyd's Rep. 437.

234. *Phoenix General Insurance Co. v. Halvanon Insurance Co. Ltd* [1985] 2 Lloyd's Rep. 599; *Alfred McAlpine v. BAI Insurance* [2001] 1 Lloyd's Rep. 437.

235. *Cox v. Backside* [1995] 2 Lloyd's Rep. 437, 462, *per* Sir Thomas Bingham MR; *K/S Merc-Scandia XXXXII v. Certain Lloyd's Underwriters* [2001] E.W.C.A. Civ. 1275, paras 22 and 30, *per* Longmore LJ; [2001] 2 Lloyd's Rep. 563, 572.

236. *K/S Merc-Scandia XXXXII v. Certain Lloyd's Underwriters*, *ibid.*

new categories, but it is also clear that a much more conservative approach is to be adopted to the application of the doctrine to the post-contractual phase compared with that adopted in relation to the pre-contractual phase.[237] There is no duty of good faith in relation to an underwriter's contractual right of cancellation,[238] nor in matters relating to the risk once the contract has been concluded.[239] And again no duty of good faith arises when an assured gives information in response to a request made by the underwriter and in circumstances when there exists no right to demand the information.[240]

The great policy issue which arises in connection with the post-contract application of the duty of good faith concerns the question of remedy. If the duty arises out of s.17, the only remedy is avoidance. Once a contract of marine insurance has been established and has begun to regulate relations between the parties, the impact of the remedy may be particularly harsh. Because the effect of avoidance is to return the parties to the *status quo ante* the impact of the remedy, beyond providing a response to the immediate breach of good faith, may operate to undo earlier and honest settlements agreed by the parties under the terms of the policy. A breach of the duty of good faith late in the period of the cover may consequently have disastrous consequences for an assured. The question is whether such consequences would be just.[241] 1.132

In addressing this question, the judges have identified a number of guiding principles, all of which encourage caution.[242] First, in the face of a breach of duty by an assured, the object of the law is not to punish the assured. Second, to give too wide a recognition to the post-contract application of the duty has the potential to be unfairly advantageous to underwriters, for it may provide them with disingenuous opportunities to escape from their contracts. Third, in developing the law, regard should be had to the principle of proportionality between the nature of the breach and the consequence flowing from it. Fourth, once the parties are into a contractual relationship it must be borne in mind that it is open to them to make contractual provision for the consequences of breach, and even in the absence of such express provision there may be available ordinary contractual remedies, including rescission. Fifth, the availability of a contractual remedy does not of itself exclude the remedy of avoidance. The latter remedy continues to be available if justified by reference to considerations of public policy and over-riding needs of justice. 1.133

The cautious approach to the post-contract development of the doctrine has had its effects. In making a claim there is no breach of duty unless it can be established that the assured has acted fraudulently.[243] The same is true where the assured fails to 1.134

237. *Manifest Shipping Company Ltd v. Uni-Polaris Shilling Company Ltd and Others, The Star Sea, supra per* the speeches of Lords Hobhouse and Scott.

238. *Niger Co. Ltd v. Guardian Assurance Co. Ltd* (1922) 13 Ll.L.R. 75; *New Hampshire v. MGN* [1997] L.R.L.R. 24, 58–62.

239. *Cory v. Patton* (1872) 7 Q.B. 304.

240. *Iron Trades Mutual Insurance Co. Ltd v. Componkia de Seguros Imperio* [1991] 1 Re L.R. 213, 224.

241. *The Star Sea, supra, per* the speech of Lord Hobhouse.

242. The principles communicated find expression in the speech of Lord Hobhouse in *The Star Sea, ibid.* and the judgment of Longmore LJ in *K/S Merc-Scandia XXXXII v. Certain Lloyd's Underwriters, supra.* See also *Pan Atlantic Insurance Co. Ltd v. Pine Top Insurance Co. Ltd* [1995] 1 A.C. 501, 549, *per* Lord Mustill.

243. *The Star Sea, supra.*

discharge an obligation to give information to the underwriter.[244] Misrepresentations or omissions or other forms of culpable conduct not amounting to fraud will not suffice. Fraud is also defined very narrowly as an absence of honest belief.[245] Where the conduct of an assured is both a breach of contract and of the duty of good faith, the Court of Appeal has recently held that the remedy of avoidance is only available if the underwriter is entitled to accept the contractual breach as repudiatory.[246]

1.135 In the context of the broader legal developments it is the recognition of the applicability of the general doctrine to contractual variations and renewals which provides the closest analogies with h/c clauses. In this context, the concept of a variation is probably to be construed somewhat generally and there would appear to be little difficulty in characterising the effect of the invocation of a h/c clause as working a variation by way of establishing additional cover. But variations of the kinds here recognised, though they are negotiated after the original contract of insurance is agreed, do not represent post-contractual activity such as making a claim or communicating information under or in accordance with the terms of the original policy. The variations are effected by entering into a new contract. This is clearly so in relation to a renewal, and it is equally the case, though a little less clearly, in the case of a variation. These categories, therefore, do not provide genuine examples of the doctrine of utmost good faith applying to the post-contract phase. The doctrine is being applied to the pre-contract phase leading to the establishment of the new contract, with the consequence that in the event of breach of duty what is lost by electing avoidance is either the renewed contract or the new contract working the variation to the original. In both instances the original contract remains untouched.[247]

1.136 The same approach is applicable to h/c clauses. The way h/c clauses may be analysed is considered in the final section of this contribution.[248] It is there suggested that a h/c clause represents a new contract between the parties, and, if not a new contract, in the alternative a severable category of cover in the original contract. If this represents a correct approach it opens the way to the application of the doctrine of utmost good faith in the same way as it applies to renewals and variations, with s.17 and the specific statutory duties set out in ss.18–20 applicable. It is this position which seems to be anticipated in the *Style* and *Mosse* cases, and it results, in the event of breach of duty, in the remedy of avoidance being restricted to the new contract or the severable part establishing the additional cover.[249]

1.137 An implication of the applicability of the duty of utmost good faith when invoking a h/c clause is that the assured is under particular obligations to disclose all material information and not to make material misrepresentations. Sections 18 and 20 are relevant, but in all likelihood subject to certain qualifications. In the first place the concept of materiality, as defined in sub-section (2) of both sections, is to be restricted

---

244. *K/S Mere-Scandia XXXXII v. Certain Lloyd's Underwriters, supra.* In *The Star Sea, supra,* Lord Scott at para. III, said of the post-contract duty, "Unless the assured has acted in bad faith he cannot . . . be in breach of a duty of good faith, utmost or otherwise".

245. *The Michael* [1979] 2 Lloyd's Rep. 1, 21–22, *per* Roskill LJ.

246. *K/S Merc-Scandia XXXXII v. Certain Lloyd's Underwriters* [2001] E.W.C.A. Civ. 1275, para. 35, *per* Longmore LJ; [2001] 2 Lloyd's Rep. 563, 575.

247. *Ibid.*, para. 31.

248. Under the title, "A Final Question of Legal Analysis", para. 1.141 *et seq.*

249. *Supra*, para. 31.

to the held covered risk. Second, information is material if it would influence the judgment of a prudent insurer in fixing the additional premium and/or determining the conditions on which the additional cover is to be provided. Third, since the insurer is already obliged to provide the additional cover, if demanded, information relating to whether the additional risk should be accepted is not material, but information which helps the underwriter to decide whether the additional risk falls within the terms of the h/c clause is material. Fourth, given the circumstances which may prevail when an assured gives notice of a held covered event and also the conditions precedent the additional cover which must be satisfied, it may be that the concept of deemed knowledge pursuant to s.18(1), and which has been developed in the context of the standard pre-contractual application of the doctrine, may require some modification.

Support for the approach developed in the text may be derived from the judgment of Hobhouse J (as he then was) in *Iron Trades Mutual Insurance Co. Ltd v. Companhia de Seguros Imperio.*[250] In a dictum which is capable of being applied to h/c clauses the following guiding principles are expressed: *1.138*

"1.89 When there is an addition to the contract, as where it is varied, there can be a further duty of disclosure but only to the extent that it is material to the variation being proposed. If the addition does not alter the contractual rights there will be no fact that is material to disclose and the same will apply if a variation is favourable to the insurer. It will only be when the insurer is being asked to take on some additional risk and/or needing to reassess the premium or terms of cover that disclosure of further facts could be material and, even then, the facts to be disclosed are only those which are material to what the insurer is being asked to do. . . ."

Of course, a wider obligation of disclosure may arise if there is an express obligation to do so under a term of the primary insurance contract.

Materiality, in its adjusted sense, is not in itself sufficient to make available the remedy of avoidance. It must also be established that the underwriter was induced to provide the additional cover, though in this regard the underwriter is assisted by a favourable supporting presumption.[251] The requirement of inducement is not expressly stated in ss.18(1) and 20(1), but it is implied.[252] *1.139*

As for the consequences of breach of the duty of utmost good faith in invoking a h/c clause it is becoming increasingly certain that it is the additional cover alone which may be avoided. The early cases are inconclusive, though, with these cases in mind, Longmore LJ has recently observed, "although it is settled that good faith must be observed, it is never suggested that lack of good faith in relation to a matter held covered by the policy avoids the whole contract of insurance".[253] Incidental judicial comment has also found this possibility unpalatable[254] and understandably so for it would colour the law as penal and offend against the principle of proportionality. That avoidance does not have this wider effect is now rendered virtually certain *1.140*

---

250. [1991] 1 Re L.R. 213.
251. *St Paul Fire and Marine Co. (UK) v. McConnell Dowell Constructors Ltd* [1995] 2 Lloyd's Rep. 116.
252. *Pan Atlantic Insurance Co. Ltd v. Pine Top Insurance Co. Ltd* [1995] 1 A.C. 501.
253. *K/S Merc-Scandia XXXXII v. Certain Lloyd's Underwriters, supra*, para. 22, p.571.
254. *Manifest Shipping Company Ltd v. Uni-Polaris Shipping Company Ltd and Others, The Star Sea* [1997] 1 Lloyd's Rep. 360, 370, *per* Leggatt LJ.

because of the way h/c clauses may be construed, and also because of the very clear analogy with the way the law is developing in relation to contractual variations of the original policy risk, with avoidance limited to the variation. The effect of a h/c clause when invoked is to extend the original policy cover, which is quite clearly a variation. The fact that the variation is brought about by a contractual facility in the original contract does nothing to change matters.

1H A FINAL QUESTION OF LEGAL ANALYSIS

1.141 Although h/c clauses are familiar in practice and unambiguously valid and effective as legal agreements, nonetheless they appear never to have been the subject of close legal analysis. Both judicial and academic analytical comment is conspicuously absent, in all probability because the issue has not arisen as a central question in litigation. As a result, how the effect of the invocation of a h/c clause is to be understood in terms of legal analysis remains an uncertain issue. Nevertheless, the question is one of significance, possibly of growing significance, and what follows is an attempt to fill the void.

1.142 A h/c clause is undoubtedly a valid contract but the question remains how is the contract established and what is the nature of the established contract? There are several possible responses to this question.

1.143 First, it is possible to view the h/c provision as an integral part of the initial contract on policy terms. As such, the additional cover made available may be viewed as just one category of cover, albeit of a contingent and prospective nature, arising under the contract of insurance. The cases in their generality appear to assume this approach, but they are far from conclusive for in none of them was the question here addressed being considered directly. The difficulty confronting this line of reasoning is that a contract is recognised in connection with an agreement, the hallmarks of which are futurity, conditionality, unilateralism and which contemplates further negotiation and the settlement of new terms. The additional cover may or may not come into existence at a future date. All depends on the election of the assured, though the underwriter is without any choice in the matter provided the assured acts in accordance with the terms of the h/c clause. Nevertheless, in the event of the cover being invoked, the assured is aware that there may arise an obligation to agree amended terms. Notwithstanding the peculiarities and difficulties of the situation, it will be suggested later in the text that a h/c clause does establish an immediate contract between the parties, though of a unilateral character.

1.144 A second possible analysis is to view the additional cover as founded on a distinct unilateral contract of marine insurance, sometimes characterised as an "if" contract.[255] Under this analysis, the h/c clause is perceived as an offer made by the underwriter to provide, if demanded, additional cover in accordance with the terms and conditions specified in the clause. Beyond being unilateral, the offer is also

---

255. See, *United Dominions Trust (Commercial) Ltd v. Eagle Aircraft Services Ltd* [1968] 1 W.L.R. 74, 85–86, *per* Diplock LJ (CA).

irrevocable. The underwriter is bound to maintain the offer for as long as the h/c clause is capable of being invoked by the assured, which period may extend beyond the duration of the initial insurance contract. The assured accepts the offer and provides consideration by giving a valid notice as specified in the clause, but it is for the assured to elect whether or not to claim the benefit of the additional cover. The effect of giving notice is to establish a contract which thereafter is the basis of the additional cover. In giving notice, the assured also promises, subject to any express terms the parties may agree, to pay a reasonable additional premium and/or to agree reasonable amended terms, and in so doing provides consideration.[256]

The third possible analysis amounts to a hybrid of the two just discussed, and it is the analysis which provides the most convincing answers to the questions posed earlier. It is suggested that a h/c clause establishes an immediately binding obligation in the contract of marine insurance which the parties have entered into, but of a particular character. Whereas most of the contractual terms create bilateral obligations, the h/c clause is different for initially it creates a unilateral obligation requiring the underwriter to provide the specified additional cover if demanded by the assured.[257] Under this analysis a h/c clause is not perceived as a classical "if" contract, but as a variant form in the nature of a unilateral contractual obligation. The analysis appears to fit the practical application of h/c clauses and also explains the respective legal positions of the parties. It also serves a wider purpose by providing a rational solution to the difficulties associated with the application of the doctrine of utmost good faith to h/c clauses.[258] 1.145

Adopting this hybrid analysis, the effect of a h/c clause is that the underwriter undertakes a contractual obligation to provide additional cover if the assured so demands by giving notice. Initially only the underwriter is under a binding obligation. It does not become an obligation requiring performance until notice is given, and if notice is not given it never becomes an active obligation. The obligation is irrevocable, the irrevocability being contractual in character and derives from either the proper construction or an implied term of the h/c clause. It is also probable that the underwriter is under an implied obligation not to put it out of his power to perform his undertaking should it be triggered by notice.[259] 1.146

Until notice is given, the assured is under no obligation whatsoever. There is no obligation to invoke the h/c provision in the event of the happening of a held covered event, and there is no breach of contract if the assured decides not to do so. The giving of notice is the unilateral act of the assured and it is also done at the election of the assured.

But once notice is given, both parties are subject to immediate obligations. The underwriter is obliged to provide the promised additional cover. There is no option in the matter and failure to do so amounts to breach of contract. The assured is obliged to agree any specified conditions precedent, usually relating to additional premium

256. For textbook commentaries on unilateral contracts, see, *Chitty on Contracts* (Vol. 1, General Principles) 28th edn., paras 2–071 to 2–078. Treitel, *The Law of Contract* (10th edn.) pp.35–39, 138–139.

257. *United Dominions Trust (commercial) Ltd v. Eagle Aircraft Services Ltd*, *supra* p.86, *per* Diplock LJ (CA).

258. Considered *infra*.

259. *Cf. Little v. Courage Ltd*, *The Times*, 6 January 1995, *per* Millet LJ (a case concerning an "option").

and amended terms of cover. But the underwriter is not necessarily under a contractual obligation to insist on additional premium and/or amended terms. This is sometimes made clear by the inclusion of the words "if demanded" in h/c clauses, but even in the absence of such express words, the same result is likely to follow as a matter of construction. An underwriter who does not insist on amended terms of cover is not in breach of contract, nor can it subsequently be argued that conditions precedent to the additional cover have not been satisfied.

1.147 The outcome of the proper contractual performance of a h/c clause is the provision of additional cover on amended terms, if required. The question next arises as to the legal basis of the additional cover? Is it based on a new and distinct contract, as results from the exercise of an option or right of pre-emption or right to sell-back?[260] Or does it amount to the materialisation of a contingent cover provided by the marine insurance contract?

1.148 As a matter of practice, it probably does not matter which analysis is adopted, but the legal nature and workings of h/c clauses appear to favour the former. When the unilateral offer is accepted, there is established a new contract which is distinct from, but yet closely associated with, the initial contract. The new contract may have its own special terms, but subject to such special terms, the terms of the original will be incorporated. The additional cover is provided by a new contract which extends on the cover provided by the original contract. They are, quite obviously, two closely related contracts and together they provide the cover contracted for. For the purposes of construction they would no doubt be treated as one, and a policy issued in respect of the original marine insurance contract would probably serve as a policy for the new contract.

But even if this analysis is erroneous and the additional cover is analysed as a category of contingent cover provided by the marine insurance contract, as a question of construction the category would seem to be sufficiently distinct to justify its being analysed as a severable part of the contract.

1.149 A significant advantage of the suggested analysis is that it avoids potential difficulties relating to the application of the doctrine of utmost good faith to h/c clauses, which have been considered earlier in the text.[261] It is clearly the case that the doctrine applies to h/c clauses, and presently this appears to be justified on the general ground that the invocation of a h/c clause produces a variation to the policy cover. The suggested analysis supports and adds weight to this approach, for what is the additional cover other than a variation by way of an extension of the original policy cover.

It is in relation to the consequences of breach of the duty of utmost good faith that the suggested analysis produces clarity and the solution which most commentators appear anxious to achieve, namely that only the additional cover should be avoided. If the additional cover is based on a new contract then the position becomes quite straightforward. What is in issue is a matter of pre-contract good faith and beyond s.17, ss.18–20 apply, with the remedy of avoidance restricted to the new contract.

---

260. *Cf. Shiloh Spinners Ltd v. Harding* [1973] A.C. 691; *Greene v. Church Commissioners for England* [1974] 1 Ch. 467; *United Scientific Holdings Ltd v. Burnley BC* [1978] A.C. 904; *Trustees of the Chippenham Golf Club v. North Wiltshire DC* (1992) 64 P. & C.R. 527.

261. *Supra*, under the title "Application of the Doctrine of Utmost Good Faith", para. 1.121 *et seq.*

The complications associated with breach of the post-contract duty of utmost good faith do not arise.

Even if the alternative analysis applies, with the additional cover analysed as a severable category of contingent cover provided under the terms of the original contract, in the event of breach of the duty of utmost good faith it is that severable part alone which is avoided.[262] Under both lines of reasoning the original policy cover is unaffected by breach of the duty of utmost good faith in invoking the h/c clause.

Often a h/c clause will also amount to a waiver or an election, as a necessary prelude *1.150* to the establishment of additional cover. Such will be the case when the h/c clause holds the underwriter covered, notwithstanding the existence of circumstances which, had there been no h/c clause, would have automatically terminated cover or entitled the underwriter to avoid or terminate the insurance contract or to reject a claim made under the policy.

A clear example is provided when the effect of a h/c clause is to hold covered in *1.151* the event of a breach of warranty.[263] In the absence of the clause, and subject to the express policy terms, a breach of warranty automatically terminates cover without the requirement of an election on the part of the assured. It is nonetheless the case that a breach of warranty may be waived by the underwriter and cover maintained. Where the parties have agreed a held covered provision, which is invoked by the assured, it must be the case that the agreement also amounts to a waiver of the breach of warranty. But if the h/c agreement is not invoked, then there is no waiver. The possibility of h/c clause being invoked proactively presents no difficulty, for a waiver may be prior or subsequent to a breach of warranty.

The analysis is slightly different when a h/c clause holds covered notwithstanding *1.152* the breach of a term which is a condition precedent a claim under the policy, or of a term which is a condition in the traditional contractual sense, or in the event of a serious breach of an intermediate term;[264] or holds covered notwithstanding an event which renders the policy voidable.[265] In all of these various circumstances, the remedy of rejecting the claim or of accepting the breach as repudiatory or of avoiding the contract is not automatic, but depends on the underwriter electing to take that course. If the election is not exercised, then the right to reject the claim or to repudiate or avoid the contract is lost. The existence of an applicable h/c clause which is invoked by the assured must represent an election on the part of the underwriter to affirm liability for the claim or the validity of or the existence or continued existence of the marine insurance contract. The election leaves untouched any right to damages the underwriter may possess.

262. The author of Arnould's *Law of Marine Insurance and Average*, Vol. III, Sixteenth edn., para. 50 at p.37 also views severability as a possible solution to the question surrounding the ambit of avoidance.

263. Discussed *supra* under the title "Breach of Warranties", para. 1.65 *et seq.*

264. Discussed *supra* under the title "Breach of policy terms not being warranties", para. 1.75 *et seq.*

265. Discussed *supra* under the title "Voidable Risks", para. 1.56 *et seq.*

CHAPTER 2

INCORPORATION OF TERMS INTO REINSURANCE AGREEMENTS

PROFESSOR ROB MERKIN

2A THE USES AND ABUSES OF INCORPORATION

The term of a commercial contract may be carefully negotiated and devised *2.1* specifically by the parties to meet their requirements. If the subject-matter of the contract is unique, then there is no real alternative. However, most commercial contracts fall into clearly defined categories within clearly defined markets, and the pressure to use "off the peg" terms has proved to be irresistible over the years. If lawyers are involved at the drafting stage – and this will rarely be the case unless there is some special feature involved – their training and instincts will lead them towards what has worked in the past. If lawyers are not involved, those in the market responsible for preparing contracts exhibit exactly the same tendency. This is for the most part an efficient use of resources where a direct match is appropriate. Beyond that point, however, dangers begin to emerge. In a number of contexts, the desire to cut corners has led not just to the adoption of terms previously used in the same type of contract but the adoption of terms previously used in related but nevertheless quite distinct forms of contract. This is potentially serious, not least because of: (a) the risk of inconsistency between the express terms and the adopted terms which were designed for other purposes;[1] and (b) the possibility that the adopted terms have acquired a special meaning in the market in which they were originally designed which is not conveyed on their face.

The dangers are compounded the further that the process is taken. The next step may be the wholesale incorporation by reference into one contract of terms and conditions set out in another contract. Even if the contracts are identical in terms of subject-matter,[2] risks are minimised but not eliminated. If the contracts are not identical, then experience has shown that disputes are inevitable. There are numerous contexts in which incorporation is adopted as the usual method of contracting. It is commonplace for the terms of a charterparty to be incorporated into bills of lading. Equally, in the case of construction contracts, the terms of the head contract may be incorporated into sub-contracts. Incorporation has its attractions, as in these situations the subject-matter of the contracts – the goods to be supplied or the works to be completed – are likely to be the same, and rights and liabilities at one level of contracting are intended to be replicated at the other levels. The courts have indeed adopted a "benevolent" view of this approach to contract formation.[3] However, incorporation has proved in practice to give rise to major difficulties. Many of the principles developed by the courts have been worked out in the context of the purported incorporation of arbitration clauses.

2.2 First, it is necessary to determine which of the terms in the primary contract have been incorporated into the secondary contract. This will turn upon an analysis of the wording of both the primary contract and the secondary contract. If there is to be incorporation, then ideally there should be express reference to the term to be incorporated, although there are cases which demonstrate that even this will fail if it is not possible to identify the relevant clause in the primary contract.[4] The practice, however, is to rely upon general words of incorporation, for example, by reference in the secondary contract to the incorporation of the "terms and conditions" of the primary contract. Here, it is necessary to examine that contract to see precisely what is meant by its terms and conditions. An arbitration clause has consistently held not to be a term or condition but rather an ancillary contract in its own right,[5] so that general

1. Those responsible for drafting contracts are, of course, perfectly capable of producing awe-inspiring inconsistencies within a document, even where it is specifically stated to be self-contained. See, for recent illustrations: *Paul Smith Ltd v. H & S International Holding Ltd* [1991] 2 Lloyd's Rep. 127; *Shell International Petroleum Co. Ltd v. Coral Oil Co. Ltd* [1999] 1 Lloyd's Rep. 72; *M H Alshaya Co. WLL v. Retek Information Systems Inc.* 2000, unreported.

2. If they are not, it follows that terms in one contract which relate to a specific subject matter not forming part of the other contract will not be carried across into that other contract. For an insurance illustration, see *Union Camp Chemicals Ltd v. Ace Insurance SA-NV* [2002] Lloyd's Rep. IR (forthcoming) in which a primary layer policy contained terms relating to public liability and employers' liability, whereas the excess layer policy – which incorporated the terms of the primary layer policy – related only to public liability. HHJ Thornton QC held that terms relating only to employers' liability did not form a part of the excess layer policy.

3. *Federal Bulk Carriers Inc. v. Itoh & Co. Ltd, The Federal Bulker* [1989] 1 Lloyd's Rep. 103, *per* Bingham LJ.

4. As in *HIH Casualty & General Insurance Ltd v. New Hampshire Insurance Co.* [2001] E.W.C.A. Civ. 735 [2001] Lloyd's Rep. IR 596, where the reference in the secondary contract to a "cancellation clause" in the primary contract failed on the basis that there was no clause meeting that description in the primary contract.

5. *Cf.* now Arbitration Act 1996, s.7.

words of incorporation will not carry it across.[6] The policy basis here is that an arbitration clause deprives the parties to it of access to the courts, and express agreement rather than implication by incorporation is required for this purpose. The same reasoning has been adopted by way of extension in relation to exclusive jurisdiction clauses,[7] choice of law clauses[8] and time-bar clauses,[9] and it is certainly open for argument that other clauses which may have substantial consequences for the rights of the parties – which may not be identified until the point arises in the course of proceedings – should fall to be treated in the same way. At the other extreme, however, there is authority for the proposition that a term which is implied into the primary contract may by general words of incorporation be carried across into the secondary contract if the term is appropriate to that contract.[10] The dangers of relying upon generalised incorporation are, therefore, all too apparent.

Second, the contract from which incorporation is to be effected has to be identified. 2.3
This point may arise where a head charter is followed by a sub-charter, and bills of lading issued purport to incorporate the terms of the "charterparty", as it then becomes necessary to choose between the two.[11] There is a general presumption in English law that a reference of this type refers to the head charter rather than the sub-charter,[12] and it has equally been held that a reference to the terms of the "original" in a retrocession agreement means the direct policy rather than the reinsurance,[13] although in the shipping context the rule has more recently been doubted in Canada[14] and the argument that the terms of the charterparty under which the goods were being carried rather than the head charterparty ought to be looked at as the source for incorporation has been accepted. The point may also arise where the contract containing the clause to be incorporated is itself incomplete.[15]

Third, there may be inconsistency between the incorporated terms and the agreed 2.4
terms. The general approach of the courts in this situation is to give priority to what

6. The authorities on this point are numerous and not fully consistent. The most important are: *T W Thomas & Co. Ltd v. Portsea Steamship Co. Ltd, The Portsmouth* [1912] A.C. 1; *The Njegos* [1936] P 90; *The Elizabeth H* [1962] 1 Lloyd's Rep. 172; *The Merak* [1964] 2 Lloyd's Rep. 527; *The Annefield* [1971] 1 All E.R. 394; *The Rena K* [1978] 1 Lloyd's Rep. 545; *The Varenna* [1983] 2 Lloyd's Rep. 592; *The Federal Bulker* [1989] 1 Lloyd's Rep. 103; *Aughton Ltd v. M F Kent Services Ltd* (1991) 57 BLR 1; *Giffen v. Drake and Scull* 33 Con L.R. 84; *The Nerano* [1994] 2 Lloyd's Rep. 50; *Partenreederei M/S Heidberg v. Grosvenor Grain and Feed Co. Ltd, The Heidberg* [1994] 2 Lloyd's Rep. 287; *Excess Insurance Co. Ltd v. Mander* [1995] LRLR 358; *Trygg Hansa v. Equitas* [1998] 2 Lloyd's Rep. 439; *The Delos* [2001] 1 Lloyd's Rep. 703; *Cigna Life Insurance Co. of Europe SA-NV & Ors v. Intercaser SA de Seguros y Reaseguros* [2001] Lloyd's Rep. IR 821.

7. *AIG Group (UK) Ltd v. The Ethniki* [2000] Lloyd's Rep. IR 343. See *infra*.

8. *Gan Insurance Co. Ltd v. Tai Ping Insurance Co. Ltd* [1999] Lloyd's Rep. IR 229, affirmed [1999] Lloyd's Rep. IR 472. See *infra*.

9. *OK Petroleum AB v. Vitol Energy SA* [1995] 2 Lloyd's Rep. 160.

10. *HIH Casualty and General Insurance v. New Hampshire Insurance* [2001] Lloyd's Rep. IR 224 affirmed as regards general principles by the Court of Appeal [2001] E.W.C.A. Civ. 735, [2001] Lloyd's Rep. IR 596.

11. A further possibility is that the contract referred to does not exist: see *Modern Buildings Wales Ltd v. Limmer and Trinidad Co. Ltd* [1975] 1 All E.R. 549.

12. *The San Nicholas* [1976] 1 Lloyd's Rep. 8; *Navigazione Alta Italia SA v. Svenska Petroleum AB, The Nai Matteini* [1988] 1 Lloyd's Rep. 452.

13. *Pine Top Insurance Co. Ltd v. Unione Italiana Anglo Saxon Reinsurance Co. Ltd* [1987] 1 Lloyd's Rep. 476.

14. *Thyssen Canada Ltd v. Mariana Maritime SA* 2000, unreported.

15. *Cigna Life Insurance Co. of Europe SA-NV & Ors v. Intercaser SA de Seguros y Reaseguros* [2001] Lloyd's Rep. IR 821.

has actually been agreed over what has been purportedly incorporated.[16] This approach is, of course, of little use where two sets of inconsistent terms are incorporated into a contract.[17]

2.5 Fourth, the incorporated terms may be linguistically incompatible with the contract into which they have been incorporated. In some situations the terms of the primary contract may make express reference to disputes which might arise under the secondary contract, in which case the construction of the incorporated terms[18] is made relatively easy. However, in other cases they may be wholly incompatible, and after an uncertain start[19] the courts have allowed themselves to engage in "manipulation" of the incorporated term to make it fit the secondary contract, so that the word "charterparty" in an arbitration clause has been converted to "bill of lading" for the purposes of incorporation,[20] and equally "insurance" has been converted to "reinsurance" to the same end.[21] However, manipulation is not possible if the incorporated provisions would have to be rewritten or if they make no sense in the incorporated context in which they appear, in which case the terms have to be disregarded.[22]

2.6 Finally, the meaning of the incorporated terms has to be considered. The issue here is whether the meaning of the terms in the primary contract is carried across to the secondary contract where the context may be different, or whether the meaning is treated as not having changed. Where the two contracts are intended to be back to back in that they form parts of a coherent chain, then there is obviously little justification in regarding the process of transmission as one which changes meanings:[23] if the subject-matter is different, the meaning of the words in their original context may be a neutral consideration.

2.7 It might be thought that the legal difficulties which are created by incorporation

16. *Franco-Hungarian Insurance v. Merchants Marine Insurance* 1888, unreported; *Adamastos Shipping Co. Ltd v. Anglo-Saxon Petroleum Ltd* [1959] A.C. 133; *Denny, Mott & Dickson Ltd v. Lynn Shipping Co. Ltd* [1963] 1 Lloyd's Rep. 339; *The Merak* [1964] 2 Lloyd's Rep. 527; *Lovelock v. Exportles* [1968] 1 Lloyd's Rep. 163; *Sabah Flour and Feedmills Sdn Bhd v. Comfez Ltd* [1988] 2 Lloyd's Rep. 18; *CNA International Reinsurance v. Companhia de Seguros Tranquilidade* [1999] Lloyd's Rep. IR 289.

17. *Central Meat Products Co. Ltd v. McDaniel Ltd* [1952] 1 Lloyd's Rep. 562.

18. A rather different question is whether such reference is of itself sufficient to give rise to incorporation into the secondary contract where the secondary contract contains no more than general words of incorporation. There are *dicta* to the effect that an arbitration clause in a charterparty which refers to disputes under bills of lading will be regarded as incorporated into a bill of lading even where the incorporating words in the bill of lading do not refer to arbitration. See: *The Merak* [1964] 2 Lloyd's Rep. 527; *The Annefield* [1971] 1 All E.R. 394. Contrast *The Federal Bulker* [1989] 1 Lloyd's Rep. 103. The point was left open in *The Nerano* [1994] 2 Lloyd's Rep. 50 and *The Delos* [2001] 1 Lloyd's Rep. 703.

19. *Hamilton & Co. v. Mackie & Sons* (1889) 5 TLR 677; *Miramar Maritime Corporation v. Holborn Oil Trading Ltd* [1984] A.C. 676.

20. *The Rena K* [1979] 1 All E.R. 397; *The Nerano* [1994] 2 Lloyd's Rep. 50; *The Delos* [2001] 1 Lloyd's Rep. 703.

21. *CNA International Reinsurance v. Companhia de Seguros Tranquilidade* [1999] Lloyd's Rep. IR 289; *HIH Casualty and General Insurance v. New Hampshire Insurance* [2001] Lloyd's Rep. IR 224, reversed on this point by the Court of Appeal, [2001] E.W.C.A. Civ. 735 [2001] Lloyd's Rep. IR 596.

22. *Home Insurance of New York v. Victoria-Montreal Fire* [1907] A.C. 59; *Skips A/S Nordheim v. Syrian Petroleum Co. Ltd* [1983] 2 Lloyd's Rep. 592; *Balli Trading Ltd v. Afalona Shipping Co. Ltd* [1993] 1 Lloyd's Rep. 1; *Municipal Mutual Insurance Ltd v. Sea Insurance Co. Ltd* [1996] LRLR 265, partially reversed on other grounds [1998] Lloyd's Rep. IR 421; *HIH Casualty and General Insurance v. New Hampshire Insurance* [2001] Lloyd's Rep. IR 596.

23. *Mann v. Lexington Insurance Co.* [2001] Lloyd's Rep. IR 179, *per* Waller LJ at para. 39.

would militate against its use. In the real world, however, this is not the case, and incorporation is rigidly adhered to by those responsible for the preparation of contracts. A psychologist[24] could doubtless explain the precise reasons for this and could suggest how it could be prevented. The role of the lawyer is to undo the damage flowing from incorporation. This chapter is concerned with the experience of incorporation of the terms of direct insurance policies into facultative reinsurance contracts. This practice is almost universal in the London market, and is achieved by the briefest wording, consisting of a front page "Slip Policy" attached to the direct insurance the only main substantive term of which is the "full reinsuring clause" under which the terms of the reinsurance are stated to be "as original" and the reinsurer agrees to follow the settlements of the reinsured. As will be seen, all of the dangers set out above have been experienced by the market in its adherence to this procedure, but only partly overcome.

2B THE NATURE OF FACULTATIVE REINSURANCE

2B.1 The role of reinsurance

Reinsurance is in essence insurance of insurance. Reinsurance would appear to be 2.8
as old as insurance itself.[25] Early reinsurance contracts apparently took the form of further insurance upon the insured subject-matter procured by the insurer from another insurance company, and the only difference between two classes of contract was that, at most, the word "reassurance" would be substituted for "assurance" in a standard form contract, so that an underwriter would not necessarily be aware whether he was a direct insurer or a reinsurer.[26] This was of little real significance to the validity of the contact, in the light of the principle earlier devised by the courts that the nature of an insurable interest was not a material fact which had to be disclosed.[27] Closer examination of leading cases in the nineteenth century indeed reveals that they involved reinsurance rather than insurance.[28] Nevertheless, as early as 1807, in *Delver v. Barnes*,[29] Mansfield CJ was able to define reinsurance as "a new assurance effected by a new policy on the same risk which was before insured in order to indemnify the underwriters from their previous subscriptions".

The form of reinsurance described in the above paragraph has come to be known as 2.9
"facultative", i.e. reinsurance taken out by an insurer on a single risk accepted by him from a direct policy holder and requiring an independent assessment of the risks involved by the reinsurer. The insurer accepts the risk, retains an agreed proportion of

24. Or perhaps Scott Adams. See, *The Dilbert Principle* (1999).
25. The first recorded marine contract has been dated at 1370, and the practice appears to have been widespread by the seventeenth century. See, Golding, *The Law and Practice of Reinsurance*, 4th edn., 1968; Golding, *The History of Reinsurance*, 1927.
26. *Mackenzie v. Whitworth* (1875) LR 10 Ex 142.
27. *Crowley v. Cohen* (1832) 3 B & Ad 478.
28. See, *Dalby v. India and London Life Assurance Co.* (1854) 15 CB 365: had the reinsurance aspects of this case been apparent to the court, the development of the life insurance industry might well have taken a very different turn.
29. (1807) 1 Taunt 48.

it for its own account[30] by way of deductible and reinsures the surplus, possibly subject to financial limits.[31] As the subject-matter of the insurance and the reinsurance are the same, the market has taken the view that reinsurance contracts can be formed simply by the incorporation of the direct wording into the reinsurance: that practice is the focus of this essay. Most direct risks are, however, reinsured by means of treaty, a form of reinsurance which was rather later to develop[32] and which need here be described only briefly. A treaty consists of a framework contract under which the reinsurer agrees to accept risks of a given class and size which are ceded by the reinsured. The obligations to accept risks and to cede them may be compulsory or optional on one or both sides, but the essence of the arrangement is to provide at least a facility and more commonly a guaranteed mechanism to allow liabilities[33] under large numbers of direct policies to be reinsured. Treaties may be "proportional" in the sense that the reinsured retains a proportion of the risk, or "non-proportional". It has long been clear in England that, even though proportional contracts resemble co-insurance or partnership, and in many cases are designed to replicate co-insurance, the reinsurance contract is autonomous and the direct policy holder has no cause of action against anyone other than the direct insurer,[34] in that the reinsured accepts a deductible and cedes the remainder to the reinsurer.[35] Treaties, unlike facultative contracts, are long and complex documents which do not rely upon the incorporation of direct insurance wordings. The placing and administraton of a facultative contract is obviously more expensive and time-consuming than the operation of a treaty, and facultative reinsurance tends to be used for very large risks which fall outside treaty financial limits or which are non-standard and thus require detailed consideration at the underwriting stage.

2.10 Reinsurance has many legitimate objectives.[36] The most important are the following:

(a) Reinsurance increases the underwriting capacity of a direct insurer, allowing him to accept substantial risks which would not otherwise have been insurable but for the guarantee provided by reinsurance. While co-insurance between direct insurers can achieve the same purpose, reinsurance provides an alternative – and in many cases a supplementary –

30. This does not necessarily preclude the insurer from reinsuring its deductible elsewhere, although the reinsurer may insist that the insurer retains a part of the risk as a guarantee against careless underwriting. The key point is that the deductible is the trigger for the reinsurer's liability: see *Kingscroft Insurance Co. v. Nissan Fire & Marine Insurance Co. Ltd (No. 2)* [1999] Lloyd's Rep. IR 603.

31. In which case it may be necessary to find other reinsurance to cover this excess layer.

32. The first recorded treaty dates from 1821.

33. The reinsured liabilities need not be all of those accepted by the reinsured. For example, reinsurance cover may be restricted to specific forms of liability within the general coverage provided by the insurer.

34. *Re Norwich Equitable Fire Assurance Society* (1887) 57 LT 241, the first English case on treaty reinsurance.

35. The nature of proportional (surplus, quota share) treaties and non-proportional (excess of loss, stop loss) is expertly analysed by Carter, *Reinsurance*, 3rd edn. For the operation of the market, see Kiln, *Reinsurance in Practice*, 3rd edn., 1991.

36. And illegitimate objectives as well. It would appear that in the eighteenth century there was gambling by reinsurance, in that a vessel would be insured at one premium and then reinsured at a different premium, thereby allowing speculation on the rise and fall of premiums. It was for this reason that marine reinsurance was banned by s.4 of the Marine Insurance Act 1745, and was permitted only following the repeal of that section by the Revenue (No. 2) Act 1864.

device. Reinsurance may also allow an insurer to expand both the amount and classes of its business more quickly than might otherwise be the case.

(b) Reinsurance enables an insurer to stabilise results over a period of time, and protects the insurer from sudden and violent fluctuations in profitability – and indeed solvency – should there be a catastrophe which causes substantial losses falling disproportionately on the insurer. Again, a large number of small losses exceeding the number which might statistically be expected may expose the insurer in the absence of reinsurance. The key point is, therefore, stability. The role of reinsurance in guarding against insolvency is recognised by the EC regulatory structure for insurers, which demands adequate reinsurance to protect the required solvency margin.

(c) Reinsurance allows countries without highly-developed insurance markets to spread their losses internationally.

(d) Reinsurance is a useful mechanism for overcoming regulatory problems. The laws of some jurisdictions permit only local insurers to accept risks, although the reality is that the local insurer's capacity is too limited to carry all liability: the solution in such a case is for the local insurer to insure, and then to reinsure up to 100 per cent in other markets. Although the reality is a fronting arrangement,[37] the legal position is that the insurance and reinsurance contracts are autonomous. Reinsurance pools, whereby a group of reinsurers agree to accept direct risks of specified types in agreed individual proportions, operate in the same way. The underwriting agent charged with the management of the pool is empowered[38] to use individual members of the pool as "fronting" companies: the front chosen will be one which complies with local licensing requirements, and the front can then reinsure within the pool so that losses can be spread by insurance and reinsurance rather than by co-insurance.

2B.2 Defining the nature of facultative reinsurance

It is a vexed question whether reinsurance is insurance at all. International practice is far from consistent on the point,[39] and it has been held by both the House of Lords and the European Court of Justice that reinsurance is not "insurance" for the purpose of the special jurisdiction rules applicable to insurance contracts in the Brussels Convention 1968 and the Lugano Convention 1989. In *Agnew v. Lansforsakrings-bolagens AB*[40] the House of Lords was of the view that there was no need to treat reinsurance as insurance in this context, given that the purpose of the insurance rules was to provide a measure of consumer protection. The speech of Lord Millett is of particular significance, as he expressed the view that the distinction between the two 2.11

37. Captive insurers, i.e. insurers wholly owned by industrial concerns who insure primarily risks run by those concerns, also reinsure in the open market for the same reasons.

38. The limits of such power may be disputed: *Companhia de Seguros Imperio v. Heath (REBX) Ltd* [2001] Lloyd's Rep. IR 109.

39. See *What is Reinsurance*, AIDA Working Paper No. 1, 1998, a comparative survey conducted by the AIDA Reinsurance Working Party of the treatment of reinsurance in different jurisdictions.

40. [2000] Lloyd's Rep. IR 317.

forms of contract was not simply that reinsurance was always commercial[41] and the risks were always large, whereas insurance could be consumer by nature, but rather because insurance and reinsurance were conceptually different. Direct insurance protected the insured against extraordinary risks outside the ordinary course of events. Reinsurance was concerned with the management of risks which it was in the ordinary business of both parties to underwrite, and was in essence a professional hedging operation. This analysis anticipated the views of the ECJ in *Group Josi Reinsurance Co. SA v. Universal General Insurance Co.*,[42] where much the same approach was adopted.

The *Agnew* and *Group Josi* cases merely provide an answer to a specific question, and ought not to be taken as authority for the general proposition that reinsurance is something other than insurance. Almost every reinsurance case decided in England proceeds on the basis that the rules governing insurance contracts apply to reinsurance,[43] particularly the principle of utmost good faith which in English law is confined to insurance contracts,[44] and also that reinsurance is insurance for regulatory purposes.[45] Assuming, therefore, that reinsurance is insurance, a further question of classification of facultative contracts arises. Three alternatives may be considered: (a) reinsurance is a *sui generis* form of insurance; (b) reinsurance is to be classified by reference to the direct policy which is covered by it; and (c) reinsurance closely resembles liability insurance and is to be treated as such.

2.12 It is suggested that classification (c) is the correct one, and that facultative reinsurance is in essence reinsurance of the liability of the direct insurer under a contract of insurance with the assured.[46] The earlier discussion of the purposes of reinsurance, coupled with the comments of Lord Millett in *Agnew*, make it clear that the purposes of reinsurance are quite different from those of direct insurance. Reinsurance is concerned with stability, capacity and loss spreading. Insurance is concerned with providing a fund to meet one or more contingencies which may affect the assured's personal or business interests. While both forms of contract regulate financial loss, reinsurance has no necessary connection with the nature of the loss suffered by the direct assured other than in the obvious respect that such loss will form the basis of the reinsured's claim against the reinsurer. The reinsurer is not concerned with the direct risk but only with the liability of the reinsured for it. If the reinsurance excludes particular forms of loss – as is the case with a marine reinsurance against total loss only – then the fact that the insured subject-matter has been damaged is of no

41. It has been described as "insurance between consenting adults": Barlow Lyde & Gilbert, *Reinsurance Practice and the Law*, looseleaf, para. 1.1.

42. Case C-412/98 [2001] Lloyd's Rep. IR 483.

43. See, e.g., *Delver v. Barnes* (1807) 1 Taunt 48; *Re Norwich Equitable Fire Assurance Society* (1911) 104 LT 254; *Law Guarantee Trust and Accident Society v. Munich Reinsurance Co.* [1912] 1 Ch 138; *China Traders Insurance Co. v. Royal Exchange Insurance Corporation* [1898] 2 Q.B. 187; *Re London County Commercial Reinsurance Office* [1922] 2 Ch. 67.

44. *L'Alsacienne Premiere Societe v. Unistorebrand International Insurance AS* [1995] LRLR 333. Note, however, that a particular problem arises with non-obligatory treaties, which are best regarded as contracts "for" insurance rather than contracts "of" insurance, in that they merely facilitate rather than create contracts: *HIH Casualty and General Insurance Ltd v. Chase Manhattan Bank* [2001] Lloyd's Rep. IR 191 reversed in part [2001] Lloyd's Rep. IR 703.

45. *Bedford Insurance Co. Ltd v. Instituto de Resseguros do Brasil* [1984] 1 Lloyd's Rep. 210; *Stewart v. Oriental Fire and Marine Insurance Co* [1984] 2 Lloyd's Rep. 109; *Phoenix General Insurance Co. of Greece v. ADAS* [1986] 2 Lloyd's Rep. 552. See also the authorities cited in fnn.47–49 below.

46. This is also the view of Professor Carter, *op cit* at pp.3–4.

significance to the reinsurer. It is also irrelevant to reinsurance whether the direct policy is indemnity (property, liability and the like) or non-indemnity (life), as in either case the reinsurer is required to pay to the insurer the amount for which the insurer has become liable to the direct assured: the nature of the underlying insurance has no implications for the obligations of the reinsurer. Modern reinsurance arrangements, including alternative risk transfer, operate wholly independently of the direct policy.

Regrettably, at least as far as the present author is concerned, the English cases have on the whole failed to recognise the true nature of reinsurance. The problem stems from a series of cases decided in the late nineteenth and early twentieth centuries which involved facultative wordings referring to the subject-matter insured under the direct policy. In the light of wording of this type, which doubtless reflected market understandings of the time, it is hardly surprising that the conclusion reached in those cases was that a direct policy conferred upon the insurer an insurable interest in the insured subject-matter, and it was the interest in the subject-matter rather than liability for it which was being reinsured. As was said by Buckley LJ in *British Dominions General Insurance v. Duder*,[47] a case involving the reinsurance of a vessel: 2.13

"[A] contract of reinsurance is a contact which insures the thing originally insured, namely the ship. The reinsured has an insurable interest in the ship by virtue of his original contract of insurance. The thing insured, however, is the ship, and not the interest of the insurer in the ship by reason of his contract of insurance upon the ship."

This reasoning led the courts to conclude that a reinsurer could not avoid a policy for non-disclosure of the fact that contrary to his belief it was one of reinsurance rather than direct insurance, as the subject-matter was the same in both cases,[48] and that the reinsured could recover no more than the value of the insured subject-matter.[49] The view that reinsurance was simply a further insurance on the subject-matter of the direct contract was seemingly adopted by Chalmers in his drafting of the Marine Insurance Act 1906. Section 9(1) provides that "The insurer under a contract of marine insurance has an insurable interest in his risk, and may re-insure in respect of it".

It might be thought that this analysis of the nature of a reinsurance contract is somewhat artificial and unnecessarily complicated. It is obviously far simpler to say that the reinsured is reinsuring its liability rather than that the insurer, by virtue of an insurable interest in the subject-matter, is able to insure the subject-matter under a contract of reinsurance. However, the approach adopted in the early cases has persisted. In a series of decisions involving the question whether a treaty reinsurer has to be authorised to carry on the individual classes of direct business which it has reinsured, or whether it is sufficient to be authorised as a liability insurer, the courts have concluded, with one notable exception,[50] that the proper construction of the 2.14

47. [1915] 2 KB 394, at p.400. See also *Nelson v. Empress Assurance Corporation* [1925] 2 K.B. 281.
48. *Mackenzie v. Whitworth* (1875) 1 Ex D 36.
49. *Uzielli & Co. v. Boston Marine Insurance Co.* (1884) 15 Q.B.D. 11, a difficult case as the Court of Appeal appears to have allowed the reinsured to recover more than an indemnity (see Butler and Merkin, *Reinsurance Law*, chapter B.2.2); *British Dominions General Insurance Co. Ltd v. Duder* [1915] 2 K.B. 394.
50. The decision of Adrian Hamilton QC in *D R Insurance Co. v. Seguros America Banamex* [1993] 1 Lloyd's Rep. 120.

relevant legislation is that reinsurers are to be treated as carrying on the individual classes of direct business in which they are involved.[51] While it might be thought that the wording of the legislation demands that construction,[52] the result has generally been the same even where the matter at stake has been purely contractual. The point was addressed directly by the Court of Appeal in *Toomey v. Eagle Star Insurance Co. Ltd*;[53] Hobhouse LJ specifically rejected the notion that a reinsurance contract was one of liability insurance, and instead was an insurance of the reinsured's insurable interest in the subject-matter of the direct policy. That analysis has been adopted in later cases,[54] although there have been isolated illustrations of judges taking the view that reinsurance is liability cover[55] or at least reserving their position on the point.[56]

2.15 It is somewhat curious that, while there have been conflicting views expressed as to the nature of a reinsurance policy, the courts have readily adopted identical rules between liability insurance and reinsurance in relation to the right to recover. It is clear law that the assured under a liability policy is entitled to recover only by proving his loss, which can be done by means of a judgment or arbitration award against him or under a settlement which is binding on the insurer.[57] Exactly the same principles apply to the right of a reinsured to recover from his reinsurer.[58] Unless there is a judgment or arbitration award, or a settlement which is binding on the reinsurer (either because the reinsured can demonstrate that actual legal liability would have been faced but for the settlement,[59] or that the reinsurer has agreed by means of a "follow the settlements" clause to accept liability for bona fide and businesslike settlements[60]), the reinsured cannot seek indemnity for any payment which he has made or for which he has become liable to pay.[61] This, if nothing else, clearly demonstrates the liability nature of reinsurance cover.

---

51. *Glasgow Assurance Corporation v. Welsh Insurance Corporation* 1914 SC 320; *Attorney General v. Forskringsaktieselskabet National of Copenhagen* [1925] A.C. 639; *Re NRG Victory Reinsurance Ltd* [1995] 1 All E.R. 533; *Re Friends' Provident Life Office* [1999] Lloyd's Rep. IR 547.

52. The present legislation, the Financial Services and Markets Act 2000 and the regulations made thereunder, makes numerous and specific references to reinsurance.

53. [1994] 1 Lloyd's Rep. 516. See the discussion of this case in Barlow Lyde & Gilbert, *Reinsurance Practice and the Law*, paras 15.2.8.7 and 22.4, where it is pointed out that the real ratio of this case was that the contract under consideration – stop loss reinsurance – was not strictly reinsurance at all but rather was a contract to pay for accumulated losses rather than individual claims.

54. *Baker v. Black Sea and Baltic General Insurance Co. Ltd* [1996] LRLR 353 (CA – the issue did not arise on appeal to the House of Lords); *Commercial Union Assurance Co. v. NRG Victory Reinsurance Ltd* [1998] Lloyd's Rep. IR 439; *CNA International Reinsurance Co. Ltd v. Companhia de Seguros Tranquilidade SA* [1999] Lloyd's Rep. IR 289.

55. Sir Roger Ormrod in the Court of Appeal in *Forsakrings Vesta v. Butcher* [1986] 2 Lloyd's Rep. 179.

56. Lord Mustill in *Charter Reinsurance Co. Ltd v. Fagan* [1996] 2 Lloyd's Rep. 113.

57. *West Wake Price & Co. v. Ching* [1956] 2 Lloyd's Rep. 618; *Post Office v. Norwich Union Fire Insurance Society* [1967] 2 QB 363; *Socony Mobil Oil Co. Inc. v. West of England Ship Owners Mutual Insurance Association Ltd, The Padre Island* [1987] 2 Lloyd's Rep. 529; *Bradley v. Eagle Star Insurance Co.* [1989] 1 A.C. 597; *Cox v. Bankside Members Agency Ltd* [1995] 2 Lloyd's Rep. 437.

58. Unless the policy can be construed as covering other forms of loss, as was the case in *Toomey v. Eagle Star Insurance Co. Ltd* [1994] 1 Lloyd's Rep. 516.

59. *Commercial Union plc v. NRG Victory Reinsurance Ltd* [1998] Lloyd's Rep. IR 439.

60. *Insurance Co. of Africa v. Scor (UK) Reinsurance Co. Ltd* [1985] 1 Lloyd's Rep. 312; *Hill v. Mercantile and General Reinsurance Co. Ltd* [1996] LRLR 341. See the discussion below.

61. For a comparative study, see *Follow the Settlements*, AIDA Reinsurance Working Party Paper No. 3, 1998.

2B.3 The optimal terms of a facultative reinsurance contract

It is of crucial importance to the notion of incorporation to classify reinsurance correctly. If reinsurance is regarded as no more than a further insurance on the original subject-matter, albeit based on the reinsured's separate insurable interest in that subject-matter conferred by reason of the fact that it is an insurer, then some support may be derived for an argument for incorporation of the terms of the direct policy into the reinsurance, although even on this approach incorporation has in practice been shown not to work satisfactorily: this is considered in more detail below. However, it the submission made earlier is correct, and that what is really at stake in a facultative contract is no more than an insurance of the reinsured's liability, it follows that the differences between insurance and reinsurance are more significant than might otherwise be thought and that incorporation has to be regarded with much greater suspicion than it has to date been afforded.[62] 2.16

One way to test the efficacy of incorporation is to consider what a liability policy typically contains. Although there is no standard format, it is possible to divide the terms of a liability policy as follows: (1) the insuring clause, setting out the liabilities of the assured for which the insurer accepts responsibility (negligence, breach of contract, etc), and the financial limits of cover; (2) exclusions from cover; (3) obligations of the assured. These will cover obligations such as payment of the premium, duties during the currency of the policy in relation to the risk and conditions setting out the procedures to be followed in the event of a claim against the assured; (4) provisions relating to the defence of any claim against the assured, including the insurer's liability for defence costs and the right of the insurer to take over the defence or to settle or authorise settlements; and (5) ancillary provisions, including applicable law and arbitration or choice of forum. The policy reflects the potential liabilities of the assured towards third parties, and sets out a framework for dealing with claims against the assured which fall within the scope of the policy. 2.17

The needs of a facultative reinsurance contract are identical: (1) the liabilities faced by the reinsured have to be defined; (2) the limits of cover have to be specified; (3) the obligations of the reinsured in relation to presenting claims to the reinsurer have to be set out; (4) claims handling by the reinsured, in particular the rights of the reinsurer to take over the defence of the claim by the assured and to settle or authorise settlements, has to be clarified; and (5) jurisdiction and choice of law issues have to be resolved. 2.18

2B.4 The appropriateness of incorporation from the direct policy

It is well established that there is a strong presumption of back-to-back cover between a direct policy and the reinsurance contract relating to it. That presumption is based on the notion that the reinsured intends, by effecting reinsurance, to transfer the major part of the risk of liability for an insured loss[63] to the reinsurer. Indeed, in 2.19

62. The cases on the meaning of reinsurance are discussed by O'Neill and Wolonecki, *The Law of Reinsurance*, paras 1–22 to 1–30: the authors conclude that the correct classification is largely irrelevant, although accept in para. 1–30 that the link between the insurance contract and the reinsurance contract is strengthened if the reinsurer can be regarded as having insured the "same thing".

63. This excludes defence costs unless the contract otherwise provides: *Baker v. Black Sea and Baltic General Insurance Co.* [1998] Lloyd's Rep. IR 327.

Vesta v. Butcher[64] Lord Griffiths expressed the view that cover would be treated as matching in the absence of some special contract between the parties excluding certain risks from the coverage of the reinsurance. The application of the back-to-back principle has led the courts: to treat the risks covered by the insurance and the reinsurance as identical;[65] to construe the duration provisions of the two contracts as matching;[66] and to give the same effect to the warranties in the reinsurance contract so as to accord with that applicable to the same warranties found in the direct policy.[67] There are only two situations in which the presumption of back-to-back cover has no application. The first is where the reinsurance agreement is in non-proportional treaty form, as here the interests of the reinsured and the reinsurer are readily distinguishable.[68] As facultative contracts are by their nature proportional, this is of no significance to the present discussion. Second, if there is a clear and express difference between the two contracts, possibly arising from individual negotiation of the reinsurance, then there is no room for the presumption of back-to-back cover in respect of the points of difference. The reinsurance agreement may, for example, provide for specific commencement and duration dates which differ from those of the direct policy[69] or it may be restricted to reinsuring liability for particular forms of direct loss.[70]

2.20 The presumption of back-to-back cover recognises the obvious overlaps between the demands of a facultative reinsurance contract and the direct policy underlying the reinsurance. What, then, is the purpose of incorporating the terms of the direct policy into the reinsurance? Such incorporation has superficial attraction in that it confirms the nature of the relationship between the reinsurer and reinsured, but it is the submission of the present author that the concurrencies between the insurance and the reinsurance are confined to the insuring clause, and that wholesale incorporation does more harm than good. Let it be supposed that the direct policy is one on a ship and that there is a desire to achieve back-to-back cover as regards the risks insured against by the reinsured. What is the role of incorporation? It is helpful to consider the constitutent elements of facultative reinsurance contract identified above:

(a) The insuring clause. Given that there is a presumption of back-to-back cover between the direct policy and the reinsurance independently of any

64. [1989] 1 Lloyd's Rep. 331.

65. *Reliance Marine Insurance Co. v. Duder* [1913] 1 KB 265; *Citadel Insurance Co. v. Atlantic Union Insurance Co. SA* [1982] 2 Lloyd's Rep. 543; *Abrahams v. Mediterranean Insurance and Reinsurance Co. Ltd* [1991] 1 Lloyd's Rep. 216; *Mann v. Lexington Insurance Co.* [2001] Lloyd's Rep. IR 179; *HIH Casualty and General Insurance Ltd v. New Hampshire Insurance Co.* [2001] Lloyd's Rep. IR 225, approved in principle by the Court of Appeal [2001] E.W.C.A. Civ. 735 [2001] Lloyd's Rep. IR 596.

66. *Commercial Union Assurance Co. plc v. Sun Alliance Insurance Group plc* [1992] 1 Lloyd's Rep. 475.

67. *Vesta v. Butcher* [19898] 1 Lloyd's Rep. 331, although this case turned on the ruling that the reinsurance did not contain any warranties of the type alleged, as these appeared only in the direct policy and had not been incorporated; *Groupama Navigation et Transport v. Catatumbo CA Seguros* [2000] 2 Lloyd's Rep. 340.

68. The leading authority on this point is *Axa Reinsurance (UK) plc v. Field* [1996] 2 Lloyd's Rep. 233, where the House of Lords refused to construe differently worded aggregation provisions in the direct policy ("originating cause") and in the reinsurance ("event") as being back to back. See also *American Centennial Insurance Co. v. INSCO Ltd* [1996] LRLR 407.

69. See, *Youell v. Bland Welch & Co. (No 1)* [1992] 2 Lloyd's Rep. 127; *Municipal Mutual Insurance Ltd v. Sea Insurance Ltd* [1998] Lloyd's Rep. IR 421.

70. *Street v. Royal Exchange Assurance* (1914) 19 Com Cas 330 (total loss only).

incorporation of insuring terms, it is difficult to see what purpose incorporation achieves other than confirming the intentions of the parties in this regard. If Lord Griffiths is right, then only the presence of a special provision in the reinsurance restricting the operation of back-to-back cover would suffice to defeat the presumed intention of the parties.

(b) The exceptions clause. There is no need to incorporate the exceptions clause in the direct policy into the reinsurance, for the simple reason that if an exception in the direct policy is applicable then the reinsured cannot face liability and the reinsurance does not attach as the reinsured cannot prove its loss.

(c) Obligations of the assured. If the assured breaks a condition or warranty in the direct policy, the effect of which is to confer upon the reinsured the right to deny liability, then the terms of the reinsurance are immaterial: if the reinsured chooses to pay despite the existence of a valid defence, its payment is *ex gratia* and it cannot prove its loss. If that breach does not provide a defence, then the reinsured has proved its loss and *prima facie* the reinsurer has to pay, unless of course the reinsurer has inserted terms of its own into the reinsurance which confer a defence in those very circumstances. However, unless the exclusion is very clearly worded, it may well be overriden by the presumption of back-to-back cover.[71] The point, therefore, is that the incorporation of the direct terms into the reinsurance policy adds nothing, and merely gives rise to the possibility – which indeed arose in *Vesta v. Butcher*[72] – that if the laws applicable to the direct policy and the reinsurance are different as regards the effect of a breach of a policy term, the reinsurer may not face liability whereas the reinsured may face liability. Plainly, the fortuitous application of different applicable laws ought not to defeat the presumption of back-to-back cover, and in *Vesta v. Butcher* it was not permitted to do so,[73] but what is apparent is that the problem arises only because of incorporation.

(d) Defence of the claim. The processes for dealing with direct claims and reinsurance claims are quite different. In a first party marine policy on a vessel, issues of defending claims from third parties do not arise, and to face liability the reinsured has to be satisfied that the loss of the ship is a genuine one and the loss was caused by an insured peril. At the reinsurance level, by contrast, the liability nature of the contract means that the reinsured has to prove its loss, which it does by demonstrating either an obligation to pay under the direct policy or at least a bona fide and businesslike settlement which triggers the reinsurer's liability under a follow the settlements clause. If there is a follow the settlements clause, the incorporation into the reinsurance of the claims conditions in the direct policy makes little sense: if the assured has not complied with the necessary conditions, the reinsured is not liable in any event, and if he has and the reinsured's liability is established, then it is difficult to see why the reinsured should have to jump

71. *Groupama Navigation et Transport v. Catatumbo CA Seguros* [2000] 2 Lloyd's Rep. 340.
72. [1989] 1 Lloyd's Rep. 331.
73. See *infra*.

through the same procedural hoops as the direct assured. It is perfectly open to the reinsurer to impose conditions upon the right of the reinsured to reach settlements – in the form of claims co-operation and claims control clauses – and such terms are perfectly adequate to protect the reinsurer as they have been held to "emasculate" any obligation to follow settlements.[74]

(e) Choice of law, jurisdiction and arbitration. There is no need for the reinsurance to incorporate any choice of law clause in the direct policy,[75] as the presumption of back-to-back cover means that the law applicable to the direct cover will necessarily determine the scope of the reinsurance cover.[76] As regards jurisdiction clauses and arbitration clauses, there is no particular reason to suppose that any jurisdiction and arbitration arrangements agreed between the assured and the reinsured are appropriate at the reinsurance level, and as noted earlier there is a strong presumption against the incorporation of these types of clause from one contract into another by the mere use of general words of incorporation.

2.21 The general conclusion that may be derived from these considerations is that the objective of back-to-back cover can perfectly easily be achieved without recourse to any concept of incorporating the terms of the direct policy into the reinsurance. In *HIH Casualty and General Insurance Ltd v. New Hampshire Insurance Co.*[77] incorporation and the presumption of back-to-back cover were regarded by David Steel J as alternative methods of reaching the same result, namely, that the reinsurers were entitled to the benefit of a term implied into the direct policy. Here, the assured, LDT, had loaned money to two film production companies: the loan was to be repaid from the profits flowing from the films. The slips for the two policies stated that six films and ten films respectively would be made. The policies themselves did not refer to the numbers of films involved, although David Steel J ruled that the slips had been incorporated into the policies, rendering the number of films involved warranties in the policies: even if that was wrong, David Steel J held in the alternative that it would have been appropriate to imply warranties to that effect. As the learned judge pointed out, without commitments of this type there would have been no obligation for any films to be made at all, converting the policies from insurances against shortfall of profits from an agreed number of films into unconditional and on demand performance bonds under which no films need be made but the insurers would remain liable. The further issue was whether the warranties/implied terms applied to the reinsurance, which David Steel J regarded as having been made back-to-back with the insurance, with the insurance operating as a fronting operation for the reinsurance. David Steel J held that it was appropriate in the circumstances to disregard reservations as to incorporation and to hold that the reinsurance contracts contained the same warranty, and in the alternative the presumption of back-to-back

74. *Insurance Co. of Africa v. Scor (UK) Reinsurance Co. Ltd* [1985] 1 Lloyd's Rep. 312; *Gan Insurance Co. Ltd v. Tai Ping Insurance Co. Ltd (No. 2)* [2001] Lloyd's Rep. IR 667. See *infra*.

75. *Gan Insurance Co. Ltd v. Tai Ping Insurance Co. Ltd* [1999] Lloyd's Rep. IR 472.

76. *Vesta v. Butcher* [1989] 1 Lloyd's Rep. 331; *Groupama Navigation et Transport v. Catatumbo CA Seguros* [2000] 2 Lloyd's Rep. 340; *Ace Insurance Co. SA/NV v. Zurich Insurance Co* [2001] Lloyd's Rep. IR 504.

77. [2001] Lloyd's Rep. IR 224.

cover produced the same result. On appeal to the Court of Appeal, David Steel J's conclusion that the warranties had been incorporated into the reinsurance agreement was affirmed in a single sentence. The Court of Appeal did not rely upon the presumption of back-to-back cover, as it was clear from the arguments before the Court of Appeal that the reinsurers were not prepared to accept the assumption that the insurance and reinsurance agreements were formed on a back-to-back basis and that the arrangement was akin to a fronting arrangement. Rix LJ, delivering the only reasoned judgment in the Court of Appeal, was content to assume that there was overall back-to-back coverage, based on the fact that many of the key terms of the two contracts – interest, type, premium, amendment provisions – were common. However, the decision did not turn on this point, and indeed Rix LJ derived support for his working assumption of back-to-back coverage from the very fact that general words of incorporation were contained in the reinsurance. It is submitted that nothing in Rix LJ's approach weakens the autonomy of the principle of back-to-back cover, particularly as the case concerned only preliminary issues and the existence of back-to-back cover had not been one of them.

Even if it is right that incorporation is the proper approach to achieving back-to-back cover, rather than that principle operating independently, there is nevertheless no reason to allow incorporation of anything other than the cover provided by the direct policy. Other terms and conditions in the direct policy are not designed for reinsurance and ought therefore, it might be thought, to have no part to play. Two further questions are addressed in the following discussion: how did the notion of incorporation develop in the first place, and what problems has it produced? 2.22

2C THE DEVELOPMENT OF THE CONCEPT OF INCORPORATION

2C.1 Market wordings

The current practice in the London market for the making of a facultative reinsurance contract is to append to the direct policy a cover page, often headed "Slip Policy".[78] That cover page is a reinsurance agreement in its own right, and will normally contain a "full reinsurance" clause. The wording is not always the same, but the following is typical: 2.23

> "Being a reinsurance of and warranted same gross rate, terms and conditions as and to follow the settlements of the company. . . ."

Two quite different issues are here being addressed. The first is the statement that the "gross rate, terms and conditions" of the reinsurance are the same as those of the direct policy. The second is that the reinsurer will follow the settlements of the

78. To make it clear that the slip is the policy and that no further wording will be issued.

reinsured. The modern wording has been in use since the 1920s, and was the successor[79] of an earlier formulation:

> "Subject to the same terms and conditions as the original and to pay as may be paid thereon."

Once again, the same two concepts – the terms of the reinsurance policy and the obligation of the reinsurer to pay – are being addressed. The meaning of the phrases "pay as may be paid thereon" and the more recent "follow the settlements", is of some relevance to the present discussion as it forms part of an entire clause and thus possibly throws some light upon the meaning of the remainder of that clause. It is nevertheless sufficient to note that "pay as may be paid thereon" was construed as meaning that the reinsured was entitled to be indemnified by the reinsurer before making actual payment to the reinsured[80] but proof of the reinsured's liability as a matter of law was required[81] and the words did not in any way expand the reinsurer's liability to meet claims which were expressly excluded by the terms of the reinsurance.[82] The change of wording from "pay to be paid" to "follow the settlements" was prompted by a desire to ensure that a reinsurer would be bound by a settlement reached by the reinsured in a bona fide and businesslike fashion even though it later proved that the reinsured could have contested liability as a matter of law, e.g. for fraud by the assured or on the proper construction of the policy: the cases decided in the wake of that change have established the draftsman's success in achieving this objective.[83]

---

79. Another formulation adopted in the marine market purported to render the reinsurer liable for total loss, constructive total loss or arranged/agreed/compromised total loss. The authorities were inconsistent on the question whether words of this type were sufficient to bind the reinsurer to follow a settlement which did not as a matter of law involve a total loss: *Bergens Dampskibs Assurance Forening v. Sun Insurance Office Ltd* (1930) 37 Ll LR 175; *Gurney v. Grimmer* (1932) 44 Ll LR 189.

80. *Martin v. Munich Assurance Co.* 1891, unreported; *Re Eddystone Marine Insurance Co, ex parte Western Insurance Co. Ltd* [1892] 2 Ch 423. There are *dicta* in *Fireman's Fund Insurance Co. v. Western Australian Insurance Co. Ltd* (1928) 138 LT 108 to the contrary, but these can scarcely stand in the light of the ruling of the House of Lords in *Charter Reinsurance Co. Ltd v. Fagan* [1996] 1 Lloyd's Rep. 113.

81. *Chippendale v. Holt* (1895) 1 Com Cas 197; *St Paul Fire and Marine Insurance Co. v. Morice* (1906) 22 TLR 449; *Fireman's Fund Insurance Co. v. Western Australian Insurance Co. Ltd* (1928) 138 LT 108; *Merchants' Marine Insurance Co. Ltd v. Liverpool Marine and General Insurance Co. Ltd* (1928) 31 Ll LR 45. In *Western Assurance Co. of Toronto v. Poole* [1903] 1 KB 376 Bigham J suggested, *obiter* that once the reinsured's liability had been established, the reinsurer was required to pay as may be paid without the opportunity to dispute *quantum*. That distinction was doubted in *Gurney v. Grimmer* (1932) 44 Ll LR 189 and *Versicherungs und Transport AG Daugava v. Henderson* (1934) 49 Ll LR 252, but approved in *Hong Kong Borneo Services Ltd v. Pilcher* [1992] 2 Lloyd's Rep. 593.

82. *Marten v. Steamship Owners' Underwriting Association Ltd* (1902) 71 LJKB 718; *Western Assurance Co. of Toronto v. Poole* [1903] 1 K.B. 376. The decision in *Uzielli & Co. v. Boston Marine Insurance Co.* (1884) 15 Q.B.D. 11 is seemingly to the contrary, and has over the years defied rational explanation. *Cf.* Lord Hoffmann in *Charter Reinsurance Co. Ltd v. Fagan* [1996] 1 Lloyd's Rep. 113 at p.122. For brave attempts see: O'Neill and Wolonecki, *The Law of Reinsurance*, para. 7–06; Butler and Merkin, *Reinsurance Law*, Chapter C.1.2.

83. Despite an uncertain start: see *Garthwaite (Liberia) Ltd v. Port of Manchester Insurance Co. Ltd* [1930] 37 Ll LR 194; *Versicherungs und Transport AG Daugava v. Henderson* (1934) 49 Ll LR 252. However, the binding effect on the clause in the event of a bona fide and businesslike settlement is now settled law: *Excess Liability Insurance Co. Ltd v. Matthews* (1925) 31 Com Cas 43; *Insurance Co. of Africa v. Scor (UK) Reinsurance Co. Ltd* [1985] 2 Lloyd's Rep. 312; *Hiscox v. Outhwaite* [1991] 2 Lloyd's Rep. 54; *Charman v. Guardian Royal Exchange Assurance plc* [1992] 2 Lloyd's Rep. 607; *Municipal Mutual Insurance Ltd v. Sea Insurance Co. Ltd* [1996] LRLR 265; *Hill v. Mercantile and General Reinsurance Co. plc* [1996] LRLR 341.

2C.2 "Same terms and conditions"

The key phrases in the full reinsurance clause are "subject to the same terms and conditions as original" and the succeeding "warranted same gross rate, terms and conditions". It does not appear to have been suggested in the cases that the two formulations bear any different meaning. That said, the latter wording on its face appears to be directed not towards incorporating the terms of the direct policy into the reinsurance but rather to ensuring that the terms of the direct policy were no different to those actually agreed with the reinsurer. This point emerges from a series of cases involving direct insurance, where the assured, having procured an initial direct policy subsequently obtained a second direct policy which was warranted to be on the same terms as the original. The effect of the warranty was to allow the second insurer to deny liability in the event that there were variations between the first and second policies, e.g. as to the rate of premium payable.[84] The origins of the clause do not appear to have featured in the arguments raised in more recent cases on incorporation in reinsurance cases, and it has simply been assumed that they have the same incorporating effect as their predecessor. Adoption of direct language for reinsurance purposes again makes the point that facultative reinsurance has typically been viewed as no more than a further policy on the original subject-matter. 2.24

Although it is not possible to be certain exactly when the phrase "subject to the same terms and conditions as original" was first used, it appears from the arguments in *Re Eddystone Marine Insurance Co.*[85] that it was familiar in the London market in the second half of the nineteenth century and that its purpose was to ensure that the reinsurer's liability matched that of the reinsured by means of incorporation. As Walton QC explained in argument in *Re Eddystone*, "the original policies may perhaps not be at hand, or cannot be copied in, so the incorporation of the terms of the original policy is effected by putting in this form". This statement suggests that the reinsurer might not have been in possession of the direct policy but as a matter of market practice would nevertheless have been prepared to follow the reinsured's liabilities.

The reference to incorporation is, however, the key point. It will be recalled that at the beginning of the twentieth century facultative reinsurances were framed as being further insurances on the subject-matter of the direct insurance, and this was the analysis generally adopted by the courts. It would, therefore, have made perfect sense for a reinsurer simply to adopt the wording of the direct policy as his own, particularly if that wording was not available to him at the time of placement. A further pointer towards an intention to incorporate might be that, if the sole purpose of the overall clause "subject to the same terms and conditions as the original and to pay as may be paid thereon" had been to require the reinsurer to pay on proof of the reinsured's liability, then that purpose would have been achieved by the final words "to pay as may be paid thereon", and the opening words "subject to the same terms and conditions as the original" would have been otiose. It might of course be pointed out that this argument relies upon hindsight, as the meaning of "pay to be paid thereon" was not discussed by the courts until long after the clause had become widely used: it 2.25

84. *Barnard v. Faber* [1893] 1 Q.B. 340; *Walker & Sons v. Uzielli* (1896) 1 Com Cas 492; *Bancroft v. Heath* (1901) 17 TLR 425.

85. [1892] 2 Ch. 423.

was not confirmed until *Re Eddystone Marine Insurance Co.*[86] in 1892 that the reinsurer was required to make payment on proof of the reinsured's liability rather than payment by the reinsured, and until *Chippendale v. Holt* in 1895[87] that actual liability had to be shown. The point nevertheless remains that the almost certain purpose of the clause was to effect some form of incorporation of the terms of the direct policy into the reinsurance. If Walton QC was right, incorporation may well have been intended to relate to the entirety of the direct policy.

2.26 Whatever the intention, the bulk of cases decided in the early part of twentieth century showed a healthy sceptical attitude to the possibility of incorporation. The courts were plainly concerned with the problem that, if incorporation were accepted, there could be a problem in reconciling the incorporated terms with the express terms and indeed with the very nature of a reinsurance contract. Nevertheless, it has gradually come to be accepted, particularly since an influential concession to that effect in *Vesta v. Butcher* in 1989,[88] that formulations such as "subject to the same terms and conditions as original" – which in modern practice in some instances has been abbreviated to just "as original" – have an incorporating effect. While there have been powerful voices of protest,[89] the objections have in recent years been primarily directed not to any denial of incorporation but rather to the adverse consequences that incorporation has had for certainty and contract construction.

2D THE MODERN LAW ON INCORPORATION

2D.1 Principles governing incorporation

2.27 The principles determining incorporation that can be gleaned from the cases were restated by David Steel J in *HIH Casualty and General Insurance Ltd v. New Hampshire Insurance Co.*[90] and adopted on appeal by the Court of Appeal without argument:[91]

Incorporation of a specific term (or condition) is only achieved if the term:

(i) is germane to the reinsurance;
(ii) makes sense, subject to permissible "manipulation", in the context of reinsurance;
(iii) is consistent with the express terms of the reinsurance;
(iv) is apposite for inclusion in the reinsurance.

These conditions are not fully mutually exclusive, but the general theme can be readily ascertained. A term will be carried across by express words of incorporation if it can be made to work in the reinsurance agreement to which it relates. Incorporation applies not just to the scope of coverage, but to all parts of the direct policy insofar as

86. *Ibid.*
87. (1895) 1 Com Cas 197.
88. [1991] 1 Lloyd's Rep. 331.
89. Notably their Lordships, led by Lord Griffiths, in *Vesta v. Butcher*.
90. [2001] Lloyd's Rep. IR 224, at p.234.
91. *HIH Casualty & General Insurance Ltd v. New Hampshire Insurance Co.* [2001] E.W.C.A. Civ. 735 [2001] Lloyd's Rep. IR 596.

they can be made sense of at the level of reinsurance. Just how these conditions have worked in practice will be considered in the following paragraphs.

An initial point to note here is that the concept of incorporation encompasses three separate concepts which have not always been kept distinct. First, incorporation may do no more than operate as a statement in the reinsurance of the reinsured's rights under the direct policy, setting out the terms and conditions of the reinsured's liability and thus the reinsurers' liability (on the basis that the reinsurers are obliged to indemnify the reinsured for any loss within the direct policy). Second, incorporation may have the effect of bringing the terms of the direct policy into the reinsurance, so that those terms are applicable as between reinsurer and insurer in exactly the same way as between insurer and assured. Thus, if the direct policy states that the assured must claim against the insurer/reinsured within 14 days of damage to the insured subject-matter, then incorporation requires the insurer/reinsured to make a claim against the reinsurer within the same time period.[92] Third, incorporation may have the effect of allowing the reinsurer to rely upon breaches of the terms of the direct policy by the assured. Description of the third process as "incorporation" is misleading. If the assured has broken the direct policy in a way which gives the reinsured a defence, then the reinsurer is not liable on the simple ground that any acceptance of liability by the reinsured is *ex gratia* and thus outside the scope of the cover provided by the reinsurance. Accordingly, there is no need to resort to incorporation at all in this situation. Nevertheless, some of the cases proceed on the basis that the reason that the reinsured cannot recover is that the assured's obligations have been incorporated into the reinsurance. The true issue to be determined on incorporation is the choice between the first two situations outlined above, i.e. whether incorporation operates as no more than a statement of the reinsurers' obligation to follow the liabilities or settlements of the reinsured, or whether it operates to insert a term in the reinsurance which has effect as between reinsurers and reinsured. That question itself depends upon the nature of the term incorporated. 2.28

2D.2 Incorporating coverage

2D.2(i) Coverage contained in the direct policy

Incorporation has, historically at least, had its greatest impact by ensuring that the coverage of the direct policy and the reinsurance are back-to-back. As has been commented at various points in this chapter, the notion of back-to-back coverage can operate perfectly satisfactorily without the incorporation of the terms of the direct policy into the reinsurance. The earliest cases can indeed be explained on this basis. However, it gradually became the position that the phenomenon of back-to-back coverage was explained by incorporation. The concept of incorporation has its origins in, and was developed by, a series of marine decisions. In *Joyce v. Realm Marine Insurance Co. Ltd*[93] a direct marine cargo voyage policy insured cargo on its outward voyage to Africa and on its homeward voyage to a port of discharge in the UK. The 2.29

92. This example illustrates the inappropriateness of incorporation. If the nature of facultative reinsurance is that it is liability cover, then what the reinsurer should be concerned with is not the original loss but rather the manner in which it is dealt with by the reinsured.

93. (1872) LR 7 Q.B. 580.

policy specifically stated that cargo on board the vessel on arrival at the first port of discharge in Africa was, for a period of 24 hours, deemed to be on its homeward voyage. The reinsurance, which was made after the vessel had arrived in Africa, provided cover only for the homeward voyage "from the loading thereof" but was otherwise stated in the reinsuring clause to be "subject to all clauses and conditions of the original policy". Cargo was damaged by fire at a time when it was deemed to be on its homeward voyage by virtue of the extension clause, and the reinsured – itself clearly liable for the loss – argued that the reinsurers were liable by virtue of the extension clause. The court agreed. Lush J held that the words of incorporation affected the interpretation of the phrase "from the loading thereof", and allowed it to be construed as covering the constructive loading contemplated by the extension clause in the direct policy. Blackburn J relied on what would today be regarded as a presumption of back-to-back cover, bolstered by the reinsuring clause. Although the reasoning is not always clear, the reinsuring clause words were regarded not as directly incorporating the words of the direct policy but rather as providing the correct interpretation of the meaning of the reinsurance. If this is right, then the reasoning would seem to be impeccable.

2.30 Subsequently, however, incorporation began to be regarded as the explanation of back-to-back cover. In *Franco-Hungarian Insurance Co. v. Merchants Marine Insurance Co.*,[94] a direct time policy on a vessel contained a held covered clause which automatically extended the insurance on the vessel, despite the termination of the policy period, until she reached the port of Marseilles. That risk had been reinsured by a local French company, reinsured with the claimants and subsequently retroceded to the defendants. The retrocession was stated to be "subject to the terms and conditions of the original policy". The vessel was lost in the period covered by the held covered clause, and the issue before Day J was whether that clause took effect in the retrocession. Day J held that it did not, apparently because the retrocession was a self-contained time policy and that it was not possible to incorporate the terms of the direct policy – including the held covered clause – into it. Leaving aside the difficulty in reconciling the outcome with *Joyce*,[95] there was a perceptible shift from reliance on back-to-back cover to reliance on incorporation, with the result that if incorporation were not possible then there could be no back-to-back cover. That analysis was confirmed in *General Insurance Co. of Trieste Ltd v. Corporation of the Royal Exchange*.[96] Here, the direct policy on cargo covered the cargo during loading and thereafter. Cargo on each lighter during the course of loading was deemed to be a separate risk. The liability under this policy was reinsured and retroceded. The retrocession provided that its coverage was "warranted free of all average" (i.e. total loss only) but was "subject to the terms, clauses and conditions of the original policy". Cargo on board the vessel was destroyed by fire, but cargo in the course of being loaded and still in lighters was unaffected. The retrocessionaires denied liability as there had been only a partial loss of the cargo: the retrocedents argued that the provision in the direct policy that the cargo on each lighter was a separate risk had been incorporated into the

94. *Shipping Gazette*, 7 June 1888.

95. Regrettably, the report of *Franco-Hungarian v. Merchants Marine* is insufficiently detailed for it to be ascertained whether *Joyce* was referred to.

96. (1897) 2 Com Cas 144.

retrocession, with the result that there had been a total loss of a distinct part of the cargo. Mathew J upheld the retrocedant's argument, and ruled that the clauses in the direct policy were part of the retrocession and were to be read in conjunction with the "free of all average" warranty, limiting its effects in the case of a total loss of a part.

Marten v. Nippon Sea and Land Insurance Co. Ltd[97] was a further step in the same process. The direct insurance covered a cargo under a voyage policy from Liverpool to Guayaquil, and included a warehouse to warehouse clause extending the coverage under the policy until the cargo was discharged and safely landed, including all risks of inland transport for delivery to the consignee. The reinsurance was expressed to apply until the cargo was discharged and safely landed, and was otherwise "subject to the same clauses and conditions" as the direct policy. The cargo was lost while in a customs warehouse. Bigham J held that the reinsurers were not liable for the loss, but on the narrow ground that a customs warehouse was not within the scope of the direct policy as it was to be treated as the consignee's warehouse, so that there had been safe delivery. On the wider issue, the learned judge accepted that the warehouse to warehouse clause had been incorporated into the reinsurance: it was a customary clause in a marine policy, and the reinsurers ought to have appreciated that it was in the direct policy. It is not clear from this reasoning whether the reinsuring clause was the justification for incorporation, whether incorporation took effect directly into the reinsurance as it was a marine policy in its own right, or whether the principle of back-to-back cover required the implication of direct policy terms which were generally found in the underlying direct policy. Whichever is correct, the language used was that of incorporation, and the only qualification was that the terms should be a common one. Bigham J adopted much the same reasoning in *Charlesworth v. Faber*,[98] ruling that a held covered clause in a direct marine hull time policy was commonplace and ought to be regarded as having been incorporated into the reinsurance. In *Charlesworth*, Bigham J distinguished *Franco-Hungarian Insurance Co. v. Merchants Marine Insurance Co.* on the basis that the extension clause in that case had not been shown by the evidence to be one in common usage. 2.31

The common usage exception to incorporation was applied by Mathew J in *Maritime Insurance Co. v. Stearns.*[99] This case concerned a direct voyage cargo policy on the transport of coal from Newcastle to various ports in Scandinavia. The policy contained a held covered clause, stating that in the event of deviation[100] the insurance was to continue subject to an additional premium being paid. There was deviation, in the form of delay,[101] and an increased premium was paid to the reinsured. Following a loss, the issue was whether the reinsurers were liable given that they had reinsured "subject to the same terms and conditions as the original policy". Mathew J held that there had been no incorporation, as the held covered clause had not been shown to be a common one in direct policies of the present type and accordingly that the reinsurers were not liable. 2.32

97. (1898) 3 Com Cas 164.
98. (1900) 5 Com Cas 408.
99. [1901] 2 K.B. 912.
100. Which would otherwise have discharged the insurers: Marine Insurance Act 1906, s.46.
101. Which is treated by the Marine Insurance Act 1906, s.48, as a discharging event in its own right, although it remains closely aligned to deviation: see Marine Insurance Act 1906, s.49 for the defences common to both deviation and delay.

2.33 The conclusion which may be drawn from the early marine cases is that the common law at this stage accepted that reinsuring wordings such as "terms and conditions as original" were to be treated as incorporating the coverage of the direct policy even though that coverage was in some way extended beyond that expressed to be the case in the reinsurance. The only specific qualification[102] was that the incorporated term had to be one in general usage, so that the reinsurer was not taken by surprise by the inclusion of the coverage provisions of a direct policy the terms of which the reinsurer may not have seen. It is submitted that this reasoning is defective, and that the cases could more rationally have turned simply on the notion of back-to-back cover.

2.34 If incorporation is set aside for the purposes of discussion, then it is the essence of the notion of back-to-back that the reinsurer is liable for all losses within the standard terms of the direct policy. If there are unusual risks for which additional premium has been taken by the reinsured but not by the reinsurers, then it almost goes without saying that, if those terms have not been disclosed to the reinsurer, the reinsurance can be avoided for non-disclosure given the premium-sensitivity of coverage provisions.[103] If they have been disclosed and the reinsurer has chosen to reinsure on that basis, then there is waiver and the reinsurer's liability necessarily follows. An alternative route to the same conclusion is that the reinsurer cannot under the back-to-back principle be liable for loss resulting from extended circumstances as the reinsured has only paid for back-to-back coverage consistent with the usual coverage of a direct policy of that type. The point remains that incorporation is not relevant to the discussion.

2.35 By contrast, if incorporation is the basis upon which the scope of the reinsurer's liability is established, it becomes difficult to see upon what basis unusual risks should be excluded from incorporation. After all, phrases such as "all terms and conditions as original", if they are words of incorporation, are not on their face restricted in their application. It thus becomes necessary to imply an "unusual terms" limitation. Moreover, if the reinsurer has had sight of the direct policy, and that will generally be the case in the modern market as the reinsuring clauses are attached to that document, then once again, it is difficult for the reinsurer to argue that he ought not to be bound by the terms of the direct policy simply because they are unusual. In short, incorporation is an unnecessary and artificial explanation of why the reinsurer is or is not liable, as the case may be.

---

102. There was, presumably, a further restriction in that the terms of the direct policy could not be permitted to override the express terms of the reinsurance, although they could certainly require a different interpretation of them, as is demonstrated by *Joyce v. Realm*. See, however, the comments of David Steel J in *HIH Casualty and General Insurance Ltd v. New Hampshire Insurance Co.* [2001] Lloyd's Rep. IR 224, at para. 49, expressing the view that it is possible for the terms of the reinsurance to be overridden by incorporated terms. The citation of *Marten v. Nippon* and *Charlesworth v. Faber* in support of that proposition would appear not to be strictly correct, as in those cases there was no obvious inconsistency.

103. See *Property Insurance Co. Ltd v. National Protector Insurance Co. Ltd* (1913) 108 LT 104, in which Scrutton J held that a policy would be voidable on this ground, but went on to hold that the phrase "subject without notice to the terms and conditions as the original policy" operated as a waiver of the right to avoid.

2D.2(ii) Incorporating waiver of defences provisions

A clause whereby the reinsured agrees to waive defences against the direct assured is by its nature akin to a coverage term, as it extends the reinsured's liability to situations in which the reinsured would otherwise have been off risk. If such a clause is incorporated into the reinsurance, assuming that the requirements for incorporation are met, a further question arises as to how the clause is intended to operate at the reinsurance level. Let it be supposed that the clause waives the right of the reinsured to avoid the direct policy for non-disclosure or misrepresentation, and the clause is then incorporated into the reinsurance. The possible effects of the clause as incorporated into the reinsurance are threefold: 2.36

(i) The clause may simply be recognising that the reinsured faces liability at the direct level, and that – in accordance with the reinsurers' obligation to indemnify the reinsured on proof of the reinsured liability – the reinsurers cannot refuse to pay if the reinsured has been unable to rely as against the assured on an utmost good faith defence which would otherwise have been available to the reinsured. In this way, incorporation means that the clause operates as little more than a form of "follow the settlements" provision, binding the reinsurers to indemnify the reinsured for its contractual liability. If that is the extent of the effect of incorporation, then it adds nothing to the ordinary obligation of the reinsurers to indemnify the reinsured for losses for which the reinsured is liable. Incorporation thus achieves nothing.

(ii) The clause may have effect at the reinsurance level by recognising that the presentation of the risk made to the reinsured would have been more or less the same as that made to the reinsurers: the same brokers are likely to have been operating at both levels, and the same placing information will have been made available. Indeed, if the arrangement is by way of fronting, there may have been a common presentation. Accordingly, the clause operates at the direct level by depriving the reinsured of its utmost good faith defence against the assured, and it operates at the reinsurance level by depriving the reinsurers of their utmost good faith defence against the reinsured, but only in respect of a presentation which was common to both reinsured and reinsurers. It might be thought that this is no more than an extension of the obligation of the reinsurers to indemnify the reinsured for losses within the scope of the direct policy. The fact that the reinsured has been deprived of an utmost good faith defence should not – on ordinary back-to-back principles – allow the reinsurers to plead at the reinsurance level the very defence which the reinsured cannot rely upon at the direct level. Cases such as *Forsakrings Vesta v. Butcher* and *Groupama v. Catatumbo* indirectly support the proposition that reinsurers ought not to have the benefit of their independent defence, whether or not the waiver provisions have been incorporated.[104]

104. However, the decision of the House of Lords in *Hill v. Mercantile and General Reinsurance Co. plc* [1996] LRLR 341 leaves open the analogous point of whether a follow the settlements clause which allows the reinsured to prove its loss by a bona fide and businesslike settlement deprives the reinsurers of their independent right to rely upon the identical wording of the insuring or exclusion provisions of the

(iii) The clause may operate as a reinsurance clause in its own right. Thus, the reinsurers, by incorporating the waiver of defences clause, have thereby waived defences which they would otherwise have had as against the reinsured, irrespective of whether the defence covered the same ground as that waived at the direct level. By way of illustration, if the assured has misstated the geographical extent of the direct risk to the reinsured, and the reinsured has passed on that information to the reinsurers while adding its own independent misrepresentation as to the numerical extent of the direct risk, the reinsurers cannot avoid the policy for the geographical misstatement neither can they – because of the incorporation of the waiver clause and its independent operation at the reinsurance level – rely upon the numerical misstatement. If (iii) is to be achieved, there will inevitably have to be some manipulation of the wording of the clause to make it fit into the reinsurance context.

2.37 Accordingly, interdependent issues both as to the fact of incorporation and the effect of incorporation arise in this context. In *HIH Casualty and General Insurance Ltd v. New Hampshire Insurance Co.*,[105] the direct policies contained a waiver of rights clause under which the reinsured agreed that it would not seek to avoid or rescind the policy or to reject any claim on the basis of misrepresentation or non-disclosure by the assured, the financiers of a film production scheme. The reinsured retained a right of recourse, by way of subrogation, against the producers themselves in the event of loss of rights under the clause. David Steel J, applying *Marten v. Nippon* and *Charlesworth v. Faber*, concluded that the clause had been incorporated into the reinsurance by the formulation "all terms, clauses and conditions as original":[106] (1) the clause was germane to reinsurance, in that it was equivalent to a clause affecting coverage and was not merely a collateral term such as an arbitration clause, choice of law clause or jurisdiction clause;[107] (2) the clause made sense in the reinsurance context, as it could be made referable to reinsurance only by minor "manipulation", substituting the word "reinsurance" for the word "insurance"; (3) the term did not contradict any of the express terms of the reinsurance agreement; and (4) the clause was not inapposite, particularly since the insurance was in essence a fronting arrangement for the participating reinsurers. The outstanding question was whether the waiver of rights clause was so unusual as to be incapable of incorporation. David Steel J, while not going quite as far as accepting the principle that unusual terms cannot be the subject

reinsurance agreement to defeat the reinsured's claim. The author's view is that a bona fide and businesslike settlement under a follow the settlements clause defeats all defences on policy wording both at direct level and (insofar as the wording is the same) at the reinsurance level, as otherwise the follow the settlements clause is deprived of all meaning, but the point is widely disputed.

105. [2001] Lloyd's Rep. IR 224, at p.234.

106. David Steel J also concluded, albeit tentatively, that the clause had been incorporated by the express words "Cancellation Clause as Original Policy" in the reinsurance slip. The Court of Appeal reversed the first instance decision on this point, holding that the waiver of defences clause was not by its nature a cancellation clause: it was not by its title referred to as a cancellation clause, and its substance was to prevent avoidance *ab initio* for breach of the duty of utmost good faith rather than post-contract cancellation. Accordingly, the reference to a "Cancellation Clause" simply failed to have content. Rix LJ did accept, however, that if he had been wrong on the point, there would remain questions as to how the clause could operate at the reinsurance level with or without manipulation of its wording.

107. See *infra*.

of general words of incorporation, held that the appropriate test was whether it was fair in the circumstances to hold the reinsurers bound by the clause.[108] In his view this was the case, given the back-to-back nature of the contracts, the fact that the clause was not unique, the terms of the direct insurance had been available to the reinsurers by means of the placing broker's files, and the reinsurers would have had the right to avoid the reinsurance had there been material non-disclosure. In deciding that the clause had been incorporated, David Steel J implicitly assumed that the clause had some independent effect at the reinsurance level, as he rejected the reinsurers' argument that the clause was no more than a form of follow the settlements clause (possibility (a) above). However, he did not go on to distinguish between possibilities (b) and (c).

The Court of Appeal, on appeal in *HIH*,[109] gave detailed consideration to the effect of incorporation as well as the fact of incorporation, and what emerges from the decision is that it is impossible to divorce David Steel J's tests for the fact of incorporation from the further question as to what the clause means at the reinsurance level. As far as the fact of incorporation was concerned, Rix LJ (speaking for the Court of Appeal) upheld David Steel J's decision that the waiver of rights clause had been incorporated into the reinsurance: 2.38

(i) The clause was germane to reinsurance. Rix LJ rejected the suggestion by the reinsurers that a clause could be germane only if it related to the risk, as there were cases in which other forms of clause had been incorporated.[110] He also denied that the waiver of rights clause could be allied with clauses which were comparable to arbitration, jurisdiction and choice of law clauses, as it was also an ancillary provision which survived the termination of the main contract.

(ii) The term could be given content at the reinsurance level. This raised the separate issue of what content it could be given, a point discussed below.

(iii) The clause was not inconsistent with any term of the reinsurance agreement. The only issue here was whether the waiver of rights was inconsistent not with the terms of the contract but rather with the common law right of the reinsurers to avoid the agreement for breach of the duty of utmost good faith. Once again, Rix LJ felt that inconsistency could only be tested once the meaning of the clause at the reinsurance level had been ascertained.

(iv) The clause was apposite in the reinsurance context. Again, this raised the question of the effect of the clause at the reinsurance level.

Rix LJ also considered the question whether the allegedly unusual nature of the waiver of rights clause precluded incorporation. There was no appeal against the principles adopted by David Steel J, although it was argued by the reinsurers that

108. Following the general principle laid down for all contracts in *Interfoto Picture Library Ltd v. Stiletto Visual Programmes Ltd* [1989] Q.B. 433.

109. *HIH Casualty & General Insurance Ltd v. New Hampshire Insurance Co.* [2001] E.W.C.A. Civ. 735; [2001] Lloyd's Rep. IR 596.

110. See, in particular, *CNA International Reinsurance Co. v. Companhia de Seguros Tranquilidade SA* [1999] Lloyd's Rep. IR 289, discussed *infra*.

the clause was sufficiently unusual to be regarded as not incorporated. Rix LJ accepted David Steel J's conclusion from the evidence that such clauses were unusual but not unknown, and that the clause was not to be regarded as unconscionable or unfair or incapable of incorporation by general words. The real question was whether the reinsured had broken its duty of disclosure by failing to inform the reinsurers of the existence of the clause, but as that was not one of the preliminary issues nothing more could be said on the point.

2.39 The real issue in *HIH* was what the clause actually meant once incorporated into the reinsurance. As noted above, David Steel J rejected the argument that the clause as incorporated meant no more that that reinsurers were required to follow the reinsured's settlements where the waiver of rights clause defeated the reinsured's defences against the assured ((i) above). He did not go further and choose between (ii) and (iii) above. Rix LJ, by contrast, focused on this matter. He ruled that the clause went as far as (ii), that in the event of a common presentation to the reinsured and the reinsurers, by reason of the waiver clause neither could rely upon the right of avoidance. However, Rix LJ refused to give the clause effect (iii), i.e. an independent provision which prevented the reinsurers from avoiding the reinsurance contract for any breach of duty by the reinsured unconnected with the presentation at the direct level. This refusal was based upon the inability of the court to manipulate the wording of the waiver of rights clause, for two reasons. First, on purely linguistic grounds, the clause was not capable of manipulation as there were references in the clause to named parties. Second, giving the clause independent effect at the reinsurance level would have resulted in cover which was not back-to-back. At the direct level, if the assured was in breach of duty, the reinsured had waived its rights against the insured financiers but retained a right of recourse against the producers. By contrast, if the clause had effect as between reinsured and reinsurers, any breach of duty by the reinsured which had no connection with anything said by the assured or the producers would deprive the reinsurers of their rights but would not confer upon them any right of recourse against the producers, as the producers would have done nothing wrong. Accordingly, the wording of the clause could not be manipulated, and it took effect in the reinsurance in its unmanipulated form. In that form, the clause provided that the reinsured was liable despite any breach of the duty of utmost good faith by the assured, and the reinsurers were under the same obligation to the reinsured in respect of the same breach of duty.

2.40 It is submitted that the same result could have been achieved in *HIH* without the need to resort to incorporation at all. The reinsurers had agreed to reinsure on a back-to-back basis, and were thus liable to indemnify the reinsured if the reinsured was itself liable, subject to the obligation on the reinsured to prove its loss. A clause inserted by the insurer waiving the right to avoid the policy as against the assured was plainly material to the reinsurance risk, and if it had not been disclosed then the reinsurers would have themselves been able to avoid for want of a fair presentation. In short, the combination of utmost good faith and back-to-back cover would have been quite sufficient to deal with any problems. David Steel J's conclusion was that the purpose of the parties was to achieve back-to-back cover, and this could be achieved by incorporating the clause into the reinsurance policy but manipulating its wording. The Court of Appeal held that the same could be achieved by incorporating the clause in an unmanipulated form. The present author's view is that the same would have followed without incorporation, confirmed by the presence of a follow the settlements clause which deprived the reinsurers of the right to challenge any settlement by the reinsured as long as it was made on legal liability *under the terms of the direct policy* (taking into account the waiver of rights) or was a bona fide and businesslike settlement of liability. This analysis sidesteps any need to discuss whether an unusual term is to be regarded as incorporated from the direct policy into the reinsurance, and if it is incorporated whether its wording is to be manipulated, as the only question becomes whether that clause, if not disclosed to the reinsurers, is material to the reinsurance risk. David Steel J indeed recognised that a term which had been incorporated into a reinsurance policy – on the basis that it was not sufficiently unusual – could well give rise to a right of avoidance if its existence had not been disclosed to the reinsurer, and it was this very point which led Rix LJ to reserve his opinion on the question whether an unusual term could be regarded as incorporated. This curious dichotomy arises because the same question is being asked for two different purposes: is the clause sufficiently unusual not to have been incorporated; and if it is incorporated, is it sufficiently unusual to demand disclosure? Surely the point need be addressed only once, in the latter context which is in any event overriding. It will also be noted that a key consideration in determining whether incorporation has taken place is whether the insurance and reinsurance are back-to-back. If the contracts are back-to-back, why is it necessary to ask the further question?

2D.2(iii) Amendments to coverage

An additional question which has arisen in relation to the phrase "subject to the same terms and conditions as original" is whether it can bind the reinsurers to changes in coverage agreed to by the reinsured but without reference back to the reinsurers. First principles dictate that it is necessary to look at whether the reinsurer has agreed to run the risk of alterations to the direct cover, and that may in turn depend upon the premium payable. The general principle applied in direct insurance cases is that an insurer is required to accept liability for increases in,[111] but not changes to the nature of,[112] the risk, unless the policy provides to the contrary.[113] However, this principle is not necessarily automatically applicable in the reinsurance context, particularly where the reinsured has accepted an increased premium to accept the varied risk, as it might be thought that the reinsurer has the right to receive the same proportionate increase to run the new risk.[114] It may be, therefore, that the principle of back-to-back cover will assist the reinsured only in respect of immaterial changes to 2.41

111. *Toulmin v. Inglis* (1808) 1 Camp 421; *Shaw v. Robberds* (1837) 6 Ad & El 75; *Pim v. Reid* (1843) 6 Man & G 1; *Thompson v. Hopper* (1856) 6 EB & E 172; *Mitchell Conveyor & Transport Co. v. Pullbrook* (1933) 45 Ll LR 239.

112. *Hadenfayre Ltd v. British National Insurance* [1984] 2 Lloyd's Rep. 393.

113. Such clauses are traditionally construed very narrowly: *Glen v. Lewis* (1853) 8 Ex D 607; *Baxendale v. Harvey* (1859) 4 H & N 445; *Shanley v. Allied Traders Insurance Co.* (1925) 21 Ll LR 195; *Mint Security v. Blair* [1982] 1 Lloyd's Rep. 188; *Exchange Theatre Ltd v. Iron Trades Mutual* [1983] 1 Lloyd's Rep. 674; *Kausar v. Eagle Star* [2000] Lloyd's Rep. IR 154.

114. It is most unlikely, in the wake of *The Star Sea* [2001] Lloyd's Rep. IR 247 that reinsurers could avoid the policy for breach of a post-contractual obligation to disclose an increase in risk and to pay additional premium.

the risk. The question then arises whether reinsuring words alter this position. The cases on the point have turned not on the argument that the new policy terms are incorporated into the reinsurance, but rather on the different point as to whether the reinsuring words on their true construction operate to bring the new or varied cover within the scope of the reinsurance. The answer has consistently been that policy changes are not protected by reinsurance.

2.42 In *Lower Rhine and Wurttemburg Insurance Association v. Sedgwick*,[115] the defendant underwriters insured the hull and cargo of a vessel under two time policies for 12 months. The defendants reinsured a reinsurance with the claimants, stated to be on the same terms and conditions as the original. A space in the printed reinsurance form for the insertion of the identities of the direct policies had been left blank. During the currency of the reinsurance the first of the direct policies came to an end and the other was cancelled, and they were replaced by a new direct policy at a higher premium and on a lower valuation, but otherwise on the same terms. Following the loss of the vessel, the reinsurers paid the sums due under the reinsurance, but in the present action sought to recover the payments on the basis that the reinsurance had not extended to the replacement cover. The defendant insurers successfully resisted the claim before Kennedy J, the learned judge ruling that the blank in the reinsurance meant that the reinsurers had agreed to insure whatever direct policies were in force at the relevant time providing that they complied with the terms of the reinsurance. The Court of Appeal disagreed, and held that a reinsurance covered the liabilities of direct underwriters under policies which were in place at the date of the reinsurance, and not liabilities under future policies. The blank was regarded as an oversight rather than an intention to cover future policies on different terms. There was, however, supplementary argument on the effect of the words "subject to the same clauses, terms and conditions as the original policy", and whether they would have incorporated new direct policies into the cover provided by the reinsurance had the terms of those policies been unchanged: A L Smith LJ felt that the new policies would have been covered, whereas Collins LJ was of the view that the words applied only to the coverage provided under the original policies. This dispute was subsequently resolved in favour of A L Smith LJ's analysis.[116]

2.43 The *Sedgwick* case was followed by McCardie J in *Norwich Union Fire Insurance Society Ltd v. Colonial Mutual Fire Insurance Co. Ltd*,[117] which involved a variation to a direct hull policy whereby the agreed value of the vessel was reduced from £313,000 to £225,000. The reinsurance, which was as ever written as being subject to the terms and conditions of the original policy, was against total loss only: the revalution had the obvious effect of increasing the prospects for a constructive total loss in the event of damage to the vessel. McCardie J held that the variation discharged the reinsurers, as there was no difference in principle between the issue of a new policy and the variation of an existing policy, and the "incorporating" words could not affect this outcome as they were not appropriate to increased risks. *Norwich Union* was itself followed by

115. [1899] 1 Q.B. 179.

116. *Scottish National Insurance Co. Ltd v. Poole* (1912) 107 LT 687, although in that case it was held that the original policy had not been cancelled and replaced. *Poole* was followed on the latter point in *Emanuel & Co. v. Andrew Weir & Co.* (1914) 30 TLR 518.

117. [1922] 2 K.B. 461.

David Steel J in *HIH Casualty and General Insurance Ltd v. New Hampshire Insurance Co.*, the only authority in the line not involving marine insurance.[118] In that case there was an express clause in the reinsurance under which the reinsured agreed to consult and obtain reinsurers' agreement to all amendments to the terms of the direct policies, and David Steel J regarded that clause as a warranty, the effect of which was to give contractual force to *Norwich Union* in that any amendment material to the risk would trigger the operation of the clause. This conclusion was upheld on appeal to the Court of Appeal.[119]

2D.3 Incorporating claims conditions

2D.3(i) Practical considerations

The notion that the provisions of one insurance policy can be incorporated into another on the same risk was recognised at the turn of the twentieth century, with the conclusion that a breach of the terms of the first policy entitled the insurers under the second policy to deny liability.[120] There is nothing particularly surprising or contrary to principle about this. The problem arose when there was an attempt by reinsurers to transfer the concept across to facultative reinsurance, on the apparent assumption that the reinsurance agreement was no more than a further policy on the original subject-matter. The courts proved to be highly doubtful of this further proposition. 2.44

It was pointed out above that claims conditions in direct policies and in reinsurance agreements have different objectives and are framed in terms which reflect those differences. The insurer under a direct policy is concerned to have prompt notice of any loss so that its causes can be investigated and possible subrogation rights against third parties investigated, and will then seek to ensure that the assured takes all necessary steps to prove its loss by providing receipts, invoices and the like. At the reinsurance level the reinsurer is primarily interested in the question whether the reinsured has properly accepted liability to the assured. This is perhaps of less significance in the absence of a follow settlements clause, as the reinsured must prove that the direct loss was covered by the policy as a matter of fact and as a matter of law. It is of more significance to a reinsurer to monitor the settlement process between reinsured and assured where there is a follow settlements clause, as the reinsured is entitled to be indemnified in respect of a settlement unless the reinsurer can demonstrate that the settlement was not not bona fide and businesslike.[121] It is now accepted that the reinsurer can protect itself by means of a claims co-operation clause (under which the reinsured is required to co-operate with the reinsurer in negotiating with the reinsured, particularly by keeping the reinsurer informed as to progress and seeking the reinsurer's consent to any settlement) or a claims control clause (under which the reinsured simply passes control of negotiations to the reinsurer. The cases 2.45

118. [2001] Lloyd's Rep. IR 224.

119. *HIH Casualty & General Insurance Ltd v. New Hampshire Insurance Co.* [2001] E.W.C.A. Civ. 735 [2001] Lloyd's Rep. IR 596.

120. *Sulphite Pulp Co. Ltd v. Faber* (1895) 11 TLR 547; *Beauchamp v. Faber* (1898) 3 Com Cas 308. For a more recent example, see *Hong Kong Borneo Services Ltd v. Pilcher* [1992] 2 Lloyd's Rep. 593.

121. *Insurance Co. of Africa v. Scor (UK) Reinsurance Co. Ltd* [1985] 1 Lloyd's Rep. 312.

have made it clear that the claims co-operation and claims control clauses prevail over the reinsurer's obligation to follow settlements, so that if co-operation or control constitutes a condition precedent to the reinsurer's liability the reinsured will be unable to recover unless there has been due compliance by the reinsured even if the loss can be independently proved.[122] There is now some authority on the steps required to comply with a claims co-operation or claims control clause.[123]

2.46 If a reinsurance contract is silent on claims co-operation, and simply purports to incorporate the terms of the direct policy into the reinsurance, there are powerful arguments in favour of the proposition that either incorporation is not appropriate, or that if it is appropriate it operates only to bring into the reinsurance agreement a statement of the situation in which the reinsured does or does not face liability (i.e., it operates as a follow the settlements clause). The reasons for not giving the clause independent effect as between reinsurers and reinsured are as follows. First, claims provisions have different functions in direct and reinsurance contracts, particularly where the direct policy is against first party loss rather than liability; it has already been argued that reinsurance is liability insurance by its nature. Second, there are established[124] claims co-operation and claims control wordings in use for facultative reinsurance contracts, and these are both appropriate to reinsurance and their relationship with follow settlements clauses has been resolved by the courts. Third, a reinsurer who chooses not to adopt the simple device of inserting into the slip an appropriate clause – it would probably suffice just to add the words "claims co-operation clause" – should surely not be allowed to benefit from his own slackness by being allowed to take advantage of a clause in the direct policy which was devised for different purposes and which may fit at best imperfectly into the reinsurance regime.

2D.3(ii) The early analysis

2.47 The first case in which the point was discussed in detail was *Home Insurance Co. of New York v. Victoria-Montreal Fire Insurance Co.*[125] Here, property belonging to the Canadian Pacific Railway had been insured by a Canadian company, Western. Western reinsured 20 per cent of their liability with a US company, Home Insurance; in turn Home, retroceded a part of its liability to another Canadian company, Victoria-Montreal. The original insurance was in the form of a New York fire policy, and stated that no suit could be brought on the policy "unless commenced within twelve months after the fire". The agreement had been converted into reinsurance and retrocession by the insertion of the prefix "re-" on the word "insurance", and the policy had been appended to a typewritten slip which set out various claims conditions of its own. It was common ground that none of the 20 or so clauses in the fire policy seemed to be of any relevance to reinsurance or retrocession. The issue before the Privy Council was whether the suit clause was applicable as between Home

122. *Insurance Co. of Africa v. Scor (UK) Reinsurance Co. Ltd* [1985] 1 Lloyd's Rep. 312; *Gan Insurance Co. Ltd v. Tai Ping Insurance Co. Ltd (Nos 2 and 3)* [2001] Lloyd's Rep. IR 667.
123. *Gan Insurance Co. Ltd v. Tai Ping Insurance Co. Ltd (Nos 2 and 3)* [2001] Lloyd's Rep. IR 667.
124. Although it is true to say that there is no single wording which operates in the London market.
125. [1907] A.C. 59.

and Victoria-Montreal. In an opinion scathing of the contractual documents, Lord Macnaghten, speaking for the Privy Council, ruled that the suit clause had not been incorporated into the retrocession: the typewritten slip was complete in itself and there was no need to incorporate the terms of the direct policy into it; none of the other terms of the direct policy were relevant to the retrocession and the parties could not have intended just one of the terms to be incorporated; and the suit clause operated unreasonably in the retrocession as Home had no control over when a claim would be made against it and thus might be defeated by dilatory conduct on the part of the direct assured or Western. His Lordship continued:

"It is no doubt possible to read the sentence prescribing suits and actions, divorced from its immediate context, into the contract of [retrocession]. . . . It is difficult to suppose that the contract of [retrocession] was engrafted on an ordinary printed form of policy for any purpose beyond the purpose of indicating the origin of the direct liability on which the indirect liability, the subject of the [retrocession]would depend, and setting forth the conditions attached to it . . .. [A]ccording to the true construction of the instrument, so awkwardly patched and so carelessly put together the condition in question is not to be regarded as applying to the contract of reinsurance. To hold otherwise would . . . be to adhere to the letter without paying due attention to the spirit and intention of the contract."

It is noteworthy that Lord Macnaghten was prepared to accept that incorporation was possible, but that it was not appropriate in the circumstances even though there was nothing actually inconsistent with the clause in the typed slip.

2D.3(iii) The current approach

Subsequent cases on the point have adopted an ad hoc clause-by-clause approach rather than a principled objection to incorporation of claims conditions. In *Vesta v. Butcher*[126] the direct policy contained a claims control clause under which the assured was precluded from making any payment or reaching any settlement with a third party without the consent of the reinsured. This clause obviously related to liability rather than first party claims, but as the policy was purely against first party loss appears to have been included by error and was beyond all doubt irrelevant to the actual claim made by the assured for storm damage. Nevertheless, the case proceeded on the assumption – based on concession – that the terms of the direct policy were incorporated into the reinsurance. Hobhouse J at first instance held that the reinsured had proved its loss as a matter of Norwegian law so that the clause was immaterial to the claim, but the notion that the clause was at all relevant to the reinsurance is a disturbing one, and Hobhouse J refused a late application for an amendment to the pleadings so that the correctness of the concession could be litigated. The matter did not resurface in the appeals to the Court of Appeal and the House of Lords, and in those courts the concession held good. As will be seen below, its correctness was nevertheless strongly doubted by Lord Griffiths in the House of Lords, on the ground that incorporation of direct policy terms was inapppropriate to reinsurance. 2.48

Incorporation of claims conditions was rejected by Moore-Bick J in *Municipal Mutual Insurance Ltd v. Sea Insurance Ltd*,[127] relying on the comments of Lord 2.49

126. [1989] 1 Lloyd's Rep. 331.
127. [1996] LRLR 265, reversed in part on other grounds [1998] Lloyd's Rep. IR 421.

Griffiths in *Vesta v. Butcher*. *MMI* involved the facultative reinsurance of a direct policy covering the liability of the Port of Sunderland Authority in respect of damage caused to property belonging to third parties. The direct policy provided that all accidents and claims had to be reported to the reinsured immediately and confirmed in writing, and the reinsured had the right to take over the conduct of any proceedings brought by, or negotiations with, third parties. The reinsurance, which was in excess layers, was in typically brief form, and contained a reinsuring clause providing: "follow their settlement. Conditions as underlying". The reinsurers argued that the notice provision had been incorporated into the reinsurance by reason of the words "as underlying", with the result that the reinsurers could not be liable unless the reinsured had served notice on them and had allowed them to take over the conduct of the negotiations with the assured. Waller J rapidly dismissed this argument. In his view, the words "as underlying" did not necessarily operate to import the terms of the direct policy into the reinsurance and require the court to adapt those incorporated terms to give them sense at the reinsurance level. In his view, the notice provision and a claims control provision would be difficult to work, given that they were designed to deal with disputes between the assured and the reinsured. Moreover, the existence of excess layers of reinsurance raised the question of which reinsurers would have to be notified and which of them would have the right to take over the proceedings.

2.50 These decisions demonstrate a fairly consistent and sceptical attitude to incorporation, and perhaps make surprising the lengths to which Clarke J was prepared to go in *CNA International Reinsurance Co. v. Companhia de Seguros Tranquilidade SA*,[128] although in all fairness to the court it would have been a challenge to any draftsman to devise contracts as chaotic and inappropriate as those presented to Clarke J. The objective of the various transactions was to insure the promoters of a series of concerts to be given by Placido Domingo against losses caused in the event of the cancellation of any concert. The direct policy was issued by the defendant, a Portuguese insurer, and was in Portuguese. It was a curious mix of local and London terms. The local terms were incorporated from the insurer's own "General Civil Liability Policy", which was unfortunate as the policy was not one against liability but rather against first party loss. The London terms expressly incorporated were Lloyd's contingency and non-appearance wordings. This hybrid was reinsured by the claimants in London. It was apparent that the direct policy was more or less a fronting operation for the London market: the reinsurance was for 90 per cent of the defendant's liability and had indeed been placed before the insurance. The intention of the parties was clearly to achieve back-to-back cover. The reinsurance agreement was in the form of a slip policy, setting out the interest of the assured and then providing that its conditions were "as per Lloyd's Contingency Policy".

2.51 Placido Domingo was forced to cancel a concert in Lisbon due to the illness of his mother. A claim was made by the assured which was settled by the defendant, and in the present proceedings the claimant reinsurers sought declarations as to the content of the insurance and reinsurance policies. The issues at the direct level related to disclosure and to claims. The local terms contained provisions avoiding the insurance in the event of non-disclosure and misrepresentation, and also a claims control

128. [1999] Lloyd's Rep. I.R. 289.

clause. The contingency wording itself contained provisions relating to non-disclosure and misrepresentation, and a claims procedure. The non-appearance wording contained more limited disclosure provisions. Clarke J held that the local terms had been expressly incorporated into the direct policy and were, so far as possible, to be given effect even though they were designed for liability cover. Of more interest to the present discussion, however, is Clarke J's approach to the reinsurance. The learned judge held that the two contracts were to be construed back-to-back, and that it was necessary to adapt the terms of the direct policy to fit the reinsurance even though they were originally drafted for the purposes of insurance. He then considered various of the incorporated terms to seek to make sense of them. His conclusions, in summary, were as follows.

(i) The claims conditions imposed on the assured, setting out the procedure for claims to be made, were incorporated into the reinsurance, by the device of substituting "reinsured" for "assured". The obligations imposed were not onerous, nor were they repugnant to a reinsurance contract.
(ii) A condition precedent in the direct policy which required notice of loss to be given to persons designated in the schedule to that policy had no application to reinsurance, as there was no reinsurance policy and no schedule.
(iii) A condition precedent in the direct policy which prevented the assured from admitting liability was neither inappropriate nor repugnant to the reinsurance agreement, and took effect by allowing the reinsurers to control the negotiations between the reinsured and the assured. Clarke J did accept that any admission of liability by the reinsured would not have been binding on the reinsurers in any event, given the absence of a follow settlements clause in the reinsurance, but nevertheless felt that meaning could be given to the clause as a whole at the reinsurance level.

The meticulousness of the reasoning cannot disguise its artificiality. It is submitted that it would have been equally open to the court to rule that, in the absence of any follow settlements and claims co-operation or claims control clause in the reinsurance, the reinsured would be able to recover under the reinsurance by establishing that as a matter of fact and a matter of law it was liable to the original assured, and the reinsurers had no right to intervene in the settlement process. The effect of Clarke J's decision was to confer rights upon the reinsurers which they had not sought in any readily comprehensible manner. Clarke J could have reached this conclusion either by: (a) denying incorporation entirely; or (b) allowing incorporation, but not giving the incorporated clause any independent effect at the reinsurance level but simply treating it as a statement of the terms and conditions on which the reinsured faced liability under the direct policy, thereby delimiting the circumstances in which the reinsurers were obliged to follow the reinsured's settlements.

2D.4 Incorporating other contractual obligations

2D.4(i) The incorporation principle

The approach of the courts to the incorporation of claims conditions is applicable 2.52
also to other policy terms or obligations imposed upon the assured. The earliest

relevant decision is that of the Privy Council in *Australian Widows' Fund Life Assurance Society Ltd v. National Mutual Life Association of Australasia Ltd.*[129] The direct policy in this case was a life insurance in the sum of £5000 with profits on one Moran, issued by National Mutual Life. There was a policy recital to the effect that had lodged with National Mutual Life a proposal, a declaration and a personal statement all of which were stated to be the basis of the contract. There were express provisions as to proof of any claim. National Mutual Life reinsured with Australian Widows' Fund under a without profits policy which contained different provisions as to proof of death, payment of premiums and days of grace. The proposal for the reinsurance contained a recital to the effect that the statements contained in the proposal, declaration and personal statement were the basis of the reinsurance and were incorporated into it. There was a further clause in the proposal specifying that the reinsurance was made "on the same terms and conditions" as the contract between Moran and National Mutual Life. Following Moran's death, National Mutal Life paid the sum assured to his estate and sought indemnification to the reinsurers. Australian Widows' Fund denied liability on the basis that Moran had made deliberate false statements sufficient to allow National Mutual Life to avoid the direct policy, and that Australian Widows' Fund's liability under the reinsurance was conditional on the truth of those statements.

It is apparent to modern eyes that the only question which could arise in this case was whether the reinsurers were bound to follow the settlement of the reinsured: in the absence of any follow the settlements clause in the reinsurance, the reinsured would have to prove that they had no defence against Moran's claim as a matter of law; with a follow the settlements clause, the reinsured would have to prove that they had acted in a bona fide and businesslike fashion in deciding to make payment and that they had not acted purely *ex gratia*. However, the arguments actually put to the Privy Council were more convoluted, as it had been conceded by Australian Widow's Fund that the effect of the "same terms and conditions" provisions in the reinsurance proposal was to incorporate the terms of the direct policy into the reinsurance, thereby conferring a discretion on the National Mutual Life as to settlements. Lord Haldane LC, delivering the opinion of the Privy Council, was far from satisfied that the concession to the effect that there had been any such incorporation was correct, but that even if incorporation was assumed, such incorporation could not be permitted to contradict the express terms of the reinsurance agreement. Given that the reinsurance had its own terms as to claims, it would have been contrary to all canons of construction to reject or modify the express terms so that the reinsurance could be made to conform to the direct policy. At most, incorporated terms could only operate subject to the implicit qualification "except as herein otherwise provided". The reinsurers were on this basis entitled to rely upon the declaration made to them by the reinsured as to the truth of Moran's statements.

The arguments and the reasoning in this case are not always transparent, but what does emerge is that (a) the entire notion of incorporation was far from being established, and (b) even if there was incorporation, it would not be permitted to contradict the express terms of the reinsurance or to import terms which had no

129. [1914] A.C. 634.

relevance to reinsurance. These principles were overlooked in the arguments put to the House of Lords in what is undoubtedly the leading case on back-to-back cover, *Vesta v. Butcher*,[130] and led to their Lordships delivering speeches which they plainly believed were based on misconceptions.

The claimants, Norwegian insurers, had issued a direct policy on a fish farm. That contract was governed by the law of Norway. The claimants reinsured with the defendant underwriters in London under a facultative reinsurance governed by English law. The reinsurance consisted of the usual cover page to which was appended the direct policy, and the statement that it was a "reinsurance of and warranted same gross rate and terms and conditions and to follow the settlements of the insurer. The notion of aquacultural insurance of this type had been devised by London brokers, and the brokers had been instrumental in establishing the chain of contracts. It was the undoubted intention of the parties that the cover should be back-to-back. The direct policy contained a "twenty-four hour watch" warranty, under which the assured warranted that continuous surveillance of the fish farm would be maintained, and the assured was also obliged to maintain detailed stock records. The defences of the fish farm were damaged in a serious storm and many of the fish were lost. At the time of the loss there was no surveillance in place, but the evidence showed that surveillance could not have prevented the loss from occurring. Also, the obligation to maintain stock records had not been adhered to. These breaches of contract did not have the effect of discharging the claimants from liability to pay the claim, as under Norwegian law[131] a breach of warranty provides a defence only where it is causative of the loss. The reinsurers nevertheless refused to pay. Their argument was that the full reinsurance clause had operated to import the terms of the direct policy into the reinsurance, so that there were warranties on the part of the reinsured that the assured would comply with its surveillance and stock control obligations. The incorporation point was the subject of a concession, and the case proceeded on the basis that the reinsured had warranted compliance.[132] The conundrum to be resolved was, therefore, that under Norwegian law the reinsured was liable to the assured to pay for the losses caused by the storm, whereas under English law the breaches of warranty by the reinsured provided a defence to the reinsurers irrespective of causation.[133] 2.53

A resort to first principles resolves the problem with little difficulty if incorporation is disregarded. The reinsurance was back to back with the direct policy, and the reinsurers were required to indemnify the reinsured in respect of settlements and also established loss: as it was not disputed that the reinsured was liable to the assured, then the reinsurers' liability ought to have followed as a matter of course. However, the complication that the warranties had been incorporated into the reinsurance

130. [1989] 1 Lloyd's Rep. 331.

131. And indeed the law of most jurisdictions other than England.

132. A late attempt by the brokers (who faced liability to the reinsured in the event of the reinsurance not responding to the loss) to reopen the incorporation point by means of amendment was refused by Hobhouse J.

133. A rule which was to be condemned by the House of Lords in *Vesta*. However, it was subsequently determined by the House of Lords in *The Good Luck* [1991] 2 Lloyd's Rep. 191 that where there is a breach of warranty the risk terminates automatically, so that it is not just causation that is irrelevant – automatic termination takes effect irrespective of whether there has been a loss.

undermined this obvious solution. It was seemingly not argued that even if the warranties were to be regarded as incorporated, the effect of incorporation was no more than a statement in the reinsurance of the circumstances in which the reinsured faced liability to the reinsured, thereby delimiting the circumstances in which reinsurers were required to provide indemnification. Either an absence of incorporation, or incorporation in this more restrictive sense, would have rendered the reinsurers liable without more.

Hobhouse J, the Court of Appeal and the House of Lords were at one in finding that the reinsurers were not liable, but the judgments and speeches are complicated by the notion that the warranty formed part of the obligations between reinsured and reinsurers. Hobhouse J's decision rested on the overriding effect of the presumption of back-to-back cover: while it was the case that different laws applied to the two contracts, it was appropriate to apply Norwegian rules of construction to the warranties in the reinsurance, to ensure back-to-back cover. This is a novel[134] and flexible approach to conflict of laws rules, designed to meet the needs of the case, although it is to be noted that Hobhouse J was not prepared to take the more extreme step of ruling that the reinsurance – being a contract negotiated in London and evidenced by London market forms – was governed by Norwegian law.[135] In the Court of Appeal Neill and O'Connor LJJ adopted much the same reasoning as that of Hobhouse J. Sir Roger Ormrod preferred to rely upon an implied term in the reinsurance agreement that the reinsurer would, irrespective of the reinsured's breach of warranty, remain liable on a back-to-back coverage basis. The House of Lords all but rejected the notion that the direct terms had been incorporated into the reinsurance and was precluded from deciding the case on simple back-to-back principles. Lord Templeman, whose reasoning was adopted by Lords Bridge and Ackner, all but disregarded the conflict of laws issues raised by incorporation and held that the presumption of back-to-back cover ensured that the reinsurers had to indemnify the reinsured. Lord Griffiths, by contrast, focused on the incorporation issue and expressed regret that it had not been fully argued. His Lordship heavily criticised the "inelegant and ungrammatical" terminology of the reinsurance agreement, doubted whether the terms of the direct policy had been incorporated due to their irrelevance to reinsurance and went on to conclude that, despite his extreme reluctance to so hold, even if those terms had been incorporated the back-to-back principle meant that the reinsurance had to be read in accordance with Norwegian law. Lord Lowry came to the same conclusion.

2D.4(ii) The current approach

2.54 The effect of *Vesta v. Butcher* is to refuse to allow the incorporation of terms from the direct policy into the reinsurance to defeat the back-to-back principle, thereby confirming the primacy of that principle. Conversely, the principle of back-to-back coverage may well require the courts to pay particular regard to the terms of the direct policy as an aid to the construction of the terms of the reinsurance itself. In *Groupama*

134. Hobhouse J admitted as much.

135. Although he would have taken that step had there been no other way of achieving back-to-back cover.

Navigation et Transports Continent SA v. Catatumbo Ca Seguros[136] the defendant insurers provided hull and machinery insurance on a fleet of vessels belonging to a Venezuelan company. That policy was governed by Venezuelan law, and incorporated classification provisions under which class was guaranteed and the policy was to terminate on change of class. The claimant reinsurers had subscribed to a facultative reinsurance in slip policy form covering 50 per cent of the reinsureds' liability. The reinsurance was expressly governed by English law, stated "all terms, conditions, warranties, additional premiums, return premium as original" and specifically stated "Warranted existing class maintained". Two vessels in the fleet were damaged in a heavy storm, and it transpired that neither had been classed at that or any other time. The defendants nevertheless accepted liability, as under Venezuelan law breach of warranty did not provide a defence unless causative of the loss. The claimants' position in the present proceedings, for negative declaratory relief, was that they were entitled to rely upon the warranty in the reinsurance, and that in accordance with English law breach of that warranty prevented the risk from attaching. The Court of Appeal, affirming the judgment of David Steel J, held that the reinsurers could not rely upon breach of the reinsurance warranty. David Steel J[137] ruled that, as the contracts were back to back, *Vesta v. Butcher* demanded that the reinsurance warranty had to be construed in accordance with the meaning to be ascribed to the insurance warranty. He also took the view that the "as original" provision was an incorporating clause which was consistent with the presumption of back-to-back cover: it is noteworthy that he did not go so far as to suggest that the insurance warranty had been incorporated into the reinsurance in place of the warranty expressly agreed. The Court of Appeal relied upon both back-to-back cover and incorporation. As to the back-to-back cover, the Court of Appeal was satisfied that the two contracts were back to back despite various differences between them not just in the warranties but also as regards claims procedures. As to incorporation, the Court of Appeal held that the direct warranties had been incorporated and it was necessary to ascribe the same meaning to them in the insurance and the reinsurance. If that was right, then the express warranty in the reinsurance could not itself have any different meaning.

The decision and the reasoning are not beyond dispute. First, the existence of differences between the two contracts, and in particular the adoption of the express warranty in the reinsurance, might well have been taken as cogent evidence of an intention to oust that presumption. What persuaded the Court of Appeal otherwise was that the incorporated and express warranties were not inconsistent or incompatible, and that it was not unknown for there to be repetitive language in reinsurance agreements given the way that the market operated and in particular the uncertainty of reinsurers as to whether the direct wording contained appropriate warranties capable of incorporation into the reinsurance. The argument here is of course circular, given that the reinsurers had in fact chosen to use their own wording: that was not thought to be sufficiently different to oust the presumption of back-to-back cover. Second, *Groupama* takes a step further than *Vesta*, as the latter decides that incorporated terms are to be construed back-to-back whereas the former decides 2.55

136. [2001] Lloyd's Rep. I.R. 141.
137. [2000] Lloyd's Rep. I.R. 434.

that express reinsurance wording should be disregarded where there are incorporated terms. Finally, there was surely no need to resort to incorporation to justify the outcome. If the insurance and reinsurance were back to back, then it would surely have been sufficient to construe the English warranty consistently with the Venezuelan warranty, rather than to carry the Venezuelan warranty into the reinsurance contract and then to apply Venezuelan principles of construction to it while at the same time disregarding the English warranty.

2D.5 Incorporating dispute resolution provisions

2.56 Whatever doubts may arise in relation to the incorporation of claims conditions and other terms of the direct policy, the courts have drawn the line at dispute resolution clauses. It is of interest to note that the language used in some of these cases deprecates the entire notion of incorporation.

2D.5(i) Arbitration clauses

2.57 The root case on this point is *Pine Top Insurance Co. Ltd v. Unione Italiana Anglo Saxon Reinsurance Co. Ltd*,[138] and it demonstrates both the dangers and the difficulties of incorporation. Here, the insurer had issued a number of travel policies conferring cover for medical expenses being incurred. Those policies contained arbitration clauses setting out brief procedures appropriate to the nature of disputes likely to arise and to the amounts likely to be at stake. Liabilities had been reinsured with the defendant reinsurers under a slip which stated in the usual way "all terms and conditions as original", although there was a far more elaborate arbitration clause appended to the slip. The defendants retroceded their liability to the claimants, again under a slip stating "all terms and conditions as original". The issue between the claimants and the defendants was whether disputes arising between them were subject to arbitration. Two questions arose: was the "original" referred to the reinsurance or the direct travel insurances; and, whichever was being referred to, was there incorporation of any of the terms of that contract, including the arbitration clause? Gatehouse J was of the view that the word "original" was referring to the terms of the first policies in the chain, i.e. the travel insurances.[139] Having reached that point, Gatehouse J found very little in the travel policies which was appropriate for incorporation into a retrocession other than the insuring provisions: that was of particular significance for the arbitration clause, which had no relevance to retrocession. Even if that was wrong and the original had been the reinsurance, Gatehouse J was not satisfied that it was right to regard an arbitration clause in one contract to be incorporated into another. At one level the outcome of this case is no real surprise, as there is much authority to the effect that arbitration clauses are *sui generis* as regards incorporation,[140] but of wider significance is the reluctance of Gatehouse J to accept that the phrase "all terms and conditions as original" had any

138. [1987] 1 Lloyd's Rep. 476.
139. The point is nevertheless open to doubt: see fn.12, *supra*.
140. See the discussion of incorporation, *supra*.

incorporating effect other than in respect of insuring provisions. It may be commented, that if that is right, then given that insurance and reinsurance are to be construed back-to-back, incorporation as a concept is misguided.

Pine Top has been followed in two more recent cases. In *Excess Insurance Co. v. Mander*[141] the issue was whether an arbitration clause in a reinsurance agreement had been incorporated into the retrocession relating to it, by reason of the full reinsuring clause "all terms, clauses, conditions and warranties as original". Colman J, following the bills of lading cases, held that an arbitration clause was not a condition but rather a self contained contract, and that it was not to be regarded as incorporated in the absence of express wording. This decision does not take the matter much further, as the nature of reinsurance incorporation did not need to be considered. Finally, in *Trygg Hansa Insurance Co. Ltd v. Equitas Ltd*,[142] Judge Jack QC applied the established rule that an arbitration clause is not to be regarded as incorporated from one contract into another simply by general words of incorporation which did not refer specifically to the clause. The possibility of incorporation was not questioned, and the only real issue in the case was whether the supervening implementation of the Arbitration Act 1996 had changed the law on the incorporation of arbitration clauses, a proposition denied by Judge Jack.[143] In Judge Jack's view, the fact that the reinsurer had seen the direct policy and had appreciated that it contained an arbitration clause was immaterial to this conclusion. 2.58

It may be that too much attention should not be paid to the arbitration cases, given that they turn upon principles developed in relation to arbitration clauses rather than reinsurance agreements, but the judgment of Gatehouse J in *Pine Top* is in broader terms and cannot be lightly dismissed. 2.59

2D.5(ii) Exclusive jurisdiction clauses

An exclusive jurisdiction clause, like an arbitration clause, removes from the claimant the right to sue in any court of competent jurisdiction and confines him to proceeding in the agreed forum. The analogy between arbitration and exclusive jurisdiction is a close one, and the cases have uniformly refused to authorise the incorporation of exclusive jurisdiction clauses from direct policies into reinsurance agreements by the use of general words of incorporation. In the earliest decision, that of Tuckey J in *Arig Insurance Company Ltd v. Sasa Assicurazione Riassicurazione SpA*,[144] the reinsurance agreement stated "Policy wording as original", and it was argued that this wording was effective to carry across a clause in the direct policy conferring exclusive jurisdiction on the courts of the "place of the residence or office of 2.60

141. [1995] LRLR 358.

142. [1998] 2 Lloyd's Rep. 439. See also *Cigna Life Insurance Co. of Europe SA-NV & Ors v. Intercaser SA de Seguros y Reaseguros* [2001] Lloyd's Rep. IR 821, where the issue was not incorporation from insurance to reinsurance but rather from other terms which had not at that stage been agreed to.

143. The key provision of the Arbitration Act 1996, s.6(2), provides that "the reference in an agreement to a written form of arbitration clause or to a document containing an arbitration clause constitutes an arbitration agreement if the reference is such as to make that clause part of the agreement". Judge Jack QC was doubtless correct to rule that there had been no change in the law. The opening words of this provision would appear to challenge the common law requirement for express reference, but the concluding words plainly refer back to common law requirements for incorporation.

144. 1998, unreported.

the Contracting Party", the Italian policy holder. Tuckey J held that the clause was not incorporated into the reinsurance. Article 17 of the Brussels Convention 1968, which demanded consensus between the parties if an exclusive jurisdiction clause was to override the other jurisdictional rules in the Convention, had not been satisfied, as the general words of incorporation were not a sufficiently clear demonstration of consensus.

2.61 This approach was confirmed by Colman J and the Court of Appeal in *AIG Group (UK) Ltd v. The Ethniki.*[145] The direct policy in this case insured a factory in Athens owned by Hellenic Arms Industry Sam and contained a clause under which the parties agreed to submit to the exclusive jurisdiction of the courts of Athens. The reinsurance, placed in London and doubtless governed by English law, provided that its conditions were "as original". The factory was seriously damaged by an earthquake, and reinsurers sought declarations of non-liability in the English courts. The reinsured argued that the action could not be brought in London, given that the exclusive jurisdiction clause in the direct policy had been incorporated into the reinsurance. Had that clause been incorporated into the reinsurance agreement, then Art. 17 of the Brussels Convention 1968 would have removed jurisdiction from any court other than the courts of Athens. Colman J and the Court of Appeal rejected the argument that there had been incorporation and that the English courts had jurisdiction.[146] Colman J placed some emphasis upon the facts that the direct policy had not been seen by the reinsurers when the reinsurance slip was scratched, and that the reinsurance agreement was governed by English law so that there would have been little sense in allowing disputes under it to be litigated in Greece.[147] However, the clinching considerations in the view of the learned judge were that general words were not normally to be construed as being sufficient to incorporate an arbitration clause from some other contract, and that an exclusive jurisdiction clause was indistinguishable in its effects. The Court of Appeal agreed, and held that their general words were not sufficient to incorporate an exclusive jurisdiction clause both as a matter of English law, and also – more significantly – as a matter of EC law evidenced in the authorities emanating from the European Court of Justice on the requirements for consensus demanded by Art. 17.

Although the case was not concerned primarily with the specific issue of incorporation from insurance contracts into reinsurance contracts, both Colman J and Evans LJ in the Court of Appeal expressed the view that the effect of

145. [1999] Lloyd's Rep. IR 221, affirmed [2000] Lloyd's Rep. IR 343.

146. There was also an issue in the case as to whether the English court had jurisdiction in the face of the rule in Art. 2 of the Brussels Convention that a person domiciled in the EC must be sued in the Contracting State of his domicile. Colman J and the Court of Appeal went on to rule that the case fell within the derogation in Art. 5(1) of the Convention, which confers jurisdiction of the courts of the Contracting State in which the performance of the "obligation in question" was due. It was ruled that the obligations in question in the present case were to be performed in England.

147. The latter proposition is open to doubt. *Vesta v. Butcher* [1989] 1 Lloyd's Rep. 331 makes it very clear that insurance and the reinsurance are to be construed back-to-back, so that the meaning of the English policy would follow from the meaning ascribed to the direct policy by the Greek court. On that basis, it would make perfectly good sense for both contracts to be adjudicated in the same forum. See *Ace Insurance SA-NV v. Zurich Insurance Co.* [2001] Lloyd's Rep. IR 504, in which the Court of Appeal on *forum non conveniens* grounds stayed English proceedings on the interpretation of a reinsurance agreement governed by English law partly on the basis that its meaning would depend upon the meaning of the direct policy, which was governed by New York law.

incorporating words was to ensure that the substantive cover provided by the two contracts matched, and that they had no application to clauses which, in the words of Evans LJ,[148] do "nothing to define the risk" and were "wholly inappropriate to disputes arising between insurers and reinsurers under the reinsurance contract.

The *Ethniki* decision was followed by Moore-Bick J in *AIG Europe SA v. QBE International Insurance Ltd*,[149] a decision which confirms that in a case governed by the Brussels Convention 1968 the principle of non-incorporation of exclusive jurisdiction clauses is bolstered by the requirements for the making of an exclusive jurisdiction clause set out in Art. 17 of the Convention. The claimants were the material damage and consequential loss insurers of Aerospatiale under a direct policy which contained an exclusive jurisdiction clause.[150] Facultative reinsurance was placed with the French branch of the defendants through the agency of Luxembourg brokers. The reinsurance contained the usual full reinsurance clause, "All terms, clauses and conditions as original and to follow the original in all respects including settlements". A dispute arose at the reinsurance level as to the cancellation of the contract, and the reinsureds commenced proceedings in England. The reinsurer asserted that the exclusive jurisdiction clause had been incorporated into the reinsurance and sought a stay of the proceedings so that they could be resolved in France. Moore-Bick J held that the necessary consensus for an exclusive jurisdiction agreement demanded by Art. 17 of the Brussels Convention 1968 had not been demonstrated. In his view, the requirements of Art. 17 had to be considered only in relation to the words used by the parties, and not by looking to the presumed or actual intention of the parties or to the surrounding commercial considerations: resort could be had to the factual matrix only where the words used by the parties were unclear. Here, the words were clear. It had been established by *Ethniki* and other cases that the full reinsurance clause did not operate to incorporate all of the terms of the direct policy, and an exclusive jurisdiction clause – being ancillary to the main provisions of the contract – was not carried across from the direct policy to the reinsurance by mere general words of incorporation. On this basis the English courts had jurisdiction over the action by virtue of the English domicile of the reinsurer.[151] 2.62

Two additional comments of Moore-Bick J are noteworthy. First, Moore-Bick J was of the view that the background commercial considerations all pointed towards France as the appropriate place for the dispute to be determined: the reinsurance agreement was made in France between what were in effect two French companies, and the agreement itself was in French. However, these considerations were not permitted to colour the basic principle that an exclusive jurisdiction clause is not incorporated without express reference to it in the reinsurance agreement. Second, even if incorporation was in principle possible, there remained the problem of reconciling the wording of the clause with the dispute at the reinsurance level. Moore-Bick J accepted that the well-established practice of manipulation of the

148. [2000] Lloyd's Rep. IR 343, at p.351.
149. [2002] Lloyd's Rep. IR 22.
150. There were actually two clauses, entitled "Arbitral Procedure" and "Law and Jurisdiction", although Moore-Bick J held that the true nature of the clauses was to confer exclusive jurisdiction on the French courts for a process which was judicial rather than arbitral.
151. Under Art. 2 of the Brussels Convention.

wording could overcome that problem in many cases, but was less easy if the dispute resolution clause provided for a procedure which the reinsured and reinsurer were unlikely to have agreed to, e.g. compulsory judicial mediation. The difficulties of manipulation were in themselves an indication that the clause was inappropriate for incorporation.

2D.5(iii) Choice of law

2.63 If the insurance and the reinsurance are back-to-back, the decision in *Vesta v. Butcher* means that it is largely irrelevant whether the reinsurance is governed by English law or by the law applicable to the direct policy if that is not English law, as the reinsurance is to be construed in accordance with the law applicable to the direct policy. It was partly on this basis that the Court of Appeal in *Ace Insurance SA-NV v. Zurich Insurance Co.*[152] exercised its discretion to stay English proceedings involving a reinsurance agreement governed by English law but reinsuring a Texas law direct policy.[153] Principles of English law are only of real significance, therefore, where they relate to matters other than the construction of terms which have to be construed on a back-to-back basis and affect, e.g., the right of the reinsurers to avoid the reinsurance for non-disclosure or misrepresentation[154] or to rely upon clauses which are contained in the reinsurance agreement but not in the direct policy, e.g. claims co-operation provisions.[155] In these situations it may remain necessary for an English court to determine whether the reinsurance is governed by English law, as that finding will confer jurisdiction upon the court under CPR r. 6.20 to hear an action involving the reinsurance so that the decision as to whether or not the action should be heard in England can be made. The question that then arises is whether an express choice of law clause in the direct policy is incorporated into the reinsurance by general words of incorporation. This point arose in *GAN Insurance Co. Ltd v. Tai Ping Insurance Co. Ltd.*

2.64 This case concerned a direct policy expressly governed by Taiwanese law on a building under construction in Taiwan. The insurer's liability was reinsured on the London market under a facultative slip policy which at a number of different points was stated to be "as original", "original wording" and "per local standard . . . policy wording". The slip policy did not contain any express choice of law clause, although it did require the reinsurers to follow the reinsured's settlements subject to a claims co-operation clause. Following a fire for which the reinsured accepted liability, the reinsurers commenced proceedings in the English courts seeking a declaration of

152. [2001] Lloyd's Rep. IR 504.

153. The Court of Appeal was also heavily influenced by a permissive jurisdiction clause conferring jurisdiction on the courts of Texas.

154. This was the position in *Tiernan v. Magen Insurance Co.* [2002] Lloyd's Rep. IR (forthcoming), where the key issue was whether the brokers responsible for placing the London market reinsurance on an Israeli direct policy were acting for the reinsured (the position under English law) or the reinsurers (the position under Israeli law). Longmore J perceived a danger that Israeli law might be applied to this issue by the Israeli court. See also *GAN Insurance Co. Ltd v. Tai Ping Insurance Co. Ltd* [1999] Lloyd's Rep. IR 472 (misrepresentation and non-disclosure on placement).

155. One of the issues in *GAN Insurance Co. Ltd v. Tai Ping Insurance Co. Ltd* [1999] Lloyd's Rep. IR 472.

non-liability in that the reinsurers were entitled to avoid the policy for misrepresentation or non-disclosure and that there had been a breach of the claims co-operation clause. The main head of jurisdiction put forward by the reinsurers was that the reinsurance was governed by English law. Cresswell J and subsequently the Court of Appeal rejected the reinsured's claim that the reinsurance was governed by Taiwanese law by virtue of the incorporation of the direct choice of law clause into the reinsurance. The primary consideration was that the choice of law clause was inappropriate to the reinsurance, and accordingly could not be regarded as incorporated. As Beldam LJ pointed out, reinsurers were not to lose the benefit of English law applicable to placements simply because the direct policy happened to contain a choice of law clause nominating the law of some other place.[156] Further, it was far from clear on the facts that the direct policy and the reinsurance were intended to be back-to-back, given that the risk had been presented to the insurers and the reinsurers in different ways and that the terms of the two agreements reflected those differences. Cresswell J and the Court of Appeal further held that it was appropriate for the issues to be resolved in England, given that Taiwanese law had no relevance to those issues.

2E CONCLUSION

The discussion above leads the author to a number of conclusions. First, the notion of incorporation of the terms of a direct policy into a facultative reinsurance developed from wordings in widespread use in the late Victorian period, at which time there was a general assumption that reinsurance was a further insurance on the direct risk insured. Mature understanding of the operation of a facultative policy, gathered through market development and experience, demonstrates that a facultative contract is by its nature a liability cover and ought to be treated as such. Second, it is wholly inappropriate to incorporate the terms of a direct policy into a facultative reinsurance: the underlying policy may have nothing to do with liability insurance, and it surely cannot be sensible to attempt to treat the terms of a business interruption or fidelity policy as if they were designed for reinsurance. The cases decided at the end of the nineteenth century and the beginning of the twentieth century provide authority for incorporation only of insuring clauses: ancillary terms, including notice provisions, have not been treated as incorporated. Third, incorporation is simply not necessary. The presumption of back-to-back cover is enough to protect the reinsured against constructions of the insuring provisions of the reinsurance which are contrary to the intentions of the parties. This chapter attempts to show that incorporation has added nothing to the presumption of back-to-back cover as regards insuring clauses. Fourth, incorporation creates commercial uncertainty. The cases demonstrate that exactly when a term can be regarded as incorporated is an uncertain process: some judges are prepared to engage in "manipulation" to allow the term to fit; other judges 2.65

156. A consideration which is given even greater force where the reinsurance is placed in advance of the direct policy.

are prepared to reject incorporation as inappropriate given the express terms or nature of the reinsurance or to allow incorporation but only so that the rights and duties of the reinsured are set out in the reinsurance; and there are categories of cases – involving choice of law, arbitration and jurisdiction clauses – where incorporation is denied as a matter of policy even though the conditions for incorporation otherwise appear to have been met. Finally, incorporation is simply bad practice on the part of brokers and reinsurers. There can surely be little excuse for the London market refusing to develop the minimal wordings required to set out the terms of a facultative cover, dealing expressly with claims obligations and the effect of breaches of provisions of the direct policy. It surely cannot be right for the determination of policy terms to take place at the claims stage rather than at the underwriting stage.

It is submitted that there is little justification for the English courts continuing to encourage laziness by allowing the parties responsible for preparing a reinsurance contract to emerge unscathed from failure to agree coherent and relevant terms. Clarke J in *CNA International Reinsurance Co. Ltd v. Companhia de Seguros Tranquilidade SA*[157] all but rewrote the reinsurance contract for the parties, in a brave attempt to ascertain exactly what the parties could possibly have intended. Judges should not be put into that position, and should not tolerate it when they are. If there are no agreed terms, then there are no terms and the reinsurer is required to indemnify the reinsured on proof of liability or, in the case of a follow settlements clause, to pay in respect of a bona fide and businesslike settlement.

157. [1999] Lloyd's Rep. IR 289.

CHAPTER 3

VALUED POLICIES

PROFESSOR HOWARD N. BENNETT

3A INTRODUCTION

Section 27(1)–(3) of the Marine Insurance Act 1906 provides as follows: *3.1*

"(1) A policy may be either valued or unvalued.
(2) A valued policy is a policy which specifies the agreed value of the subject-matter insured.
(3) Subject to the provisions of this Act, and in the absence of fraud, the value fixed by the policy is, as between the insurer and assured, conclusive of the insurable value of the subject intended to be insured, whether the loss be total or partial."

This contribution considers the valued policy and the significance of an agreed valuation within the law of marine insurance.

3B WHETHER THE POLICY IS VALUED: SUM INSURED v. AGREED VALUE

In determining whether a policy is a valued policy, a distinction needs to be drawn between a sum insured and an agreed value. A sum insured delimits the financial scope of cover; it states the maximum potential liability of the insurer under the policy. It also, consequently, affects the level of premium and provides the basis for *3.2* the operation of average in the event of under-insurance.[1] A sum insured, however, is of no evidential value in determining the value of any insured property. An agreed value, in contrast, is, by virtue of s.27(3) of the Marine Insurance Act 1906, conclusive evidence of the insurable value of the insured property so valued and, as such, it plays a crucial role in determining the precise amount of the insurer's liability under the policy. Indeed, it is determinative of the value of the subject-matter insured for all purposes under the policy. Thus, where a policy warrants that a certain percentage or amount shall remain uninsured, the percentage or amount is calculated against the agreed value.[2]

3.3 Whether a particular sum of money represents an insured value or an agreed value is a matter of construction of the policy in question. In *Wilson v. Nelson*,[3] the policy stated that the insured property "shall be valued at as under", the last two words being added in handwriting. The only further statement in the body of the policy about the subject-matter insured was a statement that the insurance covered freight warranted to be free from capture and seizure. However, the sum "£1,300" was written in the margin of the policy. The Court of Queen's Bench held that the policy was unvalued. The sum of £1,300 could not, without more, be construed except as a sum insured. To constitute an agreed value, additional wording linking the sum to the value of the insured property (such as "so valued" or "valued at same") would generally be required. Similarly, where a policy covering absence of a lecturer on a lecture tour provided simply that underwriters would pay in respect of specified losses "not exceeding the sum of £100" for each lecture missed, the policy was not a valued policy.[4]

3.4 In *Kyzuna Investments Ltd. v. Ocean Marine Mutual Insurance Association (Europe)*,[5] the schedule to a yacht policy contained a "sum insured" and the main insuring clause provided that the underwriters would indemnify "up to the amounts and/or limits contained herein". The policy provided that whether the yacht had become a constructive total loss should be calculated by reference to "the sum appearing in the schedule hereto as the value of the insured property". The policy also incorporated the Institute Yacht Clauses 1.11.85, which refer to "the insured value" in clauses concerned with unrepaired damage and constructive total loss.[6] It was argued, construing the policy as a whole, that the sum insured in the schedule had to be read as an agreed value. Thomas J accepted that references in the Institute clauses to "insured value" did mean agreed value. However, given the clear authority that a sum insured denoted merely a ceiling on the indemnity recoverable, he held that a clear expression of intention was required to transform a figure expressed as a sum insured into an agreed value. Such an expression of intention was not present. The presence

1. *Reynolds v. Phoenix Assurance Co. Ltd* [1978] 2 Lloyd's Rep. 440, 450.
2. *General Insurance Co. of Trieste Ltd. v. Cory* [1897] 1 Q.B. 335 (although on the facts a policy that *prima facie* covered the balance warranted uninsured was held not to break the warranty because financial difficulties of an insurer rendered the real value of one policy considerably less than its face value).
3. (1864) 33 LJQB 220.
4. *Blascheck v. Bussell* (1916) 33 TLR 74.
5. [2000] Lloyd's Rep. IR 513.
6. Institute Yacht Clauses 1.11.85, Clause 16 (unrepaired damage), 17 (constructive total loss). Equivalent clauses are found in the Institute Hulls clauses. See also the "Total Loss Clause" in the Institute Freight clauses.

in the policy of clauses that depended for their operation on an agreed value was insufficient. They could not transform a sum insured into an agreed value and, in the absence of an agreed value, simply did not apply. Moreover, the wording of the main insuring clause strongly indicated an unvalued policy.

The policy may always provide that a sum insured is also to operate as an agreed value. In *Elcock v. Thomson*,[7] a policy on a mansion and adjoining buildings contained a sum insured but provided also that, "The sum set opposite each item in this specification has been accepted by the underwriters and the assured as being the true value of the property insured and in the event of a loss the said property will be assumed to be of such value and will be assessed accordingly". The measure of indemnity was accordingly calculated on a valued policy basis. 3.5

3C THE MEASURE OF INDEMNITY

The primary significance of the agreed value under a valued policy is its pivotal role in ascertaining the measure of indemnity payable in respect of both total and partial losses. In principle, the measure of indemnity under an indemnity insurance policy is the actual loss sustained, subject to any contractual ceiling on recovery,[8] and any proposition that would result in the assured recovering a greater or lesser sum is wrong as incompatible with the indemnity nature of the contract.[9] In the context of marine insurance, however, the concept of indemnity assumes a particular meaning since the measure of indemnity never seeks to compensate the assured for the actual loss sustained.[10] If the policy is unvalued, the assured is placed back in the financial position occupied as at the inception of risk: the measure of indemnity is calculated by reference to the insurable value of the insured property and the insurable value is the value of the property at the time of inception of the risk.[11] Where the policy is valued, then, by virtue of s.27(3) of the Marine Insurance Act 1906, the agreed value is "as between the insurer and assured, conclusive of the insurable value of the subject intended to be insured". The agreed value, by contract as supported by statute, becomes the basis on which indemnification is calculated. The contract remains one of indemnity, but of indemnity according to its terms. 3.6

In practice, the agreed value usually exceeds the actual value, sometimes significantly so. This benefits both parties.[12] The assured is dispensed from the need to prove the insurable value[13] and is able to insure for a sum sufficient to permit replacement of the insured property or discharge outstanding financial obligations attached to the acquisition of the insured property and/or secured thereon. In *Glafki Shipping Co. SA v. Pinios Shipping Co. No. 1 (The Maira) (No. 2)*,[14] a loan secured by a mortgage on a ship required insurance for 130 per cent of the total amount secured by 3.7

7. [1949] 2 K.B. 755.
8. *Leppard v. Excess Insurance Co. Ltd* [1979] 2 Lloyd's Rep. 91.
9. *Castellain v. Preston* (1883) 11 Q.B.D. 380, 386.
10. *Goole & Hull Steam Towing Co. Ltd v. Ocean Marine Insurance Co. Ltd* [1928] 1 K.B. 589, 594–595.
11. Marine Insurance Act 1906, s.16.
12. *Thames and Mersey Marine Insurance Co. Ltd v. Gunford Ship Co. Ltd* [1911] A.C. 529, 548–549.
13. *Lidgett v. Secretan* (1871) LR 6 CP 616, 627.
14. [1985] 1 Lloyd's Rep. 300; affd. [1986] 2 Lloyd's Rep. 12, 17.

the mortgage. By the time of subsequent renewal, the ship was in fact worth $4,875,000 while the amount of insurance required by the loan was just under $12 million. The ship's managers procured insurance for $10 million. When the ship was a total loss, the managers were held liable for the shortfall, even though the indemnity was sufficient to repay the outstanding mortgage liabilities and the uninsured balance represented a windfall to the assured. The arbitrator observed that insurance for 30 per cent above mortgage liabilities was common practice even where the value of the insured ship was considerably below those liabilities. This practice was endorsed by the courts.

A high agreed value benefits the insurer as well. Most obviously, the agreed value is factored into premium calculations. Moreover, in policies that contain a franchise clause,[15] the higher the agreed value the fewer claims an insurer will have to process. Moreover, provided an express contractual term makes the agreed value the standard for a constructive total loss, a higher agreed value will commensurately reduce the danger of liability for such a loss.[16]

3.8 Indemnification by reference to the agreed value clearly represents a departure from a true indemnity principle.[17] The departure, however, was sanctioned by the courts on the ground of commercial convenience. An analogy was also drawn with liquidated damages clauses in general contract law.[18] Although damages for breach of contract are, in principle, compensatory for loss actually sustained by reason of the breach, the law permits the parties, within the limits of the penalty jurisdiction, to establish the measure of damages by express contractual term. There was no reason to deny a similar contractual freedom to parties to insurance contracts.

3.9 The full impact of an agreed value on the measure of indemnity will now be explored in the context of underinsurance, total losses and partial losses.

3C.1 Underinsurance

3.10 An assured is not obliged to insure property for its full value. In order to obtain a lower premium or to spread cover between a number of insurers, the assured may decide to insure for only a proportion of the property's value, actual or agreed. In such a case, s.81 of the Marine Insurance Act 1906 provides as follows:

> "Where the assured is insured for an amount less than the insurable value or, in the case of a valued policy, for an amount less than the policy valuation, he is deemed to be his own insurer in respect of the uninsured balance."

In consequence, liability for any loss has to be apportioned between the insurer and the assured in the same proportion as the value covered by the policy bears to the value uninsured and retained by the assured. Thus, if property with an insurable value of £100 is insured under an unvalued policy for £80, the insurer will be liable for 80 per cent of the measure of indemnity for any loss, whether total or partial. The same result would follow for a valued policy where the agreed value was £100.

---

15. See, for example, the Institute freight clauses.
16. Discussed *infra*, text following fn.88.
17. "In a valued policy, what is valued is the subject-matter of the insurance, and not the amount of the loss": *City Tailors Ltd v. Evans* (1921) 38 TLR 230, 234 *per* Atkin LJ.
18. *Irving v. Manning* (1847) 1 HLC 287, 307.

Underinsurance also arises where the agreed value is less than the actual value. So far as damage to the insured property is concerned, such underinsurance is irrelevant since the conclusiveness of the agreed value as between assured and insurer precludes the insurer from relying on the underinsurance. However, such underinsurance becomes relevant in the context of liability insurance where the liability is determined according to the actual value. 3.11

In *Steamship Balmoral Co. Ltd v. Marten,*[19] a ship with an actual value of £40,000 was insured under a valued policy with an agreed value of £33,000. The ship's contribution to general average and salvage was adjusted at £530 8s 8d on the basis of the ship bearing a contributory value of £40,000. The assured argued that the hull insurer was liable for the full amount of the ship's contribution provided the amount of that contribution did not exceed the agreed value. The insurers contended that the underinsurance of the ship had to be reflected in liability for general average and salvage so that the assured should recover such proportion of the adjusted contribution as the agreed value bore to the contributory value. The House of Lords held in favour of the insurers. A majority of the House had no doubt that the adjusters were correct to employ the true value of the ship as the contributory value, rather than the agreed value, since the latter could only bind the parties to the insurance contract. However, the agreed value had to apply in all questions of indemnity on the policy. Lord Shand was adamant: "There is no exception".[20] By underinsuring, the assured retained a proportion of the risk in return for a lower premium and that carried through to all aspects of the insurers' liability. Thus, according to Lord Brougham:[21] 3.12

"Based, as the amount of a salvage award invariably is, upon the true contributory value of the ship and the property saved, I cannot conceive anything more unreasonable or unjust than that an owner should seek to recover from an underwriter salvage based upon a value far in excess of its insured value, and so get the benefit of an insurance (without paying the premium) largely in excess of the smaller value which as between themselves they have agreed for all purposes of the policy to treat and be bound by as if it were the real value."

Moreover, according to Lord Lindley, the assured's argument misunderstood the function of an agreed value:[22]

"To say that the whole value, as fixed in the policy, is insured, and then to treat the assured as fully insured, appears to me misleading. The contract is not fully to insure the shipowner up to a certain limit, but to insure him on the footing that his ship is to be taken to be of the value of [the agreed value] for the purpose of ascertaining what is payable under the policy."

In other words, an agreed value is not the same thing as a sum insured. It is not merely a limit on liability, but also the yardstick by which all measures of indemnity are to be calculated.

3C.2 Total loss

Unless the policy otherwise provides and subject to underinsurance, in the event of a total loss the measure of indemnity under a valued policy is stated by s.68(1) of the 3.13

19. [1902] A.C. 511.
20. At 515.
21. At 518.
22. At 522.

Marine Insurance Act 1906 to be the agreed value. The assured is entitled to this sum regardless of whether it exceeds the actual loss.[23] Apart from s.68(1) itself, this result is achieved as follows.

3.14 As already noted, even in the absence of an agreed value, the assured under a marine policy is indemnified not by reference to the actual loss sustained but by reference to the insurable value. In the case of a total loss, the measure of indemnity is a sum equal to the insurable value.[24] However, under a valued policy, the agreed value is conclusive as between the assured and insurer of the insurable value of the subject-matter insured.[25] Thus, if adherence to the indemnity principle induced one to look behind the agreed value, marine insurance law would direct one not to the actual loss but to the insurable value and that, in the context of valued policies, would take one back to the agreed value.[26]

3.15 In consequence of the conclusiveness of the agreed value between assured and insurer, and its resultant function as the measure of indemnity for a total loss under a valued policy, the assured may well receive a measure of indemnity that bears little connection to the scale of the actual loss. An emphatic and oft-cited example is provided by *Barker v. Janson*,[27] which concerned a hull policy with a sum insured of £6,000 on a ship with an agreed value of £8,000. At the time of conclusion of the contract, the ship had already been so badly damaged by a storm that the cost of repairs would have exceeded the ship's value once repaired. She had, therefore, a market value of nil. The assured did not know of the casualty or its consequences when taking out the insurance. The ship was subsequently destroyed by an insured peril. Calculated by reference to diminution in market value of the insured ship by reason of the casualty, the actual loss was nil. The insurers, however, were held bound by the agreed value and, therefore, liable for £6,000.

3C.3 Partial loss

3.16 A partial loss in marine insurance raises the question of how the actual loss sustained is to be related to the agreed or insurable value. The issue is perhaps unnecessarily complicated since the salient common law principles were clearly articulated by Lord Mansfield in 1761 in *Lewis v. Rucker*.[28] However, while cargo and freight insurance appear to have had little difficulty in accepting these principles, generating clear and specific law for codification in the Marine Insurance Act 1906, hull insurance has proved more resistant. Consequently, it is convenient to examine, first, partial loss of goods, second, partial loss of freight and, third, damage to ships.

23. By way of contractual exception, where a ship insured under a time policy sails "with an intention of being (a) broken up, or (b) being sold for breaking up", the measure of indemnity for any subsequent casualty is limited to the market value of the ship as scrap at the time of the loss: Institute Time Clauses Hulls (1.10.83), Clause 1.3; (1.11.95), Clause 1.5. For criticism, see Hudson, *The Institute Clauses* (3rd edn., LLP, London, 1999), pp.93–94.

24. Marine Insurance Act 1906, s.68(2).

25. *Ibid.*, s.27(3), codifying *Lewis v. Rucker* (1761) 2 Burr. 1167, 1171 *per* Lord Mansfield: "The effect of the valuation is only fixing, conclusively, the prime cost. If it be an open policy, the prime cost must be proved: in a valued policy, it is agreed".

26. *Irving v. Manning* (1847) 1 HLC 287, 307.

27. (1868) LR 3 CP 303.

28. (1761) 2 Burr. 1167, discussed *infra*.

3C.3(i) Partial loss of goods

The rules governing the measure of indemnity for partial loss of goods are found in s.71 of the Marine Insurance Act 1906. A distinction is drawn between total loss of a part of the goods insured and damage to some or all of the goods. Under an unvalued policy, a total loss of a part yields a measure of indemnity of the insurable value of the part lost.[29] In case of a total loss of a part under a valued policy, the assured receives the proportion of the agreed value that the insurable value of the goods lost bears to the insurable value of the whole insured.[30] To the extent that there is no total loss of a part but, instead, insured goods arrive damaged, the proportion of value lost is determined by expressing the diminution in the wholesale value of the goods by reason of their damaged condition at the port of destination as a proportion of the wholesale value they would have had if undamaged. The assured is then entitled to that proportion of the agreed value or insurable value.[31] 3.17

Section 71 is in large measure a codification of the judgment of Lord Mansfield in *Lewis v. Rucker*,[32] in which the assured unsuccessfully argued that the measure of indemnity for damaged goods under a valued policy should be determined by simply subtracting the actual value of the goods in their damaged condition from the agreed value. Lord Mansfield, however, pointed out that such a basis of assessment would involve the insurers in the rise and fall of the market. This would offend against the very nature of a contract of cargo insurance:[33] 3.18

> "Insurance is a contract of indemnity against the perils of the voyage: the insurer engages, so far as the amount of the prime cost, or value in the policy, 'that the thing shall come safe'; he has nothing to do with the market; he has no concern in any profit or loss which may arise to the merchant from the goods. . . ."

In consequence, according to Lord Mansfield, a total loss of the whole or a part should pay a measure of indemnity equal to the agreed or insurable value or corresponding part thereof, regardless of the market value of that which has been lost and of such part as may remain. However, in a case of damage to a part, the agreed or insurable value could not determine the measure of indemnity directly. Nevertheless, if one could determine the proportion of value lost, one could then apply that proportion to the agreed or insurable value. Subtracting the actual damaged value of the goods at the port of destination from the market value the goods would have had if undamaged and expressing the resulting figure as a proportion of the undamaged value gave the proportion of the agreed or insurable value that the insurer undertook would arrive safely. This method of incorporating the agreed value or insurable value into the calculation of the measure of indemnity will be termed the "proportion method".

Although *Lewis v. Rucker* itself concerned a valued policy, Lord Mansfield's judgment embraced unvalued policies and later case law had no hesitation in 3.19

29. Marine Insurance Act 1906, s.71(2).
30. Marine Insurance Act 1906, s.71(1). See, for example, *Anstey v. Ocean Marine Insurance Co. Ltd* (1913) 19 Com. Cas. 8.
31. Marine Insurance Act 1906, s.71(3).
32. (1761) 2 Burr. 1167.
33. At 1170.

confirming the application of the principles stated by Lord Mansfield to unvalued policies.[34]

3C.3(ii) Partial loss of freight

3.20 Where there has been a partial loss of freight, the measure of indemnity again responds to either the insurable or agreed value through the proportion method. Again, the Marine Insurance Act 1906 is clear. Section 70 provides that the assured receives the proportion of the insurable or agreed value that corresponds to the proportion of the whole freight at risk that has been lost.

3.21 *The Main*[35] concerned a policy on return freight at and from New Orleans with an agreed value of £5,500. This was a reasonable valuation at the date of conclusion of the contract. However, the ship was damaged on the outward voyage, necessitating a delay while repairs were carried out. During this period, the freight rates from New Orleans suffered a considerable decline. Ultimately, the ship sailed with a full cargo generating freight of £3,250, of which £925 was paid in advance and not, therefore, at risk. The ship and freight at risk were totally lost by an insured peril. Since the agreed value reflected freight on a full cargo, but some of the freight was not at risk, this was a case of partial loss.[36] The assured's actual loss was £2,325. The insurers, however, were held bound to pay not the actual loss but the appropriate proportion of the agreed value.

3C.3(iii) Damage to ships

3.22 The measure of indemnity in the case of damage to a ship is addressed in part by s.69 of the Marine Insurance Act 1906. Four situations may be distinguished according to whether and to what extent the damage has been repaired before the policy expires[37] and whether the ship has been sold in her damaged condition before that time.[38]

3.23 First, where the damage has been fully repaired, the measure of indemnity is the reasonable cost of repairs, not exceeding the sum insured in respect of any one casualty. Second, where the damage has been partly repaired before the expiry of risk, the measure of indemnity for those repairs is again their reasonable cost. In addition, the assured is entitled to the reasonable depreciation in the value of the vessel arising from the unrepaired damage, provided that the aggregate amount does not exceed the indemnity payable had the damage been fully repaired. Third, where the ship has not been repaired and has not been sold in a wholly unrepaired state during the currency of the policy, the measure of indemnity is the reasonable depreciation arising from the damage, again not exceeding the amount payable in the case of full repair. These three situations are addressed by s.69(1)–(3) respectively.

3.24 The Marine Insurance Act 1906 does not address the question of the measure of

34. *Usher v. Noble* (1810) 12 East 639.
35. [1894] P. 320.
36. See further *infra*: "Loss of a proportion of the valued property".
37. That the relevant time is when the policy expires was established in *Lidgett v. Secretan* (1871) LR 6 CP 616. See also *Helmsville Ltd v. Yorkshire Insurance Co. Ltd (The Medina Princess)* [1965] 1 Lloyd's Rep. 361, 517; *Kusel v. Atkin (The Catariba)* [1997] 2 Lloyd's Rep. 749, 756–757.
38. This second criterion emerges from the Marine Insurance Act 1906, s.69(3).

indemnity where the ship is sold wholly or partly unrepaired during the currency of the policy. In such a case, where the Act is silent as to the measure of indemnity, s.75(1) directs ascertainment of the measure "as nearly as may be" in accordance with principles deployed in the Act. To the extent that expenditure has been incurred on repairs, the measure of indemnity is evidently the reasonable cost of repairs.[39] However, in respect of the unrepaired damage, the Act is silent, but in *Pitman v. Universal Marine Insurance Co.*,[40] it was held by Lindley J and affirmed by a majority of the Court of Appeal that the measure of indemnity should reflect the depreciation in the value of the ship by reason of the casualty.

In three out of the four situations considered by the Act and the case law, therefore, the measure of indemnity for damage to a ship involves the reasonable depreciation in the value of the vessel. Two questions arise. First, how is the depreciation actually sustained to be calculated? A choice falls to be made between the reasonable depreciation in the value of the vessel and the estimated reasonable cost of repairing the damage. Second, must the depreciation thus determined then be related to the agreed or insurable value, depending on whether the policy is valued or unvalued, in order to calculate the measure of indemnity for which the insurer is liable, and, if so, how exactly should that value be included in the calculation? 3.25

The first question, the method of calculation of reasonable depreciation, was settled before the advent of the Marine Insurance Act 1906. In *Lidgett v. Secretan*,[41] a ship sustained damage that remained partially unrepaired on expiration of the policy. The insurers argued that the assured was entitled only to indemnification in respect of the cost of such repairs as had been undertaken. The Court of Common Pleas held, however, that the assured was entitled in respect of unrepaired damage to depreciation as reflected in the diminution in the market value of the vessel at the time the policy expired. The cost of repairs necessary to restore the vessel could be considered only to the extent that it shed light upon the amount of diminution in market value.[42] 3.26

In *Pitman v. Universal Marine Insurance Co.*,[43] a ship insured under a valued policy was severely damaged so that she was uneconomic to repair.[44] Consequently, after some minor repairs, she was sold in a substantially unrepaired state. The question for decision was how to assess the measure of indemnity. The assured contended for a proportion of the agreed value based on the estimated cost of repairs.[45] The insurer argued for depreciation calculated by a simple subtraction of the value of the ship in her damaged condition (the damaged value) from her value in an undamaged condition (the sound value). 3.27

At first instance, in respect of the first question posed above, Lindley J, relying on

39. Although the loss may already have been compensated in whole or in part by a higher sale price.
40. (1882) 9 Q.B.D. 192.
41. (1871) LR 6 CP 616.
42. At 626–627.
43. (1882) 9 Q.B.D. 192.
44. It seems clear that the ship was a constructive total loss, but the insurers resisted a claim on that basis and the subsequent claim and litigation were pursued on the basis that the ship was a partial loss.
45. The estimated cost of repairs was subject to a customary discount of one-third to reflect the replacement of old with new. The resulting figure needed to be adjusted to reflect the defendant insurer's share of the risk (ship insured for £1,000 against an agreed value of £3,700). When applied as a proportion of the agreed value, that produced the sum claimed by the assured.

Lidgett v. Secretan, rejected the estimated cost of repairs as a basis for the measure of indemnity and held that the assured was entitled to depreciation. The estimated cost of repairs was again stated to be relevant only as evidence of the value of the depreciation in the absence of more cogent evidence.[46] In the case of a sale, however, the assured could not claim an actual loss greater than the difference between the sound value of the ship and the sale price.[47] The second question posed above, the relevance of the agreed value to the measure of indemnity, appears not to have been the subject of argument before the court. However, in giving judgment, Lindley J departed from the method of computation proposed by the insurer. He held, without reference to authority,[48] that the actual loss would have to be expressed as a proportion of the sound value of the ship at the port of distress and that proportion then applied to the agreed value in the case of a valued policy or the insurable value in the case of an unvalued policy (the proportion method).[49] The matter was then remitted to arbitration for determination of the precise sum to be paid by the insurers, with costs being reserved pending that determination. Thus, while rejecting the assured's cost of repairs basis for calculating the measure of indemnity, Lindley J did not simply give judgment for the insurers. If he had concurred with the principles advanced by the insurers then, since they had paid into court a sum equal to a measure based on those principles, he would have given judgment for the insurers and awarded them costs.

The assured appealed, arguing for a measure of indemnity based on the estimated cost of repairs. By a majority, the Court of Appeal rejected the appeal. The case thus resolves the first question posed above firmly in favour of a measure of indemnity based on depreciation. The Court of Appeal was not asked to consider whether the measure of indemnity for depreciation should reflect the agreed or insurable value. Brett LJ, who dissented on the issue before the Court, cited without demur textbook authority that unambiguously espoused the proportion method.[50] Jessel MR appears to have understood Lindley J as having adopted the insurers' method of calculating depreciation, ignoring the agreed value, and seemingly approved that method. That interpretation of the first instance judgment is, with respect, unsustainable. Cotton LJ

46. At 201. In *Goole & Hull Steam Towing Co. Ltd v. Ocean Marine Insurance Co. Ltd* [1928] 1 K.B. 589, 595, MacKinnon J stated as follows:

"As regards partial loss of ship by particular average loss, the convention is that you are to estimate the depreciation not in the way that depreciation is estimated in the case of goods, because that is impracticable; but you are to estimate the depreciation in terms of the cost of repairs. The assured need not actually do the repairs; if he does not do them, then you are to estimate the cost, instead of taking down what he spent upon them."

With respect, that is clearly inconsistent with prior authority.

47. At 202. The insurer can always contend that the ship was sold at an unreasonably low price.

48. For example, *Lewis v. Rucker* (1761) 2 Burr. 1167 (discussed *supra*) and *Usher v. Noble* (1810) 12 East 639 that establish the proportion method as correct in the context of damaged cargo with respect to valued and unvalued policies respectively.

49. At 201.

50. At 209, referring to Arnould, *Law of Marine Insurance* (5th edn., Stevens & Sons, London, 1877).

did not attempt to address the question of depreciation in a comprehensive fashion,[51] although there are passages in his judgment that, read out of context, might suggest an assessment of depreciation by pure market values.[52]

Subsequently, in *Steamship Balmoral Co. Ltd v. Marten*,[53] Lord Lindley (as he had by then become) stated that calculation of the measure of indemnity for depreciation as a proportion of the agreed value had been "assumed" to be correct at first instance in *Pitman*, an assumption "not questioned" on appeal. In the light of the above discussion of the judgments in *Pitman*, it is suggested that the first instance judgment does a little more than assume the involvement of the agreed value, while the judgment of at least Jessel MR is not wholly devoid of questioning of the first instance view. 3.28

The relevance of the agreed value next arose in the post-Act, non-marine case of *Elcock v. Thomson*.[54] A mansion and adjoining buildings damaged by fire were insured under a fire policy containing an agreed value of £106,850. Before the fire, the value of the buildings was £18,000. After the fire, their damaged value was £12,600. Reinstatement would have cost about £40,000. Since reinstatement had not been effected and the property had not been sold during the currency of the risk, had the insured property been a ship the applicable provision would have been s.69(3). The assured argued for a measure of indemnity assessed by subtracting the actual damaged value from the agreed value. This was the approach rejected by the House of Lords in *Marten*, albeit in a different context, as misunderstanding the nature of an agreed value. Alternatively, it was contended that, applying the principle in s.69(3), one should apply the proportion method, yielding on the facts just under one third of the agreed value.[55] The insurers argued that the agreed value should be ignored. They contended that the principle of the conclusiveness of the agreed value, as stated in s.27(3), was subject to other provisions of the Act, and that s.69(3) contained such an exception under which depreciation was calculated according to market values alone. Alternatively, if the measure of indemnity had to reflect the agreed value, the correct percentage was the proportion the cost of reinstatement bore to the cost of constructing new buildings. 3.29

Morris J rejected the insurers' arguments on the interpretation of s.69(3). The subsection provided for indemnification by reference to reasonable depreciation. It did not state that depreciation was to be calculated ignoring the agreed value and thereby enunciate an exception to s.27(3). On the contrary, according to Morris J:[56]

> "Indemnification for reasonable depreciation must in my judgment take into account any agreed valuation. Such agreed valuation is the corpus out of which depreciation takes place and by reference to which the depreciation must be measured."

51. Thus, he expressly left open the issue of whether in assessing actual loss, the sound value should be taken at the port of origin or the port of distress since this did not arise for decision, the value on the facts being unaffected by the place at which assessed. Since the relevance of the agreed value likewise did not arise for decision, it is difficult to read his judgment as intended to resolve that issue either.
52. At 218–219.
53. [1902] A.C. 511, 521.
54. [1949] 2 K.B. 755.
55. A further possible measure, not advanced very strongly, was the cost of reinstatement.
56. At 762.

Moreover, nothing in the Marine Insurance Act 1906 was inconsistent with the principle laid down, in the opinion of Morris J, by Lindley J and "the majority of the Court of Appeal" in *Pitman*, namely that sale of a damaged ship during the currency of the policy entitled the assured to indemnification for depreciation in the value of the ship assessed by applying the proportion of depreciation in the actual value to the agreed value. Since there was no reason to apply a different approach to depreciation in the context of non-marine property insurance, the assured's alternative argument was correct.

3.30 The computation of the measure of indemnity for depreciation was again in issue in the s.69(3) case of *Irvin v. Hine*.[57] Without reference to authority,[58] Devlin J held that s.27(3) required the measure of indemnity to be based upon the agreed value. Consequently, he rejected one argument of the insurers, namely that depreciation should be calculated by taking the actual sound value of the ship and subtracting the actual damaged value. A final decision on the precise method of calculation was not, however, required. On the facts, the assured's formula of the agreed value less the damaged value (rejected by Morris J in *Elcock* and by Lord Lindley in *Marten*) and the insurers' alternative espousal of the proportion method (adopted by Lindley J in *Pitman* and Morris J in *Elcock*) both yielded a figure in excess of the s.69(3) ceiling figure of the estimated cost of repairs.

3.31 The question of depreciation next arose before the Supreme Court of New York in *Compania Maritime Astra SA v. Archdale (The Armar)*.[59] Judge Rabin followed *Elcock*, noting also *Pitman* and *Irvin*, in calculating the measure of damage for depreciation as a percentage of the agreed value equal to the percentage of actual depreciation.

3.32 Further consideration in the English courts at first instance level came in *Kusel v. Atkin (The Catariba)*.[60] In the context of deciding whether the agreed value capped the indemnity recoverable in a case of successive partial losses,[61] as a matter of common law Colman J clearly espoused the proportion method of calculating the measure of indemnity for depreciation. He explained the relationship between depreciation, repair costs and the agreed value as follows:[62]

> "The measure of indemnity in respect of an unrepaired partial loss is based upon the reasonable depreciation of the vessel, but that is subject to the reasonable cost of repairing the damage. The *Castellain v. Preston*, (1883) 11 Q.B.D. 380, indemnity principle works in this way. If the partial loss has diminished the sound value of the vessel the assured has sustained a loss measured by the reduction in value unless he could have mitigated that loss by restoring the value of the vessel by means of repairs costing less than the reduction in value. In that case, the true loss is obviously the cost of the repairs that he would carry out and not the reduction in value.
>
> Where, however, the value of the vessel has been fixed by the policy, depreciation must clearly be calculated not by reference exclusively to the sound value but by reference to the insured value. That is because the parties have by their contract agreed to treat the insured value as the yardstick for all loss measurements for which the value of the vessel is a relevant factor. . . ."

57. [1950] 1 K.B. 555.
58. *Elcock v. Thomson* was cited in argument but not referred to in the judgment.
59. [1954] 2 Lloyd's Rep. 95, 101–102.
60. [1997] 2 Lloyd's Rep. 749.
61. *Infra*, text to fn.73 *et seq.*
62. [1997] 2 Lloyd's Rep. 749, 755.

This, of course, leaves the question of exactly how the agreed value is to be reflected in the measure of indemnity. For Colman J, *Pitman* at first instance, "not disturbed by the majority in the Court of Appeal which upheld his judgment",[63] *Elcock* and *The Armar* were all authority in favour of the proportion method. Indeed, for Colman J:[64]

> "It is difficult to see how as a matter of principle one could otherwise relate the actual depreciation of the vessel to the policy value. ... The [proportion] method ... is entirely consistent with the express limit on recoverable loss imposed by reference to the policy value. If there is 100 per cent depreciation in sound value which exceeds insured value, it must be correct in principle, that apart from the cost of repairs, the assured's recovery should be limited to 100 per cent of the insured value."

This is true, but it does not, with respect, explain why the question left unanswered in *Irvin*, namely whether one should reflect the agreed value by the proportion method or by simply subtracting the damaged value from the agreed value, should be resolved in favour of the proportion method. Nor does it address the case where less than 100 per cent depreciation in sound value exceeds the agreed value. In such a case, why can the assured not recover up to the agreed value? Answers are, however, provided by case law already discussed. 3.33

The reason why the judgment of Colman J does not answer these questions is because it appears to confuse the concepts of sum insured and agreed value.[65] A sum insured caps the potential liability of an insurer. Where actual loss (whether or not in the form of depreciation) exceeds the sum insured, the assured's recovery cannot be greater than the sum insured. However, as Lord Lindley pointed out in *Marten*,[66] an agreed value is different from and more than a sum insured. The conclusiveness of the agreed value means that it too operates as a limit on recovery, but an agreed value has a far greater significance, operating as the conclusively agreed basis for all measures of indemnity. The reason why the proportion method is correct for depreciation is because the agreed value is the financial embodiment of the subject-matter insured. The insurer undertakes that that value will be safely preserved against the insured perils. The bargain is not to indemnify for actual loss to property in accordance with market values over which the insurer has no control. The bargain is to indemnify for loss of that abstract value. As Lord Mansfield explained in *Lewis v. Rucker*, the insurer does not undertake to pay more on a falling market or the assured to take less on a rising market, and insulation of the measure of indemnity against market values is ensured by a rule that where part of the value of an insured ship is lost, the assured is entitled to part of the conclusive representation of the full value of that ship.[67]

It was noted above that s.75 of the Marine Insurance Act 1906 directs that, in cases where the Act is silent, the measure of indemnity should be determined as nearly as may be in accordance with the provisions the Act does contain. As already seen, the Act expressly adopts the proportion method in calculating the measure of indemnity 3.34

63. *Ibid.*
64. At 756.
65. See also *infra*, fn.72.
66. *Supra*, text to fn.22.
67. This reasoning was articulated in the context of valued cargo policies in *Lewis v. Rucker* (1761) 2 Burr. 1167 (expressly rejecting an argument that the measure of indemnity for damage to cargo under a valued policy should be assessed by subtracting the damaged value from the agreed value) and accepted for unvalued cargo policies in *Usher v. Noble* (1810) 12 East 639.

for partial loss of goods and freight. It might, therefore, be argued that s.75 would direct adoption of the proportion method of calculating depreciation, which is merely a form of partial loss of a ship. However, while the possibility of drawing an analogy between goods and ships was raised in argument in both *Elcock* and *Irvin*, the rules on measure of indemnity for damaged goods did not form part of the reasoning of the judge in either case. Indeed, as a matter of statutory interpretation, while the clear adoption of the proportion method in relation to goods and freight is clearly persuasive, it is far from compelling. The starting point adopted by s.69 for the measure of indemnity for damage to ships is the cost of repairs. This is indemnified pound for pound. The assured recovers the actual, out of pocket, reasonable cost of repairs undertaken. The assured does not recover such proportion of the agreed or insurable value as the cost of repairs bears to the sound value of the ship. It is consequently arguable that the failure by the Act in the context of damaged ships clearly to incorporate the agreed or insurable value and to do so through the proportion method is deliberate. This is not to argue that the courts are wrong to assess depreciation in the way they do, merely that the Marine Insurance Act 1906 does not point in that direction as clearly as might be thought.

3.35 Whatever inference is to be derived from the Act, it is nevertheless clear that the courts have as a matter of common law approved the incorporation via the proportion method of the agreed or insurable value into the measure of indemnity for depreciation. This was clearly the view of Lindley J in *Pitman* and such reservations as may perhaps be found in the judgments of the Court of Appeal in that case, particularly that of Jessel MR, have not persuaded later courts. The judgment on depreciation in *Elcock*, albeit in respect of a non-marine policy, is unequivocal and indistinguishable from hull insurance as a matter of principle. Moreover, it was adopted in the US marine insurance case of *The Armar*, and was endorsed, albeit *obiter*, in the English marine insurance case of *The Catariba*.

3.36 One, perhaps curious, consequence of the courts' approach is that, where damage is partly repaired before the policy expires, the measure of indemnity in respect of the repaired damage will ignore the agreed or insurable value, while that for the unrepaired damage will incorporate the agreed or insurable value through the proportion method.

3.37 Ultimately, however, the measure of indemnity is a matter for contract. In this respect, as in most others, the provisions of the Marine Insurance Act 1906 are merely default rules, applied only in the absence of contrary intention. Clause 18 of the Institute Time Clauses Hulls (1.10.83 and 1.11.95) provides as follows:

> "*18 Unrepaired Damage*
>
> 18.1 The measure of indemnity in respect of claims for unrepaired damage shall be the reasonable depreciation in the market value of the Vessel at the time this insurance terminates arising from such unrepaired damage, but not exceeding the reasonable cost of repairs.
>
> 18.2 . . .
>
> 18.3 The underwriters shall not be liable in respect of unrepaired damage for more than the insured value at the time this insurance terminates."

3.38 By contract, therefore, the insurers persist with the approach to depreciation repeatedly argued unsuccessfully before the courts. The contractual approach is identical to that of the common law in that, first, depreciation is assessed by reference to the time when the policy expires and, second, the assured cannot recover more than the agreed value at that time or the reasonable cost of repairs. However, the contractual approach departs from the common law by assessing depreciation purely by reference to market values. The market value of the vessel in its damaged condition at the time the policy expires is subtracted from the market value the vessel would have had at that time if undamaged. This does not vary if the vessel is sold unrepaired before the policy was otherwise due to expire, since such a sale automatically terminates the policy.[68]

The reason why insurers persisted in rejecting the approach of the common law was the tendency for agreed values to exceed actual values. Thus, on the facts of *Elcock* for example, the assured's loss in terms of market value was £5,400, representing a fall in market value of just under one third. Incorporating the agreed value by the proportion method, however, produced a measure of indemnity of £32,055. Although the estimated cost of reinstatement presumably placed a ceiling of £40,000 on the measure of indemnity regardless of the proportion of market value lost, the common law approach inflated the insurers' liability considerably. Since high agreed values for vessels are common, such inflation would not be untypical in hull insurance and was unacceptable to hull insurers.[69] 3.39

3D SUCCESSIVE LOSSES

Although the sum insured represents the limit on an insurer's liability in respect of any one casualty befalling the insured property, the possibility of the property suffering more than one casualty raises the prospect of the aggregate of the measures of indemnity for the successive losses exceeding the sum insured. Section 77 of the Marine Insurance Act 1906 addresses this situation as follows: 3.40

> "(1) Unless the policy otherwise provides, and subject to the provisions of this Act, the insurer is liable for successive losses, even though the total amount of such losses may exceed the sum insured.
> (2) Where, under the same policy, a partial loss, which has not been repaired or otherwise made good, is followed by a total loss, the assured can only recover in respect of the total loss. . . ."

The basic rule, laid down in sub-section (1), is that the insurer is liable for the full measure of indemnity for each and every loss regardless of the aggregate total. To that basic rule, sub-section (2) then creates an exception.

The principles codified in s.77 are simply specific manifestations of the indemnity principle. Sub-section (1) will apply in either of two situations. First, a partial loss may be remedied at least to some extent and then followed by a total loss. In such a case, the assured is in fact out of pocket through having incurred expenditure to remedy that partial loss in whole or in part and has in addition sustained a total loss of the property and is entitled to indemnification for both losses.[70] Second, the insured 3.41

68. Institute Time Clauses (Hulls) 1.10.83, Clause 4; 1.11.95, Clause 5.
69. See O'May, *Marine Insurance Law and Policy* (Sweet & Maxwell, London, 1993), pp.446–448.
70. *Le Cheminant v. Pearson* (1812) 4 Taunt. 367.

property may sustain successive partial losses that the assured remedies. The insurer will be liable in full for each loss, irrespective of the aggregate total of the measures of indemnity.[71] The assured is in fact out of pocket in respect of the full aggregate loss and there is no reason in principle why full recovery should be denied. Section 77(1) provides that the insurer's cumulative liability is not limited to the sum insured and it has been held that under a valued policy the agreed value is similarly no limit to recovery for successive remedied partial losses.[72]

3.42 To the extent, however, that successive partial losses are unrepaired and the policy is a valued policy, the insurer's cumulative liability will be confined to the agreed value. In *Kusel v. Atkin (The Catariba)*,[73] a yacht insured under a valued policy was damaged, first, by running aground and, second, by a hurricane. At the time the policy expired, no repairs had been carried out in respect of either casualty. By virtue of s.69(3) of the Marine Insurance Act 1906, the measure of indemnity in respect of unrepaired damage under a valued policy is the reasonable depreciation in the value of the vessel attributable to that damage. Colman J held that under a valued policy this depreciation had to be calculated as a proportion of the agreed value.[74] Consequently, if the vessel sustained 100 per cent depreciation in sound value in a sum in excess of the agreed value, the assured's recovery would be limited to a sum equal to the agreed value.[75] Moreover, depreciation was assessed by reference to the time of expiry of the policy. Consequently, where successive unrepaired losses had been incurred, the assured's actual loss was the cumulative depreciation caused by the various casualties as reflected in the vessel's market value at the time of expiry of the policy. Depreciation was, accordingly, to be calculated on a cumulative basis rather than separately in respect of each casualty and then aggregated.[76] Since one cannot sustain more than 100 per cent depreciation and since the agreed value is conclusive evidence of the full value of the insured property, it follows that the measure of indemnity for successive unrepaired losses cannot exceed the agreed value.[77]

3.43 Section 77(2) operates by way of a proviso to sub-section (1) and codifies the doctrine of merger of loss whereby an unrepaired partial loss is said to merge into a

71. *Brooks v. MacDonnell* (1835) 1 Y. & C. 500, 515.

72. *Kusel v. Atkin (The Catariba)* [1997] 2 Lloyd's Rep. 749, 757–758. Colman J held in favour of liability unlimited by the agreed value on the basis of s.77(1), evidently reading "sum insured" as meaning agreed value. There is, however, no discussion on this point and the judgment is hard to sustain on this application of the sub-section. This construction of the phrase is inconsistent with the terminology of other provisions of the Marine Insurance Act 1906 when referring to the agreed value (see, for example, ss.27, 68, 70, 71) and with the clear view of the phrase "sum insured" adopted in the context of insurance policy wording in *Kyzuna Investments Ltd. v. Ocean Marine Mutual Insurance Association (Europe)* [2000] Lloyd's Rep. IR 513 (*supra*, text to fn.5 *et seq.*). It is, therefore, suggested that the judgment is incorrect in invoking s.77(1) but correct on the substantive issue as a matter of common law.

73. [1997] 2 Lloyd's Rep. 749.

74. *Supra*, text to fn.60 *et seq.*

75. At 756.

76. At 757.

77. The Institute clauses reproduce this principle as a contractual provision. Thus, Institute Time Clauses Hulls (1.11.95), Clause 18.3 provides that "The Underwriters shall not be liable in respect of unrepaired damage for more than the insured value at the time this insurance terminates". The reference in Clause 18.1 to "claims" for unrepaired damage indicates that Clause 18.3 applies whether the unrepaired damage is the product of one casualty generating a claim or a number of such casualties: *Kusel v. Atkin (The Catariba)* [1997] 2 Lloyd's Rep. 749, 758.

subsequent total loss that occurs during the currency of the policy.[78] Again, this doctrine is merely an articulation of the indemnity principle. Given that the insured property has become a total loss, the assured will receive the measure of indemnity for a total loss.[79] In the case of a valued policy, that measure is, of course, a sum equal to the agreed value. Since that measure represents full indemnification for the loss of the insured property, the indemnity principle will deny the assured any recovery in respect of the earlier partial loss unless the assured is in fact out of pocket through having incurred expenditure to remedy that partial loss in whole or in part. As already seen, if the assured incurs expenditure in repairing a damaged vessel that is subsequently lost, the insurer will be liable for the cost of repairs in addition to the indemnity for the total loss.[80] However, to the extent that the damage remained unrepaired at the time of the total loss, the insurer will not be liable for the reasonable depreciation arising from the unrepaired damage. The assured is not out of pocket in respect of repairs and a vessel that has become a total loss has sustained 100 per cent depreciation and cannot sustain any more.[81]

3E CLASSIFICATION OF THE LOSS SUSTAINED

The impact of the agreed value upon the measure of indemnity, as discussed in the previous section, follows from the classification of the loss sustained as either total or partial. The agreed value does not, however, impact upon this preliminary issue. Subject to contrary intention, whether a loss is total or partial is a question of fact, involving an assessment of the nature and extent of loss or damage in fact sustained. 3.44

The (absence of) role of the agreed value in classifying the loss sustained has arisen in the context of, first, constructive total loss and, second, loss of a proportion of the valued property.

3E.1 Constructive total loss

A constructive total loss arises in circumstances where the insured property is not an actual total loss but under the circumstances it is commercially sensible to treat the property as a total rather than a partial loss for the purpose of determining the measure of indemnity.[82] Most commonly, a constructive total loss arises where insured property has been so damaged that it would not be economic to repair. With respect to valued policies, the question is whether the economic viability of repairs should be judged by reference to the agreed value or the market value of the insured 3.45

78. The insurer's liability crystallises on expiry of the risk, so that a subsequent total loss cannot produce a merger: *Lidgett v. Secretan* (1871) LR 6 CP 616.

79. Assuming the insurer is liable under the terms of the policy for the loss that has occurred. Where the insurer is not liable for the total loss, there is no merger under s.77(2) but the merger remains effective at common law: *British & Foreign Insurance Co. Ltd v. Wilson Shipping Co. Ltd* [1921] 1 A.C. 188.

80. *Supra*, text to fn.70.

81. *Livie v. Janson* (1810) 12 East 648; *British & Foreign Insurance Co. Ltd v. Wilson Shipping Co. Ltd* [1921] 1 A.C. 188; *Kusel v. Atkin (The Catariba)* [1997] 2 Lloyd's Rep. 749, 757.

82. For the full statutory definition, see Marine Insurance Act 1906, s.60. This may be modified by contract: see, for example, Institute Cargo Clauses (A), (B), (C), Clause 13.

property.[83] The answer consistently espoused by the common law and now enshrined in the Marine Insurance Act 1906 is that the market value, not the agreed value, is the standard for determining whether there is a constructive total loss. While the agreed value is conclusive as between the parties with respect to all questions relating to the quantification of the measure of indemnity for losses covered by the policy, whether the insured property has sustained a partial or total loss is not affected by whether the policy is valued or unvalued. The question of economic viability of repair is merely another way of asking whether, under particular circumstances, the property has sustained a partial or total loss.

3.46 The primacy of the market value in this context was first articulated in *Allen v. Sugrue*.[84] A vessel insured under a valued policy was so damaged that it would have cost about £1,450 to repair. The agreed value was £2,000 but the market value of the repaired vessel would have been less than the cost of repairs. The Court of King's Bench held the insurer liable for a total loss. The same issue arose in *Young v. Turing*[85] and again the question of whether the loss was total or partial was held to depend upon the market value of the repaired vessel and not the agreed value. Lord Abinger CB, delivering the judgment of the Exchequer Chamber, drew a clear distinction between the factual question of whether the loss is total or partial and the impact of the contractual valuation upon the measure of indemnity.[86]

3.47 The issue was conclusively settled in *Irving v. Manning*.[87] A vessel insured under a valued policy with an agreed value of £17,500 was so damaged as to be rendered unseaworthy. If repaired so as to be seaworthy once more, the vessel would have been worth £9,000, but the necessary repairs would have cost £10,500. The House of Lords summoned the judges and accepted their unanimous advice that the vessel was a total loss. Under an unvalued policy, uneconomic repairs equated to a total loss and there was no reason why the position should be different under a valued policy. The purpose of the agreed value was simply to avoid disputes about quantum of sums payable. Reference was made to cases of damage to goods where the extent of the loss is determined by depreciation in market value. Only once this factual extent of loss is determined is the agreed value introduced to determine the precise measure of indemnity.[88]

3.48 The settled position of the case law was duly codified in s.27(4) of the Marine Insurance Act 1906. Subject to contrary provision in the policy, the agreed value is not conclusive in determining whether the insured property has sustained a constructive total loss. As already noted, however, agreed values tend to be higher than actual values, sometimes considerably so. Were the agreed value to be used in constructive total loss calculations, insurers would be less frequently liable for the total loss measure of indemnity. Consequently, the Institute hulls clauses provide that "[i]n ascertaining whether the Vessel is a constructive total loss, the insured value

83. The question of economic viability arises also where the assured has been deprived of possession of the insured property. There is a constructive total loss where the cost of recovering the insured property would exceed its value once recovered: Marine Insurance Act 1906, s.60(2)(i)(b).

84. (1828) 8 B. & Cr. 561.

85. (1841) 2 Man. & Gr. 593.

86. At 601.

87. (1847) 1 H.L.C. 287.

88. *Lewis v. Rucker* (1761) 2 Burr. 1167, discussed *supra*, text to fnn.32 *et seq.*

shall be taken as the repaired value" and "[n]o claim for constructive total loss based upon the cost of recovery and/or repair of the Vessel shall be recoverable hereunder unless such cost would exceed the insured value".[89] As a result, where a ship is a constructive total loss by reason of being in fact uneconomic to repair but the cost of repairs does not exceed the agreed value, the assured will have to undertake the uneconomic repairs before the policy expires or, under the terms of the Institute clauses as already discussed, accept compensation for depreciation based on the lower actual value.

3E.2 Loss of a proportion of the valued property

The fact that a policy is valued cannot transform a loss of a part into a total loss. The agreed value is recoverable by the assured only where the whole of the interest valued has been lost. In other words, the agreed value is, by virtue of s.27(3) of the Marine Insurance Act 1906, conclusive evidence of the value of the insured interest, but the assured must still demonstrate what loss the insured interest has sustained and the measure of indemnity for a total loss is payable only where the assured proves there has been a total loss of that interest. Thus, s.75(2) of the Marine Insurance Act 1906 provides, *inter alia*, that: "Nothing in the provisions of this Act relating to the measure of indemnity shall . . . prohibit the insurer . . . from showing that at the time of the loss the whole or any part of the subject-matter insured was not at risk under the policy." 3.49

In *Forbes v. Aspinall*,[90] a vessel sailed to Haiti with cargo for barter. A valued policy was taken out on return freight. After exchanging some of the cargo for fifty-five bales of cotton, the vessel sailed in search of further return cargo but was lost before any could be obtained. The insurer paid in respect of the freight lost on the bales of cotton, but the assured claimed a sum equal to the full agreed value. The Court of King's Bench adamantly rejected that claim and held that the assured was entitled only to an appropriate proportion of the agreed value. Delivering the judgment of the Court, Lord Ellenborough stated as follows:[91] 3.50

> "The object of valuation in a policy is to fix by agreement between the parties an estimate upon the subject insured, and to supersede the necessity of proving the actual value, by specifying a certain sum as the amount of that value. . . . The valuation, however, in the case of goods, looks to all the goods intended to be loaded; and in the case of freight, it looks to freight upon all the goods the ship is intended to carry upon the voyage insured: and if by the perils insured against in a valued policy on goods, part only of the goods intended to be covered be lost, the valuation must be opened, and the assured can only recover in respect of that part: and so, if by the perils insured against the freight of part only of the goods to be carried be lost, the assured can only recover in respect of that loss, according to the proportion which that part bears to the whole sum at which the entire freight was estimated in the valuation."

Consequently, where a valued policy is taken out on 500 hogsheads of sugar, the vessel sails with only 100 hogsheads and the vessel and cargo are subsequently lost, the assured will recover 20 per cent of the agreed value. Since the valuation is fixed on the basis of a full cargo, there is no total loss of the interest valued. Any argument that

89. Institute Time Clause (Hulls) (1.10.83 and 1.11.95), Clause 19; Institute Voyage Clauses (Hulls) (1.10.83 and 1.11.95), Clause 17. See also the "Total Loss Clause" of the Institute freight clauses.
90. (1811) 13 East 323.
91. At 326–327.

the assured should be entitled to a sum equal to the agreed value on the basis of a total loss of the cargo that in fact was on board notwithstanding that only part of the interest valued was lost would offend against the indemnity principle.[92]

3.51 The principle of apportionment of the agreed value established in *Forbes v. Aspinall* was applied in two subsequent cases, also of freight insurance. In *Williams v. North China Insurance Co.*,[93] valued policies were taken out on freight and a separate policy was obtained on advances against freight. When the vessel and cargo became a total loss, the latter policy was paid in full. The assured then claimed a sum equal to the agreed value under the freight policies without giving credit for the indemnity obtained under the advances policy. As a matter of construction, it was held that the interest valued and insured under the freight policies included advances against freight. Consequently, credit had to be given through an apportionment of the agreed value in the freight policy, entitling the assured to such proportion of the agreed value as was attributable to the true freight with advances deducted.[94] In *The Main*,[95] freight in the sum of £3,250 was insured by the defendants under a valued policy with an agreed value of £5,500. However, £925 was paid in advance and was never at risk under the policy. The plaintiffs collected £3,250 under other policies and claimed £1,500 from the defendants. Gorell Barnes J held that the agreed value of £5,500 had to be apportioned to reflect the part of the freight not at risk, yielding an agreed value of £3,889,[96] the defendant's liability being limited to the balance of that apportioned value.

3.52 Notwithstanding the reference by Lord Ellenborough in *Forbes v. Aspinall* to re-opening the valuation, the legal response to part of the valued interest not being at risk does not involve a re-opening of the agreed value. That remains conclusive as between the insurer and assured as a valuation of the entirety of the interest the insurer contracts to cover. The legal response consists of an apportionment of the agreed value and not the setting of a new agreed value reflecting updated knowledge of relevant circumstances.[97] Accordingly, s.27(3) states specifically that the agreed value is conclusive "whether the loss be total or partial", and the courts will not permit an agreed value to be re-opened under the disguise of apportionment. In *Loders & Nucoline Ltd. v. Bank of New Zealand*,[98] a contract for the sale of goods on CIF terms required insurance in the value of the contract price plus 5 per cent. The contract price included an element attributable to freight that was payable only at destination by the buyer.[99] The seller tendered a policy that was held not to comply with the contract in that, *inter alia*, it was for an amount that excluded the freight element. The seller, argued, however, that this breach occasioned no loss since the value recoverable could not have included freight not at risk. The argument failed. How the

92. At 328.
93. (1876) 1 CPD 757.
94. See especially Mellish LJ at 769. This was a case of double insurance of the advances, rendering the freight insurers liable in contribution to the advances insurers.
95. [1894] P. 320, 329.
96. $\frac{925}{3250} \times 5500 = 3889$
97. At 324. See also *Burnand v. Rodocanachi, Son & Co.* (1880) 5 CPD 424, 426–427.
98. (1929) 33 LL. L. Rep. 70.
99. It was, therefore, deducted from the invoice price: p.74.

contract price (and, therefore, the value under the policy) was calculated was irrelevant to the question of what interest was in truth at risk. On the facts, the freight element was included as part of the price of the goods. That was a matter for the parties to the sale contract. In a cargo policy, apportionment of the agreed value would occur only in the event of a shortfall in shipment of the quantity of goods on which the value was calculated.

The essential principle in *Forbes v. Aspinall* is, it is suggested, clear and correct. An agreed value on cargo or freight is based on a full cargo or freight for a full cargo. It does not involve an undertaking to pay a sum equal to the agreed value in the event of the total loss of whatever cargo or freight is at risk at any moment during the currency of the policy. Where the casualty causes a loss of part only of the interest valued, the measure of indemnity should be calculated according to the principles governing partial loss under valued policies, so that the assured recovers an appropriate proportion of the agreed value.[100] The application of those principles is, however, confined by practicality. Calculation of the appropriate proportion of the agreed value assumes that it can be determined with tolerable certainty what proportion of the true value of the interest that is the subject of the agreed value was at risk. The mathematics were clear in *Williams* and *The Main*, but such is not always the case. In the report of *Forbes v. Aspinall* itself, it is stated that the insurer "settled for the freight of the 55 bales of cotton", but not on what basis.[101] On the facts, the value was calculated for a complete cargo, but the ship was lost before a complete cargo had been procured. What that cargo might have comprised, or indeed whether a full cargo could have been obtained, was unknown.[102] What proportion, in financial terms, of the final cargo was represented by the lost cotton was, therefore, pure speculation. This was not, however, a matter the court had to decide. 3.53

A similar problem arose in *Rickman v. Carstairs*[103] in the context of a valued policy on return cargo from Africa. At the time of the loss, the vessel had on board some of her outward cargo and some return cargo. A further portion of her return cargo was awaiting loading. The assured sought to recover in respect of both outward and return cargo. The Court of King's Bench held that the policy covered only return cargo, and that, following *Forbes v. Aspinall*, the assured could not be entitled to a sum equal to the full agreed value. The problematic nature of the required calculation was noted:[104] 3.54

"It is true that there will be some difficulty in making the proper calculation as to the sum to be paid, on the supposition that the subject of insurance is the full homeward cargo; because, on such a voyage, it is not easy to say what the value of a full home cargo will be; nor what proportion of a full cargo is on board at the time of the loss."

The Court was not, however, asked to determine and did not state how on the facts the true proportion was to be ascertained.

The difficulties in calculation were ultimately confronted in *Tobin v. Harford*.[105] 3.55

100. Marine Insurance Act 1906, ss.70, 71 (many of the principles thereby codified being established by the apportionment cases). The sections are discussed *supra*: "Partial loss of goods"; "Partial loss of freight".
101. (1811) 13 East 323, 324.
102. At 331–332.
103. (1833) 5 B. & Ad. 651.
104. At 665 *per* Denman CJ, delivering the judgment of the Court.
105. (1863) 13 CB (NS) 791; affd. (1864) 34 LJCP 37.

Return cargo was insured under a valued policy that provided that 24 hours after arrival on the outward voyage, outward cargo was to be considered as return cargo. The agreed value was £8,000. The vessel arrived and unloaded 57 per cent of the outward cargo. More than 24 hours later but before loading any fresh cargo, she was lost together with the remaining 43 per cent of the outward cargo. The assured claimed for a sum equal to the agreed value as on a total loss. The Court of Common Pleas, in a judgment affirmed by the Exchequer Chamber, held that the facts revealed only a partial loss. With respect to the appropriate measure of indemnity, the Court, alert to the problems mentioned in *Rickman v. Carstairs*, stated as follows:[106]

> "If the value of the whole of the intended cargo was a datum, the partial loss would be adjusted by the common proportion; but, where the value of the whole of the intended cargo cannot be ascertained, the proportion which the part lost bears to the whole cannot be known, and the mode of estimating a partial loss under a valued policy cannot be adopted.
>
> Under these circumstances, we think that the assured would be entitled to the ordinary indemnity as under an open[107] policy underwritten for 80,001."

In other words, where the proportion of the interest valued in the policy that has in fact been lost cannot be determined, the agreed value loses its evidential relevance. It is conclusive evidence as between the parties of something that has not been lost and what has been lost is of an unknown relationship to what was valued. All that can be done under those circumstances is to calculate the measure of indemnity on an unvalued basis, subject to a maximum liability of the agreed value, which becomes, in effect, a sum insured.

3.56 *Tobin v. Harford* was followed in *Denoon v. Home & Colonial Assurance Co.*[108] A vessel carried a mixture of cargo and passengers. The assured procured a valued policy on freight valued at £2,000 in the sum of £1,000.[109] His intention was to insure only the freight attributable to the cargo and not the passage money payable in respect of the passengers. That, however, was not communicated to the insurers. The vessel was subsequently wrecked, resulting in a total loss of the cargo and its freight, but nearly all the passengers were saved and reached their destination so that their passage money was paid. The assured claimed for a sum equal to the agreed value on the basis that there had been a total loss of the insured interest. The insurer contended that freight, in the policy in question, included the passage money so that liability was confined to a partial loss calculated by reference to an apportioned agreed value.[110] Willes J held that as a matter of construction the policy did not include the passage money so that there had been a total loss of the insured freight. However, valuation of freight in a valued policy referred, in the absence of contrary intention, to a full cargo, which there had not been on the facts. Consequently, apportionment of the agreed

106. At 803 *per* Williams J, delivering the judgment of the Court.

107. "Open" in this context means unvalued.

108. (1872) LR 7 CP 341.

109. The assured thereby underinsured to the extent of one half, remaining his own insurer for that half share: Marine Insurance Act 1906, s.81.

110. The calculation would have worked as follows. The freight on the rice was £1,412. The total passage money was £1,944. A total loss of £3,356 (all freight and passage money) would have paid £1,000 under the policy. The assured had in fact lost all the freight on the rice and £64 16s passage money, a total of £1,476 16s out of £3,356. The measure of indemnity would, therefore, have been that proportion of £1,000.

value was required, but, in the absence of a value for a full cargo,[111] there was no basis to compute the correct proportion. The policy was, therefore, treated as an unvalued policy on freight with a sum insured of £1,000. On the facts, the lost freight was worth £1,412, rendering the insurers liable, by reason of the 50 per cent underinsurance, in the sum of £706.

3.57 A further problem is to determine the threshold at which the principle in *Forbes v. Aspinall* first operates. Where a valuation of freight or cargo is calculated by reference to a full cargo, at what point in the loading stage is a full cargo reached for the purpose of the principle? On the assumption that a full cargo of freight would be worth £100,000, how many pounds short of that figure need the freight fall before apportionment under *Forbes v. Aspinall* is required?[112] The cases give little guidance. In *Tobin v. Harford*,[113] it was stated that "the valuation applies to what is substantially a full cargo, and not to any quantity of goods substantially less than a full cargo".[114] In *Denoon v. Home & Colonial Assurance Co.*,[115] Willes J stated that the assured would have recovered for a total loss of freight "if there had been no passengers, or so few as not substantially to interfere with the amount of the cargo".[116] The threshold to be passed for recovery in accordance with the agreed value without apportionment is, therefore, that the interest in fact at risk should be not substantially less than the interest valued. However, what precisely is meant by substantial remains to be elucidated.

3F SUBROGATION

3.58 Where a casualty generating a claim under an insurance policy is caused by a third party under such circumstances as to render that third party also liable in respect of the loss caused, the assured has a choice whether to sue the third party or claim under the policy. If the assured elects to claim under the policy, the existence of the right to sue the third party is no defence. This produces a difficulty. On the one hand, the nature of insurance as a contract of indemnity demands that the assured should not be permitted the double recovery that would follow from the assured recovering against both the insurer and the third party. On the other hand, were the third party's liability reduced to the extent that the assured recovered indemnity under the policy, the third party would receive a wholly unmeritorious windfall. The doctrine of subrogation provides the solution. Once the insurer has paid the assured, the insurer is entitled to exercise all the assured's rights and remedies against the third party.[117]

3.59 An agreed value becomes relevant to the operation of the doctrine of subrogation

111. Thus, according to Willes J (at 351): "It is not stated, and we must conclude could not be stated with certainty, what the total freight would have been had the vessel been filled up with cargo, or that there might not possibly have been a full cargo the freight of which would not have exceeded £2,000."
112. The question was raised, *arguendo*, in *Rickman v. Carstairs* (1833) 5 B. & Ad. 651, 659.
113. (1863) 13 CB (NS) 791.
114. At 802 *per* Williams J, delivering the judgment of the Court of Common Pleas.
115. (1872) LR 7 CP 341.
116. At 351.
117. Marine Insurance Act 1906, s.79.

where the actual loss exceeds the agreed value. In the absence of an agreed value, the assured is entitled to control the third party action (to be *dominus litis*) and is entitled to priority over the insurer with respect to any proceeds of the action. Thus, suppose an assured sustains loss of £100, is paid £70 under a policy and recovers £50 in an action against the third party responsible for the loss. Since, subrogation is designed to prevent unjust enrichment through double recovery, and since there is no double recovery until the assured has received an extra £30, in principle[118] the assured is entitled to control the litigation against the third party and is entitled to first dip into the proceeds to make up the shortfall in indemnification. The assured, therefore, receives £30, leaving the insurer the remaining £20.[119] Where, however, the policy is valued and the shortfall between the indemnity under the policy and the assured's actual loss results from the agreed value being less than the market value at the time of loss, the conclusiveness of the agreed value as between insurer and assured precludes the assured from alleging any shortfall in indemnification.[120]

3.60 *North of England Iron Steamship Insurance Association v. Armstrong*[121] arose out of the total loss by collision of a vessel insured under a valued policy. The agreed value was £6,000 and the vessel was insured for that sum. The insurers duly paid £6,000. The real value of the vessel, however, was £9,000. The assured recovered £5,000 from the owners of the other vessel involved in the collision. On general principles, the assured should have been entitled to make up the shortfall in indemnification out of those damages, receiving £3,000. The presence of an agreed value, however, meant that, as against the insurer, the assured was precluded from claiming any shortfall in indemnification with the result that the entire £5,000 went to the insurers. Similarly, in *Thames & Mersey Marine Insurance Co. v. British & Chilean Steamship Co.*[122] a vessel insured for its agreed value of £45,000 was rendered a total loss by collision. The insurers paid the agreed value, but the assured remained out of pocket because the true vessel of the vessel was £65,000. Scrutton J followed *Armstrong* in holding that the agreed value gave the insurers priority with respect to damages recovered from the owners of the other vessel. It was irrelevant that the quantum of damages reflected the true value of the vessel.[123]

3.61 The two cases just discussed concerned total losses. The impact of an agreed value in a case of partial loss was considered in *Goole & Hull Steam Towing Co. Ltd v. Ocean Marine Insurance Co. Ltd.*[124] A vessel insured for the agreed value of £4,000 incurred collision damage costing £5,000 to repair. The assured recovered £2,500 damages from the owners of the other vessel and claimed from the insurers the remaining

118. Subject to any contrary indication in the policy, as arises where the shortfall stems from a deductible: *Lord Napier and Ettrick v. Hunter* [1993] A.C. 713; Institute Time Clauses (Hulls) (1.10.83 and 1.11.95), Clause 12.3.

119. Authority supporting the assured's priority includes *Re Driscoll* [1918] 1 IR 152; *Arthur Barnett Ltd v. National Insurance Co. of New Zealand Ltd* [1965] N.Z.L.R. 874; *Ledingham v. Ontario Hospital Services Commission* (1979) 46 DLR (3d) 699.

120. *Burnand v. Rodocanachi Sons & Co.* (1882) 7 App. Cas. 333, 335.

121. (1870) LR 5 Q.B. 244.

122. [1915] 2 K.B. 214.

123. On the irrelevance to the significance of the agreed value as between insurer and assured of a different basis for assessment of liability as between assured and a third party, see also *Steamship Balmoral Co. Ltd v. Marten* [1902] A.C. 511, discussed *supra*, text to fnn.19 *et seq.*

124. [1928] 1 K.B. 589.

£2,500 by which the assured was in fact out of pocket. The insurers, however, argued successfully that their liability was limited to the difference between the sum recovered and the agreed value, namely £1,500. The measure of indemnity for the damage could not, under s.69 of the Marine Insurance Act 1906, exceed the sum insured in respect of any one casualty, which in a valued policy will be the agreed value unless the policy states to the contrary.[125] Put another way, had the assured claimed initially on the policy, following the total loss cases discussed above, the insurers could not have been liable for more than £4,000, and, having received that sum, the assured could not then have disputed full indemnification, leaving the insurers entitled to the third party damages. The assured could not alter the financial position as between insurer and assured simply by claiming first against the third party.[126]

While it is, therefore, clear that the insurer is entitled to priority with respect to the proceeds of any third party action once the assured has been indemnified to the extent of the agreed value,[127] a question remains as to entitlement to any surplus proceeds remaining once the insurer has recouped in full the indemnity paid to the assured. As a matter of general principle, the assured is entitled to any such surplus.[128] The third party action belongs to the assured: subrogation operates merely to prevent unjust enrichment in the form of double recovery from the insurer and the third party. Once the insurer has recouped in full the indemnity paid to the assured, there can be no such double recovery and the fact that the action is the assured's must give the assured any surplus proceeds. It is hard to see how the presence of an agreed value in the policy can alter that result. The conclusiveness of the agreed value as to the value of the insured property dictates the amount of compensation to which the assured is entitled before the law considers double recovery to arise. The presence of an agreed value does not transform the subrogation to the assured's rights and remedies into an assignment to the insurer of those rights and remedies.[129] Consequently, an agreed value says nothing about priority between assured and insurer once the assured has in the eyes of the law been fully indemnified and the insurer has also received full reimbursement. The assured has a claim to the surplus because the surplus is part of the proceeds of a cause of action that remains the assured's. The insurer has no claim to the surplus. 3.62

While the assured's entitlement to the surplus would appear to be clear as a matter of principle, as a matter of authority a slight doubt persists. A statement of Cockburn CJ in *North of England Iron Steamship Insurance Association v. Armstrong*[130] appears to 3.63

125. Mackinnon J placed reliance on the wording of s.79(2) of the Marine Insurance Act, which provides for subrogation in cases of partial loss once the assured has been indemnified "according to this Act", thus importing the conclusiveness of the agreed value through s.27(3). Such reasoning may be valid. However, the fact that s.79(1), which provides for subrogation in cases of total loss, contains no equivalent wording does not, as already seen, prevent the agreed value from operating conclusively in cases of total loss.

126. See, *North of England Iron Steamship Insurance Association v. Armstrong* (1870) LR 5 Q.B. 244, 249, where Cockburn CJ described any such argument as "altogether monstrous".

127. Either by the insurer or by a combination of insurance money and some of the proceeds of the action.

128. *Yorkshire Insurance Co. v. Nisbet Shipping Co. Ltd* [1962] 2 Q.B. 330.

129. An insurer to whom the assured has assigned the benefit of the third party claim acquires rights to the entirety of the proceeds: *Compania Columbiana de Seguros v. Pacific Navigation Co.* [1965] 1 Q.B. 101, 121.

130. (1870) LR 5 Q.B. 244.

suggest that an insurer who indemnifies for a total loss under a valued policy becomes entitled to the entirety of any third party proceeds. On the facts of *Armstrong*, the assured received the agreed value from the insurer and recovered from the third party a sum less than the agreed value. There was, therefore, no surplus. Cockburn CJ observed that had the assured first recovered against the third party, the indemnity recoverable from the insurer would have been *pro tanto* reduced. Since, as against the insurer, the assured could not claim to have lost more than the agreed value, the assured would have been entitled only to the balance of the agreed value after taking into account the third party proceeds. He then continued as follows:[131]

> "Therefore, though it certainly startles one a little that the underwriters, who have only paid [the agreed value], shall, if the vessel should prove to be equal to that [agreed value], or worth more, get all that can be recovered in respect of the loss of the vessel, yet still, I think that is an incident which arises from this novel form of policy, in which the value of the vessel is taken at a fixed sum as agreed between the parties."

3.64 The statement that insurers would take the entirety of the proceeds even where the ship was worth more than the agreed value suggests that the surplus would accrue to the insurers. However, to the extent that the dictum is intended so to suggest, it appears to have been prompted by confusion between the concepts of subrogation and abandonment together with an exaggeration of the consequences of abandonment.[132] An insurer who pays on a total loss is entitled by virtue of the indemnity principle to whatever remains of the insured property and any rights attached to that property. A hull insurer under a valued policy who pays the agreed value is, therefore, entitled to whatever remains of the ship and, for example, to any freight in the course of being earned at the time of the total loss and that is subsequently earned.[133] A cause of action against a third party responsible for the casualty, however, is personal to the assured in the sense that, while it may be expressly assigned to the insurer, it does not automatically attach to the insured property and pass with it. In contrast to abandonment, subrogation of course merely provides the insurer with access to the assured's cause of action against the third party and involves no transfer of that right to the insurer. Consequently, to the extent that the *dictum* of Cockburn CJ in *Armstrong* is intended to suggest that the insurer should be entitled to surplus proceeds in valued policies, it should not be followed.

3G DOUBLE INSURANCE

3.65 Double insurance arises "[w]here two or more policies are effected by or on behalf of the assured on the same adventure and interest or any part thereof".[134] There is

---

131. At 249.

132. See Cockburn CJ at 249–250 and Lush J at 251; *Thames & Mersey Marine Insurance Co. v. British & Chilean Steamship Co.* [1915] 2 K.B. 214, 221 (*dicta* in *Armstrong obiter* and based on confusion with abandonment); *Goole & Hull Steam Towing Co. Ltd v. Ocean Marine Insurance Co. Ltd* [1928] 1 K.B. 589, 598 (*dictum* of Cockburn CJ in *Armstrong* "can only be right if it rests upon the cession of property to the underwriter upon payment for a total loss" and, therefore, certainly inapplicable in cases of partial loss).

133. *Case v. Davidson* (1816) 5 M. & S. 79, affd. (1820) 2 Brod. & B. 379. The right to such freight is, however, waived by the Institute hulls clauses.

134. Marine Insurance Act 1906, s.32(1).

nothing unlawful in insuring the same interest more than once, but the prospect of multiple indemnities tempting the assured into conniving at losses induces insurance law to deny any measure of double recovery.[135] The solution is to permit the assured to recover against the various insurers in such order as the assured elects, but to limit the assured overall to indemnification of the loss sustained in accordance with the principles of insurance law. To the extent that any insurer is called upon to pay the assured more than a due share, that insurer is then entitled to pro rata contribution from the other insurers. The result is to deny the assured double recovery while preserving equity among the insurers, placing the main risk of insurer insolvency on the insurers.

Valued policies raise the question of when double recovery arises. Suppose that a vessel insured under two valued policies is in fact worth more than either of the agreed values taken individually. Two possible rules may be contemplated. First, each policy may be regarded as providing that the assured cannot recover more than the agreed value stated in that policy from any source. Consequently, any sums recovered under other policies have to be credited against the agreed value under that policy and the assured is confined to recovering under that policy the balance, if any, of the agreed value stated in that policy. Second, the agreed value may be regarded as definitive of the value of the insured property for the purpose only of claims on that policy. Consequently, while the assured may not recover more on an individual policy than the agreed value stated in it, cumulatively the assured is entitled to recover the full market value of the vessel subject to an upper limit of the aggregate of all the agreed values. In the former view, double recovery would depend on the agreed value under the policy in question. In the latter, it would be judged against the market value of the insured property. 3.66

The issue first arose in *Bousfield v. Barnes*.[136] A ship was insured under two valued policies containing agreed values of £8,000 and £6,000. The first policy was subscribed for £6,000 and the second for £600. The ship was totally lost and the second policy paid in full. The assured then sought to recover under the second policy, adducing evidence that the true value of the ship was in excess of £8,000. The insurer argued that payment on the first policy of a sum equal to the agreed value under the second precluded the assured from claiming any further sum under the second. However, Lord Ellenborough held that the assured was not so precluded: 3.67

> "I think the valuation in this policy is only conclusive in settling a loss upon it between the assured and the underwriters who have subscribed it, without taking into consideration what has been transacted between the assured and third persons. ... [I]t is not enough for the underwriters on a particular policy to shew that the assured has received from another quarter the amount of the valuation in that policy, unless this amounts in point of fact to a complete indemnity."[137]

Bousfield v. Barnes, therefore, decided in favour of the second rule outlined above in a case of policies containing different agreed values. 3.68

In *Irving v. Richardson*,[138] a ship was valued at £3,000 under each of two valued

135. *Godin v. London Assurance Co.* (1758) 1 Burr. 489, 492.
136. (1815) 4 Camp. 228.
137. At 229–230.
138. (1831) 1 M. & W. 153.

policies with sums insured of £1,700 on one policy and £2,000 on the other. The assured was a mortgagee of the ship for a sum less than £3,000. The ship was lost and the assured recovered in full under both policies, the second insurer being unaware of the first policy. On discovery thereof, the second insurer sought restitution to the extent the assured had recovered cumulatively in excess of the agreed value. The ship was in fact worth more than the cumulative recovery. The primary issue in the case was whether the policy covered only the assured's interest as mortgagee or also that of the mortgagor. The assured contended that both interests were covered and that, following *Bousfield v. Barnes*, he was not limited under the second policy to the balance of the agreed value under that policy. The second insurer won, the assured being held liable to repay £700. The case was decided on a finding of fact by the jury that the assured had insured only as mortgagee of the ship. However, Lord Tenterden CJ stated that, had it been necessary, he would have considered *Bousfield v. Barnes* as distinguishable on the basis that the agreed values in the present case were the same. In such a case, in his opinion, the assured could not recover beyond that sum.

3.69 The true rule in cases where valued policies on the same interest contain the same agreed value arose for decision in *Morgan v. Price*.[139] Two valued policies on a ship each contained an agreed value of £2,500. The ship was lost. Payment of £2,500 under one policy was held to constitute satisfaction under both. Once the assured had been indemnified in the sum of £2,500, no claim could then be made on a policy that conclusively valued the lost ship at £2,500. There appears to have been no claim that the true loss exceeded £2,500, but the tenor of the judgments provides no grounds for belief that such a claim would have made any difference.

3.70 The question arising in the light of *Morgan v. Price* was whether a distinction could endure depending upon whether the valued policies contained the same agreed value or different agreed values. The issue was resolved in *Bruce v. Jones*.[140] A ship was insured under four valued policies with various agreed values and subscribed for various sums.[141] The ship was lost and the assured recovered a total of £3,126 13s. 6d. under three of the policies. The insurers under the remaining policy contended that the assured had to credit this amount against the policy's agreed value of £3,200. Counsel for the insurer referred to *Bousfield v. Barnes*, but argued that this decision failed to take proper account of the agreed value. Counsel for the assured submitted that the insurer was not entitled to any deduction in respect of sums recovered under other policies or was liable for the balance of the average of the four agreed values. The Court of Exchequer held in favour of the insurer. The conclusiveness of the agreed value with respect to both insurer and assured was decisive. Just as the fact that the insured property might in fact be worth less than the agreed value could not avail an insurer, so an assured could not be heard to say that the property was in fact worth more. Consequently, once and to the extent that the assured had been indemnified, regardless of the source of that indemnity, insurers were *pro tanto* discharged. That other policies might value the property differently was irrelevant to issues of

139. (1850) 4 Exch. 615.
140. (1863) 1 H. & C. 769.
141. The figures for the four policies were as follows: (1) agreed value of £3,000, subscribed for £725; (2) agreed value of £3,000, subscribed for £500; (3) agreed value of £5,000, subscribed for £3,450; (4) agreed value of £3,200, subscribed for £2,400. The litigation concerned the fourth policy.

indemnification as between the insurer and the assured on the policy in question. Perhaps curiously, none of the judgments refer to *Bousfield v. Barnes*, cited in argument, although the court was clearly rejecting the approach adopted by Lord Ellenborough.

One consequence of the decision in *Bruce v. Jones* is said to be that the amount recovered by an assured may vary according to the order in which claims are made under the policies. It is, however, difficult to see why this should be the case. Ultimately, the assured will recover according to the highest agreed value. If the assured claims first against the policy with the higher agreed value, his indemnity according to that value will be higher than the indemnity in principle recoverable under the policy with the lower value. Consequently, in any subsequent proceedings under that other policy, the assured will be precluded from alleging that any loss remains to be indemnified and will recover nothing. If the assured claims in reverse order, he will recover, first, according to the lower agreed value and, second, according to the higher value but only subject to giving credit for the indemnity recovered under the first policy. Again, therefore, the net result is that the assured will recover according to the higher agreed value. The amount recovered in *Bruce v. Jones* itself would have varied according to the order in which claims were made but only because, for reasons that are not explained, the assured's claims under the first three policies yielded in each case less than the agreed value in the policy.[142] 3.71

The decision in *Bruce v. Jones* did not win universal approval. The following year, in *Wilson v. Nelson*,[143] freight was insured under a number of policies. Insurers argued that their policy was valued and that a sum equal to the agreed value had already been recovered by the assured under other policies. The assured's loss exceeded the alleged agreed value. The Court of Queen's Bench found in favour of the assured on the basis that the policy was not valued,[144] but Shee J stated that even if the policy had been valued he would still have favoured the assured. Expressing support for *Bousfield v. Barnes*, he stated that in cases of double insurance and valued policies, the assured ought to recover against the balance of the true loss.[145] 3.72

However, notwithstanding any such reservation, the approach of *Morgan v. Price* and *Bruce v. Jones* was codified without qualification in the Marine Insurance Act. By virtue of s.32(2): 3.73

> "Where the assured is over-insured by double insurance:
> (a) The assured, unless the policy otherwise provides, may claim payment from the insurers in such order as he may think fit, provided that he is not entitled to receive any sum in excess of the indemnity allowed by this Act;
> (b) Where the policy under which the assured claims is a valued policy, the assured must give credit as against the valuation for any sum received by him under any other policy without regard to the actual value of the subject-matter insured. . . ."

It is suggested that the stance of the common law codified in the Act is correct. The

142. In respect of the first three policies, the assured recovered £492 6s 6d, £684 7s and £1,950 respectively. Had the assured claimed against the fourth policy before the third, the value of the final claim would have been the cumulative balance of the higher agreed value of £5,000, rather than the cumulative balance of £3,200. Insolvency of some participating insurers and uncertainty as to the law on double insurance are two possible explanations for the quantum of recovery on the first three claims.

143. (1864) 33 LJ Q.B. 220.

144. *Supra*, text to fn.3.

145. At 223.

approach of Lord Ellenborough in *Bousfield v. Barnes* treats an agreed value as a sum insured in the double insurance context. As clarified by subsequent nineteenth century case law, however, the conclusiveness of the agreed value is pervasive.

3H RE-OPENING AN AGREED VALUE

3.74 Given that an agreed value is designed to dispense with the need for an assured to prove the true, market value of any loss, it follows, as has been seen, that an insurer cannot object to indemnifying according to the agreed value merely because that value exceeds, even considerably, the true loss in fact sustained. It does not, however, follow that an agreed value can never be re-opened. This final section is concerned with the circumstances under which an insurer can challenge an agreed value.

3.75 As discussed in a previous section, the presence of an agreed value does not prevent the insurer from challenging an alleged total loss as in truth partial. *A fortiori*, valued policies remain subject to the requirement of an insurable interest.[146] Section 75 of the Marine Insurance Act 1906, part of which was considered previously, also provides that nothing in the statute is to "prohibit the insurer from disproving interest wholly or in part". Mere over-valuation, however, even if excessive, does not render a policy a wager,[147] but over-valuation will provide a defence where it amounts to fraud or a material non-disclosure. Section 27(3) of the Marine Insurance Act provides that the conclusiveness of the agreed value is subject to the provisions of the Act and to the absence of fraud. It is now clear that the relevant statutory provisions include those concerned with pre-formation utmost good faith.[148]

3.76 In *Thames and Mersey Marine Insurance Co. Ltd. v. Gunford Ship Co. Ltd*,[149] Lord Shaw observed that "[w]here there is heavy over-valuation fraud is, *a priori*, not very far to seek". However, he continued to note that commercial concerns may render "intelligible and legitimate" an insurance valuation "going much beyond" the market value of the insured property. Indeed, the fraud exception to the conclusiveness of the agreed value has been more often stated[150] than applied. A rare example is provided by *Haigh v. De La Cour*[151] where the assured induced the insurer to agree to a value on cargo by producing forged invoices and bills of lading.

3.77 More commonly, excessive over-valuation has been challenged as a breach of a pre-formation duty of utmost good faith. To invoke non-disclosure, it must be shown that the assured knew of the over-valuation or should have known it in the ordinary course of business,[152] that it was material according to the standard of the prudent underwriter,[153] and that its non-disclosure induced the actual underwriter into the

146. *Lewis v. Rucker* (1761) 2 Burr. 1167, 1171; *Shawe v. Felton* (1801) 2 East 109, 116; *Lidgett v. Secretan* (1871) LR 6 CP 616, 629;

147. *Glafki Shipping Co. SA v. Pinios Shipping Co. No. 1 (The Maira) (No. 2)* [1984] 1 Lloyd's Rep. 660, 667.

148. *Inversiones Manria SA v. Sphere Drake Insurance Co. plc (The Dora)* [1989] 1 Lloyd's Rep. 69, 92.

149. [1911] A.C. 529, 542.

150. For example, *Lidgett v. Secretan* (1871) LR 6 CP 616, 629; *Elcock v. Thomson* [1949] 2 K.B. 755, 760.

151. (1812) 3 Camp. 319.

152. Marine Insurance Act 1906, s.18(1).

153. *Ibid.*, s.18(2) as construed in *Pan Atlantic Insurance Co. Ltd v. Pine Top Insurance Co. Ltd* [1995] 1 A.C. 501.

contract.[154] In *Ionides v. Pender*,[155] cargo with a true value of less than £8,000 was insured under a valued policy with an agreed value of about £14,000. Additional policies worth a further £2,500 were also concluded. The highest over-valuation saw Russian spirits worth £973 valued at £2,800. The assured sought to justify this through the prospect of a heavy Russian duty the imposition of which would bridge the gap. Uncontested evidence was given that over-valuation to such an extent was regarded by insurers as material. Once the over-valuation exceeded 25–30 per cent, insurers would regard the valuation as speculative, so that insurers either would decline the risk or charge a higher premium. The judge left the question of whether on the facts the valuation was excessive to the jury, instructing them "not to find the valuation excessive unless they thought the goods were valued with an addition of profit greater than could be expected to be realised under any circumstances which could be reasonably contemplated".[156] The jury found that the over-valuation was not fraudulent but was material. The Court of Queen's Bench dismissed an application for a new trial on the ground of a misdirection with respect to over-valuation. If anything, the direction was "perhaps ... too favourable to the assured, as it makes the question, whether there is an excessive valuation or not, depend on whether the valuation was so high as to amount in part at least to a wager".[157] Consequently, once the valuation enters the realm of "speculation", the transaction is invalid as a wager while a lesser degree of "excessive" over-valuation suffices to give rise to a good faith defence.

Non-disclosure of a material over-valuation was present also in *Gooding v. White*[158] where cargo probably worth no more than £2,000 was insured for £5,000. In *Thames and Mersey Marine Insurance Co. Ltd. v. Gunford Ship Co. Ltd*,[159] a combination of policies on hull, freight and disbursements produced a cumulative over-valuation of £21,800 on a true value of £11,400 that the House of Lords had little hesitation in holding material. In *Piper v. Royal Exchange Assurance*,[160] a yacht purchased by the assured for £1,000 was insured initially for £2,000 with the valuation subsequently being increased on renewal to £2,500. Roche J held that the assured had in fact overpaid for the yacht, but was prepared to accept that the initial valuation, albeit optimistic, was not commercially excessive and did respond to the price the assured hoped to obtain on a desired re-sale. However, by the time the value was increased, the assured had repeatedly failed to re-sell the yacht, and was fully aware of her condition and that a value of £2,500 was at least double her true value. This over-valuation was material and should have been disclosed. 3.78

A contrast may be drawn with *Inversiones Manria SA v. Sphere Drake Insurance Co. plc (The Dora)*.[161] The assured purchased a yacht and insured her under a policy with an agreed value in the sum of the purchase price of $480,000. Phillips J found that this agreed value was $80,000 higher than her market value. However, expert evidence 3.79

154. *Pan Atlantic Insurance Co. Ltd v. Pine Top Insurance Co. Ltd* [1995] 1 A.C. 501.
155. (1874) LR 9 Q.B. 531.
156. At 536 *per* Blackburn J, delivering the judgment of the Court of Queen's Bench.
157. *Ibid.*
158. (1913) 29 TLR 312.
159. [1911] A.C. 529.
160. (1932) 44 LL. L. Rep. 103.
161. [1989] 1 Lloyd's Rep. 69.

established that "an assured insuring a yacht will put forward the value he subjectively believes the yacht to have. More particularly, the purchaser of a yacht will naturally insure the yacht for the price he pays".[162] In the light of this expert evidence, he concluded that "where a yacht owner insures for the price he has paid, a discrepancy between the insured value and the open market value is not material".[163]

3.80 It is noteworthy that the preferred formulation in the context of an inflated agreed value generally is non-disclosure of the excessive over-valuation rather than misrepresentation of the true value, although in *The Dora* Phillips J referred to "the representation made as to the value of *Dora*".[164] It is suggested that non-disclosure is, indeed, the more appropriate analytical tool in this context. Viewed as a representation, a difficult question arises as to the content and nature of the statement. Clearly, insurance law accepts that a value put forward as an agreed value is not necessarily the market value. As already seen, an assured may legitimately over-value in order to finance replacement of the insured asset or to discharge mortgage indebtedness and provide a margin in addition. The value advanced amounts more to a proposal for a basis for indemnification in the event of an insured casualty rather than either a statement of fact as to the market value of the property or even a statement of the assured's opinion of a legitimate basis for indemnification in the light of the market value of the ship.[165] The difficulty is demonstrated most graphically by *The Glafki*[166] where, it will be recalled, the courts had no difficulty in accepting the validity of an over-valuation in excess of $7 million. In percentage terms, the value that should have been insured amounted to approximately 240 per cent of the market value of the ship. The difficulty, however, is eased when viewed through the lens of non-disclosure. The assured is obliged to disclose "every material circumstance" and an excessive over-valuation is clearly a "circumstance".

31 SUMMARY

3.81 It might be helpful to summarise the main points of the above discussion of agreed values and valued policies.

(a) An agreed value represents a conclusive agreement between insurer and assured for all purposes concerning measure of indemnity as to the value of the subject-matter insured. It must be distinguished from a sum insured, which represents merely a ceiling on recovery.

(b) An agreed value will commonly exceed the market value of the insured property as at the time when the insurance contract is concluded. In any

162. At 92.

163. *Ibid.*

164. *Ibid.*

165. Moreover, in *Economides v. Commercial Union Assurance Co. plc* [1998] Q.B. 587 the Court of Appeal held that the Marine Insurance Act, s.20(5) rendered a statement of opinion actionable in insurance contract law only if fraudulent, precluding an insurer from arguing, in appropriate circumstances, that the assured impliedly represented the existence of reasonable grounds to support the opinion. *Sed quaere.* See Bennett, "Statements of Fact and Statements of Belief in Insurance Contract Law and General Contract Law" (1998) 61 MLR 886, and for a sign of possible judicial disquiet, see *Sirius International Insurance Corp. v. Oriental Assurance Corp.* [1999] Lloyd's Rep. 343, 351.

166. [1985] 1 Lloyd's Rep. 300, affd. [1986] 2 Lloyd's Rep. 12, discussed *supra*, text to fn.14.

event, it will not fluctuate thereafter to reflect an appreciating or depreciating market value.

(c) The conclusive nature of the agreed value on questions of indemnity between insurer and assured persists even with respect to indemnification for third party liabilities assessed on a market value basis.

(d) In cases of total loss, the measure of indemnity is the agreed value, regardless of the actual market loss sustained by the assured.

(e) In cases of partial loss of goods or freight, the measure of indemnity is the appropriate proportion of the agreed value.

(f) In cases of damage to ships, the measure of indemnity is either the reasonable cost of repairs or, where the damage is not repaired by the time the policy expires, the reasonable depreciation in the value of the ship at that time. At common law, such depreciation is assessed by reference to the appropriate proportion of the agreed value, although the Institute hulls clauses assess depreciation purely by reference to market value.

(g) In principle, successive losses are recoverable even where the aggregate loss exceeds the agreed value. However, to the extent that successive partial losses are indemnified by reference to depreciation, the agreed value will cap the indemnity recoverable for unrepaired damage simply because insured property cannot depreciate by more than 100 per cent. An unrepaired partial loss will merge into a subsequent total loss.

(h) An agreed value is, in principle, irrelevant to the question of what loss has been sustained. In particular, as a matter of common law, the question of whether repair or recovery of the insured property is economically viable is determined by reference to market values, although the Institute hulls clauses provide for determination by reference to the agreed value. Furthermore, where only part of the subject-matter insured is at risk at the time of the casualty, the measure of indemnity is calculated by reference to the corresponding proportion of the agreed value. Where, however, what proportion was at risk cannot be ascertained, the policy will be treated as unvalued.

(i) The agreed value determines the operation of the doctrine of subrogation. The insurer is entitled to priority with respect to proceeds of third party litigation once the assured has received indemnification equal to the agreed value. The assured is precluded from claiming as against the insurer that a total or partial loss has occasioned financial loss in excess of the agreed value. However, any surplus remaining after the insurer has been reimbursed in full belongs to the assured.

(j) In cases of double insurance, any claim under a valued policy must give credit against the agreed value in that policy for any sum received under any other policy regardless of whether the policies in question share the same agreed value.

(k) The presence of an agreed value does not dispense with the requirement of an insurable interest. However, over-valuation of that interest will not afford the insurer a defence in the absence of fraud or material non-disclosure.

CHAPTER 4

THE ELEMENTS OF INSURABLE INTEREST IN MARINE INSURANCE LAW

NICHOLAS LEGH-JONES QC

4A INTRODUCTION

The requirement that the assured must possess an insurable interest in the subject-matter of a marine insurance is inherent in the fundamental and long-established principle that a contract of marine insurance is one of indemnity.[1] Only if the assured possesses an interest in the subject-matter can the insurance perform its function of affording him an indemnity against loss in the event of the subject-matter being lost or damaged by marine perils,[2] and the absence of an interest will provide the insurer with a defence to payment.[3] An insurable interest is also required for a different reason, namely, to prevent the insurance from being deemed to be a contract by way of gaming or wagering and in consequence void.[4] Where the assured possesses no interest whatsoever in the thing insured, an insurance thereon is no more than a wager on whether harm will come to it. The presence of an interest accordingly differentiates insurance from wager.[5] The absence of any interest in the subject-matter of a wager other than that created by the bet itself is at the heart of the common *4.1*

1. Marine Insurance Act 1906, s.1.
2. *Wilson v. Jones* (1867) LR 2 Ex. 139, 150 *per* Blackburn J; *Lucena v. Craufurd* (1806) 2 Bos. & Pul. (NR) 269, 302 *per* Lawrence J.
3. *Macaura v. Northern Assurance* [1925] A.C. 619, 632 *per* Lord Sumner.
4. Marine Insurance Act 1906, s.4.
5. *Wilson v. Jones* (1867) LR 2 Ex. 139, 146 (Willes J), 150 (Blackburn J).

law definition of a wagering contract given by Hawkins J in *Carlill v. Carbolic Smoke Ball Company*,[6] namely:

> "one by which two persons, professing to hold opposite views touching the issue of a future uncertain event, mutually agree that, dependent upon the determination of that event, one shall win from the other, and that other shall pay . . . a sum of money . . .; neither of the contracting parties having any other interest in that contract than the sum or stake he will so win or lose. . . ."

4.2 The Marine Insurance Act 1906 devotes 12 sections to the subject of insurable interest.[7] Even in 1906 many of the decisions which these sections were intended to codify were already elderly, and it may be argued that the space devoted to insurable interest fails to reflect its insignificance in current law. The subject nonetheless deserves study. The Act preserves the requirement of interest, reinforced by the contractual stipulation for an insurable interest contained in the Institute Cargo Clauses.[8] Despite, or perhaps because of, their antiquity, the extent to which the modern law remains anchored to the pre-Act authorities is uncertain, and this in turn affects the definition of insurable interest in non-marine property insurance law, which is rooted in the early marine insurance decisions. In this chapter the author starts by examining the development of the statutory prohibition of wagering policies and the formulation of the definition of insurable interest codified in s.5 of the Marine Insurance Act 1906. These are treated separately because an insurance which escapes the statutory definition of a wagering contract is not necessarily one in which the assured therefore possesses a valid insurable interest in the subject-matter. Section 5 leads to the question of whether the courts are free to change the law in the absence of an amending statute, and the problems attendant on a radical revision of the traditional definition of insurable interest.

4B GAMING AND WAGERING POLICIES

4B.1 The advent of the wager policy

4.3 It is sometimes said[9] that insurable interest was devised after the statutory ban on gambling policies in order to provide a means of distinguishing the insured sheep from the wagering goats. This appears not to be historically correct. Well before the passing of the Marine Insurance Act 1745, English law had accepted the doctrine of European mercantile law that the contract of marine insurance was a contract of

6. [1892] 2 Q.B. 484, 490–491, aff'd. [1893] 1 Q.B. 256 and described as "the classic definition of wagering" by Hobhouse J in *The Maira (No. 2)* [1984] 1 Lloyd's Rep. 660, 667. The defendant had submitted that any contract created by the celebrated smoke ball advertisement was rendered void by the Gaming Act 1845.

7. Section 4 (avoidance of gambling policies), s.5 (definition), s.6 (time at which interest to be shown), ss.7–14 (particular categories of insurable interest), and s.15 (consequences of a disposition of interest in the agreed subject-matter).

8. Clause 11.1.

9. For example, "The whole law as to what amounts to an insurable interest and when it is required, is derived from the statutory avoidance of wagering contracts". *Lonsdale & Thompson v. Black Arrow* [1993] Ch. 361, 368; "Insurable interest, a notion created to deal with a problem of gaming contracts rather than a problem of insurance. . . .": Professor R Grime, *Modern Law of Marine Insurance* (LLP, London) (1996), Chapter 3, p.135, fn.170.

indemnity requiring the assured to have an interest in the thing insured.[10] Yet at some stage, believed by Park[11] to be shortly after the Revolution of 1688, insurers began to issue marine insurance policies in which they expressly waived proof of the assured's interest or alternatively admitted that he possessed interest.[12] A common wording in such policies was "interest or no interest".[13] By agreeing a policy in this form the parties signified their intention not to make an insurance upon interest but to wager regardless of it, and such wagers under the guise of insurance were called gaming and wager policies. It is unclear when the courts agreed to enforce them. In the late seventeenth century case of *Goddard v. Garrett*[14] Chancery's reaction was hostile:

> "Take it that the law is settled, that if a man has no interest and insures, the insurance is void . . . and the reason the law goes upon, is that these insurances are made for the encouragement of trade, and not that persons unconcerned in trade, nor interested in the ship, should profit by it."

A hundred years later Sir James Mansfield CJ could say only that, "Wager policies at last came to be legal, nobody knows how, contrary to common sense".[15] Lord Hardwicke LC, who sat in the King's Bench before his time in Chancery, provides more illumination in his comment that, "The common law leant strongly against these policies for some time, but being found beneficial to merchants, they winked at it".[16] Seeing that the common law courts' practice was to enforce wagers, albeit reluctantly, unless it was against the public interest to do so in a given case[17] their attitude towards wager policies is perhaps understandable. At any rate the eighteenth century law reports disclose a number of cases[18] in which the courts allowed claims for a total loss under wager policies written "on interest or no interest", "free from average", and "without benefit of salvage". Given the absence of an interest in the insured ship these policies were inevitably on total loss only, the assured could never tender abandonment or confer a right to salvage in the event of a loss, and he was not able to sue and labour.[19] Not only were such policies enforced, but the very concept of a total loss by capture was redefined to accommodate the wagering character of the insurance. Such policies were interpreted as being a bet on the event of the insured vessel being taken and her voyage disrupted, so that her subsequent recapture and restoration to her owner thereafter did not entitle the insurer to say that the loss was 4.4

10. *Lucena v. Craufurd* (1802) 3 Bos. & Pul. 75, 101; (1806) 2 Bos. & Pul. (NR) 269, 296 and 300–302; Park, *A System of the Law of Marine Insurances* (8th edn., 1842), Chapter 14, p.557.

11. Park, *op.cit*, p.552.

12. *Depaba v. Ludlow* 1 Com. Rep. 360; *Lucena v. Craufurd* (1802) 3 Bos. & Pul. 75, 101; (1806) 2 Bos. & Pul. (NR) 269, 296, 321–322.

13. *Depaba v. Ludlow supra*; *Assievedo v. Cambridge* (1710) 10 Mod. Rep. 77; *Pond v. King* (1747) 1 Wils. 191; *Dean v. Dicker* (1746) 2 Str. 1250. Others are noted in the report of *Fitzgerald v. Pole* in (1754) 4 Bro. Parl. Cas. 439, 445–446.

14. (1692) 2 Vern. 269.

15. *Cousins v. Nantes* (1811) 3 Taunt. 513, 522.

16. *Sadlers' Company v. Badcock* (1743) 2 Atk. 554, 556.

17. *Good v. Eliot* (1790) 3 TR 693, 695; *MacGillivray on Insurance Law* (9th edn., Sweet & Maxwell Ltd, London 1997) paras 1–15 to 1–16.

18. *Depaba v. Ludlow*; *Pond v. King*; *Dean v. Dicker*, fn.13 *supra*, distinguished in *Goss v. Withers* (1758) 2 Burr. 683, a case of insurance upon interest. Others are cited by Park, *op. cit.* at pp.159–165.

19. *Cousins v. Nantes* (1811) 3 Taunt. 513, 524; *Edwards v. Motor Union* [1922] 2 K.B. 249, 255, citing *Kulen Kemp v. Vigne* (1786) 1 TR 304, 308.

adeemed, the assured never having owned her in the first place.[20] By 1745, therefore, English law had come to recognise two kinds of marine insurance policy. The first was the traditional mercantile or "common" policy, a contract of indemnity made upon interest. The second was the wager policy, the same in form, but not a contract of indemnity because, as Lord Mansfield said, there was no interest upon which a loss could accrue.[21]

4B.2 The Marine Insurance Act 1745

4.5 However beneficial the wager policy might appear to merchants, Parliament took a different view. In 1745 an Act[22] was passed to prohibit the making of insurances on British ships—"interest or no interest, or without further proof of interest than the policy, or by way of gaming and wagering, or without benefit of salvage to the assurer; and that every such insurance shall be null and void to all intents and purposes".[23] The preamble to the Act stated that the making of such insurances had been "productive of many pernicious practices", which it then proceeded to list. The mischief which the Act sought to remedy was not the evil of gambling in itself, but rather the effect that this wagering was having upon the country's trade and commerce.[24] The main objections to it were that it encouraged the fraudulent and deliberate loss of vessels and cargoes in furtherance of wagers upon their safe arrival, which in turn endangered the lives of seamen and the solvency of underwriters, and that it facilitated the carrying out of illicit trades and smuggling of contraband. The Act contained a number of important exceptions to the general prohibition. These underlined the character of the Act as a pragmatic measure to protect the country's merchant fleet, trading laws, and nascent insurance industry.

4.6 Wager policies on foreign ships and cargoes were still permitted.[25] The reason was later said to have been the difficulty of bringing witnesses from abroad to prove interest.[26] Arnould thought this was an inadequate explanation. [27] One can only say

20. In *Fitzgerald v. Pole* (1754) 4 Bro. Parl. Cas. 439 the House of Lords declined to interpret an insurance upon a privateer in this way, it being (unusually) a hull insurance written upon interest.

21. *Lowry v. Bourdieu* (1780) 2 Dougl. 468, 470. A similar opinion was expressed by Buller J in *Kulen Kemp v. Vigne* (1786) 1 TR 305, 309.

22. 19 Geo. 2, c.37.

23. Section 1.

24. *Murphy v. Bell* (1828) 4 Bing. 567, 569–571 *per* Best CJ.

25. *Thellusson v. Fletcher* (1780) 1 Dougl. 315; *Lucena v. Craufurd* (1806) 2 Bos. & Pul. (NR) 269, 322. If the policy was in the common form, and not ppi, then it was still necessary to aver and to prove interest in the foreign ship or cargo—*Lucena v. Craufurd, ubi cit; Cousins v. Nantes* (1811) 3 Taunt. 513, disapproving the contrary opinion of Lord Kenyon CJ in *Craufurd v. Hunter* (1798) 8 TR 13. The curious case of *Kulen Kemp v. Vigne* (1786) 1 TR 304 concerned a ppi policy made by foreign cargo interests on the safe arrival of the carrying vessel at Marseilles. Arnould suggests that the court's denial of the assured's claim rested on the fact that it was a ppi policy—*Marine Insurance Law* (16th edn., Stevens, London 1981) Vol. I, para. 385. The real reason, it is submitted, was the ship's failure to proceed to Marseilles when able to do so after her release from capture by the Spaniards. The court held that the assured under a wager policy undertook to perform all that the true owners of the ship could have done in the same situation. Lord Mansfield described this as the "fatal objection", p.308. This conforms to the opinion of Marshall, *Law of Insurance* (3rd edn., Joseph Butterworth, London 1823) p.127, n.(a) and pp.695–696.

26. *Lucena v. Craufurd* (1806) 2 Bos. & Pul. 269, 322 *per* Lord Eldon.

27. Arnould, *Law of Marine Insurance* (2nd edn., 1857), p.332.

that the laudable aim of protecting the British merchant marine did not require the protection of its competitors. Second, s.2 of the Act permitted wager policies to be made on English privateers fitted out solely to cruise against the king's enemies. It was later said that the reason for this was that the large numbers of crew carried on these vessels would frustrate any attempt to plan a deliberate sinking or capture and keep it a secret.[28] This again is most probably not the whole explanation. The Crown derived much benefit from the activities of licensed privateers, which provided sailors with useful training in naval warfare, and which brought in much bullion to the royal coffers.[29] It did not wish to discourage investors from incurring the considerable expense of crewing and equipping a ship in preparation for a "cruise" by restricting their ability to insure against the risk of failure. A common policy on the adventure could not adequately indemnify the investor against an unprofitable cruise.[30] As regards cargo, no interest could be shown in an identified cargo either on board at the start of the voyage or to be laden in the course of it. As regards the ship, she might be captured and detained for a time but the policy would neither cover the loss of such booty as might have been taken during that time nor treat the ship as a total loss. The practice had, therefore, developed of insuring the ship's capacity to cruise for a fixed period of, say, three or four months, under a valued policy dispensing with proof of the profits the ship would have made if she had remained fit to cruise for that whole period.[31] One wonders if these privateer policies were the first English time policies. They anticipated the rationale of the modern loss of earnings insurance policy.

Third, s.3 of the Act permitted the continued use of wager policies on cargoes 4.7
shipped from the dominions of Spain and Portugal, a trade in which Lord Hardwicke believed they had first started.[32] Park claimed that under the law of those countries only Spanish subjects could engage in the trade, which made it necessary for all trading documents to be made out in the names of Spaniards,[33] and accordingly proof of interest by English assureds had to be limited to the production of the policy itself. Marshall, however, claims that British subjects did import goods from Spain and Portugal in their own names and the real reason for the use of ppi policies was the need to conceal the true nature of the trade.[34] It was a clandestine, contraband trade in bullion, the export of which was forbidden by the laws of those countries.

The aim of s.1 of the Act was to prohibit the use of insurance wordings which 4.8
dispensed with proof of interest by evidence extraneous to the policy itself. By

28. *Murphy v. Bell* (1828) 4 Bing. 567, 569.

29. Privateers were licensed by the Crown through the issue of Letters of Marque and were regulated by the Convoys and Cruizers Act 1708: Richard Hill, *The Prizes of War* (Sutton Publishing Ltd, Stroud 1998), pp.7–9.

30. See counsel's submission in *Fitzgerald v. Pole* (1754) 4 Bro. Parl. 439, 446.

31. The policy construed in *Pond v. King* (1747) 1 Wils. 191 appears to be an example of this kind of insurance.

32. *Sadlers' Co. v. Badcock* (1743) 2 Atk. 554, 556.

33. *Op. cit.*, Vol. 2, p.593.

34. *Law of Insurance* (3rd edn., Joseph Butterworth, London 1823) p.124 n.(a). The same reason is given by Buller J in *Andrée v. Fletcher* (1787) 2 TR 161, 164–165, and by Kent, Commentaries (14th edn., 1896) Vol. 3, p.265. *Da Costa v. Firth* (1766) 4 Burr. 1966 is a case within this exception to the 1745 Act. It concerned a consignment of bullion shipped in an iron trunk from Lisbon to Falmouth, and insured under an open ppi cover on "goods and merchandises", which was lost in December 1763 off Falmouth and then "fished up" in April 1765 after the assured had been paid for a total loss. The insurers claimed a refund of the policy monies, but the court refused it, saying that they were to have the salvage under what was described as a "mixed policy", partly wager and partly open, in order to support the entitlement to salvage.

inserting the words "or by way of gaming and wagering" into the list of forbidden phrases, it permitted the courts to declare void policies which were not expressly written without interest, but which were shown to be wagers without an underlying interest. *Kent v. Bird* is an example.[35]

4B.3 The Marine Insurance Acts 1906–1909

4.9 The current law governing wager policies is contained in s.4 of the 1906 Act,[36] supplemented by s.1 of the Marine Insurance (Gambling Policies) Act 1909.[37] Section 4(1) provides that every contract of marine insurance by way of gaming or wagering is void. Section 4(2) provides that a contract of marine insurance is deemed to be a gaming or wagering contract in two instances. The first is where the assured does not have an insurable interest as defined by the Act and the contract is entered into with no expectation of acquiring it.[38] The second is where a policy is made "interest or no interest" or "without further proof of interest than the policy itself" or "without benefit of salvage to the insurer"[39] or subject to any other like term.[40] Such policies will be referred to compendiously as "ppi policies".

4.10 The 1906 Act does more than codify the previous law on gaming and wagering policies. It declares void not only ppi policies expressly dispensing with proof of interest but also all marine insurances which are shown in evidence to fall within the definition in s.4(2)(a). It is unclear whether the words "where the assured has no interest as defined by this Act" in s.4(2)(a) refer to interest at the time the contract is made or at the time of loss, when s.6(1) requires it to be shown. The use of the present tense in the words "and the contract *is* entered into" suggests the former.[41] This construction leads to the curious result that an assured who lacked interest at the outset, and never expected to acquire it, is not redeemed by the subsequent unexpected acquisition of interest before loss, despite compliance with s.6, although the likelihood of an assured acquiring interest by the time of loss when he had no expectation of doing so is no doubt remote. Policies on foreign ships and cargoes

35. (1777) 2 Cowp. 583. This was a wager between a ship's surgeon and a passenger and it is difficult to see why Lord Mansfield described it as an insurance which was consequently void under the 1745 Act. Reinsurances were also thought to promote a species of gaming, and were prohibited under s.4 of the Act unless the insurer was dead or insolvent: see *Andrée v. Fletcher* (1787) 2 TR 161.

36. 6 Edw. 7 c.41. The 1745 Act was repealed by the Second Schedule of the Act.

37. 9 Edw. 7 c.12. Section 2 of the 1909 Act provides that the two Acts may be cited together as the Marine Insurance Acts 1906 and 1909.

38. Section 4(2)(a).

39. Section 4(2)(b). A proviso permits policies to be made "without benefit of salvage" in cases where the nature of the subject-matter rules out the possibility of abandonment. Such cases were said to be outside the ambit of the 1745 Act—*Lucena v. Craufurd* (1806) 2 Bos. & Pul. (NR) 269, 311—such as insurances on freight, bottomry and *respondentia*.

40. Full interest admitted ("fia") is an example—see the pre-Act decision of *Berridge v. Man On Insurance Co.* (1887) 18 Q.B.D. 346. A ppi policy is avoided by s.4(2)(b) regardless of whether the assured possesses an interest: *Cheshire v. Vaughan* [1920] 3 K.B. 240. There are several American decisions in which the court has treated a ppi policy as an ordinary indemnity policy if interest was shown and there was no intent to wager: *Brown v. Merc. Marine Insurance Co.* 152 Fed. Rep. 411 (1907, CCA 9); *Hall v. Jefferson* 279 F.392 (1921, SDNY); *Cabaud v. Fed. Ins.* 37 F.2d 23 (1930, CCA 2); *The Hai Hsuan (No. 2)* (1958) 2 Lloyd's Rep. 578 (DC Md).

41. This is the view taken in Arnould, *Law of Marine Insurance* (16th edn., 1981), para. 390.

come within s.4, and the Act, unlike its predecessor,[42] applies to Ireland. Exemptions no longer relevant to twentieth century trading conditions are discarded, such as policies on privateers[43] and Iberian bullion cargoes.

Whereas ppi policies had previously been adjudged illegal as well as void,[44] all gaming or wagering policies are now pronounced void. One reason for this was that by this time it was customary to use ppi policies in cases where assureds possessed an interest, either valid in law or at least in a bona fide business sense, but where proof of the quantum of that interest might be complex and difficult.[45] Another reason may have been that the Gaming Act 1845[46] was content to declare gaming and wagering contracts to be void and not illegal. In this respect the comment of McCardie J in *John Edwards & Co. v. Motor Union Insurance Co.*,[47] that Parliament had placed a ppi policy on much the same footing as a wager on a horserace, seems apposite. Parliament might not applaud betting on the horses, but did not seek to ban it, and the punters could expect to collect their winnings, albeit without the assistance of the law. 4.11

There was, however, a less benign side to ppi policies. The ppi clause facilitated fraud and gambling by persons who had neither interest nor an expectation of acquiring it.[48] This was believed to lead to the same evil which had concerned Parliament in 1745, deliberate attempts to procure the insurance monies, thereby jeopardising the lives of seamen and the safety of commercial cargoes.[49] The subsequent enactment of the 1909 Act[50] suggests that the avoidance of ppi policies and other wager policies was thought to be an insufficient disincentive to their continued use for harmful speculation.[51] The Act was intended to penalise this kind of gambling policy while not penalising the use of a wager policy for unexceptional business purposes. Moving the first reading of the Bill in April 1909[52] the President of the Board of Trade, Winston Churchill, acknowledged the convenience and utility of ppi policies when the assured possessed a bona fide interest in the subject-matter, and stood to benefit from the safe arrival of a ship as opposed to its loss. He did not want to prohibit them altogether. What could not be tolerated was their use for speculative gambling by those without an interest and who stood to gain only from a loss of ship and cargo. Underwriters still paid claims on all ppi policies with the same invariable 4.12

42. *Keith v. Protection Marine Insurance Co.* (1882) 10 L.R. Ir. 51.
43. Letters of Marque were not issued to privateers after the Napoleonic Wars: Arnold-Baker, *Companion to British History* (Longcross Press, Tunbridge Wells, 1996), p.1030.
44. At first there was judicial disagreement: *Lowry v. Bourdieu* (1780) 2 Dougl. 468. By the end of the next century it was resolved: *Allkins v. Jupe* (1877) 2 C.P.D. 375; *Gedge v. Royal Exchange Assurance Co.* [1900] 2 Q.B. 214.
45. *Cheshire v. Vaughan* [1920] 3 K.B. 240, 252 *per* Scrutton LJ.
46. 8 & 9 Vict. c. 109, s.18.
47. [1922] 2 K.B. 249, 255.
48. *Cheshire v. Vaughan* [1920] 3 K.B. 240, 252 *per* Scrutton LJ.
49. [1920] 3 K.B. 240 at 251 *per* Bankes LJ.
50. 9 Edw. 7 c.12.
51. In *Thames & Mersey Marine Insurance Co. v. Gunford Ship Co.* [1911] A.C. 529, 543 Lord Shaw remarked that the case before him suggested that the policy of the 1906 Act, the abolition of gambling involving danger to life and property at sea, had not been much furthered by the avoidance of gambling policies in the 1906 Act. The use of ppi increased value insurances is now forbidden by Clause 22.2 of the ITC(H) and Clause 20.2 of the IVC(H) 1995.
52. H.C. Debs. 1909, vol. 3, cols. 1676–1680.

regularity that they paid under insurances subject to legal enforcement,[53] allowing speculators to gamble on the lives of seamen, the safety of cargoes, and the reputation of the British merchant marine. There had been a number of suspicious casualties in recent years from which speculators without interest had profited greatly under ppi policies. The 1909 Act was intended to stop this use of wager policies by making it a criminal offence.

4.13 The Act accordingly makes it an offence to effect what it calls "contracts by way of gambling on loss by maritime perils", which it deems to arise in two contingencies. The first is when any person effects a contract of marine insurance without having any bona fide interest, direct or indirect, either in the safe arrival of the ship in relation to which the contract is made or in the safety or preservation of the subject-matter insured, or a bona fide expectation of acquiring such an interest.[54] The second is where any person employed by the owners of a ship, not being a part owner, effects a ppi insurance in relation to the ship.[55] On conviction the assured is liable to imprisonment for a term not exceeding six months or to a fine not exceeding level 3 on the standard scale, and to forfeiture of any monies received under the insurance.[56]

4.14 The Act deals most severely with employees of owners of ships (other than part owners) who effect ppi policies on their employers' ships. They are deemed without more ado to have committed an offence, and proceedings can be instituted without affording them an opportunity to show that they possessed an interest or expectation of it. Presumably, it was thought desirable to treat with severity those who were in a position to influence the outcome of their wagers. But a person outside s.1 (1)(b), including a part owner, will be found guilty under s.1(1)(a) only if, when effecting the insurance, he lacked a bona fide interest and an expectation of getting one. The part owner's ppi policy is presumed to be a gambling policy unless he proves the contrary,[57] but he receives the protection which s.1(4) gives to all persons charged under s.1(1)(a), namely, the requirement that no proceedings are to be brought before he has had the opportunity to show interest or expectation of it. A part owner who has effected a ppi policy as a bona fide increased value insurance on his ship thus avoids criminal proceedings. The gambler without semblance of interest does not.

4.15 The 1909 Act appears to invalidate the simple proposition that all gaming and wagering policies are void, because it most probably makes them additionally illegal if they come within the definition of contracts by way of gambling on loss by maritime perils. Although the 1909 Act does not in terms prohibit such contracts, it is arguable that it impliedly does so by making it an offence to effect them.[58] If this is right it might

53. The same point was made in the *Gunford Ship* case by Lord Robson, [1911] A.C. 529, 550. The policy in that case antedated the 1909 Act.

54. Section 1(1)(a).

55. Section 1(1)(b). This sub-section applies to any insurance made on the terms to which s.4(2)(b) of the 1906 Act applies.

56. Section 1(2). The same penalties are visited on the insurer and broker involved in the transaction if they knew that the insurance was a contract for gambling on marine losses. "Owner" includes a charterer—s.1(8).

57. Section 1(5).

58. This is Arnould's view, *Law of Marine Insurance* (16th edn., 1981), para. 389. "The sole question is, whether the statute means to prohibit the contract", *Cope v. Rowlands* (1836) 2 M. & W. 149, 157 *per* Parke B, approved by Kerr LJ in *Phoenix General Insurance Co. v. ADAS* [1988] Q.B. 216, 268. The 1909 Act is entitled, "An Act to Prohibit Gambling on Loss by Maritime Perils".

be thought to have a bearing upon whether the court in a civil case ought to take the point that the policy sued upon is, for instance, a ppi policy when the insurer has not relied upon that ground of defence. In *Gedge v. Royal Exchange Assurance Corporation*,[59] the assured sought to enforce a ppi policy which was a mere wager upon whether a steamship would reach Yokohama before the time at which new import duties came into force. Insurers did not plead a defence based on the 1745 Act then in force, but Kennedy J declined to entertain the claim because the insurance was illegal, being prohibited by that Act.[60] It may be doubted that the distinction is of practical significance. It is likely that a court would follow the *obiter* opinions expressed by Bankes and Scrutton LJJ in *Cheshire v. Vaughan*[61] that it must have been the intention of Parliament in 1906 to make all gaming and wagering policies unenforceable at law, being contracts contrary to public policy. If so, a court should give effect to that public policy whether or not the defendant relied on the statute. Otherwise it would be necessary to examine the nature of the assured's interest in order to see whether he could successfully be prosecuted under the 1909 Act. On the other hand, authority suggests that the distinction between a void insurance and an illegal one is important in determining whether the assured can recover his premium for failure of consideration,[62] and s.84(3)(a) of the 1906 Act supports it.

4B.4 Valued policies

Valued policies *per se* were not avoided by the 1745 Act, although they could be said 4.16
to offer another means to wager on the loss of property at sea. It depended on the wording of the valuation clause. If it went to the extent of dispensing with all proof of interest, then it was void under the Act,[63] but if it merely dispensed with proof of the quantum of the assured's interest, it was not.[64] Since the Act applied mainly to policy wordings which relieved the assured from proof of any interest,[65] this was not such a fine distinction as might appear at first sight. The repeal of the 1745 Act afforded an opportunity to classify agreed value policies containing an excessive over-valuation of the subject-matter insured as a species of contracts by way of gaming and wagering. It was of course settled, more controversially, that mere over-valuation did not breach the principle of indemnity and could not be re-opened,[66] but it might have been

59. [1900] 2 Q.B. 214.

60. The insurers pleaded concealment of material facts, and want of insurable interest independently of the ppi clause. Kennedy J distinguished *Buchanan v. Faber* (1899) 4 Com. Cas. 223, 227n. where Bigham J agreed after consultation with Mathew J, and with the parties' consent, to try a claim on a ppi policy as if that clause was deleted. That course could not assist the assured in *Gedge*, who admitted they lacked interest.

61. [1920] 3 K.B. 240, 251, 255. In *Luckett v. Wood* (1908) 24 TLR 617 the Div. Ct. refused to adjudicate upon a bet on a horserace where the defendant did not plead the 1845 Act.

62. In *re London County Commercial Reinsurance Office Ltd* [1922] 2 Ch. 67, 85; *Re Cavalier Insurance Co. Ltd* [1989] 2 Lloyd's Rep. 430, 449.

63. *Murphy v. Bell* (1828) 4 Bing. 567; *Berridge v. Man On Insurance Co.* (1887) 18 Q.B.D. 346.

64. *Grant v. Parkinson* (1782) 3 Dougl. 16; *Lewis v. Rucker* (1761) 2 Burr. 1167.

65. If the agreed value exceeded the true value of the interest by a margin consistent only with an intention to wager, the insurance could have been avoided by the prohibition on insurances by way of gaming or wagering in s.1 of the Act, as Lord Mansfield seems to have thought – *Lewis v. Rucker, supra*, at p.1171 – but the Act was in practice confined to cases where there was no real interest at all, as he later said in *Glover v. Black* (1763) 3 Burr. 1394, 1400.

66. *Irving v. Manning* (1847) 1 H.L. Cas. 287; Marine Insurance Act 1906, s.27.

possible to classify agreed value policies as wager policies if the agreed value exceeded the quantum of the overall loss which the assured could ever possibly sustain in the event of a casualty. At all events the opportunity was not taken, and it is plain from the wording of s.4(2)(a) of the 1906 Act that the presence of an insurable interest in the subject-matter prevents an insurance upon it from being one by way of gaming and wagering, however excessively it is over-valued.[67] Arnould suggests that such a policy could nevertheless be void for being a contract of insurance by way of gaming and wagering within s.4(1) of the 1906 Act.[68] This presumes that s.4(2) is not exhaustive. The judgment of Hobhouse J in *The Maira (No. 2)*[69] is authority against the proposition, and it is in any case very unlikely that Parliament can have intended to classify an insurance made upon interest as a species of wagering policy when the presence of an interest would take it outside the definition of a wager for the purposes of s.18 of the Gaming Act 1845.[70] The presence of an interest would also take it outside s.1(1)(a) of the 1909 Act. It follows that the Marine Insurance Acts 1906 and 1909 do nothing to prevent gambling on the loss of maritime property through the medium of excessive over-valuation by those who possess an interest in it, so long as the insurance is not on ppi terms. In the case of overvaluation by one with interest, the underwriter will be left to rely where appropriate on the assured's wilful misconduct under s.55(2)(a) of the 1906 Act or, if he was unaware of the over-valuation, on a defence of non-disclosure of a material fact suggesting that the adventure was speculative in nature,[71] or on the defence that the subject-matter was fraudulently over-valued with the intention of cheating the insurers.[72]

4C INSURABLE INTEREST

4C.1 *Lucena v. Craufurd* and the definition of insurable interest

4.17 The common law definition of insurable interest which formed the basis of the statutory definition in s.5(2) of the Marine Insurance Act 1906 requires the assured to have a legal relationship to the subject-matter of the insurance, in consequence of which he may benefit from its safety and suffer detriment from its loss. As insurance law developed during the reign of George III, there were different opinions held as to what constituted a valid interest. In particular, some judges expressed the view that a reasonable expectancy of benefit from the safe arrival of ship or cargo entitled a person to insure it whether or not he had a title or right to it.[73] This divergence of

67. *The Maira (No. 2)* [1984] 1 Lloyd's Rep. 660, 667. The wager point was not appealed. It was held that managers were in breach of lawful instructions to insure a ship worth less than $5m. for $12m, and were held answerable in damages—[1985] 1 Lloyd's Rep. 300; [1986] 2 Lloyd's Rep. 12.

68. *Law of Marine Insurance* (16th edn., 198l) Vol. 1 paras 385 and 427.

69. [1984] 1 Lloyd's Rep. 660, 667–668.

70. 8 & 9 Vict. c. 109.

71. *Ionides v. Pender* (1874) LR 9 Q.B. 531.

72. *Thames & Mersey Marine Insurance Co. v. Gunford Ship Co.* [1911] A.C. 529, 542.

73. *Le Cras v. Hughes* (1782) 3 Dougl 91; *Curling v. Long* (1797) 1 Bos. & Pul. 636, 637; *Wolff v. Horncastle* (1798) 1 Bos & Pul 323, 324. In *Camden v. Anderson* (1794) 5 T.R. 711 Lord Kenyon left open the question whether a party might insure an expectation without possessing a legal interest in the subject insured. In *Lucena v. Craufurd* (1806) 2 Bos & Pul (NR) 269, 321, Lord Eldon said that there were "many cases" in which a moral certainty of benefit had been said to constitute insurable interest.

opinion was especially important in relation to such subjects of insurance as anticipated profits and commissions. In *Lucena v. Craufurd*[74] the topic of insurable interest was, to use the expression of one counsel in the case, "exhausted" [75] in the course of litigation in five courts over a period of some eight years. It established at the highest level the enduring principle that an insurable interest in property required a legal relationship between the assured and the property which was the subject of the insurance. The actual decision turned on the terms of a statutory commission granted to the assureds, and the facts of the case are, therefore, of some significance.

The dispute arose out of the response by the British Government to the capitulation of the United Provinces to the French Armee du Nord in January 1795. On 19 January the tricolour was carried triumphantly into Amsterdam and the *stadholder,* Prince William of Orange, fled to England. The "Patriot" (revolutionary) Party welcomed the French as a means to overthrow the existing constitution but hoped that the United Provinces would be allowed to be neutral in the war between France and Britain. Paris in fact had a different agenda, but Britain did not want to declare war on the Dutch, her former allies, and thereby provoke them to become active belligerents in alliance with France.[76] The Government decided to encourage Dutch subjects to come to Britain together with their property. By Orders in Council made on 16–21 January 1795, the king in effect offered to warehouse and secure Dutch property coming into British ports, whether from Dutch ports or on ships bound for the United Provinces, and to keep it for the benefit of its owners. On its being found that Dutch ships and cargoes were not coming voluntarily into UK ports, another Order in Council was made in February 1795 directing the Royal Navy and English privateers to seize Dutch property encountered at sea and to bring it forcibly into British ports to enjoy the royal offer of safe-keeping. This measure, being taken for the protection of the realm, was within the scope of the royal prerogative, but the enforced detention and possible disposal of property belonging to neutrals was thought not to be. Hence an Act of Parliament[77] was passed, empowering the Crown to appoint three or more Commissioners to take into their possession such Dutch ships and cargoes as "had been, or might be thereafter detained in, or brought into the ports of this Kingdom", and "to manage, sell, or otherwise dispose of the same to the best advantage" in accordance with instructions given by the Crown. 4.18

On 15 June 1795, the King issued a Commission[78] to one Craufurd and four others appointing them Commissioners of Dutch property in accordance with the Act. Meanwhile, Captain Essington of His Majesty's ship *Sceptre,* together with several East Indiamen, had captured eight Dutch merchantmen homeward bound from East Asia and Africa, and had taken them to St Helena. On 2 July 1795 these ships began their voyage to British ports under armed escort. On learning of this on 15 August 4.19

74. References are given *infra*.
75. R. Carr, *arguendo,* in *Routh v. Thompson* (1809) 11 East 428.
76. Lord Eldon recalled later that it had been uncertain whether the Dutch were "finally reduced" to French domination: (1806) 2 Bos. & Pul. 269, 318. In fact, the capitulation of the United Provinces was complete by February 1795, as the British Government well knew: *Cambridge History of British Foreign Policy* (1922) Vol. 1, p.255; Simon Schama, *Patriots and Liberators* (1977) p.192. On 16 May, the Dutch concluded an alliance with France by which they re-entered the war on the French side.
77. 35 Geo. 3, c.80. The relevant section, 21, is reproduced in (1798) 8 T.R. 13.
78. Cited in (1802) 3 Bos. & Pul. 75, at pp.78–79.

1795 the Commissioners effected a marine policy in their own names on the usual terms upon the ships, lost or not lost, for the voyage from St Helena to London. Four ships were lost by perils of the sea at different times while on the voyage, the last casualty, to the *Zeelelye,* occurring on 20 September 1795. On 15 September, the Crown had declared war on the United Provinces in response to their conclusion of a formal alliance with France on 16 May, and this had the effect of vesting property in the ships in the Crown itself. The surviving ships were directed to Ireland, then still a separate kingdom and outside the scope of the commission. They were then dealt with as lawful prize under the prerogative, the disappointed Commissioners being appointed as prize agents on behalf of the Crown to dispose of them. The Commissioners claimed on their insurance in respect of the ships which had been lost. The insurers declined to pay on the ground of want of an insurable interest.

4.20 The assureds' claim was first brought in the King's Bench before Lord Kenyon and a jury. He directed the jury to find a verdict for the Commissioners on the first count declared, which averred that they possessed an interest in all the ships. In doing so he was following the outcome of another action brought earlier by the assureds against another underwriter on the same policy in the case of *Craufurd v. Hunter*[79] in which the question of interest had been argued at length. Lord Kenyon there himself had described the insurers' defence as "unconscientious", and the Court of King's Bench[80] held that the assureds possessed an interest. They were in the character of trustees or prize agents or consignees, because by the terms of their commission the ships could not come to anyone else other than them. There appears at that stage to have been no real scrutiny of the Commissioners' powers. In the *Lucena* case the jury found for the insurers on all the remaining counts, including the second one averring interest to be in the king.

4.21 The case was then argued three times in the Exchequer Chamber,[81] and argument came to focus more upon the terms of the assureds' commission. They argued that as a general rule, where nothing stood between the assured and possession of the insured property but the perils insured against, he had a good interest, and submitted that a contingent and reasonable expectation of benefit from its arrival was enough. Baron Graham spoke for a majority of the judges in upholding the verdict.[82] Accepting that a mere expectation of probable interest was insufficient to constitute insurable interest, he held the Commissioners to have an actual interest vested in them as trustees, which nothing but the perils of the seas could prevent from being reduced into possession. Chambre J dissented.[83] His analysis of the assureds' commission led to the conclusion that they lacked any right or power over the ships before their actual arrival in England, and that there were indeed several contingencies besides perils of the seas standing between them and possession of the ships.

4.22 The case now went to the House of Lords, who first took the advice of the judges on eight questions formulated by Lord Eldon.[84] The fifth question posed the issue of

79. (1798) 8 T.R. 13.
80. Lord Kenyon CJ, Ashurst, Grose and Lawrence JJ.
81. (1802) 3 Bos. & Pul. 75, 80.
82. *Ibid.*, at 93.
83. *Ibid.*, at 99.
84. (1806) 2 Bos. & Pul. (NR) 269, 274–278.

whether the assureds had a valid insurable interest. Eight judges, led by Baron Graham, opined that they had a contingent interest or, put another way, an inchoate right founded on an existing title, which would be perfected by occupancy.[85] Although Lord Mansfield's judgment in *Le Cras v. Hughes* was described as a case of "mere expectation" that had stood for 24 years, this was done only to show that the present assureds had a stronger case, based on their contingent legal interest.[86]

Chambre and Lawrence JJ dissented. Chambre J again held that the ships had not become objects of the assureds' commission at the times of loss, and that this made it impossible for them to possess an interest of any kind. They had only a naked expectation of concern or benefit which, as it turned out, would have been unfulfilled.[87] Lawrence J's justly celebrated judgment is often cited for its lucid definition of an insurable interest in property: 4.23

> "A man is interested in a thing to whom advantage may arise or prejudice happen from the circumstances which may attend it . . . and where a man is so circumstanced with respect to matters exposed to certain risks or dangers, as to have a moral certainty of advantage or benefit, but for those risks or dangers, he may be said to be interested in the safety of the thing. To be interested in the preservation of a thing, is to be so circumstanced with respect to it as to have benefit from its existence, prejudice from its destruction. The property of a thing and the interest deviseable (derivable) from it may be very different: of the first the price is generally the measure, but by interest in a thing every benefit and advantage arising out of or depending on such thing may be considered as being comprehended."[88]

This part of his judgment is sometimes interpreted as authority[89] for the proposition that a factual expectation (moral certainty) of benefit from the continued existence of property is a valid ground of an insurable interest in it, but this reading of the judgment takes the passage out of context. In this part of his judgment, Lawrence J sought to establish two propositions, (1) that ownership of property was not the only source of interest in it, and (2) that there had to be sufficient certainty of the assured's benefit from the safety of the property. The definition was not intended to be complete in itself, because it lacks a criterion of "moral certainty". This is supplied by the remainder of the judgment, in which he applied his broad definition to the facts. From this, one sees that he agreed with the reasoning of Chambre J. The touchstone of moral certainty of benefit is the assured's possession of a legal right to, or power over, the insured property. No other criterion of moral certainty is offered. Had their commission granted a power and control to the Commissioners over all Dutch ships detained at sea by order of the king, and which did not depend on whether they

85. *Ibid.*, at 289.
86. *Ibid.*, at 294.
87. *Ibid.*, at 298–300.
88. *Ibid.*, at 302.
89. *Macaura v. Northern Ass. Co.* (1925) N.I. 141, 157; *The "Moonacre"* [1992] 2 Lloyd's Rep. 503, 511; *Mark Rowlands v. Berni Inns* [1986] 1 Q.B. 211, 228; *Glengate-KG Properties v. Norwich Union Fire Insurance Society* [1996] 1 Lloyd's Rep. 614, 621, 626; *Constitution Insurance Co. of Canada v. Kosmopoulos* (1987) 34 DLR (4th) 208, 216; Bennett, *Law of Marine Insurance* (OUP, Oxford, 1996), p.17; Merkin, *Insurance Contract Law*, Vol. 1, para. A.4.1–19, Kluwer, Kingston on Thames; Hartnett & Thornton, *Insurable Interest in Property*, 48 Col. Law Rev 1162 (1948). The author admits to having followed this interpretation: *MacGillivray on Insurance Law* (9th edn., 1997), paras 1–46; 1–116. By contrast, both Bovill CJ in *Ebsworth v. Alliance Marine Insurance Co.* (1873) LR 9 C.P. 596, 617, 621, and Walton J in *Moran, Galloway v. Uzielli* [1905] 2 K.B. 555, 561–562, regarded the House of Lords as having adopted the reasoning of Lawrence J.

arrived in port, then they would have had an interest before the safe arrival of the ships, but it did not. The Commissioners, he said, were not like trustees, or consignees able to insure on their own account, because they lacked any right to or property in the ships at the times of loss.[90] Accordingly, the Commissioners could have no interest in the ships until such time as they acquired rights over them by virtue of their commission. The ground of his disagreement with the majority was not that the Commissioners could not prove a sufficient likelihood of benefit, but that they could not have an interest at a time when they had no right in or responsibility for the insured ships.

4.24 The disagreement between the majority and minority was, therefore, not whether factual expectation of benefit from property was *per se* a good ground of insurable interest in it, but whether it could be deduced from the evidence that the Commissioners had a legal right in or over the ships at the times of their respective losses. Since the majority had accepted in their answers to other questions[91] that the king could restore them to their Dutch owners even after their safe arrival in England, and that he could divert them to Ireland beyond the scope of the commission, the assureds' claim was becoming difficult to sustain.

4.25 Lord Eldon gave the leading speech in the House of Lords. Essentially he accepted the advice of Chambre and Lawrence JJ. He first analysed the relationship of the assureds' commission to the royal prerogative, and concluded that the intention of Parliament had been to limit the powers of the commissioners so as not to fetter the prerogative. Consequently, the king retained the power both to direct the ships to Ireland (a separate kingdom outside the commissioners' jurisdiction) or to restore them to their Dutch owners. In the event of war being declared against the Dutch, he acquired title to them and could treat them as prize. It was never intended that the assureds should have had any legal power or control over the ships during the voyage. Events had shown that their expectation of having custody of the ships was frail. This answered the argument accepted by the majority in the Exchequer Chamber that nothing but the perils of the sea could prevent the assureds from reducing the ships into possession and it also made their assertion of an interest depend on expectation alone.

Lord Eldon continued by rejecting expectation of benefit, however strong, as a criterion of interest:

> "In order to distinguish that intermediate thing between a strict right, or a right derived under a contract, and a mere expectation or hope, which has been termed an insurable interest, it has been said in many cases to be that which amounts to a moral certainty. I have in vain endeavoured however to find a fit definition of that which is between a certainty and an expectation; nor am I able to point out what is an interest unless it be a right in the property, or a right derivable out of some contract about the property, which in either case may be lost upon some contingency affecting the possession or enjoyment of the party."[92]

He believed that moral certainty was a nebulous criterion, and one which would open the door to an undesirable multiplicity of insurances by those without legal nexus with the insured property, such as everyone in a port who stood to receive a

90. (1806) 2 Bos. & Pul. (NR) 269, 306–307.
91. Questions 1 and 2.
92. (1806) 2 Bos. & Pul. (NR) 269, 321.

benefit from the arrival of a ship.[93] Another ground of objection, which Lord Eldon did not mention, but which was developed by Lord Ellenborough in a later case,[94] was that recognition of an insurable interest based upon expectation offended the fundamental principle of indemnity. I will revisit these points below in the context of s.5 of the Marine Insurance Act 1906.

On Lord Eldon's advice,[95] the House directed a new trial so that the question of interest could be investigated afresh and all the original counts be re-opened. On any view it had been wrong to direct the jury to award damages in respect of the *Zeelelye*, because the Crown alone had possessed title to her as enemy property after the proclamation of war five days before her loss. Moreover, if as the assureds had argued, they were acting in the character of Parliamentary agents for the benefit of the Crown, it seemed logically to follow that interest really lay in the Crown as their principal. That had been the averment laid in the second count, and we are told by Park, who was counsel for the assureds, that the court made it plain in argument that their best case lay here.[96] A retrial would enable the assureds to litigate their best title instead of being restrained to a futile one.[97] A second trial duly took place at which additional evidence was called and a verdict was found for the Commissioners on the second count. The jury was directed by Lord Ellenborough that the assureds should succeed, apparently on the basis that the insurance had been made for the account and benefit of the king and that he had ratified and adopted it. An appeal taken by consent directly to the House of Lords in 1808 was dismissed without reasons and without calling on counsel for the Commissioners.[98] 4.26

4C.2 The development of insurable interest before the Marine Insurance Act 1906

During the nineteenth century, the courts applied Lord Eldon's definition in cases where insurable interest was disputed. It was enlarged, perfectly logically, to include instances where the assured was liable to bear the cost of loss and damage to insured property, such as when goods in transit were at the risk of their buyer after shipment.[99] In the great majority of cases, the established categories of commercial interests concerned in maritime commerce could be accommodated within that doctrine. Captors, for example, could no longer acquire an interest in captured ships and cargoes by virtue of a well-founded expectation of a grant of prize by the Crown,[100] 4.27

93. *Ibid.*, at 324.

94. *Routh v. Thompson* (1809) 11 East 428.

95. (1806) 2 Bos. & Pul. (NR) 269, 326. Lord Erskine and Lord Ellenborough CJKB delivered short concurring speeches.

96. Park, *op. cit.*, Vol 2, Chapter 14, p.572.

97. (1806) 2 Bos. & Pul. (NR) 269, 328, *per* Lord Ellenborough CJKB. The decision to order a re-trial was interpreted by Wilson J. in *Constitution Insurance Co. of Canada v. Kosmopoulos* (1987) 34 DLR 208, 216, as making the preceding reasoning *obiter*, but in truth the order was the direct consequence of the decision that the Commissioners had no insurable interest.

98. Details of the retrial proceedings appear in the report of the second appeal to the House of Lords in (1808) 1 Taunt. 325.

99. *Anderson v. Morice* (1876) 1 App. Cas. 713; *Colonial Insurance Co. of New Zealand v. Adelaide Marine Insurance Co.* (1886) 12 App. Cas. 128.

100. This had been a second ground of Lord Mansfield's decision in *Le Cras v. Hughes* (1782) 3 Dougl. 81.

but only if the relevant Prize Act gave them a special property in their booty, albeit subject to possible divestment of that title by the king or the prize court, or if it could be said that they were under a contingent liability to account to third parties for the seizure and custody of the relevant prize.[101] Consignees possessed an insurable interest in cargoes awaited by them only if they had a right under an existing contract to deal with them at least partly for their own benefit on arrival or were liable to account for their loss in transit by an insured peril, but not if they were "naked consignees" as the Commissioners had been.[102] In the latter case they should insure on behalf of their principals. Mortgagees possessed a charge over the ship as their security, which gave them an interest in it.[103] Their medieval precursor, the lender on bottomry, also possessed a special interest entitling him to insure his borrower's ship. Because the ship was hypothecated to him as security for the due repayment of his loan, and because the borrower's obligation depended upon the safe outcome of the adventure, he possessed a security right in the ship and would suffer the loss of his right to repayment of principal and maritime interest in the event of its loss.[104] The lender on *respondentia* seems not to have had a security right in the borrower's cargo, because the cargo owner was usually free to trade it, but could rest his insurable interest in it on the term of his bond which made the safe arrival of cargo a condition of his right to be repaid.[105] Vendors and purchasers of goods possessed an insurable interest depending on whether at the time of loss these were at their risk or they had property in them, a criterion producing some "very nice and subtle distinctions" in certain cases.[106]

4.28 One area in which the ambit of insurable interest was expanded was that of freight. It was established at an early stage that the right to freight was a separate subject-matter of insurance distinct from an insurance upon ship.[107] Consistent with the ruling in *Lucena v. Craufurd* an insured shipowner had no insurable interest in potential future freights to be earned on carrying prospective cargoes not yet contracted for.[108] These were mere expectancies. The question much discussed in the

101. *Routh v. Thompson* (1809) 11 East 428, interpreting *Le Cras v. Hughes* as a case where the captors acquired a special property under the Spanish Prize Act 19 Geo. 3, c.67; *Stirling v. Vaughan* (1809) 11 East 619; *Boehm v. Bell* (1799) 8 T.R. 154. In *Devaux v. Steele* (1840) 6 Bing. (NC) 358, concerning the loss of a bounty expected to be paid by the French government on whale catches, Tindal CJ doubted the authority of *Le Cras v. Hughes* but said that in any event it could only apply where the expectation was never known to fail.

102. *Seagrave v. Union Marine Insurance Co.* (1866) LR 1 CP 305; *Ebsworth v. Alliance Mar Insurance Co.* (1873) LR 8 CP 596.

103. *Irving v. Richardson* (1831) 2 B & Ad. 193; *Samuel v. Dumas* [1924] A.C. 431, 444 (equitable interest where the charge had not been registered).

104. Where the bond fails to charge the ship with repayment or does not oblige the lender to bear the risk of her loss, it will not be a valid bottomry bond and the lender will have no interest: *The Heinrich Bjorn* (1885) 10 PD 44; *Stainbank v. Fenning* (1851) 11 CB 51; *Stainbank v. Shepard* (1853) 13 CB 418.

105. Park, *op.cit.*, Vol. 2, Chapter 22, p.869; Arnould, *Law of Marine Insurance* (2nd edn., 1857) Vol. 1, p.299. As early as 1802 bottomry and *respondentia* were said to be rarely used in England: Marshall, *Law of Insurance* (1802), Preface to 1st edn. It is curious that the Marine Insurance Act 1906 devotes a whole section (10) to these archaic interests.

106. *Gilman v. Supple* (1858) 11 Moo., PC 551, 566, cited by Blackburn J in *Anderson v. Morice* (1875) LR 10 C.P. 609, 618.

107. *Thompson v. Taylor* (1795) 6 TR 478; *Camden v. Anderson* (1798) 6 T.R. 709.

108. (1806) 2 Bos. & Pul. (NR) 269, 326 *per* Lord Eldon; *Knox v. Wood* (1808) 1 Camp 543; *Stockdale v. Dunlop* (1840) 6 M. & W. 224, 231–232; *Scottish Shire Line v. London & Provincial Marine Insurance Co.* [1912] 3 K.B. 51, 64–67.

case law was the time at which the hope of getting freight became a right capable of being an insurable interest. By 1870 it was established that a shipowner with a contract under which he was to earn freight possessed an inchoate interest in it so soon as he had taken steps and incurred expenses towards earning it, so that in the case of charter freight the owner had an interest in it once the ship had begun her ballast voyage.[109] The requirement that the assured should have a right to the subject-matter of the insurance on freight was satisfied by the existence of a contract entitling him to earn it. As Lord Abinger said in *Stockdale v. Dunlop*,[110] "The cases of freight presuppose a contract capable of being enforced". By the end of the century it was being suggested that the existence of an engagement to earn freight was sufficient in itself to create an interest in the freight so contracted, regardless of whether the shipowner had taken steps referable to its performance, and Arnould regarded it as certainly arguable although not yet established law.[111] The subsequent recognition of a ship's earning capacity as a separate species of pecuniary interest was to dispense with the precondition of a contract but this development in the insurance of future earnings belongs to the twentieth century, and is not an insurance on freight strictly speaking.[112]

The rule that insurable interest required a right to or over the subject-matter of the insurance posed a potential difficulty for insurances against loss of profits anticipated from the sale of cargo. Unless the assured had a resale contract which entitled him to realise a sum in excess of his purchase price, he could not be said to have any right to the profit.[113] Moreover, to permit the assured to recover an indemnity referable to the value of the cargo at its destination appeared to contradict the standard measure of indemnity for loss of cargo, which was based upon its prime cost at the outset of the adventure, a rule designed to protect insurers from being answerable for fluctuations in market values.[114] The latter difficulty was met by agreeing a value for the cargo which covered the contracted or expected profit to be made on its resale.[115] The insurance was said to be on cargo valued at a sum which included the assured's interest in the profits. In the cases decided before *Lucena v. Craufurd*,[116] the courts appeared willing to allow that the assured had an interest in the profits if they were "certain" by reason of prior contractual arrangements[117] or even if a profit was "pretty 4.29

109. *Barber v. Fleming* (1869) LR 5 Q.B. 59.
110. (1840) 6 M. & W. 224, 232.
111. Arnould, *Law of Marine Insurance* (16th edn., 1981) para. 362, following earlier editions.
112. It was foreshadowed by *dicta* of Walton J in *Manchester Liners v. British and Foreign Marine Insurance Co.* (1901) 7 Com. Cas. 26, and developed in *obiter dicta* of Lord Wright in *Robertson v. Petros Nomikos Ltd* [1939] A.C. 371, in turn applied in *Papadimitriou v. Henderson* [1939] 64 Ll.L. Rep. 345. The assured under a loss of earnings insurance may use a valuation provision to preclude inquiry into predicted income, but must prove that, but for an insured casualty, the vessel would have been deployed in the market: *The Capricorn* [1995] 1 Lloyd's Rep. 622, 641.The idea of insuring the revenue earning capacity of a ship was not new, as witness the ppi policies on the capacity of a privateer to cruise.
113. *M'Swiney v. Royal Exchange Assurance* (1849) 14 Q.B. 646 was such a case—see Parke B. at pp.659–660.
114. *Lewis v. Rucker* (1761) 2 Burr 1167; *Usher v. Noble* (1812) 12 East 639.
115. *Grant v. Parkinson* (1781) 3 Dough 16; *Hodgson v. Glover* (1805) 6 East 316, 320; *Usher v. Noble* (1812) 12 East 639.
116. (1906) 2 Bos. & Pul. (NR) 269.
117. *Grant v. Parkinson* (1781) 3 Dougl. 16.

certain" to be gained, judging by prior experience in an established trade.[118] In *Lucena v. Craufurd* itself the insurance was construed as one on ship and cargo, and not on profits anticipated to be made by the Commissioners from their stewardship,[119] but opinions were expressed *obiter* on loss of profits insurance. Lord Eldon said that an assured could not insure against loss of hoped for profits to be made from the sale of cargoes which he had still to acquire, this being an expectation upon an expectation, and he reserved his opinion upon the legitimacy of loss of profits insurances as a whole.[120] The judges advising the House, however, took the view that this type of cover was both usual and fulfilled a legitimate commercial need.[121] In subsequent decisions insurances against loss of profits were reconciled with Lord Eldon's formulation of insurable interest by treating profit as an element of increased value possessed by the goods, an "excrescence" upon the goods, as it was put, which was invariably and properly covered by the cargo-owner under an agreed valuation placed upon them.[122] It being already established that valuations were binding and did not offend against the 1745 Act so long as there was some interest in the subject-matter, this device dispensed with the necessity to demonstrate a legal right to the profit itself. It was sufficient to show title to the goods or a binding contract for their purchase under which property in them would later vest.[123] Where the policy was unvalued, it was necessary as a part of proof of loss to show that a profit would have been realised if the goods had arrived in safety.[124]

4.30 As will be seen, there were at least two decisions before the Marine Insurance Act 1906 which were difficult to reconcile with the definition of insurable interest given in *Lucena v. Craufurd*.

4C.3 Definition of insurable interest in the Marine Insurance Act 1906

4.31 Insurable interest is defined in s.5:

> "(1) Subject to the provisions of this Act, every person has an insurable interest who is interested in a marine adventure.[125]
> (2) In particular a person is interested in a marine adventure where he stands in any legal or equitable relation to the adventure or to any insurable property[126] at risk therein, in consequence of which he may benefit by the safety or due arrival of insurable property or

118. *Barclay v. Cousins* (1802) 2 East 544; *Henrickson v. Margetson* (1802) 2 East 551, fn.(a), decided in 1775.

119. This was the subject of the eighth question put to the judges.

120. (1806) 2 Bos. & Pul. (NR) 269, 321.

121. *Ibid.* at 313. Lawrence J had earlier supported the legitimacy and importance of insurances on profits in *Barclay v. Cousins, supra.*

122. *Hodgson v. Glover* (1805) 6 East 316, 320; *Eyre v. Glover* (1812) 16 East 218, 220; *Stockdale v. Dunlop* (1840) 6 M&W 224, 232–233; *M'Swiney v. Royal Exchange Assurance* (1849) 14 Q.B. 634, 661; *Smith v. Reynoulds* (1856) 1 H&N 221; followed in *Berridge v. The Man on Sea Insurance Co.*(1887) 18 Q.B.D. 346.

123. *Stockdale v. Dunlop* (1840) 6 M. & W. 224. It was later held that the buyer of a cargo under a valid contract of purchase could insure his "special interest" in the profit expected to be made under a concluded contract for resale: *M'Swiney v. Royal Exchange* (1894) 14 Q.B. 634, 661; *Halhead v. Young* (1856) E. & B. 312, 324.

124. *Eyre v. Glover* (1812) 16 East 218.

125. Defined in Marine Insurance Act 1906, s.3.

126. *Ibid.*

> may be prejudiced by its loss, or by damage thereto, or by the detention thereof, or may incur liability in respect thereof."

4.32 The section does not itself require proof of interest but provides a definition. Section 6 of the Marine Insurance Act 1906 requires proof of interest at the time of loss, upholding the common law rule established in *Rhind v. Wilkinson*[127] that in the absence of a valid insurable interest at the time of loss the assured cannot enforce the contract of insurance. By contrast the Life Assurance Act 1774 prohibits insurances without interest upon lives and other events but does not attempt a definition. It can be seen from a comparison of ss.4 and 5 of the Marine Insurance Act 1906 that a marine insurance contract may fall outside s.4 and escape being void as a gaming or wagering contract while still being unenforceable for want of a valid insurable interest.[128] A contract made by an assured who possesses no interest at the outset, but has a bona fide expectation of acquiring one, falls outside the definition of a wagering contract in s.4(2) and also outside that of a gambling policy in s.1(1)(a) of the Marine Insurance Act 1909, but if the expectation remains unfulfilled at the time of loss, the insurance will be unenforceable for want of a valid interest.[129] Thus the C&F purchaser in *Anderson v. Morice*[130] failed to recover for loss of part of a cargo which was in the course of being loaded pursuant to his purchase contract when the carrying vessel unexpectedly sank, because he could not show insurable interest at the time of its loss. He had every expectation, however, of acquiring title to the entire cargo in the course of an ordinary commercial contract, and it could scarcely be suggested that his insurance was void for being a wager. It is, with respect, incorrect to say that if an assured is not gaming and wagering he must possess a good insurable interest.[131]

4.33 A reading of s.5 itself shows that the definition which it provides is not exhaustive. The effect of the words "in particular" in s.5(2) is to make that sub-section merely illustrative of the broad statement in s.5(1), and thereby to create the impression that an insurable interest can be supported in unspecified circumstances lying without s.5(2). Until the Bill[132] was in Committee in the House of Commons in 1906, there were two limbs to s.5(2). Section 5(2)(a) consisted of a provision substantially similar to the current s.5(2). It was followed by a sub-section 5(2)(b) which provided that:

> "A prospect of loss or gain which is not founded on any right or liability in, or in respect of, the subject-matter is not insurable."

4.34 Both these two sub-sections were preceded by the words "In particular". For undisclosed reasons the Committee amended the section by deleting sub-section 5(2)(b).[133] The House accepted this and other amendments on the third reading of

127. (1810) 2 Taunt. 237.

128. This applies equally to non-marine insurance: *Macaura v. Northern Assurance* [1925] A.C. 619. The defence of lack of a valid interest is entirely separate from a defence that the insurance is a wager: see Lord Sumner at p.632.

129. Chalmers, Marine Insurance Act 1906 (10th edn., 1993), p.9.

130. (1876) 1 App. Cas. 713.

131. This is the view of Arnould, *Law of Marine Insurance* (16th edn., 1981), Vol. 3 (1997), para. 332, following *dicta* by Mr A.D. Colman QC, Deputy Judge, in *The Moonacre* [1992] 2 Lloyd's Rep. 501, 510.

132. The Marine Insurance Bill introduced in the 1906 session of Parliament was sent to the Commons Standing Committee on Law, and Courts of Justice, and Legal Procedure. It is document no. 95 in the HC Bills and Papers for that session.

133. The Committee's Report, printed on 1 May, lists the amendments voted in committee but gives no account of the discussions leading to them. It is document no. 150 in the HC Papers for the session.

the Bill, and passed it.[134] In one sense it made little difference. Sub-section 5(2)(a) had stated that interest in a marine adventure was established by a legal relationship between the assured and the adventure or insurable property at risk in it, in consequence of which the assured gained from its safety and suffered from its loss. Sub-section 5(2)(b) had merely stated the converse, that if there was no legal relationship, interest could not be founded upon expectation of benefit or detriment alone. The authorities cited by Chalmers and Owen in support of the predecessor of sub-section 5(2)(b) in their first edition of *A Digest of the Law of Marine Insurance* (1901)[135] re-appeared in the third edition (1907) as authorities which by implication supported s.5(2) of the Act as enacted.[136] On the other hand, the removal of sub-section 5(2)(b) may have been intended to make it easier to accommodate within s.5 certain decisions which were not easy to reconcile with established doctrine.

4.35 One such case may have been *Wilson v. Jones*.[137] The assured was a shareholder in the Atlantic Telegraph Company which was formed to carry out "a novel and speculative enterprise involving great risk and uncertainty,[138] namely, to establish a telegraph across the Atlantic by laying a cable over the seabed from Ireland to Newfoundland using Brunel's mammoth steamship, the *Great Eastern*.[139] He took out an all risks insurance against the failure of the project. This was construed to be an insurance on the profits expected to be made from the success of the venture through the consequent rise in value of his shares. The gain was valued, by agreement, as £10 per share on 20 shares, and so £200 in all. The venture failed when the cable broke, and a claim was made on the policy. On the insurers' appeal from the Court of Exchequer[140] to the Exchequer Chamber a point was taken that there was no valid insurable interest in so speculative an adventure. It was argued that the profits were but an excrescence on the shares, and the shares were not exposed to marine perils. The Court held that the assured had a valid interest in his expected profits, relying on *M'Swiney v. Royal Exchange Assurance Co.*[141] That was a very different case, however. The assured insured his profits to be made on a cargo of rice to be shipped from India. He had purchased it, and had resold on a forward contract at considerable profit before shipment, thereby establishing a legal right to an ascertained profit upon safe arrival of the cargo. Part of the cargo already loaded was lost by perils of the seas, and the remainder could not be shipped on the same vessel, so that the resale contract was not fulfilled. His claim failed because the policy did not provide adequate coverage, but his interest in the profits was adjudged good in principle. By contrast, the assured in *Wilson v. Jones*[142] had merely a title to shares which were likely to yield a gain if the venture was a success. He had no right or title in respect of the adventure itself or in

134. Parl. Deb. Vol. 161 (4th ser.) 1906, Cols. 1557–1559.
135. At p.9.
136. At p.10. They are preceded by the comment that, conversely, a prospect or possibility of loss which is not founded on any right or liability in or in respect of the subject-matter insured is not insurable.
137. (1867) LR 2 Ex. 139.
138. Willes J, (1867) LR 2 Ex. 139, 144.
139. It was the first time that a profitable use was found for the cavernous holds of this leviathan. Another cable was later laid successfully, and she went on "like some industrious spider, to weave a web of cables round the world": LTC Rolt, Isambard Kingdom Brunel (1957) p.307.
140. (1866) LR 1 Ex. 193.
141. (1849) 14 Q.B. 634; 646.
142. (1867) LR 2 Ex. 139.

insurable property at risk therein. Arnould regards the decision as one of doubtful authority,[143] while Chalmers suggests that it dispensed with the need to show a proprietary or contractual right in the subject-matter.[144]

Another decision doubted by Arnould was *Moran, Galloway & Co. v. Uzielli*.[145] 4.36
The assured were the UK agents of a foreign single-ship company. They were owed a considerable sum by the shipowners for advances made by them on account of disbursements for ship's purposes. The company's ship, the *Prince Louis*, performed a cargo carrying voyage from Vancouver to Cardiff. The assured took out a voyage policy on disbursements against the risk of total loss of the ship. The ship was severely damaged on her voyage by bad weather and was declared a constructive total loss after arrival at Cardiff. The assured claimed on their policy and the insurers pleaded want of insurable interest. Walton J held that they possessed a valid insurable interest in the ship because upon its arrival they were entitled under the Admiralty Court Act 1840 to arrest it by commencing *in rem* proceedings to recover their debt. Although they possessed no lien or other legal security right in the ship at the time of loss, nonetheless it was their de facto security for repayment. The court accepted that an expectation of benefit from the arrival of the ship was insufficient, and that an interest in it recognised by law had to be shown. The assured were held to possess at the date of loss an existing right which entitled them to arrest the ship upon her arrival and so obtain security for prompt payment.

Although the decision seems commercially reasonable, the court's reasoning is difficult to support. The assured's status as creditors of the shipowners gave them a right in law to arrest the ship on arrival, but this could hardly be described as a legal title to or right in the ship itself at the date of loss. It might well be described as merely a reasonable expectation of obtaining a legal interest in the ship in the future.[146] In the language of the Marine Insurance Act 1906, it is hard to see how the assured stood in any legal or equitable relationship to insurable property. Perhaps the decisions in both this case and *Wilson v. Jones* should be supported on a wider principle consistent with ss.3 and 5 of the Marine Insurance Act 1906. A marine adventure itself may be the subject-matter of an insurance, as opposed to insurable property at risk therein.[147] These cases could be taken as authority for the proposition that, where a person is legally entitled to acquire a right to insurable property or to realise a pecuniary benefit dependent only upon the successful conclusion of a marine adventure, he has an insurable interest in that adventure.

143. Arnould, *Law of Marine Insurance* (16th edn., 1981) para. 328, commenting that it is difficult to see how the decision can be reconciled with that in *Macaura v. Northern Assurance* [1925] A.C. 619. Lord Summer at p.630 distinguished it as a case on profits. Lord Buckmaster described it as a case where the shareholder's interest was in the adventure, a view shared by Chalmers: *Digest of Marine Insurance* (2nd edn., 1903) p.2, (10th edn., 1993) p.11.

144. *Marine Insurance Act* (10th edn., 1993) p.11.

145. [1905] 2 K.B. 555.

146. Arnould accordingly regards the case as wrongly decided: *Law of Marine Insurance* (16th edn., 1981) Vol. 1, para. 337.

147. Marine Insurance Act 1906, s.3(1).

4C.4 Relaxation of the requirement of "legal relationship"

4.37 When Parliament provided that s.5(2) of the Marine Insurance Act 1906 was merely illustrative of a wider concept of insurable interest expressed in s.5(1),[148] did it mean to empower the courts to develop new heads of insurable interest in cases outside s.5(2)? It may be argued that such must have been the purpose of the amendment to the Bill in Standing Committee, despite the ambivalence in the wording of the section.[149] However, the Act is a codifying measure, as its preamble states, and clear words are needed to attribute to Parliament an intention either to alter the law itself or to invite alterations to it which represent a significant departure from the previous law.[150] Even if that difficulty were overcome, there remains the further obstacle of appellate precedents. The requirement of a legal interest in the insured subject-matter has been affirmed in several decisions of the House of Lords, most notably *Macaura v. Northern Assurance Co.*,[151] and attempts to pray in aid the illustrious authority of Lawrence J in support of its abolition are, it has been submitted above, a misinterpretation of his views.[152]

4.38 Supposing, however, that consideration were to be given to legislative reform of the doctrine of insurable interest in marine insurance, and that it were to be proposed that the requirement of a legal relationship to the subject-matter was to be dispensed with, then the reasons for the present rule would have to be examined more closely than hitherto. Lord Eldon, it will be recalled, gave two reasons for it. The first was the difficulty of defining a "moral certainty" in any other way. There is much force in this objection. It has never been explained in what way the adjective "moral" qualifies the word "certainty". Presumably it means something falling short of absolute certainty. In *Lucena v. Craufurd* both Lawrence J[153] and Lord Eldon[154] seem to have been using the phrase as equivalent to "extremely likely", or "practically certain". In the non-marine insurance case of *Whitehead v. Hullett*[155] counsel told the court that the assured was "morally certain" that he had taken insured property out of the safe where it was kept. The assured himself later testified that he was "sure" of it. The court commented that he was "more definite" about it in evidence than his counsel

148. In the present context the words, "In particular", cannot be interpreted as meaning "Additionally" as they have been construed in s.60(2): Lord Wright in *Rickards v. Forestal, etc. Co.* [1942] A.C. 50, 84.

149. Professor Grime has happily described the wording of the section as "language which contains a degree of (perhaps creative) imprecision": *Modern Law of Marine Insurance* (1996), p.136.

150. *Polurrian SS Co. v. Young* [1915] 1 K.B. 922, 936; *Samuel v. Dumas* [1924] A.C. 431, 451.

151. [1925] A.C. 619. The decisions on insurable interest in cargo are all based upon the need to show a legal right in, or liability for, the insured cargo: *Anderson v. Morice* (1876) 1 App. Cas 736; *Inglis v. Stock* (1885) 10 App. Cas. 263.

152. In any event the requirement of a legal relationship was adopted by the House of Lords in accepting the advice of Lawrence and Chambre JJ (1806) 2 Bos. & Pul. (NR) 269.

153. (1806) 2 Bos. & Pul. (NR 269, 302. In *Barclay v. Cousins* (1802) 2 East 544, 547 he referred to a "moral certainty" of profit in the sense of "probable", based on past experience in the trade. Similarly, in *Macaura v. Northern Assurance Co.*, Andrews LJ described moral certainty as "at best a highly probable expectation" (1925) N.I. 141, 157.

154. *Ibid.*, at p.324, speaking of the heir at law's expectation of inheriting property.

155. (1946) 79 Ll.L. Rep. 410. Another variant is "legal certainty" as submitted by losing counsel *arguendo* in *Macaura v. Northern Assurance* [1925] A.C. 619, 622. It was also used by Lord Denman CJ in *M'Swiney v. Royal Exchange* (1849) 14 Q.B. 634, 645, to describe the prerequisite of interest in expected profits. He was reversed on appeal.

had been in opening. The use of this phrase as a test of the insurability of an expectation would create considerable uncertainty.[156]

Lord Eldon's second reason was that the test of moral certainty of benefit from the preservation of insured subject-matter would result in a multiplicity of insurances upon the same property. This is probably a less weighty objection now than in the formative years of the London insurance market, although it does lead to problems in assessing the measure of indemnity to which such assureds are entitled in respect of an uncontracted-for benefit. 4.39

The greatest obstacle to the adoption of expectation of benefit as a ground of insurable interest is the cardinal principle of indemnity itself. The point was made by Lord Ellenborough CJKB in *Routh v. Thompson*,[157] where he held that expectation of a grant of prize by the Crown was not a sufficient ground of insurable interest in captured ships. The principle of indemnity was intended to provide an assured with compensation for his actual loss. If the assured had no legal title to the insured property at the time of loss, but recovered the insured value of the property as if he were its legal owner, then there was a real risk that he was over-indemnified, for he might never have acquired it. To allow a full indemnity is to overlook that the insurer is conceding that the expectation of benefit would have been fulfilled. The alternative is to indemnify the assured for the loss of a chance, something which Lord Ellenborough was not prepared to contemplate because of the evidentiary difficulties in trying to evaluate it. Even if the Crown would provide evidence as to whether it would have remunerated the captors, the evidence would not be satisfactory because the Crown would be trying to estimate what it would have done in a situation which, owing to the loss of the ships, *ex hypothesi* never arose in practice. 4.40

It may be said in answer that today the courts do award damages for the loss of a chance, and Lord Ellenborough overestimated the difficulties. Moreover, we have come to realise that the contract of marine insurance is not a perfect contract of indemnity.[158] Nonetheless, to allow expectation of benefit to be a ground of insurable interest in marine property would even today confront insurers with real difficulties. 4.41

Let us take as an example[159] the assured who is negotiating to buy a ship. He decides to insure it against marine perils in the expectation that the negotiations will succeed and the ship will be his. Before the deal is struck, the ship becomes a total loss. The negotiations terminate, and a claim is brought. 4.42

The first point to note is that, as was the case with the old "interest or no interest" insurances referred to above, the assured cannot tender abandonment, and nothing can be abandoned to the insurer on payment, because the assured does not own the ship. Similarly, there can be no attempt to sue and labour, and no rights of

---

156. The Supreme Court of Canada adopted "moral certainty" as a self-standing criterion of insurable interest in property in *Constitution Insurance Co. of Canada v. Kosmopoulos* (1987) 34 DLR 208, 226, without giving its own definition of the phrase.

157. (1809) 11 East 428.

158. *Irving v. Manning (1847) HL Cas. 287, 307*; *Goole & Hull Steam Towing Co. v. Ocean Marine Insurance Co.* [1928] 1 K.B. 589, 595, referring to Marine Insurance Act 1906, s.16

159. The example given is adapted from the non-marine case of *Truran Earthmovers v. Norwich Union Fire Insurance Society* (1976) 17 S.A.S.R. 1.

subrogation. The rule[160] that an assured need not disclose the precise nature of his interest would need to be revised. Second, supposing that the policy contains an agreed value, or the actual insured value of the ship is be taken as the basis of the indemnity, what account is to be taken of the fact that the assured is seeking to be paid the value of the ship without having paid the purchase price? Although there has not been an actual recovery of compensation to diminish the assured's loss, there has been a corresponding benefit in the removal of the prospective obligation to pay for the ship. Only if the purchase price was lower than the agreed value, or actual value, is there any direct pecuniary loss at all. Third, if in such cases the insurer is to indemnify the assured against the loss of the opportunity to buy the ship, how is the court to assess the probability of the assured concluding a purchase? Even with willing co-operation from the seller, no realistic estimate of the reliability of proposals from other buyers can be made. Compared to the genuine need of the putative vendor to obtain indemnity against the loss of his ship which he now cannot sell, the nature of the expectant purchaser's speculative interest seems scarcely to merit protection.

4.43 The facts in *Stockdale v. Dunlop*[161] provide material for a second illustration. The assured insures a cargo on its voyage to a discharging port in his country. He might have no existing enforceable contract with its owner to buy it, perhaps no agreement at all, but bases his interest on a reasonable expectation of the seller honouring his unenforceable promise or, as the case may be, concluding a sale ex quay. The ship is lost with the cargo on board. Once there is evidence that other potential purchasers were interested in bidding for the cargo on its arrival, the difficulties noted above all appear in relation to the claim. Supposing that the other would-be purchasers have also insured the cargo, the notion that all of them might recover an indemnity on the basis of its insurable value makes a nonsense of the principle of indemnity, while the evidentiary and other problems of achieving any consistent evaluation of the loss of the chance to buy it appear insurmountable.

4D CONCLUSIONS

4.44 (i) The concept of insurable interest developed not merely to distinguish indemnity insurance from wager policies, but also to satisfy the requirement of the indemnity principle itself that the assured should suffer a loss against which he can be indemnified. That in turn, as Lawrence J recognised in *Lucena v. Craufurd*,[162] involves a satisfactory degree of certainty that, had the insured property not been lost or damaged, the assured would have benefited, and English law has adopted the requirement of a legal relationship between the assured and the insured subject-matter as the criterion of that degree of certainty. The rules of marine insurance now enshrined in the Marine Insurance Act 1906 concerning valuation of the

160. *Mackenzie v. Whitworth* (1875) LR 10 Ex. 142, 148. The insurer may of course ask for particulars of the intending assured's interest in the *res*.

161. (1840) 6 M. & W. 224. The purchase contract in this case was unenforceable for want of a written memorandum.

162. (1806) 2 Bos. & Pul. (NR) 269, 302.

assured's interest, the measure of indemnity, and the rights of an insurer to recoup what he has paid to indemnify the assured have all developed on the assumption of that legal nexus. If that is removed, and factual expectation of benefit or loss is substituted as the sole criterion of insurable interest, these rules will not always function satisfactorily in their present form.

(ii) It is true that the test of legal relationship cannot invariably establish that the assured would certainly have benefited if the insured subject-matter had not been lost, since a defeasible title to insured property is a good source of interest.[163] Equally, cases can arise where there is a virtual certainty of benefit even in the absence of a legal nexus with the subject-matter, as the case of *Moran, Galloway v. Uzielli*[164] demonstrates. Perfection is no doubt unattainable but the present concept of insurable interest has worked tolerably well in marine insurance, whatever its shortcomings in non-marine insurance, especially life insurance,[165] and it is difficult to support a case for radical reform of s.5 of the Marine Insurance Act 1906.

(iii) It is submitted, however, that the courts are free to develop a new sub-head of insurable interest in a marine adventure within the ambit of s.5(1) of the Marine Insurance Act 1906, by which a valid insurable interest is held to exist in cases where the acquisition of a property right or other benefit to which the assured is entitled in law or in equity is dependent solely upon the successful outcome of a marine adventure, albeit the assured possesses no legal or equitable right to, or in, insurable property prior to its conclusion. The recognition in s.5 that the marine adventure itself can be the subject-matter of an insurance,[166] with which the assured can have a legal relationship as opposed to one with insurable property at risk therein, makes it possible for the courts to hold that assureds like the creditors in *Moran, Galloway & Co. v. Uzielli*[167] and the shareholder in *Wilson v. Jones*[168] can insure against the loss of benefits dependent upon its safe conclusion. The warehousemen in *Cheshire v. Vaughan*,[169] who were granted the right to warehouse cargoes of nitrate destined for certain ports, would also possess an interest in the marine adventure under which such a cargo was declared

163. Marine Insurance Act 1906, s.7; *Boehm v. Bell* (1799) 8 T.R. 154; *Stirling v. Vaughan*(1809) 11 East 619, 628.

164. [1905] 2 K.B. 555.

165. The shortcomings of the Life Assurance Act 1774 lie outside the ambit of this chapter. While the Australian Insurance Contracts Act (Cth) 1984 has abandoned the need to show a legal or equitable interest in property in general non-marine insurances, it left marine insurance law subject to the English law definition of insurable interest in s.11 of the Marine Insurance Act (Cth) 1909, which repeats s.5 of the Marine Insurance Act 1906. The New Zealand Insurance Law Reform Act 1985 is also expressed not to apply to the Marine Insurance Act 1908. The Australian Law Reform Commission has now recommended (1) that the requirement to show a legal or equitable interest in property insured under a marine policy be abolished and (2) that the section of the 1909 Act which avoids gaming and wagering policies be repealed – Recommendation 28 of the Review of the Australian Marine Insurance Act in the ALRC Report No. 91, dated April 2001.

166. This possibility was recognised in *Wilson v. Jones* (1867) LR 2 Ex. 139, although the court construed the insurance in that case as one on profits.

167. [1905] 2 K.B. 555.

168. (1867) LR 2 Ex. 167.

169. [1920] 3 K.B. 240. The court did not decide whether the assured possessed an interest, since the policy was written on ppi terms, and was therefore void.

for discharge at such ports. Additional support for the above proposition can be derived from *Piper v. Royal Exchange Assurance*[170] in which Roche J said *obiter* that the purchaser of a ship who had no insurable interest in her on her delivery voyage because she was at the risk of the vendor, probably possessed an interest in her safe arrival which might have been insured as distinct from the ship herself. This was really another way of describing an insurance on the outcome of the marine adventure in question. Unlike the Commissioners in *Lucena v. Craufurd*,[171] the assureds in these cases had a legal entitlement to their respective benefits which was not dependent upon the occurrence of other events outside their control and liable to occur after the safe arrival of the vessel concerned. The recognition of this sub-category of insurable interest, it is submitted, is consistent with the principles codified in s.5 of the Marine Insurance Act 1906.

170. (1932) 44 Ll. L. Rep. 103,116.
171. (1806) 2 Bos. & Pul. (NR) 269.

CHAPTER 5

MARINE WARRANTIES: OLD RULES FOR THE NEW MILLENNIUM?

DR BARIS SOYER

5A INTRODUCTION

A marine warranty is defined by s.33(1) of the Marine Insurance Act 1906 (the Act) as a term of the contract by which the assured makes a "promise" to the underwriter. The promise which forms the subject-matter of a marine warranty consists of an undertaking by the assured that some particular thing shall or shall not be done, or that some condition shall be fulfilled, or whereby he affirms or negatives the existence of a particular state of facts.[1] *5.1*

1. The term "warranty" has different meaning in different areas of contract law. In fact, the term has been described as "one of the most ill-used expressions in the legal dictionary" by Lord Greene in *Finnegan v. Allen* [1943] 1 K.B. 425, at 430. In its most traditional non-insurance sense, it is to be understood as meaning a term of the contract, the breach of which entitles the aggrieved party to damages but not a right to treat the contract as repudiated. (*Dawsons Ltd v. Bonnin* [1922] 2 A.C. 413. See also Sale of Goods Act (SOGA) s.61(1)). The term "warranty" is also used to refer to certain guarantees given by the retailer under a sale contract. It should be borne in mind that under the Consumer Transaction (Restrictions on Statements) Order SI 1976 No. 1813, as amended by SI 1978 No. 127, such a guarantee offered by a retailer cannot take away or diminish any rights which the consumer would otherwise have under the SOGA 1979, and the guarantee document must also include a statement advising the consumer that the warranty is in addition to his statutory or common law rights. It has become common in recent years for retailers to offer their customers, particularly to those who buy technical equipment, the opportunity of buying a so-called "extended warranty". This will commonly give the customer, in return for payment, a guarantee that the cost of repairs will be covered for a certain period of time. Although types of scheme often called "warranties" they are in fact a sort of insurance against mechanical breakdown, and this is the

5.2 Warranties are said to serve a very significant function in the law of insurance. A contract of insurance is one whereby the insurer promises in return for a money consideration (premium) to pay the assured a sum of money or provide him with some corresponding benefit, upon the occurrence of one or more specific events (risk).[2] Accordingly, determining the scope of the risk is an essential element as far as the insurer is concerned and incorporation of a warranty into the contract helps the insurer to rate the risk properly and adjust the premium accordingly. In case of the assured not complying with a warranty, the risk initially undertaken by the insurer is altered. That is why the insurer is afforded a valuable defence in such a case.

5.3 Almost all legal principles regarding the warranty regime were developed by Lord Mansfield, who became Chief Justice of King's Bench in 1756, by considering similar rules adopted in Continental Codes.[3] The rules were later transferred into the Marine Insurance Act 1906[4] by Sir Mackenzie Chalmers, the co-author of the first Bill of the Act. This is not an extraordinary situation considering that the intention of the Act was to codify the existing law without making any alteration. Therefore, the rules regarding marine warranties have been in force for more than two hundred years. Over the years the warranty regime has been subject to numerous criticisms from various authorities and, in particular, there are pleas to alter the remedy afforded in case of breach of a marine warranty. The objects of this chapter are twofold. First, to describe the current legal regime in relation to marine insurance in the light of recent case law.[5] Then, to evaluate the need for reform in this area by taking various factors, both legal and non-legal, into account.

5B. CURRENT WARRANTY REGIME

5B.1 Types of marine warranty

5.4 According to the Act, a marine warranty can be express or implied.[6] Express warranties are those written in the policy. Section 35(1) of the Act clearly provides that no formal or technical wording is required for the creation of an express warranty. An express warranty can be created with any kind of wording provided that the parties' intention is to give warranty status to the clause in question. The words "warranty" or "warranted" are, therefore, not essential in order to create an express warranty. Accordingly, in *Aktielskabet Greenland v. Janson*,[7] a clause worded "No

better way of describing them. In order to harmonise legal rules in member states and ensure a uniform minimum level of consumer protection in the context of the internal market on certain aspects of the sale of consumer goods and associated guarantees, an EC Directive has recently been made: EC Directive 99/44 on Certain Aspects of Sale of Consumer Goods and Associated Guarantees. This Directive has been transposed into English law by The Stop Now Orders (EC Directive) Regulations SI 2001 No. 1422.

2. *Prudential Insurance Company v. Inland Revenue Commissioners* [1904] 2 K.B. 658.
3. For a detailed analysis on the development of marine insurance in England, see Martin, *The History of Lloyd's and of Marine Insurance in Great Britain*, 1876 (London: Macmillan).
4. See ss.33–41 of the Marine Insurance Act 1906.
5. For a detailed analysis on marine warranties, see Soyer, *Warranties in Marine Insurance* 2001, London: Cavendish). This book is the joint winner of the Cavendish Book Prize 2001 for Outstanding Legal Scholarship.
6. See s.33(2) of the Marine Insurance Act 1906.
7. (1918) 35 TLR 135.

mining timber carried", was held to be an express warranty. Similarly, in *J Kirkaldy & Sons Ltd v. Walker*,[8] Longmore J did not hesitate to afford warranty status to a clause which, without using the word "warranted", required the insured vessel to be surveyed for towage purposes and then to be condition-surveyed.[9] To determine whether the parties intended to create an express warranty is not an easy task. This process can be quite problematic if the words used are ambiguous and make it very difficult to derive the presumed intention of the parties. The courts may use some internal and external aids when determining whether there is an intention to warrant.[10] Their starting point would, presumably, be ascertaining whether the clause in question possesses the characteristic properties of a promissory warranty stated in s.33(1) of the Act. To this end, they must determine whether the assured in the clause had undertaken that some particular thing shall or shall not have been done or that some condition shall have been fulfilled or whereby he had affirmed or negatived the existence of a particular state of facts. The courts may also consider the substance of the clause in question to see if it is fundamental to the contract, bearing in mind its relation to the risk, its business purpose, and whether it would be unfair to leave the insurers without a defence to a claim.[11]

---

8. [1999] Lloyd's Rep. IR 410.

9. More recently, in *HIH Casualty & General Insurance Ltd v. New Hampshire Insurance Co. et al.* [2001] 2 All E.R. (Comm) 39 a clause in a film finance insurance policy, which required the assured to complete six film projects, was held to be an express warranty by the Court of Appeal even though the term "warranty" was not used. Similarly, in the same case, the following clause in the reinsurance policy was held to be an express warranty:

"The Reinsured hereon agrees to consult and obtain Reinsurer's agreement to all amendments and alterations to the terms, clauses and conditions of the Original Policy."

10. Recently, Lord Hoffmann in *Investors Compensation Scheme Ltd v. West Bromwich Building Society* [1998] 1 W.L.R. 896, at 912–913, introduced a new approach to the interpretation of contractual terms from a contextual point of view. His Lordship is of the opinion that the meaning of a contractual term is not necessarily to be obtained from the literal meaning of the words used. An external factor could assist the court in this context. Therefore, a contractual term could be construed according to the interpretation of a reasonable person in possession of the background knowledge available to the parties. The "factual matrix" is a wide concept and extends to anything which affects the manner in which the wording would have been understood by a reasonable man. Colman J, in *Zeus Tradition Marine Ltd v. Bell (The Zeus V)* [1999] 1 Lloyd's Rep. 703, reversed on different grounds [2000] 2 Lloyd's Rep. 587, CA, formulated Lord Hoffmann's "factual matrix" view from an insurance perspective. According to Colman J, the meaning of insurance terms could be ascertained by interpreting their ordinary and natural meaning established by the terms themselves and by evidence of the "factual matrix". In this respect, extrinsic evidence is admissible, but only when the words can, on ordinary principles of construction, have more than one meaning. Expert evidence is, also, admissible in insurance cases to demonstrate the meaning of particular words or phrases even where no custom is alleged. Despite the lack of any reported case in this area, it is submitted that Lord Hoffmann's "factual matrix" view as modified by Colman J, is going to have an impact on interpretation of marine warranties in future. In fact, "factual matrix" analysis played a crucial role in construing a "non-avoidance clause" in a professional liability policy in *Kumar v. AGF Insurance Ltd* [1999] Lloyd's Rep. IR 147. *MDIS Ltd v. Swinbank* [1999] Lloyd's Rep. IR 516, CA, is another non-marine insurance case where Lord Hoffmann's analysis has been adopted.

11. Rix LJ, in *HIH Casualty & General Insurance Ltd v. New Hampshire Insurance Co. et al.* [2001] 2 All E.R. (Comm) 39, at 67, laid down the tests, which could be applied in deciding whether a term is an express warranty or not, in the following way:

"It is a question of construction, and the presence or absence of the word 'warranty' or 'warranted' is not conclusive. One test is whether it is a term which goes to the root of the transaction; a second, whether it is

5.5 Although no specific form is necessary to create an express warranty, s.35(2) of the Act requires a warranty to be included in or written upon the policy or contained in some document incorporated by reference into the policy.[12] A warranty may be written in any part of the policy, either at the top or bottom[13] or transversely on the margin[14] or on the back.[15] In the Lloyd's Marine Policy (MAR 91) a separate section has been allocated for the insertion of special conditions and express warranties and it has been stated that they form part of the policy. Therefore, no dispute arises in modern policies as to whether the warranty has been inserted into the policy or not.

5.6 The London marine insurance market operates on the slip placing system. After taking instructions from the proposer, the broker prepares the slip containing all the particulars of the proposal necessary to allow underwriters to make a decision whether or not the risk is acceptable and at what premium. The slip forms the basis of any negotiations, which may take place between the broker and underwriter and is submitted to the leading underwriter. If the leading underwriter is willing to provide cover, he writes their name on the slip and further states on the slip the amount of liability that is to be undertaken. The slip is presented to various underwriters by the broker until the requisite level of subscription is obtained. On full subscription, the broker prepares policy wording which is submitted to the assured and leading underwriter for approval on behalf of the following market. The wording is then presented to the Lloyd's Policy Signing Office, which issues a single policy on behalf of all the contributing underwriters, representing the terms and conditions set out in the slip.[16] Therefore, after the issue of the policy, two documents, namely the slip and policy, come into existence regarding a single underwriting transaction.

5.7 Problems are likely to occur in cases where the inter-relationship between the slip and policy is not specified clearly. Can an express warranty which appears in the slip but is not expressly referred to in the policy be regarded as a term of the insurance contract? Put another way, is it possible to use the slip in construing the terms of the contract between the parties? The relationship between the slip and policy was considered by the Court of Appeal in *Youell v. Bland Welch & Co. Ltd*, particularly in the judgment of Beldam LJ.[17] That case concerned a contract of reinsurance at Lloyd's. Although it was common ground that the slip was superseded by a formal policy, the reinsurers submitted that the slip could be looked at as an aid to the construction of the policy. This submission was rejected mainly on two grounds. First, attention was drawn to an older case, *Ionides v. Pacific Fire & Marine Insurance*

descriptive of or bears materially on the risk of loss; a third, whether damages would be an unsatisfactory or inadequate remedy."

12. The origins of the rule in s.35(2) of the Marine Insurance Act 1906 could be traced to the judgments of Lord Mansfield in *Bean v. Stupart* (1778) 1 Dougl. 11 and *Pawson v. Watson* (1778) 2 Cowp. 786.

13. *Blackhurst v. Cockell* (1789) 3 TR 360.

14. *Bean v. Stupart* (1788) 1 Dougl. 11 and *Kenyon v. Berthon* (1788) 1 Dougl. 12(n).

15. If written on the back, it should be referred to on the face of the policy, since if the policy is apparently complete on the face of it, the assured's attention might never have been directed to the back and he would be entitled to accept what appeared on the face as constituting the whole contract between the parties.

16. Section 22 of the Marine Insurance Act 1906 asserts that in the absence of a marine policy the contract is inadmissible in evidence. The effect is that in the event of a dispute neither party may introduce or allude to the contract of marine insurance in court or arbitral proceedings.

17. [1992] 2 Lloyd's Rep. 127 at 140–141.

Co.,[18] said to determine the rule on this point. There a problem arose because the policy named the vessel in which the insured cargo was to be carried as the "*Socrates*", whereas the vessel in which the cargo had actually been shipped and lost, was the "*Socrate*". The question was whether the slip could be used to assist in finding the parties' true intention. In the light of the prevailing stamp duty expressed in a duly stamped policy,[19] Kelly CB observed that the slip was not admissible to prove a legally binding contract of marine insurance or to affect in any way the construction of such a contract. Beldam LJ viewed the admissibility of the slip to be governed by s.89 of the Act.[20] The use of the words "as heretofore" in that section indicated to Beldam LJ that the admissibility of a slip was governed by the state of law as it stood at the date of codification. As far as his Lordship was concerned, the state of law was expressed in *Ionides v. Pacific Fire & Marine Insurance Co.*[21] The other reason why the slip could not be used in construing the policy, according to Beldam LJ was the possible infringement of parol evidence rule[22] by virtue of which "parol testimony cannot be received to contradict, vary, add to or subtract from the terms of a written contract, or the terms in which the parties have deliberately agreed to record any part of their contract".[23] In fact, Beldam LJ stated his preference for a rule of law on this point founded in the parol evidence rule.[24]

Those remarks made in *Youell v. Bland Welch & Co. Ltd* do not form binding precedent that where a prior contract is followed by a further contract, or where in an insurance context a slip has been followed by the policy, there is a rule of law which makes it inadmissible to consider the terms of the prior contract, or that the parol evidence rule has the same effect. The reason for this is that in *Youell*'s case it was 5.8

18. (1871) LR 6 QB 674 aff'd (1873) LR 7 QB 517.

19. At one time, a slip could not be given in evidence for any purpose whatsoever. However, that had changed by the Customs and Inland Revenue Act 1867. Sections 7 and 9 of that Act provided that no contract of marine insurance could be valid unless expressed in a policy, and that no policy could be given in evidence unless duly stamped. The rule, which in marine insurance required a "policy" in due course became embodied in s.22 of the Marine Insurance Act 1906. It was only under the Finance Act 1959 that such a policy became valid even though not stamped.

20. This section provides:

"Where there is a duly stamped policy, reference may be made, as heretofore, to the slip or covering note, in any legal proceedings."

21. A similar view was also expressed by Hobhouse J (as he then was) in *Punjab National Bank v. de Boinville* [1992] 1 Lloyd's Rep. 7, at 13, where he said:

"But in the present case there is no claim for rectification and no allegation of mistake. Accordingly, in my judgment, it is not proper to look at the slip or other anterior document. If they disclose a different intention to that which is contained on the policy itself, they are irrelevant unless there is also a claim for rectification. The parties' contentions must stand or fall by the terms of the policy document itself – subject always to taking into account documents which are referred to in or incorporated into the policy, and the general principle of construing any document taking into account the surrounding circumstances."

22. It should be noted that the first instance judge, Phillips J, had a similar approach [1990] 2 Lloyd's Rep. 423 on this point. Also, in *St Paul Fire & Marine Insurance Co. (UK) Ltd v. McConnell Dowell Constructors Ltd* [1993] 2 Lloyd's Rep. 503 Potter J applied the parol evidence rule again in refusing to look outside the policy for the terms of the risk insured.

23. *Bank of Australasia v. Palmer* [1897] A.C. 540, *per* Morris LJ, at 545.

24. Similarly Hobhouse J (as he then was) in *Punjab National Bank v. de Boinville* [1992] 1 Lloyd's Rep. 7, at 12, could be read as stating that there is a rule of law that – "once a policy has been issued, that is the document that contains the terms of the contract".

common ground that the policy in question was intended to supersede the slip so accordingly all these statements were *obiter dictum*. Recently, the Court of Appeal in *HIH Casualty & General Insurance Ltd v. New Hampshire et al*[25] had an opportunity to re-examine the relationship between the slip and policy. Rix LJ considered it dangerous to build, as Beldam LJ did in his *obiter dicta* in *Youell*'s case, on the single case of *Ionides* that a slip could never be used to assist in the construction of a policy. His Lordship regarded the *Ionides* case as "unique", bearing in mind the fact that at the time it was decided there were numerous statutory restrictions and controversy surrounding use of the slip for any purpose. His Lordship was of the opinion that due to these factors the Court was anxious to show that the use for which the slip was admitted into evidence was limited. Furthermore, whether s.89 of the Act attracts the restrictive interpretation adopted by Beldam LJ may also be doubted. The intention of this section seems to confirm that reference to the slip may be made as established before the passing of the Act. Accordingly, construing this provision in the way Beldam LJ did would inevitably reduce the significance of the slip, which is an outcome contradicting the general idea behind this section. It is, also, somehow old-fashioned to approach this issue armed with the parol evidence rule that evidence is not admissible to vary or contradict the words of a written contract. The modern approach of the House of Lords is that, on the positive side, evidence should be admitted of the background, surrounding circumstances, factual matrix and genesis to the contract.[26]

Thus, Rix LJ suggests that, instead of developing a conclusive rule of law on this point, the relationship between the slip and policy must be determined bearing in mind the intention of parties in the light of surrounding circumstances. According to his Lordship, three different situations could arise. First, the policy could be intended to supersede the slip. In such a case, it may in most cases be useless to try to construe the policy by reference to the slip. Where the policy is identical, its construction can stand on its own feet, and in any event its construction should be undertaken primarily by reference to its own overall terms. Where the policy differs from the slip, *prima facie*, the difference is a deliberate decision to depart from the earlier wording, which again provides no assistance. Second, the policy could be intended to live together with the slip, to the extent that this is possible, but where this is not possible it may well be proper to regard the policy as superseding the slip. Finally, the policy may be intended to be incorporated into the slip, in which case it is *prima facie* the policy which may have to give way to the slip in the event of inconsistency. Therefore, it is clear that in second and third situations, an express warranty, which appears in the slip but not in the policy, could be, nevertheless, regarded as a part of the insurance contract. In fact this was held to be the case in *HIH Casualty & General Insurance Ltd v. New Hampshire Co. et al* where the re-assured (HIH) had underwritten two film finance insurance policies under which the assured was LDT. HIH, then, obtained reinsurance cover from various reinsurers. The reinsurance policies were subject to all terms, clauses and conditions as underlying ones. In the original agreement between HIH and LDT, there was an express warranty in the slips to the effect that a slate of six or ten films would be made. The same provision did not appear in

25. [2001] 2 All E.R. (Comm) 39.
26. *Investors Compensation Scheme v. West Bromwich Building Society* [1998] 1 All E.R. 98.

the underlying policies. At the end of the insurance period, LDT suffered a loss of US$ 31 million and was indemnified by HIH, which sought to recover in the three actions contributions towards some 80 per cent of that sum under the reinsurance agreements. The reinsurers refused to indemnify HIH. One of their defences was that there was an express warranty in the underlying policies with regard to the completion of the full state. Accordingly, it could be concluded that the reinsurance contracts contained the same warranty and breach of this warranty afforded a defence to the reinsurers. The central issue here was whether the insurance and reinsurance contracts contained an express warranty which appeared in the slip but not mentioned in the policies. The answer of the Court of Appeal to this question was positive. There was nothing in the formal policy suggesting that the wording of the slip had been superseded. Furthermore, since certain aspects of the agreement, e.g. the maximum cover for each film, were not referred to in the formal policy, the structure of the insurances would have made sense only if the slip was taken as the basis of the agreement. Therefore, the slips needed to be read together with the policies and accordingly the express warranty was held to be part of the contract.

Unlike express warranties, implied warranties do not appear in the policy; but are tacitly understood by the parties to be present. They are implied by law from the circumstances within which the bargain was effected.[27] There are three warranties implied by the Marine Insurance Act 1906, namely, warranty of seaworthiness (ss.39(1)(2)(3)(4)); warranty of cargo-worthiness (s.40(2)) and warranty of legality (s.41). 5.9

The warranty of seaworthiness is implied in a voyage policy,[28] whatever be the subject-matter insured.[29] The warranty, therefore, applies whether the policy is on ship, goods, freight or any property exposed to a maritime peril.[30] Similarly, in cases where the cargo insurance contracts are effected on an "open cover" basis,[31] the implied warranty of seaworthiness would still apply to each overseas shipment embraced within the open cover, because each adventure relates to a separate voyage. Thus, each certificate of insurance issued under an open cover will be subject to s.39(1) of the Act. 5.10

According to s.39(4) of the Act, the insured vessel is seaworthy "when she is reasonably fit in all respects to encounter the ordinary perils of the seas of the adventure insured".[32] Two points emerge from this definition. First, the implied 5.11

27. Implied warranties are not present in any areas of insurance law except marine insurance. There is, for example, no implied warranty in fire insurance that the premises are well built and incorporate fire precautions.

28. For the definition of a voyage policy see s.25(1) of the Marine Insurance Act 1906.

29. Section 39(1) of the Marine Insurance Act 1906 declares in general terms that:

"In a voyage policy there is an implied warranty that at the commencement of the voyage the ship shall be seaworthy for the purpose of the particular adventure insured."

30. For the definition of maritime peril see ss.1 and 3 of the Marine Insurance Act 1906.

31. An open cover is an agreement whereby the underwriter undertakes to insure all shipments or interests of the assured for certain voyages or trades, either at specified rates of premium, or at rates to be arranged. The underwriter is notified by the assured, when the shipments are made, of the interests attaching to the cover.

32. This definition is derived from the celebrated case of *Dixon v. Sadler* (1839) 5 M & W 405, affirmed (1841) 8 M & W 895, where Baron Parke defined "seaworthiness" in the following terms:

warranty of seaworthiness is very far reaching; it does not just cover the structure and manning of the vessel but extends to the smallest details on board, such as the accuracy of the charts[33] and sufficiency of medicine.[34] Second, the concept of "seaworthiness" is relative in a number of respects.[35] For instance, seaworthiness varies according to the voyage to be undertaken.[36] The extent of the seaworthiness obligation may also differ for the same voyage at different seasons. A ship, for example, may be seaworthy for a summer voyage but unseaworthy for the one undertaken in winter as she is not in a condition to overcome perils to be anticipated on a winter voyage, such as light ice. The extent of the obligation can also be different for the same voyage at the same season. In one American case[37] it was held that although the vessel was seaworthy for that voyage in ordinary weather at that season, she was unseaworthy as she left the port without being fitted to cope with the hurricane, which was announced to approach. Moreover, the extent of the warranty may vary for the same voyage at the same season according to whether the ship is loaded with one kind of cargo or another.[38]

5.12 It is clear from s.39(1) of the Act that the implied warranty of seaworthiness needs to be satisfied at the commencement of the voyage. There is no warranty that a ship originally seaworthy for the voyage insured shall continue to be seaworthy or that the master and crew shall do their duty during the voyage. The negligence and misconduct of master or crew after the voyage has commenced, therefore, is no defence to an action on the policy where the loss has been immediately occasioned by the perils insured against. In other words, the assured makes no warranty that the ship shall continue to be seaworthy throughout the voyage.[39]

5.13 Apart from the seaworthiness warranty, s.40(2) of the Act implies a warranty of cargoworthiness in voyage policies effected on goods and other movables.[40] This sub-section defines "cargoworthiness" as being reasonably fit to carry the goods or other movables to their destination. Cargoworthiness means in the first place that the vessel is in a fit state to receive the contractual cargo. Therefore, the warranty would not be satisfied where the vessel's holds needed fumigating or cleaning before

---

"... it is clearly established that there is an implied warranty that the vessel shall be seaworthy, by which is meant that she shall be in a fit state as to repairs, equipment, crew and in all respects to encounter the ordinary perils of the voyage insured, at the time of sailing upon it."

33. *The Irish Spruce* [1976] Lloyd's Rep. 63.

34. *Woolf v. Claggett* (1806) 3 Esp. 257

35. *Steel v. State Line SS Co.* (1877) 3 App. Cas. 72.

36. See *Cohen (G) Sons & Co. v. Standard Marine Insurance Co. Ltd* (1925) 41 TLR 232 where a ship without steam power was held to be seaworthy for a tow from England to Germany.

37. *Texas & Gulf SS Co. v. Parker* 263 Fed. Rep. 864.

38. *Stanton v. Richardson* (1874–5) LR 9 CP 39.

39. *Berman v. Woodbridge*, (1781) 2 Dougl. 781; *Eden v. Parkinson* (1781) 2 Dougl. KB 732; *Watson v. Clark* (1813) 1 Dow. 336; *Busk v. Royal Exchange Assurance Co.* (1818) 2 B & Ald. 73 and *Biccard v. Shepherd* (1861) 14 Moo. PC 471.

40. The Marine Insurance Act 1906, Schedule 1, rule 17 of the Rules for Construction of the Policy provides:

"The term goods means goods in the nature of merchandise, and does not include personal effects or provisions and stores for use on board."

being in a fit state to receive cargo.[41] In order to be considered cargoworthy, a ship must also be equipped to carry the particular kind of cargo, which she has contracted to carry.[42] If, for example, the cargo is frozen meat, then the refrigerating machinery, holds etc, must be in proper order, efficient and fit to receive and carry that particular cargo. Similarly, a vessel intended for the carriage of grain in bulk must be supplied with sufficient separation cloths and adequate shifting boards.

The implied warranty of legality is laid down in s.41 of the Act. Accordingly, there 5.14
is an implied warranty that the adventure insured is a lawful one, and that, so far as the assured can control the matter, the adventure shall be carried out in a lawful manner. No distinction has been made between voyage and time policies in respect of the application of the implied warranty of legality. Therefore, where the policy covers a ship for a period of time, the implied warranty is imposed for each voyage on which the ship embarks. Similarly, the implied warranty of legality is incorporated, by law, in the marine insurance policy covering each separate interest in a common maritime adventure. This means s. 41 applies whether the subject matter of the insurance is ship, cargo, freight or anything else.[43]

As can be seen, s. 41 of the Act imposes two types of obligation on the part of the assured. The marine adventure insured must not only be legal at the inception of the policy[44] but it must be performed legally, so far as the assured can control the matter.[45] In cases where the assured has no control over the illegality and accordingly the implied warranty is not broken, he will be entitled to recover loss caused by illegality of the performance of the adventure, as long as it is caused by an insured peril.[46] For example, if the illegality is on the part of the master or crew, the assured is entitled to recover on the basis of the insured peril of barratry.[47] Finally, it should be borne in mind that the further performance of an adventure which is lawful at the outset, might become unlawful later as a result of a change of events, such as outbreak of war.[48] In such a case, the assured must abandon the voyage. If he persists in an adventure, this will lead to an illegality in the performance of the adventure and he will be in breach of the implied warranty of legality.[49]

---

41. In *Tattersall v. National SS Co.* (1884) 12 Q.B.D. 297, for example, a vessel which had carried cattle with foot-and-mouth disease was not properly cleansed and disinfected before a fresh lot of cattle were received on board. When these consequently caught the disease, it was held that the cargoworthiness warranty was breached. See also *Ciampa v. British India SN Co.* [1915] 2 K.B. 774 and *Compañia de Naviera Nedelka v. Tradex International (The Tres Flores)* [1973] 2 Lloyd's Rep. 247.

42. See *Maori King (Cargo Owners) v. Huges* [1895] 2 Q.B. 550 and *The Waikato* [1899] 1 Q.B. 56.

43. Movables, passage money, commission, profit, loan, disbursements or any liability to a third party may also be the subject matter of a marine insurance contract under s.3(2)(a)/(b)/(c) of the Marine Insurance Act 1906.

44. A marine adventure could be regarded as "illegal" by various means, i.e. by statute, common law, prize law, orders made by the Queen and other international rules.

45. In *Ingham v. Agnew* (1812) 15 East 517, although the adventure insured was lawful at its outset, it was not performed legally as the assured sailed without a convoy in violation of a statute which prohibited sailing without a convoy.

46. *Carstairs v. Allnutt* (1813) 3 Camp. 497 and *Wilson v. Rankin* (1865) LR 1 Q.B. 162.

47. The term "barratary" has been defined in the Marine Insurance Act 1906, Schedule 1, rule 11 as "including every wrongful act wilfully committed by the master or crew to the prejudice of the owner, or, as the case may be, the charterer".

48. *Sanday & Co. v. British & Foreign Marine Insurance Co. Ltd* [1915] 2 K.B. 781.

49. *Sanday & Co. v. British & Foreign Marine Insurance Co. Ltd, ibid.*, at 788, *per* Bailhache J.

5B.2 Nature of marine warranties

5.15 Whether express or implied, a warranty is a term in a marine insurance contract. The legal principles underlying this contractual term has been laid down by the case law and the Act and they apply equally to both types of warranty. The object of this section is to scrutinise these rules, and thereby to clarify the legal character of this contractual term and in this way distinguish it from other terms of a marine insurance contract.

5.16 One of the main features of the marine warranty regime is that the obligation undertaken by a marine warranty must be exactly (strictly) complied with. Accordingly, no motive and no necessity will provide an excuse. The exact compliance rule was introduced into marine insurance contracts by Lord Mansfield in *Pawson v. Watson*.[50] A couple of years later the rule was applied in *De Hahn v. Hartley*,[51] where an express warranty, which required the insured vessel to sail with at least 50 hands or upwards, was held to be breached when the insured vessel sailed with 46 crew members on board, although six more joined soon after departure.[52] The doctrine was later embodied in s.33(3) of the Act by Sir Mackenzie Chalmers.[53]

It has been stated in *Overseas Commodities Ltd v. Style*[54] by McNair J, that the harsh consequences of the exact compliance doctrine could be mitigated by the adoption of the *de minimis non curat lex* rule.[55] In that case, the assured shipped two consignments of tinned pork from France to London under an all risk policy of insurance underwritten by the insurers. The policy contained a warranty, which required that all the tins should be marked by the manufacturers verifying their date of manufacture. When the tins were delivered, many of them were found to be rusty or broken and much of the pork was either condemned or sold off cheaply. The assured claimed on the policy but the insurer rejected the claim on the basis that, as many of the tins did not have the date of manufacture upon them, the warranty was breached. The court ruled that lack of such marks on many of the tins amounted to breach of warranty and thus the underwriters were not liable. However, McNair, J said:[56]

"Being satisfied that, as regards both policies, a substantial number of tins – *well exceeding any tolerance that could be disregarded under the de minimis rule* – were not marked with a code which

50. (1778) 2 Cowp. 785.

51. (1786) 1 TR 343.

52. See also, *Hore v. Whitmore* (1778) 2 Cowp. 784; *Earle v. Harris* (1780) 1 Doug. KB 357 and *Sanderson v. Busher* (1814) 4 Camp. 54n.

53. Being one of the features of warranties, the exact compliance doctrine is certainly not the one which distinguishes them from other terms of an insurance contract. For example, conditions in insurance contracts which deal with particular matters, also need to be exactly complied with, a substantial performance only being insufficient. In other words, if the condition goes to details, those details must be literally fulfilled and it is no defence for the assured to assert that such details are immaterial. Accordingly, in *Conn v. Westminster Motor Insurance Association Ltd* [1966] 1 Lloyd's Rep. 407, CA, where a condition in motor insurance policy requiring the assured to take all reasonable steps to maintain the insured car in efficient condition, was held to be broken since two of its front tyres were in a deplorable state.

54. [1958] 1 Lloyd's Rep. 546.

55. In cases where this rule applies non-performance or defective performance of a commercially insignificant amount has no legal consequence.

56. [1958] 1 Lloyd's Rep. 546, at 558. [emphasis added]

enabled the true and correct date of manufacture to be established, I have no option but to hold that the breach of the express warranty affords the underwriters a complete defence in this action."[57]

The other feature of the marine warranty regime, as expressed in s.33(3) of the Act, is that the insurer is discharged from liability in case of breach of a marine warranty even though the warranty breached is not material to the risk. This rule, in fact, implies two things. First, it means that an express warranty, even though it might not affect the risk in any manner, must be literally complied with.[58] Accordingly, breach of a premium warranty which requires the assured to make regular payments, is sufficient to discharge the insurer from further liability; despite the fact that the payment made by the assured could have no effect on the risk insured against.[59] Furthermore, it also implies that even though the warranted event concerns things which could be material in a general way, whether the particular breach by the assured has any material effect on the case in question is irrelevant. This point could be illustrated with a celebrated case, *Yorkshire Insurance Co. Ltd v. Campbell.*[60] There the insurance was on a horse against marine perils and risks of mortality during a sea voyage, and it was described in the proposal form as – "Bay gelding by Soult X St Paul (mare) 5 years". The pedigree as stated was incorrect and the Privy Council held that since on its construction the description of the horse was a warranty, the inaccuracy provided the insurers with a defence to the owner's claim when the horse died on the voyage. The pedigree of the insured horse could have a bearing on its temperament and thus its ability to withstand a marine voyage, but there was no evidence in the case that the horse's actual pedigree adversely affected in this regard or it had made no difference in the actual circumstances of the loss. However, the fact that there was a breach of warranty in the case was sufficient to discharge the insurer from liability.[61] 5.17

One of the most controversial features of the warranty regime is the rule which provides the insurer with a defence even though the loss may not have been in the remotest degree connected with the breach of warranty. This severe rule was first applied in *Hibbert v. Pigou*[62] where a ship warranted to sail with convoy had in fact sailed without it and went down in a storm. Even though breach of warranty had no link with the loss, in other words the loss would have still occurred had the warranty been complied with, the underwriter was held not liable for this loss.[63] Although this 5.18

57. However, it should be born in mind that in commercial law the application of this rule is rather limited and the breach should involve only a trivial part of the whole undertaking.

58. In *De Hahn v. Hartley* (1786) 1 TR 343 at 345 Lord Mansfield said:

"It is perfectly immaterial for what purpose a warranty is introduced, but, being inserted, the contract does not exist unless it be literally complied with."

59. The premium warranty has recently become subject of litigation in *Chapman v. Kadirga Denizcilik ve Ticaret* [1998] Lloyd's Rep. IR 377, CA.

60. [1917] A.C. 218.

61. See also *Blackhurst v. Cockell* (1789) 3 TR 360 to the same effect.

62. (1783) 3 Doug. KB 213.

63. See also *Christian v. Ditchell* (1797) Peake's Add. Cas. 141; *Wedderburn v. Bell* (1807) 1 Camp. 1; *Foley v. Tabor* (1861) 2 F & F 663 and *Lane v. Nixon* (1866) LR 1 CP 412.

rule has not been expressly stressed in the Marine Insurance Act 1906, by virtue of s.91(2)[64] it is an established rule.

5.19 Once a marine warranty has been breached, it is irrelevant whether the warranty is later complied with. This rule has been stressed in s.34(2) of the Act and has been derived from cases decided in the eighteenth and nineteenth century. For instance, in *De Hahn v. Hartley*,[65] when the insured vessel commenced the intended voyage, the warranted number of crew were not on board. The warranted number of crew had been recruited before the vessel sailed on the leg of the voyage during which the casualty occurred. However, it was ruled by Lord Mansfield that once the warranty was breached it was immaterial whether it was remedied later. Similarly, in *Quebec Marine Insurance Co. v. Commercial Bank of Canada*[66] the vessel was insured for a voyage at and from Montreal to Halifax, Nova Scotia. After leaving Montreal, her boiler, which had been defective from the outset, became unmanageable when seawater entered and she had to seek refuge nearby in order to effect repairs. The repairs were duly made but, soon after resuming her voyage, she encountered severe weather and was lost. The Privy Council ruled that the assured were in breach of the implied warranty of seaworthiness and the insurers were not liable under the policy even though the defect was remedied before the loss occurred.

5.20 Section 34(1) of the Act is another provision, which emphasises the strict nature of the warranty regime. Accordingly, apart from the exceptions mentioned in this sub-section, no defence would excuse breach of a marine warranty.[67] The first case where non-compliance with marine warranties could be excused is when the warranty ceases to be applicable to the circumstances of the contract by reason of a change of circumstances. At first sight, the scope of this exception seems to be extensive. However, evaluating the example provided by Sir Mackenzie Chalmers himself, in the commentary for the Marine Insurance Act 1906[68] it could be observed that it has only a limited application. According to the co-author of the Act, if during war a warranty to sail with a convoy at a future time from some foreign station were inserted, the intervention of peace before the period at which the ship was so to sail would excuse the necessity of compliance. Thus, under this sub-section, in cases where a warranty was incorporated into the policy for a particular reason, the assured will be excused for not complying with it provided that the reason which made parties agree on such a warranty ceases to exist after the attachment of the policy. In this respect, the exception expressed in this sub-section seems to be an implication of the celebrated Latin maxim *cessante ratione, cessat lex*.[69] If this analysis is accurate, then it

64. This sub-section reads as follows:

"The rules of common law including the law merchant, save in so far as they are inconsistent with the express provisions of this Act, shall continue to apply to contracts of marine insurance."

65. (1786) 1 TR 343.
66. (1870) LR 3 PC 234.
67. This rule has been stressed in Mustill and Gilman (eds), *Arnould's Law of Marine Insurance and Average Vol. 2*, 1981, 16th edn., at para. 687, in the following way:

"No cause, however sufficient; no motive however good, no necessity, however irresistible, will excuse non-compliance with a warranty."

68. Chalmers and Archibals, *The Marine Insurance Act 1906* (3rd edn., London: Butterworths 1922).
69. With the reason of the law ceasing, the law itself ceases.

can be concluded that this exception has no application as far as implied warranties are concerned since it is very unlikely that the reason behind an implied warranty will cease to exist during the currency of the policy. Furthermore, non-compliance with a warranty is excused in cases where compliance with the warranty is rendered unlawful by any subsequent law. It is an established rule of law that if a man agrees to do a thing which is lawful at the time, but an Act of Parliament comes in and hinders him from doing it, the agreement is repealed.[70] The second exception expressed in s.34(1) of the Act 1906 could be regarded as a reflection of this principle on the marine warranties regime.

5B.3 Consequences of breach

Both express and implied warranties can be further classified according to the time of undertaking. Certain warranties undertake that a given state of affairs will be satisfied or avoided at some time after the inception of the risk. A warranty of this type could also be referred to as a "warranty as to future events". The warranty of seaworthiness which is implied in respect of voyage policies by s.39(1) of the Act and most express warranties, such as locality warranties,[71] are examples of warranties of this type. Some warranties, on the other hand, relate in time to the circumstances at the inception of the risk. In such a case, the warranted event or condition must be complied with at some time before the risk attaches. For instance, the Act implies a warranty of seaworthiness in respect of a voyage policy on hull which attaches "at and from" the place named in the policy. Section 39(2) of the Act requires such a vessel to be reasonably fit to encounter the ordinary perils of the port at the commencement of the risk. Express warranties can also be drafted to cover a period before the attachment of the risk. For instance, an express warranty of neutrality requires the vessel to be warranted neutral to have such a character at the commencement of the risk.[72] The classification of warranties according to the time of undertaking is far from being a pragmatic one. The consequences of breach of a marine warranty depend on the nature of the warranty breached, whether it is a warranty which is related to a period after or before the attachment of risk. 5.21

The legal effect of breach of a marine warranty, which relates to a period after the attachment of the risk, has been spelt out in s.33(3) of the Act in the following way: 5.22

> "... the insurer is discharged from liability as from the date of the breach of warranty, but without prejudice to any liability incurred by him before that date."

The meaning and scope of this sub-section had not been subject to judicial analysis until *Bank of Nova Scotia v. Hellenic Mutual War Risks Association (Bermuda) Ltd (The Good Luck)*[73] reached the House of Lords at early 1990s. *The Good Luck* was insured with the defendant P & I club (Hellenic Mutual War Risks Association (Bermuda)

70. *Brewster v. Kitchin* (1698) 1 Ld. Raym. 321
71. With a locality warranty the assured undertakes either that the insured vessel will navigate within the confines of a specified area or she will not navigate in specific waters or beyond a specified point.
72. See s.36 of the Marine Insurance Act 1906.
73. [1991] 2 Lloyd's Rep. 191, hereinafter referred to as *The Good Luck*.

Ltd) and mortgaged to the plaintiff bank (Bank of Nova Scotia). As required by the mortgage, the benefit of the insurance was assigned to the bank, and the club gave a letter of undertaking, whereby the club promised to advise the bank promptly if they should "cease to insure" the ship. The rules of Hellenic Mutual War Risks Association contained an express warranty prohibiting the insured vessel from entering certain declared areas. These were areas of such extreme danger that it was not considered acceptable by the club that they should cover vessels entering these areas. If an owner wanted such cover while his vessel was in a prohibited area special arrangements had to be made. The owners of *The Good Luck* were in the practice of sending the vessel into prohibited areas but neither the club nor the bank were informed. The managers of the club later discovered what was going on but they neither took any steps to deter the owners of *The Good Luck* from carrying on, nor informed the bank of what they had discovered. On her last voyage, *The Good Luck* was sent to part of the Arabian Gulf in breach of warranty. However, this time she was not that lucky! While in the Arabian Gulf she was hit by Iraqi missiles and became a constructive total loss. Both club and bank knew of the total loss, but whereas the club discovered the breach of warranty, the bank negligently did not investigate the possibility.[74] In the mistaken belief that the loss was covered, the bank made further loans to the shipowners. In view of the breach of warranty, the insurance could not be enforced, but the bank brought an action against the club for having failed to give prompt notice that they had ceased to insure the ship. Accordingly, it was contended that the club was in breach of the letter of undertaking given by them to the bank.

The bank relied on a number of grounds one of which gave rise to a serious and intense judicial examination of s.33(3) of the Act. It was argued that by virtue of this sub-section, breach of warranty brought the vessel's insurance to an end automatically and accordingly the insurer was in breach of the express provisions of the letter of undertaking in failing to notify the bank as to such a breach. Accepting this contention, Hobhouse J (as he then was) ruled in favour of the bank. The Court of Appeal, on the other hand, allowed the appeal on the basis that s.33(3) of the Act does not provide that a breach of warranty terminates the contract of insurance. Drawing support from some academic texts, reports and a *dicta* in a prior case, the Court of Appeal assimilated breach of warranty to a breach of condition in general contract law. Accordingly, breach of warranty does not terminate the insurance contract automatically but gives the insurer an opportunity to do so. Reversing the Court of Appeal's decision, the House of Lords held that breach of a warranty of this nature automatically discharges the insurer from liability from the date of breach.

Accordingly, the club was in breach of the letter of undertaking as, once they decided to rely on breach of warranty defence, they were automatically discharged from further liability from the moment *The Good Luck* entered the prohibited area.

5.23 The reason for the conflict between the Court of Appeal and House of Lords could be explained by the existence of various interpretations of s.33(3) of the Act adopted by different texts. Without a doubt, before the enactment of the Act, breach of a marine warranty was held to have similar consequences to breach of a condition in

74. The bank was of the opinion that an arrangement was made between the owners and the club to keep the vessel insured while she was in the prohibited areas.

general contract law.[75] This is probably the reason why in all editions of books written by Sir Mackenzie Chalmers, one of the co-authors of the Bill which preceded the Marine Insurance Act 1906, the following commentary appears:[76]

"It is often said that breach of a warranty makes the policy void. But this is not so. A void contract cannot be ratified, but a breach of warranty in insurance law appears to stand on the same footing as the breach of a condition in other branch of contract."

Also, there is authority suggesting that breach of a non-marine warranty entitles the insurer to repudiate the contract.[77] In all these cases, pre-Act marine authorities and comments made by the co-author of the Act seemed to play a crucial role. Similarly, all the other texts[78] and reports[79] cited by the Court of Appeal refer to these sources when equating the effect of breach of a marine warranty with a breach of condition in general contract law. However, all the sources mentioned above, including the books written by Sir Mackenzie Chalmers, ignore the possible impact of s.33(3) of the Act when commenting on the effect of breach of a marine warranty. Perhaps this sub-section was intended to alter the common law position in respect of breach of a warranty. This could be seen clearly if different provisions of the Act are interpreted as a whole. Some provisions of the Act adopt the use of "avoidance". If, for example, the utmost good faith be not observed by either party the contract may be avoided by the other by virtue of s.17. Similarly, if the assured fails to disclose a material fact or makes a material misrepresentation in the course of pre-contract negotiations, the insurer may avoid the contract.[80] A further group of provisions, including s.33(3), on the other hand speaks of discharge from liability.[81] As can be seen, different consequences have been afforded for breach of different provisions of the Act. Therefore, if the parliamentary draftsman had had intentions of retaining the common law position in respect of breach of a warranty, a different wording for s.33(3) would have been adopted. Indeed, at one stage during its chequered passage to the statute book,[82] the second sentence of s.33(3) of the Bill read: "... if it be not so complied with, the insurer may avoid the contract". The fact that s.33(3) was enacted in the present form indicates that the Parliamentary draftsman intended to change the common law position in respect of the effect of breach of warranty.[83] The following speech of Swinfen-Eady LJ, in *Sanday & Co. v. British & Foreign Marine Insurance*

75. *De Hahn v. Hartley* (1786) 1 TR 343.

76. *A Digest of the Law Relating to Marine Insurance* (1901 1st edn.; 1903 2nd edn.) and *The Marine Insurance Act 1906* (1907 1st edn.) with subsequent editions in 1913, 1922 and 1932.

77. *CTN Cash & Carry Ltd v. General Accident Fire & Life Assurance Corporation Ltd* [1989] 1 Lloyd's Rep. 299.

78. See Parkington, Legh-Jones, Longmore and Birds (eds.), *MacGillivray and Parkington on Insurance Law Relating on All Risks Other Than Marine* (1988 8th edn.), (London: Sweet & Maxwell), para. 790.

79. For example, in paragraph 8 of The Fifth Report of the Law Reform Committee on *Conditions and Exceptions in Insurance Policies*, Cmnd 62, 1957, London: HMSO, Lord Mansfield's *dicta* in *De Hahn v. Hartley* (1786) 1 TR 343 was cited as authority when equating breach of a warranty in insurance law with breach of a condition in general contract law.

80. See ss.18(1) and 20(1) of the Marine Insurance Act 1906 respectively.

81. See, s.45(2) of the Marine Insurance Act 1906, for example, which provides that if there is a change of voyage the insurer is discharged from liability as from the time of change. See also ss.46 and 48 of the MIA 1906.

82. The Marine Insurance Act of 1906 had been first introduced into Parliament in 1894 and was re-introduced many times thereafter with variations in its language.

83. The intention of the Parliament was presumably to give a different legal character to marine insurance warranties due to the role they play in accessing the risk undertaken.

Co.[84] in relation to principles of construing a codifying act, also supports the notion that s.33(3) of the MIA altered the common law position:

"The proper course is in the first instance to examine the language of the statute, and to ask what is its natural meaning, uninfluenced by any considerations derived from the previous state of law, and not to start with inquiring how the law previously stood."

Presumably, when the Bill was drafted the intention was to retain the common law position for breach of a warranty and accordingly entitle the insurer to repudiate the contract in case of breach of a marine warranty. The final wording of s.33(3), however, made this impossible and the authorities and academic commentaries on the issue paid no attention to this development. Accordingly, Lord Goff was quite accurate to suggest that the Court of Appeal was "led astray by passages in certain books and other texts".[85]

Had the effect of breach of a marine warranty which relates in time to a period after the attachment of the risk been equated with breach of a condition, the insurer would have been discharged from future obligations, but rights and liabilities of the insurer which had arisen before the breach would have remained unaffected.[86] The automatic discharge remedy afforded by *The Good Luck* does not change this position. The only difference is that, in the former, in order to achieve the legal consequences mentioned above the insurer was required to elect to repudiate the contract and, until this repudiation occurs, the contract would be in force. However, under the rule adopted by Lord Goff, the insurer is discharged from liability automatically as soon as the breach occurs, but this discharge does not mean that the contract comes to an end at that moment. According to Lord Goff, the contract remains on foot for certain purposes, i.e. liability to pay a premium.[87]

5.24 The legal position on this point has recently been illustrated in *J A Chapman & Co Ltd v. Kadirga Denizcilik ve Ticaret.*[88] In that case the assured had warranted that instalments of the premium would be paid on given dates, but had fallen behind. It was held that the late payment of a single instalment brought the risk to an end, so that the insurer could never be liable for future losses whereas the assured remained under an obligation to continue to make payments. This, of course, assumes that the risk is indivisible and does not run from instalment to instalment.[89] Delivering the Court of Appeal's judgment on this point, Chadwick LJ, said:[90]

"The fact that the successive instalments are due and payable on dates which occur at three monthly intervals during the term of the policy does not, in my view, lead to the conclusion that the premium, which comprises the aggregate of those instalments, is itself divisible between successive three month periods."

If the risk was held to be divisible, the position would be different. In such a

84. [1915] 2 K.B. 781 at 786.
85. [1991] 2 Lloyd's Rep. 191, at 202.
86. See *Leslie Shipping Co. Ltd v. Welstead* [1921] 3 K.B. 420 where in a time charterparty the shipowner was entitled to recover arrears of hire charges due but unpaid up to the date of the shipowner's acceptance of the repudiation. See also *Chatterton v. Maclean* [1951] 1 All E.R. 561 and *Hyundai Heavy Industries Co. Ltd v. Papadopulos* [1980] 1 W.L.R. 1129.
87. [1991] 2 Lloyd's Rep. 191 at 202.
88. [1998] Lloyd's Rep. IR 377.
89. See s.84(2) of the Marine Insurance Act 1906.
90. [1998] Lloyd's Rep. IR 377, at 389.

scenario, the insurer would have been entitled to the part of the premium, which fell due before the breached occurred. It should, however, be borne in mind that determining whether the risk is divisible is a rather problematic task and the existence of commercial useage in that area could be a decisive factor. In *Meyer v. Gregson*[91] a ship insured "at and from Jamaica to Liverpool, warranted to sail on or before the first of August", did not sail until 1 September, so that, by this breach of warranty, the insurer was off risk. The assured, however, contended that the risk was divisible, and had attached upon the ship while she lay in port at Jamaica before 1 August; he, however, gave no proof of a useage of trade to consider such risks divisible, or to make a rateable return of the premium for the risk after leaving the island. Under these circumstances, the court held that there could be no apportionment.[92]

When a marine warranty which relates in time to circumstances at the inception of the risk, is breached; the effect of such a breach cannot be determined by virtue of s.33(3) of the Act. This is because by the time such a warranty is breached, the insurer is not on risk. Accordingly, he could not be discharged from liability. Breach of a marine warranty which relates in time to circumstances at the inception of the risk will result in the insurer never coming on risk. In *Woolmer v. Muilman*[93] the insured vessel was warranted neutral and was lost by perils of the sea. In the trial, there was evidence to the effect that she was not neutral property and Lord Mansfield said:[94] 5.25

> "This was no contract, for the man insured neutral property and this was not neutral property."

Similarly, in a non-marine case, *Thomson v. Weems*,[95] compliance with a warranty of this type was considered as "a condition precedent" to the attaching of the risk by Lord Blackburn. There, the assured in a life policy had warranted the accuracy of the statements made by him in the proposal form. When the evidence clearly proved that the assured's statement as to his temperance in his habits was untrue, the policy was held null and void. The fact that breach of a warranty of this type prevents the contract from coming into existence might have an impact on the position of the premium paid in advance. In such a case, it seems likely that the premium is refundable due to total failure of consideration unless the assured acted fraudulently.[96]

5B.4 Waiver of breach

The term "waiver" is generally used in the law of insurance to describe an intentional act which relinquishes a right or privilege otherwise afforded to the insurer either by statute or contract.[97] As examined in the previous part, in case of breach of a 5.26

91. (1784) 3 Dougl. 402.
92. *Cf. Gale v. Machell* 2 Park Ins. 797 where the risk was held to be divisible in an "at and from policy" due to the existence of a commercial useage.
93. (1763) 3 Burr. 1419.
94. (1763) 3 Burr. 1419, at 1420.
95. (1884) 9 App. Cas. 671, at 684.
96. See s.84(1) of the Marine Insurance Act 1906.
97. *Hoxie v. Howe Insurance Co.* (1864) 32 Conn. 21.

breach of a marine warranty the insurer is either discharged from liability automatically or prevented from coming on risk.[98] The commercial realities may require the insurer to waive the breach of warranty[99] and accordingly withdraw a right which is afforded by the Act.[100]

5.27 Such a waiver may take place either before or after the occurrence of the breach. With an express term, which appears in the policy, the insurer may agree in advance not to rely on breach of a warranty as a defence. In marine insurance, this kind of clause usually intends to waive breach of implied warranties, i.e. warranties of seaworthiness or cargoworthiness, which are incorporated into the policy by the Act.[101] The language employed in a term of this type must be "*express*, *pertinent* and *apposite*" in order to achieve the desired result.[102] The loose drafting of such a clause was one of the main reasons for litigation in *HIH Casualty & General Insurance Ltd v. New Hampshire Insurance et al.*[103] There, one of the issues raised was whether the breach of warranty in the underlying contract was waived with an express term. The reinsurers contended that the re-assured (HIH) was not liable to the underlying assured (LDT) on various grounds, some of which can be categorised as coverage issues and some of which can be categorised as breach of warranty issues. It was the case of HIH that one of the clauses which appeared in the underlying contract had waived breach of warranty and accordingly there was no defence to LDT's claim. This ultimately would mean that the reinsurer would not have had a defence against HIH. The clause in question was worded as:

> "To the fullest extent permissible by applicable law, the Insurer hereby agrees that it will not seek to or be entitled to avoid or rescind this Policy or reject any claim hereunder . . . on the grounds of . . . non-disclosure or misrepresentation by any person or any other similar grounds. The Insurer irrevocably agrees not to assert and waives any and all defences and rights of set-off and/or counterclaim (including without limitation any such rights acquired by assignment or otherwise) which it may have against the Assured or which may be available so as to deny payment of any amount due hereunder in accordance with the express terms hereof."

The Court of Appeal, affirming David Steel J's judgment,[104] held that this clause was not sufficient to waive breach of warranty. The subject matter of the first sentence is "non-disclosure or misrepresentation". In other words, the type of defence attempted to be excluded by this clause is extra-contractual. On the other hand, breaches of warranty are breaches of the contract itself. Accordingly, they could not be regarded as constituting "similar grounds". As for the second sentence, HIH contended that the word "defences" should be read separately from the rest and

98. The former is the case for warranties which relate to a period after the attachment of the risk, and the latter is the effect of breach for warranties which relate to a period before the attachment of the risk.

99. See s.34(3) of the Marine Insurance Act 1906.

100. Various factors, such as the commercial importance to the insurer of retaining the particular assured as a client or the climate in the market, might require the insurer to take such a step.

101. Note that breach of the implied warranty of legality cannot be waived, as the issue is one of public policy rather than private contract. See *Gedge & Others v. Royal Exchange Assurance Corporation* [1900] 2 Q.B. 214.

102. *Quebec Marine Insurance Co. v. Commercial Bank of Canada* (1870) LR 3 PC 234, at 243.

103. [2001] 2 All ER (Comm) 39. Facts of this case have already been pointed out while evaluating the incorporation of express warranties into insurance contracts.

104. [2001] Lloyd's Rep. IR 224.

accordingly included "breach of warranty defences". The Court of Appeal rejected this argument as well. Rix LJ summarised the view of the Court of Appeal:[105]

"In my judgment, however, it is much more natural to read [the word defences] as part of the overall phrase 'defences and rights of set-off and/or counterclaim'. It is natural to think of a set-off as a defence (even if it can also be thought of as a right), and a counterclaim as a right (even if it may also give rise to a defence). In my view the word 'defences' is primarily connected with 'set-off' and the word 'rights' is primarily connected with 'counterclaim'. In any event, it is plain that a set-off may give a defence, and that is sufficient to explain the language of the sentence. Moreover, that explanation would be consistent with the closing language of the sentence – 'so as to deny payment of any amount due hereunder in accordance with the express terms hereof'. If there was prima facie a good claim ('amount due hereunder' etc), a defence of set-off or a right of counterclaim might result in a valid denial of payment of a sum otherwise due. Where, however, a breach of warranty occurs before a loss within the cover, it is difficult to say that that breach provides a defence against an amount 'due hereunder in accordance with the express terms hereof'. It would be more natural to say that by reason of the breach of warranty there was nothing due, and that that was so precisely because of the contract's 'express terms'."[106]

Fortunately, express clauses which are incorporated into Institute Cargo Clauses are capable of waiving breach of warranties of seaworthiness and cargoworthiness in an unambiguous manner. The reason behind such a practice is clear. A cargo policy is effected between the cargo interests[107] and the insurer. Insisting on the implied warranties of seaworthiness and cargoworthiness creates injustice for the cargo interest, as he has usually no means of knowing the state of the vessel carrying his goods. Standard Institute Clauses on cargo, accordingly, waive breach of these warranties with the following wording:[108] 5.28

"The Underwriters waive any breach of the implied warranties of seaworthiness of the ship and fitness of the ship to carry the subject matter insured to destination, unless the Assured or their servants are privy to such unseaworthiness or unfitness."

As can be clearly seen, the insurer, with an express term, precludes himself from relying on breach of implied warranties of seaworthiness and cargoworthiness provided that the cargo interests and their servants are not aware of that state of the vessel.

Breach of a marine warranty could also be waived beforehand by the use of held covered clauses, which are usually, but not invariably, drafted subject to two conditions: that immediate notice be given to the insurer and that any variation in conditions or additional premium be agreed.[109] With these clauses, the insurer agrees, prior to a breach of warranty, not to take any action against the assured if he chooses to operate the clause by satisfying the conditions stated above. Put another way, the 5.29

105. [2001] 2 All ER (Comm) 39 at 71.

106. For similar problems caused by vague wording of waiver clauses see *HIH Casualty v. Chase Manhattan Bank* [2001] Lloyd's Rep. IR 191 and *Kumar v. AGF Insurance Ltd* [1999] Lloyd's Rep. IR 147.

107. This person is either the cargo owner or consignee, depending on the terms of the original sales contract.

108. See cl 5.2 of ICC (type A, B and C).

109. Clause 3 of Institute Time Clauses (Hulls) (1995) is a typical held covered clause:

"Held covered in case of any breach of warranty as to cargo, trade, locality, towage, salvage services or date of sailing provided notice be given to the Underwriters immediately after receipt of advices and any amended term of cover and any additional premium required by them be agreed."

general object of such a clause is to give the assured the right to elect to maintain cover in circumstances when otherwise it would be terminated by the insurer.[110]

5.30 The broad wording of s.34(3) of the Act allows the insurer to waive the breach of a marine warranty even after such breach occurs. When breach of warranty was equated to breach of a condition in general contract law,[111] after the occurrence of such breach, the insurer had a right to affirm or repudiate the contract. Had he affirmed the contract, he would have been deemed to elect to waive breach of a marine warranty. Put another way, waiver of a warranty by election was an option available to the insurer under the remedy available. At that time, silence or delay to act after a warranty is breached could mean that the insurer had elected to waive breach of a warranty.[112]

Has the automatic discharge remedy adopted by the House of Lords in *The Good Luck* changed the legal position in relation to waiver by election? Certain leading academic studies[113] suggest that the remedy of automatic discharge makes it impossible to apply waiver by election in the context of breach of warranty. An assured who wishes to contend that the insurer has waived a breach of warranty, according to these studies, must establish waiver by estoppel, which invariably means equitable estoppel. This view has recently found judicial support. In *J Kirkaldy & Sons Ltd v. Walker*[114] Longmore, J said:[115]

"Section 33 of the Marine Insurance Act provides for the insurer to be discharged from liability as from the date of breach of warranty. It is, therefore, apparent that no question of election arises although by s.34(3) the insurers may waive the breach. Since the breach of warranty does not give rise to any election by the insurer e.g. to choose to keep the contract on foot, the doctrine of waiver by election has no application."[116]

5.31 Waiving breach of a marine warranty by means of estoppel is rather different to waiver by election. First, although an unequivocal presentation on the part of the insurer is required in both of them, the nature of this presentation is different in character in the two cases. Accordingly, in order to found waiver by election the conduct itself or the circumstances must demonstrate objectively or unequivocally that the insurer is making an informed choice of not alleging breach of warranty; in the context of estoppel, on the other hand, it is sufficient that the conduct demonstrates an unequivocal choice to the effect that the breach of warranty defence is not going to be relied on.[117] In this respect, issuing or renewing the policy after the breach of

110. The legal nature and scope of these clauses have been evaluated by Professor Thomas in Chapter 1 of this book.

111. *CTN Cash & Carry v. General Accident Fire & Life Insurance Corporation* [1989] 1 Lloyd's Rep. 299.

112. *Allen v. Robles (Compagnie Parisiene de Garantie, Third Party)* [1969] 1 W.L.R. 1193 and *Wahbe Tamari & Sons and Jaffa Trading Co. v. Colprogenca – Socidade General de Fibras Gabes e Products Colonial Ltd* [1969] 2 Lloyd's Rep. 18.

113. Clarke, *The Law of Insurance Contracts* (1999 3rd edn., London: LLP), at para. 20–7A; Longmore, Birds, Owen (eds.), *MacGillivray and Parkington on Insurance Law* (1997 9th edn. London: Sweet & Maxwell), at para. 10–98.

114. [1999] Lloyd's Rep. IR 410

115. *Ibid.*, at 422.

116. More recently, Aikens J, in *Brownsville Holdings Ltd and Another v. Adamjee Insurance Co. Ltd (The Milasan)* [2000] 2 Lloyd's Rep. 458, hereinafter referred to as *The Milasan*, at 467, expressed the same view.

117. See comments made by Mance J, in *Insurance Corporation of the Channel Islands Royal Insurance (UK) Ltd v. The Royal Hotel Ltd and Others* [1998] Lloyd's Rep. 151, at 162. The difference between waiver by election and waiver by estoppel in this context has also been pointed out by Lord Goff in *Motor Oil Hellas*

warranty or in some cases advice given by the insurer to the assured about loss prevention in future (after the warranty is breached) may amount to an unequivocal representation which is sufficient to found waiver by estoppel. Second, being a concept of equity, the law of estoppel[118] looks chiefly at the situation of the person relying on the estoppel.[119] As a consequence of this, the knowledge of the person sought to be estopped could be immaterial. Therefore, in cases where the insurer makes an unequivocal representation to the effect that he intends to keep the contract on foot and there are difficulties in establishing that the insurer or his agents had knowledge of the breach, an estoppel might nevertheless arise.[120] Finally, in order to establish the existence of a promissory estoppel, it is essential to show that the assured acted in reliance on the promise of the insurer that the legal rights arising from the breach of the warranty would not be enforced.[121] Pure reliance is not sufficient, as a final element the assured must prove that he has suffered detriment as a result of the insurer's representation.[122]

As a final point, it should be borne in mind that after the adoption of the automatic discharge remedy, silence or delay to act after a warranty is breached could not constitute a sufficiently unequivocal representation so as to found waiver on the part of the insurer. The insurer is now automatically discharged from liability in case of breach of a warranty and his silence or failure to act shows that he has elected to rely on the defence afforded to him and has no intentions of waiving this remedy. 5.32

5C. CRITICAL ASSESSMENT OF THE WARRANTY REGIME: A CASE FOR REFORM?

5C.1 Unfairness arising from harshness of the automatic discharge remedy

As stated earlier, the remedy of automatic discharge afforded by s.33(3) operates in cases where a marine warranty is breached regardless of the existence of a causal link between the breach and loss. This could lead to unfair results as far as the assured is 5.33

(Corinth) Refineries SA v. Shipping Corporation of India (The Kanchenjunga) [1990] 1 Lloyd's Rep. 391, at 399:

"... Furthermore, the representation itself is different in character in the two cases. The party making his election is communicating his choice whether or not to exercise a right, which has become available to him. The party to an equitable estoppel is representing that he will not in future enforce his legal rights. ..."

118. Since estoppel is an equitable remedy, it will not assist a party who is himself guilty of continuing misconduct. Accordingly, the assured could not allege that the insurer is estopped from relying on breach of warranty in cases where he has committed fraudulent activities after the representations being relied upon are made. For a similar case in a different context, see *Baghbadrani v. Commercial Union Assurance Co.* [2001] Lloyd's Rep. IR 94.

119. *Craine v. Colonial Mutual Fire Insurance Co.* [1920] 28 CLR 305, at 327, *per* Isaacs J.

120. There must still be some concern with the insurer's knowledge, however, for, if the assured believes that the insurer is unaware of his breach of warranty, he will find it difficult to convince a court that he justifiably relied on the insurer's not pleading a breach, of which the insurer was unaware, and that the insurer had been estopped.

121. *M'Millan v. Accident Insurance Co.* 1907 SC 484. This point has recently been stressed once again by Aikens J, in *The Milasan* [2000] 2 Lloyd's Rep. 458, at 467.

122. *Western Canada Accident & Guarantee Insurance Co. v. Parrot* (1921) 61 SCR 595. For instance, not seeking alternative cover was held to be sufficient to establish detriment in *Hargett v. Gulf Insurance Co.* 55 P 2d 12.

concerned. For example, let us assume that a dry-dock was insured for a period of 12 months and in the policy it was warranted by the assured that a condition survey would have been carried out within 30 days after the commencement of the policy. The survey was carried out 45 days after the commencement of the policy; however, 10 months later the insured dry-dock was lost as a result of a storm. It is obvious that the express warranty in the policy was breached since the survey was delayed for 15 days. Such a warranty is clearly intended to prevent an increase of risk of casualties. However, its breach, in our hypothetical scenario, had no effect whatsoever on the occurrence of loss. The loss would still have occurred even though the condition survey had been carried out within 30 days after the attachment of the policy. Nevertheless, when the assured makes a claim for total loss, it is likely that his claim would be rejected on the ground of breach of warranty. This hypothetical scenario illustrates that the current warranty regime creates unfairness for the assured as the insurer is provided with an opportunity to deny liability on technical grounds.

5.34 It has been submitted that in practice, particularly in hull insurance, insurers have a tendency of not relying on breach of warranty defence where the breach has not affected the claim.[123] However, the recent case law is to the contrary. In *The Milasan*[124] the insurer relied on an express warranty which required professional skippers and crew to be in charge at all times. While having a professional skipper and crew in charge at the time of loss, during the currency of the policy for a period of two months, there was no one whose sole and exclusive job was nominally that of master of the vessel. Breach of this express warranty had surely not affected the claim, but, nevertheless, was successfully raised by the insurer in *The Milasan*.[125] Therefore, it is not an accurate observation that insurers do not rely on breach of warranty defence if there is no link between the breach and loss. Particularly in cases where loss of the vessel is regarded as "suspicious", the insurer usually adopts all possible defences available, including breach of warranty defence even though there is no link between breach and loss, in order to strengthen his position.

5C.2 Intervention of courts and further complexities caused

5.35 Construction is the only weapon courts have against the draconian remedy afforded for breach of a marine warranty. It has been observed that courts developed various techniques of construction to relieve the harsh effects of the rule requiring strict compliance with warranties. These techniques, despite achieving fairness from the assured's point of view, create a great deal of uncertainty in this area. The restrictions imposed by the courts on the effects of warranty provisions through construction and problems caused thereby will be examined in this section.

5.36 Courts sometimes construe insurance policy provisions which might be viewed or intended by insurers as warranties to be some other type of coverage term, usually suspensory provisions or terms delimiting (describing) risk. The effect of a suspensory provision is that the operation of the policy is suspended for the period

123. Brown, *Marine Insurance: Hull Practice (Vol. 3)*, (1993 2nd edn. London: Witherby), at p.427.

124. [2000] 2 Lloyd's Rep. 458

125. Apart from breach of warranty defence, the insurer successfully relied on wilful misconduct of the assured defence and a number of negative defences.

when the circumstances specified in the clause are not satisfied. Accordingly, the insurer is not liable for any loss which occurs during this period but, unlike breach of warranty, the validity of the insurance contract is not affected and the cover reattaches as soon as the original position is restored. Whether a provision is a warranty or a suspensory provision should be ascertained by interpreting the language used in the clause in question. The clause is a warranty if it contains a promise made by the assured. On the other hand, a clause which determines the scope of the contract by describing the boundaries of cover, should be regarded as a suspensory provision. Accordingly, in *Riverside Landmark Corporation v. Northumberland General Insurance*,[126] where a policy of marine insurance contained the words "covering whilst being towed in tandem by Irving Tug TBA from Quebec City to Tampico, Mexico", it was the view of the Canadian court that the words were descriptive of the risk and the policy was not invalidated, but the cover was suspended during the period when the vessels in question were not towed in tandem.[127]

The judgment of the Supreme Court of Canada in *Case Existological Laboratories Ltd v. Foremost Insurance Co. et al (The Bamcell II)*[128] has caused a great deal of confusion in identifying the nature of insurance provisions. *The Bamcell II* was a converted chip barge, used in oceanographic experiments. She was operated by compression of air, which could be admitted or released through valves on deck. Raising or lowering the air pressure caused the stern of the barge to rise or fall, thus allowing the *Bamcell II* to float or float off certain modules used in experiments. The vessel sank during daytime, as a result of the negligence of an employee who opened the air valves and failed to close later. The marine policy in the case contained the following clause: 5.37

"Warranted that a watchman is stationed on board the Bamcell II each night from 2200 hours to 0600 hours with instructions for shutting down all equipment in an emergency."

Such a watchman was never stationed on board the *Bamcell II* from the day after the inception of the policy until the accident. The underwriters gave evidence at the trial that this clause was intended to be a warranty and the risk was accepted on the basis that the assured would strictly comply with it. Accordingly, they contended that since the assured never placed a watchman on board from the first day after the inception of the risk, the warranty was breached and the insurer was discharged from liability under the policy from that moment even if the loss was unconnected with such a breach.

In the British Columbia Court of Appeal,[129] Lambert JA, concluded that the clause was a suspensory provision and not a warranty. The assured was, accordingly, allowed to recover under the policy as the loss occurred during daytime and not

126. [1984] 8 CCLI 118.

127. Clause 9 of Institute Container Clauses (Time) (1.1.87) is as an example of clauses of this type. This clause stipulates that each container is covered, including whilst on deck, within the sea and territorial limits specified in the Schedule. This means that the cover is suspended when the container is in port or at sea but outside the territorial limits specified in the Schedule and if it is damaged while in these areas the insurer is not liable at all. The cover, however, reattaches as soon as the container is at sea and in the territorial limits specified in the Schedule.

128. 133 DLR (3d) 727; affirmed by the Supreme Court of Canada [1983] 2 SCR 47 (sub nom *Century Insurance Co. of Canada v. Case Existological Laboratories Ltd)*, hereinafter referred to as *The Bamcell II*.

129. 133 DLR (3d) 727.

between the hours stated in the clause. When reaching this decision, he cited the following passage from *MacGillivray & Parkington on Insurance Law*:[130]

"Clauses of this nature are sometimes referred to as 'warranties descriptive of the risk' or 'delimiting the risk.' This usage is not an accurate one, but it serves as a remainder that a court may be prepared to construe a clause as one descriptive of the risk even though the word 'warranty' or 'warranted' appears in it, as where a car was 'warranted used only for the following purposes.' That case illustrates the point that there is no magic in the word 'warranted' which is frequently used with considerable ambiguity in policies."

5.38 The primary cases relied upon by the editors of *MacGillivray & Parkington* in the above passage concerning suspensory provisions, are the cases of *Farr v. Motor Traders' Mutual Insurance Society Ltd*[131] and *Provincial Insurance Co. Ltd v. Morgan & Foxon.*[132] In *Farr v. Motor Traders' Mutual Insurance Society Ltd,*[133] the assured ran a taxi business, using two taxis. On applying for insurance for the use of these vehicles, he warranted in the proposal form that each vehicle would be driven for only one shift each day. The policy was issued in February 1918 and the statement remained true until August 1918, when one of the taxis was driven for two shifts for one day or a little longer. Later, after this practice had ceased, an accident occurred. It was held that the term in question was a suspensory provision and not an express warranty, so that the assured was entitled to recover for an accident happening at a time when the term was being complied with. Similarly, in *Provincial Insurance Co. Ltd v. Morgan & Foxon*[134] the proposal form contained a clause which warranted that the insured lorry was to be used only for carrying coal. It was, in fact, occasionally used to carry timber instead of or as well as coal. The lorry had an accident shortly after offloading a quantity of timber. The Court of Appeal (whole conclusion was upheld by the House of Lords), held that the clause was not a warranty but a clause delimiting the risk. Accordingly, the insurers were held liable as the lorry had not been carrying timber when damaged.[135] Admittedly, there is a similarity between these two cases and *The Bamcell II* in the sense that the obligations in question required compliance on a routine or repeated basis. Nevertheless, the author believes that *The Bamcell II* can be distinguished from both of these cases. The common feature in *Farr v. Motor Traders'* and *Provincial Insurance Co. Ltd v. Morgan & Foxon* is the fact that the provisions in question were breached only for a short period of time. By contrast, in *The Bamcell II* the assured was in breach of the clause in question from the beginning of insurance period until the date of loss. In fact, he had never complied with the provision and had no intentions of complying with it.

5.39 In the Court of Appeal, Lambert, JA, suggested that in order to determine the status of the clause in question, the intention of the parties when incorporating it into the policy must be observed. He accordingly said:[136]

"[T]he parties cannot have intended that if the watchman was late one night, or even missed a

130. (1975 6th edn.), at pp.263–264.
131. [1920] 3 K.B. 669.
132. [1933] A.C. 240, HL.
133. [1920] 3 K.B. 669.
134. [1933] A.C. 240, HL.
135. See also *Roberts v. Anglo-Saxon Insurance Co.* (1927) 27 LIL Rep. 313.
136. 133 DLR (3d) 727, at 740–741.

night, then the insurers should be discharged from liability for the remainder of the term of the policy. . . . [I]t is my opinion that the clause in this case under the heading of 'special conditions' is a clause which limits the risk and not a true warranty which discharges the insurer. The limitation on the risk has no effect in this case."[137]

This observation, which makes sense in the first instance, is subject to some severe objections. Lambert JA has not cited any authority or given any explanation to support this statement. With all respect to his decision, the author is of the opinion that the presumed intention of parties when incorporating the clause in question cannot be ascertained simply by judging its fairness. As was stated by Hobhouse J (as he then was) in *Cooke and Arkwright v. Hayden*:[138]

"It is not the courts' function, by process of construction, to make for the parties a reasonable contract which they have not made for themselves."

The assured in *The Bamcell II* was in a position to bargain the conditions of the insurance contract. If he had doubts about the fulfilment of the obligations stated in the clause, he should not have agreed in the first place. Besides, he was in breach of the said clause from the beginning of the insurance period and never had any intentions of complying with it. Thus, defining the clause in question as a clause delimiting the risk would mean rewarding the assured, who had not judged his position accurately and was in breach of an obligation he undertook continuously from the inception of the policy.[139]

For a considerable amount of time, it was thought that *The Bamcell II* would not 5.40
find support in English courts so the distinction between warranties and other similar terms would remain clear. However, recent developments in non-marine insurance are to the contrary. In *Kler Knitwear Ltd v. Lombard General Insurance Co. Ltd*[140] Morland J, by citing *The Bamcell II*, held that a clause by which the assured warranted that the sprinkler systems at its premises shall be inspected within 30 days of renewal was a suspensory provision and not a warranty. In this case, the assured had renewed a property and business interruption policy, which contained the clause mentioned above. The inspection was carried out 60 days late and almost two months later the assured's premises suffered storm damage. When the assured sought to recover under the policy for damage to raw materials and finished goods and for disruption of business, the insurer asserted that the claim was barred for breach of warranty.

The reason behind the judgment of Morland J is clear. Had the clause in question been regarded as a "warranty" the assured would have been put into an odd position as the insurer would have been entitled to reject the claim even though no link

137. Richie J, in the Supreme Court of Canada, concurring with the findings of Lambert JA, said, [1983] 2 SCR 47, at 55–56:

"The clause would only have been effective if the loss had occurred between 2200 hours and 0600 hours, and it was proved that there was no watchman stationed aboard during these hours. To this extent, the condition contained in the clause constituted a limitation of the risk, but it was not a warranty."

138. [1987] 2 Lloyd's Rep. 579 at 582.

139. This clause seems to satisfy all the tests highlighted by Rix LJ, in *HIH Casualty & General Insurance Ltd v. New Hampshire Insurance Co. et al.* [2001] 2 All E.R. 39. The term seems to go to the root of the transaction as the issue regulated by it is a safety issue. As a result of this, it bears materially on the risk of loss. Finally, damages would be an inadequate remedy if a loss is occasioned due to lack of such a watchman on board.

140. [2000] Lloyd's Rep. IR 47

between the breach and loss existed. In order to justify his judgment, Morland J cited the *dicta* of Saville LJ in *Hussain v. Brown*[141] where he said:

> "... it must be remembered that a continuing warranty is a draconian term. As I have noted, the breach of such a warranty produces an automatic cancellation of cover, and the fact that a loss may have no connection at all with that breach is simply irrelevant. In my view, if the underwriters want such a protection, then it is up to them to stipulate for it in clear terms."

5.41 There is no doubt that the use of the term "warranted" does not necessarily indicate that the clause in question is a warranty.[142] On the other hand, clauses very similar, both in structure and function, to the one in *Kler Knitwear Ltd v. Lombard General Insurance Co. Ltd* have always been regarded as warranties. For instance, the wording of the Condition Survey Warranty produced by the Joint Hull Committee[143] is very close to the one in *Kler Knitwear Ltd v. Lombard General Insurance*. This warranty reads as:

> "Warranted vessel be subject to a Condition Survey, at owner's expense, by the Salvage Association within thirty days and all recommendations complied with.
> It being understood that the surveyor's recommendations may include the necessity that this survey be upgraded to a Structural Condition Survey (JH 722) as per warranty attached."

5.42 Similarly, there was no dispute as to the warranty status of a clause which was designed to perform a very similar function and worded in a similar manner in *J Kirkaldy & Sons Ltd v. Walker*.[144] The clause in question read:

> "Towage of the vessel to be undertaken by TSA Tugs Ltd, Towage approval survey – applies to both tows – and condition survey to be performed by Surveyor Peter Curtis and all recommendations complied with prior sailing."

5.43 Furthermore, there is a significant distinction between *Kler Knitwear Ltd v. Lombard General Insurance* and suspensory provision cases such as *Farr v. Motor Traders' Mutual Insurance Society Ltd* and *Provincial Insurance Co. Ltd v. Morgan & Foxon*. In the former, the obligation in the clause was to do a specified single act within a specified time while in latter cases the obligation which was broken related to compliance on a routine or repeated basis.

5.44 Therefore, it is clear that there is a new trend amongst judges to seek alternative interpretations for clauses which broadly resemble warranties. However, this approach is adopted at the expense of the fine distinction which exists between warranties and suspensory provisions. Without a doubt, clauses intending to impose a warranty status are going to be challenged more often in future in the light of *The Bamcell II* and *Kler Knitwear Ltd v. Lombard General Insurance* and this would create more uncertainty in this area.

5.45 Even though there is no dispute as to the warranty status of a clause in question, it has been observed on numerous occasions that the courts are ready to interpret the obligations imposed by warranties narrowly in order to overcome the strictness of the

141. [1996] 1 Lloyd's Rep. 627, at 630.

142. However, it must not be thought that the use of these words are of no importance. They may be good evidence of the parties' intention to create an express warranty. As was stated in *Ellinger & Co. v. Mutual Life Insurance Co. of New York* [1905] 1 K.B. 31, the use of the word "warranted" shows *prima facie* that the parties understood that a breach of it should be a permanent or temporary bar to the insurer's liability.

143. JH 115 (1993)

144. [1999] Lloyd's Rep. IR 410.

exact compliance doctrine. For instance, in *Hide v. Bruce*[145] an express warranty, which required the insured vessel to commence the intended adventure with 20 guns, was held to be satisfied, even though there were 20 guns but not the men necessary to work them on board. Similarly, it was held in *Muller v. Thompson*[146] that a warranty that the vessel would carry a particular cargo did not preclude the assured from carrying additional cargo. This type of interpretation causes two types of problem. First, adopting a narrow construction for warranties might lead to results which contradict the main policies behind insurance. From the insurer's point of view, risk prediction is one of the main elements of insurance and the premium is adjusted according to the extent of the risk undertaken. Since warranties serve a function of determining the extent of the risk, interpreting them narrowly will, though unintentionally, make the insurers undertake a risk which they would not have accepted or would have accepted with a higher premium had they known that such a construction for the express warranty would have been adopted. Second, the law in this area becomes elusive due to the contradicting interpretations adopted.

To sum up, it is obvious that the continuing intervention of courts by adopting alternative interpretations to warranty provisions occurs due to the harshness of the remedy adopted in case of breach of a warranty. For instance, in *The Bamcell II* it would not have been necessary to classify the clause requiring a watchman to be on board every night as a clause delimiting the risk, had the breach of warranty not had draconian results. In that case, there was no link whatsoever between the breach of watchman clause and the loss of the barge. The same could be said for *Kler Knitwear Ltd v. Lombard General Insurance*. The fact that the survey of the sprinkler system was 60 days late could not have contributed to the storm damage. The warranty regime, and particularly the opportunity afforded to the insurer to deny liability even though there is no link between the breach, should be reconsidered in order to prevent further complexities being added to law by means of contradictory interpretation techniques. 5.46

5C.3 Position of London marine insurance market: significance of legal rules in competition for market share

The law of marine insurance is a part of commercial law. Commercial law has a certain peculiarity. It grows and succeeds when it is closely related to the commercial practices that it seeks to serve. This has been the case for marine insurance law as well and the interrelation between the market and the lawyers – both legislators and judges – has been constant and productive throughout the years. For this reason, it is not possible to evaluate the possibility of a reform in this area without considering the position of the market. 5.47

Statistics reveal that the London market's leading position in the marine insurance business has been under threat for some time. While 31.2 per cent of the world's marine insurance business was written in London market in 1991, this figure came down to 27 per cent in 1994. The drop continued and by 1997 the London market's 5.48

145. (1773) 3 Doug. K.B. 213.
146. (1811) 2 Camp. 610.

share of world marine insurance business was down to 21 per cent.[147] There are a number of factors behind this decline. One reason is that many countries today prevent direct insurance business from being placed outside their own national markets for foreign exchange reasons.[148] This is particularly the case for cargo insurance, and as a result of this more business has been retained by local markets.[149]

5.49 Another reason is the cautiousness of the underwriters in the London market after the bad underwriting years of the late 1980s. Numerous catastrophes which occurred during those years[150] made the underwriters more selective in accepting insurance. In the early 1990s, underwriters in the London market chose not to provide cover for certain types of vessel, usually those involving high risks. In this way, the market missed the opportunity of expanding its capacity to the developing countries.[151]

5.50 However, the main reason for the London market losing its market share is intense competition coming from other markets, including France, Germany, Switzerland, Italy, Scandinavia and the USA.[152] There are reports suggesting that the Norwegian insurance market in particular managed to get a bigger share of the world's hull business. The success of the Norwegian market lies mainly in the fact that it has succeeded in developing strong links with different interests around the world and attracting a great deal of foreign business.[153] Without a doubt, the hesitation of the London market in underwriting insurance for high risks in the early 1990s played a crucial role in the success of the Norwegian market; however, it is submitted that its main advantage was the assured-friendly legal rules adopted in insurance policies.[154] Marine insurance business has an international character and the figures which compose the demand side of this business are quite flexible in choosing the market in which they will obtain cover. Their main interest lies in obtaining the lowest available market rate on the best terms possible. In this respect, provided that the premium rate is compatible with other rival markets, insurance conditions are an important element

147. The figures have been obtained from Association of British Insurers, *Insurance: Facts, Figures and Trends* (1997, 1998, 1999 and 2000).

148. See the paper delivered by Jenkins, "Forecasting Changes in the World's Marine Insurance Market and Predicting London's Place in it in the Long Term", at a conference on the Marine Insurance Market, organised by IIR Ltd, in 1996.

149. For instance, in Hong Kong marine insurance market, a country which with strict regulations prevents certain type of insurance being placed in other markets, cargo business has increased by HK $362.5m between 1991 and 1993. The figures are taken from, DYP Group Newsletters, *Marine Business From Around the World* (1995) Marine Insurance Report No. 136, p.125.

150. The losses of Piper Alpha, Exxon Waldez, Hurricane Hugo, Philips Petroleum and Arca Baker occurred in 1988 and 1989.

151. For instance, according to the statistics compiled by the UNCTAD secretariat on the basis of data supplied by Lloyd's Maritime Information Services (London), the gross tonnage of vessels owned by developing countries of Asia has increased by 44.8m (an increase of 279.2 per cent) in 16 years, from 1980–1996. During the same period, the gross tonnage of vessels owned by developing countries of America and Europe has shown an increase of 7.2 and 0.5m respectively. (Source: UNCTAD, *Review of Maritime Transport 1997*, RMT(97/1)).

152. Association of British Insurers, *Insurance: Facts, Figures and Trends*, November 2000, at p.30.

153. Marine insurance markets which intend to extend their market share usually attempt to attract foreign business.

154. This point has been stressed on numerous occasions by Professor Hans Jacob Bull, when the author found an opportunity to consult him during the Marine Insurance Conference organised by The European Institute of Maritime and Transport Law at Antwerp in November 1999. Professor Bull was the chairman of the Committee, which revised the Marine Insurance Plan of 1964 and drafted the Norwegian Marine Insurance Plan (NMIP) of 1996

in the competition for market shares.[155] A recent example, which shows the relation between insurance conditions and marine business underwritten, can be given from hull practice. In 1995, the Institute of London Underwriters published the new version of ITCH. These clauses contain more stringent provisions, from the assured's point of view, and offer a better regime for underwriters than the 1983 version.[156] However, mainly due to the current soft nature of the London market, these clauses have not been popular. The insurers cannot insist on these clauses because the assured usually threatens to go to an alternative market which offers better conditions. Today, a large number of policies in the London market are still written or renewed on the 1983 version of the clauses. Therefore, it can be concluded that selling harder conditions in a soft market is a difficult thing to do and, by analogy, it could be argued that the nature of insurance conditions are quite significant in marine insurance business. They can, indeed, be used as a tool to attract more business to a market.

Norwegian law does not have the concept of warranties, but the function that they 5.51
serve, namely determining the scope of risk, is achieved by specific and general alteration of risk provisions.[157] Compared to the warranty regime, these provisions provide a fairer regime for the assured. In case of breach or alteration of risk provisions the insurer is entitled to a defence only when there is a serious link between breach of these provisions and loss.[158] The same is also true for other aspects of marine insurance law. For example, the good faith duty of the assured is less stringent in Norwegian law than in English law.[159] Accordingly, it is no exaggeration to state that the fact that Norway's insurance provisions protect the assured's interest more than English law, both in terms of marine warranties and in other areas, helped to increase the market share of the Norwegian marine insurance market. This situation had been foreseen long ago by Antony Diamond QC, in his lecture delivered at the Third Annual Lecture of the Institute of Maritime Law of the University of Southampton on 31 October 1985 where, after examining the current regime of English marine warranties, he concluded:[160]

155. See, the paper delivered by Honka, "Harmonisation of Hull Insurance Contracts in Light of Seaworthiness and Safety Regulations", at Marine Insurance Symposium organised jointly by Comité Maritime International, Norwegian Maritime Law Association and Scandinavian Institute of Maritime Law at Oslo in June 1998. This paper could also be found in the book published by the Scandinavian Institute of Maritime Law, *MarIus 242* (1998) at p.165.

156. For a detailed analysis of the 1995 version of Institute Time Clauses (Hull), see Chapman and Jaffe [1996] IJOSL 202.

157. See the paper delivered by Wilhelmsen, "The Marine Insurance System in Civil Law Countries – Status and Problems", at Marine Insurance Symposium organised jointly by Comité Maritime International, Norwegian Maritime Law Association and Scandinavian Institute of Maritime Law at Oslo in June 1998. This paper could also be found in *MarIus 242* (1998) at p.15.

158. For example, §3–22 of the NMIP 1996 reads:

"The insurer is not liable for loss that is a consequence of the ship not being in a seaworthy condition, provided that the assured knew or ought to have known of the ship's defects at such a time that it would have been impossible for him to intervene."

159. According to §3–3 of the NMIP 1996 in case of non-disclosure during negotiations, other than fraudulent, the insurer will be liable for loss if the loss cannot be attributed to the undisclosed circumstances and if it could be assumed that the insurer would have effected the insurance although on other conditions.

160. Diamond [1985] LMCLQ 25 at 42.

"I referred at the beginning of this lecture to the common interest of all three groups, the market-place, the academics and the legal practitioners that the law of insurance should develop so that it meets the needs of the present and future and so that it provides for a fair distribution of rights and obligations as between assured and insurer. If the law fails to do this, then other rival centres of insurance will undoubtedly succeed where we have failed."

5.52 For many years any attempt to change the current warranty regime has been opposed on the ground that it would be undesirable to disturb the basis of legal certainty in English law by making substantial changes to the Marine Insurance Act 1906, in view of London's position as a leading centre for marine insurance in a competitive international market.[161] However, the analysis carried out above, reveals that a reform in the warranty regime would help the market to retain its leading position in the world's marine insurance business. In other words, a reform in the warranty regime would give the underwriters operating in the market the weapon required to fight against the competition coming from other markets.

5.53 In practice, it is quite common to see the modification of the remedy afforded in case of breach of a warranty by means of clauses drafted for this purpose.[162] This shows that the market elements have realised the problems caused by the warranty regime. What probably needs to be done is to reform the whole regime and give underwriters operating in the market a boost to attract more foreign business to the market.

5C.4 Position in other common law jurisdictions: winds of change

5.54 Non-marine warranties have gone through a transformation in some common law jurisdictions over the past two decades. For example, the Australian Insurance Contracts Act (ICA) 1984, which applies to all insurance contracts apart from marine, has introduced a different regime for warranties. Section 54(1) of the ICA 1984 denies the insurer a right to avoid liability simply by relying on a breach of warranty or some other condition of the insurance contract. Instead, this section provides that the insurer is limited to a reduction in liability to the assured by an amount representing the extent to which the insurer's interests were prejudiced. Termination is available under s.54(2) where the breach could reasonably be regarded as being capable of causing or contributing to a loss. Section 54(3) denies the insurer the right to terminate where the act was necessary to protect a person or property or where it was not reasonably possible for the assured to do the act. Similar developments have also taken place in New Zealand.[163]

5.55 Marine insurance law has been seen as "unique" and the reform of marine

161. See The Law Commission, *Insurance law: Non-Disclosure and Breach of Warranty*, Law Com No. 104, 1980, London: HMSO, at pp.14–18.

162. See *Martin Maritime Ltd v. Provident Capital Indemnity Fund Ltd (The Lydia Flag)* [1998] 2 Lloyd's Rep. 652 where suspension of the cover was made the remedy for not complying with an express warranty of seaworthiness.

163. See, s.11 of the Insurance Law Reform Act 1977 which provides:

"... the insured shall not be disentitled to be indemnified by the insurer by reason only of such provisions of the contract of insurance if the insured proves on balance of probabilities that the loss in respect of which the insured seeks to be indemnified was not caused or contributed to by the happening of such events or the existence of such circumstances."

warranties has not been considered in those jurisdictions. However, things have started to change over the last few years. For example, after numerous debates, Australia responded to the requests of pleasure craft owners by removing these craft from the scope of the Marine Insurance Act 1909 (Cth) (MIA) and treating insurance on them as a matter of general insurance.[164] Accordingly, breach of a warranty in a yacht policy does not automatically discharge the insurer from further liability any more.[165] More significantly, in January 2000, the Attorney-General asked the Australian Law Reform Commission to review the Marine Insurance Act 1909, taking into account the desirability of having a regime consistent with international practice in marine insurance, and whether any change might result in a competitive disadvantage for the Australian insurance industry. The Commission was also required to draft any appropriate legislation and an explanatory memorandum to give effect to its recommendations. The Commission responded with a report published on 30 April 2001.[166] This report recommends reform in many areas of marine insurance, and marine warranties are on the top of the reform list.[167] Warranties are discussed at length in Chapter 9 of the Report, where the Commission recommends the abolition of the concept. Whether this recommendation will lead to any alteration in law or not remains to be seen. However, it is a clear indication that a war against the draconian remedy adopted in cases of breach of marine warranty has been officially declared in Australia. A similar attitude towards marine warranties can be seen in Canada. It is a known fact that in the Canadian marine insurance market, certain modifications are made in marine policies effected for pleasure craft and most provisions of the Marine Insurance Act, including the one on breach of warranty, are contracted out. Moreover, *The Bamcell II*, clearly indicates that Canadian courts are prepared to adopt alternative interpretations to the warranty regime for the sake of achieving fairness for the assured. It is only in very rare circumstances that a Canadian court will find a marine policy to contain a promissory warranty. These circumstances will essentially be limited to situations where the warranty is material to the risk and the breach has a bearing on the loss.[168] The fact that courts relied heavily on *The Bamcell II* in a number of cases to give the clause in question a status other than a marine warranty could be used to support this argument. For instance, *The Bamcell II* was applied by the British Columbia Supreme Court in *Federal Business Development Bank v. Commonwealth Insurance*,[169] where it found that the clause "Warranted vessel to be laid up at the north foot of Columbia Street" was not a warranty since the parties did not intend it to be strictly complied with.[170]

These recent developments illustrate that a rebellion against the draconian remedy adopted in case of breach of a marine warranty has commenced in some other 5.56

164. See s.9(A) of the ICA 1984, which applies to contract of insurance entered into on or after 30 April 1998.

165. See s.54 of the ICA 1984.

166. The Australian Law Reform Commission, *Review of the Marine Insurance Act 1909*, Report No. 91, 2001. This report could be found at http://www.austlii.edu.au/au/other/alrc/publications/reports/91/.

167. The report also recommends substantial reforms on duty of utmost good faith, insurable interest, subrogation and some amendments to various sections of the Marine Insurance Act 1909.

168. See, the paper delivered by Giaschi, "Warranties in Marine Insurance", at a conference organised by Association of Marine Underwriters of British Columbia, Vancouver in April 1997.

169. (1983) 2 CCLI 200.

170. See also, *Shearwater Marine Ltd v. Guardian Insurance Co.* (1997) 29 BCLR (3d) 13.

common law jurisdictions. Being the nation which gifted the world an impressive statute in the area of marine insurance, it could be argued that the UK is under a moral obligation to take the first step and correct the parts of this Act which do not reflect the realities of the twenty-first century. Surely the regime of marine warranties is one of the areas which is in need of reform. A reform in English law would, without a doubt, be followed by other common law countries, since the resistance of the marine insurance industry which is against a change in law in those countries will be broken. Put another way, a reform in English law in this area will have a dual role. It will not only correct the deficiencies in its legal system, but also show the way forward to other jurisdictions which adopted its law.

5D. REFORM OF THE WARRANTY REGIME: THE WAY FORWARD

5.57 The previous section dealt with the need for reform. In this section, the author will analyse the possible extent of any reform. It is believed that the most effective way of reforming the law on marine insurance warranties is through statutory change.[171] Such reform would not only balance the relationship between the assured and insurer, but also be effective in showing the shift in the attitude of English marine insurance law towards the assured to the rest of the marine insurance world. In this way, it would assist English marine insurance law to retain the reputation which it has gained over many years in the eyes of international businessmen.

5.58 There are, however, certain obstacles facing legislative reform. It is a known fact that different elements in the market place, underwriters, assured, brokers, do not like governmental interference in market practice. Every time the possibility of such interference arises, they immediately forget their differences and agree on one thing if nothing else; namely, that parliamentary interference in commercial affairs is likely to be ill-formed at worst, or irrelevant at best, and is always unjustified.[172] Accordingly, legislative reform in this area is possible only if the market elements change their attitudes and welcome governmental interference. It is clear that certain market elements, particularly the assured and underwriters, have reasons to accept governmental interference in this case. The assured would surely welcome a reform which will afford them a better position and the underwriters would not wish to lose ground in the competition with other rival markets. There is, however, as indicated by Clarke,[173] a further problem which needs to be overcome in order to achieve legislative reform in this area. Parliament, with members who are subject to re-election, prefers to spend time and energy on legislation that is attractive to a significant section of the electorate. Put another way, there is almost no political will to force reform in the area of marine warranties, which is seen as something that is not

171. Statutes drafted to correct particular defects of existing legal institutions have been referred to as legislative microsurgery by Beatson [1997] CLJ 291, at 301.

172. Diamond [1985] LMCLQ 25, at 28.

173. See the paper delivered by him, "The Marine Insurance System in Common Law Countries – Status and Problems", at Marine Insurance Symposium organised jointly by Comité Maritime International, Norwegian Maritime Law Association and Scandinavian Institute of Maritime Law at Oslo in June 1998. This paper could also be found in, *MarIus 242* (1998) at p.63.

particularly relevant to the person in the street. However, the insurance industry, especially a large group of insurers who see their long-term benefit in reform, possesses the political power to inspire Parliament to put such a reform on its agenda.[174]

It is believed that most of the criticisms made to the current warranty regime could be avoided, if the insurer's right to rely on the breach of warranty defence is restricted. In other words, a link between the breach and loss needs to be established in order to achieve a fairer regime.[175] One could object to such a reform, contending that this would result in the erosion of safety standards by removing or reducing the incentive for compliance with warranties many of which are in the nature of undertakings on the part of the assured to observe precautions. Such an argument could be disputed on three grounds. First, many assureds observe prescribed precautions not out of any considerations relevant to their rights against the insurers but simply because they wish to preserve their property from loss or damage. Second, in most cases, observing prescribed precautions and protecting the subject-matter insured could be cheaper for the assured than facing litigation. Finally, it is not appropriate to make any direct link between public policy issues, such as erosion of safety standards and the contents of private marine insurance contracts. Such public policy issues are better left to national and international regulation. 5.59

In order to restrict the effect of the breach of warranty defence, the insurer might be required to show something more than mere violation of a marine warranty. A detailed analysis of other legal systems reveals that this could be achieved in two ways. One is that the insurer could be requested to demonstrate that the breach of warranty has increased the risk (*increase of risk criteria*).[176] The other is that the breach of warranty must contribute to the loss if violation is going to afford the insurer a defence. In other words, a causal link between the breach and loss needs to be established (*causal link criteria*).[177] It is believed that adoption of the latter approach is going to achieve the desired results in a less problematic manner. The reasons for choosing this measure over the "*increase of risk*" criteria need to be evaluated a bit further. 5.60

Adoption of increase of risk criteria could cause some further complexities. First of all, there could be a problem in identifying the meaning of "increase of risk". Does the term "risk" refer to a net risk, in which case an increase from the specified circumstances constituting a violation may be offset by decreases achieved. Or does it instead refer only to the effects of a breach, without regard to offsetting changes of 5.61

174. The Financial Services and Markets Act 2000 is a recent example illustrating how the commercial interest could accelerate the legislation making process.

175. The exact compliance rule, despite the lack of causal link between breach of a marine warranty and loss, has been regarded as "one of the less attractive features of English insurance law" by Lord Griffiths in *Forsikringsaktieselskapet Vesta v. Butcher* [1989] 1 All E.R. 402, at 406.

176. In some American states breach of warranty is not a defence for the insurer unless it increases the risk. *Windward Traders Ltd v. Fred S James & Co. of NY* 855 F 2d 814 (11th Circuit 1988); *Fireman's Fund v. Cox* 742 F Supp. 609 (MD Fla. 1989) (Florida Law); *United States Fire Insurance Co. v. Liberati* [1989] AMC 1436 (ND Cal. 1989) (California Law).

177. Some American courts construing marine insurance policies apply the rule that for breach of warranty to afford a defence to the insurer, the breach must be the *proximate cause* of loss. *Thann Long Partnership v. Highlands Insurance Co.* [1995] AMC 203 (5th Circuit 1994); *Home Insurance Co. v. Ciconnett* 179 F 2d 892 (6th Circuit 1950); *Coffey v. Indiana Lumberman's Mutual Insurance Co.* 372 F 2d 646 (6th Circuit 1967).

circumstance? Presumably, a narrower meaning than the total of all risks under the policy is intended. The kinds of change in circumstances which an assured might raise in mitigation of a violation are countless, and case-by-case comparative evaluation of total risk would be extremely expensive and wasteful. Furthermore, such an approach would make law fairly unpredictable. Even though it is assumed that we are concerned with only substantial increases in risk which arise from specific violations regardless of changes in net risk from all circumstances, the core question still needs to be answered. Is an increase of risk to be determined from the point of view of a standard or typical effect of a specific violation upon the risk assumed under policies of a given type, or from the point of view of the effect of the violation upon the risk assumed under the individual policy, taking into account all the particulars of the situation of that policy holder? While the latter seems like a more appropriate approach, as it incorporates subjective measures into the test, there could still be some situations where determining whether the risk has increased is not an easy question to answer. For instance, suppose in a hull policy there is an express warranty which requires the insured vessel to be subject to a condition survey within 30 days after the inception of the risk by the Salvage Association. If the vessel is made subject to a condition survey by another Association and is lost two days after this survey due to severe weather conditions, would the insurer be entitled to resist the claim on the grounds of breach of warranty? Even though the insurer succeeds in demonstrating an increase of risk arising as a result of breach of a warranty, this time another problem arises. Is a short period of increase sufficient to give the insurer a right to rely on the breach of warranty defence or should the increase persist for some substantial period of time? In the hypothetical scenario illustrated above, would a delay of one day in having the survey made be sufficient for the insurer to use the breach of warranty defence? If this were the case, then the solution would be very similar to the current regime, as the insurer would be given an opportunity to rely on a technical ground to deny liability. If, on the other hand, the increase should persist some substantial amount of time, litigation is bound to arise as to the meaning of the term "substantial amount of time". Could we, for example, assume that the risk has increased for a substantial amount of time if the condition survey is delayed by four days?

5.62 As can be seen, adoption of "increase of risk" criteria is not the ideal solution in establishing a link between breach and loss. A fairer warranty regime could be achieved by inserting a new sub-section to s.33 of the Act, stating that in cases where breach of a warranty is followed by a loss, the insurer is precluded from relying on s.33(3), if the assured, on a balance of probabilities, proves that the loss in respect of which he seeks to be indemnified was not caused or contributed to by the breach.[178]

Modification of s.33 of the Act in this manner would help the balance between the assured and insurer to be established. The insurer, in cases where the breach of warranty has caused or contributed to loss, will be discharged from further liability and in this way will be protected against serious alterations of the agreed coverage. The assured, on the other hand, will be given an opportunity to be indemnified,

178. A similar solution has been adopted by s.11 of the New Zealand Insurance Law Reform Act of 1977, which applies to non-marine insurance.

despite the breach of the warranty, in cases where he could show that there is no causal link between the breach and loss.

It should be noted that the proposed amendment to s.33 of the Act has no impact on cases where the breach of warranty does not cause any loss. Accordingly, in such a case, the insurer could still rely on s.33(3) to be discharged from further liability automatically, as soon as a warranty is breached. This situation could be justified by the fact that the insurer should not be compelled to continue to cover assureds who have committed breaches of warranty. This solution does not create any "unfairness" from the assured's point of view, because after he receives notification from the insurer stating that the latter wishes to terminate the insurance relationship, the assured has time to arrange new insurance cover. That the insurer is entitled to discharge himself automatically from liability in cases where no loss follows breach of a warranty is self-evident and needs not to be restated in s.33(3). *5.63*

The effect of the proposed amendment can be illustrated with a hypothetical scenario. Let us assume that in a cargo policy an express warranty requires the insured cargo, which would be carried on deck, to be surveyed immediately after loading. The survey is not carried out and the cargo is washed overboard during a storm. Expert reports reveals that the loss has occurred partly due to severe weather conditions and partly because the deck cargo was not secured properly, a defect which could have been identified had the cargo been condition surveyed. In such a case, there is no doubt that breach of warranty has contributed to loss. Accordingly, the insurer could be discharged from liability. In other words, the amendment to s.33 of the Act would not come to the rescue of the assured whose breach, to a certain degree, caused the loss. However, the position would have been completely different in a case where the above-mentioned cargo was partially lost as a result of fire which started in the engine room of the vessel and was then washed abroad during a storm. In such a case, the assured would be entitled to rely on the amended version of s.33 to claim partial loss for his cargo. The breach of warranty did not contribute to the partial loss, which occurred as a result of fire. However, the assured would not be able to claim indemnity for total loss of the cargo as breach of warranty in such a case contributed to the loss. *5.64*

The suggested modification of s.33 of the Act could be criticised on two grounds. It could be argued that such an alteration would cause further complexities in law and prolong litigation, since the courts will be asked to identify the causal link between breach and loss. Admittedly, this will impose an extra task on the parties and the courts; however, it can be argued that such a price is not too high considering the fact that it will lead to a fairer warranty regime. Furthermore, case law suggests that when applying other affirmative defences, e.g. s.55(2)(a) and 39(5) of the Act, where the courts are asked to determine whether the loss is attributable to a certain act, wilful misconduct of the assured, or to a certain state, unseaworthiness, they have not experienced any serious difficulties in dealing with the causation issue.[179] *5.65*

179. For example, in the application of s.39(5), the main problem is proving that the assured had knowledge about the unseaworthiness; identifying whether that particular unseaworthiness has caused loss is usually more straightforward. See *Manifest Shipping & Co. Ltd v. Uni-Polaris Insurance Co. Ltd & La*

5.66 Furthermore, one could argue that since the assured is under the burden of proof to show that breach has not caused or contributed to loss in order to preclude the insurer from relying on s.33(3), this will cause a flood of litigation because the insurer will deny liability even in cases where the loss is not connected to the breach. Anybody who brings such an argument is completely unaware of the realities of the market practice. The marine insurance market is a place where the insurer's reputation is largely dependent on the way he treats the assured. Without a doubt, any insurer who prefers to adopt such a course of action will not be approached again by many brokers. Also, there is no evidence to suggest that a flood of litigation has resulted in New Zealand from the passage of the Insurance Law Reform Act 1977, which adopted a similar solution.

5.67 As examined earlier, s.34(2) of the Marine Insurance Act 1906 provides that once a warranty is breached, it is not a defence to the assured that the breach has been remedied before loss. There is no doubt that this provision is in harmony with the automatic discharge rule adopted by s.33(3). However, once the automatic discharge rule is modified to the extent that the insurer is precluded from relying on it in cases where there is no causal link between the breach and loss, it is obvious that s.34(2) is going to be redundant. In a case where breach of warranty is remedied before loss, the assured will be able to recover in the absence of a causal link between remedied breach and loss. In this respect, adoption of a causal link requirement requires the repeal of s.34(2). Again, this point could be illustrated with a hypothetical scenario. Say there is an express warranty in a yacht policy requiring the insured vessel to be laid up and out of commission on 1 November; if the insured vessel was laid up on 4 November and became a total loss on 7 November, due to a fire started in the marina, the assured would be indemnified as the breach of warranty has not contributed to the loss. Accordingly, the new test enables the assured to be indemnified for breaches which have been remedied and have not contributed to the loss and this makes the existence of s.34(2) pointless.

5.68 A final point has to be made as to the extent of a possible reform in this area. Certain authorities are of the opinion that the context of warranties must be removed completely from marine insurance law[180] and certainly this was the view taken by the Australian Law Reform Commission in its recent report. However, such a dramatic measure might create more unfairness for the assured than the current regime. If the warranty regime is scrapped from marine insurance law, insurers would incorporate certain clauses in the standard policy form in order to fill the gap which would arise. These clauses would take the role of express and implied warranties and the legal consequence for breach of them would also be provided in the relevant clauses. In the light of freedom of contract, there is nothing preventing the insurer from adopting a legal consequence which has the same legal effect as the current warranty regime, or is even harsher. This possibility has been forecast by the Australian Law Reform

---

Réunion Européne (The Star Sea) [1995] 1 Lloyd's Rep. 651, [1997] 1 Lloyd's Rep. 361, CA, [2001] Lloyd's Rep. 389, HL.

180. See the paper delivered by Hare, "The Omnipotent Warranty: England v. The World", at International Marine Insurance Conference organised by the European Institute of Maritime and Transport Law at Antwerp in 1999. This paper can also be found in, Huybrechts, Hooydonk and Dieryck (ed.), *Marine Insurance at the Turn of the Millennium*, Vol. 2 (1999) at p.37.

Commission. In order to overcome this potential problem, the Commission in its report recommends that the abolition of the concept of warranties should be supplemented with a further reform. In place of warranties, the amended Marine Insurance Act should permit the parties to incorporate express terms into policies to deal with issues which are currently covered by warranties. A breach by the assured of an express term would entitle insurers to be relieved of liability to indemnify the assured for loss where the breach is causative of that loss. In the absence of such a term, breach of the contract will entitle the insurer only to such relief as may be available under the general law of contract, which would be generally the award of damages. Despite offering a sensible solution, the author is of the opinion that the reform advocated by the Australian Law Reform Commission is not one which would be welcomed by the London insurance market. First, such a reform requires drafting of a large number of clauses and this might take a considerable amount of time. Second, the regime proposed puts serious restrictions on the freedom of contract principle since the parties are prohibited from drafting express clauses in the way they would like. It is a known fact that the market does not like governmental interference to this extent and surely would object severely to such a restriction. Finally, the notion of warranty has come to underpin the London insurance market, and insurers would not be prepared to lose a privilege which they have enjoyed for over two centuries. Therefore, expecting modest alterations in the warranty regime, as highlighted earlier in this part, would be more realistic than expecting the whole regime to be scrapped.

5E CONCLUSION

The notion of warranty not only has a role in determining the extent of the risk for 5.69
the underwriter but also has come to underpin the London insurance market. The last decade saw the clarification of the effect of breach of a marine warranty by the House of Lords. The unfairness arising from the strict compliance doctrine has become more apparent after the adoption of the "automatic discharge" remedy. There is evidence to suggest that the courts are looking for alternative interpretations in order not to allow the insurer to deny liability in cases where breach of warranty and loss are not connected. This could be seen as a development which could cause further complexities in the law. The position of the London marine insurance market and recent developments in other jurisdictions emphasise the need for a reform in this area in the near future. Such an attempt, however, must overcome technical and political obstacles and might require a massive effort. Also a reform like the one advocated above could, despite making law fairer, bring new problems, i.e. it could be problematic to identify the causal link between the loss and breach. However, it should be borne in mind that change is not made without inconvenience, even from worse to better.[181] Also, the fact that such a reform would result in a competitive advantage for the London insurance market must be a relevant consideration.

181. Samuel Johnson, *Dictionary of the English Language* (1755), Preface.

Commission, [illegible] to overcome this practical problem. The Commission in its report recommends that [illegible] the concept of [illegible] [illegible] in a [illegible] in respect of warranties, as [illegible] [illegible]. All should [illegible] [illegible] with [illegible]. Therefore, [illegible] [illegible] [illegible] [illegible] [illegible] [illegible] [illegible] [illegible] [illegible] [illegible] [illegible].

[illegible] OF DESIGN

The [illegible] of warranty not only [illegible] determining the extent of the [illegible] of the insurer but also [illegible] [illegible]. The last development was the [illegible] of the [illegible] of breach of a marine warranty by the House of Lords. [illegible].

[illegible]

CHAPTER 6

THE QUEST FOR SEAWORTHINESS: A STUDY OF US AND ENGLISH LAW OF MARINE INSURANCE

*DR SUSAN HODGES**

6A INTRODUCTION

"[T]here is nothing in matters of insurance of more importance than the implied warranty that a ship is seaworthy when she sails on the voyage insured; and I have endeavoured, both with a view to the benefit of commerce and the preservation of human life, to enforce that doctrine. . . ." *6.1*

Per Lord Eldon, *Douglas v. Scougall* (1816) 4 Dow 269 at 270.

Indeed, no other warranty in the law of marine insurance of the US and England is more revered than or has attracted as much attention as the implied warranty of seaworthiness. It is described by a well-known US author as "the single most important warranty in the law of marine insurance" and "an essential prerequisite of cover".[1] Its significance lies in the fact that it is to all intents and purposes a defence which an insurer may rely upon, in the event of its breach, to reject a claim of an assured for indemnity for loss or damage sustained by the subject-matter insured. The undertaking has been variously described as the "foundation of the contract"[2]

* *The author would like to thank GL Leigh for his helpful comments and for proofreading an earlier draft of this article.*

1. Schoenbaum, *Key Divergences Between English and US Law of Marine Insurance: A Comparative Study*, Published in the US, Cornell Maritime Press, 1999, p.159.

2. *Per* Baron Martin, *Gibson v. Small* (1853) 10 ER 499 at 506, and Senator Verplanck, *US Ins. Co. v. Ogden* SC 15 Wend. 535.

and the "foundation for the underwriter's promise",[3] endorsing the importance of the notion of seaworthiness.[4]

6.2 The objective of this article is to analyse the "undertaking" of seaworthiness applicable to policies on hull under both US and English law, and in particular to highlight the main differences in their nature, scope, extent and effect. The word "undertaking" (as opposed to "warranty") is used here in the lay sense without any of the legal connotations generally associated with the classification of legal terms under ordinary English contract law. Further, under English law it is not correct, in a time policy, to describe the undertaking of seaworthiness as a "warranty", for the Marine Insurance Act 1906 does *not* imply a warranty of seaworthiness in such a policy. In fact, the Act is categorical in its declaration in the opening line of s.39(5) that: "In a time policy there is no implied warranty that the ship shall be seaworthy at any stage of the adventure." Thus, the undertaking of seaworthiness in a time policy is not couched in terms of a *warranty* (or as a particular species of contractual term imposing an obligation or requiring the performance of an act), but as an exemption under which an insurer is freed from liability for a particular loss if the terms of the subsection are met.

6.3 As the character of the undertaking is fundamentally different in a time and a voyage policy, it is necessary to divide this chapter into two main parts: Part A will examine the implied warranty of seaworthiness applicable in a voyage policy, and Part B on the undertaking of seaworthiness in a time policy, on hull. Suffice it here to say that in a cargo policy, the general rules applicable in relation to the undertaking of seaworthiness have been modified by cl. 5 of the Institute Cargo Clauses (A), (B) and (C) and will not be discussed.[5]

PART A: VOYAGE POLICY

6A.1 The implied "warranty" of seaworthiness

6.4 In a voyage policy of insurance on hull, the undertaking of seaworthiness is clearly defined as a "warranty" under both American and English law. In the US, the implied warranty is a part of their general maritime law,[6] whereas in England it is embodied

3. Arnould, *Law of Marine Insurance and Average*, 16th edn., 1981, Vol. 2, para. 708.

4. Deutsch and Hammond, *Marine Insurance Policies: The Implied Warranty of Seaworthiness,* IJC, 1963, p.89, describe it as "It is a cardinal rule of marine insurance that a vessel must . . . be seaworthy".

5. In the early days, the "seaworthiness admitted" clause was often inserted in a policy to negate the operation of the warranty of seaworthiness implied by law. The purpose of cl.5 is essentially to exclude the application of the implied warranty of seaworthiness (as set out in s.39 of the Marine Insurance Act 1906) by waiving any breach of the implied warranty of seaworthiness in advance.

6. Unlike England, the US does not have an Act codifying their case law on marine insurance. Over the years, suggestions have been put forward that an American Marine Insurance Act should be enacted: see, e.g., Cattell, *An American Marine Insurance Act: An Idea Whose Time Has Come*, 1995 Tul. Mar. L.J. 1 and Schoenbaum, *Warranties in the Law of Marine Insurance: Some suggestions for Reform of English and American Law*, 1999 Tul. Mar. L.J. 267.

in case law and statutory law as s.39(1) of the Marine Insurance Act 1906.[7] Both legal regimes are clear that a *warranty* of seaworthiness is implied in every voyage policy at the commencement of the insured voyage, and that there is no warranty of continuing seaworthiness during the course of the insured voyage. Classified as a *warranty*, it has, of course, to bear all the attributes that the law (common law and statutory law) has ascribed to such a term.

A ship may be insured for a voyage "at and from" or "from" a particular place. In the case of the former, the ship has to be port-worthy (to encounter the ordinary perils of the port) whilst she is at that port,[8] and also seaworthy when she sets sail from that port. In a "from" policy,[9] she has only to be seaworthy at the commencement of the voyage from that port. Once the ship has sailed in a seaworthy condition the policy will attach, and there is no warranty of continuing seaworthiness that she shall be seaworthy during the course of the voyage. The legal position was summarised in *Gibson v. Small*,[10] by the learned Baron Parke, as follows: "It is also perfectly clear that, in our law, there is no other warranty of seaworthiness in a voyage-policy, than that the ship is seaworthy at the commencement of the voyage. There is no warranty in the law of England that the vessel shall continue seaworthy after the voyage has commenced". 6.5

In both countries, the meaning of "seaworthiness" is essentially the same[11] (at least in relation to commercial contracts) and the implied warranty is absolute in nature in the sense that no defence whatsoever is available to the assured in the event of a breach. In England, this principle is firmly cast in the vintage case of *The Mills Frigate*,[12] and in the US, it is enshrined in 1895 in the celebrated case, *The Caledonia*.[13] But even before *The Caledonia*, the rule was applied in 1803 in *Barnewell v. Church*.[14] In *Bullard v. Roger Williams Insurance Co.*,[15] Judge Curtis decided that, "It is not a contract that the owner will use diligence to make his vessel, but an absolute warranty that she is seaworthy . . .". 6.6

Both legal regimes apply the rule that no causal connection needs to be shown 6.7

7. Section 39(1): "In a voyage policy there is an implied warranty that at the commencement of the voyage the ship shall be seaworthy for the purpose of the particular adventure insured." At one stage in the history of the law of seaworthiness, it was thought (by Lord Abinger) that a warranty of seaworthiness was implied by the use of the term "good ship" appearing in some of the older policies. This myth was dispelled by Baron Parke in *Small v. Gibson* 16 Q.B. 141 who ruled that the term "good ship" is neither an express nor an implied warranty of seaworthiness.

8. See s.39(2) and rule 3 of Rules for Construction of Policy.

9. See s.39(1) and rule 2 of Rules for Construction of Policy.

10. 10 ER 499 at 517, HL. See also *Dixon v. Sadler* (1839) 5 M&W 405.

11. It is observed that under US law, the meaning of seaworthiness is much more unpredictable when it is applied in relation to personal injury claims brought by seafarers. US courts have bent backwards in their endeavours to protect seamen, their "little darlings" of the Admiralty court, so much so that they have pushed the frontiers of the notion almost beyond its limits, embracing situations which English law would not recognise as defects amounting to unseaworthiness.

12. *Mills v. Roebuck*, reported in a footnote in *Gibson v. Small* (1853) 10 ER 499 at 501. See also *Forshaw v. Chabert* (1821) 3 Br. & B. 158, *Douglas v. Scougall* (1816) 4 Dow. 278 and *Wedderburn & Others v. Bell* (1807) 1 Camp. 1.

13. 157 US 124 (1895). Though a case dealing specifically with a carriage dispute, it is often cited as *the* authority establishing the general principles of the implied warranty of seaworthiness applicable in contracts of affreightment and marine insurance (for both time and voyage policies).

14. 1 Caines 217; 2 Am. Dec. 180 (N.Y. 1803).

15. 1 Curt. 148 at 155.

between the breach and the loss; in other words, the loss does not have to be attributable to or be proximately caused by unseaworthiness for the legal effects of its breach to operate. To this extent, it is correct to say that:[16] "As to voyage policies of insurance, the American law is identical to the English rules". But that is as far as the similarities go. Though both countries apply essentially the same principles to many aspects of the warranty, they do however differ on a fundamental point, viz. the legal effects attendant on its breach. Another variance can also be detected in relation to the courts' attitude towards suspension of the policy as the effect of a breach of a warranty. This part will, therefore, focus only on these two aspects of the law of warranties.

6A.2 Legal effects of breach

6.8 Though the undertaking of seaworthiness is regarded as a "warranty" in both jurisdictions, each has however prescribed its own rule relating to the legal effects for its breach; the divergence presumably is due as much to the difference in their understanding of the word "warranty" as it is to the somewhat chaotic state of US law in this regard, which has been engendered by the controversial rule laid down in the notorious *Wilburn Boat*[17] case. In 1955, much to the dismay of almost the entire legal fraternity, the Supreme Court held that there is no federal law on insurance warranties and that each State should therefore apply its own law (if any) on the matter. The judgment was construed by State courts to mean that they had been given *carte blanche* authority to formulate any rule they might deem fit. The opening of the floodgates produced a proliferation of divergent rules on the subject. With this hint of what is to come in the ensuing discussion of US law, it is necessary first to trace the development of English law, to examine how case law has over the years handled the legal effects of a breach of a warranty, express and implied.

6.9 The legal expression "warranty" has for some time caused confusion in this area of law.[18] However, the meaning of the word is now, in the light of the House of Lords' pronouncement in *The Good Luck*,[19] firmly established. A feature which has never been in doubt is that the term "warranty" in insurance is used in a sense wholly different to that commonly understood in general contract law, where a breach afforded the innocent party with only a right to sue in damages with no right of avoidance of the contract. Though the point in dispute was in relation to an *express* warranty, the judgment is nevertheless applicable to *all* warranties, express or implied.

16. See Schoenbaum, *Key Divergences Between English and American Law of Marine Insurance: A Comparative Study* (Cornell Maritime Press, 1999), p.167.

17. *Wilburn Boat Co. v. Fireman's Fund Insurance Co.* 348 U.S. 310, 75 S. Ct. 368 (1955).

18. The courts in England will not be tied down to nomenclature, and if they think that the term "warranty" is misplaced, they may construe it as something else, for example as a suspensive condition: see *Roberts v. Anglo-Saxon Insurance Association Ltd* (1926) 26 Ll L Rep 154. However, it is true to say that so far this flexibility has not been applied to a warranty of seaworthiness and there are particularly good policy reasons why it should not be.

19. [1991] 2 Lloyd's Rep. 191, HL.

During the eighteenth and nineteenth centuries, it was originally thought, in cases such as *Woolmer v. Muilman*,[20] *De Hahn v. Hartley*[21] and *Wedderburn v. Bell*,[22] that a breach of an insurance warranty rendered the contract void or void *ab initio*. Early US law followed suit and this is evident in *The Caledonia*,[23] where Chief Justice Fuller cited with approval the words of Parsons, an eminent US author of the nineteenth century, who stated that: 6.10

> "This warranty is strictly a condition precedent to the obligation of insurance; if it be not performed, the policy does not attach; and if this condition be broken, at the inception of the risk in anyway whatever and from any cause whatever, *there is no contract of insurance*, the policy being *wholly void*." [emphasis added]

In similar vein, Judge Curtis in *Bullard v. Roger Williams Insurance Co.*[24] reiterated that it is "an absolute warranty that she is seaworthy, and if broken the policy is made void". In *Gregoire v. Underwriters at Lloyd's*,[25] the legal position was described thus: "In a voyage policy, the owner of the vessel warrants the seaworthiness of his vessel at the time it sets out on the voyage. If the vessel is not seaworthy at this time, the entire policy is void and no recovery can be had under the policy even for losses not directly attributable to the lack of seaworthiness". In *Jones v. Insurance Company*,[26] mutual mistake was given, which words were presumably used as a mere figure of speech, as the excuse for holding the contract void: "If the assured does not make her seaworthy at first, she is not a vessel, not capable of being navigated; and the contract being made under mutual mistake, the consequence follows, that the subject matter, respecting which the insurance was made, *did not exist*, and neither party is bound".

Thus, during the nineteenth century, US law was in this respect in harmony with English law: both jurisdictions regarded the implied warranty as absolute, a breach of which was capable of rendering the contract void. Whether a breach of a warranty, express or implied, can render a policy *void* is certainly questionable. But if such is the effect, it will have a bearing on the question as to a return of premium, which would in turn call for an examination of the subject of a failure consideration. This will then require a discussion of a wider question, when is an insurance contract formed or concluded?

In England, however, the insurance warranty soon developed into a "condition" (as understood in general contract law), the breach of which was held to entitle the insurer the right to *avoid* the contract.[27] The Court of Appeal in *The Good Luck*[28] confirmed the avoidance rule. For a period of time prior to the Law Lords' ruling in the case, an insurance warranty was regarded by English law as a term of the contract, the breach of which would give the innocent party the option to *avoid* the contract. In 6.11

20. (1763) 1 Wl. Bl. 427; 3 Burr. 1419.
21. (1786) 1 TR 343.
22. (1807) 1 Camp 1.
23. 157 U.S. 124 at 131 (1895).
24. 1 Curt. 148 at 155.
25. 559 F. Supp. 596; 1982 AMC 2045 (D. Alaska 1982).
26. 13 F. Cas. 982 (1852). Though the comment was with reference to the implied warranty of seaworthiness in a time policy, it is nevertheless relevant to the present discussion on the same warranty implied in a voyage policy.
27. See Clarke, *The Law of Insurance Contracts*, LLP, 1997, p.545.
28. [1989] 2 Lloyd's Rep. 238 at 259, CA.

spite of the clear definition given to the term "warranty" in s.33 and its unequivocal language declaring that the insurer is to be "discharged from liability", the Court of Appeal still felt the need to cling on to the avoidance rule, which the law has specifically reserved for a failure to observe utmost good faith, non-disclosure and misrepresentation.[29] The position taken by the appeal court towards the void or void *ab initio* rule is understandable: the sentiments of the appeal court are captured in the words of Lord Justice May who strongly felt that:[30] "It would be contrary to principle if the assured were able by his unilateral act to bring the contract to an end; and it would be more surprising if breach of warranty (which might in itself be *insignificant* or *immaterial*) were to have this result".[31]

The statement of Lord Justice May was made with reference to an *express* warranty.[32] By no stretch of imagination can the notion of seaworthiness be ever described as "insignificant" or "immaterial". The fact that the law has deemed it fit to mandate that a warranty of seaworthiness be implied in every voyage of insurance must in itself be forceful, if not conclusive evidence that it is a matter the performance of which is significant and material to the risk. Unless the implied warranty of seaworthiness has been expressly negated or overridden by an unambiguous term in the policy, it will be upheld to the letter. Thus the reservation expressed by Lord Justice May, though it may be pertinent to some *express* warranties, is difficult to support in relation to the implied warranty of seaworthiness.

The Court of Appeal in *The Good Luck* put to rest the "void" rule and in its place gave an insurer the milder option of avoidance, only for it to be demolished by the House of Lords, when Lord Goff declared that a warranty is a "condition precedent" to which is attached the consequence of automatic discharge.[33]

6A.2(i) A condition precedent

6.12 Lord Goff in the same case pronounced[34] that the adjective "automatic" is to be read before the word "discharged" in s.33(3). He said:[35]

> "Those words are clear. They show that discharge of the insurer from liability is automatic and is not dependent upon any decision by the insurer to treat the contract of insurance as at an end. . . . Section 33(3) of the Act reflects what has been described . . . as the inveterate practice in marine insurance of using the term "warranty" as signifying a *condition precedent*." [emphasis added]

---

29. See Marine Insurance Act 1906, ss.17, 18(1) and 20.

30. [1989] 2 Lloyd's Rep. 238 at 259, CA.

31. Emphasis added. See Birds, *The Effect of Breach of an Insurance Warranty*, 1991 LQR 540.

32. But the point is, if an *express* term of a contract is "insignificant" or "immaterial", the court does not have to classify it as a warranty. The court is always at liberty to interpret a contractual term in whatever way it deems fit, without, of course, losing sight of the intention of the parties, which must always be respected. And if the intention of the parties is to incorporate a *warranty*, then, however immaterial it may be to the risk, neither should have any cause to complain on the grounds that its breach has produced the unpalatable outcome set by the law. Further, it is also necessary to remember that s.33(3) has clarified that an insurance warranty does *not* have to be material to the risk, and provided that an "intention to warrant" may be inferred, it will be construed as a warranty the breach of which will now, in the light of *The Good Luck*, automatically discharge the insurer from liability.

33. For an analysis of *The Good Luck*, see Clarke, *Breach of Warranty in the Law of Insurance* [1991] LMCLQ 437.

34. With the concurrence of the other members of the House.

35. [1991] 2 Lloyd's Rep. 191 at 202, HL.

Therein lies the death knell of the rule of avoidance and the proud emergence of that of automatic discharge. As the undertaking of seaworthiness is in a voyage policy framed as a "warranty", here and in the US, the term has now to be viewed in this light. And though the ensuing discussion is with specific reference to voyage policies, it is nonetheless also relevant to any policy of insurance where a warranty of seaworthiness is implied by law or is incorporated as an express term of the contract. Whether labelling it as a "condition precedent" has in any way helped with our understanding of the legal consequences of its breach is another matter; but the case has clarified beyond doubt that the right of avoidance of the contract is no longer good law in England.[36]

However, it is interesting to note that US cases have also called the implied warranty of seaworthiness a *condition precedent*. In *Berwind v. Greenwich Insurance Company*,[37] Judge Charles F Brown referred to the implied warranty of seaworthiness thus: "It is a condition precedent to the risk and, if the vessel is not seaworthy, the policy does not attach". In the same year, in *Plummer v. Insurance Company of North America*,[38] Judge Bird noted, albeit with reference to a time policy, that: "The technical warranty of seaworthiness is satisfied as a condition precedent if at the inception of the risk the vessel be staunch, strong, tight . . . and provided to meet the ordinary perils of the adventure in contemplation". The judge cited Phillips[39] with approval, whose statement was to the effect that: "Whether a policy is for a voyage or period of time, the construction of this warranty is the same as to compliance being a *condition precedent* at the outset . . . ". In similar vein, Parsons notes that, "[t]his warranty is strictly a *condition precedent* to the obligation of insurance; if it be not performed, the policy does not attach. . . ".[40] Though most of the cases that have dealt with the issue were time policies, the law in this regard should be the same, as a warranty of seaworthiness is implied by US law not only to voyage but also time policies. The same principles should logically apply to all warranties, express or implied, and whether the policy be for a voyage or for a period of time. 6.13

The reason why the risk does not attach is because the time for the compliance with the warranty of seaworthiness coincides with the time for the inception of the risk. In a voyage policy, it is the commencement of the insured voyage and in a time policy, on a particular hour and date when the policy is to take effect. Thus, if the warranty is not fulfilled at the inception of the risk, the policy does not attach. And if the policy does not attach, obviously the insurer cannot be made liable for *any* loss sustained by the assured. Thus, the insurer is effectively discharged from liability for the loss or for any future loss which the vessel should suffer. For want of a better expression, such a policy is a "non-starter" in the event of such a breach. 6.14

But the above does not explain the effect which the breach has upon the contract as a whole. In other words, does the contract still exist or is it void? Or is it merely suspended with the possibility of policy re-attaching when the breach is cured? As 6.15

36. Described by Hodgin, *Insurance Law, Text and Materials* (Cavendish Publishing 1998), p.318, as follows: "The short answer to the effect of a breach of a promissory warranty is that the insurer is discharged from liability automatically and irrespective of any decision by him."
37. 21 N.E 1511 (N.Y. 1889).
38. 95 A. 605 (Me. 1915).
39. A well-known early US author: 1 Phil. Ins. 730.
40. Cited in *The Caledonia* 157 U.S. 124 at 131 (1895).

mentioned, the answers to these questions would, of course, have a bearing on the important matter of a return of premium.

In a very recent comparative study of US and English marine insurance law, Schoenbaum explains that:[41] "The breach of this warranty *had* similar consequences to English law except that certain American cases termed the coverage of the policy 'suspended', opening the possibility for cure". In the latest edition of his textbook, he states:[42] "Breach of warranty allows the insurer to *avoid* the contract in a manner similar to nondisclosure or misrepresentation". This suggests that in the US the rule of avoidance is still being applied side by side with the rule of a suspension of the policy.

6.16 A recent account of the law can be found in *The Papoose*[43] where, with confidence, the Court of Appeal, State of Maryland, stated: "For under the American Rule, unlike the English, there is an implied warranty of seaworthiness in a time policy. A consequence of this is that if the vessel is unseaworthy – as *M/V Papoose* assured was – at the time the insurance attaches, the breach absolutely avoids the policy. Existing spectacular unseaworthiness kept the policy from becoming effective". And then in a footnote, the court states that: "If there is any breach of a warranty the policy is *null and void*, and . . . the underwriters are relieved of their liability notwithstanding the loss is not connected with the breach or the breach is cured prior to the loss". It is difficult to imagine how a contract can be voidable and at the same be "null and void": they are contradiction in terms. Further, the fact that a policy may be prevented from becoming effective is another matter altogether, distinct from saying that the contract does not exist.

6A.2(ii) A "promissory" condition precedent

6.17 Confusion can arise in the use of the term "condition precedent". According to Treitel,[44] the term, like the word "condition", is "chameleon-like", capable of referring to a host of meanings. For the purpose of the present discussion, the pertinent question is whether the implied warranty of seaworthiness is a *contingent* condition precedent or a *promissory* condition precedent?[45] The answer to this is crucial in deciding whether a return of premium is possible in the event of a breach of the implied warranty, or condition precedent. For if the implied warranty of seaworthiness is a *contingent* condition precedent, the very existence of the contract is dependent upon the happening of that event, and the contract is not binding until that event/contingency occurs. On the other hand, if it is a *promissory* condition precedent, the contract is already binding and provides the foundation upon which the warranty is based.

It is one thing to say that a breach of the condition precedent will free or "automatically discharge" the assured from liability and future liability under the policy, and quite another to say that the contract is void. If a breach of the implied

41. *Key Divergences between English and American Law of Marine Insurance: A Comparative Study* (Cornell Maritime Press), 1999, p.166.

42. *Admiralty and Maritime Law,* West Group, 2000, 3rd edn., p.938.

43. 1969 AMC 781 (5th Cir. 1969).

44. *The Law of Contract* (Sweet & Maxwell 10th edn., 1999) p.58.

45. See Treitel, *"Conditions and Conditions Precedent"* 1990, LQR, Vol. 106, p.185.

warranty is capable of rendering the contract void, as suggested by some of the cases, then the insurer will presumably have to return any sums of money (premiums) that have been paid by the assured as consideration of the contract.

As will be seen, the implied warranty of seaworthiness under English law is clearly a *promissory* condition precedent: the assured has to fulfil his promise (to provide a seaworthy ship) before the insurer's *liability* can accrue. The provision of a seaworthy ship is not a condition precedent for the existence or validity of the contract, but a condition precedent to the liability of insurer. Whether referred to as a "warranty" or a "condition precedent", a breach of the warranty of seaworthiness cannot, as will be seen, be regarded as having the effect of rendering the contract void.

6A.2(iii) Return of premium?

Only where the "policy is void, or is avoided by the insurer as from the commencement of the risk" is a return of premium allowed by s.84(3) of the Marine Insurance Act 1906. If the policy is rendered void by reason of the breach, the assured would be entitled under this section to demand for a return of premium. Section 84 of the Act, on return of premium, is captioned as "Return for failure of consideration". Thus, it is relevant to inquire whether there is a failure of consideration in such an event. To answer this question effectively, it is necessary to know when an insurance contract is clinched or concluded. A contract of marine insurance is not like a typical contract, such as a sale of goods, where an exchange of consideration, namely performances or obligations, has to take place between the parties before the contract can come to life. 6.18

One point of view can be found in the ancient case of *Christie v. Secretan*,[46] where the court appeared to be amenable to a return of premium. Modern academics, however, have suggested otherwise. On such matters, we can always safely rely on Treitel for guidance. He states that:[47] 6.19

> "In a contract of insurance against loss the position is that the performance of one party (i.e., payment of premium by the assured) is exchanged for the promise of the other (the insurer), and in the great majority of cases this promise is not performed at all because the event insured against does not occur. The occurrence of this event is thus a contingent condition precedent of the insurer's liability to pay, while on breach of the 'warranty' he is discharged from his conditional promise even before the event occurs."
>
> ". . . there is no total failure of consideration as he had the benefit of the insurer's promise for some time."

Thus, the consideration for the premium paid by the assured is the *promise* given by the insurer to indemnify him in the event of a loss or damage sustained by a *seaworthy* ship. There is no total failure of consideration, as the assured has had the benefit of the insurer's *promise* that he would be indemnified should a loss or damage sustained by a seaworthy be caused by a peril insured against.

---

46. 8 TR 192. The court states: "The warranty of seaworthiness is implied from the nature of the contract of insurance. The consideration is paid, in order that the owner of a ship which is capable of performing her voyage, may be indemnified against certain contingencies; and it supposes the possibility of the underwriter's gaining the premium; but if the ship be incapable of performing her voyage, there is no possibility of the underwriter's gaining the premium; and if the consideration fails, the obligation fails."

47. *The Law of Contract* (Sweet & Maxwell, 10th edn., 1999) pp.787 & 977.

6.20 With similar astuteness and even greater clarity, Clarke has also laboured on the point. His observation is that:[48] "An insurance warranty is not part of the consideration and, if broken, the insurer is not substantially deprived of what he contracted for – which is premium. The insurer wants the warranty in his contract not for it own sake but in order to limit the risk and so limit the burden or extent of his own promise of cover". More pointedly, he observes that, "A warranty is part of an insurance contract, and *its breach assumed the existence of a contract* which obliged the insurer to undertake the warranty".[49] The fact of the matter is, a warranty needs a pre-existing contract to give it life.

The primary obligation (indemnity) of the insurance contract does not accrue until the warranty is fulfilled. But this is not to say that the contract does not exist until the warranty of seaworthiness is complied with. In this regard, it may be helpful to note that the implied warranty of seaworthiness is nothing like terms such as "subject to satisfactory mortgage", "subject to satisfactory survey" or "subject to satisfactory references" where no contract is formed until the stipulated condition is fulfilled.

6.21 The US case of *Plummer v. Insurance Company of North America*[50] seems to have the finger on the pulse when it ruled that the assured was not entitled to ask for a return of premium:

> "We do not understand that the plaintiff seeks, in the event that the defendant is not found liable on the policy, to recover back the premium paid [by the] defendant, either in whole or in part, as suggested may be the case by plaintiff. We need only state that where the policy has once attached (it is admitted that the policy was in full force and effect at the time the yacht filled) and the risk is entire, there can be no such recovery. . . ."

6.22 It is submitted that much of the confusion in this regard is brought about by the unqualified use of the term "condition precedent". An insurance warranty is a promissory, and not a contingent, condition precedent. The undertaking of seaworthiness in a voyage policy is a *warranty*, which is known in insurance law as a promissory condition precedent to the *liability* of the insurer. To put it in another way, the seaworthiness of the ship is a promissory condition precedent to the assured's right to indemnity under the policy: it is not a condition precedent or a prerequisite for breathing life into the contract. The primary obligation (indemnity) of the contract does not accrue until the warranty is fulfilled; but this is not say that the contract does not exist until the warranty of seaworthiness is fulfilled or that it is brought to an end by reason of its breach.

6.23 To sum up the legal position, reference must to be made to the succinct words of Lord Goff:[51]

> "Here we are concerned with a promissory condition precedent, contained in an *existing* contract of insurance, non-fulfilment of the condition does not prevent the contract from coming into existence. What it does (as s.33(3) makes plain) is to discharge the insurer from liability as from the date of the breach. Certainly, it does not have the effect of avoiding the contract *ab initio*. Nor strictly speaking, does it have the effect of bringing the contract to an end."

---

48. *The Law of Insurance Contracts* (LLP, 3rd edn.) p.522.
49. Emphasis added.
50. 95 A. 605 at 608 (Me.1915).
51. [1991] 2 Lloyd's Rep. 191 at 202, HL.

It may be difficult to fathom from this how a contract can still exist when the insurer is automatically discharged from all future liability. The irresistible question is, does an assured still have to continue to pay premium when the insurer is discharged from liability and the contract is to all intents and purposes no longer on foot? If he is to continue to pay premium, the crucial question is, what is the consideration for that premium? Lord Goff explains:[52]

"It is possible that there may be obligations of the assured under the contract which will survive the discharge of the insurer from liability, as, for example, a continuing liability to pay a premium. Even if, in the result, no further obligations rests on either parties, it is not correct to speak of the contract being avoided; and it is, strictly speaking, more accurate to keep to the careful chosen words in s.33(3) of the Act, rather than to speak of the contract being brought to an end, though that may be the practical effect."

Lord Goff in his judgment rejected in clear terms avoidance of the policy *ab initio* on breach of warranty; he said that the insurers were automatically discharged from liability. And he made it clear that the contract itself remained in some sort of spectral existence to enable an unpaid premium to be collected, although an accrued right of that kind normally survives the discharge of any contract at common law. The message is that the policy is not "avoided" or that it is wise not to use that verb at all in this context. Perhaps "metamorphosed" serves the purpose, with the right shade of meaning.

The author's reply to this is, more to the point, should an assured be allowed to demand a return of premium or to stop the payment of premium when he himself has committed a breach of a vital term of the contract? The constant willingness on the part of the insurer to indemnify him in the event of a loss has neither waned nor ceased. The assured has effectively, by the breach, rendered it impossible for the insurer to fulfil his side of the bargain. The primary obligation (indemnity) of the insurance contract does not accrue until the warranty is complied with. If the legal position were otherwise, it will mean that an assured can unilaterally bring the contract to an end and demand a return of premium by deliberately committing a breach of the warranty.

The apparent dangers of a failure to appreciate the implications and significance of 6.24
terms such as "conditions" and "condition precedents" is evident in the case of *Bentworth Finance Ltd v. Lubert*,[53] albeit a case concerning a hire-purchase agreement. The Court of Appeal held that there was an implied *suspensive condition* that the log-book of a motor-car should be provided.[54] The effect of the breach was briefly described by Lord Denning MR as follows:

"In the circumstances I think the contract did not come into operation. The provision of the log-book was a condition on which the very existence of the contract depended. It was, in technical language, a suspensive condition. Until the log-book was provided, there was no contract of hire-purchase at all. No instalments, therefore, fell due."

---

52. *Ibid.*
53. [1968] 1 Q.B. 680, CA.
54. Briefly, a finance company (plaintiff) had entered into a contract with the first defendant for the hire-purchase of a motor-car. When the plaintiffs delivered the car, they failed to deliver the log-book whereupon the defendants refused to pay any instalments under the contract. The plaintiffs repossessed the car and sued the defendants, *inter alia*, for arrears of instalments.

Carniegie's[55] criticisms of the court's description of the effect of the breach are perfectly justifiable and clearly worthy of recollection, as they serve as a warning against the careless use of terms. Applying the rule *mutatis mutandis* to seaworthiness, it would read as: Until a seaworthy ship is provided, there is no contract at all. Carniegie is of the opinion that it would be misleading to say that the contract never came into operation at all. He felt that the case is best construed on the basis that: "It would be a suspensive condition of the contract that the log-book should be produced to the extent that the liability of the hire-purchaser only, and not the whole contract, would be conditional on the provision of the log-book".

American judges, as will soon be revealed, will undoubtedly find the above rule of suspension attractive. This, therefore, conveniently leads us to the next line of inquiry, namely the applicability of the rule of suspension in the event of a violation of the implied warranty of seaworthiness.

6A.3 A suspensive condition precedent under US law?

6.25 American judges, academics and lawyers have always found the English rule of literal compliance (a hallmark of an insurance warranty) harsh and objectionable, so much so that they have employed the term "forfeiture" to describe the premature termination of the contract. Reference need only be made to *Goldman's*[56] and *Vances's*[57] articles to realise that, at least in relation to express warranties, US judges are repelled by the strict rule of exact compliance and its attendant effect of "forfeiture" (the equivalent of our rule of automatic discharge). US courts have, whenever possible, construed express warranties as terms the breach of which would lead to a suspension, rather than a termination of the policy.[58] It has even construed a breach of an *express* warranty of continuing seaworthiness as capable of giving rise to a suspension of the policy.[59] The crucial question is, can the same effect of suspension be applied to a breach of an *implied* warranty of seaworthiness? It would indeed be odd if one set of rules is to apply for breach of an express, and another for an implied warranty of seaworthiness. The suspension rule will be returned to when the "negative burden" of the American Rule is discussed.

Instead of applying the rule of automatic discharge, the US has adopted a flexible approach to the problem. They have applied either the avoidance rule or the suspensive rule when considering a breach of an *express* warranty. As far as the author is aware, there does not appear to be any US case declaring that a breach of the *implied* warranty of seaworthiness in a voyage policy will yield the effect of suspension.

It appears that the inclination of the US judiciary is to treat, whenever possible, express warranties as a suspensive condition precedent, with the effect that the policy or the liability of the insurer may be switched on when the warranty is complied with and switched off when it is not. Such an approach, whether applied to an express or

---

55. An Implied Condition in Motor-Car Hire-Purchase, 31 MLR 78.
56. "Breach of Warranty in US Marine Insurance", 1985, Insurance Counsel Journal, p.60.
57. "The History of the Development of the Warranty in Insurance Law", 1911, Yale Law Journal, Vol. 7, 523.
58. E.g. the "watchman", the "laid up" and towage warranties.
59. See *Aguirre v. Citizens Casualty Co. of New York* 441 F. 2d 141 (5th Cir. 1971).

implied warranty, would go against the very fibre of English law of marine insurance warranties, for the Act has specifically laid down that a breach of a warranty cannot be cured, and the moment it is breached the insurer is automatically discharged from liability. Further, the conservatism of English marine insurance law would find the suspensive rule, when applied to seaworthiness, disconcerting, too uncertain and unpredictable to be acceptable.

PART B: TIME POLICY

The duty to provide a seaworthy ship in a time policy on hull has generated many more problems, both in this country and the US, than the warranty of seaworthiness implied in a voyage policy. English law on the subject is encapsulated in s.39(5) of the Act, while US law is supposedly circumscribed in the "American Rule" laid down in the celebrated case of the *Spot Pack*,[60] where the Fifth Circuit, through Judge Brown, took the opportunity to redefine the law of seaworthiness applicable to time policies. Before proceeding to discuss the Rule and to comment on the discord between US and English law, it would be useful first to set forth the principles of English law, which is serene when compared to its US counterpart. 6.26

6B SEAWORTHINESS UNDER ENGLISH LAW

There are two limbs to s.39(5). The first simply declares that there is no implied warranty of seaworthiness in a time policy, and the second, which for convenience will be referred to as the "privity" rule, describes the role which seaworthiness plays in a time policy. 6.27

6B.1 No implied warranty of seaworthiness in a time policy

First, the introductory words of s.39(5) boldly disclaim that: "In a time policy there is no implied warranty that the ship shall be seaworthy at any stage of the adventure". As it is self-explanatory, little need be said about it save that it originated from the celebrated case of *Gibson v. Small*,[61] where a panel of nine distinguished judges was specially invited to debate and advise the law lords on the fundamental issue of whether a warranty of seaworthiness is implied in a time policy. Seven were against and two were in favour of implying a warranty in a time policy. After a long and hearty battle of wits, the House of Lords was able to provide a host of reasons to explain why it would be neither sensible nor practicable to impose a warranty of seaworthiness on a time policy.[62] With the praiseworthy aim of certainty and uniformity, Lord Campbell CJ decided "against the implied condition in *all* cases of time-policies". He felt that it would be more expedient and "most desirable that in commercial 6.28

60. *Saskatchewan Government Insurance Office v. Spot Pack, Inc.* 242 F. 2d at 388 (5th Cir. 1957).
61. (1853) 4 HL Cas 352; 10 ER 499, HL.
62. Prior to *Gibson v. Small* 10 ER 499, HL, it was assumed that a warranty of seaworthiness was implied in both time and voyage policies.

transactions there should be plain rules to go by, without qualification or exception".[63] Such a blanket rule would save the court having to agonise over the issue of whether a condition of seaworthiness is to be expected of a ship which is at sea at the inception of the risk, her condition being beyond the control or knowledge of her owner. In such a case, it does not lie within the power of the assured to remedy any defects of unseaworthiness which the ship might suffer.[64] Though Lord St Leonards was in general agreement with Lord Campbell that no warranty of seaworthiness is to be implied in time policies, he was, however, prepared to allow an exception to be made to the rule. He said:[65] "If, however, a ship were to sail on a particular voyage, and a time-policy was effected, instead of a policy on the intended voyage . . . I think that a condition could be implied that the ship was seaworthy at the commencement of the voyage". As will be seen, US courts have grasped upon this sentiment and have used it as the basis of their rule.

6.29 Not long after *Gibson v. Small* was decided, the matter was laid to rest for all time in *Dudgeon v. Pembroke*, where Lord Penzance in the House of Lords announced that:[66]

> "... The case of *Gibson v. Small*, supplemented as it was by the two cases of *Thompson v. Hopper* and *Fawcus v. Sarsfield*, must be considered to have set at rest the controversies on this subject, and to have finally decided that the law does not, in the absence of special stipulations in the contract, infer in the case of a time policy any warranty that the vessel at any particular time shall have been seaworthy."

Regardless of whether the ship is at sea or in port at the time of the inception of the risk, the cardinal rule is that under no circumstances is a warranty of seaworthiness to be implied in a time policy governed by English law. The wisdom of the law lords is now enshrined in s.39(5).[67]

6.30 There is of course nothing in law prohibiting the parties from departing from the general rule laid down in s.39(5) by incorporating an *express* warranty of seaworthiness in the policy. Provided that an intention to warrant may be inferred, the express clause (warranty) may be in any form of words.[68] The recent case of *The Lydia Flag*[69] has demonstrated the efficacy of an *express* warranty of seaworthiness in a time policy

63. *Ibid.*, at 527. Another reason which influenced the court's decision was given by Erle J (at 512): "... it being now settled that the term 'seaworthy' when used in reference to marine insurance, does not describe absolutely any of the states which a ship may pass through . . . but expresses a relation between the state of the ship and the perils it has to meet in the situation it is in".

64. The other side of the coin was referred to by Lord Campbell CJ thus (at 527): "I have hesitated more upon the question whether, when a timepolicy is effected upon an outwardbound ship lying in a British port where the owner resides, a condition of seaworthiness is to be implied".

65. 10 ER 499 at 524, HL.

66. (1877) 2 App Cas 284 at 293–294, HL.

67. The phrase "at any stage of the adventure" appearing in s.39(5) of the Act is to remove any doubt which one might have regarding the applicability of the warranty when the ship is in port at and after the inception of the policy.

68. See s.35(1) of the Act.

69. *Martin Maritime Ltd v. Provident Capital Indemnity Ltd* [1998] 2 Lloyd's Rep. 652. For an analysis of this case, see Hodges, *Express warranties of seaworthiness in time policies: A comparative Analysis of US and English law*, JMLC, 2001, Vol. 32, no. 1, p.95.

on hull.[70] As will be seen, much depends upon the wording of the express clause, which has to be construed in order that its scope and intention can be ascertained.

6B.2 The privity rule

The heart of s.39(5) however lies in its second part which states that "where, with the privity of the assured, the ship is sent to sea in an unseaworthy state, the insurer is not liable for any loss attributable to unseaworthiness". As worded, this is clearly *not* a warranty in any shape or form, as its purpose is to exempt an insurer from liability for any loss that is attributable to such unseaworthiness to which the assured is privy. In the words of Lord Justice Roskill in *The Eurysthenes*:[71] 6.31

"... But the subsection goes on to free underwriters from liability in the case of a loss by unseaworthiness under a time policy if, notwithstanding the absence of any warranty of unseaworthiness [sic], the assured had been privy to sending the ship to sea in an unseaworthy state."

Not surprisingly, litigation has centred itself on the meaning of the phrases "privity of the assured" and "attributable to unseaworthiness". What exactly is meant by the word "privity" was considered very recently by the House of Lords in *The Star Sea*.[72] The kindred question as to whose knowledge or privity within a corporate structure is to be considered that of "the assured" was also examined by the House, although the matter had been given a thorough airing in the Court of Appeal.[73]

6B.2(i) Meaning of "privity"

The meaning of the word "privity" received judicial attention all the way to the House of Lords. Though a simple word, which any lay person would without hesitation say is synonymous to "knowledge", there is more than meets the eye, as the cases of *The Eurysthenes* and *The Star Sea* have illustrated. For a proper understanding of the rule established in *The Star Sea*, it is necessary to have some insight into the facts of the case: the parties were in agreement that *The Star Sea* was unseaworthy and that the assured did not have actual knowledge of her defective condition, which manifested itself in more ways than one, not all of which are relevant to the present discussion. The two material respects in which she was found to be unseaworthy were related to her ability (or rather her inability) to deal with fires that might arise on 6.32

70. Just as it is possible for the parties in a voyage policy to negate the warranty of seaworthiness implied by s.39(1), it is also possible for the parties in a time policy to insert an express warranty of seaworthiness in spite of the statutory declaration that there is no implied warranty of seaworthiness in such a policy. Besides *The Lydia Flag*, there does not appear to be any other English reported authority concerning an express warranty of seaworthiness in a time policy.

71. *Compania Maritima San Basilio SA v. Oceanus Mutual Underwriting Ass'n (Bermuda) Ltd.* [1977] 1 Q.B.D. 49 at 76, CA. The report says "any warranty of unseaworthiness" but clearly either his Lordship or perhaps the learned law reporter nodded.

72. [2001] 1 Lloyd's Rep. 389, HL.

73. For a study of the rules of attribution and this aspect of *The Star Sea*, see Hodges, "The Legal Implications of the ISM Code: Insurance and Limitation of Liability", [2000] IJIL, 39, pp.52 & 53 and Hodges & Hill, *Principles of Maritime Law* (LLP, 2001) at p.586.

board; the first pertained to her "structural inadequacy" – the defective condition of her engine room dampers rendered it impossible to seal the engine room in the event of a fire. The second concerned the incompetence of the master to deal with fire. Because of his "massive ignorance", he was oblivious of how the CO_2 system on board worked. *The Star Sea* was rendered a constructive total loss when she was wholly consumed by a fire, the extent of which could have been easily contained had the dampers been effective and her master competent. The loss having been due to fire (an insured peril), it was *prima facie* recoverable from the insurer; the real point at issue was the extent of the liability of the insurer: was he also liable for the *additional* damage sustained by the vessel that led her to become a constructive total loss? In other words, the problem was whether the additional damage sustained by her was "attributable to" unseaworthiness. It needs to be stressed that the trial judge, Mr Justice Tuckey, found that the additional damage was brought about by a combination of *both* aspects of unseaworthiness.

As the assured company had no actual knowledge of the incompetence of the master, the controversy was whether it had constructive knowledge of his incompetence. Thus, the House had to inquire whether the assured had "blind-eye" knowledge, which is equivalent to constructive knowledge, of the master's incompetence.

6B.2(ii) Blind-eye knowledge and suspicion

6.33 The House of Lords, agreeing with Lord Denning in *The Eurysthenes*,[74] reaffirmed that the notion of "privity" envisaged in s.39(5) covered not only positive knowledge but also blind-eye knowledge. The House was clear that blind-eye knowledge can only arise if an assured is suspicious of the defective condition of the ship and has deliberately refrained from finding out more about it. In emphasising the distinction between negligence and suspicion, the House cited with approval from the judgment of Lord Justice Leggatt in the Court of Appeal:[75]

> "Negligence there may have been in failing to ensure that the master was instructed, but 'suspicion' in the minds of any of the relevant individuals that an incompetent master might be used was simply not established."

In the House of Lords, Lord Clyde's account of the law on blind-eye knowledge is most illuminating:[76]

> "Blind-eye knowledge in my judgment requires a conscious reason for blinding the eye. There must be at least a suspicion of a truth about which you do not want to know and which you refuse to investigate. . . . I am not able to spell out of the judgment of Mr Justice Tuckey . . . any finding that the assured . . . suspected any incompetence on the part of the master of *Star Sea*, let alone any suspicion of his incompetence in the particular respect which mattered. That is sufficient to dispose of this part of the case; but in any event there is no finding of a suspicion on the part of the insured of the defective state of the dampers which contributed to the loss."

Equally informative is the speech of Lord Hobhouse:[77]

74. [1976] 2 Lloyd's Rep. 171, CA.
75. [1997] 1 Lloyd's Rep. 360, CA.
76. [2001] 1 Lloyd's Rep. 389 at 391, HL.
77. *Ibid.*, at 395.

"The use of the words 'suspicion' and 'belief" are indicative of the strength of the suspicion that is required. . . . The illuminating question therefore becomes 'why did he not inquire?' If the Judge is satisfied that it was because he did not want to know for certain, then a finding of privity should be made. If, on the other hand, he did not enquire because he was too lazy or he was grossly negligent or believed that there was nothing wrong, then privity has not been made out."

Lord Scott's crisp and categorical statement reads thus:[78]

"It is common ground – and if it is not, it should be – that an imputation of blind-eye knowledge requires an amalgam of suspicion that certain facts may exist and a decision to refrain from taking any steps to confirm their existence."

All the judges talked in terms of "suspicion" as the decisive criterion. But how is this suspicion to be discovered, when even the Devil knows not the thoughts of man? According to Lord Hobhouse, the test is subjective and not objective, meaning that the court is not concerned with the frame of mind of the prudent shipowner, but only with that of the assured. He said:[79] "The test is subjective: Did the assured have direct knowledge of the unseaworthiness or an actual mind which the law treats as equivalent to such knowledge?" With similar inclination, Lord Scott remarked:[80] "I do not, myself, see how a failure to think about the facts, and hence a failure to realise their implications, can afford the basis for a finding of blind-eye knowledge". 6.34

With due respect, the author submits that matter must surely rest upon whether the suspicion of the assured *ought* to have been aroused, rather than whether his suspicion is *in fact* aroused. If the suspicion of an ordinary prudent shipowner ought to be aroused, then it should not lie within the power of the particular assured to aver, save for very powerful reasons, that his suspicion was not aroused by the facts and circumstances of the case. In this regard, the author submits that the judgment of Lord Justice Roskill in *The Eurysthenes*, in the Court of Appeal, is more acceptable and realistic:[81] 6.35

"If the facts amounting to unseaworthiness are there staring the assured in the face so that he must, *had he thought of it*, have realised their implications upon the seaworthiness of his ship, he cannot escape from being held privy to that unseaworthiness by blindly or blandly ignoring those facts or by refraining from asking relevant questions regarding them in the hope that by his lack of inquiry he will not know for certain that which any inquiry must have made plain beyond possible doubt." [Emphasis added]

The tenor of his speech appears to suggest that an objective test is to be applied. Lord Hobhouse, however, felt that the phrase "had he thought of it" should not be construed as proposing an objective test.

Not surprisingly, Lord Scott has expressed approval of the distinction drawn by Lord Blackburn, in *Jones v. Gordon*,[82] between a person who was "honestly blundering and careless" and a person who "refrained from asking questions, not because he was an honest blunderer or a stupid man, but because he thought in his 6.36

78. *Ibid.*, at 413.
79. *Ibid.*, at 395.
80. *Ibid.*, at 414.
81. [1976] 2 Lloyd's Rep. 171 at 184, CA.
82. (1877) 2 App. Cas. 615 at 629. Emphasis added.

own secret mind – I suspect there is something wrong, and if I ask questions and make further inquiry, it will not longer be my suspecting it, but my knowing it, and then I shall not be able to recover". But the fact is, how does one know what is and what is not in the shipowner's "secret mind"? Only by the employment of the objective test can one ascertain whether it is plausible or reasonable for a person *not* to think (in his secret mind) that there is something wrong. Should not one be suspicious of those who are not suspicious when they ought to be suspicious?

On Lord Scott's choice of Nelson as analogy,[83] it would be far safer for Nelson (since he knew what he was going to see was the truth) to be lazy, to do nothing or pretend to be stupid than to place the telescope to his blind eye. In displaying conduct of utter indifference, he can never be accused of harbouring any suspicion or to have knowledge of the truth. In the words of Lord Scott, if "he did not enquire because he was too lazy or he was grossly negligent or believed that there was nothing wrong, then privity had not been made out".

6.37 Such talk is to encourage slovenly and unprofessional behaviour. It does little to promote safety at sea or the preservation of human life. In truth, it would be highly dangerous for any shipowner to think too much about the seaworthiness of his ship, for should he spare a thought on the matter, he could well be deemed to have turned a blind eye. The result of the application of the subjective test would be to punish the attentive and the vigilant, and to reward the lazy, slovenly and uncaring shipowner. Surely it cannot be right anyway to reward an obtuse fool, nor to burden an insurer with the need to engage in a deep psycho-analysis of his shipowning clients or their managing directors. The criterion of the notional prudent and honest shipowner is the only sensible and safe basis.

6B.2(iii) Privity to one or both aspects of seaworthiness?

6.38 The next inquiry is, does the assured have to be privy to *both* aspects of the unseaworthiness of the vessel before the insurer can be exonerated from liability? Or would the assured's privity to just *one* of the two (or more) aspects of unseaworthiness be sufficient? The author has dealt with this issue elsewhere[84] and maintains that the decision of Justice Tuckey, in the first instance, is more acceptable.

It is interesting to note that in *The Star Sea*, the lawyers for the insurer had *conceded* that the assured had to be found to be privy to *both* aspects of unseaworthiness before their client can be freed from liability. Why the concession was made is unclear, for it means that an assured who is privy to one aspect of unseaworthiness would still be able to claim under the policy. The generality of the wording of s.39(5) does not suggest that such is the case.

Though Lord Hobhouse had touched on the issue, he was not prepared to commit himself one way or other, except to say that, as the matter of the correctness of the concession was not argued, he had to decide the case on that basis – hinting perhaps

83. [2001] 1 Lloyd's Rep. 389 at 413, Lord Scott stated: "Nelson at the battle of Copenhagen made a deliberate decision to place the telescope to his blind eye in order to avoid seeing what he knew he would see if he placed it to his good eye".

84. See "Seaworthiness and safe ship management", [1998] IJIL 162, where the author contends that "the privity of the assured to *any one* aspect of unseaworthiness to which the loss is attributable will exonerate the insurer from liability . . .".

that the matter was arguable? With similar brevity, Lord Scott, who also found it difficult to ignore the concession, appears to hold the view that the suspicion or realisation of any *one* aspect of the unseaworthiness would suffice, provided, of course, that the test of causation is satisfied. Provided that the assured is privy to *any* one aspect of unseaworthiness to which the loss is attributable, it is contended that the insurer should not be made not liable for the loss. Without impugning the reasons (whatever they were) for the concession, it must be made categorically evident that it cannot be a valid precedent. The law can so easily take and keep to a wrong turning in an ambiguous situation of this kind.

6B.2(iv) "Attributable to"

Unlike a warranty (express or implied) of seaworthiness where causation is irrelevant, a causal link between the defect and the loss has to be established before the privity rule (under s.39(5)) may be invoked. Though the rule of proximate cause is to be generally applied for the purpose of resolving a dispute regarding the cause of a loss, the Act allows exceptions to be made to the rule.[85] The fact that s.39(5) has chosen to use the term "attributable to", and not the standard expression "proximately caused by", to describe the casual connection between the unseaworthy defect and the loss, indicates that the expressions must mean different things. An insurer is freed from liability if the loss is "attributable to" such unseaworthiness to which the assured is privy. 6.39

The tentacles of the term "attributable to" are far more menacing than those of "proximately caused by". In law, "proximate cause" is a precise and technical concept, whereas "attributable to" is a blunt term which any person would take to mean simply as "caused by". The term "attributable to" is much wider in scope and will ensnare any loss which is in some measure (however minor or remote) brought about or contributed to by the unseaworthiness. A loss which is *proximately* and *solely* caused by unseaworthiness would simply be not recoverable by reason of that fact that unseaworthiness is not an insured peril. The author contends that in such a case, there is no need to inquire whether the assured is privy to the unseaworthiness. Regardless of privity, such a proximate sole cause of loss is simply not recoverable.[86]

According to Mr Justice Roche in *George Cohen, Sons and Co. v. Standard Marine Insurance Co.*,[87] "it is enough if a matter of unseaworthiness, being a matter to which the assured is privy, is a cause, or part of the cause, of the loss". In using "attributable to" as the causal rule, a wider net is cast in s.39(5). Should the unseaworthiness to which the assured is privy contribute in any way to the loss, the insurer would be exempted from liability. English law has carefully chosen a less specific criterion for the privity rule; compared to the rule of proximate cause, such a less demanding gauge of causal connection will naturally operate to the detriment of the assured. 6.40

85. Sections 39(5) and 55(2)(a) are exceptions to the rule. The opening words of s.55(1) read as: "Subject to the provisions of this Act . . . the insurer is liable for any loss proximately caused by a peril insured against . . .". For a fuller discussion of the law of causation applicable in marine insurance, see Hodges, *Cases and Materials on Marine Insurance Law*, Cavendish Publishing, 1999, Chapter 8.

86. See Hodges, *Cases and Materials on Marine Insurance Law* (Cavendish Publishing, 1999) at pp.137–138.

87. (1925) 21 Ll. L. Rep. 30.

6B.2(v) "Such" unseaworthiness

6.41 It has been suggested in *Thomas v. Tyne and Wear Steamship Freight Insurance Association*[88] that this part of the sub-section should be read as if the word "such" appears before "unseaworthiness". Thus, only a loss that is attributable to "such unseaworthiness" to which the assured is privy will free the insurer from liability. The reason for the insertion is to accommodate the scenario where the ship may be unseaworthy in more ways than one, some aspects of which the assured may not be privy to. The foregoing is, of course, based on the premise that the loss is proximately caused by an insured peril. For if it were not, there would be no reason to inquire into the privity of the assured. Thus, for the sub-section to bite, the loss must first be brought under the policy as one which is *prima facie* recoverable, as a loss proximately caused by an insured peril, before any need to establish the privity of the assured can arise.

In this case, the arbitrator's finding, that the unfitness of the hull was the sole cause of loss, was accepted by the court. And in spite of the fact that unseaworthiness was not, and it can never be, an insured peril, Mr Justice Atkin held the insurers liable on the basis that the assured was not privy to this particular aspect of unseaworthiness. The author strongly contends that as the loss was not proximately caused by an insured peril, it was simply not recoverable regardless of whether the assured was or was not privy to the condition of unseaworthiness.[89]

6B.2(vi) An exception of liability

6.42 As was seen, s.39(5) does not impose a continuing obligation or warranty on the part of the assured to ensure that the ship is seaworthy at the commencment of each and every voyage undertaken during the currency of the time policy. The "privity" rule is not a warranty of *continuing* seaworthiness: it is not even a warranty. It is a statutory exception of liability for unseaworthiness. This was made clear in *Sadler v. Dixon*,[90] where the court held that the assured was only obliged to ensure that the ship was seaworthy (provided with a competent master and crew) at the inception of the time policy.

6.43 In summing up, under English law, there is no implied warranty of seaworthiness at the inception of the time policy, neither is there a warranty of continuing seaworthiness after the attachment of the policy. Though a loss may be proximately caused by an insured peril and therefore recoverable, an assured may still be denied his right to be indemnified under the policy if he is found privy to the particular unseaworthiness to which the loss is attributable. The foregoing assumes that the assured is able successfully to claim an insured peril as the proximate cause of loss, because even non-privity unseaworthiness is not, and cannot under any known form of policy, be an insured risk.

88. [1917] K.B. 938.
89. For a further discussion of this case, see Hodges, *Cases and Materials on Marine Insurance Laws* (Cavendish Publishing, 1999) p.351.
90. 151 ER 1303 (Ex 1841).

6C THE "AMERICAN RULE"

In the US, the law on seaworthiness in relation to time policies is commonly referred to simply as the "American Rule", which was crystallised in the productive year of 1957 when the subject was examined by Judge Brown of the Fifth Circuit in *Saskatchewan Government Insurance Office v. Spot Pack Inc.* (the *Spot Pack* case)[91] and, two months later, in *Tropical Marine Products, Inc v. Birmingham Fire Insurance Co. (The Sea Pak)*.[92] Judge Brown redefined US law on the subject of seaworthiness in a time policy thus:[93] 6.44

"... [T]he American Rule, in a rare departure from a determined course of parallel uniformity ... implies for a time policy, as does the English Rule as of the commencement of the voyage for voyage policies ... a warranty of seaworthiness as of the very moment of attachment of the insurance.

And, unlike the English Rule which limits the warranty to the commencement of the voyage, the American Rule takes it somewhat further to extend, in point of time, a sort of negative, modified warranty. ... It is, rather, stated in the negative that the Owner, from bad faith or neglect, will not knowingly permit the vessel to break ground in an unseaworthy condition. And, unlike a breach of warranty of continuing seaworthiness, express or implied, which voids the policy altogether, the consequence of a violation of this 'negative' burden is merely a denial of liability for loss or damage caused proximately by such unseaworthiness".

In *The Sea Pak*, the gist of the rule was phrased in more concise terms as follows:[94]

" ... the owner's obligation under a Time Policy, as was this one, is extremely limited: the vessel is seaworthy at the attachment of the insurance, but henceforth it is a sort of negative warranty, i.e., the owner or those in privity with him will not knowingly send the vessel to sea in a deficient condition."

Indeed, after having restated the American Rule with some confidence in *The Spot Pack*, Judge Brown then immediately proceeded to question its status,[95] tracing its birthplace to the early case of *Union Insurance Company of Philadelphia v. Smith*,[96] where Judge Blatchford, in 1888, pronounced that:[97] 6.45

"In the insurance of a vessel by a time policy, the warranty of seaworthiness is complied with if the vessel be seaworthy at the commencement of the risk; and the fact that she subsequently sustains damage, and is not properly refitted at an intermediate port, does not discharge the insurer from subsequent risks or loss, provided such loss be not the consequence of the omission.

A defect of seaworthiness arising after the risk, and permitted to continue from bad faith or want of ordinary prudence or diligence on the part of the insured or his agents, discharges the insurer from liability for any loss which is the consequence of such bad faith, or want of

91. 1957 AMC 655 at 661 (5th Cir. 1957).
92. 1957 AMC 1946 (5th Cir. 1957).
93. For the purposes of clarity and of highlighting the two separate limbs of the American Rule, the author has taken the liberty to split the speech of Judge Brown into its two natural parts.
94. 1957 AMC 1946 at 1951 (5th Cir. 1957).
95. Judge Brown said (at 662): "... there seems to have been slight critical awareness that the policy in *Union* contained not alone an express warranty of seaworthiness, but an express exclusion of loss caused by unseaworthiness ...".
96. 124 U.S. 405 (1888).
97. The author has also separated Judge Blatchford's speech into two parts for the purpose of discussion.

prudence or diligence, but does not affect the contract of insurance as to any other risk or loss covered by the policy and not caused or increased by such particular defect".

Judge Blatchford's account of the law, though remarkably positive in its terms, has, however, been doubted on the grounds that the time policy under consideration contained an *express* exception of liability for unseaworthiness.[98] It has been pointed out, on more than one occasion, that his comments were made by way of *obiter* and, therefore, do not stand on the firmest of foundation.[99] Though perceived as *obiter dictum*, the rule has, nonetheless, been acknowledged as the "accepted standard for time policies".[100]

6.46 There are clearly two parts to the American Rule, both of which have engendered a number of problems. The American Rule differs from English law in two fundamental ways. First, US law implies a warranty of seaworthiness at the time of the inception of the risk (when the policy attaches), whereas English law is resolute that no such warranty is under any circumstances to be implied in a time policy.[101] This warranty implied by US law is sometimes referred to as the "pre-attachment" warranty of seaworthiness.

Second, once the initial implied warranty has been observed and the risk has attached, the American Rule will then imply "a sort of negative, modified warranty"[102] in that the assured will not (from bad faith or neglect) knowingly permit the vessel to leave port in an unseaworthy state. This rule, inappropriately called a "warranty", is sometimes also inaptly referred to as the "post-attachment" warranty. Its English counterpart, the privity rule, contained in s.39(5) has already been discussed.

6C.1 The implied pre-attachment warranty of seaworthiness

6.47 There is an abundance of case law confirming the existence and applicability of the implied pre-attachment warranty of seaworthiness in a time policy.[103] In spite of their awareness of the problems (set out in *Gibson v. Small*) associated with implying a warranty of seaworthiness in a time policy, the majority of American judges were

98. The policy expressly excepted liability, *inter alia*, for loss caused by "all unseaworthiness".

99. See, e.g., *New York & PRSS Co. v. Aetna Insurance Co.*, 204 F. 255 at p.258 (2nd Cir. 1913) where Judge Ward observed that "Mr Justice Blatchford in *Union Insurance Co. v. Smith* ... seems to have assumed that there is an implied warranty at the beginning of the risk under a time policy. The observation was not necessary to the decision of the case, because the policy under consideration contained an express exception of losses caused by unseaworthiness".

100. See *Texaco Inc. v. Universal Marine Inc.* 400 F. Supp. 311, 323, 1976 AMC 226 (E.D. La. 1975).

101. Langhauser, "Implied Warranties of Seaworthiness: Applying the Knowing Neglect Standard in Time Hull Insurance Policies", 39 Me. L. Rev. 443 at 444 (1987) refers to the divergence as follows: "Although American admiralty law strives to remain harmonious with English admiralty law, American courts have, in a rare departure from favoured uniformity, deviated from the English rule for implied warranties of seaworthiness in time hull marine insurance policies".

102. Whether this is in fact a true insurance *warranty* in the strict sense of the word is a matter of some importance that needs to be examined.

103. As early as 1803, the case of *Barnewall v. Church* 1 Caines 217; 2 Am. Dec. 180 (N.Y. 1803) laid down the general rule that, "There is, in *every* insurance, an implied warranty that the ship shall be seaworthy when the risk commences" [emphasis added]. No distinction was drawn between time and voyage policies in this regard. In 1831, in *Paddock v. Franklin Insurance Co.*, 28 Mass. (11 Pick.) 226 at 231 (1831), Chief Justice Shaw said: "[T]he general rule that the ship must be seaworthy at the inception of the risk, in order to make the policy attach, and charge the underwriter with the risk, probably would be applied

happy to depart from the English rule and imply a warranty of seaworthiness at the commencement of the risk in a time policy. But, there were also judges who have refused to acknowledge the existence of the warranty, and an avid opponent to the pre-attachment warranty is Judge Frank who, in *New York, New Haven and Hartford Railroad Company v. Gray*,[104] in passing mentioned that the "Appellees [underwriters], had correctly disclaimed of an implied warranty of seaworthiness, since these are time policies".[105] But interestingly enough, in the same eventful year of 1957, the same court (Second Circuit) had decided otherwise in *McAllister Lighterage Line v. Insurance Company of North America*[106] that: "With a term policy of insurance the warranty of seaworthiness arises at the time when the insurance becomes effective. . . . It is clear that implied in every policy of hull insurance is a covenant of seaworthiness".[107] This change of heart of the Second Circuit could be due to the fact that the *McAllister* case was decided after the decision of *The Spot Pack*. More recently, in *The Papoose*,[108] the validity of the pre-attachment warranty was endorsed by Judge Brown, who was afforded a further occasion to reiterate that, "under the American Rule, unlike the English, there is an implied warranty of seaworthiness in a time policy".[109]

One American writer, Pritchett, has pointed out that,[110] "the status of the first part of the 'American Rule' remains in a state of uncertainty"; but he has acknowledged that the view expressed in the *Gray* case is of the minority and that the "weight of authority in the US supports the existence of a warranty at the time of attachment". On the other hand, McGlone's research has led him to the finding that,[111] "The 6.48

in this, as in all other cases, being a necessary incident to the contract". See also *Jones v. Insurance Co.*, 13 Fed. Cas. 982; Fed. Cas. No. 7,470 (E.D. Pa. 1852); *Plummer v. Insurance Co. of North America* 95 A. 605 (Me. 1915); *Fisch v. Insurance Co. of North America* 130 A. 2d 891 (Superior Ct. N.J. 1957); *The M/V Papoose* 409 F. 2d 974, 1969 AMC 781 (5th Cir. 1969); *Texaco Inc. v. Universal Marine Inc.* 400 F. Supp. 311, 323, 1976 AMC 226 (E.D. La. 1975); *Lemar Towing Co. Insurance v. Fireman's Fund Insurance Co.* 352 F. Supp. 652, 1973 AMC 1844 (E.D.La. 1972); and *Gregoire v. Underwriters at Lloyd's* 559 F. Supp. 596, 599, 1982 AMC 2045 (D. Alaska 1982).

104. 1957 AMC 616, 621; 240 F. 2d 460 (2d Cir. 1957); cert. denied, 353 U.S. 966 (1957), henceforth referred to simply as the "*Gray*" case. See also *New York & PRSS Co. v. Aetna Insurance Co.* 204 Fed. 255 at 258 (2d Cir. 1913) where Judge Ward seemed to favour the English position of denying an implied warranty of seaworthiness to a time policy. In the more recent case of *Gregoire v. Underwriters at Lloyd's* 1982 AMC 2045, Judge Fitzergerald of the District Court of Alaska expressed his desire to see US law in harmony with English law in this regard. His sentiments in relation to the pre-attachment warranty were expressed thus: "Under the American Rule, the owner warrants absolutely the seaworthiness of his vessel at the time the policy attaches. This is the aspect of the implied warranty that has been most heavily criticised. . . . I do not need to consider this warranty here, however, since the Underwriters concede that the *Rex* was seaworthy at attachment".

105. As the issue was not argued, this remark is itself *obiter*, because the vessel (a carfloat) was lost by reason of sea perils after the risk had attached. Surely, if there was no evidence of unseaworthiness at the inception of the risk, it would be futile for the insurer to argue that an implied warranty of seaworthiness is applicable.

106. 244 F. 2d 867 (2d Cir. 1957).

107. The *McAllister* case was decided in May 1957, after the decision of *The Spot Pack* in March 1957; whereas the judgment in the *Gray* case was decided in January 1957.

108. 1969 AMC 781 (5th Cir. 1969).

109. See also the general remarks of Chief Justice Fuller in early case of *The Caledonia* 157 U.S. 124 (1895), referred to *supra*.

110. Pritchett, "The Implied warranty of seaworthiness in time policies: The US View" [1983] 2 LMCLQ 195 at 207 & 208.

111. McGlone, "Marine Insurance and the Implied Warranty of Seaworthiness" 1975 21 Loyola Law Review 960 at 964.

scanty authority on which the American Rule is based has led some authors to conclude that there is no implied warranty of seaworthiness in time policies, and especially no implied warranty of continuing seaworthiness". Healy, even more explicit, observes that:[112] "[t]he true US rule applicable to time policies seems to be that there is no implied warranty of seaworthiness, even when the insured vessel is in port when the risk attaches". However, Judge Cardozo in *The Traffic*[113] would like to think that "the question may still be open".[114] But as will be seen from case law, the balance appears to tip in favour of implying a warranty of seaworthiness, albeit a qualified version, to a time policy.

6.49 Speaking of the preponderant view, the question that immediately springs to mind, when applying the implied warranty to a time policy, is, how is the warranty to be complied with if the ship is at sea at the moment of the attachment of the risk? Further, is the implied warranty also to be applied if the ship is in port (any port) at the time of the inception of the policy? This then raises two further related questions: first, does the warranty apply only if the ship is, at the inception of the risk, in a home port or does it also apply if she is in a foreign port? Second, what is the position if proper repair facilities are not available in the port (at home or abroad)? And to take the matter even further, is the residence of the assured a relevant consideration?

6.50 These problems, which had plagued the minds of many of the earlier English judges, were the main reasons that led to their refusal to infer a warranty of seaworthiness in a time policy in the first place.[115] The sticking-points were described by Lord Campbell, in *Gibson v. Small*, as follows:[116]

> "There is a broad distinction which may always be observed between time-policies and voyage-policies; but when you come to subdivide time-policies into such where the ship is in a British port and where the ship is abroad, and still more if the residence of the shipowner is to be inquired into and regarded, there would be a great danger of confusion being occasioned by the attempted classification."

With such warning of the complexities involved, we can now anticipate, with some trepidation, the kind of problems which US law is likely to find in imposing an *unqualified* pre-attachment warranty of seaworthiness in a time policy.

6.51 The first part of the American Rule is stated in general terms, nothing is mentioned about the circumstances when the warranty is to apply, the nature of the warranty or the legal effects of its breach. Though the rule is worded in unconditional terms, it did not deter American judges from limiting its application to specific situations. The possibilities for its application are manifold and before we can proceed to discuss them, it is best first to eliminate the particular incidence when the warranty will *not* be implied.

112. Healy, "The Hull Policy: Warranties, Representations, Disclosures and Conditions", 41 Tul. L. Rev. 245 at 253 (1967).

113. 159 N.E. 87; 1928 AMC 174 (N.Y. 1927).

114. There was no need for him to close the subject because the policy he had to consider contained an express warranty of seaworthiness.

115. Perhaps the British should be thankful for small mercies: see Anderson, "The Evolution of the Implied Warranty of Seaworthiness in Comparative Perspective", 17 J. Mar. L. & Com. 1 at 22, (1986) where he noted that: "The lack of clarity in the US decisions as to when and with what effect a warranty of seaworthiness will be implied a time policy in a sense vindicates the practical solution reached in *Gibson v. Small*".

116. [1853] 10 ER 499 at 527, HL.

6C.1(i) Ship at sea at the inception of the policy

American law in the main accepts the notion that a warranty of seaworthiness is not to be implied in a time policy that attaches when the ship is at sea. This was confirmed in *Jones v. The Insurance Company*;[117] *Rouse v. The Insurance Company*;[118] *Plummer v. Insurance Company of North America*;[119] *Capen v. Washington Insurance Company*[120] and *The Zilliah*.[121] The *Capen* case is apparently regarded as the first in the US to have accepted the notion that, in a time policy effected on a vessel at sea, there is no implied warranty at the inception of the risk.[122] In *Henjes v. Aetna Insurance*,[123] it was perceived that in such cases "the insurer takes her as she may be", because "the legal and equitable considerations" are entirely different when the vessel is in port, as opposed to when she is at sea.[124] The rationale for the rule was recorded by Chief Justice Bigelow in *Hoxie v. Pacific Mutual Insurance Company* as:[125] 6.52

"It is easy to see a good reason for holding that a policy on time, effected on a vessel when at sea, does not include any warranty of her seaworthiness at the commencement of the risk. In such case, the insurance is on a 'vessel in an unknown sea in an unknown state'. The assured has no means of knowing her actual condition, or, if she is injured and out of repair, of restoring her to a condition of seaworthiness. Both parties enter into the contract with a full knowledge of these facts. It would not only be pushing a rule of law to an unreasonable extent to say that under such circumstances the assured undertakes to warrant his ship, of the condition and circumstance of which he can know nothing, to be then seaworthy for any purpose, but it would be contrary to the manifest intent and understanding of the parties. In such cases, the circumstances attending the making of the contract of insurance tend directly to rebut any implication of a warranty of seaworthiness at the inception of the risk."

6C.1(ii) Ship in port at the inception of the policy

On realising that it would neither be appropriate nor reasonable to imply a warranty of seaworthiness to a ship when she is at sea at the time of the attachment of the risk, the courts then went about exploring the possibility of invoking the warranty when the 6.53

117. (1852) 2 Wallace Jr. 278. Judge Grier expressed his preference for a qualified warranty of seaworthiness thus: "It may be true, also, that there is in a time policy a warranty of seaworthiness at the commencement of the risk, so far as lay in the power of the assured to effect it, so that if the ship had met with damage before, and could have been repaired by the exercise of reasonable care and pains, and was not, the policy would not attach".

118. 3 Wall (Pa.) 367 (3rd Cir. 1862). In this case, the court decided that a warranty of seaworthiness is implied if the vessel is in her *home* port at the inception of the risk. The judge took pains to distinguish the rule in *Gibson v. Small*, stating that as the ship was on a distant ocean at the date of the policy, the case did not answer the question of whether the warranty is implied if she were in a port at the inception of the risk.

119. 95 A. 605 (Me. 1915), where Judge Bird said: "In the United States the great weight of authority is to the effect that, except in cases when at the inception of the risk the vessel is at sea, there is an implied warranty of seaworthiness in time policies".

120. 66 Mass. 518.

121. 1929 AMC 166 at 168, where the judge was categorical that, "... if the vessel is at sea at that time, there is no warranty that she is then seaworthy".

122. This was noted by Chief Justice Bigelow in *Hoxie v. Pacific Insurance Co.* 7 Allen 211 (1862).

123. 132 F. 2d 715 (2d Cir.), cert. denied, 319 U.S. 760 (1943).

124. See also *Sorenson & Neilson v. Boston Insurance Company* 1926 AMC 241, 10 F. (2d) 563, where District Judge Soper was of the opinion that "were it not for the fact that in many cases the owner is not in a position to inform himself of the condition of his vessel and to remedy it if defective" the law would have implied a warranty of seaworthiness to a time as it does for a voyage policy. See also *The Zilliah* 1929 AMC 166, discussed *infra*.

125. (1863, 7 Allen) 89 Mass. 211.

insured ship is *in port* at the time of the inception of the policy,[126] only to create further confusion in the law. In the oft-cited early case of *Berwind et al v. Greenwich Insurance* Company,[127] the court stated in general terms that:

> "In every case of marine insurance by a general policy covering all perils of the sea, where the vessel insured is in port, there is an implied warranty that the vessel is seaworthy at the inception of the policy. It is a condition precedent to the risk, and, if the vessel is not seaworthy, the policy does not attach."

This comment seems clear enough in suggesting that at the precise moment when the policy attaches and the insured ship is in port, the warranty of seaworthiness will be implied. Support for this can also be found in *The Papoose*,[128] as the "spectacular unseaworthiness" of the vessel existed when the ship was in port at the time when the policy attached. It is significant to note that no mention was made of whether the ship had to be, at the critical moment, port-worthy and/or seaworthy. No clue was given about the location of the port: does the warranty apply if the vessel is in a foreign place at the time of the inception of the policy? Also, there was no clarification whether the port, home or abroad, has to be equipped with proper repair facilities.

The purpose of implying a warranty whilst a ship is in port at the attachment of the risk is captured in the early case of *Jones v. Insurance Company*[129] as:

> "It may be true, also, that there is in a time policy a warranty of seaworthiness at the commencement of the risk, so far as lay in the power of the assured to effect it, so that if the ship had met with damage before, and could have been repaired by the exercise of reasonable care and pains, and was not, the policy would not attach."

6.54 In *Rouse v. The Insurance Company*,[130] the court settled one aspect of the problem in ruling that the warranty of seaworthiness is implied in the event when the vessel is lying in her *home* port at the time the insurance was made. The facts of the case were especially appropriate for stirring the implied term, as the policy was "for one year commencing on the 27th day of December, 1860, at noon . . . on a steamboat named the *Commerce*, then lying in the port of Baltimore . . . ". The intention of the parties was that the policy was to attach on her present voyage from Baltimore. After undergoing some repairs, the boat entered upon her first voyage on 10 March 1860 and foundered at sea without encountering any exceptional weather. It was found that the ship was unseaworthy when she set sail from Baltimore. Judge Grier, who was clearly not in favour of an all-embracing rule – that a warranty of seaworthiness is not to be implied in all time policies – ruled against the assured. The basis of his decision was phrased as follows:

> "It is true, it is a time policy, but it is not on a vessel in a distant ocean, or in parts unknown, where the parties have contract without a knowledge of her situation, and with a premium paid for assuming the risk of her seaworthiness at the time by the underwriter."

126. *Cf.* Healy, "The Hull Policy: Warranties, Representations, Disclosures and Conditions", 41 Tul. L. Rev. 245 at 253 (1967), who holds the view that there is no implied warranty of seaworthiness even when the insured vessel is in port when the risk attaches.

127. (1889) 114 N.Y. 231.

128. 1969 AMC 781 (5th Cir. 1969).

129. 3 Fed. Cas. 982; Fed. Cas. No. 7, 470 (E.D. Pa. 1852).

130. 3 Wall (Pa.) 367 (3rd Cir. 1862).

A mention has to be made of the judgment of Judge Ward in *New York & PRSS Co. v. Aetna Insurance Company*,[131] which is frequently cited as authority for the principle that the implied warranty is applicable if the ship is in port at the inception of the policy. His comments were: 6.55

> "Our courts seem to take the view that although there may be no implied warranty of seaworthiness, still if the vessel is in a port where repairs may be made, or equipment and supplies obtained, the insured cannot recover for any loss caused by the want of due diligence in making repairs and obtaining equipment or supplies."

The above statement is ambiguous, as it is capable of more than one interpretation. It may be construed to mean that a warranty of seaworthiness may be implied in a time policy only if the ship is in a port where repairs may be made at the time of the time of the inception of the risk. And it may also be read as declaring a blanket rule that under no circumstances is a warranty of seaworthiness implied in a time policy. Was the judge trying to limit or qualify the initial warranty to vessels which are in port – where repair facilities are available – at the time of the inception of the risk? Or was he advocating the rule that no warranty of seaworthiness at all exists in a time policy and that unseaworthiness is only relevant in the event of a loss caused by the want of due diligence on the part of the assured in failing to take advantage of available repair facilities. The latter part of the statement sounds remarkably similar to the so-called "negative modified warranty" of the American Rule, where causation is clearly an essential feature. There appears in the statement to be a conflation of two concepts. It is significant to note that, if a *warranty* of seaworthiness is to be implied, even if it is limited to a certain circumstance, the issue as to the cause of loss would be irrelevant. In the event of a breach of *any* warranty, causation is totally immaterial.

The "in port" rule was given a thorough examination in the case of *The SS Natalie*.[132] The facts of the case are particularly pertinent to the present discussion, because there were two time policies of insurance in the case, one of which had attached when the ship was in port and a later policy when she was at sea. After conducting a survey of US cases on the subject, the court arrived at the conclusion that a warranty of seaworthiness is implied in a time policy only if the vessel is at the inception of the risk in a port where repair facilities are available. The court stated: 6.56

> "In the United States, however, the law is settled that if the insured vessel is in a port where there are repair facilities when the time insurance becomes effective, there is an implied warranty of seaworthiness *on sailing from that port*, and breach of that implied warranty of seaworthiness relieves Underwriters of liability." [emphasis added]

It is significant to note that the warranty of seaworthiness does not have to be fulfilled until such time when the vessel leaves the port. Thus, the time of the attachment of the risk and the time when the warranty is to be complied with do not coincide. The vessel, if she is in a port with repair facilities at the time of the attachment of the policy, has to be seaworthy (as in the case of a voyage policy) only at

131. 204 Fed. 255 at 258 (2d Cir. 1913). See also *Hoxie v. Pacific Mutual Insurance Co.* 89 Mass. 211 (1863), where the insured vessel was, at the time of the inception of the policy, at an intermediate foreign port which was fully equipped with full repair facilities.

132. 1959 AMC 2379 (Mount, Arb.)

the commencement of the voyage. Consequently, the warranty of seaworthiness does not apply at the time of the attachment of the policy, but at a later time, when the ship sets sails on a voyage. Once again, we can sense a reluctance on the part of a judge who has refused to treat time policies differently from voyage policies. No mention is made about her port-worthiness whilst she remains in the port.

6.57 The plot, however, thickens with the case of *Hoxie v. Pacific Mutual Insurance Company*[133] where the vessel was under repair in Bermuda (a foreign port) when her owner obtained a hull policy on her for one year. A few days after she was repaired, she sailed from Bermuda and ten months later, after several intervening voyages, she sank. The court held that as the policy was effected on the vessel whilst she was in port, before she set sail from Bermuda, the assured had to comply with not only the warranty of port-worthiness, but also that of seaworthiness at such time when she set sail from Bermuda. A new trial was ordered in order to determine whether she was seaworthy on sailing from Bermuda. The court held that:

> "... on the facts disclosed at the trial ... there was an implied warranty of seaworthiness in the policy declared on, in analogy to that which would exist under similar circumstances in a policy for a voyage; and that the insurance having been effected on a vessel while in port, to take effect from a certain day, which was before she sailed thence, the warranty includes seaworthiness for port as well as seaworthiness in setting out therefrom, as in the policy at and from a particular place."

The *Hoxie* case has extended the implied pre-attachment warranty to a vessel that is in a foreign port where there are "ample means and opportunities of putting the vessel in a state of complete repair, and of fitting her in all respects for sea to when the policy attaches". Even though the court was inclined not to imply a warranty of seaworthiness to a vessel which is at sea at the time of the inception of the policy, it was not prepared to go all the way, as England has done, of laying down an absolute disclaimer. For a proper understanding of the subject, much is to be gained from examining the rationale of the US approach which was set out in the following terms:

> "The main ground on which the Court of Queen's Bench seems to have gone in deciding that there is no warranty of seaworthiness whatever, under any circumstances, in any time policy, is the inconvenience which might be occasioned in applying the doctrine to certain cases of insurance on time which might arise. But this inconvenience, which we do not deny might sometimes exist, is far less in our judgment than would be created by the anomaly of an absolute denial of one of the great principles of marine insurance, in its application to an entire class of contracts which are almost precisely analogous to those in which it is uniformly and rigorously applied."

6.58 Another authority which has buttressed the position taken in the *Hoxie* case is *The Zilliah,*[134] where the court held that:

> "The warranty of seaworthiness in a time policy is complied with if the vessel is seaworthy at the commencement of the risk, *Union Insurance Co. v. Smith* ... but that the weight of authority in this country is to the effect that, if the vessel is in port at the time of the commencement of the risk, there is an implied warranty of seaworthiness for the port risk and that before sailing the vessel will be made seaworthy for the voyage. But if the vessel is at sea at that time, there is no

133. (1863, 7 Allen) 89 Mass. 211.
134. 1929 AMC 166 at 168.

warranty that she is then seaworthy. Nor, in the absence of any statutory provision, is there a warranty that the vessel will be seaworthy at the commencement of subsequent voyages."

A keen determination not to differentiate between a time and a voyage policy is reflected in the above two cases. If a time policy is effected while the ship is in a port (at home or abroad) where repairs may be carried out, two warranties are inferred: she has to be port-worthy while she is port, and seaworthy when she commences on her voyage.

In imposing a twin burden on the assured, the judges have effectively converted a time policy into a voyage policy. Under English law, a voyage policy that attaches while the ship is in port, namely in an "at and from" policy, has to be port-worthy[135] and seaworthy.[136] In the light of this, it would be to the advantage of an assured to arrange for his ship to be at sea at the time when he takes up the policy, for in such a situation, no warranty of port-worthiness or seaworthiness will be implied. With due respect, American judges appear to have taken the matter a little too far. It is one thing to imply the warranty at the inception of the risk, but quite another to extend its application beyond that specific time set by the policy for the attachment of the risk. 6.59

Some American judges have introduced a new dimension to the American Rule. Surely, the attachment of risk in a time policy must take place at a precise time on a particular date specified in the policy. Assuming that "port-worthiness" is subsumed as an aspect of "seaworthiness",[137] the above view has effectively extended the moment of the attachment of a time policy from a single to two specified points in time.

It is worthwhile considering the matter from the other side of the coin, as Judge McAlliser had done in *Merchants' Insurance Company of Chicago v. Morrison*.[138] The policy under consideration was placed on 1 April 1869 while the vessel was still in the Port of Muskegon undergoing repairs. She was insured from 1 April; she remained in port until 10 April when, being laden with a cargo of lumber, set upon a voyage to Chicago. She continued to be engaged in the lumber trade between those ports until the 8 October when she was consumed by a fire, not the result of unseaworthiness. The pivotal issue before the court was based on the insurers' argument that she was unseaworthy at the time she set out upon her first voyage on 10 April. After setting out the facts of the case, Judge McAlliser framed the issue with admirable clarity as follows: 6.60

"Under these circumstances, did the law imply a warranty that the vessel should be seaworthy when she set out upon her *first* voyage from that port; and was it requisite that she was seaworthy at that time, in the sense of that term as applied to voyage policies, in order to make the policy attach and charge the insurer for a subsequent loss by fire not arising from want of seaworthiness?" [emphasis added]

His answer was blunt: "We think not. To so hold would not be the mere recognition of a condition to the policy by implication of law, and in respect to which the contact was silent, but would be to vary its terms and legal effect". The thrust of his reasoning, which is most convincing, was that:

---

135. See s.39(1)
136. See s.39(2).
137. As is cargoworthiness, which is always recognised in the law of carriage of goods by sea as a feature of seaworthiness.
138. 14 Am. Rep. 93.

"It would lead to great embarrassment if the vessel owner cannot obtain a policy like that in question without its being arbitrarily subjected to the same rules incident to voyage policies. Aside from the circumstance of the vessel being ice-bound for several months, is the further circumstances, that much of the commerce upon the lakes is carried on between ports which are not remote from each other. Hence, voyages are short and quickly and frequently made. In such case there would be an obvious inconvenience in the use of voyage policies. This inconvenience, together with the other peculiarity of navigation upon the lakes we have mentioned, dictate the propriety of seeking a substitute for the usual voyage policy, in another form of contract which, in the very necessities of the case, must be substantially different."

The judge felt very strongly that the assured had the right to obtain a (time) policy which is "untrammelled with the incident which the law attaches to a voyage policy". This is clearly a decision in favour of upholding the distinction between a policy that is governed by "the motion of the earth" and one by "the motion of the ship". Though the judge was clear in his mind that "the vessel must be seaworthy ... at the commencement or inception of the risk, in order that the policy attach and charge the insurer", he had failed to elaborate whether port-worthiness or seaworthiness was the standard expected of the ship on 1 April. As the ship was undergoing repairs on 1 April right through to the 10 April when she set sail, she could not have been seaworthy on 1 April; at best, she must have been port-worthy.[139]

6C.1(iii) No warranty of continuing seaworthiness

6.61 It has also been suggested in the US, albeit half-heartedly, that the implied warranty applies at the beginning of *each* and *every* voyage undertaken during the currency of the time policy.[140] If this proposition is upheld, it would place an assured in a much more onerous position than if he had taken up a voyage policy, where there is no shadow of a doubt in law, both here and in the US, that there is no warranty of continuing seaworthiness in such a policy.

6.62 In *American Insurance Co v. Ogden*,[141] this specific question was put to the court, to which its answer was: "In ordinary cases, the implied warranty of seaworthiness only applies to the commencement of the adventure, or risk, and not to any intermediate port of destination during the continuance of the adventure, or voyage . . . ". In even clearer terms, another judge, Senator Wagers, stated that: "The implied warranty of seaworthiness attaches as a condition at the commencement of the risk, and not at *every port* at which the vessel puts in during her voyage. If she be seaworthy at the commencement of her voyage, the implied warranty is answered".[142] The court, however, took great pains to explain the difference between implying a *warranty* of continuing seaworthiness and the requirements of the "negative warranty" of the second part of the American Rule. Senator Verplanck, with equal panache noted:

139. There was clear evidence that she was thoroughly overhauled and, therefore, seaworthy when she set out upon her voyage on 10 April.

140. See, e.g., *The Companion* 1929 AMC 693, where the defendants (insurer) contended that the vessel was unseaworthy at the commencement of and during the last voyage performed under the time policy. But as the vessel was found to be seaworthy at the commencement and during the voyage in question, the issue of whether such an implied term exists in a time policy was not discussed.

141. S.C. 15 Wend. 535.

142. Emphasis in original text.

"But there cannot possibly be an implied warranty of the fact of unbroken and continual seaworthiness, for that would be in contradiction to the very object of the policy, which is to insure against perils and damages, such as must occasionally render the vessel not seaworthy."

In *The Zilliah*,[143] the Minnesota Supreme Court was also clear that, though an implied warranty of seaworthiness is to be implied at the commencement of the *first* voyage, there is in the absence of any statutory provision, no implied warranty that the vessel will be seaworthy at the commencement of subsequent voyages. 6.63

6C.1(iv) An absolute warranty?

Save for confirming that the pre-attachment warranty is similar to the English warranty of seaworthiness applicable at the commencement of the voyage for voyage policies, the American Rule has not explicitly clarified whether the pre-attachment warranty is "absolute" in nature in the sense that there is no defence available to the assured in the event of its breach. Under English law, the warranty of seaworthiness implied by common law, both for marine insurance and contracts of affreightment, is always absolute in its terms.[144] In relation to a voyage policy, the matter is firmly established in the very early case of *The Mills Frigate*, discussed above. Moreover, framed as a warranty, its breach cannot be cured[145] and English common and statutory laws will not hear of any excuse for its non-compliance. As spelt out in s.33(3), the name of the game is exact or literal compliance. As there does not appear to be any litigation on the subject, we may probably safely assume that the implied warranty in time policies is similar in character to the same implied in a voyage policy under English law. 6.64

6C.1(v) Legal effects of breach

Except for stating that the pre-attachment warranty is similar to the English warranty of seaworthiness applicable to a voyage policy, the American Rule has not expressly clarified whether a violation of the implied pre-attachment warranty in a time policy will achieve the same result as for a violation of the same warranty in a voyage policy. However, the American Rule, in its comparison between the effects of a breach of a warranty of *continuing* seaworthiness, express or implied, with that of a breach of the "negative modified warranty", has indicated that a breach of the former "voids the policy altogether".[146] In the first place, Judge Brown's reference to the implied warranty of *continuing* seaworthiness is curious, as neither English nor US law has implied such a warranty of continuing seaworthiness to a time or a voyage policy. A party, if he so wish, may of course incorporate such an express warranty into the contract, but such is not implied by law. Is it supposed to be read that, since the implied obligation to furnish a seaworthy ship at the inception of the risk is also a 6.65

143. 1929 AMC 166 at 168.

144. In *Lyons v. Mells* 5 East. 428, it was held that breach of the implied warranty of seaworthiness in a charterparty is absolute.

145. See s.34(2).

146. The point the judge was probably trying to make was that, whereas a breach of a *warranty* (express or implied) will render the contract void, a breach of the post-attachment duty or the negative burden will result only in a denial of liability for loss or damage caused by such unseaworthiness.

warranty, its breach will, as in the case of a breach of a warranty of continuing seaworthiness, render the contract void?[147]

6.66 To recapitulate, in England, the terms "void" and "void *ab initio*" were used in the early days to describe the legal effects of a breach of a warranty. English law then moved on to the rule of avoidance and now applies the rule of automatic discharge as the legal effect for a breach of a promissory warranty.[148] As the implied pre-attachment warranty of seaworthiness is similar in nature to that implied at the commencement of the voyage in a voyage policy, the effects attendant upon a breach should logically be the same for both. Various expressions, such as "void",[149] "void *ab initio*", voidable[150] "discharge" and even "suspension" have been freely used by American judges to describe the effect of a breach of their pre-attachment warranty.

6.67 In *Merchants' Insurance Company of Chicago v. Morrison*,[151] Judge McAllister noted, though by way of *obiter*, that:[152]

> "... it is the general rule that the vessel must be seaworthy in the sense mentioned, at the commencement or inception of the risk, in order that the policy attach and charge the insurer. Seaworthiness at the commencement of the voyage is a condition precedent, and, if it does not then exist, the policy is *void*, and the insurers are not responsible for a subsequent loss, even if it arises from another cause." [Emphasis added]

6.68 Except for the use (misuse?) of the word "void", the effect, as described, is the same as that applied by English law in relation to a breach of any warranty, including that of the implied warranty of seaworthiness in a voyage policy. The wording of the first part of the statement is in general terms suggesting that the effect of a breach of a pre-attachment warranty is the same whether the policy be for a voyage or for a period of time. Though the warranty of seaworthiness is depicted as a *condition precedent* to the attachment of the risk, as in the case of *The Good Luck*, the US court nevertheless held the policy to be *void*. The embellishment in the remaining part of the sentence, that "the insurers are not responsible for a subsequent loss, even if it arises from another cause", clarifies that the insurer is discharged from all further liability. Perhaps, we should not read too much into the word "void", as it could be used in a loose sense (and not in the strict legal sense as understood under English contract law) to mean simply that as from the date of the breach, the insurer is no longer liable to indemnify the assured for any further loss under the policy.

6.69 *The Papoose*[153] may generate confusion, as both expressions, "avoid" and "null and void", appear in the judgment. In the main part of the text, the court stated that:

---

147. At the time when this statement was made, English law was already applying the avoidance rule.

148. See *The Good Luck* [1991] 2 Lloyd's Rep. 191, HL discussed *supra*.

149. See, e.g., *Bullard v. Roger Williams Insurance Co.* 1 Curt. 148; *The Caledonia* 157 U.S. 124 (1895) and *Paddock v. Franklin Insurance Co.* 11 Pick 227. In *Gregorie v. Underwriters at Lloyd's* 559 F. Supp. 596; 1982 AMC 2045, the judge notes that: "Breach of the first warranty *voids* the entire policy irrespective of proximate cause between the condition and a subsequent loss."

150. See, e.g., *The Papoose* 1969 AMC 781 (5th Cir. 1969); *Lemar Towing Co. Inc. v. Fireman's Fund Insurance Co.* 352 F. Supp. 652 (ED la. 1972), 1973 AMC 1844 (ED La. 1972); aff'd 471 F. 2d 609 (5h Cir. 1973), 1973 AMC 1843; cert. denied, 414 U.S. 976, 1974 AMC 1891 and *New York & PRSS Co. v. Aetna Insurance Co.* 1929 AMC 166.

151. 14 Am. Rep. 93 (1871). See also *Paddock v. Franklin Insurance Co.* 11 Pick 227, where the Chief Justice Shaw referred to the policy as being "wholly annulled" to describe a breach of the implied warranty.

152. As the judge was of the view that there is no pre-attachment of seaworthiness in a time policy at the commencement of the first voyage, his observation can only be *obiter*.

153. 1969 AMC 781 (5th Cir. 1969).

"For under the American Rule, unlike the English, there is an implied warranty of seaworthiness in a time policy. A consequence of this is that if the vessel is unseaworthy . . . at the time the insurance attaches, the breach absolutely *avoids* the policy. Existing, spectacular unseaworthiness kept the policy from becoming effective."

At the time when this case was decided, avoidance was regarded by English law as the appropriate remedy. Later, a footnote, states:

"See 45 C.J.S., Insurance, sec 650, at 555 'If there is any breach of a warranty the policy is null and void, and . . . the underwriters are relieved of their liability notwithstanding the loss is not connected with the breach or the breach is cured prior to the loss'."

As no commentary was offered, it is difficult to pin down what the real rule is. But three years later, in the *Lemar* case,[154] the court cited *The Papoose* with approval as having laid down the rule that "the breach avoids the policy".[155] 6.70

However, there is another group of cases which neither uses the word "void" nor "voidable" to describe the effects of a breach of the warranty. And though these cases were decided long before *The Good Luck*, it is interesting to note that the line of thought is similar to that expressed by Lord Goff. Further, it is also to be observed that the implied warranty was consistently referred as a "condition precedent", the term used by Lord Goff to define the nature of an insurance warranty. The decision of *US Insurance Company v. Ogden*,[156] emanating from a court suitably named as the "Court for the Correction of Errors of New York", referred to the implied warranty as a "condition" the breach of which, as Judge Senator Verplanck has accurately pointed out:

". . . *discharges* the entire responsibility of the insurer, whether the loss incurred by in any way the consequence of such special defect of seaworthiness or not. It is an obligation *strictissimi juris*; it goes to the foundation of the contact. . . . The first [referring to the pre-attachment implied warranty of seaworthiness] is a stipulation as to a present fact, always required and understood as a *condition precedent*, on which the contract depends; and when that is executed, the contract attaches, and the assured has fully performed that part of his stipulation." [Emphasis added]

The case is directly on point, as the statement was made with specific reference to the pre-attachment warranty of seaworthiness in a time policy.

In simple terms, the court, in *Berwind et al. v. Greenwich Insurance Co.*,[157] stated that: "there is an implied warranty that the vessel is seaworthy at the inception of the policy. It is a *condition precedent* to the risk, and, if the vessel is not seaworthy, the policy does not attach." Aside from saying that the policy does not attach and, therefore, the assured would not be able to claim under it, the court did not clarify the effect the breach has upon the contract as a whole. 6.71

With even greater lucidity and precision, Chief Justice Shaw in *Capen v. Washington Insurance Co.*[158] has defined the legal consequences that will arise in the event of a violation of the pre-attachment warranty thus:

154. 352 F. Supp. 652 (ED la. 1972), 1973 AMC 1844 (ED La. 1972); aff'd 471 F. 2d 609 (5h Cir. 1973), 1973 AMC 1843; cert. denied, 414 U.S. 976, 1974 AMC 1891.

155. See also *New York & PRSS Co. v. Aetna insurance Co.* 1929 AMC 166 where the court in passing commented that: "The breach of warranty of seaworthiness avoid a policy".

156. 15 Wend. 535 (1838).

157. 21 N.E. 1511 (N.Y. 1915).

158. 12 Cush. 517.

"Again, such a warranty, on the part of the assured, is not merely a stipulation on his part, that he will be responsible for the direct consequence of its breach; but according to the old peculiar doctrine of warranty in the English common law, it is a rigorous, unbending condition precedent, which admits of no equivalent, and no substitute, and no excuse for a strict literal performance."

". . . that a warranty is a strict condition precedent to the further liability of the insurer, so that from the time of the breach, he is absolved from all obligations to pay any loss, arising from any cause. . . ."

The last comment bears a close resemblance to Lord Goff's rule of automatic discharge in *The Good Luck.* Such is the acute foresight of a learned nineteenth century American judge.

6.72 It is fair to say that when describing the effects of a breach, US judges have not been particularly careful in their choice of words. Though various technical terms were used, the general effect which all the judges were trying to portray was that the insurer is to be released from liability as from the date of the breach. Thus, we should probably overlook the carefree use of terminology.

As can be seen, US law has not evolved in a consistent or systematic way. The above survey of US case law can only bring home to English lawyers a realisation that they owe a great deal to the learned Lord Campbell. We can all sigh with relief that English law has taken a pragmatic approach, for in so doing, it has avoided all the pitfalls and problems (described above) which the US has to wrestle with in choosing to imply a warranty of seaworthiness in a time policy.

6.73 There are differences of opinion in the US as to the exact extent of the pre-attachment warranty in time policies. Some judges have categorically refused to acknowledge the existence of the implied warranty in a time policy, by reason of the fact that such a short and sharp rule is trouble-free and easy to apply. Whether there is any real justification for distinguishing between time and voyage policies in this regard is, of course, another matter altogether. But the rule is founded upon convenience and, as can be seen, there are advantages in taking the easy way out. Further, it would bring US law in harmony and conformity with English law.

Another approach is to imply a qualified warranty of seaworthiness at the inception of the risk, but only if the ship is in a port where repair facilities are available. However, the judges who have taken this stand, as case law has revealed, are not totally clear about the precise moment when the warranty has to be fulfilled and the standard of fitness that has to be attained, namely whether the ship has to be port-worthy or seaworthy, or both.

A third avenue is to have a free and easy rule, or more accurately, no fixed rule as such, but to let the facts and circumstances of a particular case govern the outcome of the case. This is by no means a satisfactory way of dealing with the problems, as parties to the contract need to know in advance and for certain what their obligations are and when they are to be performed. In the absence of a clear declaration one way or the other, either from Congress or the bench, it would generate an increase in the volume of litigation. Parties to the contract should know for certain what the law expects of them at the time when they take up a policy and not when they appear before the court.

6.74 American law is inconsistent and uncertain. To hazard a guess, it is perhaps fair to say that the popular view in the US is that, where a ship is at the inception of the risk at sea or is in a port where proper repair facilities are *not* available, the implied warranty will not apply; in such an event, the insurer has to take the ship as he finds her.[159] One US author is content to accept the legal position thus:[160]

> "The American cases did recognise special circumstances, which were rather more the rule than the exception, in which the warranty could be implied: where, at the inception of the risk, the vessel was in a port, domestic or foreign, where proper maintenance and repairs could be accomplished".

But above all, the position is best described in the *Capen* case by the learned Chief Justice Shaw in the following terms:[161]

> "But the doctrine of implied warranty of seaworthiness, has not yet, we believe, been authoritatively applied to policies on time, though the contrary has not yet been fully established, and it has often been supposed to apply, from its analogy to voyage policies."

Though intimated in the nineteenth century, the author believes (looking at the subject as an outsider) that the conclusion still holds true today.

If the philosophy for imposing the implied warranty is to ensure that a shipowner is 6.75 punished for his sins, in sending an unseaworthy ship to sea, the same result is by and large achieved in the rule encompassed in the negative burden or its English counterpart laid down in the privity rule (s.39(5)).

English law is conscious that there is no such thing as a perfect or foolproof rule of law; this was made patently clear from the arguments tendered in *Gibson v. Small*.[162] A compromise is, therefore, struck in s.39(5) and in rejecting the implied warranty, the law enjoys the virtues of certainty and clarity: its inflexibility avoids the need of having to make exceptions.

However, it should be pointed out that the above difficulties encountered by the Americans in relation to the implied warranty will be relevant under English law if a time policy incorporated an unconditional *express* warranty of seaworthiness at the inception of the risk. Fortunately for Mr Justice Moore-Bick in *The Lydia Flag*,[163] the question did not arise, because the vessel was found to be seaworthy at the inception of the policy, which contained an express pre-attachment warranty of seaworthiness.

US law in this regard is clearly in desperate need of clarification and refinement. The only way out of the maze is to start with a clean slate, and that means codification in the form of federal law, as has been the call of many US lawyers.

6C.2 "A sort of negative, modified warranty" of seaworthiness

Unlike the pre-attachment warranty of seaworthiness, the validity of the second 6.76 part of the American Rule, the "negative warranty" or "negative burden" has never been doubted. It has been consistently applied by the courts, though various interpretations have been given regarding its extent and scope. One of the major

159. See *Capen v. Washington Insurance Co.*, 66 Mass. (12 Cush.) 517 (1853) and *Henjes v. Aetna Insurance Co.*, 132 F. 2d 715, 719, 1943 AMC 27 (2d Cir.), cert. denied, 319 U.S. 760 (1943).

160. Anderson, "The Evolution of the Implied Warranty of Seaworthiness in Comparative Perspective", 1986 JMLC 1 at 17.

161. 12 Cush. 517.

162. (1853) 4 HL Cas 352; 10 ER 499, HL.

163. [1998] 2 Lloyd's Rep. 652.

issues that needs to be addressed is the standard of conduct required by the negative burden. Another equally important question that calls for an answer is, is the so-called warranty in fact a warranty? To be more precise, does it spell out a warranty of continuing seaworthiness, the non-compliance with which will attract the legal effects normally attendant upon a breach of such a contractual term? Until this question is answered, the term "negative burden", a neutral term, is preferred and will be used in the ensuing discussion.

If the negative burden is not a warranty, it will be necessary to consider whether it is identical or similar to the English privity rule discussed earlier. But before we can proceed to make comparisons, it is necessary to examine US cases that have defined the fundamental features of the American Rule. First, the meaning of the requirement that the owner will not from bad faith or neglect "knowingly" permit the vessel to break ground in an unseaworthy condition has to be analysed. Second, the rule of causation that is applied has to be considered. Finally, the legal consequences for its breach, the most significant aspect of the Rule, will be studied. The last two considerations are described in the American Rule in a single sentence to the effect that: "the consequence of a violation of this 'negative' burden is merely a denial of liability for loss or damage caused proximately by such unseaworthiness".

6C.2(i) The standard of knowledge and/or negligence?

6.77 The wording of the American Rule on the negative burden is unclear on a number of issues, one of which is the standard of conduct required to satisfy the Rule. It seems to suggest that knowledge is its main ingredient, but it also talks about bad faith and negligence. Thus, besides knowledge, there also appears to be the requirement that the assured must have either acted in bad faith or have been negligent. Bad faith is, of course, much more difficult to prove and, therefore, not surprisingly, there is hardly any case law on the subject. The question that remains therefore is, will proof of negligence alone exonerate the insurer from liability or has negligence to be coupled with knowledge? In other words, is the test that of knowledge *or* negligence, or knowledge *and* negligence? The ambiguity and complexity of the Rule was pointed out in *Gregoire v. Underwriters at Lloyd's*[164] as follows:

> "Most confusion surrounding this second part of the American Rule springs from the ambiguous language 'the Owner, from bad faith or neglect, will not knowingly permit the vessel to break ground in an unseaworthy condition'. The unfortunate juxtaposition of 'neglect' and 'knowingly' leaves it unclear whether the standard being proposed requires actual knowledge of the unseaworthy condition of the vessel by the owner as in the English rule, or whether the owner's mere negligence is enough."

6.78 According to the judge in *L & L Marine Service v. Insurance Company of North America*,[165] there are juxtaposed "two and arguably three different standards of intent".

A study of case law will reveal that there is evidently more than one standard being applied in the US. There is a cluster of cases that advocate the "knowledge" standard; the authorities that support this standard would naturally lean to English law for

164. 1982 AMC 2045.
165. 796 F. 2d 1032 at 1035 (8th Cir. 1986).

support. Another group of cases favours the "negligence" standard where the exercise of due diligence is expected of the shipowner. And there is a third category of cases which proposes a combination of both knowledge and neglect as the test to be applied – the "knowing neglect" standard – though this appears to be confined to cases relating to express warranties of seaworthiness and due diligence exclusion clauses.[166] One need only have a glimpse of Langhauser's well-researched article to realise the state of chaos that US law has found itself in, in this regard.[167]

6C.2(ii) The knowledge standard

In the early case of *Starbuck v. New England Marine Insurance Company*,[168] in 1837, there can be found a brief comment to the effect that in order to throw the risk upon the assured, "the master must have known, or have had reason to believe, that there was a defect". Not only was knowledge the sole test applied, but the knowledge of the *master* was considered sufficient to deny the assured the right of recovery.[169] Citing the English privity rule with approval, the court in the *Gregoire*[170] case also applied "knowledge" as the criterion; this is evident in its remark that:[171] "Where however, the owner of a vessel or those in privity with him send their vessel to sea *knowing* it to be unseaworthy, the insurer is not liable for damages proximately caused by unseaworthiness". 6.79

In *The Sea Pak*,[172] Judge Brown reiterated that "the owner or those in privity with him will not *knowingly* send the vessel to sea in a deficient condition".[173] This should not come as a surprise, as it was decided in the same year and by the same court that formulated the American Rule in *The Spot Pack*. 6.80

In *The Spot Pack*, the assured, though he was aware of the defective condition of the circuit breaker, was allowed to recover under the policy, because he did not know that that defect rendered the vessel unseaworthy. As such, the court could not regard him as having *knowingly* permitted (either through bad faith or neglect) an unseaworthy ship to be sent to sea. It is interesting to note that the court took the view that the owner was entitled to assume that his master was competent; accordingly, the owner was not charged with the neglect committed by the master in failing to reinstall the

166. As much hinges upon the wording of the particular express warranty or the exclusion clause, it would be futile to speculate whether this criterion is applicable to the negative burden. See *Texaco Inc. v. Universal Marine Insurance*. 400 F. Supp. 311, 1976 AMC 226 (E.D. La. 1975); *Insurance Company of North America v. Board of Commissioners* 733 F. 2d 1161, 1985 AMC 1460 (5th Cir. 1984) and *L & L Marine Serv. v. Insurance Co. of N. America* 796 F. 2d 1032, 1987 AMC 2283 (8th Cir. 1986), cert. denied, 479 U.S. 1065, 1987 AMC 2407 (1987).

167. "Implied Warranties of Seaworthiness: Applying the Knowing Neglect Standard in Time Hull Policies", Me. L. Rev. 39 (1987).

168. 19 Pick. 198 (1837).

169. Whether the knowledge of the master may be imputed to the shipowner for the purpose of liability under s.39(5) is arguable. The subject of attribution will not be discussed here, see *supra* note 73.

170. 1982 AMC 2045 at 2051. Emphasis added.

171. *Ibid.*, at 2051.

172. 247 F. 2d. 116 (5th Cir. 1957). The insurer's defence was that the loss resulted from the owner's failure to discover a leak.

173. In another Fifth Circuit decision, *DJ McDuffie, Inc. v. Old Reliable Fire Insurance Co.* 1979 AMC 595 (ED La. 1979); aff'd. 1980 AMC 1836, cert. denied, 449 U.S. 830, 1980 AMC 2099, the court stated: "the insurer owner will not knowingly or in bad faith allow the vessel to go to sea in an unseaworthy condition."

circuit breaker.[174] The House of Lords in *The Star Sea* would of course approve of the stand taken by the judges in *The Spot Pack*,[175] the effect of which is that, if there is nothing to arouse the suspicion of an assured as regards the competence of their master, no constructive knowledge will be imputed to them. The point made is that an assured is entitled to rely on the professional skill and judgment of the master and is, therefore, not expected to possess the requisite knowledge about matters concerning the safety of the ship. As can be seen, "knowledge" is the test envisaged by the court in *The Spot Pack*.

6C.2(iii) The negligence standard

6.81 With equal force and frequency, US law has also applied the negligence standard as the decisive consideration to the question of liability. In 1838, in *US Insurance Company v. Ogden*,[176] Senator Verplanck noted that, "... any subsequently occurring defect of seaworthiness, does not discharge the insurers from any loss or damage not ascribed to want of due diligence ...".

6.82 The origin of the negative burden rule, it has been said, is derived from *Union Insurance Company of the City of Philadelphia v. Smith*,[177] where Judge Blatchford, after citing a long line of cases to support his proposition, confirmed the legal position as follows:

> "A defect of seaworthiness arising after the commencement of the risk and permitted to continue from bad faith or want of ordinary prudence or diligence on the part of the insured or his agents discharges the insurer from liability for any loss which is the consequence of such bad faith, or want of prudence or diligence. ..."

No mention is made of any requirement of "knowledge". But, as pointed out earlier, the standing of this authority has been consistently doubted as not having the *gravitas* of a precedent.

A year later, a similar yardstick was employed in *Berwind et al. v. Greenwich Insurance Co.*,[178] where the implied covenant was said to impose upon the insured "the duty of active diligence to keep the vessel in good order and in a seaworthy condition". Similarly, in *Plummer v. Insurance Company of North America*,[179] the assured was denied the right to claim under a time policy, because he was found to have been negligent in failing to ensure that the seacocks were closed before the vessel set sail. On the evidence, the assured (acting as master) did not know that the seacocks were open when she was launched at the shipyard. He had assumed that they would be closed contrary to the usual practice. Judge Bird adopted the "negligence" standard and said that: "The result of such lack of care on the part of the insured is, as

174. The defective circuit-breaker was repaired and placed on board, but was not reinstalled.

175. 1957 AMC 655 at 664, the question was framed as: "Specifically, what reason was there why the Owner should have anticipated that the competent Master would not have required the competent Engineer to perform this simple task? None ...".

176. S.C. 15 Wend. 535.

177. 124 U.S. 405 (1888).

178. 21 N.E. 151 at 152 (N.Y. 1889).

179. 95 A. 605 (Me. 1915).

we have seen, to relieve the insurers from any liability for a loss which is the consequence of such want of prudence or diligence".

Last but not least, attention has to be given to the case of *Lemar Towing Co. Inc. v. Fireman's Fund Insurance Co.*[180] as it is particularly useful for the purpose of comparison with English law. As in the English case of *The Star Sea*, the vessel was sent to sea with an incompetent master. The US court held that, as the unseaworthiness had resulted from the "owner's *neglect* in failing to determine the qualification and competence of the crew", the assured had no right of claim under the policy. It is observed that the court had also uttered some remarks about knowledge, that "to escape liability by way of this contention the underwriter must prove that the shipowner had *knowledge* of this unseaworthy condition, if in fact it did exist, and that said condition was the proximate cause of the loss".[181] In the light of this statement, it is curious why the judge did not investigate whether the owners, in fact, had *knowledge* (actual or constructive) of the incompetence of the master and crew. Instead, he applied only the negligence standard and ruled that "... such unseaworthiness proximately resulted from the owners' *neglect* in failing to determine the qualification and competence of the crew to man the vessel for the intended voyage before its commencement". By English law, as expounded in *The Star Sea*, such a loss would be recoverable, as negligence, however gross, will not bar the claim of an assured, if he had no actual knowledge or suspicion (constructive knowledge) that his crew is incompetent. 6.83

It may be said, from the tenor of the speeches delivered by some of the judges who support the negligence standard, that the requirement appears to be couched more in terms of a duty (to exercise due diligence) rather than as a basis for an exception of liability.[182] Under English law, no duty whatsoever is imposed on the assured at any stage of the adventure to make the ship seaworthy. All that he has to ensure is that he is not "privy" to the particular unseaworthiness to which the loss is attributable.

The above survey of case law demonstrates that there is no fixed rule in America laying down the level of conduct required by the negative burden. It is difficult to say which one is the preponderant view, as both have been applied with equal enthusiasm. But if the general view, that the negative burden stems from English law, is correct, then, the test of knowledge has to prevail.[183] However, at the end of the day, the scales seem to hang in the balance. 6.84

US authors seem to be in general agreement that the knowledge standard is to be applied. Schoenbaum,[184] for instance, notes that: "In actual operation, the 'American' rule for time policies is similar to MIA s 39(5)". Cattrell[185] states that, "only when the owner is *aware* that a ship was sent to sea in an unseaworthy condition

180. F. Supp. 652 at 653 (ED La. 1972); aff'd 1973 AMC 1843, 471 F. 2d 609 (5th Cir. 1972), cert. denied, 414 U.S. 976, 1974 AMC 1891.

181. *Ibid.*, at 660.

182. Similar to the obligation to exercise due diligence to make the ship seaworthy under Article III, rule 1 of the Hague-Visby Rules.

183. In the *Gray* case, 1957 AMC 616 at 622, Judge Frank was of the opinion that the negative burden is similar to s.39(5), suggesting that the test to be applied is privity or knowledge.

184. *Key Divergences Between English and US Law of Marine Insurance: A Comparative Study* (Cornell Maritime Press, 1999) p.169.

185. "An American Marine Insurance Act: An Idea Whose Time Has Come", 1995 Tul. Mar. L.J. 1 at 46.

can the insurer avoid liability for any loss attributable to that unseaworthiness". The fact that McGlone[186] has throughout his article used the words "knowledge" and "privity", without question, suggests that knowledge must be the accepted or preferred test. Langhuaser's sentiments can be found in his summing up that:[187] "Adoption of an actual knowledge standard will, in addition to serving the shipowner's needs fairly, achieve the desired uniformity with English admiralty law".

6C.2(iv) Proximately caused by or attributable to?

6.85 As was seen, the causal connection required by English law for their privity rule is that the loss must be "attributable to" such unseaworthiness to which the assured is privy. In the US, both phrases "proximately caused by" and "attributable to" have been used to link the cause with the defect. Perhaps US law does not draw a distinction between the terms and they are used interchangeably as if they were synonymous.

6.86 In *The Spot Pack*, Judge Brown applied the causal rule of "proximate cause", that "the consequence of this 'negative' burden is merely a denial of liability for loss or damage caused *proximately* by such unseaworthiness".[188] Whereas in the *Capen*[189] case, the learned Chief Justice, possessed with a deep insight into the subject of causation, phrased the formula as:

> "If she is not in that condition [of seaworthiness], and shall suffer sea-damage, it will be impossible to say that it is not *attributable* in whole or in part, to the insufficiency of the vessel. If the evidence should tend to show, that the loss was caused partly by extraordinary stress of weather and partly by the insufficient condition of the vessel, it would be impossible for the insured to recover, because the degree of influence arising from each cause could not be measured. . . ."

He concluded with the sharp note that the assured will lose the benefit of his insurance to which such failure on his part may have "in any degree contributed" to the loss. It is obvious from his choice of the words that the causal rule of proximate cause is not the test to be applied.

6.87 In *Union Insurance Co. of the City of Philadelphia v. Smith*,[190] the required causal connection was spelt out broad terms as:

> "A defect of unseaworthiness, arising after the commencement of the risk . . . discharges the insurer from liability for any loss which is the consequence of such bad faith, or want of prudence; but does not affect the contract of insurance as to any other risk or loss covered by the policy, and not caused or increased by such particular defect."

The more popular view appears to be in line with the English rule, that any measure

186. "Marine Insurance and the Implied Warranty of Seaworthiness", 1975 21 Loyola Law Review 960.

187. "Implied Warranties of Seaworthiness: Applying the Knowing Neglect Standard in Time Hull Policies", Me. L. Rev. 39 (1987).

188. See also *Lemar Towing Co. Inc. v. Fireman's Fire Fund Insurance Co.* 352 F. Supp. 652 at 660: "However, a breach of the implied negative warranty after the policy has attached . . . only exonerates the underwriters for loss or damage proximately caused by the unseaworthy condition".

189. 66 Mass. (12 Cush.) 517 (1853).

190. 124 U.S. 405 (1888).

of contribution made by the particular defect of unseaworthiness to the loss would be sufficient to exonerate the insurer from liability.

6C.2(v) Legal effects of breach

Judge Brown in *The Spot Pack* was quick to point out that a breach of the negative burden will *not* attain the same result as a breach of an express or implied warranty of continuing seaworthiness, which, in his opinion, will "void the policy altogether". An infringement of the negative burden, he said, will result merely in "a denial of liability" only for the particular loss caused by such unseaworthiness. The legal consequence of a breach of the negative burden is dependent essentially upon how the term is classified: whether it is to be regarded as a *warranty* in the strict sense of the word or as a mere stipulation in the contract. In *Paddock v. Franklin Insurance Co.*,[191] the inquiry was pointedly framed by Chief Justice Shaw thus: 6.88

"But what shall be the consequence of a failure and breach of duty in this respect, seems not to be so well settled. Are each and all of these requisites included in the implied warranty of seaworthiness, regarded as strict conditions precedent, to the effect that if not complied with, on the part of the owner, the contract of insurance becomes wholly annulled? Or are they obligations and duties binding on the owners, and if not performed on his part, and if in consequence of such non-performance a loss happens, or by any reasonable probability may be ascribed to that cause, the effect will be, that such loss will fall upon the assured, and not upon the underwriter?"

The alternatives are vividly revealed in the question posed, and his answer was to the effect that it operates as a defence to a claim:[192]

"... after the policy has once attached, the implied warranty should be so construed, as to exempt the underwriter from all loss or damage, which did or might proceed from any cause, thus warranted against; but to hold him still responsible for those losses which by no possibility could be occasioned by peril increased or affected by the breach of such implied warranty."

It is interesting to note that in one breath, Judge Brown, in *The Spot Pack*, referred to the second duty imposed on the assured as a "warranty" and in another, as a "burden". This is indeed regrettable and has caused much of the confusion in the interpretation of the term. The expression "burden" is, of course, a more accurate and suitable description, as the judge in the *Capen*[193] case has highlighted. He hit the nail on the head in the following speech: 6.89

"If it were regarded as a technical warranty, it would, for reasons before stated, be the failure to perform a strict condition precedent, and absolve the insurer from all further obligations to pay for any loss. But treating it as a stipulation, it would leave the underwriters liable for losses for other and independent perils."

"... But that such duty was not a technical warranty, the breach of which, would wholly terminate the policy; but a merely a duty, the failure of which would discharge the underwriter from any loss arising from such want of repair."

---

191. 28 Mass. (11 Pick.) 226.

192. See also the *Jones* case, discussed *supra*, where the implication was that any contribution made by the particular defect of unseaworthiness towards the loss, though proximately caused by an insured peril, would exonerate the insurer from liability. In *American Insurance Co. v. Ogden*, the court held that "a breach of the negative burden will not discharge the insurer from subsequent risk or [of] loss, not consequent on such defect".

193. 66 Mass. 517 at 539 (1853).

6.90 In *Jones v. The Insurance Co.*,[194] the distinction between the pre-attachment warranty and the negative burden was described simply as: "The difference is this: if the vessel is not seaworthy at first, the policy never attaches; in the other case, the insurers, having become responsible, continue liable for all losses not arising from the fault of the owners".

6.91 Thus, though often called a warranty, the negative burden is not in fact a warranty but rather a stipulation excepting the liability of the insurer. It is, therefore, indeed unfortunate that the word "warranty" has been used to refer to the continuing duty imposed on the assured. This misuse in terminology has led some American judges to regard the negative burden as equivalent to an express *warranty* of continuing seaworthiness, which is known to bear the effect of either avoidance or a suspension of the policy in the event of its breach. Such an analogy was drawn in *The Papoose*,[195] where the court observed, in a footnote, that "if the warranty is complied with at the attachment, then the policy is effective and subsequent breaches merely *suspend* coverage until the breach is cured and the consequences of the breach are obliterated". *Henjes v. Aetna Insurance Co.*[196] was cited as authority in support of the proposition, when that was a case dealing with the effects of a breach of an express *warranty* that had nothing to do with seaworthiness. The controversy in the *Henjes* case was whether the tug's breach of an express *warranty* (not to tow more than one vessel) took her "completely and forever out of the coverage of the policy or merely suspended that and, if the latter, whether it reattached before the vessel was a total loss". In the circumstances of the case, the court felt that the result of a forfeiture of the policy would be too draconian and accordingly ruled that the policy was suspended until such time as the breach is cured.

6.92 Another case which is closer to home is *Thomas Aguirre v. Citizens Casualty Co. (The Esmeralda)*[197] where the policy contained an express *warranty* of continuing seaworthiness.[198] Judge Dyer had no doubt that "the owner's breach of their express warranty of seaworthiness suspended coverage under the insurance policy". The policy will reattach once the breach is remedied. It is of vital importance to note that under English law, a warranty, express or implied, cannot be remedied. This is specifically laid out in s.34(2) of the Act. Once it is breached, the policy is effectively terminated and there cannot be a suspension of the policy the life of which is to be governed by the conduct of the assured in rectifying the breach. The innocent party (insurer) may, however, intervene to revive the policy by waiving the breach.[199] Thus, if the negative burden is considered as equivalent to an express warranty of continuing seaworthiness, its breach would not bring about a suspension of the policy: such would be a contradiction in terms, as a breach of a warranty cannot be cured.

6.93 The same was held in *Smith v. Northwestern Fire and Marine Insurance Company*,

194. (1852) 2 Wallace Jr. 278.
195. 1969 AMC 781 (5th Cir. 1969).
196. 132 F. 2d 715 (2nd Cir), cert. denied, 319 U.S. 760 (1974).
197. 441 F. 2d 141, 1971 AMC 1134 (5th Cir.), cert. denied, 404 U.S. 829 (1971).
198. The express warranty stated: it is "warranted that at the inception of this policy the vessel shall be in a seaworthy condition and, thereafter, during the currency of this policy, the assured shall exercise due diligence to keep the vessel seaworthy, and in all respects fit, tight, and properly manned . . .". The insurers contended that with two, rather than three, men on board, the vessel was unseaworthy.
199. A breach of a warranty may be waived, see s.34(3).

(*The Traffic*),[200] a case that needs to be examined closely. Chief Judge Cardozo in his comparison of an express warranty of continuing seaworthiness[201] with the so-called implied negative warranty explained the effects of the breach of the latter as follows:

"We think the intention of the parties must be presumed to be that under a warranty of seaworthiness continuing beyond the inception of the risk, and during the whole of many voyages, a supervening breach shall do no more than suspend the obligation of the policy, and that the obligation shall revive when the defects have been corrected unless indeed there is an express provision that the effect of any breach shall be to end the policy forever. . . .

Nothing more than this is the consequence of a breach of the continuing *duty* to keep the vessel seaworthy imposed by the law itself in the absence of a covenant, a *duty* often spoken of as growing out of an implied warranty, though the description may be lacking in technical precision. Indeed, the breach of the implied warranty does not even suspend the risk in the absence of a casual relation between breach and loss." [emphasis added]

He then clarified that:

"Upon a breach of the continuing warranty of seaworthiness, the obligation of the contract is suspended, if the risk has once attached, and thereafter revived when the defect has been cured."

The judge seems to labour under the impression that, save for the element of causation, the effect of suspension is applicable to both an express warranty of continuing seaworthiness and the negative "duty". If a causal connection is an essential prerequisite for the negative burden, as he had pointed out, then, it cannot be regarded as warranty. The very essence of a warranty, at least under English law, is that causation is irrelevant in the event of its breach: a breach of a warranty *per se*, regardless of the cause of loss, will automatically discharge the insurer from liability and future liability under the policy.

The above trend has led *Schoenbaum* to reiterate that:[202] "The consequence of the breach of this warranty of seaworthiness is only denial of the particular claim involved; the policy remains in force but coverage is suspended until the unseaworthy condition is corrected". If this is the case, it would mean that should the vessel suffer a further loss (after having been denied recovery for the particular claim) caused solely or exclusively by an insured peril (for example, barratry or theft), that loss would also be not recoverable. That the policy will remain in force cannot be doubted, but whether it can operate to suspend the *general* (or overall) coverage of the policy is, it is contended, questionable. The above statement could perhaps be read to mean that coverage only for the *particular* loss is suspended. Under English law, the insurer would, in spite of the unseaworthy condition of the vessel, be liable for any loss proximately caused by an insured peril, provided, of course, that the particular unseaworthiness to which the assured is privy does not in any way contribute (proximately or remotely) to the loss. 6.94

The suspension rule has found a great deal of support in the US.[203] It is seen as a 6.95

200. 159 N.E. 87, 1928 AMC 174 (N.Y. 1927).

201. The express warranty read as: "warranted by the insured that the said vessel shall at all times during the continuance of this policy be tight and well found in anchors . . .".

202. *Key Divergences Between English and US Law of Marine Insurance: A Comparative Study*, (Cornell Maritime Press, 1999, p.169). It is noted that the author has cited *Thomas Aguirre v. Citizens Casualty Co. (The Esmeralda)* to support his statement.

203. See Goldman, "*Breach of Warranty in US Marine Insurance*", 1985 Insurance Counsel Journal 60.

means of softening the blow that will arise whenever a *warranty* is breached. However, it is generally invoked in the event of a violation of *express* warranties,[204] where the court has the leeway of affording the term a construction which is fair and just in the light of the facts of the particular case. Whether the same effect may be ascribed to the negative burden is doubtful, for though called a warranty, the negative burden is in reality an exception of liability. Thus, unless the negative burden is construed as an implied *warranty* of continuing seaworthiness, it is difficult to see how it can bear the effect of a general or overall suspension of the policy.

There is a whole ocean between an express warranty of continuing seaworthiness and an express exclusion or limitation of liability clause for failure to maintain a seaworthy ship. As the consequences produced by a breach of the former are devastating, it is imperative that each express clause be carefully scrutinised to ascertain whether it in fact supports a warranty. The confusion has arisen obviously because of the misuse of the term "warranty".

An insurer who subscribes to a time policy governed by US law is blessed with "a double-bottomed defence of avoidance of the whole policy and a negation of damage from an insured peril . . . ".[205] A breach of a pre-attachment *warranty* of seaworthiness will perform the "double act", while a breach of the negative burden will only free the insurer from liability for a particular type of loss, namely a loss attributable to such unseaworthiness to which the assured is privy.

204. See also *Ideal Cement Co. v. Home Insurance Co.* 210 F. 2d 937, 1954 AMC 663 (5th Cir. 1954) and *Continental Insurance Co. v. Patton-Tully Transport Co.* 212 F. 2d 543, 1954 AMC 889 (5th Cir. 1954).

205. *Per* Judge Brown in *The Spot Pack* 1957 AMC 655 at 660.

CHAPTER 7

WILFUL MISCONDUCT

JULIAN HILL

7A INTRODUCTION

Wilful misconduct is a topic often discussed in cases involving rail, road and aviation transport law, where it has been relevant to whether or not the contractor could limit liability. However, it has received less attention in the field of marine insurance where, of course, the insurer is not liable if wilful misconduct is shown. Indeed, there would seem to be considerable ambivalence as to its width in this latter area, with some judgments clearly limiting it to fraudulent claims. Yet in the recent spate of cases concerning the duty of good faith and its application to claims, little if any mention has been made in the judgments of wilful misconduct. A further aspect, particularly relevant to hull insurance, has been the recent trend whenever there is a total loss in a sensitive area of the coast for the underwriters to be criticised for insuring the ship in the first place. The market, so the cry goes, should police the sub-standard ship and shipowner. The tools for any market or underwriter doing so are limited but what there are certainly require the courts to play their part and to take a modern and robust approach, particularly to wilful misconduct and unseaworthiness cases. *7.1*

The starting point for a consideration of this subject is s.55(1) and (2)(a) Marine Insurance Act 1906. These state: *7.2*

> "(1) Subject to the provisions of this Act, and unless the policy otherwise provides, the insurer is liable for any loss proximately caused by a peril insured against, but,subject as aforesaid, he is not liable for any loss which is not proximately caused by a peril insured against.
> (2) In particular,—
> (a) The insurer is not liable for any loss attributable to the wilful misconduct of the Assured, but, unless the policy otherwise provides, he is liable for any loss proximately caused by a peril insured, even though the loss would not have happened but for the misconduct or negligence of the master or crew;".

The wording of these two sections continues to cause argument even though it could be said that much of them is a statement of the obvious. There is, for example, a clear emphasis on proximate cause in section (1). Yet sub-section (2)(a), which is the first example, refers to any loss attributable to the wilful misconduct of the assured. Are the words "attributable to" the same as proximate cause or, if not, what causal test is to be applied in construing the sub-section? If they are the same, what is the point of the particularisation, save possibly for the case where wilful misconduct is a peril insured and there is more than one assured with separate interests. The second half of sub-section (2) (a) is equally intriguing since it appears to introduce a "but for" test of causation and refers simply to "misconduct" as opposed to "wilful misconduct". The definition of barratry in Rule 11, Rules for Construction of Policy, Marine Insurance Act 1906, is worth noting in this regard, perhaps indicating that something wider is intended by the use of the one word. Again the question arises as to the point of the example if the misconduct or negligence of the master or crew referred to is not a proximate cause of the loss.

7.3 The genesis of s.55(2)(a) is perhaps to be found in the case of *Trinder Anderson & Co. v. Thames and Mersey Marine Insurance Company*.[1] The facts of the case were that the ship was run onto a reef through the negligent navigation, though not the wilful act, of the master and it was alleged by underwriters in the appeal that the master, since he was a part owner and one of the assured, could not recover under the policy. The Court found that the policy covered a loss proximately caused by a peril of the sea and that provided this was the proximate cause it did not matter if the loss was remotely caused by the negligent navigation of the master or crew or the owner himself, "always assuming that the loss is not occasioned by the wilful act of the assured". Collins LJ explained the point as follows:

"The wilful default of the owner inducing the loss will debar him from suing on the policy in respect of it on two grounds, either of which would suffice to defeat his right: first because no one can take advantage of his own wrong, using the word in its true sense which does not embrace mere negligence (see *per* Bramwell B. in *Thompson v. Hopper*); secondly, because the wilful act takes from the catastrophe the accidental character which is essential to constitute a peril of the sea".

7.4 The second of these reasons is specifically picked up in *Samuel v. Dumas*[2] where Viscount Findlay says:

"As regards the first of the two grounds referred to in this passage, it is to be observed that the mortgagee was in no way party to the fraud of the owner in the present case. The first ground would therefore be applicable to him only if in the circumstances of this case the mortgagee is to be considered as so identified with the owner whose wilful misconduct brought about the loss as to be incapable of taking advantage of it . . .
Lord Collins' second ground is in terms applicable to the present case. The loss was directly due to the wilful and deliberate act of the owner, and there was nothing of the accidental element which is essential to constitute a peril of the sea."

Later in the same judgment he goes on to make the much quoted remark explaining the reason:

"The possibility of scuttling is not a peril of the sea; it is a peril of the wickedness of man, and would have to be mentioned expressly in the policy, like barratry or pirates, in order that the assured should recover from the underwriter in respect of it."

1. *Trinder Andersen & Co. v. Thames and Mersey Marine Insurance Company* [1898] 2 Q.B. 114.
2. *Samuel v. Dumas* [1924] A.C. 431; 18 Ll. L.Rep. 211, HL.

The first part of s.55(2)(a) would seem to flow, therefore, from the first of Lord Justice Collins' reasons quoted above, whereas the second part reflects the finding in the case itself. The distinction drawn between "his own wrong" and "mere negligence" leads on to the meaning of "wilful misconduct" and whether it embraces more than scuttling or similar deliberately produced losses and this is considered later in this chapter. 7.5

It is relevant to ask whether, in view of the second reason given by Collins LJ and the speeches of the majority in *Samuel v. Dumas*, s.55(2)(a) is needed at all. In this respect it would seem to be correct that for a peril such as perils of the sea or indeed "all risks" policies[3] which require the assured to prove a peril which involves an accident or fortuity within the definition of that peril, then s.55(2)(a) should not be necessary. However in the case of other perils, such as fire, the position is different (see, for example, *Slattery v. Mance*;[4] *Schiffshypothekenbank Zu Luebeck AG v. Norman Philip Compton (The "Alexion Hope")*;[5] *Continental Illinois National Bank and Trust Co. of Chicago v. Alliance Assurance Co. Ltd*[6]). Accident or fortuity is not part of the definition with the result that the Courts have held the assured is not required to prove this. In these cases underwriters will have the burden of proving wilful misconduct and cannot simply deny that a peril has proximately caused the loss. 7.6

7B LOSS

It has been suggested that when s.55(2)(a) refers to "any loss attributable to wilful misconduct" that the reference involves a requirement that the assured have the fraudulent intention of claiming under the policy prior to the misconduct or subsequently does so; see, for example, the judgment of Colman J in *National Oilwell (UK) Ltd v. Davy Offshore Ltd.*[7] The sub-section would not, however, seem to support this approach. Clearly, the context in which an underwriter will raise a defence of wilful misconduct is that of a claim under the policy. That is obvious, but it does not follow that such a requirement becomes a part of the definition of the statutory defence. The language of both s.55(1) and (2)(a) is such as to refer to the event brought about by the peril as opposed to the financial loss following from that. The fact that it may be misconduct to scuttle one's ship with the intention of committing a fraud by claiming on the policy, whereas it may not be if there is no such fraudulent intention, is an example of the need to examine the particular facts of the 7.7

3. Compare, however, the reference by Rix J at first instance in *The State of the Netherlands v. Youell and Hayward and Others* [1997] 2 Lloyd's Rep. 440 at 454 where he refers to perils of the sea as "the exceptional case" in respect of the requirement of a fortuity. However, in respect of all risks this would seem to be too wide a comment, and it would seem it should be viewed in the context of the type of policy that was concerned in the particular case which provided not merely all risks coverage but also specific additional coverage "for all the risks excluded in Paragraph 55 Marine Insurance Act except wilful misconduct of the Assured and delay . . .". The same, therefore, as named peril coverage for these additional risks.

4. *Slattery v. Mance* [1962] 1 Q.B. 676; [1962] 1 Lloyd's Rep. 60; [1962] 1 All E.R. 525.

5. *Schiffshypothekenbank Zu Luebeck AG v. Norman Philip Compton ("The Alexion Hope")* [1987] 1 Lloyd's Rep. 60; [1988] 1 Lloyd's Rep. 311, CA.

6. *Continental Illinois National Bank and Trust Co. of Chicago v. Alliance Assurance Co. Ltd ("The Captain Panagos DP")* [1986] 2 Lloyd's Rep. 470; [1989] 1 Lloyd's Rep. 33, CA.

7. *National Oilwell (UK) Ltd v. Davy Offshore Ltd* [1993] 2 Lloyd's Rep. 582.

alleged misconduct in each case to see whether they fall within the definition of wilful misconduct. It does not import a requirement of an intention to claim into the definition or exclude the possibility that there may be wilful misconduct even if that intention is absent.

7C ATTRIBUTABLE TO

7.8 Does the sub-section require that for a defence insurers must prove that wilful misconduct was the proximate cause of the loss? The pre-Act cases suggest that this is not necessary. Wilful misconduct overrides considerations of proximate cause. The wording of the Act itself as mentioned above implies by comparison with the second part of the sub-section that a "but for" test is the appropriate one and this concept will be familiar from, for example, modern professional negligence cases. This would certainly also fit with the pre-Act cases. *Arnould*, 16th edn., in para. 786 says:

"It seems clear that the misconduct need not be the proximate cause in order for the subsection to operate, for if it were so it would be largely superfluous. It is submitted that, as in the analogous case of section 39(5) of the Act, it is only necessary that the misconduct of the assured should be one of the effective causes of the loss."

This is, however, merely to substitute two proximate causes for one, as there is no difference between effective and proximate causes. This would not seem to be logical or correct against the earlier authorities. Elsewhere, in the *Salem*[8] Lord Justice Kerr suggested in another context that the words "attributable to" did not alter the normal rules as to proximate cause. Other commentators, for example in the first volume of this work, have also indicated that "attributable to" in the section was intended to reflect what is now the view of proximate cause rather than the view that it was the cause that was last in time which prevailed at the time of the Act. However this would seem to credit the authors of the Act with a remarkable prescience and reforming spirit. It also runs foul of the comments in Arnould quoted above.

7.9 The most recent comments are those of Phillips LJ in *State of the Netherlands v. Youell and Hayward*:[9]

"I do not believe it is normally helpful, when considering the effect of negligence or misconduct on the cover afforded by a policy of marine insurance, to ask whether or not the negligence or misconduct is the 'proximate cause' of the loss. Negligence and misconduct are generic terms that apply to acts or omissions that are coupled with a particular mental element. . . . A policy of marine insurance can provide cover against 'negligence' or 'misconduct' (other than that of the assured) or exclude cover for losses attributable to such causes. In either case, the cover or exclusion will apply whether or not the negligence or misconduct is the proximate cause of the loss."

Phillips LJ also refers to *Arnould*, 16th edn., para. 763A with approval making the point that a remote cause of negligent navigation will not affect the assured's right to recover under the policy unless it is the wilful act of the assured himself. This seems to make clear that it is not necessary for the wilful misconduct to be a proximate cause of the loss. A "but for" test would seem to the author to be the most appropriate.

8. *Shell International Petroleum Co. Ltd v. Gibbs* ("*The Salem*") [1981] 2 Lloyd's Rep. 316; [1982] 1 Lloyd's Rep. 369, CA; [1983] 2 A.C. 375, HL.

9. *The State of the Netherlands v. Youell and Hayward and Others* [1998] 1 Lloyd's Rep. 236, CA.

7D WHAT IS WILFUL MISCONDUCT?

Arnould, 16th edn., para. 786 points out that there has been little discussion since 1906 of what constitutes "wilful misconduct of the assured" and after some examples goes on to say: 7.10

"In other contexts, however, the words 'wilful misconduct' have been held to apply in cases where a person deliberately undertakes some course of action, either knowing it to be wrongful so far as others are concerned or recklessly, without caring whether it be wrongful or not, and it is possible to argue that s.55(2)(a) should receive a similar construction so that the deliberate courting of a known risk, as well as deliberately bringing about a loss, would fall within its scope."

A contrast is however drawn with the persisting in a course of conduct which is in itself proper but which may have possible financial consequences to insurers. The cases referred to by *Arnould* are certainly consistent in their approach to what is wilful misconduct and there does appear to be no reason to disregard them or to take a narrower view of what is intended by s. 55(2)(a). Indeed there are good policy reasons rooted in the safety of shipping as to why the same approach should be adopted by the courts. This means that breaches of safety regulations, even minor regulations, or of accepted standards of safety, such as for example the ISM Code, should be capable of being wilful misconduct if the other elements of intention and knowledge or recklessness are present.

In the well known case of *Horabin v. BOAC*[10] the following definition is given of wilful misconduct: 7.11

"It means misconduct to which the will is a party, and it arises when the person concerned appreciates that he is acting wrongfully, or is wrongfully omitting to act, and yet persists in so acting or omitting to act regardless of the consequences, or acts or omits to act with reckless indifference to what the results may be. The same act may constitute negligence in the absence of any intention to do something wrong, but wilful misconduct if that intention is present."

In a more recent case, *Laceys Footwear Ltd v. Bowler International Freight Ltd*,[11] Beldam LJ gave the following definition: 7.12

"Few phrases have been more fully considered in decisions of the Courts than 'wilful misconduct'. The definition most usually adopted is that put forward by Lord Alverstone CJ in *Forder v. Great Western Railway Co.* (1905) 2 K.B. 532 where, with an addition, he adopted the definition of 'wilful misconduct' given by Mr Justice Johnson in *Graham v. Belfast and Northern Counties Ry Co.* (1910) 2 I.R. 13:

'Wilful misconduct in such a special condition means misconduct to which the will is party as contradistinguished from accident, and is far beyond any negligence, even gross or culpable negligence, and involves that a person wilfully misconducts himself who knows and appreciates that it is wrong conduct in the existing circumstances to do, or to fail or omit to do (as the case may be), a particular thing and yet intentionally does or fails or omits to do it, or persists in the act, failure or omission regardless of the consequences.'

Lord Alverstone continued:

'The addition which I would suggest is, "or acts with reckless carelessness, not caring what the result of his carelessness may be".'"

Beldam LJ, later in his judgment, enlarges on this last point by saying:

10. *Horabin v. British Overseas Airways Corporation* [1952] 2 Lloyd's Rep. 450.
11. *Laceys Footwear Ltd v. Bowler International Freight Ltd* [1997] 2 Lloyd's Rep. 369, CA.

"Further, a person could be said to act with reckless carelessness towards goods in his care if, aware of a risk that they may be lost or damaged, he nevertheless deliberately goes ahead and takes the risk when it is unreasonable in all the circumstances for him to do so."

7.13 It must of course be remembered that these cases are ones involving the contractual carriage of passengers or more often goods, whereas of course hull claims are concerned with the shipowner's use of his own ship. The old cases and, indeed, the more recent *National Oilwell (UK) Ltd v. Davy Offshore Ltd* case,[12] point out that there is nothing necessarily wrongful about scuttling your own property or your vessel putting to sea in an unseaworthy state. Nevertheless, the last point above made by Beldam LJ is surely the key issue. Has the owner deliberately taken a risk of loss or damage of which he is aware when it is unreasonable for him to do so? Clearly not where the owner scuttles his ship openly and for good reason. This is surely also the best explanation of the case of *Papadimitriou v. Henderson.*[13] This case involved a war risks insurance of the vessel *Ellinico Vouno*. The vessel was captured on a voyage from Odessa to Oran and a total loss was claimed from the war underwriters. They argued, *inter alia*, that the loss was contributed to by the wilful misconduct of the assured by his allowing the vessel to continue the voyage at a time when he knew that her capture was imminent. The judge found on the facts that there was no misconduct, let alone wilful misconduct in the owner performing his chartered voyage in the circumstances:

"I think it would be a very dangerous doctrine to lay down in the courts of this country that the captain of a neutral ship or the owner of a neutral ship or the owner of a ship belonging to a country not at war, is guilty of wilful misconduct if he tries to proceed with his contract voyage, simply because there is a risk of capture, as there must always be a risk of capture during a war, which is the very reason why shipowners and merchants insure against war risks."

The judge made the point that it might obviously be different if the shipowner deliberately endeavoured to get his ship captured rather than carry out the voyage. There does not, however, seem to be any support in the judgment for the statement in *Arnould* that "it seems clear that it is not enough to show that the assured realised that his conduct involved a high probability of exposure to losses covered by the policy". In fact the judge found there was no evidence to show that the vessel might be captured east of Malta where the incident took place. This was surely a case where the judge was of the view that the owner acted reasonably in the circumstances and so was not guilty of any misconduct. Unreasonable conduct involving a high probability of exposure to losses must surely be likely to be on the other side of the line.

7E PRIVITY

7.14 Privity is not, of course, mentioned in s.55(2)(a) unlike s.39(5). Is it, however, the same as wilful misconduct? In *Compania Maritima San Basilio SA v. The Oceanus Mutual Underwriting Association (Bermuda) Ltd (the "Eurysthenes")*,[14] one of the issues argued by Michael Mustill QC, as he then was, was that "privity" in s.39(5) equalled

12. See fn.7 *supra*.
13. *Papadimitriou v. Henderson* (1939) 64 Ll.L. Rep. 345.
14. *Compania Maritima San Basilio SA v. The Oceanus Mutual Underwriting Association (Bermuda) Ltd* ("*The Eurysthenes*") [1977] Q.B. 49; [1976] 2 Lloyd's Rep. 171; [1976] 3 All E.R. 243.

"wilful misconduct". It was held that it did not. Lord Denning MR said of the shipowner:

" 'Privity' did not mean that there was any wilful misconduct by him, but only that he knew of the act beforehand and concurred in it being done. Moreover, 'privity' did not mean that he himself personally did the act, but only that someone else did it and that he knowingly concurred in it."

Roskill LJ was to the same effect:

"one asks why, if 'privity' means the same as wilful misconduct, the same language was not used both in s.39(5) and in s.55(2)(a)."

and later in the judgment:

"In the context of the Act as a whole I think it is clear that 'privity' is not the same as 'wilful misconduct'. Nor is it the same as negligence or fault, whether personal or otherwise."

Thus, although sending the ship to sea in an unseaworthy state might amount to wilful misconduct it wasn't in the Lord Justice's view necessarily so. Geoffrey Lane LJ in his judgment says:

" 'Privity' means with knowledge and consent. It has, so far as I can discover, no connotation of fault."

This concept of privity has been further considered by the House of Lords in the very recent case of *The Star Sea.*[15] Here the Law Lords were considering "blind eye" knowledge within s.39(5). They passed up the opportunity to align the law in this area with modern practices in shipowning, concentrating instead on what was found in the *Eurysthenes* and interpreting it rather than reviewing it. They found that the test for blind eye knowledge was a subjective one. Lord Hobhouse said: 7.15

"The illuminating question therefore becomes 'why did he not enquire?' If the judge is satisfied that it was because he did not want to know for certain, then a finding of privity should be made. If, on the other hand, he did not enquire because he was too lazy or he was grossly negligent or believed that there was nothing wrong, then privity had not been made out."

Lord Scott said:

"There must be a suspicion of the relevant unseaworthiness, and a decision not to check. Unless there is a decision not to check, not to obtain confirmation of what is suspected, there will, in my opinion, be no privity, no blind-eye knowledge, however seriously negligent the failure to check may be."

He goes on to say that the suspicion is not a vague feeling of unease but "must be firmly grounded and targeted on specific facts. The deliberate decision must be a decision to avoid obtaining confirmation of facts in whose existence the individual has good reason to believe". It may be said that these types of thought processes may have some relevance to the normally conscientious blue chip shipowner but seem a little naïve as a test for measuring the thought processes of a shipowner who is not prepared to spend money on maintenance and is at the other end of the spectrum of shipowners. However, be that as it may, privity has been defined in the House of Lords in the context of deliberate decisions by the assured as opposed to negligence,

15. *Manifest Shipping & Co Ltd v. Uni-Polaris Insurance Co. Ltd* and *La Reunion Europeene* ("*The Star Sea*") [2001] UKHL/1; [2001] 1 Lloyd's Rep. 389, HL.

even of the most serious kind. Clearly this is the same as with wilful misconduct but, of course, there is no reference to recklessness in the speeches in the House of Lords.

7.16 The changing legal obligations on shipowners with regard to safety and seaworthiness and good practice in this regard, which are well categorised in the introduction of the ISM Code, but by no means limited to that, would not seem to be reflected at all in this latest decision of the House of Lords in the *The Star Sea*. By limiting themselves to an analysis of the *Eurysthenes* decision they seem to have rendered s.39(5) of little practical value by raising the threshold of what is and is not privity in this context. Yet the E*urysthenes* refers back to the pre-Act decisions such as *Thomson v. Hopper* and *Dudgeon v. Pembroke* where the background practices of the trade and the ships involved were very different – thus giving rise, for example, to the differences in s.39 of the Marine Insurance Act 1906 between voyage and time policies with respect to unseaworthiness – and when there was no necessary breach of any legal duty for a shipowner to trade his ship and send it to sea in an unseaworthy state. The legal and regulatory regimes under which shipowners operate today could hardly be more different and are if anything becoming more onerous in this respect. It would seem that against the decision in *The Star Sea* wilful misconduct may in unseaworthiness cases surprisingly offer a defence to a claim for underwriters where a restrictively interpreted s.39(5) does not – unlike the suggestion in the *Eurysthenes* that the latter section is wider.

7.17 Was the Court of Appeal right in the *Eurysthenes* to declare so robustly that privity was not the same as wilful misconduct? It would seem not and that Michael Mustill QC's argument had much to commend it. If one is to find any difference between s.39(5) and s.55(2)(a), it is surely in the context of the "conduct" or the "misconduct", not in the element of privity. *Arnould*, 16th edn., at para. 786 perhaps encapsulates this best when dealing with scuttling and s.55(2)(a):

> "The plainest application of the subsection is in cases where the assured has procured or connived at the deliberate casting away of the insured property in order to recover on his insurance."

The footnote to this passage reads:

> "The classic form of a plea of scuttling is that the assured 'procured or connived at' the casting away of the vessel. There appears to be no reported case proceeding clearly on the ground that the vessel was cast away with the connivance of the assured, but not at his instigation, but there can be no difference in principle between the procurement and connivance. 'It is clear that consent or privity can range from active complicity to mere passive concurrence. An owner who makes it clear that he would like to see his ship at the bottom of the sea, but does not want to know any more about it, is privy to its sinking in just the same way as Henry II was privy to the murder of Thomas a Becket when he said: "will no one rid me of this turbulent priest?" Even if the suggestion of scuttling comes from someone else and the owner implies consent by saying nothing against it, he would still be privy . . .', *per* Kerr J in *The Michael* (1979) 1 Lloyd's Rep. 55,66; affirmed, in the Court of Appeal (1979) 2 Lloyd's Rep. 1. Moreover, if the assured so to speak ratifies the scuttling of his vessel and presents the claim on a basis which he knows to be false, this is a fraudulent claim and cannot as such, be recovered: see Halsbury (4th Ed.), Vol. 25, paras 510–511; *The Michael, supra.*"

All that needs to be added to the above, which is surely correct, is that such privity is clearly within s.55(2)(a) and is indeed "wilful misconduct". This would not of course be so if the assured knew nothing of the scuttling beforehand but "ratified" it (whatever that might mean?) after the event, for then the assured would not have been privy to the event and the loss would not be attributable to his misconduct.

7F THE ASSURED

To come within the sub-section the wilful misconduct must be of the assured. Today, of course, it is commonplace to have many assured on a policy, particularly where fleets in which each vessel is normally owned by a one-ship company are concerned. Managers and indeed technical superintendence companies are often named as assured as well as the owning companies, as may also be mortgagees. When the policy is analysed there may be bundled within it many separate contracts of insurance between each assured and each separate underwriter. 7.18

"The assured" in s.55(2)(a), and generally in insurance, has consistently been held to mean the particular assured claiming under the policy. The distinction has been drawn between assureds who have a true joint interest in the property insured and those who are insuring separate interests, see, for example, *Samuel v. Dumas*;[16] *General Accident Fire & Life Assurance Corporation, Ltd and Matthew Watt Drysdale v. Midland Bank Ltd, Scoffin & Willmott Ltd, and Plant Bros Ltd*,[17] *New Hampshire Insurance Company and Others v. MGN Ltd and Others*.[18] Whilst the reasoning is clear – why should the wilful misconduct of one assured affect the separate right of another innocent assured? – the argument, and indeed the result, can seem unreal in the interconnected worlds of one ship companies, managers, technical superintendence companies and banks. 7.19

An attempt to have this area of the law reviewed was made in *State of the Netherlands v. Youell and Hayward and Others*.[19] Here, submarines were being constructed for the Dutch Navy by a building yard. There was, of course, a contract between the two regulating the building and the duties of each party. Under this contract one policy was taken out naming both the Navy as owner and the yard as builder plus co- and sub-contractors as assured. The paint applied to the submarines was incorrectly put on and cracked and fell off and the Navy sued the insurers for the cost of stripping and repainting. Both of the main assureds had the ability to claim in full and the fact that the Navy paid the yard for the repairs and claimed had the effect of removing the yard's claim. The judge at first instance (the point was not considered on appeal) considered the argument that there was here a pervasive interest – this means a "right to claim an insurable interest in the whole of the property" – in both assureds. He held that, notwithstanding this, the policy was to be construed as a composite policy with the interests of the various assureds being considered as separate and not joint. However, insofar as an assured with a pervasive interest sues for a loss which is greater in amount than his own underlying interest, to that extent he could not seek to recover free of a defence of wilful misconduct based on the wilful misconduct of the other 7.20

---

16. See fn.2 *supra*.
17. *General Accident Fire & Life Assurance Corporation Ltd and Matthew Watt Drysdale v. Midland Bank Ltd, Scoffin & Willmott Ltd, and Plant Bros. Ltd* [1940] 2 K.B. 388, CA; (1940) 67 LL. L. Rep. 218, CA.
18. *New Hampshire Insurance Company and Others v. MGN Ltd* and Others [1997] LRLR 24.
19. See fn.9 *supra*.

assured so beneficially entitled. Thus the Navy could not recover monies to which the yard would be beneficially entitled. A claim by an innocent assured based on a pervasive interest may well be affected by defences available to insurers by reason of the wilful misconduct of a co-assured. A mortgagee bank suing as an assured on hull policy for the whole insured value may well be affected in respect of any amounts in excess of the outstanding loan on the ship by reason of the wilful misconduct of the mortgagor. However, the wilful misconduct of a manager will not affect the claim of an "innocent" owner, notwithstanding any contractual arrangement between them and even if, as is often the case, subrogation rights have been waived by insurers in the policy.

In this last example, the only issue would be whether or not the owner was privy to the wilful misconduct in the sense considered above or if the manager was in fact the *alter ego* of the shipowner. This is because the sub-section only applies if insurers can show that the wilful misconduct was that of the assured personally or in the case of a company, its *alter ego*; see, for example, *The Star Sea.*[20]

7G IN CONCLUSION

7.21 In the light of the decision of the House of Lords in *The Star Sea*[20] and changes such as the ISM Code, wilful misconduct would seem to be an area of marine insurance law ripe for reconsideration. It is noteworthy, and in the author's opinion, damaging from the point of view of upholding good practice and good management of ships how far the courts have moved away from the reasoning that in 1906 resulted in the distinction between s.39(1) and s.39(5) of the Act. Yet, if anything, the reasoning behind s.39(1) has become as readily applicable to time policies today as it was to voyage policies in 1906. The main debate on s.39(1) has been one that has largely focused on causation, not privity. Clearly, wilful misconduct in the marine insurance context has over time become equated with scuttling and fraud and, as such, judges and practitioners are loathe to view it in its wider context and to find that assureds have been guilty of it. A similar although perhaps more understandable "tenderness" was previously to be found in arbitration law in respect of "misconduct" of arbitrators. In the Arbitration Act 1996 this has been overcome by changing the terminology to that of "serious irregularity". Whilst a change in terminology should not be necessary, a similar type of approach to misconduct for the purposes of s.55(2)(a) Marine Insurance Act 1906 by the Courts would in the author's view be beneficial.

20. See fn.12 *supra*.

CHAPTER 8

COUNTERCLAIMS BY MARINE INSURERS

PROFESSOR ROBERT GRIME

8A INTRODUCTION

In *British and Foreign Marine Insurance Co. v. Gaunt*[1] wool, insured against all risks from the sheep's back in Patagonia to the consignee's mills in Bradford, was found to have been wetted, possibly through the negligence of persons for whom the assured might have been responsible.[2] One argument presented by the insurers was that they might have an action for damages by way of counterclaim based upon s.78(4) of the Marine Insurance Act 1906. Section 78 deals with the rights and obligations of insurer and insured in connection with "suing and labouring".[3] Sub-section (4) provides that "it is the duty of the assured and his agents, in all cases, to take such measures as may be reasonable for the purpose of averting or minimising a loss".[4] Lord Sumner was dismissive:[5] *8.1*

"There remains an argument based on a reading of s.78, sub-s. 4, of the Act which is novel. It

1. [1921] 2 A.C. 41 (HL); [1920] 1 K.B. 903 (CA).

2. For a concise statement of the facts, see the speech of Lord Birkenhead. The damage had occurred between the sheep and Punta Arenas, where the wool was loaded aboard the overseas vessel. During that time it had been (in part) stored on baulks of timber under tarpaulin on the seashore and (in part) carried as deck cargo on small coasting vessels with little freeboard. An important issue was where the deck carriage affected the insurance, given Rule 17 of the Rules for the Construction of the Policy (Sched. 1 of the Marine Insurance Act 1906) which declares that "in the absence of usage to the contrary, deck cargo . . . must be insured specifically and not under the general denomination of goods". The House agreed with the Court of Appeal that the Rule had an interpretative and not a substantive effect. The case is, of course, primarily noteworthy as being the first major analysis of an "all risks" policy, given that the Institute of London Underwriters did not offer a standard All Risks form of cargo insurance until 1951.

3. The "suing and labouring" clause has appeared in the standard marine policy since the beginning. In its traditional form it permitted the assured and their "factors servants and assigns" to "sue, labour and travel for the defence safeguards and recovery" of the insured property, providing a separate and additional cover for the expenses thereby incurred.

4. The background and probable original purpose of s.78(4) is discussed below. It was undoubtedly inspired by the decision of the Privy Council in *Currie v. Bombay Native Insurance Co.* (1869) LR 3 PC 72, (discussed *infra*) which concerned the consequences of the assured's *failure* to "sue and labour".

5. [1921] 2 A.C. at p.65.

is one of the disadvantages of codification that new terms used or even unfamiliar sequences of propositions suggest that the law has been changed, where those familiar with the old decisions would not have suspected it. The argument affords a striking instance of this. The section obviously refers to suing and labouring. It cannot possibly be read as meaning that if the agents of the assured are not reasonably careful throughout the transit he cannot recover for anything to which their want of care contributes. The point therefore fails."[6]

8.2 Lord Sumner's exact words were adopted and used by Scrutton LJ in *Lind v. Mitchell*[7] as one reason for not permitting an underwriter a defence based upon misconduct of the assured's employees that did not amount to the defence of the "wilful misconduct *of the assured*" enshrined in the Marine Insurance Act 1906.[8]

8.3 In *La Banque Financiere de la Cite v. Westgate Insurance*,[9] a consortia of Swiss banks was persuaded to lend large sums of money to four companies controlled by Ballestero, a fraudster, for the purpose of a property development in Menorca called "Shangri-la". Shangri-la was, as ever, a myth. The primary security was a parcel of gemstones, which later proved to be worthless. As secondary security, insurance policies were specifically written to cover default by the companies and failure of the primary security. These insurances contained an exclusion for fraud. The underwriters properly refused payment on the ground of Ballestero's fraud. The banks claimed for breach of the duty of good faith by the insurers in that they had not informed the lending banks of other frauds committed by the broker who had effected the policies, of which frauds the insurers were aware. The duty of good faith is aplicable both to insurer and to assured.[10] The banks claimed damages for breach of this duty, as for a tortious act causing loss to them: they would not have advanced the money had they been properly informed. In the Court of Appeal, Slade LJ, giving the judgment of the court, rejected the argument. He was clearly concerned with the impact of the proposition upon the position of the assured, against whom such claims were likely to be made more often than against insurers:[11]

"A decision that the breach of such an obligation in every case and by itself constituted a tort

6. In the Court of Appeal, Atkin LJ had also been unimpressed. [1920] 1 K.B. at p.917: "I think that the only effect of that sub-section is to impose a duty to sue and labour – a very restricted duty compared with the general obligations contended for".

7. (1928) 32 Ll.L. Rep. 70, a case of alleged scuttling. Discussed *infra*.

8. Section 55(2)(a): "The insurer is not liable for loss attributable to the wilful misconduct of the assured, but, unless the policy otherwise provides, he is liable for any loss proximately caused by a peril insured against, even though the loss would not have happened but for the misconduct or negligence of the master and crew". For the common law origin of this distinction between "wilful misconduct" and "crew negligence", see *Trinder v. Thames and Mersey* [1898] 2 Q.B. 114.

9. [1988] 2 Lloyd's Rep. 513 (CA) and [1990] 2 Lloyd's Rep 377 (HL). At first instance (Steyn J) [1987] 1 Lloyd's Rep. 69, the case is entitled *Banque Keyser Ullmann v. Skandia (UK) Insurance Co. Ltd.* Skandia withdrew from the case before the appeal to the Court of Appeal and the bank changed its name. The case reverted to its original name in the House of Lords. To add to the confusion, Westgate Insurance was, at the time when the policies were written, called Hodge General and Mercantile Insurance Co. Nevertheless, the case usually goes under its first title and is commonly referred to as "the Banque Keyser Ullman litigation". Or, more succinctly, as "the Gemstones Case". The case is discussed in greater detail *infra*.

10. See Marine Insurance Act 1906, s.17, discussed later. The frauds committed by the broker, Mr Lee, were constituted (i) by the issue of cover notes for first and second excess layers of insurance (not written by the respondents) at the time the loan was made, when the layers were not put in place until much later, and (ii) by the issue of a cover note with regard to a third excess layer which was entirely false. The primary insurers were aware of the true facts but did not inform the banks.

11. [1988] 2 Lloyd's Rep. at p.550, col. 2. For further discussion, see *infra*.

if it caused damage could give rise to great potential hardship to insurers and even more, perhaps, to insured persons. An insured who had in complete innocence failed to disclose a material fact when making an insurance proposal might find himself subsequently faced with a claim by the insurer for a substantially increased premium by way of damages even before any event had occurred which gave rise to a claim. . . . In our judgment, it would not be right for this Court by way of judicial legislation to create a new tort, effectively of absolute liability, which would expose either party to an insurance contract to a claim for substantial damages in the absence of any blameworthy conduct."

In the House of Lords, the case was disposed of on other grounds.[12] Before that decision, however, Slade LJ's exact words were used by May LJ, in giving the judgment of the Court of Appeal in *The Good Luck*, a case very similar in its essential features.[13] The Court decided that the defendant was under a duty of good faith, or perhaps a "duty to speak",[14] but that breach of that duty did not sound in damages. The juridical basis of good faith was extensively examined[15] and May LJ concluded not only that there was no tort but also that, in most cases, the duty did not take effect as an implied term in any contract. This "free standing" duty "arose by operation of law as an incident of the contract of insurance".[16] But gave rise to no action for damages. 8.4

It would almost seem that some policy or principle is at work, a policy which includes the proposition that an insurer is not to be allowed to claim damages for breach of those very duties which are imposed for his benefit. The reasons are not made entirely clear but the proposition is stated in the firmest and baldest terms. But the immunity of assureds to insurers' actions for damages is not universally accepted. There are *dicta* in support of the opposite view.[17] More recently, in *The Star Sea*, Leggatt LJ succinctly reviewed the case law on the question of whether damages were 8.5

12. [1990] 2 Lloyd's Rep. 377. The House held that Mr Dungate, who acted for the insurers, was under no duty to disclose the particular matters to the banks. The frauds did not directly affect the primary insurance and only became known to Mr Dungate at a later stage, when the banks were negotiating a variation in the arrangements, at which stage the information related to *past* misbehaviour. The House further held that the losses suffered by the banks did not derive from the misrepresentations and non-disclosures of Mr Lee (the broker's employee), carried forward by Mr Dungate's failure to inform the banks, but from the fraud of Mr Ballestero (the primary fraudster) and would not have affected the making of the loans. "In the circumstance", said Lord Templeman, who gave the only substantial speech in the House, "it is not necessary to consider whether Hodge [later Westgate] were under a duty to disclose . . . by reason of the obligation of an insurer to deal with the proposer of the insurance with the utmost good faith". He did, however, describe the reasons given by Slade LJ as "cogent" and added, "But it may be helpful to observe that I agree with the Court of Appeal that a breach of the obligation does not sound in damages".

13. [1989] 2 Lloyd's Rep. 238 at p.263. The case concerned a claim by a bank for damages suffered by lending to a shipowner. Part of the security was a "loss payable" clause (a clause whereby in the event of a claim, the lender is paid in preference to the assured: whether such a clause, of itself, necessarily confers any legal right upon the beneficiary may be arguable) in war risk cover written by the Hellenic War Risks Association. The managers of the Association, Thomas Miller, had failed to inform the lending bank that a claim in respect of the loss of one of the shipowner's vessels was not to be met.

14. May LJ regards the "duty to speak" as separate from the "duty of good faith", being a possible tort to be derived from the circumstances which also give rise to the general obligation to observe the utmost good faith. Nevertheless, the essence of any tortious or contractual obligation of good faith must be well described as a "duty to speak". See *infra*.

15. Somewhat more extensively than in the *Gemstones Case*.

16. At p.264, col. 2.

17. See, for example, Hirst J in *The Litsion Pride* [1985] 1 Lloyd's Rep. 437, Hobhouse J in *The Good Luck* at first instance ([1988] 1 Lloyd's Rep. 514), Evans J in *The Captain Panagos DP* [1986] 2 Lloyd's Rep. 511.

available for a breach of the duty of good faith and can be said to have left the matter open.[18] That case is currently under consideration by the House of Lords. Now might be a good time to consider the question of the insurer's right to claim damages from the assured in slightly wider terms than those that are likely to be considered by the House.

8B SUE AND LABOUR AND THE DUTY OF THE ASSURED; THE DUTY TO PRESERVE SUBROGATION RIGHTS

8.6 Lord Sumner's remarks in the *Gaunt* case cannot be taken quite at their face value. Section 78(4) was inserted to deal with a number of the "old decisions" to which he refers. In *Currie v. Bombay Native Insurance Co.*[19] a cargo of teak and "padouk"[20] was insured for a voyage from Moulmein, Burma, to Madras in India aboard the vessel *Northland*. It was insured against total loss only. Hardly had the voyage begun when the *Northland*, temporarily stopped, dragged her anchors, went aground and was seriously damaged. The master, who was a part-owner of the *Northland*, took his passengers back to Moulmein, returned with surveyors and, perhaps on their advice, began to strip the ship of spars, etc. He then gave notice of abandonment on two policies, one on the cargo, the other on disbursements, and sold the ship (which was apparently uninsured), cargo and stores as a single lot. He had made no attempt to discharge the cargo, which was undamaged, but the purchasers did so successfully, except for some 60 logs. The Privy Council held that the underwriters on cargo were not obliged to pay for a total loss. The reasons are clear, the reasoning opaque. "It was the duty of the Assured, or of the Captain of the *Northland* (to whom everything appears to have been left) to take some steps in accordance with the recommendations of the Surveyors to try to save the cargo."[21]

8.7 So the assured had a duty. That this was so reinforced by Lord Blackburn in what may still be the leading case on the meaning of the Sue and Labour Clause, *Aitchison v. Lohre*.[22] The object of the Sue and Labour Clause, he said, was "to encourage and induce the assured to exert themselves" rather than to provide a more perfect indemnity. When Sir Mackenzie Chalmers came to the matter of reducing the common law of Sue and Labour to a section of the new Marine Insurance Bill, it was inevitable that he should insert sub-section 4 to give effect to *Currie v. Bombay Native*

18. [1997] 1 Lloyd's Rep. 360 at p.370.

19. (1869) LR 3 PC 72.

20. "A Burmese leguminous tree, *Pterocarpus macrocarpus*, yielding a kind of rosewood; the wood itself." (Shorter Oxford English Dictionary). The court described the cargo as being "of great specific gravity". It was presumably also of high value.

21. At p.81. The Privy Council was quite hard on the Captain. He was an uninsured part owner of the ship and he was accused of "tenderness" to the ship. "When a Ship and cargo are in peril of being lost, the Captain is called upon to act for the benefit of all concerned – he is not at liberty to prefer the interests of one of the parties to another." Which duty sounds rather wider than necessary for the policy of insurance on cargo. It looks rather like the sort of duty that might be derived from the Master's rights in case of General Average.

22. (1879) 4 App Cas 755 at p.765. Lord Blackburn in the case refers to a learned analysis of the Sue and Labour engagement by Willes J in *Kidston v. The Empire Marine Insurance Co.* (1867) LR 2 CP 357, which unfortunately did not deal with the point at issue before him. These two cases effectively constituted the common law on sue and labour until *Royal Boskalis v. Mountain* [1997] 2 All E.R. 929 re-opened the matter in the twentieth century. The sue and labour clause seems rarely to provide a basis for litigation.

Insurance and the *dicta* of Lord Blackburn. The legal significance of the duty is not clear in the statute: because it was not clear in the cases.[23]

But it is clear that the duty – or rather breach of it – does have *a* legal significance. 8.8
And, *pace* Lord Sumner, it is a significance wider than "suing and labouring".[24] For in *Currie* the breach was the given reason why the insurer did not have to pay for a total loss of cargo that had been sold as a result of a casualty. Why that was so was not so clear. There are grounds for understanding the case as deciding that there simply never was a total loss.[25] But that disregards the very extensive identification and discussion of the duty of the assured, which the assured, through his *alter ego* the captain, had broken. Such discussion would have been unnecessary for that approach. It could be that a breach of duty provides a defence to a claim. But to which claims and to what extent? Is it to be understood as analogous to the right of the insurer to avoid *ab initio* for a breach of the duty of utmost good faith? That seems unlikely. Reading of the case drives one to the conclusion that the insurer is not to have to pay for losses that derive from the breach of duty. Again, why? Is it a matter of causation only, that the breach of duty was not a risk covered?[26] That would be hard to justify in many cases, perhaps in *Currie v. Bombay* itself, and it certainly was never addressed. One must, at the end, at least consider the possibility that the Privy Council might have thought that the assured was liable in damages for a breach of the duty which caused the loss. A possibility firmly ruled out as unacceptable by Lord Sumner and others.

In *The Gold Sky*[27] the issue was re-examined. The *Gold Sky* had been lost in 8.9
circumstances that led the insurers to conclude that she had been deliberately scuttled. What was certainly plain was that, when the vessel was listing and sinking, assistance from a salvage tug was refused and the salvage master was physically

23. His declared aim was "to reproduce as exactly as possible the existing law without making any attempt to amend it". So he asserted in the introduction to his *Digest of Marine Insurance* (1901), a commentary on his Marine Insurance Bill, which was first introduced into the House of Lords by Lord Herschell in 1894. The *Digest* in its second edition became *Chalmer's Marine Insurance Act*, now in its ninth edition.

24. What Lord Sumner meant by saying that sub-section 4 "obviously refers to suing and labouring" is not entirely clear. It may be that he understood it to preserve the position when there was *not* a suing and labouring clause in the contract. In *Emperor Goldmining v. Switzerland Insurance* [1964] 1 Lloyd's Rep. 348 (Sup. Ct. of New South Wales) it was held that in the absence of an express clause, the statutory duty imported an implied obligation on the insurer to meet the costs of performing that duty. Section 78(1) begins "Where the policy contains a suing and labouring clause" and sub-sections (2) and (3) both refer to consequences of the application of a "suing and labouring clause". Sub-section (4) applies "in all cases" and stands alone in not being dependent upon the existence of a clause in the policy. In *Integrated Container Services v. British Traders' Insurance* [1984] 1 Lloyd's Rep. 154, the Court of Appeal used s.78(4) as defining the ambit of "suing and labouring" – i.e., that which might fall within the duty would qualify for payment. This enabled the court to consider questions of the extent of the duty partly in terms of the impact upon the assured. See particularly the judgment of Eveleigh LJ.

25. It must be remembered that the cover was for total loss only: it was, therefore, only necessary for the court to be satisfied that there was no total loss, or no total loss attributable to a risk covered. It is not clear from the judgment which, if either, of those analyses was adopted. Nor was it, of course, necessary for the court to consider whether there might have been a *partial* loss caused by an insured peril. The facts were (a) that the timber was sold after and perhaps in consequence of the grounding of the *Northland* and not damaged by the grounding and (b) some of the timber remained in the vessel.

26. That conclusion would depend upon what was covered by the policy generally. Where, as in *Gaunt*, the cover was extensive, there would be little room for the argument. For further consideration of the "balance of risk" argument, see *infra*.

27. [1972] 2 Lloyd's Rep. 187.

pushed away by the *Gold Sky's* third engineer.[28] Deliberate sinking is not a loss by a peril of the seas and is, therefore, generally not covered.[29] To establish a loss by a peril of the seas, some fortuity must be shown.[30] Mocatta J held that, while the underwriters had not established deliberate casting away, the shipowners had not established fortuitous loss either, so the claim for a loss by perils of the seas simply failed. However, the underwriters raised, as their second and alternative defence, a counterclaim that the vessel had been lost in breach of s.78(4). Mocatta J proceeded to deal with this point. He examined all the authorities, including those after *Gaunt*. The case of *Lind v. Mitchell*[31] concerned the insurance by a mortgagee of an ice-damaged rum-runner, abandoned by her master, which later sank. At first instance, Wright J was able to distinguish the leading case of *Samuel v. Dumas*[32] and hold that the ship had not been lost by deliberate act, which was *not* a peril of the seas (there being no evidence of fraudulent intent by the master), but by the ice damage, which was. The abandonment, albeit premature, did not cause the loss.[33] The Court of Appeal upheld the decision, clearly holding that the loss was caused by a peril insured against, though exacerbated by the acts of the master and crew, and that there was no evidence of wilful misconduct by the assured. The case therefore fell squarely within the terms of s.55(2)(a) of the Marine Insurance Act 1906.[34] In that context, Scrutton LJ addressed s.78(4) and disposed of the point by referring to the remarks of Lord Sumner in *Gaunt*. This he did, said Mocatta J, "by way of parenthesis and without indicating that the point had been raised by Counsel".[35] Clearly, then, *obiter*. In *Irvin v. Hine*[36] it was argued on behalf of insurers that, since an accurate assessment of damage could not be achieved without a dry-docking survey, the claim was not maintainable because failure to arrange for such a survey constituted a breach of s.78(4). Devlin J held that it did not constitute a breach, because post-occurrence survey did not "minimise" losses.[37] Also unhelpful.

---

28. The Third Engineer, alleged by the underwriters to be "the villain of the piece", was regarded as an unreliable witness. For his further adventures, see *The Michael* [1979] 2 Lloyd's Rep. 1.

29. *Samuel v. Dumas* [1924] A.C. 431.

30. "The term 'perils of the seas' refers only to fortuitous accidents or casualties of the seas." Rules for the Construction of the Policy, Rule 7 (Marine Insurance Act 1906, Sched. 1.).

31. (1928) 32 Ll. L.Rep. 70 (CA), upholding Wright J at 31 Ll. L. Rep. 262.

32. [1924] A.C. 431. That case also concerned the position of an absolutely innocent mortgagee.

33. The vessel was also set afire by the crew, to avoid creating a danger to shipping, but there was no evidence that she was lost by fire. Had she been so lost, the resolution of the case might have been easier, since while the deliberate admission of sea-water is *not* a "peril of the seas", deliberate fire is "fire" within the meaning of the policy. See *Busk v. Royal Exchange* (1818) 2 B and Ald 73.

34. "The insurer is not liable for any loss attributable to the wilful misconduct of the assured, but, unless the policy otherwise provides, he is liable for any loss proximately caused by a peril insured against, even though the loss would not have happened but for the misconduct or negligence of the master or crew." The leading case on the issue before the Act was *Trinder v. Thames and Mersey Marine Insurance* [1898] 2 QB 114, relying on *Thompson v. Hopper* (1858) E B & E 1047 and *Dixon v. Sadler* (1839) 5 M & W 405. The last case was the case that established that negligent navigation was a peril of the seas.

35. At p.220, col 1.

36. (1950) 83 Ll. L. Rep. 162. A leading case on unrepaired damage in hull insurance. In *The Gold Sky* Mocatta J also referred to *Emperor Goldmining v. Switzerland Insurance* [1964] 1 Lloyd's Rep. 348, a decision of Manning J in the Supreme Court of New South Wales, to the effect that in a policy *without* a Sue and Labour Clause, the existence of the statutory duty contained in s.78(4), (s.84(4) of the Australian enactment of the UK Marine Insurance Act), gave an entitlement to reimbursement by the insurer of expenses incurred by the insured in discharging the duty.

37. At p.170, col 1.

Mocatta J did not find himself able to follow the simple approach that had been found sufficient by Lord Sumner, by Scrutton LJ and by Atkin J – a very impressive trio. For him, the sub-section *could* give rise to a counterclaim.[38] However, he recognised that to extend the ambit of s.78(4) to "any failure of the master and crew to act reasonably to avert or minimise a loss, when, during the currency of the cover, the subject matter insured appears about to suffer loss through an insured peril or has suffered some such loss which may increase or perhaps become total, would appear irrational".[39] His escape-route depended upon s.55(2)(a) of the Act, which distinguished between the consequences of "wilful misconduct of the assured", which were not covered, and losses "proximately caused by a peril insured against" which would not have happened "but for the misconduct or negligence of the master or crew". He proposed that, as a matter of construction of the statute, in order to reconcile two sub-sections, the master and crew should be excluded from the ambit of the phrase "the assured and his agents" in s.78(4):[40] 8.10

"While the master of the *Gold Sky*, had he entered into a Lloyd's salvage agreement . . ., would no doubt by so doing have bound the plaintiffs, I do not think it necessarily follows that, in the absence of instructions from his owners, the master of a vessel must be taken to be included within the words 'the assured and his agents' in s.78(4), so that a failure by the master to take such measures as may be reasonable will militate against his owners' claim against insurers. I think the words 'his agents' should in the context and in order to avoid an acute conflict between two sub-sections of the Act be read a inapplicable to the master or crew, unless expressly instructed by the assured in relation to what to do or not to do in respect of suing and labouring."

This is not an easy interpretation. The master and crew are generally servants, or employees, of the insured shipowner. Servants commonly have some authority as agents with regard to the protection of their employer's property, and the shipmaster most certainly has.[41] That "agents" should not include those very agents who most usually do act in this particular matter is, shall we say, rather counter-intuitive. Nor would it be easy to apply in practice. Mocatta J himself allows for one exception, when the owners have issued instructions. Which must surely include general instructions, such as, perhaps, "do not sign salvage agreements without reference to head office".[42] Other difficulties may arise.[43] Nor, as we shall see, does the interpretation assist when the modern "duty of the assured" clauses in the policy are considered. Those 8.11

38. "I think the right view to take on the facts here, if he had brought the sub-section into play, is that the defendant would be able to set off or counterclaim the £45,000 particularised, if he could prove his figures, rather than that the action should wholly fail. This conclusion is, I think, consonant with the attempt made above to reconcile the two sub-sections. It also appears to have been the view of McArthur as the position at common law: see Contract of Marine Insurance, 2nd edn. (1890)." At p.221, col. 2.

39. At p.220, col 2. Mocatta J was led to his examination through a consideration of s.55(2)(a) and therefore does not consider failures otherwise than by the crew.

40. At p.221.

41. For the general point, see, as an example, *Poland v. Parr* [1927] 1 K.B. 236. The position of the shipmaster was usually discussed in the context of necessaries and of various rights in the master to pledge ship and cargo for necessaries, including repairs and supplies to complete the voyage (*bottomry* and *respondentia*). See the treatment in *Abbott's Law of Merchant Shipping and Seamen* Chapter 3.

42. Which might possibly have been the case in *The Gold Sky*.

43. Mocatta J adverts to the problem of the owner/skipper, as occurred in *Trinder v. Thames and Mersey* [1898] 2 Q.B. 114.

expressly refer to "servants" as well as "agents".[44] And the point is *obiter*.[45] One institutional writer has concluded that Mocatta J's analysis "probably cannot be supported".[46]

8.12 Another method for avoiding the most unacceptable consequences of permitting an insurer to base a claim against an assured upon s.78(4) was offered in *O'May on Marine Insurance*.[47] It is there suggested that "the duty under s.78(4) arises after the occurrence of a casualty has created a potential loss".[48] The significance of this analysis is that a breach of duty arising after the claimable loss might lead to a reduction of the claim (as seems to have occurred, in a sense, in *Currie v. Bombay Native Insurance*, which concerned insurance against total loss only), but would not allow for a complete defence[49] to a claim (as was canvassed in *Gaunt*). So it fits the decided cases. The justification offered for the interpretation is that the traditional Sue and Labour clause opens with the words "And in case of any loss or misfortune". However, the modern clauses do not all open with similar words,[50] s.78(4) applies "in all cases",[51] and both the sub-section and the clauses apply to "averting" as well as to "minimising" losses. Attractive though the result is, the interpretation seems difficult to support as a piece of literal analysis.

8.13 There is a further aspect of the "duty of the assured". That is the obligation to preserve subrogation rights for the benefit of the insurer. On payment of a claim, the insurer is subrogated to all rights and remedies of the assured in respect of the subject of the claim. Subrogation generally applies to claims maintainable by the assured against third parties, but may be wider.[52] It is well established that the assured must not act so as to injure his insurer's rights – by releasing claims, for example. That may

---

44. ITC (Hulls) 1995 Clause 11; ICC (1982) Clause 16. Both declare that "it is the duty of the assured, their servants and agents . . .".

45. Mocatta J had already held that the loss was not recoverable as a loss by "perils of the seas".

46. *Arnould on Marine Insurance* 16th edn., para. 770.

47. 1993. This work, begun by Donald O'May, Senior Partner of Ince and Co., and a leading figure in the world of marine insurance, completed, after his untimely death, by Julian Hill, provides a most important contribution to our understanding of the law of marine insurance.

48. Page 142. See also pp.327–334.

49. The debate as to whether any entitlement of the insurer based upon s.78(4) is properly to be considered a defence or a counterclaim, is included in *Arnould on Marine Insurance* 16th edn., paragraph 770. The learned editors conclude (fn.96) that it makes little practical difference. The defence would be based upon causation, the counterclaim, it is there argued, for damages for breach of statutory duty. But see *infra*.

50. The hull and machinery policy does: "In case of any loss or misfortune, it is the duty . . ." ITC (Hulls) 1995, Clause 11. The cargo clauses do not: "It is the duty of the assured . . ." ICC 1982, Clause 16.

51. Although this phrase can, of course, be understood as applying the subsection to all insurance policies, whether or not they contain a suing and labouring clause, in contradistinction to sub-section (1) which is confined in its application to policies which *do* contain such a clause. See *Emperor Goldmining v. Switzerland Insurance*, discussed *supra*.

52. "The underwriter is entitled to the advantage of every right of the assured, whether such right consists in contract, fulfilled or unfulfilled, or in remedy for tort capable of being insisted on or already insisted on, or in any other right, whether by way of condition or otherwise, legal or equitable, which can be, or has been exercised or has accrued, and whether such right could or could not be enforced by the insurer in the name of the assured by the exercise or acquiring of this right or condition the loss against which the assured is insured, can be, or has been diminished." Per Brett LJ in *Castellain v. Preston* (1883) 11 Q.B.D. 380 at p.388. Subrogation extends to "windfalls" (*Yorkshire Insurance v. Nisbet Shipping* [1962] 2 Q.B. 330), but not to gifts (*Burnand v. Rodocanachi* (1882) 7 App. Cas. 333) nor, it would seem, to payments in respect of which the assured has no legal rights. See *The Esso Bernicia* [1989] A.C. 643.

be described in the language of duty. In *Commercial Union v. Lister*[53] a silk mill in Halifax was blown up, allegedly because of the negligence of the employees of Halifax Corporation, who had supplied gas to the mill. The insurers settled the claim[54] and sought a declaration "that they were entitled to the benefit of any right of action" and an injunction restraining the mill-owner "from prosecuting the action otherwise than for the full amount". No injunction was issued, the mill-owner having given appropriate undertakings, but Sir George Jessel MR had no doubts that the assured was under an "equitable obligation" and was not entitled "to compromise the action otherwise than bona fide".[55] It might be unwise to read too much into the use of the adjective "equitable".[56] The duty in question was "equitable" in the sense that it was asserted to be a duty to act in good faith. There is nothing in the judgments that would support the contention that the obligation derived from an equitable jurisdiction, nor that, on that account, the remedies for its breach might be restricted.

The legal nature of the obligation to preserve subrogation rights was under consideration in *West of England Fire Insurance v. Isaacs*.[57] A tenant had insured against fire and recovered on his policy. The lease contained a term whereby he might have claimed from his landlord for the consequences of the fire. His landlord died and the tenant made a settlement with the executors that covered all claims, including claims for dilapidations and did not proceed to enforce any of his rights. Collins J allowed a claim by the insurer for £100 representing the benefit lost to them through the assured's abandoning his action against his landlord. The judge "did not shrink" from dealing with the case on that basis, rather than on the basis of requiring the assured to account for money received into his hands (the proceeds of the settlement) which, in part, may have represented the loss compensated by the insurer. The facts simply did not support that analysis of the settlement. The insurer was entitled to compensation for what he had lost through his assured's failure to perform his duty: the right to participate in the assured's claim on the lease to a maximum of the amount paid by the insurer to the assured under the policy.[58] This was not a successful claim for an account of money in the hands of the assured. It was compensation. Damages in all but name. But the judgment is notable for the absence of that simple word. The assured was "under an obligation, however it is to be expressed in point of law, to make good" the "benefit" represented by the foregone claim, to the insurers.[59] 8.14

It would not be unreasonable to conclude that, while recognising that an assured 8.15

53. (1874) LR 9 Ch App 483.

54. Or most of it. The mill-owner lost £56,000, but £6,000 was loss of profit, which was not at that time considered to be insurable.

55. At pp. 486 and 484. The court refused to restrain the assured from making any compromise of the action. He remained *dominus litis*, despite the recognised interest of the insurer.

56. The insurer's subrogation rights are recognised at common law, but Equity intervenes to permit the insurer in appropriate cases to proceed in the name of the assured, and offers certain other relief, while preserving the position of the assured as *dominus litis*. See the discussion in *Castellain v. Preston*, cited *supra*.

57. [1896] 2 Q.B. 373.

58. The amount had been fixed by an agreement which had at an earlier stage involved the insurer and also the fire insurer of the landlord, who had covered the same risk in the landlord's interest. This, in the judge's view, disposed of the question of evaluating the claim on the lease: its value had been agreed.

59. At p.383. Alternative terminology, which was not used either, might be that of equitable indemnity (see, for example, *Whittington v. Seal-Hayne* (1900) 82 LT 49). Lord Haldane and Lord Dunedin in the leading case of *Nocton v. Lord Ashburton* [1914] A.C. 932 would, apparently, have allowed compensation for breach of another "equitable duty" and are unclear about whether it be damages or indemnity. The

owes to his insurer certain definable duties, a principle, or policy, is being asserted that these duties to not support ordinary claims for damages. One reason sometimes assigned for that conclusion is that these duties do not constitute simple contractual obligations. Such was certainly the view of Brett LJ in *Castellain v. Preston*, a leading case on subrogation: "that doctrine does not arise upon the terms of the contract of insurance".[60] It derived from the "fundamental principle of insurance", that of indemnity. Again, discussion of the effect of the duty contained in s.78(4) of the Marine Insurance Act 1906 has proceeded upon the basis that, although connected with a contract of insurance, it arises as a statutory duty independent of it.[61] Such analysis renders discussion of any right to damages technically rather difficult. If it is not to be damages for breach of contract, perhaps it must be tort, or more specifically, an action for breach of statutory duty.[62]

8.16 Modern marine policies, however, generally contain specific clauses dealing with the "duty of the assured". These radically alter the position. Before the reforms of 1982–1983, the Institute Time Clauses (Hulls) contained a clause designed further to explain the Suing and Labouring Clause contained in the ancient SG policy, which was then still the basis of cover in the London market. But that clause did not address the "duty of the assured".[63] The Institute Cargo Clauses, however, did, by including the "Baillee Clause":[64]

> "It is the duty of the Assured and their Agents, in all cases, to take such measures as may be reasonable for the purpose of averting or minimising a loss and to ensure that all rights against carriers, baillees or other third parties are properly preserved and exercised."

While the first part of the clause repeats exactly the words of s.78(4), the latter part makes clear the traditional purpose of the clause, which its title implies: to require the

---

distinction may be more terminological than substantive. See *infra* for further discussion. The present decision was affirmed by the Court of Appeal ([1897] 1 Q.B. 226). See also the discussion in *Arnould on Marine Insurance* 16th edn. para. 1320, which is just as careful in point of language. A care that is made more significant by the assertion (mentioned *infra*) that where the policy contains a "Baillee Clause", there *is* an action for damages.

60. (1883) 11 Q.B.D. 380 at p.387.

61. See the discussion in *Arnould on Marine Insurance* 16th edn. para. 770, in which a contrast is drawn between the *option* to sue and labour in the old clause and the obligation under the statute. It has also been pointed out by distinguished academic authors that the extent of the statutory provision, which in its terms imposes obligations upon "agents" who are not likely to be parties to the contract, is far too extensive for a contractual analysis. See Rose *Failure to Sue and Labour* [1990] JBL 190; Bennett *The Law of Marine Insurance* (1996) pp.387 *et seq.*

62. *Arnould* treats the matter as requiring consideration of an action for breach of statutory duty. The learned editors of the 16th edition do, however, keep an open mind on the general issue of whether damages are recoverable.

63. The SG policy, settled in 1779, always regarded as "a strange and incoherent instrument" (Buller J in *Brough v. Whitmore* (1791) 4 TR at p.210). It featured in Sched. 1 of the Marine Insurance Act 1906 accompanied by 17 "Rules for the Construction of the Policy" of statutory force. The suing and labouring clause, already mentioned, reads, in full, "And in case of any loss or misfortune, it shall be lawful to the assured, their factors, servants and assigns, to sue, labour and travel for, in and about the defence, safeguards, and recovery of the said goods and merchandises and ship, etc., or any part thereof, without prejudice to this insurance; to the charges whereof, we, the assurers, will contribute each one according to the rate and quantity of his sum herein insured". Clause 9 of the Institute Time Clauses (Hulls) 1963 deals with two matters arising from the clause, as extended and interpreted by s.78(1), (2) and (3) of the Marine Insurance Act 1906 – the effect of under-insurance (9(a)) and deduction of salvage after total loss (9(b)).

64. Institute Cargo Clauses 1963, Clause 9.

assured contractually to preserve subrogation rights. The learned editors of *Arnould* had no doubt that the effect of the inclusion of the Baillee Clause in a policy was to render the assured liable in damages for failing to preserve subrogation rights.[65] It would be hard to distinguish the effect of the first and second parts of the clause. The same conclusion must, in principle, be reached as regards failure to perform the "duty of the assured". Under the 1963 Baillee Clause, for the assured, or for his agents,[66] to fail to take reasonable measures is a plain breach of contract, presumptively sounding in damages.

The comprehensive and radical re-draft of the Institute marine insurance forms that took place in 1982–1983 showed significant changes in this area. Both hull and cargo forms included new "duty of the assured" clauses in similar terms. The hull and machinery clauses included:[67] 8.17

> "In case of any loss or misfortune it is the duty of the Assured and their servants and agents to take such measures as may be reasonable for the purpose of averting or minimising a loss which would be recoverable under this insurance."

The cargo clauses:[68]

> "It is the duty of the Assured and their servants and agents in respect of loss recoverable hereunder:
>
> to take such measures as may be reasonable for the purpose of averting or minimising such loss, and
>
> to ensure that all rights against carriers, baillees or other third parties are properly preserved and exercised. . . "

The immediately obvious change is the inclusion of "servants" with "agents" and "the Assured" as persons whose failures the clause is intended to cover. This turns the flank of Mocatta J's argument in *The Gold Sky*.[69] These clauses could cover the misbehaviour of the Third Engineer. With that exception, the clauses follow the terms of s.78(4) and make them contractual.[70]

The consequence is hard to avoid. Unreasonable failure by the assured to avert or minimise loss, and any failure by a cargo assured to preserve subrogation rights is a breach of contract. Breach of contract ordinarily sounds in damages. And yet we retain those strong expressions of judicial policy against the conclusion that an assured should be placed under, in effect, a continuing duty of care to avoid claims. It is unacceptable, irrational. Can the circle be squared? 8.18

65. "It is submitted that the effect of this important clause is to give the underwriter a cross-claim for damages . . ." *Arnould on Marine Insurance* (16th edn.) para. 1320.

66. To take the "privity" point (see fn.61 *supra*) the contractual duty lies upon the assured only and does not extend to agents. It does, however, impose a strict vicarious liability for the failure of those agents – and, after 1982–1983, servants.

67. ITC (Hulls) 1995 Clause 11. The 1995 amendments did not alter in any way the precursor of this clause drafted in 1983.

68. ICC 1982, A, B and C, Clause 16.

69. See *supra*. According to *O'May on Marine Insurance*, such was the intention of the draftsmen. See p.490. The author's knowledge of the background to the clauses was as extensive as his understanding of their legal significance.

70. The inclusion in the hull and machinery clauses (but not in the cargo clauses) of the introductory phrase "in case of any loss or misfortune", taken from the SG policy (which is no longer a part of the insurance cover) would give some support to the argument contained in *O'May on Marine Insurance* that, if the "duty of the assured" sounds in damages, it only does so in respect of failures occurring *after* the claimable loss. But only in hull and machinery insurance. The matter is discussed above. It is submitted that, in any case, the analysis is not convincing.

8.19 Some assistance may be gained if another route is followed. The decision of the Privy Council in *Currie v. Bombay Native Insurance*[71] may easily be understood in terms of causation. The total loss of the cargo was not caused by the stranding of the ship, which was a risk that was covered, but by the master's misconduct, which was not covered.[72] In *Lind v. Mitchell* at first instance, Wright J held that the vessel was lost by ice damage and that the subsequent hasty abandonment by the master and the firing of the ship did not disrupt that chain of causation.[73] That decision was upheld in the Court of Appeal, where consideration was also given to a further slant on the same argument.[74] The facts of the case fitted exactly into another sub-section of the Marine Insurance Act 1906, s.55(2)(a):

> "The insurer is not liable for any loss attributable to the wilful misconduct of the assured, but, unless the policy otherwise provides, he is liable for any loss proximately caused by a peril insured against, even though the loss would not have happened but for the misconduct or negligence of the master and crew."

This sub-section does two things. It declares that (unless provision is specifically made) losses attributable to the wilful misconduct of the assured are not covered. Second, it deals with a particular matter of interactive causation: where, to use old-fashioned language, the *causa causans* is an insured peril and crew negligence or misconduct appears as *causa sine qua non*.[75] In such a case, the risk is covered. But there may be many circumstances which do not involve that particular example of interactive causation and yet which are covered by the policy and which fall outside the exclusion contained in the first part of the sub-section, "wilful misconduct of the assured". Such was the case in *Gaunt*, where the terms of the policy clearly covered the events alleged to have caused the damage. That, indeed, was the basis of the decision in favour of the assured in the Court of Appeal.[76] The issue was not revisited in the speeches in the House of Lords, but the conclusion may have informed the

71. (1869) LR 3 PC 72.

72. One might go further. The insurance was against total loss only. There was no total loss. The purchasers discharged all but 60 logs. Therefore 60 logs were lost by a peril of the sea, the rest from other causes. Two partial losses.

73. (1928) 31 Ll. L. Rep. 262. The question of barratry was raised, although the underwriters asserted that barratry did not apply where the master was not appointed by the assured, the mortgagee. There may have been little in that point. See *The Minden* [1942] A.C. 50. In any case, Wright J dealt with the barratry point by concluding that, despite much suspicion, there was no compelling evidence of fraud (misconduct) by the master in abandoning the ship. That assisted his conclusion that, in effect, the abandonment was not a *novus actus interveniens*.

74. (1928) 32 Ll. L. Rep. 70. See, in particular, the judgment of Scrutton LJ.

75. Section 55, cross-headed in the Act "Included and excluded losses", is expressed entirely in terms of causation, which could be regarded as surprising. The English courts have not developed complex or subtle rules of causation. "Proximate cause", means "dominant" or "effective" cause, or "proximate in efficiency" not time. See *Ionides v. Universal Marine Insurance* (1863) 14 CB(NS) 259, *Leyland Shipping v. Norwich Union* [1918] A.C. 350, *The Coxwold* [1942] A.C. 691. For a rare, but relatively recent, case on interactive causes (not involving crew negligence) see *The Miss Jay Jay* [1987] 1 Lloyd's Rep. 32 (CA). This establishes, generally, that when one of two (or more?) interactive causes is covered, the risk is covered by the policy. *Sed quaere* when one (or more) interactive causes is *excluded*.

76. [1921] 1 K.B. 903. See particularly the judgment of Atkin LJ at p.913. The terms of the cover were: "Including all risks of craft, fire, coasters, hulks, transhipment and inland carriage by land and/or water and all risks from the sheep's back and/or station, while awaiting shipment and/or forwarding and until safely delivered into warehouses in Europe with liberties as per bills of lading". The wetting of the wool occurred either while the wool was waiting for coastal vessels and was stored by the sea on baulks of timber under tarpaulin, or while in transit as deck cargo on coasters with little freeboard.

brisk rejection by Lord Sumner of the s.78(4) point with which we started.[77] Furthermore, if there had been acts or omissions for which the assured might have been responsible, these were not confined to the "negligence or misconduct of the master and crew". Section 55(2)(a) was not at issue. It was not a matter of reconciling two sub-sections of the Marine Insurance Act 1906, as it had been for Mocatta J in *The Gold Sky*.

Even outside "all risks" insurance, the cover at issue in *Gaunt*, there are many examples of insured risks which include matters which might constitute a breach of the duty imposed by s.78(4), or, more practically, by the "Duty of the Assured" clauses in the policies. In hull insurance, the cover for "perils of the seas" covers collisions, sinkings, groundings, etc, caused by negligent navigation.[78] Even acts of lunatic irresponsibility do not prevent the loss being accounted a loss by perils of the seas.[79] In *The Zinovia*, there was a catalogue of failure, by "the Assured and their servants and agents", but still, when the ship went aground, it was held to be a loss by perils of the seas.[80] The only stopping point is provided by the decision of the House of Lords in *Samuel v. Dumas*.[81] Deliberate, or fraudulent, action is not a peril of the seas.[82] This is not simply an aspect of the "wilful misconduct of the assured". A deliberate act is not a peril of the seas, no matter who does it. On the other hand, fire is covered even when deliberate.[83] The adoption of the phrase "entry of seawater" in 8.20

77. [1921] 2 A.C. 41. The main ground of appeal related to the issue of whether the inclusion of the interpretation of the word "goods" by Rule 17 of the Rules for the Construction of the Policy in the Marine Insurance Act 1906, Sched. 1, altered the substance and rendered deck cargo not covered without specific mention. The House held that was not the case.

78. ITC (Hulls) 1995 Clause 6.1.1. "perils of the seas rivers lakes or other navigable waters". *Dixon v. Sadler* (1839) 5 M & W 405 is usually taken as the *fons et origo* of the proposition that negligent navigation is a peril of the seas. See also *Trinder v. Thames and Mersey marine Insurance* [1898] 2 Q.B. 114 and *Thompson v. Hopper* (1858) E B & E 1047.

79. See *Cohen v. National Benefit* (1924) 18 Ll. L. Rep. 199, *The La Pointe* [1989] 2 Lloyd's Rep. 536 (Canada). The most extreme case, where the ship was apparently lost through an excess of curiosity by a new and enthusiastic deckhand, is probably *The Bamcell* [1986] 2 Lloyd's Rep. 524.

80. [1984] 2 Lloyd's Rep. 264. The case makes fascinating reading. The vessel was clearly "an accident looking for somewhere to happen". But it was not, held Bingham J, wilfully cast away, the issue in the case.

81. [1924] A.C. 431. The decision on this point was reached by a majority, Lord Cave and Lord Finlay giving substantial speeches, Lord Parmoor concurring, without giving reasons, with Lord Finlay. Given his position on s.78(4), it is perhaps interesting to note that Lord Sumner gave a very strong dissent on this point. He would have allowed any incursion of seawater, not attributable to the "wilful misconduct of the assured" under s.55(2)(a), to be a peril of the seas. The decision of the majority was regarded as rather radical. Its impact on cargo insurance was unacceptable and led to an amendment of Clause 8 of the (old) Institute Cargo Clauses, to preserve the position of the cargo-owner whose property is lost aboard a scuttled ship. "In the event of loss the Assured's right of recovery hereunder shall not be prejudiced by the fact that the loss may have been attributable to the wrongful act or misconduct of the shipowners or their servants, committed without the privity of the Assured." Logically, the clause misses the point: when a ship is scuttled, the insured cargo-owners do not have a claim that may be prejudiced by the misconduct of others, they do not have a claim, since there was no "peril of the seas". The issue was examined in *The Salem* [1981] 2 Lloyd's Rep. 316, where the judges declined to be pedantic.

82. It is not entirely clear whether deliberation or fraud is required, although this is unlikely to make any difference. Both Atkin J and the Court of Appeal in *Lind v. Mitchell* (1928) 32 Ll.L. Rep. 70, discussed earlier, held that the fact that the action of the captain in abandoning and firing the ship in that case was not fraudulent (or possibly deliberate) did not break the chain of causation from the ice-damage to the final sinking.

83. See *Busk v. Royal Exchange* (1818) 2 B & Ald 73. "Fire" is covered both in hull and machinery policies (ITC (Hulls) 1995 Clause 6.1.2, "fire, explosion") and in named perils cargo insurance (ICC 1982, Forms B and C Clause 1.1.1, "fire or explosion").

Form B of the Institute Cargo Clauses in 1982 must have been carried out with the intention of avoiding the need for express exception to counter the catastrophic effects of *Samuel v. Dumas* on cargo interests.[84] Certainly an assured need not prove *how* water got in in order to establish that it did.[85] The "named perils" cargo policies contain several other risks that are likely to be interpreted in similar absolute terms.[86] Negligence at large, that is negligence which does not give rise to a loss otherwise described, is explicitly covered in hull insurance under the "Additional Perils Clause", which contains a special defence for the insurer based upon want of due diligence by the assured and others.[87] The negligence covered is that of "Master Officers Crew or Pilots"[88] and of "repairers or charterers".[89] "Barratry" involves misconduct by master or crew in breach of their obligations owed to their employers. That, too, is risk enumerated in the Additional Perils Clause of the hull and machinery policy.[90] Of course, in virtue of s.55(2)(a), none of these claims may be maintained if the loss is "attributable to the wilful misconduct of the assured", but if the sub-section is to apply, the misconduct must be "of the assured", not of his servants or agents, and it must be "wilful", not merely negligent or even reckless.[91]

---

84. Clause 1.2.3. "Entry of sea lake or river water into vessel craft hold conveyance container liftvan or place of storage". For the adjustment to the policy following *Samuel v. Dumas*, see fn.81 *supra*. The insurer is given a defence under Forms B and C, Clause 4.7, which declares, "In no case shall this insurance cover deliberate damage to or deliberate destruction of the subject-matter insured or any part thereof by the wrongful act of any person or persons". This exception, which does not appear in Form A (All risks), is primarily aimed at vandalism. But it may extend to the consequence of scuttling the carrying ship, although in such a case the "deliberation" is not specifically aimed at the cargo.

85. In contradistinction to the position when "perils of the seas" are covered when the assured must present a *prima facie* case to that effect. See *The Popi M* [1985] 2 Lloyd's Rep. 1 (hull and machinery policy).

86. In B and C, much of the standard "catastrophe cover" would seem to be effective whether or not the cargo interests were at fault in any way: 1.1.2 to 1.1.4 in both forms, "vessel or craft being stranded grounded sunk or capsized, overturning or derailment of land conveyance, collision or contact of vessel craft or conveyance with any external object other than water", although this may have little practical importance. "Jettison" is similarly absolutely covered (1.2.2 in both). In the more extensive Form B, as well as "entry of seawater", "total loss of any package lost overboard or dropped whilst loading on to, or unloading from, vessel or craft" is covered (1.3). This could easily include cases where the cargo interests, or their servants or agents, were at fault.

87. ITC (Hulls) 1995 Clause 6.2 "provided that such loss or damage has not resulted from want of due diligence by the Assured, Owners, Managers or Superintendents or any of their onshore management" (somewhat widened in the 1995 re-draft of the 1983 form). All of whom are clearly likely to be "servants or agents of the assured".

88. Clause 6.2.2. The clause was originally "The Inchmaree Clause" and inserted to counter the decision of the House of Lords in a case of that name (*Thames and Mersey Marine Insurance v. Hamilton Fraser & Co.*, *The Inchmaree* (1887) 12 App. Cas. 484). In that case a ship was damaged by the explosion of a steam pump, which had been negligently handled by an unnamed member of the ship's crew. The House held that this was not a "peril of the seas" either because such machinery failures were too remote from the sea itself or because it was caused by crew negligence. The latter proposition might have been hard to reconcile with the then well-established principle that crew negligence in navigation did not prevent the subsequent loss being attributed to a "peril of the seas" (see fn.78 above). The precise overlap, if any, between this Clause 6.2.3 and Clause 6.1 (perils of the seas, rivers, etc.) is still not entirely clear.

89. Clause 6.2.3. "Provided such repairers or charterers are not an Assured hereunder".

90. Clause 6.2.4, "Barratry of Master Officers or Crew". It was transferred into the additional perils clause in 1983, so that the underwriters might have the benefit of the "due diligence" defence. This effectively turned the flank of the decision of the Court of Appeal in *The Michael* [1979] 2 Lloyd's Rep. 1, on the burden of proof in barratry, which was unexpected in the market.

91. The word "wilful" was clearly regarded as crucial in both *Lind v. Mitchell* and *The Gold Sky*. In *The Isothel* [1985] 1 Q.L.R. 293, the Queensland Supreme Court, relying upon authority from a wide variety of sources, including the criminal law, was prepared to extend the concept of "wilful" to include gross recklessness. This development has not yet been transplanted to England.

A number of propositions may be advanced. First as to counterclaims by insurers for damages. There is no reason in principle why an insurer might not claim or counterclaim against the assured for breach of an express "duty of the assured" clause whenever the assured or his agents or servants fails to take reasonable steps to avert or minimise losses, or, in cargo cover fails to preserve subrogation rights. There is no reason to restrict the application of such clauses to events which occur after loss. In the unlikely absence of such an express clause, there is authority for the proposition that an insurer may claim compensation for losses caused to him by the assured's failure to preserve subrogation rights. It is also possible that a claim for damages might be made without an express "duty of the assured" clause, based upon s.78(4) of the Marine Insurance Act 1906, either by way of action for breach of statutory duty or implied term.[92] 8.21

On the other hand, many of the situations in which an action might be maintained are situations which expressly or by inescapable implication are covered by the risk clauses in the policy. Therein, perhaps, lies the "irrationality"[93] which led Lord Sumner, Scrutton LJ and Atkin J to the clear statement of policy which they asserted. The duty of the assured must not be allowed a general application throughout the currency of the cover, for that would allow the underwriter to resist the very cover he has afforded in the policy – and has been paid for. This provides not only a clear explanation of the decided cases, without straining interpretations, it may also provide a principle upon which cases can be decided. The contract must be construed as a whole. The counterclaim for breach of the duty of the assured may not be allowed to diminish the cover which has clearly been conferred by it. In other legal contexts, such an approach enjoys a named principle: that there should be no derogation from grant.

8C THE DUTY OF THE UTMOST GOOD FAITH

In 1766, Lord Mansfield introduced a new principle of law to insurance. It was based upon the fact that "insurance is a contract upon speculation" involving reliance ("trust") and confidence, particularly of the insurer upon the assured, but applicable to both parties. It involved the disclosure of "circumstances" and failure to do so, even by mistake, was characterised as "fraud". The consequence, that the policy be "void".[94] This principle later became known as the principle of the utmost good faith or *uberrima fides*. It was debated, refined, restricted, adapted in the case law of the nineteenth century. 8.22

By the time Sir Mackenzie Chalmers came to draft the Marine Insurance Act, in the early 1890s, Lord Mansfield's principle had thrown off a number of discrete rules. The assured, and his broker, but not the insurer, were under duties, which terminated 8.23

92. See *Arnould on Marine Insurance* (16th edn.) para. 770.

93. The word is used by Mocatta J in *The Gold Sky* [1972] 2 Lloyd's Rep. 187, at p.220, col. 1.

94. *Carter v. Boehm* (1766) 3 Burr 1905. There is a somewhat languorous debate about whether Lord Mansfield was a true innovator in this matter and whence, if anywhere, he derived his principle. Mansfield was an educated Scot and had greater opportunity than most to make use of unusual sources. There were antecedents in the common law, in equity, in the Law Merchant. He may even have been incorporating the *jus naturale*. The issue does not seem to have great importance today.

as soon as the contract was made, to disclose all material facts and not to make material misrepresentations.[95] The duties were strict: it was not necessary to show an intention to deceive and the negligence and even the actual knowledge of the assured or his broker were equally irrelevant considerations.[96] The remedy was that the insurance might be avoided at the suit of the insurer. These rules were carefully enacted as ss.18 to 21 of the Marine Insurance Act 1906. However, perhaps only for the sake of completeness, Mackenzie Chalmers also included an enactment of Lord Mansfield's original principle, as properly understood at the end of the century. Section 17 of the Act reads:

> "A contract of marine insurance is a contract based upon the utmost good faith, and, if the utmost good faith be not observed by either party, the contract may be avoided by the other party."

8.24 The section attracted little attention until 1985, when Hirst J decided *The Litsion Pride*.[97] The case concerned war risk insurance. The operation of war risk insurance depends upon the use of "Additional Premium Areas" (APAs) within which cover is only retained on extra payment. APAs are generally protected by "Trading Warranties" coupled with "Held Covered" clauses.[98] The system generally requires early notice to the insurer.[99] The *Litsion Pride* was chartered on 25 May for a voyage likely to end in an APA, she sailed on 2 July and by 9 July her owners knew her destination for certain. She entered the APA on 2 August, was damaged by hostile action on 9 August and became a total loss. The brokers[100] received on 12 August a letter dated 2 August, but postmarked 11 August, informing them of the ship's imminent entry into the APA. The previous day, they had received a telex, informing them of the casualty and explaining that the letter of 2 August had not been mailed immediately. On these facts (and others), Hirst J was able to hold that the insurers

95. Materiality, clearly the central issue, was recently revisited by the House of Lords in *Pan Atlantic Insurance Co. Ltd v. Pine Top Co. Ltd* [1994] 2 Lloyd's Rep. 427.

96. The developed rules of pre-contractual misrepresentation and non-disclosure as contained in the Act bear little relation to good faith. There is no element of fraud in the system. And fraud and bad faith are commonly seen in law as interchangeable terms.

97. [1985] 1 Lloyd's Rep. 437.

98. Because of the volatility of politics, war risk insurance is sold on an annual basis very cheaply, effectively on condition that the vessel keeps away from actual and potential wars. This is achieved by inserting Trading Warranties covering such areas, which, in virtue of s.33(3) of the Marine Insurance Act 1906, have the effect of automatically discharging the insurer "from liability as from the date of the breach of warranty, but without prejudice to any liability incurred by him before that date" as soon as the risky area described in the warranty is entered. These are accompanied by Held Covered clauses. The traditional form of a Held Covered clause is that which is found in Clause 3 of ITC (Hulls) 1995: "Held covered in case of any breach of warranty as to cargo, trade ... provided notice be given to the Underwriters immediately after receipt of advices and any amended terms of cover and any additional premium required by them be agreed". This negatives the effect of s.33(3) and allows the insurer to charge a "real" premium for the shortest possible stay within the APA that the vessel needs to do its job. This continuation is expressed to be subject to conditions. The legal position where there is a partial, but not complete, failure in such conditions could be arguable.

99. Traditionally, the notice requirement is expressed as a condition precedent to the continuation of cover – see fn.98 *supra*. However, in this case the clause dealing with APAs did not contain a condition precedent governing notice.

100. The usual "postman" in these situations.

might have a defence to the claim based upon lack of good faith.[101] Breach of s.17: a breach of good faith *after* the contract had been concluded. The "continuing duty of good faith" was born.

It is a moderately healthy child. The duty seems established in English law,[102] although there is considerable debate about its extent.[103] But its existence or extent is 8.25

101. The clauses in the insurance of the *Litsion Pride* dealing with Additional Premium Areas were not cast in the traditional form of a Held Covered clause, containing a requirement of prompt notice expressed as a condition precedent. Hirst J was unable to construe the policy so as to make prompt notice an implied condition precedent. Indeed, the policy stated "the absence of prior advice shall not affect the cover hereon". He was thus driven to s.17 to provide a defence for the insurer. However, even where the policy is expressed in different terms, it might be a nice question whether the undertaking that the insured property should continue to enjoy cover ("held covered") should not have its effect even where notice, though given, was late. Where there is no express requirement of prior notice, it is established that a Held Covered clause operates so as to continue cover on a reasonable (market) premium: see *Greenock SS Co. v. Maritime Insurance* [1903] 1 K.B. 912. As to the establishing of bad faith, Hirst J not only concluded that the crucial letter had been intentionally misdated, but found that the long correspondence between the owners and their brokers that occurred between the commencement of the voyage (which had been noticed by solicitors for the mortgagees, who had the benefit of a loss payable clause in the insurance; the solicitors contacted the brokers) and the loss of the *Litsion Pride* displayed evasiveness. There was ample evidence to support the contention that the owners had never intended to give notice to the underwriters and pay the additional premium, "if they could get away with it".

102. The idea was considered favourably (*obiter*) by Evans J in *The Captain Panagos DP* [1986] 2 Lloyd's Rep. 470, and was applied by the Court of Appeal in *The Good Luck* [1989] 2 Lloyd's Rep. 238. In the House of Lords, the issue was disposed of on other grounds, and the House "formed no view" on the duty of good faith ([1991] 2 Lloyd's Rep. 191, at p.193, col. 2, *per* Lord Goff, who gave the only substantial speech). In *Banque Financiere de la Cite v. Westgate Insurance* [1988] 2 Lloyd's Rep. 513, the Court of Appeal would have applied the duty, but it is a little unclear as to whether they considered the case as providing an example of pre- or of post-contractual nondisclosure. In the House of Lords, where the matter was disposed of on different grounds, and where no "duty to speak" in a tortious sense was found, nevertheless, Lord Templeman and Lord Bridge both agreed that an insurer owed a continuing duty of good faith and agreed with the general analysis in the Court of Appeal. In *Orakpo v. Barclays Insurance Services* [1995] LRLR 443, the Court of Appeal applied the principle, as did Potter LJ, sitting in the Commercial Court in *The Shakir III* [1997] 1 Lloyd's Rep 586. The Court of Appeal in *New Hampshire Insurance v. MGN* [1997] LRLR 24 (fidelity insurance) was rather against the continuing duty. The Court distinguished *The Litsion Pride* and would not import a continuing duty of good faith simply because the policy contained a right of cancellation. Staughton LJ relied *inter alia* upon *New South Wales Medical Defence Union v. Transport Industries Insurance* [1985] 4 NSWLR 107, in which the New South Wales Commercial Court simply refused to apply the principle contained in *The Litsion Pride*. He also made use of a well-turned quotation from Lord Sumner in *Commercial Union v. Niger Co.* (1922) 13 Ll.L. Rep. 75 that such a development "would turn what is an indispensible shield for the Underwriter into an engine of oppression against the insured". Staughton LJ commented (at p.61), "We should hesitate to enlarge the scope for oppression by establishing a duty to disclose throughout the period of a contract of insurance merely because it contains (as is by no means uncommon) a right to cancellation for the insurer". In *The Star Sea* [1997] 1 Lloyd's Rep. 360, the Court of Appeal proceeded on the basis that the continuing duty does exist, but it cannot be said that the House of Lords is precluded from taking a different view. On balance, it seems likely that the continuing duty of good faith is part of English marine (and possibly other) insurance law.

103. It has been applied to the making of fraudulent claims by the assured (*Orakpo v. Barclays Insurance Services* [1995] LRLR 443), to the operation of a Held Covered clause (*The Litsion Pride* [1985] 1 Lloyd's Rep. 439), to the exercise of a liberty to change destination in a voyage policy (*The Shakir III* [1997] 1 Lloyd's Rep. 586), to the failure by an insurer to disclose to a lending bank circumstances entitling the insurer to reject a claim (*The Good Luck* [1989] 2 Lloyd's Rep. 238), to the failure by an insurer to inform the assured of misconduct by the assured's broker (*Banque Financiere de la Cite v. Westgate Insurance* [1988] 2 Lloyd's Rep. 513). It has not been applied to the operation of an insurer's cancellation clause (*New Hampshire Insurance v. MGN* [1997] LRLR 27) nor to the false assertion of lack of privity in answer to a defence raised by an insurer based upon s.39(5) of the Marine Insurance Act 1906 (*The Star Sea* [1997] 1 Lloyd's Rep. 360). (Section 39(5) declares that where a ship is "sent to sea in an unseaworthy state with the privity of the assured", the insurer is not liable for losses attributable to that unseaworthiness.)

not the subject of this chapter, which is to address the question of what the appropriate remedy for breach of the duty might be. The Marine Insurance Act 1906 says that the contract "may be avoided" by the innocent party.[104] Is avoidance *ab initio* to be understood, or refusal of further performance as if for breach of condition? Is this the only remedy? Is there room for damages? As we have seen, on this last point, Slade LJ thought not, at least in the context of arguments presented in the *Gemstones Case*.[105] For him there seemed to be some policy or principle against insurers counterclaiming for damages. On the other hand, not only is the remedy of avoidance sometimes demonstrably inadequate to meet the needs of the innocent party whose interests have been infringed by the failure to perform the continuing duty of good faith,[106] it may on other occasions be excessive. It has been described as "Draconian".[107] Certainly, if the continuing duty of good faith is to be applied promiscuously and without restriction to all aspects of the continuing connection between the parties to an insurance contract, and if the only remedy is to be avoidance *ab initio*, or "forfeiture", then the adjective seems to be justified.[108]

8.26 The issues raised here are more complex than those raised by the Duty of the Assured Clause and the consequences of Suing and Labouring which were discussed above. There are three interlocking arguments or approaches: the tortious, the contractual and the route of equitable fraud.

8.27 That fraud is actionable as a tort at common law is well established. A person who makes a false statement intending to induce another to act and who is intentional or

104. Section 17.

105. *Banque Financiere de la Cite v. Westgate Insurance* [1988] 2 Lloyd's Rep. 513 (CA), at p.550, quoted at the beginning of this article.

106. In neither *The Good Luck* nor *The Gemstones Case* would the plaintiff have been satisfied by a right to avoid any contract or other legal relationship. Damages were the only appropriate remedy. In general it must be the case that the remedy of avoidance, so obviously apposite in pre-contractual bad faith is less useful for post-contractual breaches of the duty.

107. The term was used by Rix J in *Royal Boskalis v. Mountain* (1995), unreported at first instance, but reported in the Court of Appeal, on other matters, at [1997] 2 All E.R. 929. Rix J was quoted by Leggat LJ in giving the judgment of the Court of Appeal in *The Star Sea* [1997] 1 Lloyd's Rep 360. He used the excessive nature of the remedy as an argument for the restriction of the ambit of the continuing duty of good faith.

108. The word "forfeiture" was used by Leggatt LJ in *The Star Sea*. It is perhaps noteworthy that the alleged bad faith in that case lay in the way in which a defence in respect of a claim in respect of one ship was countered by the assured – which might be regarded as a little peripheral – while the insurance policy was a fleet policy covering all vessels operated by Kappa Shipping. If the insurers of the *Star Sea* were to have this right of forfeiture, then, on one analysis at least, all 33 or 34 vessels comprised in the cover would be retrospectively rendered uninsured for the period of the insurance and settled claims might have to be re-opened. Concerns about the broad extent of the right of rescission for pre-contractual misrepresentations in the general law of contract led to the provision in s.2(2) of the Misrepresentation Act 1967, which gives the court power to refuse rescission and award damages in lieu. See the Law Reform Committee's Tenth Report (Cmnd 1728). The learned editors of *Arnould* (16th edn. para. 626) take the view that the general provision of s.2(2) of the Misrepresentation Act 1967 cannot prevail over the specific provision of ss.18 and 19 of the Marine Insurance Act 1906. This, of course, requires understanding the Marine Insurance Act 1906 as restricting the remedy for misrepresentation to rescission, an interpretation which is disputed below. The conclusion of *Arnould* was referred to by Steyn J in *Highlands Insurance v. Continental Insurance* [1987] 1 Lloyd's Rep. 109, when he exercised his discretion under s.2(2) by refusing to allow damages in place of rescission in respect of a misrepresentation in a non-marine reinsurance contract. He offered no substantive analysis of the *Arnould* argument.

reckless as to the falsity of the statement is liable in the tort of deceit.[109] The rather broad definition of fraud for the purpose of this tort was not universally welcomed. In *Nocton v. Lord Ashburton* the House of Lords took the opportunity to suggest limits.[110] Side by side with the duty of honesty contained within the tort of deceit lay other duties, one of which was a breach of fiduciary duty.[111] This was not based upon dishonest statements intended to provoke action, but upon failure to observe fiduciary duties which might be imposed in cases of reliance. Such duties were recognised, but were not tortious.[112] They became known as "constructive fraud" or "equitable fraud" duties. It was generally asserted that breach of such duties would not ground an action for damages.[113]

In 1964, the House revisited the area, this time through the tort of negligence. In *Hedley Byrne v. Heller*[114] the House held *obiter* that there was a tort of negligent mis-statement, limited to circumstances not markedly different from the fiduciary relationship described in *Nocton v. Lord Ashburton*. The application of the new principle to statements which might have significance in the general law of contract, either because they might amount to a pre-contractual misrepresentation, or because they might constitute terms of a contract, was accepted by the Court of Appeal in *Esso v. Mardon*.[115] But certain questions of the precise relationship between tort and 8.28

109. The leading case is, of course, *Derry v. Peek* (1889) 14 App. Cas. 337. Lord Herschell said, at p.376: "First, in order to sustain an action of deceit, there must be proof of fraud and nothing short of that will suffice. Secondly, fraud is proved when it is shown that a false representation has been made (1) knowingly, (2) without belief in its truth, or (3) recklessly, careless whether it be true or false. Although I have treated the second and third as distinct cases, I think the third is but an instance of the second, for one who makes a statement under such circumstances can have no real belief in the truth of what he states. To prevent a false statement being fraudulent there must, I think, always be an honest belief in its truth". Several members of the House insisted on the difference between reckless statements that might be fraudulent and merely careless ones that could not be. It is also necessary to make clear that the defendant's state of mind as regards the truth of his statements has to be distinguished from the clear requirement that he must always *intend* that the victim act thereon. Recklessness in *this* context is as irrelevant as negligence.

110. [1914] A.C. 932. The facts of the case, which involved a solicitor who persuaded his client to engage in property speculation and, in that context, made a number of very doubtful statements, might have been argued to fall within the rubric of "*Derry v. Peek* recklessness". It is said that Lord Haldane LC was determined not to apply *Derry v. Peek* to "a positive fiduciary duty such as a solicitor's, in other words go as near as they dare to saying it was wrong, as all Lincoln's Inn thought at the time" (Sir Frederick Pollock writing to Oliver Wendell Holmes Jun., *Pollock-Holmes Letters* Vol. 1 p.215, quoted in *Salmond and Heuston on Torts*, p.441). Lord Haldane, in the case, asserted firmly (at p.953) "nothing short of proof of a fraudulent intention in the strict sense will suffice for an action of deceit". He then continued by showing that "side by side" with the law of deceit there arose other duties which had other consequences.

111. Lord Haldane was also ready to allow the tort of negligence and implied contracts covering similar contiguous ground.

112. Lord Haldane would, nonetheless, have awarded damages for their breach. Lord Dunedin would not. There was, on the facts, also the possibility of (a) liability in negligence and (b) liability for breach of a contractual obligation to exercise professional skill as a solicitor.

113. See Sealy, *Some Principles of Fiduciary Obligation* [1963] CLJ 119. Money compensation might be given, although this was often called "indemnity" rather than "damages". In the early part of this century, the judges did not seem to draw a very firm distinction.

114. [1964] A.C. 465. The relationship that gives rise to the duty in respect of statements is usually called a "special relationship". It is based on reliance and has been described as "equivalent to contract" (see the speech of Lord Devlin at p.528, quoting Lord Shaw in *Nocton v. Lord Ashburton* [1914] A.C. at p.972). The *Hedley Byrne* principle was immediately applied to a range of professional relationships involving the giving of advice. Progress was not uniformly swift, however. See *Mutual Life Assurance v. Evatt* [1971] A.C. 793 (PC) – no liability for negligent investment advice given by insurer to policyholder: *Hedley Byrne* distinguished, *Low v. Bouverie* [1891] 3 Ch. 82 applied.

115. [1976] Q.B. 801.

contract, the so-called "overlap problem", remained. In the Privy Council in 1985, Lord Scarman took a firm line, holding, effectively, that if the parties were in a contractual relationship, the contract should govern and reference to the law of tort would not assist.[116] However, in *Henderson v. Merrett* in 1994, the House of Lords seemed to take a somewhat more liberal view.[117] After a lengthy and erudite survey of the authorities, both common and civil law, Lord Goff, who gave the only substantial judgment in the case, came down on the side of alternative remedies. Where a tort duty existed in contractual relations, "unless his contract precludes him, the plaintiff who has available to him concurrent remedies in contract or tort, may choose that remedy which appears to him to be the most advantageous".[118] Additionally, the Misrepresentation Act 1967 gave a cumulative remedy in damages for pre-contractual misrepresentations that were "negligent".[119]

It is accepted that neither deceit nor s.2(1) of the Misrepresentation Act 1967 apply to anything other than positive statements and that *Hedley Byrne* does so only rarely and subject to further conditions.[120] Perhaps the most significant aspect of the obligation of good faith is that it embraces nondisclosure. It imposes some sort of

---

116. *Tai Hing Cotton Mill Ltd v. Liu Chong Bank* [1986] A.C. 80. "Their Lordships do not believe that there is anything to the advantage of the law's development in searching for a liability in tort where the parties are in a contractual relationship" (at p.107). The case concerned a defence to an action by a customer against its bank, which had paid cheques forged by a "trusted" employee. The banks claimed that the customer owed them a duty to take care by adopting effective control measures within their own business. The standard case law on the duties of the customers of banks had been set by the House of Lords in two cases, *London Joint Stock Bank v. Macmillan* [1918] A.C. 777 and *Greenwood v. Martins Bank* [1933] A.C. 51, which imposed duties only in respect of the drawing of cheques and the disclosure of known fraud. Lord Scarman took the view that if the banks wanted more protection they should stipulate for it in their contracts with their customers and could not turn to the law of tort to assist them. Lord Scarman's judgment was applied by the Court of Appeal in *National Bank of Greece v. Pinios Shipping, The Maira* [1989] 1 All E.R. 213, a case which concerned a contract governing the relations between a defaulting shipping company, a lending bank and a ship management company put in in order to safeguard the lender's interests. No duty could be derived from tort so as to make the management company liable to the owners.

117. [1995] 2 A.C. 145. The case concerned the liabilities of underwriting agents at Lloyd's insurance market to "names", some of whom were in direct contractual relations with the defendants, others of whom were not. The House, in effect, held that the presence or absence of a contractual nexus was insignificant. See also *Youell v. Bland Welch (No. 2)* [1990] 2 Lloyd's Rep. 231 (insurance broker liable to his principal in tort as well as contract) *Punjab National Bank v. de Boinville* [1992] 3 All E.R. 104 (liability of insurance brokers to confirming bank, who had the benefit of political risk insurance negotiated for the account of the exporter) and *Forsikringsaktieselkapet Vesta v. Butcher* [1988] 2 All E.R. 43 (CA) (application of the Law Reform (Contributory Negligence) Act 1945 to the comparative fault of a broker and his principal) (House of Lords decision, on other grounds, [1989] A.C. 852).

118. [1995] A.C. at p.174. The decision can be reconciled with *Tai Hing Cotton* and *The Maira*. It is not every case that gives rise to concurrent remedies, and the contract may preclude reliance on the tort remedy. Both those cases involve contracts which, when properly interpreted, did not allow for the claim (or defence) contended for by reference to the law of tort.

119. Section 2(1). Strictly, the section does not impose liability for negligent misstatement. It imposes liability as if for deceit in case of innocent misrepresentation where the defendant is unable to satisfy the court of the reasonableness of his action. Attenuated fraud with reverse burden of proof.

120. See *La Banque Financiere de La Cite v. Westgate Insurance* [1988] 2 Lloyd's Rep. 513, *per* Slade LJ at pp.556, *et seq.* The matter is considered further below. In his speech in *Bell v. Lever Bros* [1932] A.C. 161, Lord Thankerton, at p.230, somewhat tantalisingly equated non-dislosure with misrepresentation. "If there was such a duty [to disclose] there is no doubt that the failure to disclose – though innocent – amounted to a misrepresentation as to material facts which induced Lever Brothers to enter into these agreements, and which would entitle the latter to rescind them." His Lordship, of course, found that there was no duty to disclose in the case.

"duty to speak". To impose under that obligation liability for statements only would be, at the least, distortive.[121] But the point is wider. Bad faith is not negligence, nor is it *Derry v. Peek* deceit.[122] It is *sui generis*. The question is whether there is a tort of bad faith.

The issue was examined by Slade LJ, who gave the judgment of the Court of Appeal in *La Banque Financiere de la Cite v. Westgate Insurance*.[123] Steyn J, who had decided the case at first instance, had held that there was a breach of the duty of good faith, that such a breach sounded in damages, that the losses suffered by the banks were (in part) caused by those breaches and were not too remote.[124] Slade LJ was not prepared to advance a new category of legal liability. If damages were to be awarded, then bad faith must be a breach of contract or a tort. It was not a breach of contract.[125] As to tort:[126] 8.29

"There is no authority whatever to support the existence of such a tort and, quite apart from such lack of authority, there are in our judgment at least four reasons why this Court should not by its present decision create a novel tort of this nature:

First, we have already concluded that the powers of the Court to grant relief where there has been non-disclosure of material facts in the case of a contract *uberrimae fidei* stems from the jurisdiction originally exercised by the Courts of Equity to prevent imposition. The powers of the Court to grant relief by way of rescission of a contract when there has been undue influence or duress stem from the same jurisdiction. Since duress and undue influence as such give rise to no claim for damages, we see no reason in principle why non-disclosure as such should do so.

Secondly, the decision in *CTI v. Oceanus*[127] establishes that where an underwriter is seeking the conventional remedy of avoidance of the policy, the actual effect of the non-disclosure on his mind is irrelevant. . . .

Thirdly, s.17 of the 1906 Act, which imposes reciprocal obligations of good faith on both parties to such a contract, specifically gives the remedy of avoidance of the contract (and no other remedy). Likewise, s.18(1), which specifically defines the duty of disclosure falling on the assured, concludes by stating the insurer's remedy as follows:

'If the assured fails to make such disclosure, the insurer may avoid the contract.'

There is not a suggestion in any of the succeeding provisions of the 1906 Act that a breach of the obligation of good faith will give rise to a claim for damages . . .. We think the clear inference from the 1906 Act is that Parliament did not contemplate that a breach of the obligation would give rise to a claim for damages in the case of such contracts. Otherwise it would surely have said so. . . .

Fourthly, as we have already stated, in the case of a contract *uberrimae fidei*, the obligation to disclose a known material fact is an absolute one.[128]

No relevant breach of contract has been established and fraud is not alleged against Mr

121. In *Litsion Pride*, for instance, the only positive statement in the long story of evasion and concealment was the date, 2 August, which appeared on the letter postmarked 11 August, which Hirst J found to be false.

122. That may be said to be the significant decision in *Nocton v. Lord Ashburton*.

123. [1988] 2 Lloyd's Rep. 513. On appeal, the House of Lords held that the insurer's duty to disclose (duty of good faith) did not extend to the matters in question.

124. [1987] 1 Lloyd's Rep. 69. He further held that the Law Reform (Contributory Negligence) Act 1945 had no application to a breach of the duty of good faith (at p.106). See *Vesta v. Butcher* [1988] 2 All E.R. 43 (CA). He also found a breach of a duty of care in negligence. See *infra*.

125. This issue is considered *infra*.

126. At pp.550, col. 1 to 551, col.1.

127. [1982] 2 Lloyd's Rep. 280. Now overruled. See *infra*.

128. There then follows the powerful statement of policy, based upon the oppression of assured's, with which the article opened.

Dungate or Hodge.[129] We accordingly hold that if the breach by Hodge, through Mr Dungate, of its duty of full disclosure is to give rise to a claim for damages at the suit of Kusa,[130] this claim must be based on (innocent) misrepresentation or the tort of negligence."

Not all these arguments are equally strong. The second has been overtaken by events, since the House of Lords in *Pan Atlantic Insurance v. Pine Top Insurance*[131] has laid all doubts to rest by making it clear that the inducement of the particular underwriter *is* a part of the requirements for the operation of ss.18–20 of the Marine Insurance Act 1906.[132] The statutory interpretation argument (the third) is at best unconvincing. It might be retorted that the Marine Insurance Act 1906 does not *exclude* an action for damages, either. After all, ss.17, 18 and 20 all say that the innocent party *may avoid* the contract, not *may only avoid*. The fourth point, that to create a tort of bad faith would be to create a tort of strict liability, seems to be based upon a misconception.[133] It is, of course, true that the pre-contractual good faith responsibilities of the *assured* in matters of misrepresentation and nondisclosure (in marine insurance) are strict. The provisions of ss.18–20 of the Marine Insurance Act 1906 make that clear. The duties are not only strict but are also limited in point of application and of time.[134] Section 17 on the other hand is uncluttered. The decision in *Litsion Pride*,[135] whose validity underlay the decision in this case, demonstrates that one of those limitations – that as to time – does not apply. It can hardly be argued that the rest do. Section 17 does not in its terms impose strict duties. The continuing duty of good faith must be about honesty: it requires that the party does not knowingly[136] conceal information or tell lies.[137]

---

129. Mr Dungate was the employee of the insurers who failed to inform the banks of the misconduct of the broker's employee. Hodge became Westgate.

130. La Banque Keyser Ullmann SA, the original plaintiff.

131. [1995] 1 A.C. 501, overruling *CTI v. Oceanus*.

132. Before the Marine Insurance Act 1906, the matter had been in some doubt. Two great common law judges had appeared to adopt inconsistent views. Blackburn J in *Ionides v. Pender* (1874) LR 9 QB 531 taking a strictly objective view and Brett MR in *Tate and Sons v. Hyslop* (1885) 15 Q.B.D. 368 requiring the actual inducement of the particular underwriter. The Act certainly adopted an objective approach, but it could still be argued that since actual inducement was a rule of the general law of contractual misrepresentation, it was preserved by s.91(2) of the Act: "The rules of the common law, including the law merchant, save in so far as they are inconsistent with the express provisions of this Act, shall continue to apply to contracts of Marine Insurance". So thought the House in *Pan Atlantic v. Pine Top*.

133. The same misconception, that the terms of ss.18–20 can be implied into s.17, is also present in the second argument, which is now redundant.

134. That they are strict is provided for by the "deeming" provisions in s.18(1) ("the assured is deemed to know every circumstance which, in the ordinary course of business ought to be known by him") and section 19 ("an agent [to insure – a broker] must disclose . . . every material circumstance which is known to himself, and an agent to insure is deemed to know every circumstance which in the ordinary course of business ought to be known to him or communicated to him; and every material circumstance which the assured is bound to disclose . . ."); and by the objective definition of materiality in ss.18(2) and 20(2) ("a representation is material which would influence the judgment of a prudent insurer in fixing the premium or determining whether he will take the risk"). That they are limited in point of time is provided for by the use of the phrase "before the contract is concluded" in ss.18(1) and 19(1). And, of course, they apply only to the assured.

135. [1985] 1 Lloyd's Rep. 439.

136. Or possibly recklessly, on analogy with *Derry v. Peek*.

137. It must also be noted that the concept of materiality does not appear in s.17. Nevertheless, Slade LJ used the language of materiality and even sought to adapt the definition of "material" to be found in ss.18(2) and 20(2). "In adapting the well established principles relating to the duty of disclosure falling upon the insured to the obverse case of the insurer himself, due account must be taken of the rather different reasons for which the insured and the insurer require the protection of full disclosure. In our

8.30 There remains the first argument, the "equity" argument. The proposition is that the duty of good faith is an equitable duty and that, therefore, the award of damages, a common law remedy, is inappropriate. A number of points might be made. It cannot be said that the proposition is self-evident. The fusion of the jurisdictions of the courts of Law and Equity in 1873–1875 presented several possibilities of interaction between substance and remedy or procedure. It is certainly not the case that such is never possible. The "Covent Garden Case", *Duke of Bedford v. Ellis*,[138] shows the House of Lords applying an equitable procedure to common law rights and rejecting the argument that the jurisdictions should be kept distinct. More appositely, we have already seen that Collins J was prepared to allow an insurer to be awarded money compensation for the breach by the assured of his "equitable duty" to preserve subrogation rights.[139] In *Nocton v. Lord Ashburton*, discussed below, Lord Haldane was clear that the plaintiff might be compensated for a breach by the defendant of his fiduciary duty.[140] It is true, of course, that compensation for breach of equitable obligations is generally called "indemnity" rather than "damages", and that distinctions can properly be drawn.[141] But there can be no objection in principle to awarding money compensation for breach of duty on the ground that such duty happens to be one that was developed in Chancery.

8.31 But the obligation to observe good faith in insurance contracts did not, historically, derive from the Court of Chancery. It was a common law doctrine, developed by common law judges in common law courts. It is, of course, easy to confuse with analogous obligations that were developed in the Court of Chancery. Equity did relieve against impositions, by allowing rescission of legal engagements, when "fiduciaries" failed in their obligations. Such obligations are, at least, very similar to those imposed upon the parties to a contract *uberrimae fidei* and include a duty of disclosure. It is also true that the House of Lords in *Nocton v. Lord Ashburton*[142] explained fiduciary relationships in terms of reliance that were not dissimilar from those that Lord Mansfield used in *Carter v. Boehm* and then proceeded to refuse to

judgment, the duty falling upon the insurer must at least extend to disclosing all facts known to him which are material either to the nature of the risk sought to be covered or the recoverability of a claim under the policy which a prudent insured would take into account in deciding whether or not to place the risk for which he seeks cover with that insurer". While it must be the case that dishonesty in respect of quite irrelevant matters must be outside the ambit of the duty of good faith, there seems to be no good reason to import the complexities of "the prudent insured" and possibly actual inducement. Which might avoid the difficulties that have given us *CTI v. Oceanus* and *Pine Top*.

138. [1901] A.C. 1. The House reversed the decision of the Court of Appeal in *Temperton v. Russell* [1893] 1 Q.B. 435 which had held that officials of a trade union could not be sued in a representative capacity for the tort of procuring a breach of contract on the grounds that the equitable procedure was not available in matters over which the old Court of Chancery had no jurisdiction. An interesting sidelight on the decision is that the Lords gave judgment some three months after the first instance hearing in the *Taff Vale Railway Case*, which proceeded against the (unincorporated) trade union in its registered name, thus allowing the House of Lords to create a new form of quasi-corporate liability (*Taff Vale Railway Co. v. ASRS* [1901] A.C. 426. Had the timing been different, the opportunity would never have arisen.

139. *West of England Fire Insurance v. Isaacs* [1896] 2 Q.B. 373, discussed *supra*.

140. [1914] A.C. 932, at p.958: "My Lords, the conclusion at which I have arrived is that this action ought properly to have been treated as one in which the plaintiff had made out a claim for compensation either from loss arising from misrepresentation made in breach of a fiduciary duty or for breach of contract to exercise due care and skill".

141. See *Whittington v. Seal-Hayne* (1900) 82 LT 49.

142. [1914] A.C. 932.

apply a particular common law remedy thereto. However, the purpose of the House in *Nocton v. Lord Ashburton* was to delimit the tort of deceit by drawing a clear distinction between "common law fraud" and "equitable fraud". It is authority for the proposition that the latter may not be subsumed in the former so that *Derry v. Peek* deceit damages may be awarded for breach of the duties of "fiduciary relationships".[143] It is no authority for the proposition that damages may not be awarded at all in that context. Indeed, the defendant, but for time-bar problems, might have been held liable in damages to the plaintiff on other grounds.[144] And although the language, particularly in the speech of Lord Haldane, is cast in broad terms, the case is no authority on disclosure in contracts *uberrimae fidei*.

8.32 The House did have to consider disclosure in contract generally in *Bell v. Lever Bros.*[145] The case, as is well known, dealt with the question of whether two severance contracts made with company directors might be void, or voidable, because they had been negotiated in common ignorance of the fact that the appellants had engaged in activity which might have entitled the respondents to dispense with their services without compensation. The jury had found that there had been no fraud. The tort of deceit was not, therefore, available. The two grounds presented by the company were mistake and nondisclosure. Lord Atkin said:[146]

"It now becomes necessary to deal with the second point of the plaintiffs – namely, that the contract of March 19 1929 could be avoided by them in consequence of the non-disclosure by Bell of his misconduct as to the cocoa dealings. Fraudulent concealment has been negatived by the jury; this claim is based upon the contention that Bell owed a duty to Levers to disclose his misconduct, and that in default of disclosure the contract was voidable. Ordinarily the failure to disclose a material fact which might influence the mind of a contractor does not give the right to avoid the contract. The principle of caveat emptor applies outside contracts of sale. There are certain contracts expressed by the law to be contracts of the utmost good faith, where material facts must be disclosed; if not the contract is voidable. Apart from fiduciary relationships, contracts for partnerships and contracts of insurance are the leading instances. In such cases the duty does not arise out of contract; the duty of a person proposing an insurance arises before the contract is made, so of an intending partner. Unless this contract can be brought within this limited category of contracts *uberrimae fidei* it appears to me that this ground of defence must fail. I see nothing to differentiate this agreement from an ordinary contract of service."

The decision of the House was that a severance contract, which was classified for

143. See particularly the speeches of Lords Haldane and Shaw of Dunfermline.

144. The plaintiff and defendant certainly had been in contractual relations, that of solicitor and client. Both that contract (if it extended in point of time so as to cover the circumstances of the case) and the law of tort would have imposed upon Nocton a duty to exercise due care, or professional expertise, in his dealings with Lord Ashburton which, but for the problem of time-bars, would have been sufficient to dispose of the action. The claim, however, was made in the tort of deceit. The House decided that that tort did not extend to cover behaviour that fell short of a deliberate intention to mislead.

145. [1932] A.C. 161.

146. At p.227. The case was complicated by the fact that it began with thoroughgoing allegations of fraud that failed at the trial. The primary issue on appeal was, therefore, whether pleadings might be amended so as to allow mistake and nondisclosure to be pleaded. Lord Blanesborough decided the case on that ground, but agreed with Lords Atkin and Thankerton on the substantive ground. Lord Warrington of Cliffe, with whose speech Viscount Hailsham agreed, dissented from the judgments of Lords Atkin and Thankerton on the mistake point. Lord Thankerton dealt with the disclosure point rather more shortly than Lord Atkin, but agreeing in essence with him. Lord Atkin's opinion that the duty of disclosure in contracts *uberrimae fidei* is non-contractual is considered *infra*.

these purposes as the same as a service contract, was not a contract *uberrimae fidei*, and that there was, therefore, no duty of disclosure.[147]

8D TENTATIVE CONCLUSION

The purpose of this essay is not to discuss in detail the continuing development of the continuing duty of good faith. Suffice to say that the series of decisions, culminating in the decision of the House of Lords in *The Star Sea*,[148] has somewhat circumscribed the ambit of the doctrine and perhaps confined it to the operation of "held covered" clauses while treating fraudulent claims on different grounds. At first sight, it might have seemed that one solution to the problem of the "Draconian" nature of the remedy of avoidance *ab initio* of marine insurance contracts for bad faith after the inception of the risk might be the development of counterclaims for damages by insurers. The question of whether the duty should be regarded as arising from a contractual term or from an extra-contractual principle has certainly been raised, but in the context of whether the insurer's right is to avoid *ab initio* or to treat the assured as having committed a repudiatory breach, so as to reject the claim and terminate the contract.[149] And a repudiatory breach, on ordinary contractual principles would allow the innocent party to choose to affirm the contract and sue for damages for the losses deriving therefrom. But the argument cannot plausibly be made. At the inception of this development, Hirst J in *Litsion Pride*, as we have seen, asserted that the only remedy was avoidance. This assertion has not been questioned. 8.33

The position with regard to the wider "duty of the assured" as described in s.78(4) of the Marine Insurance Act 1906, and as elaborated in the relevant terms of the policies, on the other hand, seems less restricted. It is, therefore, tentatively and rather diffidently suggested that Lord Sumner's outright rejections of the possibility of counterclaims by insurers could be re-examined.

147. This proposition remains good law.
148. [2001] Lloyd's Rep. IR.
149. See *Orakpo v. Barclays Insurance Services*.

CHAPTER 9

JURISDICTION IN CONTRACTUAL DISPUTES ON MARINE INSURANCE AND REINSURANCE CONTRACTS TO WHICH THE EC JURISDICTION CONVENTION APPLIES

YVONNE BAATZ

9A INTRODUCTION

In Chapter 10 of Volume 1 of the *Modern Law of Marine Insurance*[1] issues of jurisdiction and governing law in relation to marine insurance and reinsurance contracts were considered. This contribution will consider the developments since the last volume in relation to contractual disputes in those two types of contract,[2] where the Convention on Jurisdiction and the Enforcement of Judgments in Civil and Commercial Matters 1968[3] (the "EC Jurisdiction Convention") or the EFTA 9.1

1. LLP 1996.

2. The cases considered do not necessarily involve marine insurance and reinsurance contracts and in some instances attention has been given to the position under maritime contracts as these will be relevant where the marine insurer exercises its subrogated rights under such contracts.

3. The EC Jurisdiction Convention was given the force of law in England by s.2 of the Civil Jurisdiction and Judgments Act 1982 ("CJJA") which came into force on 1 January 1987. The EC Jurisdiction Convention has been amended as a result of a number of Accession Conventions: the 1978 Convention on the accession of the Kingdom of Denmark, Ireland and the United Kingdom of Great Britain and Northern Ireland; the 1982 Luxembourg Convention on the accession of the Hellenic Republic; the 1989 San Sebastian Convention on the accession of Spain and Portugal; and the 1996 Brussels Convention on the

Convention on Jurisdiction and the Enforcement of Judgments in Civil and Commercial Matters 1988[4] (the "Lugano Convention") applies. Recent developments of note raise the important issue of whether the Conventions apply at all; whether there is a valid jurisdiction clause within Art. 17 if, for example, a reinsurance contract incorporates the terms of the primary insurance; which court should determine that question and, if there is a jurisdiction clause, whether it is appropriate to enforce that choice where there are already proceedings in another Contracting State by means of an anti-suit injunction.

The current Accession Convention to the EC Jurisdiction Convention is the 1996 Accession Convention on the Accession of Austria, Finland and Sweden, which came into force in the UK on 1 January 2001 and this contribution will focus on the provisions of that Accession Convention, unless otherwise stated. However, the EC Jurisdiction Convention will be replaced by the EC Regulation[5] except for Denmark. The EC Regulation is due to enter into force in the UK on 1 March 2002. Reference will be made to the Regulation where the provisions differ.

9B APPLICATION OF THE EC JURISDICTION CONVENTION

9B.1 Scope

9.2 The EC Jurisdiction Convention applies in civil and commercial matters subject to a number of exclusions. The first exclusion which is relevant to marine insurance and reinsurance contracts is "bankruptcy, proceedings relating to the winding-up of insolvent companies or other legal persons, judicial arrangements, compositions and analogous proceedings".[6] The second relevant exclusion is arbitration.[7] This exclusion has been interpreted by the European Court of Justice in *Marc Rich & Co.*

accession of the Republic of Austria, the Republic of Finland and the Kingdom of Sweden. The Civil Jurisdiction and Judgments Act 1982 (Amendment) Order 2000 S.I. 2000 No.1824 sets out the 1996 Accession Convention in Sched. 1 which came into force on 1 January 2001 and is the Accession Convention currently in force in the UK as at August 2001. The 1996 Brussels Convention is in force in Austria, Denmark, Finland, France, Germany, Greece, Ireland, Italy, Luxembourg, the Netherlands, Portugal, Spain, Sweden and the UK as at August 2001. See generally LA Collins, ed., *Dicey & Morris, The Conflict of Laws* (Sweet & Maxwell, London 13th edn. 2000), *Cheshire and North's Private International Law* (Butterworths, London 13th edn. 1999), A Briggs and P Rees, *Civil Jurisdiction and Judgments* (LLP, London 2nd edn., 1997) and DC Jackson, *The Enforcement of Maritime Claims* (LLP, London 3rd edn., 2000).

4. Section 3A of the CJJA (inserted by the Civil Jurisdiction and Judgments Act 1991) gives the force of law to the Lugano Convention, which is set out in Sched. 1 to the 1991 Act. It came into force in the UK on 1 May 1992. It is in force in Austria, Belgium, Denmark, Finland, France, Germany, Greece, Iceland, Ireland, Italy, Luxembourg, The Netherlands, Norway, Poland, Portugal, Spain, Sweden, Switzerland and the UK as at August 2001.

5. Council Regulation (EC) No 44/2001 of 22 December 2000 on Jurisdiction and the Recognition and Enforcement of Judgments in Civil and Commercial Matters Official Journal L 012, 16/01/2001 p.0001–0023. See the Civil Jurisdiction and Judgments Order 2001, SI 2001, No. 3929.

6. Article 1(2). See *Firswood Ltd v. Petra Bank* [1996] CLC 608 and *UBS AG v. Omni Holding AG* [2000] 1 W.L.R. 916.

7. Article 1(4).

AG v. Societa Italiana Impianti PA (The Atlantic Emperor).[8] In *Van Uden Maritime BV v. Kommanditgesellschaft in Firma Deco-Line*[9] the European Court considered whether, where parties had referred their disputes to arbitration and thus excluded the jurisdiction of the courts of any Contracting State, interim proceedings fell outside the scope of the Convention. The court considered that provisional measures are not in principle ancillary to arbitration proceedings but are ordered in parallel to such proceedings and are intended as measures of support. They concern not arbitration as such but the protection of a wide variety of rights. Therefore where, as here, the subject-matter of an application for provisional measures relates to a question falling within the scope *ratione materiae* of the Convention, the Convention is applicable and Art. 24 may confer jurisdiction on the court hearing the application even where proceedings have already been, or may be, commenced on the substance of the case and even where those proceedings are to be conducted before arbitrators.

9B.2 Application

The basic principle enshrined in the EC Jurisdiction Convention is that a defendant domiciled in a Contracting State must be sued in the courts of that State.[10] A recent Court of Appeal decision has considered the meaning of "sued". In *National Justice Compania Naviera SA v. Prudential Assurance Co. Ltd (The Ikarian Reefer (No.2))*[11] the Court of Appeal had held that the assured were not entitled to recover under their hull and machinery policy as the vessel had been deliberately run aground and then deliberately set on fire on the authority of her owners, the assured company. The underwriters were only able to recover part of their costs, as the security for costs obtained prior to trial was insufficient. Therefore, the underwriters issued a summons in the action seeking an order pursuant to s.51 of the Supreme Court Act that Mr Comninos, the director of the assured company, and a non-party to the action, be liable personally to pay its costs. The Court of Appeal inclined to the view that Mr Comninos was not "sued" as that term was used within the EC Jurisdiction Convention. "Suing" contemplates pursuing a substantive cause of action and does not relate to orders ancillary to substantive proceedings pending before a particular court. It may come as some surprise to a lay person that they are not "sued" when proceedings are brought against them for a judgment for a substantial sum for costs. 9.3

The EC Jurisdiction Convention applies where the defendant is domiciled in a Contracting State no matter where the claimant is domiciled. That view was 9.4

8. [1992] 1 Lloyd's Rep. 342. See also *The Heidberg* [1994] 2 Lloyd's Rep. 287, 298–303,; *The Xing Su Hai* [1995] 2 Lloyd's Rep. 15, 21 and 23; *Toepfer International GmbH v. Molino Boschi SRL* [1996] 1 Lloyd's Rep. 510; *Lexmar Corporation v. Nordiskskibsrederforening* [1997] 1 Lloyd's Rep. 289; *Union de Remorquage et de Sauvetage SA v. Lake Avery Inc. (The Lake Avery)* [1997] 1 Lloyd's Rep. 540; *Toepfer International GmbH v. Societe Cargill France* [1998] 1 Lloyd's Rep. 379 (CA); [1997] 2 Lloyd's Rep. 98; *Vale Do Rio Doce Navegacao SA v. Shanghai Bao Steel Ocean Shipping Ltd* [2000] 2 Lloyd's Rep. 1; 534 LMLN; and *Navigation Maritime Bulgare v. Rustal Trading Ltd (The Ivan Zagubanski)* [2002] 1 Lloyd's Rep. 106. See also on enforcement *The Heidberg* [1994] 2 Lloyd's Rep. 287; *Phillip Alexander Securities & Futures Ltd v. Bamberger* [1996] CLC 1757 discussed *infra* at paras. 9.123, 9.128, 9.129 and 9.133 and *Arab Business Consortium International Finance and Investment Co. v. Banque Franco-Tunisienne* [1997] 1 Lloyd's Rep. 531 (CA); [1996] 1 Lloyd's Rep. 485.

9. Case C-391/95, [1999] All E.R. (EC) 258.

10. Article 2.

11. [2000] 1 Lloyd's Rep. 129.

challenged by insurers in *Societe Group Josi Reinsurance Company SA v. Compagnie d'Assurances Universal General Insurance Company.*[12] There Group Josi, domiciled in Belgium, denied liability under a reinsurance contract on the grounds of misrepresentation. The Canadian insurers sued in France and the jurisdiction of the French court was challenged by Group Josi. The insurers contended that the jurisdictional rules established by the EC Jurisdiction Convention could only apply if both the claimant and the defendant were domiciled in a Contracting State. Group Josi argued that once the subject-matter of a dispute falls within the material scope of the Convention and, in particular, where the defendant is domiciled in a Contracting State, the domicile of the claimant is irrelevant. It further argued that disputes which are connected with the Community fall within its scope. A dispute will be integrated into the Community if it is covered by one of the Convention's jurisdictional rules. The European Court held that where a claimant is domiciled in a non-Contracting State that is irrelevant to the application of the EC Jurisdiction Convention, unless the Convention expressly provides otherwise.

9.5 The principle that the defendant must be sued where it is domiciled[13] is subject to a number of exceptions. Exclusive jurisdiction under Art.16; in insurance matters (Section 3 – Arts 7–12A) and consumer contracts (Section 4 – Arts 13–15) are assumed not to apply for present purposes. The Article that is of particular significance for bills of lading and thus the subrogated claims of cargo insurers, is Art. 57, which deals with the effect of other international conventions. Depending on the provisions of the other international convention, it may override the provisions of the EC Jurisdiction Convention or it may be read in conjunction with the other provisions of that Convention and will be considered in detail below.[14] Article 18 provides for a clear exception where the defendant has entered an appearance other than solely to contest the jurisdiction, in which case the court submitted to shall have jurisdiction.[15] Article 17 also provides for an important exception where there is a jurisdiction agreement which complies with the formalities set out in that Article, in which case the court chosen by the parties shall have jurisdiction.[16] Where no exception applies the claimant may have a choice of jurisdiction in addition to the court of the defendant's domicile if there is special jurisdiction under the provisions of Arts 5 and 6.[17]

12. Case C-412/98 [2000] 2 All E.R. (Comm.) 467.

13. Article 2.

14. See para. 9.

15. The European Court has recognised that Art. 18 must be interpreted as meaning that it allows a defendant not merely to contest jurisdiction but, at the same time, to submit, in the alternative, a defence on the substance of the case without losing the right to raise an objection of want of jurisdiction. *Rohr v. Ossberger* [1981] ECR 2431 and *Gerling v. Amministrazione del Tesoro dello Stato* (Case 201/82) [1983] ECR 2503. However, see *Marc Rich & Co. AG v. Societa Italiana Impianti PA (The Atlantic Emperor) (No. 2)* [1992] 1 Lloyd's Rep. 624 and *Caltex Trading Pte Ltd v. Metro Trading International Inc.* [2000] 1 All E.R. (Comm.) 108. Article 18 will apply even where there is a valid jurisdiction agreement, as entering an appearance will constitute a variation of the agreement: *Elefanten Schuh v. Jacqmain* [1981] ECR 1671.

16. See para. 9B.4.

17. See para. 9B.6.

9B.3 The insurance exception

The exception for matters relating to insurance is assumed not to apply for present purposes, on the basis that the insurance considered here falls within the definition of marine insurance covering risks in Art. 12A, so that a jurisdiction agreement is permitted,[18] or is reinsurance. 9.6

In *National Justice Compania Naviera SA v. Prudential Assurance Co. Ltd (The Ikarian Reefer (No. 2))*[19] the Court of Appeal considered the scope of the exception of matters relating to insurance. The Court of Appeal had held that the assured were not entitled to recover under their hull and machinery policy. The underwriters issued a summons in the action seeking an order pursuant to s.51 of the Supreme Court Act that Mr Comninos, the director of the assured company, and a non-party to the action, be liable personally to pay its costs. It was argued on behalf of Mr Comninos that in the event that the s.51 process was not to be considered separately from the main action for jurisdiction purposes, i.e. was ancillary to the main proceedings, then s.3 of Title II of the Jurisdiction Convention applies on the basis that the action is a matter relating to insurance. Therefore, on that basis the underwriters could bring proceedings only in Greece, the domicile of Mr Comninos. The Court of Appeal rejected that argument. It held that if the claim constituted proceedings, then it did not relate to insurance matters. If the relevant proceedings were the main proceedings, albeit they did relate to insurance matters, they had already been brought against the insurer in the UK. Thus the proceedings were brought against the insurer in compliance with Art. 8. Therefore, the insurer was not seeking to bring proceedings relating to insurance matters against Mr Comninos. 9.7

Furthermore, it is now clear law that reinsurance does not fall within the exception for matters relating to insurance in s.3. In *Societe Group Josi Reinsurance Company SA v. Compagnie d'Assurances Universal General Insurance Company*[20] the European Court of Justice held that reinsurance does not fall within these provisions. That conclusion had already been reached by the House of Lords in *Agnew v. Lansforsakringsbolagens AB.*[21] 9.8

9B.4 Jurisdiction agreement – Article 17

Article 17 of the EC Jurisdiction Convention provides that if the parties, one or more of whom is domiciled in a Contracting State, have agreed that a court or the courts of a Contracting State are to have jurisdiction, that court or those courts shall have exclusive jurisdiction. The jurisdiction agreement must satisfy certain formalities if Art. 17 is to apply. The English courts have adopted a robust approach to Art. 17. They have held that the court chosen should determine whether the formalities of Art. 17 have been satisfied, even where proceedings have been 9.9

18. See further, Chapter 10 of the previous volume of this work at pp.307–311.
19. [2000] 1 Lloyd's Rep. 129.
20. Case-412/98 [2000] 2 All E.R. (Comm.) 467.
21. [2000] 1 All E.R. 737.

commenced in another Contracting State.[22] This approach has been criticised and is discussed further below.[23]

9.10 It is now clear from the House of Lords decision in *Canada Trust Co. v. Stolzenberg (No. 2)*[24] that the standard of proof to which the claimant has to establish that there is a jurisdiction agreement is one of a good arguable case. In the Court of Appeal in *Canada Trust*[25] Waller LJ doubted that he had applied the correct standard of proof in his earlier decision in *IP Metal v. Ruote OZ SpA.*[26] There Waller J, as he then was, thought that where the argument in relation to Art. 17 is whether a consensus has been reached, that is likely to distinguish the Art. 17 situation from the Art. 5 situation. In the former situation, the court is likely to want to be more certain that the party alleging the consensus is right, because it is likely that the argument is only of relevance when jurisdiction is being decided. Thus he thought that there should be a higher threshold for a plaintiff to cross. Certainly where Art. 22 also applied the court will "want to be as clear as possible, and at least form the view that it is highly likely, that if the matter were tried out the plaintiff would succeed in his argument on the jurisdiction clause".[27] Thus, where another Contracting State is already seised, Waller J wanted to be surer that Art. 17 applied. The issue of the contract may be considered at both the jurisdiction stage and when the dispute on the merits is determined, e.g. whether there is a contract at all and, if so, what its terms are.

9B.4(i) Formalities

9.11 Article 17 has been amended by the various Accession Conventions to the EC Jurisdiction Convention. When the UK acceded to the Jurisdiction Convention in 1978, Art. 17 was amended to add a further head on which a jurisdiction clause could satisfy the formalities of Art. 17. Thus, under the 1978 Accession Convention where one or more of the parties is domiciled in a Contracting State and the court of a Contracting State has been chosen, that court shall have exclusive jurisdiction provided that the clause is either in writing or evidenced in writing, or, in international trade or commerce, in a form which accords with practices in that trade or commerce of which the parties are, or ought to be, aware. When Spain and Portugal acceded to the Convention in 1989 (by the San Sebastian Convention) further amendments were made to Art. 17 and that wording remained the same in the 1996 Accession Convention, which is the Accession Convention currently in force in the UK.[28] Thus, where the 1996 Convention applies, an agreement must be:

"(a) in writing or evidenced in writing; or
(b) in a form which accords with practices which the parties have established between themselves; or

---

22. *Denby v. Hellenic* [1994] 1 Lloyd's Rep. 320.
23. See para. 9B.5.
24. [2001] CLC 118.
25. [1998] 1 W.L.R. 547 at pp.555–559 and see also *Lafarge v. Fritz Peters* [2000] 2 Lloyd's Rep. 689 at pp.693–696.
26. [1993] 2 Lloyd's Rep. 60, 63–64.
27. *Ibid.*, p.63.
28. See fn.3.

(c) in international trade or commerce, in a form which accords with a usage of which the parties are or ought to have been aware and which in such trade or commerce is widely known to, and regularly observed by, parties to contracts of the type involved in the particular trade or commerce concerned".

The reason that the UK wanted an amendment to the EC Jurisdiction Convention was to safeguard the jurisdiction of the High Court in London, which is chosen in many international standard form contracts, including marine insurance and reinsurance contracts. The terms of such standard forms, including the jurisdiction clause, are frequently incorporated into the contract by reference, or the jurisdiction clause may be one of many printed clauses in a contract often only signed on behalf of one party.[29] English law is less strict than that of many of its European counterparts on the incorporation of terms into contracts. Thus, to take but one example, in Italy Art. 1341 of the Civil Code provides that clauses laying down particular limitations to or derogating from the jurisdiction of the courts must be specifically approved in writing. Under English law, however, a bill of lading may incorporate the terms of a charterparty which the shipper/cargo receiver has never seen. Provided that the bill of lading makes specific reference to the arbitration clause it will incorporate that clause even though the charterparty clause provides for all disputes under the charterparty to be referred to arbitration.[30]

9B.4(ii) In writing or evidenced in writing

A jurisdiction clause may be incorporated into a marine insurance or reinsurance policy by incorporating the terms of a standard form contract or by reference to terms in another contract. In *Estasis Salotti di Colzani Aimo e Gianmario Colzani v. RUWA Polstereimaschinen GmbH*,[31] the European Court held that the writing requirement is satisfied only if the reference is express and can be checked by a party exercising reasonable care. Thus the formalities of Art. 17 were satisfied in *Denby v. Hellenic*[32] as the insurance slip which incorporated the MAR form of policy, including a jurisdiction clause, was put forward by the assured's brokers and was therefore clearly in writing and consented to by both parties. Furthermore, the form was well known in international commerce in the insurance of maritime and allied risks. Evidence as to Greek law on the incorporation of clauses was irrelevant as Art. 17 is a self-contained code for deciding whether the parties have or have not agreed upon a jurisdiction clause. 9.12

29. For example, it is very common for a bill of lading to be signed by the master on behalf of the carrier but for there to be no signature by or on behalf of the shipper or consignee.

30. *Daval Aciers d'Usinor et de Sacilor v. Armare SRL (The Nerano)* [1996] 1 Lloyd's Rep. 1 and *The Delos* [2001] 1 Lloyd's Rep. 703.

31. (Case 24/76), [1976] ECR 1831. See also *WH Martin Ltd v. Feldbinder Spezialfahrzeugwerke GmbH* [1998] I.L.Pr. 794 where the Court of Appeal held that there was no jurisdiction agreement. The repair agreement containing the obligation in dispute was a separate agreement from an earlier supply agreement which did contain a German jurisdiction clause. A classic "battle of the forms" took place in *Lafarge Plasterboard Ltd v. Fritz Peters & Co. KG* [2000] 2 Lloyd's Rep. 689. As there was nothing in the buyers' printed form purchase order drawing attention to the conditions printed on the back, Art. 17 was not satisfied.

32. [1994] 1 Lloyd's Rep. 320.

9.13 In *Credit Suisse Financial Products v. Societe Generale d'Entreprises*[33] the respondents agreed to sell the appellants a "put" option. The agreement was made on the telephone. Subsequently, the appellants faxed the respondents a written revised confirmation of the deal, which the respondents signed and faxed back. This confirmation contained terms which had not been expressly referred to on the telephone, including a provision that the contract was subject to the 1992 ISDA Master Agreement. This latter agreement contained an English jurisdiction and governing law clause. Here the written contract contained an express reference to the Master Agreement. The Court of Appeal held that the judge at first instance erred in his approach that, as the respondents' employee did not have a copy of the Master Agreement in his possession and readily available to him, Art. 17 was not satisfied. The consensus necessary to satisfy Art. 17 was established.

9.14 It is very common for reinsurance contracts to incorporate the provisions of the primary insurance.[34] The English courts have recently had to consider whether the words of incorporation in the reinsurance contract are clear enough to incorporate the jurisdiction clause, whether it be an arbitration or court jurisdiction clause in the underlying insurance policy. Similar considerations apply to the incorporation of charterparty arbitration clauses into bills of lading[35] which must satisfy the formalities of ss.5 and 6 of the Arbitration Act 1996.

9.15 In *AIG Group (UK) Ltd v. The Ethniki*,[36] Colman J held that the wording of a reinsurance policy, "Wording as original", did not incorporate an ancillary provision from the primary insurance such as a jurisdiction clause conferring jurisdiction on the Courts of Athens. He considered the authorities on the incorporation of arbitration clauses. Although there might be cases where, in all the circumstances prevailing between the parties when they made their contract, it would be unrealistic to restrict the scope of incorporation to exclude a jurisdiction clause, in that case it was to be inferred that the function of the incorporating words was confined to ensuring that the substantive or subject-matter terms of the reinsurance matched the substantive or subject-matter terms of the primary cover, except where expressly provided to the contrary. The Court of Appeal upheld that decision. However, Evans LJ giving the judgment in the case, stated:

"It is clear in my judgment that the circumstances in which charterparty provisions are stated to be incorporated in a bill of lading are special and possibly unique, and they cannot give rise to any rule of construction which should apply whenever one contract incorporates the terms of another. The present case, even if it were typical of reinsurance contracts, has features which are relied upon by both parties and which could not arise in the bill of lading/charterparty context. Mr Matthews submits that the parties agreeing the reinsurance contract in London must have recognised that disputes under the insurance contract would arise in Greece and if litigation became necessary would be most likely to be decided by the courts there. On the other

33. [1997] CLC 168.

34. See Chapter 2 of this book for R Merkin, Incorporation of Terms into Reinsurance Agreements, and, in particular, paras. 2.56 to 2.62 on the incorporation of jurisdiction and arbitration clauses.

35. See generally N Gaskell, R Asariotis and Y Baatz, *Bills of Lading: Law and Contracts* (LLP, London 2000 pp.675–679 and 689–706); G Treitel and F Reynolds, *Carver on Bills of Lading* (Sweet & Maxwell, London 2001, pp.71–99) and, in particular, pp.86–89; and A Mocatta, M Mustill, S Boyd, *Scrutton on Charterparties and Bills of Lading* (Sweet & Maxwell, London, 20th edn., 1996) Article 40.

36. [2000] All E.R. (Comm.) 65 (CA); [1998] 4 All E.R. 301.

hand, as the judge noted, the reinsurance contract is probably governed by English law, and the parties to it may be thought unlikely to have intended that disputes arising under it should be decided in Greece. Neither of these factors arises in the same way in a bill of lading/charterparty case".

The distinction Evans LJ seeks to draw between the bill of lading/charterparty case and the insurance/reinsurance case is not clear cut. In both cases the carrier/insurer would like both contracts to be back to back and to have the same provisions as to jurisdiction and governing law. However, in both cases the bill of lading holder/reinsurer may want the courts of its own country to have jurisdiction.[37] Evans LJ continued:

"Nevertheless, there is one feature which the two situations have in common. In both, the parties intend that the subject-matter of the two contracts shall be the same. In the bill of lading, that the terms etc of carriage shall be those already agreed in the charterparty. In a reinsurance contract, that what may be called the scope of the insurance is identical with that in the underlying policy, particularly when the reinsurance includes a 'pay as may be paid' provision, as here. In my judgment, this is a good and sufficient reason for asking, in both contexts, what is essentially the same question: did the parties to the contract in which the general words of incorporation appear intend that their contract should include the particular term from the other contract referred to?"[38]

As the jurisdiction clause was not incorporated, Art. 17 could not apply. Article 5(1) did apply (as discussed below).[39]

The same decision was reached by Judge Raymond Jack in the context of incorporation of arbitration clauses in reinsurance contracts under the Arbitration Act 1996 in *Trygg Hansa Insurance Co. Ltd v. Equitas Ltd.*[40] Sections 5 and 6 of the Arbitration Act 1996 set out the formalities that have to be complied with for there to be a valid arbitration agreement. The reinsurer argued that the wordings for the excess of loss layers ("follow the same terms . . . as the policy of the primary insurers") incorporated the arbitration clause from the primary insurances, and that the wording of the reinsurances ("form: as original") incorporated the wording of the excess of loss insurances including the arbitration clause. The general conditions to the primary insurance, which contained the arbitration clause, were not agreed at the time that the excess of loss insurances were contracted but the case proceeded on the basis that the primary insurances were all written on the anticipated standard terms. The reinsurers relied on s.6(2) of the Arbitration Act 1996 which permitted incorporation of an arbitration clause by reference to the document containing it "if the reference was such as to make that clause part of the agreement". The reinsurers submitted that s.6 had changed the law and relied on the Report of the Departmental Committee on the Arbitration Bill to show that that was the case and that authorities on incorporation of arbitration clauses by reference under the previous legislation had been superseded. 9.16

The syndicates argued that the authorities were still relevant and that applying the

37. In bills of lading the standard form contracts often provide that the courts of the principal place of business of the carrier are to have jurisdiction, e.g. Conlinebill and Conlinebill 2000. Contrast the provisions of the latest international Convention in this area – Arts 21 and 22 of the Hamburg Rules.

38. *Ibid.*, at p.74.

39. See para. 9.49.

40. [1998] CLC 979.

general words of incorporation in the excess of loss layers would not be effective to incorporate the arbitration clause because of its special nature. Judge Raymond Jack QC held that in the absence of special circumstances, general words of incorporation were not to be treated as effective for the purposes of s.6(2) of the Arbitration Act 1996. The court could look at the Report of the Departmental Committee on the Arbitration Bill on the issue whether the existing authorities on incorporation of arbitration clauses by reference should still be applied. The report showed that it was not intended that the authorities should be put on one side. It suggested that it was for the court to apply the existing case law resolving conflicts as necessary. On the authorities the parties were not taken to have incorporated an arbitration clause which was of a special nature different from the majority of clauses in a contract, in the absence of an express indication. The words used in the excess of loss insurances did not incorporate the arbitration clause from the primary insurances, and the wording of the reinsurances would not have incorporated an arbitration clause from the excess of loss insurances. The primary insurances were in existence in *The Ethniki* at the time the reinsurance contracts were concluded, whereas in *Trygg* they were not.

9.17 A similar decision was reached by Tuckey J in *Arig Insurance Co. Ltd v. Sasa Assicurazione Riassicurazione SpA*[41] where the words of incorporation in the reinsurance contract were, "Policy wording as original".

9.18 Clearer words of incorporation were used in the reinsurance contract in *AIG Europe SA v. QBE International Insurance Ltd*, but Moore-Bick J held that they were still not effective to incorporate the French jurisdiction clause from the insurance contract.[42] The reinsurance contract provided,

> "All terms, clauses and conditions as original and to follow the original in all respects including settlements. . . ."

The insurers submitted unsuccessfully that the use of the word "all" was sufficient to incorporate the jurisdiction clauses from the insurance contract which read as follows:

> "*L. Arbitral procedure*
> In case of dispute between the insured and insurers the parties will apply to the Tribunal de Commerce in Paris who will appoint an arbitrator. The latter, with the possible collaboration of two further arbitrators appointed by the parties, will have the task of proposing an agreement acceptable to both parties.
> *M. Law and jurisdiction*
> In the event of dispute between the insured and the insurers and should the arbitral procedure referred to earlier fail to establish an agreement between the parties in the dispute, the said parties should address themselves to the French Courts which have sole jurisdiction; foreign companies which have accepted part of the risk are also subject to the jurisdiction of the French Courts and abandon all rights of appeal in their own country."

9.19 This decision may be criticised both on the basis of a European interpretation of Art. 17 and possibly by way of analogy with the bill of lading cases. On a European interpretation the judge accepted that a jurisdiction clause contained in general conditions of trading may be effectively incorporated by a general reference to those conditions provided that they are referred to expressly in the contract.[43] However, he

41. Unreported, 10 February 1998.
42. [2001] 2 Lloyd's Rep. 268.
43. *Estasis Salotti di Colzani Aimo e Gianmario Colzani v. RUWA Polstereimaschinen GmbH* [1976] ECR 1831.

went on to distinguish the incorporation by reference to a set of standard trading terms and the incorporation of the terms of one contract into another related contract between different parties. In the latter case he held that it does not necessarily follow that general words in the reinsurance contract incorporating the terms and conditions of the underlying policy can be taken as demonstrating clearly and precisely the existence of a consensus in relation to clauses which are ancillary to the substance of the contract. Then the court should construe the language of the contract in the context of its commercial background and ask itself whether a consensus is clearly and precisely demonstrated. Even if it is accepted that this further requirement is justified, and it is suggested that it is not, it may be argued that the language of this reinsurance contract did demonstrate consensus.

If we look to the bill of lading cases, in *The Merak*[44] the words "all the terms, conditions, clauses and exceptions", were effective to incorporate the charterparty arbitration clause where the latter clause provided, "any dispute arising out of this charter or any bill of lading issued hereunder, shall be referred to arbitration". In *Miramar Maritime Corporation v. Holborn Oil Trading Ltd (The Miramar)*[45] the words of incorporation were, "all terms whatsoever of the said charter". The House of Lords' decision appears to be based on the reasoning that such wording incorporated all the terms of the charterparty verbatim into the bill of lading, although the clause under consideration there related to demurrage and not arbitration. However, as the words of incorporation were general, it did not justify manipulating the wording of the charterparty clauses so as to make them apply to the bill of lading. Thus, in that case where the charterparty provided for the demurrage to be payable by the charterers, that wording could not be manipulated to impose the obligation to pay demurrage on the bill of lading holder. 9.20

Most recently, Langley J has held that wide words of incorporation are not sufficient to incorporate the charterparty arbitration clause. In *The Delos*,[46] the Ocean bills provided that all the terms whatsoever of the charter applied to the bill of lading. The charterparty arbitration clause made no reference to the bill of lading and referred any disputes under this charterparty to London arbitration. Langley J held that as the Ocean bills made no reference to the arbitration clause, the wide words of the bill of lading did not incorporate the arbitration clause. Clearly, even if they had done so, the words of the charterparty were not apt to apply to the bill of lading and could not be manipulated without a specific reference to the arbitration clause in the bill of lading. 9.21

What is not clear is whether such wide general words of incorporation would incorporate an arbitration clause provided that the wording of the arbitration clause did not require manipulation or referred to the bill of lading. Admittedly, the wording in the reinsurance contract in *AIG* is not as emphatic as in *The Miramar* as it does not use "whatsoever". Furthermore, Moore-Bick J states that the wording of clauses L and M does not require a great deal of manipulation to render it applicable to 9.22

44. [1965] P.223.
45. [1984] 2 Lloyd's Rep. 129.
46. [2001] 1 Lloyd's Rep. 703. *Cf. TW Thomas & Co. Ltd v. Portsea Shipping Co. Ltd* [1912] A.C.1. and *The Varenna* [1983] 2 Lloyd's Rep. 592. See also G Treitel and F Reynolds, *Carver on Bills of Lading* (Sweet & Maxwell, London 2001) 3–028 and 3–029 and N Gaskell, R Asariotis and Y Baatz, *Bills of Lading: Law and Contracts* (LLP, London 2000) 21.34.

reinsured and reinsurer. It is suggested that the wording "insured" and "insurers" does not need any manipulation in the context of the reinsurance contract where the reinsured is the "insured" and the "reinsured" the insurer. A possible further argument would be that the last part of clause M covers the reinsurers and where the reinsurance contract has general words of incorporation and the insurance contract by its own words applies the jurisdiction clause to the reinsurers, this validly incorporates the jurisdiction clause in the reinsurance contract.[47] The judge thought the inclusion of a mandatory conciliation clause much more apt for inclusion in an original contract of insurance than in a reinsurance contract.

9.23 The latest decision in this line of authority smacks of the English courts jealously guarding their own jurisdiction in reinsurance contracts, by rejecting the incorporation of foreign jurisdiction clauses. No doubt where the insurer is in a strong negotiating position the English courts' antipathy to the incorporation of foreign jurisdiction clauses to satisfy Art. 17 can be overcome by the use of either an express jurisdiction clause in the reinsurance contract or specific wording in the reinsurance contract. If the bill of lading cases are used by way of analogy, the words of incorporation should specifically refer to the jurisdiction or arbitration clause. In the bill of lading cases specific words of incorporation have been effective to incorporate arbitration clauses, even if it has been necessary to manipulate the wording of the charterparty arbitration clause, e.g. if it states "all disputes arising under this charterparty", so that it applies to the bill of lading.[48]

9.24 Bills of lading raise other problems as the bill of lading containing a jurisdiction clause is often issued after the contract has been concluded between the shipper and the carrier without any specific mention of jurisdiction having been made. Depending on which party has chosen the bill of lading form, the other party may not know the exact contents of a printed bill of lading. For example, some charterparties oblige the master to issue bills of lading as presented by the charterer or authorise the charterer to issue bills on behalf of the master. Furthermore, how does a jurisdiction clause, even if agreed between the shipper and the carrier, affect a third party indorsee of the bill? The original wording of Art. 17 was considered by the European Court of Justice in the context of a jurisdiction clause in a printed standard form bill of lading in *Partenreederei MS Tilly Russ v. Haven & Vervoebedrijf Nova NV*.[49] The court held that such a jurisdiction clause was an agreement in writing or an oral agreement evidenced in writing for the purposes of Art. 17 if either the agreement of the parties to the bill had been expressed in writing, or if the clause had been orally agreed by the parties before its incorporation in the bill so that the bill of lading signed by the carrier constituted confirmation in writing of that agreement, or if the bill was part of a continuing business relationship between the parties which was itself governed by general conditions including the jurisdiction clause. Furthermore, if the clause was effective for the purposes of Art. 17 as between the carrier and the shipper, it was also effective between the carrier and a holder of the bill of lading, provided that, under the

47. By analogy with *The Merak* [1965] P.223 where the charterparty arbitration clause referred not only to disputes arising out of the charterparty but also any bill of lading issued thereunder.

48. *Daval Aciers d'Usinor et de Sacilor v. Armare SRL (The Nerano)* [1996] 1 Lloyd's Rep. 1 and *The Delos* [2001] 1 Lloyd's Rep. 703.

49. [1985] 1 Q.B. 931.

relevant national law, the holder of the bill of lading succeeded to the shipper's rights and obligations under it.[50] Under English law, the rights of the holder of the bill of lading are now governed by the Carriage of Goods by Sea Act 1992 for bills of lading dated after 16 September 1992.[51]

If there is no agreement in writing or evidenced in writing and no course of dealing between the parties it may be necessary to consider whether there is a trade usage.

9B.4(iii) Trade usage

In *Trasporti Castelletti Spedizioni Internazionali SpA v. Hugo Trumpy SpA*,[52] the European Court of Justice considered the requirements that have to be satisfied under Art. 17 of the 1978 Accession Convention. In that case fruit was shipped in 1987 by Argentinian shippers under 22 bills of lading issued in Buenos Aires. The cargo was delivered in Italy to Trasporti Castelletti Spedizioni Internazionali SpA. The latter brought proceedings against Hugo Trumpy as agent of the ship and the carrier, Lauritzen Reefers A/S, in the court of Genoa on the basis that Hugo Trumpy were domiciled in Genoa. The latter contested jurisdiction as the bill of lading contained an exclusive English High Court jurisdiction clause.[53] 9.25

The jurisdiction clause was the last on the back of a printed form bill of lading. The print was small but legible. The face of the bill had been signed by both the carrier's agent and the shipper. Beneath the shipper's signature, but in larger print than the other clauses, was a reference to the conditions set out on the reverse. The Court of Genoa held that the jurisdiction clause was valid in the light of the usages of international trade, although it had not been signed by the shipper. The Genoese Court of Appeal upheld that judgment but on the ground that the shipper's signature on the face of the bills of lading implied Castelletti's acceptance of all the clauses, including those on the reverse. Castelletti appealed on a point of law, arguing that the signature of the original shipper could not have constituted acceptance of all the clauses, but only those relating to the particulars of the cargo as made clear by the position of the shipper's signature. The Italian Supreme Court of Cassation held that the signature of the original shipper could not imply consent to all the clauses of the bill of lading and, therefore, resolution of the dispute depended on the interpretation of the provision concerning international usage in Art. 17. It referred 14 questions to the European Court for a preliminary ruling. By the time the matter came before the court, the decisions in *Mainschiffahrts-Genossenschaft eG v. Les Gravieres Rhenanes*

---

50. See also *Trasporti Castelletti Spedizioni Internazionali SpA v. Hugo Trumpy SpA* Case C-159/97, [1999] I.L.Pr. 492 and *Coreck Maritime GmbH v. Handelsveem BV* Case C-387/98 [2001] CLC 550 discussed at paras. 9.29 and 9.32.

51. For bills of lading issued before that date, the Bills of Lading Act 1855 is still applicable. See, further, Sections 4B and C of N Gaskell, R Asariotis and Y Baatz, *Bills of Lading: Law and Contracts* (LLP, London, 2000).

52. Case C-159/97 [1999] I.L.Pr. 492. See also Y Baatz, "Objective Test of Validity of Jurisdiction Clauses under the Brussels Convention on Jurisdiction", [2000] ITLQ 44.

53. Which read: "The contract evidenced by this Bill of Lading shall be governed by English law and any disputes thereunder shall be determined in England by the High Court of Justice in London according to English law to the exclusion of the Courts of any other country".

(MSG)[54] and *Francesco Benincasa v. Dentalkit SRL*[55] had already answered some of the questions.

9.26 The first question related to whether Art. 17 necessarily requires the consent of the parties to the jurisdiction clause to be established. The European Court followed *MSG*. There, German owners of an inland waterway vessel claimed for damage to that vessel from the French charterers. After the negotiations for the contract the owners had sent the charterers a commercial letter of confirmation containing the following pre-printed statement: "The place of performance is Wurzburg and the courts for that place have exclusive jurisdiction". The owners' invoices also provided for that forum. The charterers did not challenge the letter of confirmation or the invoices. The European Court stated that one of the aims of Art. 17 is to ensure that there is real consent on the part of the parties. The weaker party to the contract should be protected by avoiding jurisdiction clauses incorporated in a contract by one party alone going unnoticed. However, consensus is presumed to exist where commercial practices in the relevant branch of international trade or commerce exist in this regard of which the parties are or ought to have been aware.

9.27 Although it is for the national court to decide whether commercial practices in the relevant trade or commerce are proved to exist, in *MSG* the European Court indicated that a contract concluded between two companies established in different Contracting States in a field such as navigation on the Rhine comes under the head of international trade or commerce. Whether a practice exists must not be determined by reference to the law of one of the Contracting States. Whether such a practice exists should be determined by reference to the branch of the trade or commerce in which the parties to the contract are operating. There is a practice in the branch of trade or commerce in question where a particular course of conduct is generally and regularly followed by operators in that branch when concluding contracts of a particular type.

In *Castelletti*, the parties agreed that the contracts in question formed part of international trade or commerce. In that case the European Court held that it is not necessary for a course of conduct to be established in specific countries or, in particular, in all the Contracting States. What is important is that the course of conduct is regularly followed by operators in the branch of international trade in which the parties to the contract operate. It may help to prove that a practice is generally and regularly observed by operators in the countries which play a prominent role in the branch of trade or commerce in question.

The Court further held in *Castelletti* that there is no requirement for establishing the existence of a usage that there is any particular form of publicity. However, publicity which might be given by associations or specialised bodies to the standard forms on which a jurisdiction clause appears may help to prove that a practice is generally and regularly followed.

Furthermore, the fact that numerous shippers and/or indorsees of bills of lading have challenged the validity of a jurisdiction clause by bringing actions before courts other than those chosen by the clause would not cause the incorporation of the clause

54. (Case C-106/95), [1997] All E.R. (EC) 385.
55. (Case C-269/95), [1998] All E.R. (EC) 135, noted by A Waldron, [1997] ITLQ 114.

to cease to constitute a usage, provided that it is established that it amounts to a usage which is generally and regularly followed.

In *Castelletti*, questions were raised concerning the expression "form which accords". Does the clause have to be in writing signed in any particular manner? Is it necessary to draw particular attention to the clause or is it sufficient for it to be inserted amongst numerous clauses? Must the language of the clause be related to the nationality of the parties? Are there circumstances in which the insertion of the clause in a standard form, which has not been signed by the party not involved in drawing up the clause, may be considered to be grossly unfair or even abusive? Lastly, can a usage derogate from mandatory statutory provisions adopted by certain Contracting States as regards the form of jurisdiction clauses? 9.28

The answer to all these questions depends solely on what form is consistent with the commercial usages in the branch of international trade or commerce concerned, without taking into account any particular requirements which national provisions may lay down. Contracting States cannot impose formal requirements other than those set out in the EC Jurisdiction Convention.[56]

Which party must be aware of the usage? This question is of significance in the context of bills of lading because if a bill of lading is a document of title it is transferable. Although the shipper may be the original party to the bill of lading contract with the carrier, the shipper may transfer the bill of lading by delivery and indorsement to a third party. The shipper may have been aware of any usage in the country of shipment but a third party on the other side of the world might have no knowledge of it. In *Castelletti* the European Court followed its earlier decision in *Partenreederei Ms Tilly Russ v. Haven & Vervoebedrijf NV*[57] where it had held that where a jurisdiction clause is valid under Art. 17 as between the shipper and the carrier, it can be pleaded against the third party holding the bill of lading so long as, under the relevant national law, the holder of the bill of lading succeeds to the shipper's rights and obligations.[58] As the validity of the bill of lading must be assessed by reference to the relationship between the original parties it is the awareness of those parties which must be established. The parties' nationality is irrelevant for the purposes of that investigation.[59] If the third party does not succeed to the rights and obligations of the shipper, the national court must ascertain whether the third party accepted the jurisdiction clause having regard to the requirements of Art. 17 – *Coreck Maritime GmbH v. Handelsveem BV*.[60] In that case, the European Court held that the question which national law was applicable for the purposes of determining the rights and obligations of a third party bearer of a bill of lading was not one of interpretation of the Convention and was to be determined by the national court applying its own rules of private international law. 9.29

What degree of awareness should the original parties have of the usage and should 9.30

56. *Elefanten Schuh v. Jacqmain*, Case 150/80, [1981] ECR 1671.

57. [1985] 1 Q.B. 931.

58. Under English law the "lawful holder" of a transferable bill of lading does have transferred to it the rights and obligations under the bill of lading pursuant to ss.2(1) and 3 of the Carriage of Goods by Sea Act 1992.

59. As to whether Art. 17 binds the assignee of a bank guarantee, see the *obiter dicta* of Schiemann LJ, with whose judgment Waite and Russell LJJ agreed, in *Firswood Ltd v. Petra Bank* [1996] CLC 608.

60. Case C-387/98 [2001] CLC.

any publicity be given to the standard forms containing jurisdiction clauses and, if so, in what form? In *Castelletti* the European Court relied on their earlier decision in *MSG* that actual or presumed awareness of a usage on the part of the parties to a contract can be made out, in particular, by showing either that the parties had previously had commercial or trade relations between themselves or with other parties operating in the sector in question, so that, in that sector, a particular course of conduct is sufficiently well known, because it is generally and regularly followed when a particular type of contract is concluded, so that it may be regarded as being an established usage.

As Art. 17 is silent on the means by which awareness of a usage may be proved, it is not essential that any publicity has been given by associations or specialised bodies to the standard forms containing jurisdiction clauses, although such publicity would make proof easier.

9.31 Questions were raised as to whether the parties are restricted in their choice of court. As the Convention aims to achieve legal certainty by making it possible to predict which court will have jurisdiction by fixing strict conditions as to form, there is no requirement of any link between the relationship in dispute and the court chosen. Any further review of the validity of the clause and of the intention of the party which inserted it must be excluded and substantive rules of liability applicable in the chosen court which might tend to reduce that party's liability must not affect the validity of the jurisdiction clause. In other words, the parties are free to choose whichever jurisdiction they please. A jurisdiction which has no link at all with the dispute may be advantageous in that it offers the parties greater neutrality. Furthermore, if the substantive law of one Contracting State is more favourable than another, one party may choose the courts of the first State. It is permissible to forum shop either at the choice of jurisdiction clause stage or, where there is no jurisdiction clause, at the stage of choosing where to bring proceedings.[61] The desire to forum shop could only be eliminated if there were to be a "level playing field" on substantive law within the Contracting States and similar court systems.

9.32 It is very common for standard form bills of lading to contain a formula to determine the place of the courts with jurisdiction to determine disputes. The bill of lading form may be used by parties of all nationalities and must have flexibility. Thus, the bill of lading will frequently provide that the courts of the principal place of business of the carrier shall have jurisdiction.[62] In *Coreck Maritime GmbH v. Handelsveem BV*[63] the European Court held that it is not necessary for a jurisdiction clause to be so formulated that the competent court could be determined on the wording of the clause alone. It was sufficient that the clause stated the objective factors on the basis of which the parties had agreed to choose the court or courts to which they wished to submit disputes. Those factors, which had to be sufficiently precise to enable the court seised to ascertain whether it had jurisdiction, could, where appropriate, be determined by the particular circumstances of the case.

61. *The Maciej Rataj*, Case C-406/92, [1995] 1 Lloyd's Rep. 302.
62. See, e.g., Conlinebill and Conlinebill 2000.
63. Case C-387/98 [2001] CLC 550.

It is arguable that where the EC Jurisdiction Convention applies,[64] the English courts could no longer apply the decision in *The Morviken*[65] to knock out a jurisdiction clause in a bill of lading choosing the court of another Contracting State on the ground that it is null and void under Art. III r.8 of the Hague Visby-Rules,[66] unless the Hague-Visby Rules fall within Art. 57 of the EC Jurisdiction Convention.[67] 9.33

Once it has been decided that the formalities of Art. 17 have been satisfied, it is clear that the court chosen can decide matters in relation to the validity of the contract. Thus, the European Court has held that "the national court's jurisdiction to determine questions relating to a contract includes the power to consider the existence of the constituent parts of the contract itself".[68] The European Court has held that the courts of a Contracting State which have been designated in a jurisdiction clause validly concluded under Art. 17 also have exclusive jurisdiction where the action seeks a declaration that the contract containing that clause is void. In *Francesco Benincasa v. Dentalkit SRL*[69] Mr Benincasa, an Italian national, had entered into an agreement with Dentalkit, whose seat was in Florence. By reference to Arts 1341 and 1342 of the Italian Civil Code, the parties specifically approved a jurisdiction clause in the contract which read "The courts at Florence shall have jurisdiction to entertain any dispute relating to the interpretation, performance or other aspects of the present contract" by separately signing it. Mr Benincasa brought proceedings in the German courts, where he sought to have the contract declared void on the ground that the contract as a whole was void under German law. The Landgericht Munich declined jurisdiction. Mr Benincasa appealed. The Oberlandesgericht Munich referred three issues to the European Court, including one regarding Art. 17. The courts of a Contracting State which have been designated in a jurisdiction clause validly concluded under the first paragraph of Art. 17 of the Convention also have exclusive jurisdiction where the action seeks in particular a declaration that the contract containing that clause is void. It is for the national court to interpret the clause conferring jurisdiction invoked before it in order to determine which disputes fall within its scope.[70] Thus, in *Dentalkit* it was for the national court to determine whether the jurisdiction clause covered any dispute relating to the validity of the contract. 9.34

Aikens J applied the *MSG* case in *OT Africa Line Ltd v. Hijazy (The Kribi)*.[71] In that case two actions were heard concerning bills of lading which all contained an exclusive English jurisdiction clause as follows: 9.35

"Any claim or dispute whatsoever arising in connection with the Carriage under this Bill of Lading shall exclusively be governed by English law and determined by the High Court in London."

Aikens J held that the formalities of Article 17 had been satisfied under both (b) and

64. Where the EC Jurisdiction Convention does not apply, *The Morviken* can still be applied; see, e.g., *Baghlaf Al Zafer Factory Co. v. Pakistan National Shipping Co.* [1998] 2 Lloyd's Rep. 229.
65. [1983] 1 A.C. 565.
66. Which are given the force of law by the Carriage of Goods by Sea Act 1971.
67. Discussed at para. 9.82 below.
68. *Effer SpA v. Hans Joachim Kantner* [1982] ECR 825.
69. Case C-269/95, [1998] All E.R. (EC) 135.
70. *Powell Duffryn*, Case C-214/89, [1992] ECR 1745.
71. [2001] 1 Lloyd's Rep. 76.

(c) of the San Sebastian Convention. Thus, the agreement was in a form which the parties had established between themselves. There was evidence that the form of bill of lading, and the jurisdiction clause in particular, had been much used between the shipowners and the shippers. Futhermore, there was unchallenged evidence that the form of bill of lading, including the jurisdiction clause, was one that would normally be encountered in a modern international liner service. Similar forms including English jurisdiction clauses were used by six other international shipowners or carriers. Those six included carriers on a liner basis to West Africa. The English jurisdiction clauses were regularly observed and complied with and the Liberian shippers regularly engaged in the West Africa trade. Thus, the judge concluded that the jurisdiction clause was in a form which accords with a usage of which the shipowners and the Liberian shippers are, or ought to be, aware is widely known to and regularly observed by parties to bill of lading contracts of carriage in the international liner services, including liner services between Europe and West Africa.

Furthermore, whether the receivers succeeded to the rights and obligations of the shipper was a matter for the relevant national law. In this case, Aikens J applied English law as that was the proper law of the contract of carriage and the receiver succeeded to the rights and liabilities of the shippers pursuant to ss.2 and 3 of the Carriage of Goods by Sea Act 1992.[72]

9B.5 Which court decides whether Article 17 is satisfied?

9.36 One of the key issues at the heart of the EC Jurisdiction Convention is which court has jurisdiction to determine whether the formalities set out in Art. 17 have been satisfied. What is to happen if one of the parties to the contract brings proceedings in the courts of a Contracting State other than the one chosen in the jurisdiction clause, so that that other court is first seised? The English court's attitude to this issue has been emphatic: the court *chosen* is the court which should determine whether Art. 17 is satisfied and determine the case on its merits, notwithstanding that the court of another Contracting State has been first seised. In *Denby v. Hellenic*,[73] Rix J held that the issue whether the formalities of Art. 17 have been satisfied is to be determined by the jurisdiction chosen by the parties even where proceedings have been commenced elsewhere.[74] This was the decision of the Court of Appeal in *Continental Bank NA v. Aeakos Compania Naviera SA*.[75] The Court of Appeal were so sure that they were right they refused to refer the issue to the European Court and granted an anti-suit injunction to restrain the defendant from pursuing the proceedings in the court first seised as such proceedings were in breach of the English jurisdiction clause. The issue was also not referred to the European Court in *Castelletti*, although many other issues were, presumably because the Italian court thought that it was obvious that it, the court first seised, but not the court chosen, should do so. An attempt to distinguish *Continental Bank* in *The Kribi* was unsuccessful.[76]

72. See further, K Takahashi, "Jurisdiction over direct action against sub-carrier under the Brussels Convention" [2001] LMCLQ 107 at 111 to 116.
73. [1994] 1 Lloyd's Rep. 320.
74. See *Elefanten Schuh v. Jacqmain*, [1981] ECR 1671 and in particular pp.1687–1688.
75. [1994] 1 Lloyd's Rep. 505, discussed *infra*.
76. Discussed *infra*.

An analogy with the English approach may be drawn with the putative proper law approach in relation to proper law and material validity under Art. 8 of the Rome Convention. The position may also be compared with the situation where, for example, a claimant relies on Art. 5(1) to establish jurisdiction in the place of performance of a contractual obligation. However, it is strongly arguable that this approach is wrong and that any court first seised of the case, whether or not it is the court chosen by the jurisdiction clause should determine whether the formalities of Art. 17 have been satisfied. Some support for this proposition is *Trasporti Castelletti Spedizioni Internazionali SpA v. Hugo Trumpy SpA*[77] and is discussed further below.[78] 9.37

Under the EC Jurisdiction Convention the parties have freedom to choose the court to have jurisdiction to determine their disputes.[79] If the validity of a clause is disputed, the court which determines that validity must apply only the tests set out in Art. 17 of the EC Jurisdiction Convention and no other restrictions relating to form, language, appearance, link with the dispute, national law restrictions, etc. As it is an objective test, there is much merit in its being applied by the court first seised, whether that court is the court chosen in the jurisdiction clause or not.

Article 17 further provides that where a jurisdiction agreement that satisfies the formalities required by Art. 17 is concluded by parties, none of whom is domiciled in a Contracting State, the courts of other Contracting States shall have no jurisdiction over their disputes unless the court or courts chosen have declined jurisdiction. 9.38

9B.6 No jurisdiction agreement

If there is no valid jurisdiction agreement and neither party has entered an appearance in the courts of a Contracting State, either party may seek to rely on Art. 5, or, in the case of multiple defendants such as an actual and contracting carrier, on Art. 6, or, in the case of limitation of liability, on Art. 6a. The provisions most likely to be relied on in a reinsurance claim in Art. 5 are Art. 5(1), (3) and (5). Where a claimant seeks to establish jurisdiction on the basis of one of these rules it must establish that there is a good arguable case that the dispute falls within the scope of that rule. Thus, where a party alleges that there is jurisdiction under, e.g., Art. 5(1) on the ground that the defendant is in breach of contract, the mere allegation of the existence of the contract is not enough. If the existence of the contract is in dispute the claimant must show that there is a good arguable case that there is a contract.[80] If the court holds that there is such a case at the interlocutory stage considering jurisdiction it will still have jurisdiction if it determines at the substantive trial that a contract did not exist. 9.39

---

77. Case C-159/97 [1999] ILPr 492. See also Y Baatz, "Objective Test of Validity of Jurisdiction Clauses under the Brussels Convention on Jurisdiction", [2000] ITLQ 44.
78. See paras. 9.119 to 9.120.
79. Subject to limited exceptions such as Art. 16, consumer contracts, insurance contracts, etc.
80. See *Effer SpA v. Kantner* (Case 38/81), [1982] ECR 825; *Tesam Distribution Ltd v. Schuh Mode Team GmbH* [1990] ILPr 149; and *Boss Group Ltd v. Boss France SA* [1996] CLC 1419 (all considering Art. 5(1)) and *Molnlycke AB v. Procter & Gamble Ltd* [1992] 4 All E.R. 47 (considering Art. 5(3)); *Canada Trust Co. v. Stolzenberg* [2001] CLC 118 H.L.; [1998] CLC 23.

9B.6(i) Article 5(1) – Introduction

9.40 Article 5(1) provides that a person domiciled in a Contracting State may be sued in another Contracting State "in matters relating to a contract, in the courts for the place of performance of the obligation in question". Certain principles may be stated in relation to the scope of the rule. First, as in the case of any of the derogations from the basic rule that the defendant must be sued in the courts of the Contracting State where it is domiciled,[81] the rule must be interpreted restrictively.[82] The derogation is justified on the basis that "there must be a close connecting factor between the dispute and the court with jurisdiction to resolve it"[83] and the place of performance of the obligation on which the claim is based is a sufficient link to permit the courts of that place to have jurisdiction. Both the concepts of "in matters relating to a contract" and "the obligation in question" are to be regarded as independent concepts and are not to be interpreted simply as referring to the national law of any Contracting State, as the aim of the Convention was to seek a uniform interpretation throughout the Contracting States so that each State has equal jurisdiction.[84]

9B.6(ii) Article 5(1) – Matters relating to a contract

9.41 Any claim for breach of contract,[85] e.g. breach of warranty in a marine insurance or reinsurance contract,[86] will clearly fall within this provision. This assumes there is a contractual relationship between the parties. In *Reunion Europeenne SA v. Spliethoff's Bevrachtingskantoor BV*,[87] the lead insurer brought proceedings exercising its subrogated rights for damage to pears. The pears were carried from Melbourne to Rotterdam on the vessel *Alblasgracht VOO2* under a bill of lading issued by Refrigerated Container Carriers Pty Ltd (RCC) and on their headed notepaper. RCC had its registered office in Sydney. The pears were actually carried by Spliethoff's Bevrachtingskantoor BV (the actual carrier), who were not mentioned on the bill of lading and whose registered office was in Amsterdam. The pears were discharged in Rotterdam and then carried by road under an international consignment note to Rungis in France, where the insured consignee had its registered office. The insurers sued RCC, the actual carrier, and the master of the carrying vessel, who resided in The Netherlands, in the French courts. The first issue before the European Court was

81. Article 2.

82. *Kalfelis v. Bankhaus Schroder, Munchmeyer, Hengst & Co.* (Case 189/87), [1988] ECR 5565.

83. The Report by Mr P Jenard, O.J. No. C 59/22, 5 March 1979.

84. See, e.g., *Martin Peters Bauunternehmung GmbH v. Zuid Nederlandse Aannemers Vereniging* (Case 34/82), [1983] ECR 987; *Arcado SPRL v. Haviland SA* (Case 9/87), [1988] ECR 1539; *Effer SpA v. Kantner* (Case 38/81), [1982] ECR 825; *Tesam Distribution Ltd v. Schuh Mode Team GmbH* [1990] ILPr 149 and particularly, *per* Stocker LJ, at p.165.; *Jakob Handte & Co. GmbH v. Societe Traitements Mecano-Chimiques des Surfaces (TMCS)* (Case C-26/91), [1993] ILPr 5; *Ocarina Marine Ltd v. Marcard Stein & Co.* [1994] 2 Lloyd's Rep. 524; *Gamlestaden plc v. Casa de Suecia SA* [1994] 1 Lloyd's Rep. 433; *Atlas Shipping Agency (UK) Ltd v. Suisse Atlantique Societe d'Armement Maritime SA (The Gulf Grain and El Amaan)* [1995] 2 Lloyd's Rep. 188 and *Boss Group Ltd v. Boss France SA* [1996] CLC 1419 where the Court of Appeal held that the English court had jurisdiction under Art. 5(1) where the appellant sought a negative declaration relying on the respondents' allegation that a contract existed.

85. E.g. *Fisher v. Unione Italiana de Riassicurazione SpA* [1998] CLC 682.

86. Section 33 of the Marine Insurance Act 1906. See B Soyer, *Warranties in Marine Insurance* (Cavendish Publishing Ltd, London 2001).

87. Case C-51/97, [1999] CLC 282. See A Briggs, "Claims against Sea Carriers and the Brussels Convention", [1999] LMCLQ 333.

whether the claim against the actual carrier was based on the contract of transport and whether the claim for that or any other reason fell within the scope of "matters relating to a contract" within the meaning of Art. 5(1). The European Court held that it did not. That phrase cannot be taken to refer to how the legal relationship in question before the national court is classified by the relevant national law, as Art. 5 must be interpreted independently. The bill of lading disclosed no contractual relationship freely entered into between the consignee and the actual carrier or the master of the vessel.

As the words must be given a European interpretation, this may result in there being a contractual relationship even if under the stricter English law requirements, e.g. on consideration, there would not be.[88] 9.42

The scope of the provision has resulted in much litigation and the English courts have resolved this by distinguishing between the situation where a contract is void, e.g. for illegality or *ultra vires*, and where the contract is voidable, e.g. for misrepresentation or nondisclosure.[89] Thus in *Kleinwort Benson Ltd v. Glasgow City Council*[90] a majority of the House of Lords[91] held that the bank's claim for restitution where a contract was void for *ultra vires* did not fall within Art. 5(1). However, in *Agnew v. Lansforsakringsbolagens AB*[92] a majority of the House of Lords upheld the decision of the Court of Appeal and Mance J at first instance that claims for alleged nondisclosure and misrepresentation fall within Art. 5(1). The distinction between void and voidable contracts may not appeal to a Continental lawyer who may consider matters relating to a void contract should also be matters relating to a contract within Art. 5(1).[93] 9.43

9B.6(iii) Article 5(1) – Obligation in question

The "obligation in question" is the obligation arising under the same contract and forming the basis of the proceedings commenced by the claimant.[94] It is not the obligation which characterises the contract except in relation to contracts of employment.[95] 9.44

---

88. Similar issues could arise under, e.g., the Rome Convention, which only applies to contractual disputes, and the EC Directive on Unfair Terms in Consumer Contracts (O.J. No. L95, 21.4.93, p.29).

89. See ss.17–20 of the Marine Insurance Act 1906 and the latest decision of the House of Lords on the duty of utmost good faith in *Manifest Shipping Co. Ltd v. Uni-Polaris Insurance Co. Ltd and La Reunion Europeenne (The Star Sea)* [2001] 1 Lloyd's Rep. 389 and *K/S Merc Scandia XXXXII v. Certain Lloyd's Underwriters* [2001] EWCA Civ. 1275; [2001] Lloyd's Rep. IR 802.

90. [1997] 4 All E.R. 641 (HL); [1996] 2 All E.R. 257 (CA); *Barclays Bank v. Glasgow City Council* [1994] 4 All E.R. 865 (Hirst J). See E Peel, "Jurisdiction over Restitutionary Claims" [1998] LMCLQ 145 and A Briggs, "Jurisdiction over Restitutionary Claims [1992] LMCLQ 283.

91. Lord Goff, Lord Clyde and Lord Hutton with Lord Mustill and Lord Nicholls dissenting.

92. [2000] 1 Lloyd's Rep. 317 (HL); [1997] 4 All E.R. 937 (Court of Appeal); [1996] 4 All E.R. 978 (Mance J). See HN Bennett, "Mapping the Doctrine of Utmost Good Faith in Insurance Contract Law", [1999] LMCLQ 165, 193–196.

93. *Cf.* Art.10(e) of the Rome Convention which does not have the force of law in England.

94. See *Ets. A. de Bloos SPRL v. Societe en Commandite par Actions Bouyer* (Case 14/76), [1976] ECR 1497; *Shenevai v. Kreischer* (Case 266/85), [1987] ECR 239; *The World Hitachi Zosen*, Unreported, 30 April 1997. In *Viskase Ltd v. Paul Kiefel GmbH* [1999] 3 All E.R. 362 the Court of Appeal held that an obligation to supply a machine which was reasonably fit for a known purpose, was performed at the time when the machine was supplied and therefore at the place of delivery. It was not a continuing obligation.

95. See *Ivenel v. Schwab* (Case 133/81), [1982] E.C.R. 1891 and the subsequent amendment of Art. 5(1).

9.45 In *Fisher v. Unione Italiana de Riassicurazione SpA*[96] Colman J held that where a party claimed a negative declaration that it was not bound to perform a contract on a basis which it formulated by reference to a particular obligation in the contract and that obligation was in dispute, that would be the obligation in question under Art. 5(1). Thus, where retrocessionaires sought a declaration that they were not liable under a retrocession to reinsurers because the reinsurers were in breach of a clause obliging them to retain part of the risk, the obligation in question was that to retain part of the risk and not that of the retrocessionaires to pay under the retrocession.

9.46 In *Domicrest Ltd v. Swiss Bank Corp.*,[97] Domicrest, an English company, sued a Swiss bank for payment under the bank's alleged guarantee of its Swiss customer's obligation to pay the price of goods sold to that Swiss customer. The proceedings were brought in England, in contract on the basis of Art. 5(1) alleging that the place of performance of the bank's alleged obligation to pay the price under the payment order was in England, and in tort on the basis of Art. 5(3).[98] Applying Swiss law, Rix J determined that there was a good arguable case that there was a primary obligation on the bank to pay on its own account and that obligation was to be performed in England.

9.47 In *RPS Prodotti Siderurgici SRL v. The Owners of the Sea Maas (The Sea Maas)*,[99] Rix J considered a claim for cargo damage under bills of lading. He stated:[100]

> "everything will depend on the nature of the bill of lading holder's claim. If the shipowner has misdelivered the goods at destination, then the place of performance of the obligation in question may well be at the port of discharge. If the ship is seaworthy, but the alleged failure of due diligence is some lack of care during the voyage, e.g. a failure to tighten the lashing as needed, or to maintain reefer temperatures at the appropriate level, then the place of performance of the obligation in question, viz the obligation to carry and care for the goods with due diligence, may well have occurred on the high seas, in which case there will be no special jurisdiction within Art. 5(1) and the matter must rest with Art. 2. If, however, the fundamental matter of complaint is that the shipowner never provided a seaworthy vessel, then the place of performance of the obligation would seem to me to be at the port of loading."

9.48 Where, as in *The Star Sea*,[101] the underwriters rely on the defence of unseaworthiness in a time policy under s.39(5) of the Marine Insurance Act 1906, the issue arises whether the obligation in question is the hull underwriters' obligation to pay under the hull policy or whether it is arguable that the insured has an obligation not to send the ship to sea in an unseaworthy condition. There is no obligation on the insured under a time policy in relation to seaworthiness. Unlike a voyage policy,[102] there is no implied warranty of unseaworthiness and the unseaworthiness defence is a question of causation, which provides a defence to underwriters. The same is likely to be the case in relation to the insured's failure to sue and labour[103] or wilful misconduct.[104]

9.49 Where there are a number of obligations in issue, the principal obligation will

96. [1998] CLC 682.
97. [1998] 3 All E.R. 578.
98. See para. 9.64.
99. [1999] CLC 1,336.
100. *Ibid.*, p.1,340.
101. [2001] 1 Lloyds' Rep. 389.
102. Section 39(1) of the Marine Insurance Act 1906.
103. Section 78 of the Marine Insurance Act 1906, but see, in particular, s.78(4).
104. Section 55(2) of the Marine Insurance Act 1906.

determine the court's jurisdiction.[105] In *Source Ltd v. TUV Rheinland Holding AG*[106] the plaintiffs alleged breach of contract and/or duty of care in failing to exercise reasonable skill and care in and about the preparation and supply of quality control inspection reports by German defendants in respect of goods purchased by the plaintiffs from suppliers in Taiwan and Hong Kong. The Court of Appeal held that the principal obligation for the purposes of Art. 5(1) was the inspection of the goods and not the delivery of the reports in England. Thus, the English court had no jurisdiction by virtue of Art. 5(1).

In *AIG Group (UK) Ltd v. The Ethniki*,[107] the Court of Appeal considered what was the principal obligation where the reinsurers sought a declaration of non-liability for alleged breach of the term requiring prompt notice and the provision of information, both of which were described as conditions precedent to its liability and both of which were for performance in London and in the alternative for a declaration of non-liability as to the reinsurer's duty to follow the settlements of the reassured and for damages for breach of the ascertainment of loss obligation. The Court of Appeal held that the principal obligation may be identified by considering what is the "fundamental obligation" and "the real ground of complaint".[108] The principal obligation is not the primary obligation in the sense of first in time.[109] The parties cannot select what they regard as the obligation in question by the wording of their claim. The test is an objective one and it is not within the claimant's power to make that choice but the courts. The Court of Appeal held that the principal obligation was the alleged breach of the claims control clause. That breach was the reinsurers' main point and the issues on the other obligations would only arise if the reinsurers were wrong on that point. The Court of Appeal were clear that the claims were not of equal weight, in which case there may be fragmentation of the claims in the sense that some may be heard in one State and others in another. 9.50

Fragmentation of the claims may arise where there is more than one obligation which forms the basis of the claim and none of them is the principal obligation. No difficulty will arise if all the obligations are to be performed in the same Contracting State. However, where they are to be performed in more that one Contracting State, will one Contracting State have jurisdiction to determine the claims in respect of all the obligations, or only the one to be performed in that State, or none of them? In *Leathertex Divisione Sintetici SpA v. Bodetex BVBA*,[110] the European Court had to consider Bodetex's claims for payment of arrears of commission and of compensation in lieu of notice from Leathertex. Bodetex had its registered office in Belgium and Leathertex its registered office in Italy. It was common ground between the parties that the obligation to pay commission and the obligation to pay compensation in lieu of notice were obligations of equal rank (a concession which the UK Government would not have made as it considered that of the two obligations, the obligation to pay 9.51

105. *Union Transport Group plc v. Continental Lines SA* [1992] 1 All E.R. 161; *Chailease Finance Corporation v. Credit Agricole Indosuez* [2000] 1 Lloyd's Rep. 348 (letter of credit).
106. [1997] 3 W.L.R. 365.
107. [2000] 1 Lloyd's Rep. 343 (CA); [1998] 4 All E.R. 301 (Colman J). See also *WH Martin Ltd v. Feldbinder Spezialfahrzeugwerke GmbH* [1998] I.L.Pr. 794.
108. *Union Transport Group plc v. Continental Lines SA* [1992] 1 All E.R. 161.
109. [2000] Lloyd's Insurance and Reinsurance Law Reports 343 at p.349.
110. Case C-420/97, [1999] CLC 1983.

commission was the principal one). The Belgian courts had held that the obligation to pay compensation in lieu of notice was to be performed in Belgium, whereas the obligation to pay commission was to be performed in Italy. The European Court held that the same court does not have jurisdiction to hear the whole of an action founded on two obligations of equal rank arising from the same contract when, according to the conflict rules of the State where that court is situated, one of those obligations is to be performed in that State and the other in another Contracting State. Thus, the Belgian court only had jurisdiction to determine the obligation to pay compensation in lieu of notice. Although it is unsatisfactory that the litigation should be fragmented, the solution is for the claimant to pursue all claims where the defendant is domiciled under Art. 2.

Thus, in relation to a case where underwriters sought a declaration of non-liability on the basis that the insured was in breach of the duty of utmost good faith and for breach of warranty, the obligation of disclosure would be in London if that is where underwriters are based, but the warranty might be in a different State. It is not clear whether the duty of utmost good faith, breach of which would entitle the insurer to avoid the contract, would be the principal obligation rather than the breach of warranty defence, which would only discharge the underwriters from liability as from the date of the breach. It seems that it would depend on the circumstances of each case.

9B.6(iv) Article 5(1) – Place of performance

9.52 In *Mainschiffahrts-Genossenschaft eG v. Les Gravieres Rhenanes*,[111] the European Court had to consider an oral agreement for the charter of an inland waterway vessel. If there is no valid jurisdiction clause, can an oral agreement that Germany is the place of performance, which was designed not to determine the place where the person liable is actually to perform its obligations (which was France), but solely to establish that the courts for a particular place have jurisdiction, be valid under Art. 5(1)? The European Court answered this question in the negative where the place of performance designated had no real connection with the reality of the contract. Otherwise it would be open to a party to circumvent Art. 17 and its specific requirements of form. Thus, an oral agreement on the place of performance which is designed solely to establish that the courts for a particular place have jurisdiction is not governed by Art. 5(1) but by Art. 17 and is valid only if it complies with the formalities of the latter Article.

However, where a letter of credit entitled the beneficiary to nominate the place of payment by the bank and, in consequence, the place of performance of the obligation in question, the Court of Appeal held that by nominating London as the place of payment the English courts had jurisdiction as the place of performance of the obligation in question – *Chailease Finance Corporation v. Credit Agricole Indosuez*.[112] This case was distinguished from *MSG* as there was no evidence that the choice of London by the beneficiary was made solely to establish that the English courts should have jurisdiction, whereas in *MSG* the agreement on the place of performance was

111. (Case C-106/95), [1997] All E.R. (EC) 385.
112. [2000] 1 Lloyd's Rep. 348.

designed not to determine the place where the person liable is actually to perform the obligations upon them.

In *GIE Groupe Concorde v. The Master of the Vessel Suhadiwarno Panjan*,[113] the European Court had to consider whether the expression "place of performance of the obligation in question" is to be construed as referring to the substantive law applicable under the conflict rules of the court seised or whether it must be given an independent interpretation. It held that the place of performance of the obligation is to be determined in accordance with the law governing the obligation in question according to the conflict rules of the court seised.

It is clear from *Kalfelis v. Bankhaus Schroder, Munchmeyer, Hengst & Co.*[114] that where a claimant has claims in both contract, tort and unjust enrichment simply because the court has jurisdiction to hear the contractual claim under Art. 5(1) does not give it jurisdiction to hear the claims in tort, unless it has jurisdiction on another ground[115] to hear that claim. 9.53

In *Source Ltd v. TUV Rheinland Holding*,[116] the Court of Appeal held that where the plaintiffs brought claims in both contract and tort, and could not bring their claim in contract in England under Art. 5(1),[117] they could not bring a claim in tort. See also the *obiter dicta* of Lord Gill in the decision of the Scottish Court of Session in *William Grant & Sons International Ltd v. Marie-Brizard & Roger International SA*[118] and the *obiter dicta* of Rix J in *Domicrest Ltd v. Swiss Bank Corp.*[119] 9.54

In *Domicrest Ltd v. Swiss Bank Corp.*,[120] Rix J held that Domicrest could sue in England under Art. 5(1) on its contractual claim against the bank for failure to honour a payment order. However, Domicrest also had claims in tort alleging negligent misrepresentation by the bank as to the effect of the payment order and the client's credit. Rix J held that those claims should be heard in Switzerland and in Italy where the goods had been released to the bank's customer in reliance on the bank's assurances that the bank would pay the purchase price. In view of this decision on the tort claim, and as Rix J had already held that Domicrest's contractual claims could be pursued in England, Domicrest could not pursue both its contract and tort claims in England. The solution for Domicrest, if it did not wish to pursue different aspects of the same dispute in different courts, would have been to pursue all its claims in Switzerland where the bank was domiciled. 9.55

9B.6(v) Article 6 – Multiple parties

Where there is more than one defendant, the courts for the place where any one of the defendants is domiciled are recognised as having jurisdiction.[121] 9.56

113. Case C-440/97, [1999] CLC 1976.
114. Case 189/97 [1988] ECR 5565.
115. For example, Art.5(3).
116. [1997] 3 W.L.R. 365.
117. See para. 9.49.
118. [1996] CLC 1826 at pp.1833–1834.
119. [1998] 3 All E.R. 578 at p.589.
120. [1998] 3 All E.R. 578.
121. Article 6(1). See *Kinnear v. Falconfilms NV* [1994] 3 All E.R. 42 and *Pearce v. Ove Arup Partnership Ltd* [1997] 2 W.L.R. 779; *Caltex Trading Pte Ltd v. Metro Trading International Inc.* [2000] 1 All E.R. (Comm.) 108; and *The Ikarian Reefer (No. 2)* [2000] 1 Lloyd's Rep. 129.

9.57 There must be a connection between the claims against each of the defendants. The European Court held in *Kalfelis v. Schroder*[122] that Art. 6(1) applies where the actions brought against the various defendants are related when the proceedings are instituted, that is to say where it is expedient to hear and determine them together in order to avoid the risk of irreconcilable judgments resulting from separate proceedings. It is for the national court to determine whether that is the case.

9.58 This connection is the same as that in Art. 22 of the Convention dealing with related proceedings.[123] In *Barclays Bank plc v. Glasgow City Council*[124] the Court of Appeal affirmed the decision of Hirst J at first instance and held that where there are a very large number of different plaintiffs suing different defendants in different unconsolidated actions Art. 6(1) does not apply even though the procedure of the many actions was regulated by a court order selecting lead cases in the hope that some issues common to the lead cases could be determined. See also *The Xing Su Hai.*[125]

9.59 In *Canada Trust Co. v. Stolzenberg (No. 2)*[126] the House of Lords held that the relevant time for determining domicile was at the time the writ was issued and not when it was served. In that case the writ had named all the defendants when issued and the question before the court was whether the time for determining the domicile of the person whose domicile determined the jurisdiction was either the time the writ was issued or the time that the writ was served on that person.

9.60 In *Petrotrade Inc. v. Smith*[127] the court had to consider a rather different issue, where the writ had after issue and service on the first defendant been amended to add two further defendants. Thomas J held that the relevant time under Art. 6(1) is the time at which the proceedings were originally issued and not the time at which it is sought to join the additional defendants or the time at which they are actually joined, whether by reissue of the writ or by service of that amended writ on them. In that case the plaintiff charterers alleged that their employee, Mr Smith, had been defrauding them of address commission. In September 1993, Mr Smith made a visit to London for a few days and was arrested. A condition of his bail was that he remain in England. The same month, the plaintiffs commenced proceedings in England against Mr Smith. In June 1997 the plaintiffs issued a summons to join the Alpina companies, Belgian companies, as second and third defendants to the proceedings begun in September 1993. The plaintiffs argued that joinder was permissible as Mr Smith was domiciled in England at the date of joinder in 1997, but also on the basis that he was so domiciled at the time the original proceedings were issued in 1993. If Mr Smith was domiciled in England at the time the proceedings were originally issued in 1993, then it was accepted by the Alpina companies that it was permissible to join them as additional defendants. Mr Smith's domicile was a question of fact. In determining this question of fact, the Court of Appeal had held in *Canada Trust Co. v. Stolzenberg (No. 2)*[128] that a plaintiff must show a good arguable case that a defendant is domiciled in the jurisdiction. Thomas J accepted that had it not been for the condition

122. Case 189/87 [1988] ECR 5565.
123. See paras. 9.108 to 9.110.
124. [1994] 4 All E.R. 865.
125. [1995] 2 Lloyd's Rep. 15,22.
126. [2001] CLC 118.
127. [1998] CLC 298.
128. [1998] CLC 23 upheld by the House of Lords [2001] CLC 118.

imposed as a term of his bail Mr Smith would have returned to Switzerland, where he had lived for some eight years, and the plaintiffs had not made out a good arguable case that Mr Smith was domiciled in England where his stay in England was involuntary.

In *Reunion Europeenne SA v. Spliethoff's Bevrachtingskantoor BV*,[129] the European Court had to consider whether a defendant domiciled in a Contracting State could be brought before the court of another Contracting State hearing an action against a co-defendant not domiciled in any Contracting State, on the ground that the dispute is indivisible, rather than merely displaying a connection. It held that it could not. Article 6(1) only applies if the proceedings are brought before the courts where one of the defendants is domiciled. None of the defendants was domiciled in France. The exception provided for in Art. 6(1), derogating from the principle that the courts of the State in which the defendant is domiciled are to have jurisdiction, must be construed in such a way that there is no possibility of the very existence of that principle being called into question, in particular by allowing a plaintiff to make a claim against a number of defendants with the sole purpose of ousting the jurisdiction of the courts of the State where one of those defendants is domiciled. The court went on to say that in *Kalfelis* the court had held that for Art. 6(1) to apply there must be a connection between the actions brought by the same plaintiff against different defendants of such a kind that it is expedient to determine the actions together in order to avoid the risk of irreconcilable judgments resulting from separate proceedings. As the court had also held in that case that a court which has jurisdiction over an action insofar as it is based on tort or delict does not have jurisdiction over that action insofar as it is not so based, it followed that two claims in one action for compensation, directed against different defendants and based in one instance on contractual liability and in the other on liability in tort or delict, cannot be regarded as connected. Although it is unfortunate if different aspects of the same dispute are determined by different courts, it is always open to the plaintiff to sue in the courts of the domicile of the defendant. If claims in contract and in tort are, however, not connected, the plaintiff would not be able to join all the defendants and would be obliged to have the litigation fragmented. In that event the court second seised would have a discretion to stay related actions if there were a risk of irreconcilable judgments. 9.61

In *National Justice Compania Naviera SA v. Prudential Assurance Co. Ltd (The Ikarian Reefer (No. 2))*[130] the Court of Appeal had held that the assured were not entitled to recover under their hull and machinery policy. The underwriters were only able to recover part of their costs. Therefore, the underwriters issued a summons in the action seeking an order pursuant to s.51 of the Supreme Court Act that Mr Comninos, the director of the assured company, and a non-party to the action, should be liable personally for its costs. The underwriters contended that under Art. 6(1) Mr Comninos was "one of a number of defendants" and could be sued "in the courts for the place where any one of them was domiciled", viz. in England where the underwriters were domiciled. At first instance,[131] Rix J held that Art. 6(1) did not apply to the case. The underwriters and Mr Comninos were not co-defendants and 9.62

129. Case C-51/97, [1999] C.L.C. 282. See para. 9.41 for the facts of this case.
130. [2000] 1 Lloyd's Rep. 129.
131. [1999] 2 Lloyd's Rep. 621.

this was not the sort of situation for which Art. 6 was designed. Mr Comninos appealed but not on this point.

9.63 In *The Ikarian Reefer*, the Court of Appeal also considered an argument that under Art. 6(2) the application against Mr Comninos could be regarded as "other third party proceedings" which could be brought "in the court seised of the original proceedings". Waller LJ giving the judgment of the Court of Appeal inclined to the view that a summons issued in an action relating to costs does not "sue" the non-party and therefore the EC Jurisdiction Convention did not apply. However, if that were wrong, Art. 6(2) would apply. The wording "any other third party proceedings" was entirely appropriate to cover a s.51 application for costs from a non-party. The procedure for bringing those proceedings was a matter for the English court.

9.64 At first instance in *The Ikarian Reefer*, Rix J held that Art. 6(3) did not assist the underwriters. Article 6(3) was really concerned with a counterclaim against the original claimant and the requirement that it arises "from the same contract or facts" was designed to ensure that it was not any kind of counterclaim which a defendant was permitted to bring against the claimant in the same jurisdiction but only one which was significantly connected with the original claim; even if Mr Comninos could be treated as a co-defendant to the counterclaim against the plaintiff owners for the purposes of Art. 6(1), that article would not in any event apply since the owners were not domiciled in England: and the owners' original claim could not be said to be pending once it had been determined by judgment.

9.65 Article 17 overrides Art. 6(2) – see *Hough v. P & O Containers (The Remuera Bay)*.[132]

9B.7 Other International Conventions – Article 57

9.66 Article 57 of the EC Jurisdiction Convention provides that the latter Convention shall not affect any conventions to which the Contracting States are or will be parties and which in relation to particular matters govern jurisdiction. The most widely applicable Convention in maritime claims is the International Convention relating to the Arrest of Seagoing Ships of 1952 (the "Arrest Convention"). Although marine insurers do not have a right to arrest for unpaid premiums,[133] nor do P & I Clubs have a right to arrest for unpaid calls, this area is considered in view of the fact that many marine insurers may exercise subrogated rights under maritime contracts.

The extent to which jurisdiction on the merits of a case is obtained by arrest, as opposed to merely providing security, was recognised by the Contracting States to the EC Jurisdiction and Lugano Conventions.[134] Although some of the Contracting States[135] had not ratified the Arrest Convention, they have nearly all done so.[136]

---

132. [1998] 2 All E.R. 978 discussed at para. 9.122.

133. *Gatoil International Inc. v. Arkwright-Boston Manufacturers Mutual Insurance Co. (The Sandrina)* [1985] 1 Lloyd's Rep. 181. Contrast the 1999 Arrest Convention, which is not yet in force.

134. See the foreword to F. Berlingieri, *Berlingieri on Arrest of Ships: A Commentary on the 1952 Arrest Convention* (1st edn., 1992; 2nd edn., 1996 and 3rd edn., 2000).

135. E.g. Austria, Denmark, Ireland, Finland, Norway and Sweden.

136. It came into force in Ireland on 17 October 1990; in Finland on 21 June 1996; in Norway on 1 May 1995 and in Sweden on 30 October 1993. For an analysis of the law of arrest in Norway, see T Falkanger, Part I Arrest of Ships under Norwegian Law, *Mar. Ius.* 258, 2000, p.3.

In accordance with Art. 57(2) of the EC Jurisdiction and Lugano Conventions, a court of a Contracting State which is a party to a convention which in relation to particular matters governs jurisdiction, may assume jurisdiction in accordance with that convention even where the defendant is domiciled in a Contracting State which is not a party to that convention. The court hearing the action shall, in any event, apply Art. 20 of the Lugano Convention: i.e., where a defendant domiciled in one Contracting State is sued in a court of another Contracting State and does not enter an appearance, the court shall declare of its own motion that it has no jurisdiction unless its jurisdiction is derived from the provisions of the Convention. The court shall stay its proceedings unless it is shown that the defendant has notice of the proceedings. Pursuant to Art. 27, a court of a Contracting State may refuse to recognise a judgment given by a court in another Contracting State "(1) if such recognition is contrary to public policy in the state in which recognition is sought; (2) where it was given in default of appearance".[137] *9.67*

There is a difference between the EC Jurisdiction and Lugano Conventions concerning the recognition and enforcement of judgments given by a Contracting State pursuant to jurisdiction derived from a convention on a particular matter where the defendant is domiciled in a Contracting State which is not a party to the latter Convention. Thus, Art. 57(2)(b) of the EC Jurisdiction Convention provides that judgments given in a Contracting State by a court in the exercise of jurisdiction provided for in a convention on a particular matter shall be recognised and enforced in the Contracting State where the defendant is domiciled even though that State is not a party to the convention on a particular matter. An example would be where a Contracting State has ratified the Hamburg Rules. Article 21 of the Hamburg Rules provides the cargo claimant with a choice which includes, but is not limited to, any jurisdiction chosen by the parties, and would thus override Art. 17 of the EC Jurisdiction Convention. In that event, the English courts would be obliged to recognise and enforce a judgment given in the Contracting State to the EC Jurisdiction Convention on the basis that the cargo was discharged there (pursuant to Art. 21 of the Hamburg Rules) and despite the fact that the bill of lading provided for exclusive jurisdiction of the English courts. *9.68*

By contrast, Art. 57(4) of the Lugano Convention provides that the State which is not a party to the convention on a particular matter would be able to refuse recognition or enforcement of the judgment, unless the judgment may otherwise be recognised or enforced under any rule of law in that State. Jenard and Moller emphasise that "this ground for refusal is an exception, given that paragraph 3 establishes the principle of recognition and enforcement. It does not therefore apply automatically, but is left to the discretion of the judge in the State addressed under the law of that State".[138] The Contracting State to the Lugano Convention could assume jurisdiction (e.g. on the basis that the cargo was discharged there pursuant to Art. 21 of the Hamburg Rules) against a defendant domiciled in a Lugano Contracting State even though the latter State had not ratified the Hamburg Rules (for example, at present, Denmark, Finland, Norway and Sweden apply the Hamburg Rules as *9.69*

137. See *Hendrikman v. Magenta Druck & Verlag GmbH* (Case C-78/95), [1997] 2 W.L.R. 349.
138. O.J. 1990/C189/82.

regards jurisdiction but as they have not ratified the Rules, Art. 57 may not be triggered). The courts of, e.g. Norway, would exercise their discretion in enforcement of the resulting judgment unless some other rule of the Lugano Convention gave the Contracting State giving judgment jurisdiction. The English courts would probably not object on policy grounds to such a judgment, which would be likely to impose a greater liability on the carrier than the Hague-Visby Rules,[139] except possibly where the Hamburg Rules have overridden the parties' own exclusive choice of jurisdiction.

9.70 To make sure that the English courts do have jurisdiction where the defendant is domiciled in a Contracting State, the claimant in Admiralty proceedings must actually arrest the ship,[140] unless it is a collision claim,[141] or should obtain an express agreement by the defendant to submit to the jurisdiction of the English court to avoid arrest at the same time as obtaining security. If neither Art. 18 nor Art. 17 is satisfied, cargo interests must arrest the vessel even though the shipowner has offered to provide security voluntarily and has tried through procedural means to prevent an arrest.[142] The court may not have jurisdiction in any event where there are multiple proceedings.[143]

9.71 There are a number of other conventions which deal with jurisdiction and could thus override the EC Jurisdiction Convention pursuant to Art. 57 if the requirements of the conventions have been satisfied. Examples include the Athens Convention on Carriage of Passengers and Luggage 1974, the Limitation of Liability Convention 1976 and the Hamburg Rules (Art. 21). What is not clear, however, is whether the Hague-Visby Rules would fall within the ambit of Art 57. Do they govern jurisdiction in relation to particular matters? On the face of it they do not. However, Art. III, r.8 of the Hague-Visby Rules provides that any attempt to lessen the carrier's liability is null and void and of no effect. In *The Morviken*,[144] the House of Lords held that a forum clause could have the effect of lessening the carrier's liability and, in that event, would be void. See also the decision of the European Court in *Trasporti Castelletti Spedizioni Internazionali SpA v. Hugo Trumpy SpA*.[145]

139. Which are given the force of law in the UK by s.1(2) of the Carriage of Goods by Sea Act 1971.

140. *The Deichland* [1989] 2 All E.R. 1066.

141. The International Convention for the Unification of Certain Rules Concerning Civil Jurisdiction in Matters of Collision 1952 (the "Collision Convention"), unlike the Arrest Convention, does not require an arrest to have been effected but allows an action for collision to be introduced "where arrest could have been effected and security has been furnished". See *The Po* [1991] 2 Lloyd's Rep. 206.

142. *The Prinsengracht* [1993] 1 Lloyd's Rep. 41 and *The Anna H* [1995] 1 Lloyd's Rep. 11; T. Hartley, "Jurisdiction Under Competing Conventions", [1995] LMCLQ 31. This problem was resolved under the transitional provisions of the Lugano Convention, as Art. 54A provided for there to be jurisdiction on the merits if the ship had been arrested or could have been so arrested there but bail or other security has been given. Those transitional provisions are no longer in force. Contrast the position under Art. 1(1)(b) of the Collision Convention – *The Po* [1991] 2 Lloyd's Rep. 206; Art. 5(7)(b) of the EC Jurisdiction Convention; and Art. 7 of the Arrest Convention 1999, which is not yet in force as at November 2001.

143. See *The Maciej Rataj* (Case C-406/92), [1995] 1 Lloyd's Rep. 302; *Maas Logistics (UK) Ltd v. CDR Trucking BV* [1999] 2 Lloyd's Rep. 179 and *Merzario Ltd v. Internationale Spedition Leitner Gesellschaft GmbH* [2001] 1 Lloyd's Rep. 490.

144. [1983] 1 A.C. 565.

145. Case C-159/97, [1999] I.L.Pr.492. See paras. 9.31 and 9.33.

9B.7(i) Articles 57 and 17

In *The Maciej Rataj*,[146] shipowners had commenced proceedings in Rotterdam for a declaration that they were not liable for alleged contamination of cargo. The shipowners sought a stay of English *in rem* proceedings brought by the cargo owners for damages for cargo contamination. The European Court considered the interrelationship between Arts 21, 22 and 57. The cargo owners argued that the English court had jurisdiction pursuant to the Arrest Convention and, as Art. 57 provides that the EC Jurisdiction Convention does not affect the jurisdiction under a "convention on a particular matter", Arts 21 and 22 of the EC Jurisdiction Convention had no application. That argument was rejected. If a specialised convention applies, then Art. 57 does not take the issue out of the EC Jurisdiction Convention completely but only insofar as the other specific convention covers the situation which has arisen.[147] Thus if the specialised convention does not contain any provisions as to *lis pendens* or related actions, and the Arrest Convention does not, then the EC Jurisdiction Convention, and more particularly Arts 21 and 22, determine which court should have jurisdiction to determine the disputes. Article 57 does not lead to a specialised convention and then, where that latter convention does not contain relevant provisions for the jurisdictional problem which has arisen, throw the issue back on the national law of the Contracting State, i.e. the common law. The Opinion of Advocate-General Tesauro is helpful. He describes Art. 57 not as a subordinating but as a coordinating provision, so that the provisions of the general convention fill any gaps in a convention on a particular matter. 9.72

This decision is in keeping with the spirit of the EC Jurisdiction Convention that the rules of that Convention shall apply unless there is a clear exception. Article 57 provides for an exception to the general rules, but it must be shown that the exception applies. Furthermore, the decision provides a clear pointer as to how the court would decide the interrelationship between Arts 17 and 57. In a case where there was a conflict between those two Articles, presumably one would have to ask whether the specialised convention makes provision for an agreement on jurisdiction and, if not, Art. 17 would apply. Article 2 of the 1952 Collision Convention specifically provides that the jurisdiction on the merits given by Art. 1 of that Convention shall not in any way prejudice the right of the parties to bring an action in respect of a collision before a court they have chosen by agreement, or to refer it to arbitration. Thus, where, for example, a collision occurred and the cargo owners subsequently entered into a jurisdiction agreement with the owners of the ship other than the carrying ship with whom they had previously had no contract, that agreement would be binding on them by virtue of Art. 17 if the EC Jurisdiction Convention applies.[148] Article 21 of the Hamburg Rules specifically provides that the claimant has a choice of fora in which to bring proceedings, including that of the jurisdiction agreement.[149] 9.73

Clarke J considered the position where the Arrest Convention applies and there is 9.74

146. (Case C-406/92), [1995] 1 Lloyd's Rep. 302. See A Briggs, "The Brussels Convention Tames the Arrest Convention" [1995] LMCLQ 161 and T Hartley, "Admiralty Actions under the Brussels Convention" (1995) 20 E.L. Rev. 409.
147. See Jenard and Moller C189/82 para. 83.
148. See Jackson p.129 and fn.23.
149. See also the 1999 Arrest Convention, which is not yet in force as at November 2001.

an exclusive jurisdiction agreement in a bill of lading in *The Bergen.*[150] The bill of lading expressly provided for jurisdiction in the place of business of the carrier, i.e. Germany. Clarke J held that there is a conflict between Art. 7 of the Arrest Convention and Art. 17 of the EC Jurisdiction Convention. Article 7 applies English domestic law, under which the court has jurisdiction but has a discretion whether to exercise it or to order the action to be stayed.[151] In contrast, under Art. 17 the court would be bound to hold that it had no jurisdiction. Therefore, the Arrest Convention prevailed. Clarke J did not think this decision inconsistent with the decision in *The Maciej Rataj.*[152] That was a case where two different courts had jurisdiction and the question was which court should exercise it and which decline to exercise its jurisdiction. The effect of Art. 17, where it applies, is to deprive the court of any jurisdiction at all. Thus, its effect is not that another court must decline to exercise a jurisdiction which it otherwise has, as is the case under Art. 21, but that that court must decline jurisdiction on the ground that it never had it. Therefore, Art. 17 did not apply at all to the case. Clarke J subsequently held that the English proceedings should be stayed in view of the German jurisdiction agreement.[153] The importance of this decision is that, although the final outcome may well be the same whether Art. 17 applies or English domestic law applies, the latter involves the court's discretion, whereas the former does not.[154]

9B.8 Multiple Proceedings – Articles 21 and 22

9.75 It is possible for the courts of two or more Contracting States to have jurisdiction in the same dispute. For example, the courts of the State where the defendant is domiciled may have jurisdiction under Art. 2 and the courts of the State where the obligation in dispute is to be performed may also have jurisdiction under Art. 5(1). In that event, section 8 of the EC Jurisdiction Convention provides a solution to seek to prevent multiple proceedings and thus avoid differing judgments being given in more than one jurisdiction, a situation which might lead to absurdity on enforcement of those judgments.

9.76 Article 21 of the EC Jurisdiction Convention provides that where proceedings involving the same cause of action and between the same parties are brought in the courts of different Contracting States, [155] any court other than the court first seised shall of its own motion stay its proceedings until such time as the jurisdiction of the court first seised is established. Once it has been established, any court other than the court first seised shall decline jurisdiction in favour of the latter court. Even if the requirements of Art. 21 are not satisfied, any court other than the court first seised

150. [1997] 1 Lloyd's Rep. 380.

151. The English court will exercise its discretion to grant a stay if there is a foreign jurisdiction agreement unless strong cause is shown why it should not do so – *The El Amria* [1981] 2 Lloyd's Rep. 119.

152. Case C-406/92, [1995] 1 Lloyd's Rep. 302.

153. [1997] 2 Lloyd's Rep. 710.

154. At common law, the English court has refused a stay particularly because there are multiple proceedings: see, e.g., *Citi-March Ltd v. Neptune Orient Lines Ltd* [1996] 2 All E.R. 545 and *The MC Pearl* [1997] 1 Lloyd's Rep. 566.

155. Where the States are not both Contracting States, see *forum non conveniens* at para. 9.101.

may stay its proceedings pursuant to Art. 22 where related actions are brought in the courts of different Contracting States. Actions are "related" where they are so closely connected that it is expedient to hear and determine them together to avoid the risk of irreconcilable judgments resulting from separate proceedings. Article 23 further provides that where actions come within the exclusive jurisdiction of several courts, any court other than the court first seised shall decline jurisdiction in favour of that court.[156] Under Arts 21 and 23 a stay is mandatory, whereas under Art. 22 it is discretionary.

The EC Jurisdiction Convention does not permit the court second seised to review the jurisdiction of the court first seised except in limited cases – *Overseas Union Insurance Ltd v. New Hampshire Insurance Co.*[157] 9.77

9B.8(i) Article 21 – Same cause of action

A number of different issues have arisen in relation to the interpretation of Art. 21. First, when do proceedings involve the same cause of action? In answer to that question the courts must look to the substance of the matter and not simply to the form.[158] 9.78

There may be situations where there is clearly the same cause of action because, for example, claimant A has brought the same claim against defendant B in the courts of two different Contracting States. A more likely scenario is where the parties have each commenced proceedings against each other in the courts of two different Contracting States, one, for example, alleging in one set of proceedings that the other is liable to it and the other alleging in the second set of proceedings that it is not liable. This was the situation in *The Maciej Rataj*.[159] The European Court held that the proceedings by the 9.79

---

156. This may occur, for example, under Art. 17 where the parties have chosen two alternative courts, as in *Gamlestaden*. However, see A Briggs and P Rees, *Civil Jurisdiction and Judgments* (LLP, London, 2nd edn., 1997), paragraphs 2.11.2.1.6 and 2.11.2.3 for the view that Art. 23 may not cover Art. 17 but only Art. 16.

157. Case C-351/89, [1991] E.C.R. I.-.3317. One exception is where the transitional provisions of the San Sebastian Convention apply: see *Von Horn v. Cinnamond*, Case C-163/95, [1997] All E.R. (EC) 913 distinguished in *Davy International Ltd v. Voest-Alpine Industrieanlagenbau GmbH* [1999] 1 All E.R. 103.

158. If in one set of proceedings a party seeks a declaration and in another the other party seeks damages for breach of contract, nevertheless the proceedings will involve the same cause of action if the subject-matter is the same: *The Maciej Rataj* [1992] 2 Lloyd's Rep. 552, following *Gubisch Maschinenfabrik KG v. Giulio Palumbo* (Case 144/86), [1987] ECR 4861; *Gamlestaden plc v. Casa de Suecia SA* [1994] 1 Lloyd's Rep. 433; *Grupo Torras SA v. Sheikh Fahad Mohammad Al Sabah* [1996] 1 Lloyd's Rep. 7 (CA); [1995] 1 Lloyd's Rep. 374; *Toepfer International GmbH v. Molino Boschi SRL* [1996] Lloyd's Rep. 510; *Mecklermedia Corporation v. DC Congress GmbH* [1997] 3 W.L.R. 479; *Sarrio SA v. Kuwait Investment Authority* [1997] 4 All E.R. 929 (HL); [1997] 1 Lloyd's Rep. 113 (CA); [1996] 1 Lloyd's Rep. 650; *Boss Group Ltd v. Boss France SA* [1996] 4 All E.R. 970; *Internationale Nederlanden Aviation Lease BV v. Civil Aviation Authority* [1997] CLC 43; *Maas Logistics (UK) Ltd v. CDR Trucking BV* [1999] 2 Lloyd's Rep. 179 and *Messier-Dowty Ltd v. Sabena SA* [2000] 1 Lloyd's Rep. 428. See also *Charman v. Woc* [1993] 1 Lloyd's Rep. 378, 385, reaching the same conclusion in the context of insurance contracts; L Collins, *Melanges Grossen* (1992) 385; L Collins, "Negative Declarations and the Brussels Convention" [1992] 108 LQR 545; A Bell, "The Negative Declaration in Transnational Litigation" [1995] 111 LQR 674. For a decision of the Scottish Court of Session, see *William Grant & Sons International Ltd v. Marie-Brizard & Roger International SA* [1996] CLC 1826.

159. (Case C-406/92), [1995] 1 Lloyd's Rep. 302; see A Briggs, "The Brussels Convention Tames the Arrest Convention", [1995] LMCLQ 161; T Hartley, "Admiralty Actions under the Brussels Convention", (1995) 20 E.L.Rev. 409.

shipowners for a declaration of non-liability had the same cause of action and the same object as the cargo interests' claim for damages for alleged cargo contamination. Thus, if an insurer seeks a declaration of non-liability in the English courts on the ground that the policy is voidable for misrepresentation, and the insured brings proceedings in Greece seeking judgment for an indemnity under the policy, there is the same cause of action.

9.80 Although the English courts were previously hostile to negative declarations of liability,[160] they appear to have overcome their antipathy to this remedy at least where the EC Jurisdiction Convention is concerned: see *Boss Group Ltd v. Boss France SA*[161] where the Court of Appeal accepted jurisdiction under Art. 5(1) for a declaration of non-liability. Although the plaintiff denied the existence of the contract it relied on the defendant's assertion that a contract existed. If Art. 5(1) applied it was the duty of the court to apply it. Jurisdiction under the EC Jurisdiction Convention is not a matter of discretion, nor does it depend on considerations of *forum non conveniens*. The English courts look very carefully at proceedings for negative declarations. That does not mean that caution in that regard could be used as a substantive ground for declining jurisdiction under the Convention, for that would derogate from the Convention. See also *Maas Logistics (UK) Ltd v. CDR Trucking BV*[162] and *Messier-Dowty Ltd v. Sabena SA.*[163]

9.81 One issue considered by the European Court in *The Maciej Rataj* was whether the *in personam* proceedings for a negative declaration in Rotterdam had the same object and were between the same parties as an action *in rem*, which under English law commences as an action against the *res*, i.e. the ship, and not the person who owns the ship. Once the writ *in rem* has been served and acknowledged, the action may continue both *in rem* and *in personam* or solely *in personam*. The European Court were not concerned to discuss the idiosyncrasies of English law on this latter distinction, as it held that the terms "same cause of action" and "between the same parties" have an independent meaning.[164] The two sets of proceedings did have the same cause of action and the same object. This decision does not cover the situation where the action is truly *in rem* and there is no question of the proceedings continuing either *in personam* or as a hybrid action both *in rem* and *in personam*, e.g. where the ship has been sold to a new owner and the claim, e.g. for a maritime lien, is so great that the new owner does not acknowledge service of the writ and takes no part in the proceedings, which continue only against the ship and ultimately any judgment is enforced against the proceeds of sale of the ship.[165]

9.82 More complicated situations may arise, however. A situation involving liability and limitation proceedings in different jurisdictions arose in *The Happy Fellow.*[166] The vessels *The Happy Fellow* and *Darfur* were in collision on the river Seine. The *Darfur*

160. See Sheen J in *The Maciej Rataj* [1991] 2 Lloyd's Rep. 458.

161. [1996] CLC 1419.

162. [1999] 2 Lloyd's Rep. 179.

163. [2000] 1 Lloyd's Rep. 428.

164. *Gubisch Maschinenfabrik v. Palumbo* (Case 144/86), [1987] ECR 4861.

165. *Cf.* the decision of the House of Lords in *Republic of India v. India Steamship Co. Ltd (The Indian Endurance) (No. 2)* [1997] 4 All E.R. 380.

166. [1998] 1 Lloyd's Rep. 13 (CA); [1997] 1 Lloyd's Rep. 130. See also *Dresser UK Ltd v. Falcongate Ltd.* [1991] 2 Lloyd's Rep. 557 and *The Volvox Hollandia* [1988] 2 Lloyd's Rep. 361.

was arrested at Le Havre. Seven claimants, including the owners of *The Happy Fellow*, commenced proceedings in Le Havre against the owners of the *Darfur*, which they were entitled to do, both because the collision occurred in France and because the vessel had been arrested there. After the collision the time charterers of the *Darfur*, Baco-Liner, agreed an exclusive English law and jurisdiction clause. They commenced proceedings in London claiming damages for breach of the charterparty. The owners of the *Darfur* accepted service of the writ and instituted limitation proceedings in the same court. They purported to constitute a limitation fund. Longmore J held at first instance that proceedings in France to establish liability were not the same cause of action as limitation proceedings in England. He stated:

"Once I have reached the conclusion that a shipowner's right to limit does not attach to or qualify the claimant's claim but operates to limit the extent to which an unqualified right can be enforced against the limitation fund, it must, to my mind, follow that the French proceedings do not 'involve' the same cause of action as the English proceedings. The English proceedings are at once narrower and wider than the French proceedings; narrower because the right to limit is merely procedural and does not affect the substantive rights of the French claimants and wider, because the English proceedings purport to invoke a right which is good against all possible claimants (viz. the world) whereas the French proceedings seek only to invoke rights between the parties to those proceedings. The proceedings do not, therefore, have the same 'object or cause', do not involve the same cause of action and art. 21 of the Convention has, therefore, no application."[167]

In the Court of Appeal Saville LJ, with whom Sir Stephen Brown P and Schiemann LJ agreed, stated:[168]

"I should perhaps make clear, however, that I should not be taken as having implicitly agreed with the conclusion reached by the Judge on art. 21. As a pure matter of English law, his analysis of the differences between a liability action and a limitation action cannot be faulted, but here we are dealing with a question of European law, and I would remain to be persuaded that the cause and object are not the same in the two proceedings under discussion."

It was not, however, necessary to determine that issue as Art. 22 did apply.

In *Glencore International AG v. Shell International Trading and Shipping Co. Ltd and Metro Oil Corporation*[169] Rix J commented *obiter* that he did not see why it should be held that the liability action and the limitation action involve the same cause of action for the purposes of Art. 21.[170]

In *Toepfer International GmbH v. Societe Cargill France*,[171] the Court of Appeal referred to the European Court the question whether English proceedings seeking a declaration that the commencement and continuation of proceedings before a French court constituted a breach of an arbitration agreement and an injunction restraining the defendant from continuing the proceedings in France constituted the same cause of action as a challenge to the jurisdiction of the French court, so as to require the English court to stay the English proceedings pursuant to Art. 21. The case settled before it reached the European Court. 9.83

The French version of Art. 21 refers to *"la même objet et la même cause"*. In 9.84

167. [1997] 1 Lloyd's Rep. 130, 135.
168. [1998] 1 Lloyd's Rep. 13, 18.
169. [1999] 2 Lloyd's Rep. 692.
170. *Ibid.*, p.697.
171. [1998] CLC 198. See also *The Ivan Zagubauski* [2002] 1 Lloyd's Rep. 106.

Haji-Ioannou v. Frangos[172] the Court of Appeal confirmed that the meaning to be applied to that wording is that actions have the same *cause* if they have the same facts and rule of law as their basis and actions have the same *objet* if they have the same end in view. Neuberger J held that Art. 21 did not apply to criminal proceedings in Greece and civil proceedings in England. Mr Haji-Ioannou brought proceedings in England against his former son-in-law, Mr Frangos, alleging that the defendant had been given sums of US$49m to purchase ships via one-ship companies whose shares would be held to the order of the plaintiff and that the defendant had purchased the ships but in breach of trust had retained the shares in the shipowning companies. The defendant alleged that the sums were gifts. The prosecuting authorities in Greece had investigated a complaint by the plaintiff that the defendant had appropriated shares and concluded that the plaintiff's payments to the defendants were a gift or loan and that no charges should be brought. The plaintiffs appealed to the Greek Supreme Court. The plaintiffs then brought proceedings in England claiming US$49m and claiming to be able to trace into the ships themselves. The plaintiffs contended that Art. 21 was of no use to the defendants as the Greek proceedings were criminal proceedings and were, therefore, not proceedings within the Article and not between the same parties. In order to have *locus standi* in the proceedings the plaintiffs had brought a claim for moral damages amounting to about £33. The Court of Appeal held that Neuberger J was right to hold that the action should not be stayed pursuant to Art. 21 but it did not agree with all his reasons. It held that the *cause* was the same despite the different procedures and standard of proof in Greece. However, the *objet* was not the same. The civil claim in Greece was a claim for the recovery of money. The end the proceedings had in view in England was not the simple recovery of money, but in large part the tracing of that money into the assets which were acquired with it, and the claim to a beneficial interest in those assets, based on allegations of breach of a duty of fidelity.

9.85 In *Glencore International AG v. Shell International Trading and Shipping Co. Ltd and Metro Oil Corporation*,[173] Shell commenced interpleader proceedings in London in respect of seven oil cargoes which they had bought from Metro. One of the competing claimants, Banque Trad Credit Lyonnais (France) SA ("Banque Trad"), had commenced proceedings against Shell in Paris and argued that the English proceedings against it should be stayed in view of Art. 21. It was conceded that the Paris court was first seised and that the parties were the same in the French proceedings and Shell's application for interpleader relief (as distinct from the substantive interpleader proceedings, to which Shell would not, if its request was granted, remain a party). Rix J held that the action in Paris did not have the same *cause* as Shell's application for interpleader relief because the claim by Banque Trad against Shell in England was a mere incident of the overall application, if it succeeded, and that application and Banque Trad's Paris action did not "have the same facts and rule of law as their basis". However, even if he was wrong on that, it did not involve the same *objet* as:

172. [1999] CLC 1075 (CA); [1998] CLC 61. For further discussion of the issues on *forum non conveniens* and Art. 22 see paras. 9.104 *et seq.*

173. [1999] 2 Lloyd's Rep. 692. See also *Cool Carriers AB v. HSBC Bank USA* [2001] 2 Lloyd's Rep. 22.

"In France the claim stands by itself, and the issue is Shell's liability. In England, however, Banque Trad's claim has to be seen in context, and thus viewed its *objet* is in my judgment the raising of the issue whether Shell's liability to Banque Trad, which is not in dispute, is subject to a better title possessed by another claimant."[174]

The Court of Appeal found that the cause of action in *Turner v. Grovit*[175] was the same where Mr Turner had brought proceedings in England before an industrial tribunal against Chequepoint, his former employer, and Harada, which had taken over Chequepoint, for dismissal, and CSA, another member company of the group containing Chequepoint and Harada, had brought proceedings in Spain against Mr Turner. Laws LJ stated: 9.86

"The two sets of proceedings before us are manifestly both concerned with the plaintiff's contract of employment, and in particular the circumstances of its termination. To that extent they are based on the same cause of action – that is, as the Court of Justice said in *Gubisch*, the same contractual relationship. Mr Supperstone submitted that allegations are made in the Spanish proceedings of alleged breaches of contract by the plaintiff which are quite discrete from the circumstances of the contract's termination. That is so; but every one of them could have been raised by way of counterclaim in the tribunal proceedings. In my judgment such a state of affairs demonstrates, consistently with *Gubisch*, a sufficient identity of subject-matter as well as cause of action."[176]

Laws LJ also referred to the need to regard the identity of cause of action pragmatically as well as the identity of parties. The unusual nature of this decision is commented on below. It is suggested that the decision is coloured by the fact that the Court of Appeal found that the Spanish proceedings were abusive.[177]

9B.8(ii) Article 21 – Between the same parties

As the Arrest Convention did not deal with *lis pendens* or related actions it was necessary for the European Court in *The Maciej Rataj* to consider a number of issues arising in relation to Arts. 21 and 22. One issue related to the identity of the parties to proceedings in The Netherlands and in England: does Art. 21 apply in the case of two sets of proceedings involving the same cause of action where some, but not all, of the parties are the same, at least one of the plaintiffs and one of the defendants to the proceedings first commenced also being among the plaintiffs and defendants in the second proceedings, or *vice versa*? Provided the other criteria of Art. 21 are satisfied the court second seised must decline jurisdiction only to the extent that the parties to the proceedings before it are also parties to the action previously commenced.[178] It does not prevent the proceedings from continuing between the other parties, although those proceedings may be related actions and fall within Art. 22. 9.87

In *Drouot Assurances SA v. Consolidated Metallurgical Industries*,[179] the European 9.88

174. *Ibid.*, p.699.

175. [1999] CLC 1281. Although the case went to the House of Lords [2001] UK HL 65 [2002] 1 WLR 107, this issue was not determined. See also paras. 9.100, 9.123 and 9.135 *et seq.*

176. [1999] CLC 1281, 1,299.

177. See also T Hartley, "Antisuit Injunctions and the Brussels Jurisdiction and Judgments Convention", [2000] ICLQ 166, 169, fn.17. See also paras. 9.100 and 9.135 *et seq.*

178. (Case C-406/92), [1995] 1 Lloyd's Rep. 302. See also *Blue Nile Shipping Co. Ltd v. Iguana Shipping and Finance Inc. (The Happy Fellow)* [1998] 1 Lloyd's Rep. 13 (CA); [1997] 1 Lloyd's Rep. 130 (Longmore J).

179. Case-351/96, [1998] All E.R. (EC) 483.

Court had to consider whether the owner of a vessel was the same party as the vessel's hull insurers. Drouot Assurances SA, the vessel's hull insurers, commenced proceedings in the French courts seeking a contribution to general average from the cargo owners and cargo insurers after they had paid for the refloating of a barge, the *Sequana*. The cargo owners and the cargo insurers raised an objection of *lis alibi pendens* as they had previously brought proceedings against the owner and the charterer of the vessel in Rotterdam claiming that they were not liable to contribute to general average. It was common ground that procedural rules in The Netherlands restricted the opportunity for an insurer to be party to proceedings in which the insured is involved. The European Court stated that there may be such a degree of identity between the interests of an insurer and those of its insured that a judgment delivered against one of them would have the force of *res judicata* as against the other, for example where an insurer, by virtue of its right of subrogation, brings or defends an action in the name of its insured without the latter being in a position to influence the proceedings. In such a situation, insurer and insured must be considered to be one and the same party for the purposes of the application of Art. 21. By contrast, where the interests of the insurer and its assured diverge, Art. 21 does not apply. In *Drouot* the cargo owners and their insurers made clear that they sought to have the owner of the vessel declared exclusively liable for the foundering of the vessel as it was unseaworthy. Drouot, as the insurer of the vessel, took the view that it could not be liable for the fault of its insured. In the French action, Drouot acted not in its capacity as the representative of its insured but in its capacity as a direct participant in the refloating. It was for the national court to determine whether the interests of the insurer of the vessel could be considered to be identical to and indissoluble from those of its insured. If the national court so found, Art. 21 could not apply.

9.89 The Court of Appeal applied *Drouot* in the extraordinary decision of *Turner v. Grovit*[180] where it held that there was identity of parties although the parties were legally distinct. In the latter case, Mr Turner brought proceedings before an industrial tribunal in England against his former employer, Chequepoint UK Ltd, and Harada, which had taken over Chequepoint. Towards the end of his employment Mr Turner had worked from the offices of the Spanish company in the group, CSA. The tribunal held that Mr Turner had been unfairly and wrongfully dismissed. Shortly thereafter CSA brought proceedings against Mr Turner in Spain based on an alleged contract between Mr Turner and CSA. Laws LJ, with whom Jonathan Parker J and Stuart-Smith LJ agreed, acknowledged that Harada, the English respondent, and CSA, the Spanish claimant, were distinct legal entities. Nevertheless, in a case where the court found that the Spanish proceedings were abusive, Laws LJ stated:[181]

"However for the purposes of art. 21, once it is clear (as I would hold it is) that there is an identity of cause of action and subject-matter, I do not consider that [counsel] can be heard to say that there is no identity of parties. Here the argument overlaps with that relating to abuse: the deployment of CSA, a Spanish company, as claimant in Madrid is nothing but a device to confer putative jurisdiction on the Spanish court. That is not only in the circumstances of the

180. [1999] CLC 1281. The House of Lords has referred a question of interpretation on anti-suit injunctions to the European Court [2001] UKHL 65 [2002] 1 WLR 107. See further para. 9.97 in relation to same cause of action and paras. 9.123 and 9.135 in relation to anti-suit injunctions.

181. *Ibid.*, p.1299.

case abusive upon ordinary principles of our domestic law. In addition, for this court to treat it as reality rather than the sham and pretence which it plainly is, and accordingly to deny what is otherwise the clearly established jurisdiction of the tribunal under art. 21, would in my judgment tend to undermine what Lord Goff of Chieveley has called (*Airbus Industrie GIE v. Patel* [1998] CLC 702 at p.707G; [1999] 1 A.C. 119 at p.132B):

'the primary purpose of the convention [is] to ensure that there shall be no clash between the jurisdictions of member states of the community'."

Furthermore, the European Court decision in *Drouot* was cited as authority for the proposition that the issue of identity of parties is to be regarded pragmatically. It is suggested that this is an unusual decision which is limited to its facts and, in particular, the court's finding that the Spanish proceedings were abusive. Usually the court might determine that although Art. 21 is not satisfied, Art. 22 is.

9B.8(iii) *Forum non conveniens*

The English courts have had to consider the situation whether the doctrine of *forum non conveniens* has any application where the English courts have jurisdiction under the EC Jurisdiction or Lugano Conventions. 9.90

The first scenario is where the defendant is domiciled in a Contracting State. In *Re Harrods (Buenos Aires) Ltd (No. 2)*,[182] the plaintiff minority shareholder brought proceedings in England against the majority shareholder and the company. Both the minority and majority shareholders were domiciled in Switzerland, which was not then a Contracting State. The company was domiciled in England. The majority shareholder applied for a stay on the grounds that Argentina was the appropriate forum as the company exclusively carried on its business there. The Court of Appeal held that it had a discretionary jurisdiction under the EC Jurisdiction Convention to stay or dismiss proceedings properly served on a defendant domiciled in England on the ground that the case would be more appropriately heard elsewhere in circumstances where the conflict of jurisdiction was between the English courts and the courts of a non-Convention country (Argentina), as the EC Jurisdiction Convention was intended to regulate relations only as between Convention countries. The House of Lords in that case referred the issue to the European Court, but the case was settled. In *The Nile Rhapsody*,[183] the Court of Appeal declined to refer the question whether an English court still retains the power to stay proceedings in a case where there was an exclusive Egyptian jurisdiction clause or on *forum conveniens* grounds to the European Court.[184] 9.91

The Court of Appeal has applied *Re Harrods* in *Eli Lilly and Co. v. Novo Nordisk A/S*,[185] a case concerning a Danish domiciliary, and in *Ace Insurance SA-NV v. Zurich Insurance Co.*[186] In the latter case, London reinsurers commenced proceedings against Swiss insurers, Zurich Insurance Co., in London claiming a declaration that 9.92

182. [1992] 4 All E.R. 334. Applied in *The Po*.
183. [1994] 1 Lloyd's Rep. 382.
184. *Ibid., per* Neill LJ at pp.391–392. See also the Opinion of the Advocate General C Darmon in *Brenner v. Dean Witter Reynolds* (Case C-318/93), [1995] All E.R. (EC) 278.
185. [2000] ILPr 73.
186. [2001] 1 Lloyd's Rep. 618 CA; [2000] 2 All E.R. (Comm) 449 Longmore J.

they were not liable under the reinsurance contract on the ground that there had been breaches of a warranty and claims co-operation clause. The Swiss insurers and their assignees applied for a stay of the English proceedings on the ground that Texas was the appropriate forum as there was a Texan service of suit provision. The reinsurers argued that as the Swiss insurers had submitted to the jurisdiction of the English court, the court had no jurisdiction to stay the action because the terms of the EC Jurisdiction and Lugano Conventions prohibited any reliance on the doctrine of *forum non conveniens.* It was sought to distinguish *Re Harrods* on the ground that the Swiss insurer was not domiciled in England but in another Contracting State. The case involved not just one Contracting State, but two, as proceedings had been instituted in the UK and the insurer was domiciled in Switzerland, whereas in *Re Harrods* the company alone was domiciled in a Contracting State and no other Contracting State was involved. This was not accepted as a valid distinction as it would be odd if a stay were available to a UK defendant but not to a defendant domiciled in any other Convention State. It would be even odder if an agreement to submit to the jurisdiction of a non-Convention State had to be treated as ineffective in any convention country. The Court of Appeal, therefore, dismissed the appeal against the stay of proceedings in favour of Texas.

9.93 One may compare the decisions in *Sarrio SA v. Kuwait Investment Authority* and *The Xin Yang and An Kang Jiang* and *Haji-Ioannou v. Frangos* as to the application of Arts. 21 to 23 of the EC Jurisdiction Convention and the English court's discretion on *forum non conveniens* grounds where the defendant is not domiciled in a Contracting State, but the competing jurisdictions are those of Contracting States.

9.94 *Sarrio SA v. Kuwait Investment Authority*[187] concerned a defendant incorporated in Kuwait, i.e. a non-Contracting State. The Spanish claimants commenced proceedings in Spain for payment of money owed and then commenced proceedings in England claiming damages in tort for negligent misstatement. Mance J held that, in the case of defendants not domiciled in a Contracting State, jurisdiction depended on the national rules and the English court, therefore, had a discretion as to which court was the most appropriate forum, save that an English court could not insist on exercising jurisdiction on the grounds that it was the appropriate forum in circumstances where under Arts. 21 to 23 it would be obligatory or appropriate for it as the court second seised to decline or stay the exercise of its jurisdiction where the court first seised is that of a Contracting State. Although the Court of Appeal held that Art. 21 did not apply, they approved this part of the judgment.[188] The issue was not considered when the case went before the House of Lords.[189]

9.95 In *The Xin Yang and An Kang Jiang*[190] Clarke J agreed with Mance J in *Sarrio.* He did not have the benefit of the Court of Appeal judgment in *Sarrio.* In *The Xin Yang* the defendant was not domiciled in a Contracting State. The English courts were first seised in respect of claims arising out of a collision in Holland. The defendant had subsequently brought limitation proceedings in Rotterdam. The issue was whether the English court had a discretion to stay the English proceedings where it was the

187. [1996] 1 Lloyd's Rep. 650.
188. [1997] 1 Lloyd's Rep. 113.
189. [1997] 4 All E.R. 929. The House of Lords only considered the scope of Art. 22 – para. 9.110.
190. [1996] 2 Lloyd's Rep. 217.

court first seised and the other court was that of a Contracting State or whether it was obliged to exercise jurisdiction pursuant to Art. 21 of the EC Jurisdiction Convention. Clarke J held that the English court was entitled to decline jurisdiction on the ground of *forum non conveniens* whether the alternative forum is within a Contracting State or not, as in *Re Harrods (Buenos Aires)*. As England was not the appropriate forum for the trial of the collision action and Rotterdam was clearly and distinctly more appropriate, the English proceedings were stayed. If the Rotterdam court were to take a different view of the meaning of Art. 21 and consider that it must decline jurisdiction as the jurisdiction of the English court was established, the English court could lift the stay.

In *Haji-Ioannou*, the Court of Appeal held that Mr Frangos enjoyed a special business domicile in Greece and, therefore, must be sued there under Art. 2 of the EC Jurisdiction Convention. If that was wrong, it considered whether, if proceedings are brought in England against a defendant not domiciled in another Contracting State,[191] the English court may on appropriate facts stay the proceedings or decline jurisdiction in favour of a clearly more appropriate forum in another Contracting State. It held that it is in principle open to the court to stay or dismiss proceedings even where it has jurisdiction by virtue of Art. 4. The English court would not entertain any jurisdiction in the proceedings provided that the Greek courts would accept jurisdiction. If necessary the English court would dismiss the action.[192] The Court of Appeal declined to refer the issues argued under Art. 4 to the European Court as they had found that Mr Frangos was domiciled in a Contracting State and it was not therefore necessary to have a decision on Art. 4 to give judgment. The Court further held that neither Arts. 21 nor 22 applied[193] and, as the natural forum was Greece and it was not unjust to deprive the plaintiffs of the advantage of the tracing remedies which they sought in the English proceedings, those proceedings should be stayed. 9.96

9B.8(iv) Article 22 – Related actions

A further issue considered in *The Maciej Rataj* concerned the scope of Art. 22 of the EC Jurisdiction Convention. Did that Article apply where one group of cargo owners sought damages from shipowners for loss caused to part of a bulk cargo and the owners of another part of the bulk cargo brought an action against the same shipowners for damages under separate but identical contracts? Although separate proceedings would involve the risk of conflicting decisions, they would not necessarily involve the risk of giving rise to mutually exclusive legal consequences. The European Court gave the expression "related actions" an independent and broad interpretation and held that the English proceedings were related, as the 9.97

191. Mr Frangos was domiciled in Monaco. He had been personally served with the English proceedings during his temporary presence in London for a shopping trip.
192. [1999] CLC 1075, 1089.
193. Discussed at paras. 9.95 and 9.110.

objective of Art. 22 is to avoid conflicting decisions within the Community even where the separate enforcement of each of them is not precluded by Art. 27(3).[194]

9.98 In *The Happy Fellow*[195] it was argued that a collision claim and a claim to limit in respect of that collision were inevitably related. In *Dresser v. Falcongate* it had been conceded that English proceedings by cargo claimants to establish liability and Dutch limitation proceedings were related. Longmore J also considered the comment in Dicey and Morris[196] and the *obiter dicta* of Kerr LJ in *The Volvox Hollandia*. Nevertheless, he stated:

"In spite of these authorities it does not seem to me necessarily to follow that any action in which it is alleged that a shipowner is liable must inevitably be related to any action in which a shipowner is seeking to limit his liability. If, for example, it is clear that the Court trying the liability action does not consider itself seised of the issue of limitation and the main issue in the liability action is, for example, whether a duty of care is owed by the defendant to the plaintiff, it might well be that the actions would not be related actions for the purpose of art. 22."[197]

However, on the facts of the case he held that the French proceedings and the English limitation proceedings were related for two main reasons. First, at the time of the first instance hearing the owners of the other vessel involved, the *Darfur*, had not admitted liability.[198] Thus, the issues of the failure of the *Darfur's* steering gear, the reasons for the failure and the owners' fault and the degree of such fault would be raised in the French proceedings. Very similar issues would arise in the limitation action, which would consider whether the claimant's loss resulted from the personal act or omission of the shipowners "committed recklessly and with knowledge that such loss would result" within Art. 4 of the 1976 Limitation Convention. Second, the French court would regard itself as seised of limitation as well as liability.

As Longmore J concluded that Art. 22 did apply, he, therefore, went on to consider whether to exercise his discretion to stay the limitation action against Sloman Neptun, the one party against whom a stay had been requested, and he granted that stay. Longmore J considered the fact that there was a contingent application by Baco-Liner, the time charterers of the *Darfur*, to stay the English limitation action if the action was stayed against Sloman Neptun. However, he did not think that the outcome of that application should affect the outcome of this application for three reasons: Baco-Liners's claims were relatively small; the jurisdiction agreement between the shipowners and Baco-Liner had been entered into after the collision; and

194. (Case C-406/92), [1995] 1 Lloyd's Rep. 3020. See T Hartley, "Admiralty Actions under the Brussels Convention" (1995) 20 E.L.Rev. 409, 411 for an excellent illustration of this point. See also the *obiter dicta* of Lord Gill in the decision of the Scottish Court of Session in *William Grant & Sons International Ltd v. Marie-Brizard & Roger International SA* [1996] CLC 1826, 1832–1833 and *Mecklermedia Corporation v. DC Congress GmbH* [1997] 3 W.L.R. 479.

195. [1998] 1 Lloyd's Rep. 13 (CA); [1997] 1 Lloyd's Rep. 130 (Longmore J).

196. 12th edn., pp.368–369.

197. [1997] 1 Lloyds' Rep. 130, 135–136.

198. Such an admission had been made by the time the appeal was heard. The Court of Appeal held that this should not be taken into account. Lord Saville LJ, with whom both the other appeal judges agreed, stated: "It seems to me that as a general rule, and save perhaps in the most exceptional circumstances, the question whether actions are related must be judged on the basis of the material put before the Court first concerned with this question. To allow otherwise would be to encourage appeals and thus to add to delay and expense in deciding which Court in the Community should deal with the substantive rights and obligations of the parties. This can hardly be in the interests of the proper administration of justice within the Community". ([1998] 1 Lloyd's Rep. 13, 17.)

the French court regarded itself as seised of limitation.[199] He considered but rejected the submission that the French courts do not give sufficient weight to the subjective requirement that the shipowner should personally have had knowledge that the loss would be likely to result.[200]

The Court of Appeal held that a limitation action in England and liability proceedings in France were related proceedings within Art. 22 and that the judge at first instance had clearly exercised his discretion correctly to stay the English proceedings in favour of the French courts. After the Court of Appeal decision in *The Herceg Novi*,[201] the English courts, if second seised, could not take into account the fact that the courts of the Contracting State first seised would apply a convention other than the 1976 Limitation Convention.

There is now clear authority that limitation and liability proceedings can be related proceedings under the EC Jurisdiction Convention. The court second seised will have a discretion to stay its proceedings unless other factors, such as a jurisdiction clause, prevail over Art. 22. The Court of Appeal has left open in *The Happy Fellow* whether Art. 21 can apply to liability and limitation issues, in which case the court second seised would be obliged to stay, subject to any jurisdiction agreement.

In *Sarrio SA v. Kuwait Investment Authority*[202] Lord Saville, with whom all the other Law Lords agreed, adopted a broad commonsense approach to the question whether the actions in question are related. He rejected the over-technical analysis of the Court of Appeal,[203] distinguishing as it did between primary and other issues. 9.99

In *Haji-Ioannou v. Frangos*,[204] Neuberger J held that a criminal investigation in Greece against the defendant was not a related action to English civil proceedings by Mr Haji-Ioannou claiming that the defendant had acted in breach of trust by retaining shares in one ship companies when the ships had been bought with funds advanced to the defendant to purchase the ships and to hold the shares in the one-ship companies on trust for the plaintiff. Article 22 did not apply as the substantive relief sought in the English proceedings of an equitable and tracing nature could not be pursued in Greece. The tracing remedies sought against the shipowning companies could not be sought in the Greek criminal proceedings as the shipowning companies were not parties to those proceedings. The Greek proceedings and the English proceedings could not be heard and determined together. The Greek criminal proceedings were not pending at first instance as the Greek court at first instance had held that no charges should be brought against the defendant. The court, therefore, went on to consider whether the English proceedings should be stayed on the ground of *forum non conveniens*.[205] Again, the Court of Appeal agreed with the conclusion of Neuberger J that Art. 22 did not apply, although they did not agree with all his reasoning. It referred to the decision of the House of Lords in *Sarrio*, the benefit of which Neuberger J did not have. However, it agreed that the fact that this claim in 9.100

199. *Cf. Caspian v. Bouygues* [1998] 2 Lloyd's Rep. 461.
200. *Cf. Deaville v. Aeroflot* [1997] 2 Lloyd's Rep. 67, discussed at para. 9.137.
201. [1998] 4 All E.R. 238.
202. [1997] 4 All E.R. 929. J Harris, "Related Actions and the Brussels Convention" [1998] LMCLQ 145.
203. [1997] 1 Lloyd's Rep. 217.
204. [1999] CLC 1075 (CA); [1998] CLC 61.
205. Discussed at para. 9.104.

Greece was "tacked on" as an appendage to criminal proceedings made the application of Art. 22 wholly inappropriate.

9B.8(v) Articles 21 and 22 – When is a court first seised of proceedings?

9.101 It is a question for national law to determine when a court is seised.[206] In an ordinary and straightforward case, the English court does not become seised of an action for the purposes of Art. 22 on the issue of the writ but only when the writ is served on the defendant.[207] In *The Freccia del Nord*,[208] Sheen J held that the court is seised of *in rem* proceedings when the writ is served on the ship. In *The Duke of Yare*, the Court of Appeal thought there might be exceptions to the general rule that the court is seised when the writ is served where there has been an exercise of jurisdiction by the court preceding service, e.g. to order a Mareva injunction[209] or an Anton Piller order[210] or the arrest of a ship. The Court of Appeal considered *The Duke of Yare* in *Neste Chemicals SA v. DK Line SA (The Sargasso)*.[211] There were no genuine exceptions to the rule that the date of service of the writ is the time when the court becomes seised of the proceedings. Thus, where the English court grants leave to issue a concurrent writ *in personam* for service out of the jurisdiction and/or leave to serve that writ (in this case) in Japan that limited exercise of jurisdiction does not seise the court. All three judges in the Court of Appeal doubted, *obiter*, whether the examples given in *The Duke of Yare* were exceptions to the rule that the court was seised when the writ was served because there was an actual exercise of jurisdiction, e.g. in the case of a Mareva injunction or an Anton Piller order. The Court of Appeal thought that the exercise of jurisdiction in these two cases and (*per* Peter Gibson LJ)[212] any order under Ord. 29 of the Rules of the Supreme Court made in the exercise of the court's jurisdiction to give interlocutory relief in order to preserve property in advance of service of proceedings, was only a limited provisional jurisdiction.[213]

It will, therefore, now be very important to serve the claim form to safeguard jurisdiction. A party who might traditionally have been thought of as the defendant must now be proactive and would be well advised to commence proceedings in the Contracting State most advantageous to it, where any defendant is domiciled, if necessary for a declaration of non-liability.[214] They must be careful to join in all the defendants and serve at very least one of them.[215] If a party seeks to rely on the Arrest

206. *Zelger v. Salinitri (No. 2)* [1984] ECR 2397.
207. *Dresser UK Ltd v. Falcongate Freight Management Ltd (The Duke of Yare)* [1992] 2 All E.R. 450.
208. [1989] 1 Lloyd's Rep. 388.
209. Now a freezing order under the Civil Procedure Rules.
210. Now a search order.
211. [1994] 2 Lloyd's Rep. 6.
212. *Ibid.*, at p.12.
213. See also, A Briggs, "Get your writs out?" [1992] LMCLQ 150, pp.153 and 154 approved by Gibson LJ.
214. See paras. 9.89 *et seq.*
215. In *Grupo Torras SA v. Sheikh Fahad Mohammad Al Sabah* [1996] 1 Lloyd's Rep. 7 (CA); [1995] 1 Lloyd's Rep. 374 Mance J held that the court should take the date of service on any defendant in a case of multiple defendants. This reasoning may not be in accordance with the party by party approach of the subsequent decision of the European Court in *The Maciej Rataj* and must therefore be treated with caution. Although the case went to the Court of Appeal the latter court did not need to decide the issue whether it is necessary to serve each defendant before the court is seised of proceedings against that defendant or whether it is necessary only to serve proceedings on any one of multiple defendants.

Convention to found jurisdiction, the timing of the service of the claim form *in rem* is probably a matter wholly outside the claimants' control, as it depends on the ship coming to a port within the chosen jurisdiction and being served there. A shipowner might even avoid trading to a particular jurisdiction until the court of its own choice was seised of proceedings.

The Civil Procedure Rules provide for service by fax in certain circumstances.[216] In *Molins plc v. GDSpA*[217] the Court of Appeal held that service of Italian proceedings in England by fax was not good service within the Civil Procedure Rules. Sending a letter which includes a fax number in the letterhead does not amount to a clear indication by the sender that the fax number could be used to send documents to them within Practice Direction 6 to r.6.2(i)(e) CPR. Furthermore, transmission by fax did not amount to service under the 1930 Convention Regarding Legal Proceedings in Civil and Commercial Matters. Even though the invalidity of the service could have been cured in Italy, the Italian Court was not seised until this was achieved. 9.102

The definition of the date on which a court is seised is given in Article 30 of the EC Regulation. 9.103

9B.9 Multiple proceedings and Article 17

There is clear English authority that Art. 17 is not subject to Arts. 21 or 22.[218] In *Denby v. Hellenic*,[219] the assured commenced proceedings in Greece. The underwriters brought proceedings in England for a declaration that they were entitled to avoid the insurance as they alleged misrepresentation and that they were not liable. Rix J held that Art. 17 took precedence over Arts. 21 and 22 in all situations including whether there was exclusive jurisdiction under Art. 17. In *Continental Bank NA v. Aeakos Compania Naviera SA*,[220] the Court of Appeal were confident that if Art. 17 applies, it takes precedence over Arts 21 and 22, and therefore refused to refer this issue to the European Court of Justice. The judge at first instance described Art. 17 as conclusive and Steyn LJ stated that the Article has mandatory effect. If the parties have provided for a jurisdiction agreement which satisfies Art. 17, the clause confers jurisdiction on the courts of the Contracting State so chosen, but also it deprives the courts of any other Contracting State of jurisdiction. 9.104

Banque Cantonale Vaudoise v. Waterlily Maritime Inc.[221] also concerned a loan agreement containing an exclusive English jurisdiction clause concluded for the benefit of one party only, i.e. the bank. The bank retained the right to bring proceedings in any other court with jurisdiction and had not only commenced 9.105

216. Part 6.2(i).
217. [2000] 2 Lloyd's Rep. 234.
218. This issue had been left open in the European Court of Justice decision in *Overseas Union Insurance Ltd. v. New Hampshire Co.* [1992] 1 Lloyd's Rep. 204. See also *Rank Film Distributors Ltd v. Lanterna Editrice SRL* (unreported); *Kloeckner & Co. AG v. Gatoil Overseas Inc.* [1990] 1 Lloyd's Rep. 177, 193–196; *IP Metal Ltd v. Ruote OZ SpA* [1993] 2 Lloyd's Rep. 60 (Art. 22); *IP Metal Ltd v. Ruote OZ SpA (No. 2)* [1994] 2 Lloyd's Rep. 560; *The Filiatra Legacy* [1994] 1 Lloyd's Rep. 513; and *Banque Cantonale Vaudoise v. Waterlily Maritime Inc.* [1997] 2 Lloyd's Rep. 347.
219. [1994] 1 Lloyd's Rep. 320.
220. [1994] 1 Lloyds' Rep. 505.
221. [1997] 2 Lloyd's Rep. 347.

proceedings in England to recover sums which the bank alleged were due to it under the mortgage, but also issued a petition before the court in Piraeus for the protection of its rights under the mortgage. Although the English court was first seised, the borrowers then lodged a defence to the petition and commenced proceedings against the bank in Piraeus. In these circumstances how could the risk of conflicting judgments be avoided? The bank sought an order that until final judgment in the action or further order the borrowers must not contend in the Greek courts or elsewhere that any judgment or order in the English proceedings was otherwise than conclusive and binding upon the borrowers, or take any further steps in the Greek proceedings commenced by the borrowers. Cresswell J held that Art. 17 applied to the jurisdiction agreement. There is a distinction between applications to the courts of a Contracting State for provisional/protective measures pending the determination of any dispute between the parties in the English courts and proceedings in other jurisdictions with a view to enforcing a bank's security documents. As the evidence on Greek law and procedure did not address the issue whether the bank had taken steps beyond those necessary to protect its security and retain priority; as there were complex disputes between the parties about Greek law and procedure and the Greek court would not hear the defendants' proceedings before 30 September 1997, Cresswell J ordered the speedy trial of the proceedings and fixed a trial date of 8 April 1997. He further ordered an interlocutory injunction in the terms of the first part of the order requested by the bank, as this clearly reflected the terms of the jurisdiction agreement between the parties. However, he refused the anti-suit injunction requested by the bank on the ground that all disputes arising out of the loan agreement would be determined in the English court. If necessary the bank's claims for more extensive injunctive relief could be considered at trial.

9.106 The decision in *Continental Bank* has been the subject of adverse criticism.[222] The approach of the English courts to the interrelationship between Arts 17 and 21 is not accepted throughout all the Contracting States. Thus, it may be argued that the court first seised should determine of its own motion whether there is a jurisdiction clause within Art. 17 and, if there is, stay its proceedings in favour of the court second seised. The difficulty with this divergence of views is that it may lead to conflicting judgments – a result which the Convention seeks to avoid because of the absurdities that may lead to on enforcement. Thus, the court first seised may decide that it is the court which should determine whether there is a jurisdiction clause which satisfies Art. 17 and conclude that there is not, whereas the court second seised may decide that it should determine the Art. 17 issue as the court of that State has been chosen by the parties to determine their dispute, and they may come to a different conclusion from the court first seised and decide that there *is* a jurisdiction clause which satisfies Art. 17. If the two States then reach different decisions on the merits there are two conflicting judgments, and this raises issues whether those judgments should be recognised and enforced under the EC Jurisdiction Convention.

9.107 Where the English court has granted an anti-suit injunction this may not solve the problem, as it may not be possible to serve the defendant with notice of the order (for

222. A Bell, "Anti-Suit Injunctions and the Brussels Convention", [1994] LQR at pp.204, 208; A Briggs, "Anti-European Teeth For Choice of Court Clauses", [1994] LMCLQ 158, 159, 163 and E Peel [1998] LMCLQ at pp.203, 204.

example, such an injunction is regarded as unconstitutional in Germany).[223] If the injunction is served on the defendant, but, in breach of the injunction, the defendant pursued the proceedings in the court first seised, it might not be possible to enforce the resulting judgment in England as it was obtained in breach of the English court order, but it could be enforced elsewhere. Furthermore, if the anti-suit injunction cannot be served, the defendant might seek to enforce any judgment from the court first seised in England.

Advocate-General Philippe Leger in his Opinion in *Castelletti*[224] outlines further difficulties with the English approach. If the court first seised cannot determine the validity of the jurisdiction clause but must refer that issue to the court chosen, and the court chosen determines that the clause is not valid, the court chosen would then have to send the case back to the court first seised for that court to determine whether it does indeed have jurisdiction. This would be contrary to the aims of the EC Jurisdiction Convention, one of which is to determine speedily which court has jurisdiction. 9.108

It is, therefore, critical that only one court determines the initial question as to whether the jurisdiction clause satisfies Art. 17. Which court is it: the court first seised or the court chosen? It is unfortunate that the Court of Appeal in *Continental Bank v. Aeakos*[225] did not take the opportunity to refer this issue to the European Court to have it resolved. As a consequence, in the subsequent renegotiations of the EC Jurisdiction Convention and the Lugano Convention this was one of the issues under discussion, but has not been resolved in the EC Regulation. The issue was also not referred to the European Court in *Castelletti*. There is, therefore, still no clear determination of the matter by the European Court. However, the decision in *Castelletti* certainly confirms the view of some of the Contracting States that the court first seised should answer the Art. 17 issue. The Opinion of the Advocate-General, Philippe Leger, is in favour of that solution. 9.109

It was unsuccessfully sought to distinguish *Continental Bank* in *The Kribi*.[226] *Castelletti* was not considered.

The issue of whether the English courts would stay limitation proceedings under either Arts 21 or 22 where there is an exclusive English jurisdiction agreement between two of the parties has not come directly before the English courts. In *The Happy Fellow* two of the parties had agreed English jurisdiction and the shipowners, therefore, commenced limitation proceedings in England. However, the other party to that agreement was not before the court in that case.[227] Both Longmore J at first instance and the Court of Appeal applied Art. 22 and stayed the English limitation proceedings in favour of the French courts. The decision might well have been 9.110

223. See *Phillip Alexander Securities & Futures Ltd. v. Bamberger* [1996] CLC 1757 discussed at para. 9.128 under anti-suit injunctions.

224. Discussed with reference to Art. 17 at paras. 9.25 to 9.31, 9.36 and 9.38.

225. [1994] 1 Lloyd's Rep. 505.

226. [2001] 1 Lloyd's Rep. 76.

227. See the *obiter* comments of Longmore J in *The Happy Fellow* [1997] 1 Lloyd's Rep. 130, 136, 137. The judge commented on the application by one party not privy to the jurisdiction agreement to stay the English proceedings where there was a jurisdiction clause within Art. 17. The case went to the Court of Appeal [1998] 1 Lloyd's Rep. 13 and the decision on Art. 22 was upheld, but no comment was made on Art. 17.

different had the party to the jurisdiction agreement applied for a stay of the English limitation proceedings. The position at common law has been considered in *Bouygues v. Caspian.*[228] In that case, the Court of Appeal stayed proceedings on liability in England in favour of the South African courts but refused to stay English limitation actions commenced by Caspian and Ultisol where there was an exclusive English jurisdiction clause in the towage agreement between Ultisol and Bouygues. This had the result that the liability and limitation actions would be determined by different courts.

9.111 In view of the English interpretation of the supremacy of Art. 17 over Art. 21, it is not surprising that the English court, in considering a jurisdiction agreement in the context of third party proceedings, has once again underlined the supremacy of a jurisdiction agreement and held that Art. 17 overrides Art. 6(2). In *Hough v. P & O Containers Ltd (Blohm + Voss Holding AG and Others, third parties) (The Remuera Bay)*[229] the plaintiff electrician, Hough, sued P & O Containers Ltd ("P & O"), the defendants, in England where they are domiciled. He alleged injuries while working on P & O's ship, the *Remuera Bay*, while it was in drydock in Hamburg undergoing repairs by companies within the Blohm + Voss group ("Blohm + Voss"). P & O commenced third party proceedings against Blohm + Voss in England seeking an indemnity in respect of any liability P & O incurred to the defendant. P & O relied on Art. 6(2). The repair contract between P & O and the repair yard gave jurisdiction to the courts of Hamburg. Rix J held that Art. 17 has priority over Art. 6(2). Although Rix J referred to the "divisive tendency of Art. 17 to create multiplicity of proceedings", nevertheless, the parties are entitled to enforce their contractual bargain and the risk of multiple proceedings is part of the price they pay.

9B.10 Anti-suit injunction

9.112 The English court will grant an anti-suit injunction to restrain a party from pursuing foreign proceedings where it is in the interests of justice – *Societe Nationale Industrielle Aerospatiale v. Lee Kui Jak*[230] and *Airbus Industrie GIE v. Patel.*[231] It has been argued that it is inappropriate for the English courts to grant an anti-suit injunction where the EC Jurisdiction Convention applies as the proper approach would be for the court of any other Contracting State in which proceedings had been commenced to apply the Convention and determine whether it had jurisdiction.[232] Different considerations may apply where the defendant is domiciled in a non-Contracting State and the English court applies its national law.[233] Most of the other Contracting States to the EC Jurisdiction Convention do not have the equivalent of

228. [1998] 2 Lloyd's Rep. 461.
229. [1998] 2 All E.R. 978.
230. [1987] A.C. 871.
231. [1998] 1 Lloyd's Rep. 631.
232. Most notably by A Briggs, in "Anti-suit Injunctions in a Complex World", Chapter 12 of *Lex Mercatoria Essays on International Commercial law in Honour of Francis Reynolds*, LLP 2000.
233. See Article 4 of the EC Jurisdiction Convention. For a comparison of the common law principles and the position under the EC Jurisdiction Convention, see A Briggs, *ibid.* The Chapter also contains a useful summary of the approach to anti-suit injunctions by two other common law countries: Australia and Canada.

the English anti-suit injunction.[234] This does not necessarily militate against the anti-suit injunction as the EC Jurisdiction Convention does not seek to harmonise the procedural rules of the various Contracting States. Despite a warning by the English Court of Appeal in *Phillip Alexander Securities & Futures Ltd v. Bamberger*[235] to reconsider the use of anti-suit injunctions in future, the decision has been sidelined and distinguished in *The Kribi*.[236] The Court of Appeal has gone even further in the case of *Turner v. Grovit*[237] and granted an anti-suit injunction in a case where there was no jurisdiction agreement and has asserted an inherent jurisdiction to do so in any case where there is an abuse of process. Thus, far from treating the anti-suit injunction with caution, the English courts have recently shown no reluctance to grant this remedy. The House of Lords has now referred a narrow issue concerning the anti-suit injunction to the European Court of Justice,[238] whose attitude to our somewhat eccentric English procedure may not be sympathetic.[239]

9B.10(i) Anti-suit injunction to enforce jurisdiction agreement

The issue arises most acutely where one party alleges that there is an English jurisdiction clause either court or arbitration. Most English marine insurance contracts provide for English High Court jurisdiction in their standard forms and many reinsurance contracts incorporate those jurisdiction clauses. Most P & I Club rules provide for London arbitration. Thus, enforcement of the jurisdiction agreement is a matter of great significance for the London insurance market. The great irony is that in view of the English approach to the interrelationship between Arts 17 and 21 and the fact that the English court will not wait until the court first seised has determined whether it has jurisdiction, but considers that the English court as the court chosen is the court with jurisdiction to the exclusion of all others, creates the need for an anti-suit injunction. 9.113

The problem may arise in the insurance context as follows. Goods are damaged at sea and the cargo insurers pay out the cargo interests and then exercise their subrogated rights to sue on the bill of lading. The cargo insurers are domiciled in France and they commence proceedings against not only the carriers under the bill of lading, but also commence a direct action against the P & I Club of the shipowner, the carrier under the bill of lading. The P & I Club object to the French proceedings on the ground that their Rules provide for London arbitration. Furthermore, the Rules contain a pay to be paid provision and therefore under English law the cargo insurers would have no right to recover against the P & I Club in the light of *The Fanti and The* 9.114

234. See JJ Fawcett ed., *Declining Jurisdiction in Private International Law*, Reports to the XIV Congress of the International Academy of Comparative law, Athens 1994 for a comparative study and R Asariotis, "Antisuit injunctions for Breach of a Choice of Forum Agreement: A Critical Review of the English Approach", *Yearbook of European Law* 1999/2000, OUP edn. Tridimas.

235. [1996] CLC 1757, 1789.

236. [2001] 1 Lloyd's Rep. 76.

237. [1999] CLC 1281.

238. This was done in *Toepfer International GmbH v. Societe Cargill France* [1998] CLC 198 but the case settled. See *Turner v. Grovit* [2001] UK HL 65; [2002] 1 WLR 107. See paras. 9.135 *et seq.*

239. *Cf.* the treatment of the English proceedings *in rem* in *The Maciej Rataj* where in his Opinion the Advocate General can almost be heard to be laughing at the concept of suing the *res*. His analysis was adopted by the European Court. See para. 9.92.

Padre Island.[240] These were the facts of *The Charterers Mutual Assurance Association Limited v. British & Foreign and TMM Transcap*[241] and *The Charterers Mutual Assurance Association Ltd v. ATICAM Ltd*.[242] In both cases, anti-suit injunctions were granted to restrain the cargo insurers from pursuing the French proceedings. As a general rule it is in the interests of justice to uphold an exclusive jurisdiction or arbitration clause unless there is good reason not to. Thus, in *Continental Bank v. Aeakos*[243] the Court of Appeal refused to lift an injunction restraining the borrowers from taking further steps in Greek proceedings. The injunction was to restrain a clear breach of contract and was the only effective remedy for breach of the jurisdiction agreement.

9.115 In *Aggeliki Charis Compania Maritime S.A. v. Paguan SpA (The Angelic Grace)*[244] the Court of Appeal dismissed an appeal against an injunction restraining charterers from pursuing proceedings in Italy as there was a London arbitration clause in the charterparty which was held to be wide enough to cover a collision. Millett LJ said:

> "In my judgment, where an injunction is sought to restrain a party from proceeding in a foreign Court in breach of an arbitration agreement governed by English law, the English Court need feel no diffidence in granting the injunction, provided that it is sought promptly and before the foreign proceedings are too far advanced. I see no difference in principle between an injunction to restrain proceedings in breach of an arbitration clause and one to restrain proceedings in breach of an exclusive jurisdiction clause as in *Continental Bank NA v. Aeakos Compania Naviera SA*, [1994] 1 Lloyd's Rep. 505; [1994] 1 W.L.R. 588. The justification for the grant of the injunction in either case is that without it the plaintiff will be deprived of its contractual rights in a situation in which damages are manifestly an inadequate remedy. The jurisdiction is, of course, discretionary and is not exercised as a matter of course, but good reason needs to be shown why it should not be exercised in any given case."[245]

9.116 The injunction should be sought before the foreign proceedings are too far advanced. An injunction was refused in *Toepfer International GmbH v. Molino Boschi SRL*[246] where the court proceedings in Italy had been pursued for some seven years before Toepfer applied to the English court for an injunction to restrain Molino Boschi from pursuing proceedings in Italy in breach of a London arbitration agreement. In *Donohue v. Armco Inc.*[247] it was argued that the claimant's delay of seven months in applying to the court for an anti-suit injunction was a factor to be taken into account when exercising the court's discretion. It was admitted that the defendant had not suffered any prejudice as a result of the delay and Aikens J at first

240. [1990] 2 Lloyd's Rep. 191.

241. Unreported, 15 September 1997, His Honour Judge Diamond QC.

242. Unreported, 4 April 1998, Clarke J.

243. [1994] 1 Lloyd's Rep. 505. See also *Svendborg v. Wansa* [1997] 2 Lloyd's Rep. 183; *Schiffahrtsgesellschaft Detlev von Appen GmbH v. Voest Alpine Intertrading GmbH* [1997] 2 Lloyd's Rep. 279; *Toepfer International GmbH v. Societe Cargill France* [1998] 1 Lloyd's Rep. 379; *The Charterers Mutual Assurance Association Ltd v. British & Foreign and TMM Transcap* (unreported, 15 September 1997, HH Judge Diamond QC); *The Charterers Mutual Assurance Association Ltd v. ATICAM Ltd, (unreported,* 4 August 1998, Clarke J); *Akai Pty Ltd v. People's Insurance Ltd* [1998] 1 Lloyd's Rep. 90; *Shell International Petroleum Co. Ltd v. Coral Oil Co.* [1999] 1 Lloyd's Rep. 72; *Bankers Trust Co. v. PT Jakarta International* [1999] 1 Lloyd's Rep. 910; *National Westminster Bank plc v Utrecht-America Finance Co.* [2001] CLC 442; and *Navigation Maritime Bulgare v. Rustal Trading Ltd (The Ivan Zagubanski* [2002] 1 Lloyd's Rep. 106.

244. [1995] 1 Lloyd's Rep. 87.

245. [1995] 1 Lloyd's Rep. 87,96.

246. [1996] 1 Lloyd's Rep. 510, 515–518.

247. [2000] 1 Lloyd's Rep. 579 CA; [2000] 1 All E.R. (Comm.) 425 Aikens J.

instance and a majority of the Court of Appeal[248] therefore held that the issue of delay was irrelevant.[249]

It had been thought that the English courts might be more reluctant to grant this form of injunctive relief in the future, as in *Phillip Alexander Securities & Futures Ltd v. Bamberger*[250] Leggatt LJ commented that the English courts may need to reconsider whether they grant anti suit-injunctions. Although the English courts have granted such relief on the basis that they are making an order restraining the defendant from breaching their contract and do not seek to interfere in the proceedings of the foreign court, nevertheless the courts of some Contracting States have taken a dim view of such an order and have seen it as an interference with their sovereignty. The *Bamberger* case involved several defendants and the plaintiffs alleged they were bound by arbitration clauses. Initially, an interim injunction was granted by the English court restraining some of the defendants from pursuing German court proceedings in breach of the English arbitration clause. The German court refused to serve the injunctions on the defendants in Germany on the ground that it was unconstitutional and an interference with their sovereignty. The issue then arose as to whether the English court would recognise or enforce any German judgment which was obtained by a defendant who had notice of the injunction. The Court of Appeal held that none of the arbitration clauses was enforceable and therefore the question of recognition of German judgments did not arise. The Court of Appeal agreed with Waller J at first instance that in the case of the defendants who did have notice of the injunctions before obtaining judgment in their German actions, the German judgments should by force of Art. 27(1) of the EC Jurisdiction Convention not be recognised. Where a judgment had been obtained abroad in breach of an injunction it would be contrary to public policy to enforce the judgment. Unless the apparent breaches of those parties could be excused, their German judgments would not be enforceable. The Court of Appeal agreed with the judge's exercise of his discretion not to grant declarations that the German judgments were not to be recognised and/or enforced. 9.117

Cresswell J neatly avoided granting an anti-suit injunction in *Banque Cantonale Vaudoise v. Waterlily Maritime Inc.*[251] by fixing an early trial date in the English proceedings. Thus, judgment on the substantive issues would be given in England before the Greek court considered them. 9.118

It was unsuccessfully sought to distinguish *Continental Bank* in *The Kribi*.[252] It was also argued that an anti-suit injunction is an infringement of a person's rights under Article 6 of the European Convention on Human Rights because it is intended to prevent the person from going before an "independent and impartial tribunal established by law". The Antwerp court had granted access and was in the process of deciding whether it had jurisdiction under the EC Jurisdiction Convention. Therefore, it would be unlawful for the English court to grant an anti-suit injunction which had the effect of depriving the receiver from pursuing those rights. Second, under s.3 of the Human Rights Act 1998, the court must read and give effect to s.37 of 9.119

248. Stuart-Smith and Sedley LJJ at pp.592 and 600 respectively, Brooke LJ dissenting at p.598.
249. *Ibid.*, p.447.
250. [1996] CLC 1757, 1789.
251. [1997] 2 Lloyd's Rep. 347.
252. [2001] 1 Lloyd's Rep. 76.

the Supreme Court Act 1981 in a manner that is compatible with the Convention rights. Aikens J rejected both arguments. Article 6 of the European Convention on Human Rights does not give an unfettered choice of tribunal. Otherwise, the whole of the EC Jurisdiction Convention would be incompatible with a person's Art. 6 rights if the tribunal designated by the EC Jurisdiction Convention were contrary to the litigant's choice of court. The Convention does not deal with *where* the litigant is to pursue proceedings. Therefore, the second argument also failed and there was no restriction on the courts' power to grant an anti-suit injunction under s.37 of the Supreme Court Act 1981. Furthermore, Aikens J distinguished *Bamberger*.

9.120 In *Van Uden Maritime BV v. Kommanditgesellschaft in Firma Deco-Line*[253] the European Court considered the effect of Art. 24 of the EC Jurisdiction Convention, which provides that:

> "Application may be made to the courts of a Contracting State for such provisional, including protective, measures as may be available under the law of that State, even if, under this Convention, the courts of another Contracting State have jurisdiction as to the substance of the matter."

In that case Van Uden and Deco-Line had concluded a slot/space charter agreement which contained an arbitration clause. Van Uden commenced arbitration proceedings in the Netherlands. Van Uden also sought interim relief from the Rotterdam courts and obtained a provisionally enforceable judgment that Deco-Line pay Van Uden the sum of DM377,625.35. The European Court held that where the Contracting State has jurisdiction by virtue of Art. 5(1) of the EC Jurisdiction Convention the courts of that State also have jurisdiction to order provisional or protective measures under Art. 24 without that jurisdiction being subject to any further conditions. However, where, as in this case, the parties had referred their disputes to arbitration and thus excluded the jurisdiction of the courts of any State, the question arose as to whether interim proceedings fell outside the scope of the Convention. Although arbitration is excluded from the scope of the Convention (Art. 1(4)), the court considered that provisional measures are not in principle ancillary to arbitration proceedings but are ordered in parallel to such proceedings and are intended as measures of support. They concern, not arbitration as such, but the protection of a wide variety of rights. Therefore where, as here, the subject-matter of an application for provisional measures relates to a question falling within the scope *ratione materiae* of the Convention, the Convention is applicable and Art. 24 may confer jurisdiction on the court hearing the application even where proceedings have already been, or may be, commenced on the substance of the case and even where those proceedings are to be conducted before arbitrators. The granting of provisional or protective measures on the basis of Art. 24 of the Convention is conditional on, *inter alia*, the existence of a real connecting link between the subject-matter of the measures sought and the territorial jurisdiction of the Contracting State of the court before which those measures are sought. Interim payment of a contractual consideration does not constitute a provisional measure within Art. 24 unless, first, repayment to the defendant of the sum awarded is guaranteed if the plaintiff is

253. (Case C-391/95), [1999] All E.R. (EC) 258.

unsuccessful as regards the substance of his claim and, second, the measure sought relates only to specific assets of the defendant located or to be located within the confines of the territorial jurisdiction of the court to which application is made.

9B.10(ii) Anti-suit injunction – multiple parties and jurisdiction agreement

Aeakos and *The Angelic Grace* considered a relatively straightforward position where there were two sets of proceedings in two different jurisdictions between the same parties in respect of the same contract. Recently, the courts have had to consider more complex situations involving multiple parties with claims under various different agreements. The courts have had to consider what will constitute good reason not to grant an anti-suit injunction even where there is an exclusive jurisdiction clause. The recent case law involves non-convention cases. In *Bouygues Offshore SA v. Caspian Shipping Co.*,[254] the Court of Appeal discharged an anti-suit injunction granted by Clarke J to restrain proceedings in South Africa in breach of an exclusive English jurisdiction clause where both the English and South African courts had jurisdiction to determine claims between several different parties arising both under different contracts and in tort against the South African port authority, Portnet. Only one contract contained an exclusive English jurisdiction clause. As South Africa was clearly the natural forum for the resolution of all the disputes, the English court granted a stay of the English liability proceedings in favour of South Africa but it gave effect to the English jurisdiction clause by refusing a stay of the English limitation proceedings. Evans and Mummery LJJ and Sir John Knox all agreed that, when deciding to enforce an exclusive jurisdiction clause by means of an injunction, the court should take into account the effects of such an injunction on third parties who are not parties to or entitled to enforce the contract containing the jurisdiction clause. The injunction was discharged. Sir John Knox gave three reasons for so doing: first, that South Africa was the natural forum for the resolution of the factual disputes regarding liability (although Evans LJ stated that this was of subsidiary importance when one party claims to enforce an exclusive jurisdiction clause); second, that this was the only way to minimise, if not altogether avoid, the risk of inconsistent decisions in different jurisdictions; and lastly, the argument that Bouygues should be held to its contractual bargain with Ultisol, although a strong one, was counterbalanced by the fact that Portnet was not subject to any such contractual obligation. Although the main reason for granting the injunction was to protect Ultisol's contractual right to the English limitation regime which it had successfully established before Rix J, this was not compelling in view of the contractual right to sue in South Africa for breach of the exclusive jurisdiction agreement together with the undertaking offered by Bouygues that Bouygues would only enforce any judgment against Ultisol against the limitation fund constituted by Ultisol in England. 9.121

The decision in *Bouygues* is unusual as the English court discharged an anti-suit injunction even where there was an exclusive English jurisdiction agreement. The Court of Appeal felt that it could achieve the same result for Ultisol by granting the limitation decree in England as Bouygues had undertaken not to enforce its claims against Ultisol other than against the limitation fund in England. One wonders

254. [1998] 2 Lloyd's Rep. 461.

whether, if no such undertaking had been given, the decision would still have been the same and Bouygues left to their remedy of damages in South Africa for breach of the jurisdiction agreement if the South African court did not recognise the English limitation decree.

9.122 Although in *Credit Suisse First Boston (Europe) Ltd v. MLC (Bermuda) Ltd*[255] Rix J referred to the need for caution illustrated by *Phillip Alexander v. Bamberger*, he granted an anti-suit injunction to restrain New York proceedings in breach of an exclusive English jurisdiction clause. He rejected an argument that there was good cause not to grant an anti-suit injunction to restrain New York proceedings between two parties even though it was likely that proceedings would continue in New York in respect of claims under other related agreements which did not contain an exclusive English jurisdiction clause and between other parties not bound by the exclusive jurisdiction clause. By contrast, in *Credit Suisse First Boston (Europe) Ltd v. Seagate Trading Co. Ltd*,[256] Rix J found good reason not to grant an injunction to enforce a clause which he held to be an exclusive English jurisdiction clause where the jurisdiction clause was impeached on the grounds of fraud, mistake and *non est factum* and it was alleged that the English proceedings were in breach of a Standstill agreement governed by Californian law (although who the parties to that agreement were was in dispute and being considered by the Californian court). This case also concerned a sale of Russian bonds which had been agreed over the telephone. It was alleged by the purchasers that the written confirmation sent subsequently, which contained the English jurisdiction clause, differed materially from the terms agreed on the telephone. The purchasers argued that there was mutual mistake as to the confirmed terms so that the contract was void. Alternatively, the confirmed terms had been procured by fraudulent misrepresentation so the contract was voidable and had been avoided. As it was assumed that there was a valid challenge to the terms of the contract, including the jurisdiction clause, that clause could not be relied on in pursuit of the injunction.

9.123 In *Donohue v. Armco Inc.*,[257] Armco sought to impeach an exclusive English jurisdiction clause on the ground that it was procured by fraud. Although the Court of Appeal held that the jurisdiction clause bound only some of the New York defendants and then only in relation to some of the claims, nevertheless an anti-suit injunction should be granted.

9B.10(iii) Anti-Suit injunction – no jurisdiction agreement

9.124 The broad principle underlying the jurisdiction to grant an anti-suit injunction is that it is to be exercised when the ends of justice require it. This may occur when the foreign proceedings are vexatious or oppressive.[258]

---

255. [1999] 1 Lloyd's Rep. 767.

256. [1999] 1 Lloyd's Rep. 784.

257. [2000] 1 Lloyd's Rep. 579, CA; [2000] 1 All E.R. (Comm.) 425 Aikens J.

258. *British Airways Board v. Laker* [1985] A.C. 58; *Societe Nationale Industrielle Aerospatiale v. Lee Kui Jak* [1987] A.C. 871; *Airbus Industrie GIE v. Patel* [1998] 1 Lloyd's Rep. 631; *Ascot Commodities NV v. Northern Pacific Shipping (The Irini A)* [1999] 1 Lloyd's Rep. 196; *The Irini A (No. 2)* [1999] 1 Lloyd's Rep. 189 (*per* Tuckey J, at p.194: "One of the reasons why I did not grant an anti-suit injunction was

In *Turner v. Grovit*,[259] the Court of Appeal ignored the warning to be cautious in *Bamberger* and granted an anti-suit injunction even where there was no jurisdiction clause.[260] Neither David Donaldson QC at first instance nor the Court of Appeal referred to the *Bamberger* decision. The Court of Appeal relied on a very wide inherent jurisdiction to prevent abuse of process. It is suggested that the decision is unusual and is limited to its particular circumstances, where the Court of Appeal found that the Spanish proceedings were abusive. Indeed, Lord Hobhouse giving the judgment of the House of Lords[261] described the findings of fact made by the Court of Appeal that the Spanish proceedings were launched in bad faith to vex and oppress the plaintiff as putting the case in "an exceptional category". The House of Lords referred a question of interpretation to the European Court as to whether it was inconsistent with the EC Jurisdiction Convention for the Courts of the United Kingdom to grant restraining orders against defendants who are threatening to commence or continue legal proceedings in another Convention country when those defendants are acting in bad faith with the intent and purpose of frustrating or obstructing proceedings properly before the English courts. 9.125

9B.10(iv) Article 57 and anti-suit injunctions

In *Deaville v. Aeroflot Russian International Airlines*,[262] Geoffrey Brice QC considered Art. 28(1) of the Warsaw Convention. The plaintiffs, dependants and relatives of passengers killed on an Aeroflot flight, sued Aeroflot and the manufacturer of the aircraft, Airbus Industrie, in France. In addition, in order to preserve time in England, should the French court decline jurisdiction, the plaintiffs commenced proceedings in England. The reason that the plaintiffs preferred France was that the French courts interpret Art. 25 of the Warsaw Convention on breaking the limits of liability more favourably to plaintiffs than the English courts, as the French courts adopt an objective approach and the English courts adopt a subjective approach.[263] Aeroflot challenged the jurisdiction of the French court on the ground that Art. 28(1) of the Warsaw Convention provided which courts had jurisdiction and did not include France but did include England. The defendants applied for a declaration that France did not have jurisdiction but England did, and for an anti-suit injunction restraining the plaintiffs from proceeding in France. The anti-suit injunction and the declaration were refused. Although the judge held that Arts 21 and 22 of the EC Jurisdiction Convention did not apply, there would be a stay of the English proceedings pending the French Court's decision as to whether they have jurisdiction 9.126

because the head owners did not offer to provide security for that claim here"); A Briggs, "The Unrestrained Reach of an Anti-Suit Injunction: A Pause for Thought" [1997] LMCLQ 90; R Fentiman, "Antisuit Injunctions and the Appropriate Forum" (1997) 56 CLJ 46; J Harris "Anti-suit Injunctions – a Home Comfort?" [1997] LMCLQ 413; E Peel, "Anti-suit Injunctions – The House of Lords Declines to Act as International Policeman" [1998] LQR 543.

259. [1999] CLC 1281.

260. See T Hartley, "Antisuit Injunctions and the Brussels Jurisdiction and Judgments Convention" [2000] ICLQ 166.

261. [2001] UK HL 65 [2002] 1 WLR 107.

262. [1997] 2 Lloyd's Rep. 67. See 20.176 for further discussion of this case.

263. *Ibid.*, p.70, and compare the arguments on breaking the tonnage limits under the 1976 Tonnage Limitation Convention at first instance in *The Happy Fellow* [1997] 1 Lloyd's Rep. 130, 135, 137, 138, discussed at 20.157.

where the plaintiffs were suing not only the carrier but also the manufacturer. Although under English law there was not jurisdiction in France even though there was an additional defendant, the French court might reach a different conclusion.

9C CONCLUSION

9.127 Recent case law has shown a marked reluctance on the part of the English judiciary to incorporate jurisdiction clauses into a reinsurance contract from an insurance contract without specific wording in the reinsurance contract referring to the jurisdiction clause. This case law indicates how important it is that the parties specifically address the issue of jurisdiction in their contract and do not use general terms. The ideal would be to have an express jurisdiction clause which satisfies the formalities of Art. 17 and thus avoid the delay and expense of an interlocutory skirmish on jurisdiction. The English courts remain bullish about enforcing their jurisdiction and have ignored warnings that the use of anti-suit injunctions is not appropriate within the context of the EC Jurisdiction Convention.

CHAPTER 10

MARINE INSURANCE LAW: A SAN ANDREAS FAULT BETWEEN THE COMMON LAW AND CIVIL LAW

PROFESSOR MARC A. HUYBRECHTS

10A INTRODUCTION

The title of this contribution may appear to be an exaggeration. Marine insurance in most civil law jurisdictions is not all that different from marine insurance law in the common law countries and especially in the UK. Indeed, marine insurance law traces its origins to the European continent, especially to Northern Italy, from where, in the Middle Ages, it spread to Flanders, Spain, France, Germany and England. Historically, marine insurance was basically a product of Italian commercial practice and concepts developed by the commercial courts were quickly adapted and amended by the common law courts.[1] But this development did not eliminate the civil *10.1*

1. JP van Niekerk, *The Development of the Principles of Insurance Law in the Netherlands from 1500 to 1800*, Vol. I, Juta, Cape Town 1998, 7; Chorley and Giles, *Shipping Law*, 8th edn., London, 1987, p.499.

law character and tradition of marine insurance. When Sir MacKenzie Chalmers prepared the codification of English marine insurance law, some 2000 decided cases were analysed and formed the basis of the Marine Insurance Act 1906 (MIA), a masterpiece of codification[2] in the "common law" sense of the word.

10.2 Marine insurance has never been embodied in any type of international treaty, but despite this, the practice of marine insurance is fairly universal and harmonised, particularly on account of the dominance, supremacy and accessibility of the English MIA 1906.

10.3 Many common law countries have adopted almost verbatim the UK MIA 1906. Other countries, such as the US and, to a certain extent, South Africa, have accepted its principles on the basis of the cases on which the UK statute is established. And, in a good number of other countries, marine insurance is written on the basis of the typical English policy conditions, such as the Institute Time Clauses (Hulls) and the Institute Cargo Clauses A, B and C, most of them containing a clause subjecting the policy to English law and practice.

10.4 The International Law Society launched an initiative to harmonise international marine insurance rules at the end of the nineteenth century (the Buffalo Conference 1899), which resulted in "draft" rules, known as the Glasgow Rules 1901, but they have never enjoyed any form of acceptance.[3]

10.5 In 1978 UNCTAD took an interest in Marine Insurance and in General Average and launched an initiative in favour of harmonisation, suggesting the introduction of new policy conditions that would replace the traditional S & G Policy and the various other more detailed conditions of the London market.[4] These UNCTAD rules have met with little success, except for the fact that the London market must have felt the need to overhaul the language and content of the traditional London policy conditions, for there emerged a new policy form (the MAR form), and new cargo conditions (1982) and the hull conditions (1995).

10.6 The Comité Maritime International was never very active in the field of marine insurance law, but invested all its time in more compelling subjects such as collisions, salvage, limitation of liability, maritime liens and above all transportation under bills of lading . . ., all resulting in successful conventions. However, things have since changed dramatically. After the UNCTAD attempt in 1978, a critical analysis of the present law on marine insurance was given in the Ebsworth & Ebsworth Lecture delivered by Sir Anthony Mason in 1995. Certain delicate issues were raised and substantial criticism of some of the rules of the present MIA 1906 was articulated. Some of these criticisms centred on the harshness of the rules on express and implied warranties.

2. Unlike "codification" in the common law countries, codification in the civil law tradition means a comprehensive piece of legislation reflecting some new ideas or the policies of the day; John Henry Merryman, *The Civil Law Tradition*, Stanford, 1969, pp.29–32; René David and John EC Brierley, *Major Legal Systems in the World Today*, 3rd edn., London, 1985, pp.417, 449–450.

3. John Hare, "Marine Insurance, The CMI Review Initiative", *CMI Yearbook*, 2000, p.325.

4. The 1995 Ebsworth & Ebsworth Maritime Law Lecture, Sir Anthony Mason, AC KBE, *The Future of Marine Insurance Law*, http://www.anu.edu.au/law/pub/iel/lectures/The 1995 Ebsworth Ebsworth.Mar.html, at p.3; Unctad Report TD/B/C 4/ISL, 20 November 1978 and Unctad Model Clauses on Marine Hull and Cargo Insurance, New York, 1989.

The Ebsworth Lecture also noted that the MIA 1906 was no longer adapted to certain new developments in the practice of shipping, caused by the widespread use of the container in international transport. The Ebsworth Lecture resulted in a paper by the Attorney General of Australia, proposing substantial changes to the present marine insurance law.[5]

The Scandinavian Institute of Maritime Law in conjunction with the CMI organised a conference on marine insurance in June 1998, at which various pending issues were considered. This was followed by a CMI conference in Toledo in September 2000, where the answers of the various national CMI members to a questionnaire on marine insurance sent out by the CMI working group were discussed.[6] 10.7

The CMI working group was chaired by Dr Reme of Hamburg, and had been established to find out whether and in what way marine insurance could be harmonised. 10.8

An important international conference on marine insurance was held at the University of Antwerp on 16–20 November 1999, in which 33 speakers, most of them academics and marine insurance practitioners, commented on the actual position of marine insurance law. This Antwerp Marine Conference resulted in two substantial volumes published under the title *Marine Insurance at the Turn of the Millennium*.[7] 10.9

The number of recent publications dealing with marine insurance indicates a renewed interest in the topic in Europe.[8] There are now several suggestions to introduce the concept of compulsory marine insurance for certain maritime operators.[9] 10.10

Certain international conventions, such as CLC 1969, with its amendments, and the HNS Convention, provide for a system of compulsory liability insurance.[10] And, of course, the idea of compulsory insurance is making progress despite the understandably negative attitude and reluctance of vessel operators and owners.[11]

If Europe or the World Community through the IMO or UNCTAD wants to introduce compulsory marine insurance, it would be helpful to know the marine

5. Sir Anthony Mason AC KBE, *The Future of Marine Insurance Law*, 1995 Ebsworth & Ebsworth Maritime Law Lecture, http://www.anu.edu.au/law/pub/iel/lectures/The Ebsworth Ebsworth Mar. html, at p.14.

6. Trine-Lise Wilhelmsen, "Issues of Marine Insurance, Duty of Disclosure, Duty of Good Faith, Alteration of Risk and Warranties", paper presented at CMI Toledo Seminar, 15 September, 2000, 1–84 & CMI Yearbook 2000, 332–411.

7. Marc Huybrechts (ed.), Eric Van Hooydonk and Christian Dieryck (co-eds.), *Marine Insurance at the Turn of the Millennium* (Intersentia, Antwerp, Vol. I, 1999 Vol. II, 2000).

8. IMO Legal Committee Document, LEG 76/WP and William A O'Neil, Secretary-General IMO, *Working together, IUMI, IMO and the new Millennium*, paper presented at the annual conference IUMI, Berlin, 15 September 1999; http//www.imo.org/imo/speech-l/iumi.htm; British Maritime Association, *The Role of Cargo Owners/Shippers and Marine Insurers in the Quality Shipping Compaign*, No.4, at page 8. BMLA Marine Insurance role of cargo-owners.htm.

9. Passenger ships, Athens Convention 1974. See the amendments suggested by IMO dealing with compulsory insurance and compulsory insurance in the draft international convention on civil liability for bunker oil pollution damage.

10. Commission of the European Communities, Com. (2000) 802, final communication from the Commission to the European Parliament and the Council. Measures on maritime safety following the sinking of the oil tanker *Erika*.

11. British Maritime Law Association, *ibid.*, No. 3–1–4–4, 1–4, 2–4, 5–4, 9: "Therefore, the BMLA submits there is no demonstrated need for compulsory insurance".

insurance concepts of the various legal traditions. It would be unwise for a European or an international legislator only to look at English law in its present state, without taking into account the relative merits and values of the marine insurance concepts of the other legal systems, and especially the civil law tradition, where it all started.

10.11 Moreover, for state legislators who are considering new legislation with reference to marine insurance or transport insurance, a comparative approach may be very relevant and illuminating. It is certainly worthwhile to have some knowledge of the relative values of the different legal regimes dealing with marine insurance around the world.

10.12 Given the limited extent of this contribution, the author will concentrate on the most appealing topics and differences. The structure of the chapter will, therefore, be as follows:

- (i) the formation of the contract – common law v. civil law;
- (ii) overriding principles of law/overriding principles of contract law, such as the good faith requirement, and the issue of causation;
- (iii) specific aspects of good faith:
  - (a) disclosure;
  - (b) the obligation to sue and labour / the duty to minimise losses;
- (iv) the absence of "warranties" in the civil law tradition v. warranties in the common law;
- (v) insured risks. Are the perils of the sea in the continental tradition more widely defined than the same perils in the common law? Specific perils such as barratry of the master;
- (vi) Conclusions.

10B FORMATION OF CONTRACT/THE NEED FOR AN ORIGINAL POLICY TO INSTITUTE AN ADMISSIBLE ACTION

10B.1 English law

10.13 One of the striking differences between English law and the civil law tradition is the need to submit an original policy before one can start an admissible action in court. According to s.22 of the MIA 1906:

> "The contract of Marine Insurance is inadmissible in evidence, unless it is embodied in a Marine Policy in accordance with this Act. The policy may be executed and issued, either at the time when the contract is concluded, or afterwards."

The requirement to submit the original policy relates to evidence; "at *probationem*" it is not a requirement as to the validity of contract to insure. It is even claimed that under the common law (non marine) a contract to insure need not be in writing *per se*.[12]

12. John Hare, *Shipping Law and Admiralty Jurisdiction in South Africa*, Cape Town, 1999, 666, and especially fn.9: "English Law would allow a verbal covernote or confirmation in non-marine insurance, but, because of the requirements of the 1906 Act, not in marine insurance." Quoting Ivamy, *General Principles*, 120, fn.10.

The requirement for an original policy to be submitted in order to institute an admissible action, and also the embarrassment it may cause in certain circumstances, is best understood in the light of history (namely the repealed Stamp Act 1891) and the insurance practice in the London market. Indeed, the coming into being of an insurance contract is a fairly elaborate event.

A future insured known as the "proposer" will act through a broker, presumably a Lloyd's broker. The Lloyd's broker will prepare an offer for insurance known as the "slip", upon the information given to him by the proposer. The Lloyd's broker will approach various underwriters, either acting on behalf of syndicates at Lloyd's or underwriters acting for companies, and he will try to obtain "written lines". The proposal and each such written line, when accepted, constitutes a valid contract, i.e. a contract to insure. When the slip is fully underwritten, or even underwritten beyond 100 per cent the slip and all the written lines will eventually result in the issuance of an insurance policy, either prepared by the Lloyd's policy's signing office or a similar bureau with the International Underwriters Association. 10.14

Problems may arise when a loss occurs prior to the issuance of the policy and when for some reason, such as the death of the underwriter, or the underwriter being declared bankrupt, the policy can no longer be issued. There can be little doubt that a valid contract has come into existence: the problem, however, is how to enforce it. Section 21 of the MIA 1906 states that the contract of marine insurance is deemed to be concluded when the proposal of the assured is accepted by the insurer, whether the policy be then issued or not; and, for the purpose of showing when the proposal was accepted, reference may be made to the slip or covering note or other customary memorandum of the contract, *although it be unstamped* (the words in italic were deleted by the Finance Act 1959, which repealed the Stamp Act 1891). It has been claimed that the slip is an unenforceable contract, binding in honour only.[13] 10.15

Under s.21 of the MIA 1906 it is accepted that the slip may sustain an action for specific performance (an equitable remedy) against the insurers, to obtain an order that the policy be issued. 10.16

The problem was considered by the Court of Appeal in *General Reinsurance Corporation v. Försäkringsaktiebolaget Fennia Patria* in which Kerr LJ said:[14] "The presentation of the slip by the broker constitutes the offer, and the writing of each line constitutes an acceptance of this offer by the underwriter pro tanto". As a consequence of this dictum, modern writers have suggested that most ordinary marine slips for voyage and time risks comply with the requirements of s.22 of the MIA 1906 and can be considered as policies in their own right and are, therefore, admissible in legal proceedings.[15] This conforms with modern insurance practices in which parties seek to take a short cut avoiding the issuance of a formal policy and being content with what they call a slip-policy.[16] But it has to be observed that these ship policies often make express provision for the right to demand a policy. 10.17

13. Chorley and Giles, *Shipping Law*, 8th edn., London, 1987, 534.
14. *General Reinsurance Corp. v. Forsäkringaktiebolaget Fennia Patria* [1983] 1 Q.B. 856.
15. Arnould, *Law of Marine Insurance and Average*, 1981, 16th edn., Vol. I §14, §16, §17, 9–13.
16. John Hare, *ibid.*, p.666.

10B.2 The continental approach

10.18 The starting point on the continent is similar to English law: the formation of an insurance contract is a matter of consent. In a number of jurisdictions, however, the law imposes the requirement of writing (which is not exactly the same as a policy) as a matter of evidence. It is not suggested that the absence of such formal writing results in any action being declared inadmissible. In special circumstances the absence of a writing may be remedied by additional and/or other evidence.

10.19 The French Code of Commerce of 1808 stated in section 332 that: "Le contrat d'assurance est rédigé par écrit". This Code only dealt with marine insurance. (Modern French insurance law is now to be found in the statute 67–522 of 30 July 1966 and the Decree 68–64 of 19 January 1968. Insurance law has been amended on many occasions and the reader can find the present position on the website of Legifrance.[17]) This leads dean Antoine Vialard[18] to say: "The contract of Marine Insurance is a consensual contract despite the apparent formalism laid down in section 112–2 of the statute and even if the evidence of the contract must necessarily be adduced by a written document or a writing".

10.20 The contractual documents are always considered as expressing the consensus between parties; the documents are not required for the validity of the consensus *ad idem*, nor for the very existence of the contract. In Belgium, the position is slightly different. It is a generally accepted opinion that the marine insurance contract is "*un contrat consensuel*" by which is meant that the contract comes into being by the "consensus" of parties without the requirement of special formalities.[19]

10.21 The statute, however, stipulates that a written document is necessary to prove the existence of the insurance contract, according to section 25 of the General Insurance Act of 11 June 1874. But the requirement of writing is mitigated in comparison to the written evidence rules of the civil code. Section 1341[20] of the Belgian Civil Code, which is in fact a copy of the "Code Napoleon", requires parties to execute two original copies of their contract, or as many original copies as there are parties with a different interest in the contract. However, this requirement is not imposed with reference to marine insurance, where one original copy will suffice. In addition, the second paragraph of section 25 of the Belgian General Insurance Act allows oral evidence each time there is at least the "beginning of a writing". The wording "*Commencement de preuve par écrit*" can mean a letter exchange, telegrams, telexes or printed matter emanating from the person against whom the claim is introduced.[21]

17. Legifrance, *l'essentiel du droit français*; http://www.legifrance.gouv.fr/html/frame–constitution.htm Loi 112 – Arts 2 and 3; Loi 89 – 1014 of 31 December 1989; Art. 9, Journal Officiel du 3 janvier 1990, en vigueur le 1er mai 1990: "Le contrat d'assurance est rédigé par écrit, en Français, en caractères apparents".

18. Antoine Vialard, *Droit Maritime* (Presse Universitaire de France, Paris, 1997) p.100.

19. Claude Buisseret, "Répertoire Pratique du Droit Belge", Verbo: *Assurances Maritimes*, No. 108.

20. Robert De Smet, *Traité Théorique et Pratique des Assurances Maritimes*, Paris, 1959, 75, No. 51.

21. Claude Buisseret, *ibid.*

The position in Germany[22] is basically the same. The "Handelsgesetzbuch" of 1908 deals with marine insurance in sections 778–889. These statutory provisions are generally replaced by the "Allgemeine Deutsche Seeversicherungsbedingungen" (ADS) of 1919 with various amendments. 10.22

The German Supreme Court (Bundesgerichtshof) decided on 14 October 1955 that the validity of an insurance contract is not dependent on the redaction of a writing.[23] Nowhere in the German Code or in the ADS is a requirement similar to section 25 of the Belgian statute of 11 June 1874, known as the "General Insurance Act", mentioned.[24] But, at the same time, section 784 of the German Code of Commerce says that the insurer is obliged to issue and deliver a policy to the insured, upon his demand, duly signed by the insurer and establishing the contract to insure.

According to section 14 of the ADS in a case where the policy has effectively been issued, the underwriter is not obliged to proceed with the payment of an indemnity until the original policy is submitted. But even if the original policy has been lost or destroyed, the assured still has a remedy to obtain payment from the insurer after the policy has been declared without any force ("*für Kraftlos erklärt ist*").[25]

The special German Law pertaining to insurance contracts, known as the VVG (*Versicherungsvertragsgesetz*) should also be mentioned. This statute is not made applicable to marine cargo insurance according to the specific wording of Art. 186, but is applicable to the German Inshore Transport Insurance.[26]

10B.3 Conclusion

The preceding discussion leads to the conclusion that the common law and civil law are not far apart when it comes to the formation of the contract. The existence of "*consensus ad idem*" is the decisive moment and criterion for the coming into being of a valid and binding contract. The issuance of a written document is basically an evidence rule and should not be construed as being more than that. 10.23

For this reason, the rule contained in s.22 of the MIA 1906, that an action is "inadmissible" unless an original policy in the form of the Act is produced in court, is possibly a needless exaggeration, caused by a tax concern of earlier days, i.e. the stamp duty legislation.

The solution suggested formerly, namely an equitable action seeking injunctive relief is perhaps too burdensome and complicated, i.e. special proceedings seeking

22. For a general introduction to Marine Insurance Law of Germany, see Klaus Kostka, "Marine Transport Insurance in Germany: The General German Cargo Conditions in Comparison to the Institute Cargo Clauses and Recent German Court Decisions", especially No. 1: "Introduction", and No. 2: "Governing provisions and regulations" in: Marc A Huybrechts (ed.), *Marine Insurance at the turn of the Millennium*, Vol. I, The European Institute of Maritime and Transport Law, Intersentia, 1999, 361.

23. J Sasse, *Deutsche Seeversicherung*, No. 109, Karlsruhe, 1958, No. 67 & BGH, 14 October 1955.

24. Robert De Smet, *ibid.*, Tome II, 182, No. 851.

25. Robert De Smet, *ibid.*, Tome II, 183, No. 853.

26. See Klaus Kostka, *ibid.*, 362 and website http://www.kanzlei-doehmer.de/webdoc13.htm: "Die Frage, wie eigentlicht ein Versicherungsvertrag zustanden kommt, konnte for noch nicht alzulanger Zeit recht einfach beantwortet werden. In der Regel war das Vorliegen zweier ubereinstimmender Willenserklärungen ausreichend, aber auch notwendig. Dies hat sich im Zuge der Regulierung der Versicherungsmärkte, under der ex-post Kontrolle von Vertragsbedingungen durch das Bundesaufsichtsamt für das Versicherungswezen – grundlegend geändert."

specific performance to force the underwriter to issue the original policy after which an action at common law can be initiated.

The view of modern writers is to be preferred, that the slip and written lines are policies in their own right, complying with the requirement of s.22 of the MIA 1906. The flexible approach of the civil law is also preferable in that it allows parties in certain circumstances to adduce other and additional forms of evidence if for some reason the written document has never been established or has gone astray. The stringent provision of s.22 of the MIA 1906, relating to the inadmissibility of any action, is perhaps more of an irritation to the parties than anything else.

10C SOME UNDERLYING PRINCIPLES OF THE LAW OF OBLIGATIONS AND GENERAL CONTRACT LAW

10C.1 The issue of good faith and causation

10.24 This section concentrates on some significant differences between common law regimes and civil law in relation to concepts which in the civil law tradition are very much part of the general law of obligations or contract law, whereas in the common law they are specifically dealt with in the more restricted field of marine insurance law. The two particular concepts are the duty of good faith and the issue of causation.

In common law countries the duty of good faith is very specifically dealt with in the MIA 1906. The common law has also developed the issue of causation very much within the context of marine insurance law and the insurance of war risks, establishing the concept of "*proxima causa*".

10C.2 Common law countries: the duty of utmost good faith

10.25 Numerous articles and books have been published on the issue, but for the purposes of this contribution, we can refer to the expert summaries given by Yvonne Baatz and Professor Howard Bennett.[27]

The absence of codified contract law in the common law and the specifically mentioned requirement of the duty of "utmost good faith" in marine insurance law has resulted in some remarkable consequences as to the requirement of good faith in contract law in general.

Some have defended the viewpoint that in English contract law there is not a recognised duty of good faith as such, with the exception of the marine insurance contract.[28] Others have stated that the principle of good faith is common to the entire law of contract, but that the law of (marine) insurance requires an even higher standard of honesty than usual.[29] It is not suggested that Baatz excluded other

27. Yvonne Baatz, "Utmost Good Faith in Marine Insurance Contracts", in Marc A Huybrechts (ed.), *Marine Insurance at the turn of the Millennium* (Intersentia, Antwerp, 1999, Vol. I) 15–36; Howard Bennett, *Mapping the doctrine of utmost good faith in insurance contract law*, 1999, Vol. I., LMCLQ, 165.

28. Yvonne Baatz, *ibid.*, 15.

29. Chorley and Giles, *Shipping Law*, 8th edn. (London, 1987), p.524.

possibilities, but certainly Chorley and Giles explicitly mention the principle of good faith as underpinning the entire law of contract, which is not so explicitly stated by Baatz. Apparently, the difference between general contract law and marine insurance law exists at the level of information to be provided, leading up to the contract.[30]

In the pre-contractual stage, the duty of utmost good faith is the basis of two specific duties articulated in greater detail in the statute itself, namely the duty of full disclosure and the rules in relation to misrepresentation (ss.18–20 of the MIA 1906).[31] Also, the consequence of a violation of the duty of the utmost good faith is dealt with by the statute, namely the possibility for the insurer to avoid the contract (s.17 of the MIA 1906). 10.26

Apart from these specific duties, attention is being given to whether the duty of good faith has other and larger implications than the duty of utmost good faith in the post-contractual period, i.e. during the life of the contract. Here the duty is being discussed in relation to declarations under "held covered" clauses contained in policies, the variation or alteration of the risk and fraudulent claims made by the insured against the insurer.[32]

In the US the doctrine of "utmost good faith" is broadly in line with the concept in England,[33] while the South African law tradition seems to have swung to the civil law system by throwing overboard the label or qualification "utmost", but not the principle of "good faith" as such.[34] 10.27

10C.3 Good faith in the continental law systems

In the continental law systems the starting point is that the good faith principle in the law of obligations or in contract law is a general concept and a foundation or cornerstone of any valid contract, whereas certain jurisdictions – such as France – 10.28

30. Howard Bennett, *The Law of Marine Insurance*, Oxford, 1996, p.66.

31. *Chitty on Contract*, 27th edn., 1994, para. 6–009: "Although the law will assist a party who has been induced into a contract by an inaccurate or a misleading statement, termed a misrepresentation, there is no general duty to volunteer information, even though it is evident that such information would be regarded as highly relevant by the other party in deciding whether to contract and, if so, upon what terms. Tacit acquiescence in another's self-deception does not in itself amount to a misrepresentation, provided that it has not previously been caused by a positive misrepresentation"; Anthony Mason, AC, KBE, 1995 Ebsworth Maritime Law Lecture, 4 : "Thus the duty of utmost good faith, applying to insurance contract, contrasts with the doctrine of 'Caveat Emptor', which underlay the 'Laisser-faire' approach to the general law of contracts. In English law, the issue of the duty of utmost good faith is now considered both in the pre-contractual stage as well as during the life of the contract".

32. In *The Star Sea* decision, the House of Lords has recently ruled on this issue. The duty of the utmost good faith is basically a requirement leading up to the contract and continues thereafter, but in a different form, until a claim is made in litigation or arbitration. *Manifest Shipping Co. Ltd. v. Uni-Polaris Shipping Co. Ltd and others, The Star Sea* [2001] 1 All E.R. 743.

33. Grant Gillmore, Charles Black, *The Law of Admiralty*, 2nd edn., New York, 1975, p.62, and Thomas J Schoenbaum, *Admiralty and Maritime Law* (Saint Paul, Minnesota, 1987) p.572.

34. John Hare, "Closing comments on behalf of the common lawyer", in Marc A Huybrechts (ed.), *Marine Insurance at the turn of the Millennium*, Volume II, Antwerp, 2000, p.223; John Hare, *Shipping Law and Admiralty Jurisdiction South Africa*, Cape Town, 1999, pp.687–694, quoting: "Outshoorn Municipality: Our law of insurance has no need for uberima fides and the time has come to jettison it (*Mutual and Federal Insurance Company Ltd. v. Outshoorn Municipality* 1995 (1) SA, 419, (SCH)."

have reiterated the overriding principle of good faith more specifically in their marine insurance law.

It is also claimed by some that there is no such thing as a requirement of "utmost good faith", because every contract requires the principle of good faith to be complied with in the first place. Others have stated that the requirement of good faith in marine insurance contracts is of a higher and more demanding nature than good faith in the general contract law.

Two authors, Professor Trine-Lise Wilhelmsen of the Scandinavian Institute of Maritime Law and Professor von Ziegler, have both recently published detailed examples of this debate.[35] Wilhelmsen is of the opinion that the duty of good faith is not a general concept in the marine insurance system in (all) civil law countries. Some systems, however, include the concept of good faith, such as France, Belgium and Germany.

10.29 Article 242 of the German Civil Code[36] refers to the principle of good faith in its general law of obligations. In the *Allgemeine Deutsche Seeversicherungbedingungen* the duty of utmost good faith is explicitly mentioned. The ADS is not made up of statutory provisions, but general trade conditions which have received wide application.

10.30 In French and Belgian law, the duty of good faith in contracts is embodied in s.1134 of the Civil Code. The third part of s.1134 states that contracts must be performed in good faith. It is admitted that the requirement of good faith operates in the pre-contractual stage and also in conducting negotiations the parties have a duty of good faith; the opposite of that would be a *culpa in contrahendo*, which is a special form of delict or tort. Once the contract is formed, the duty of good faith comes into play with reference to the implementation of the contract and the interpretation of contractual clauses in cases of doubtful meaning. Later the duty of good faith again comes into play when parties want to exercise their contractual rights; and an abusive exercise of these contractual rights is condemned as a violation of the duty of good faith.[37]

10.31 Wilhelmsen comes to the conclusion that the requirement of good faith in Belgium, Italy, Spain, China and Venezuela is said to be a general requirement for all contracts, but not defined by an explicit provision of law (if one wants to ignore s.1134 of the civil code, which could hardly be more specific). It is indeed true that the sanction for a violation of the good faith requirement is very much determined by judge-made law and that the consequences of a violation can take the form of the annulment of the

35. Trine-Lise Wilhemsen , "Issues of Marine Insurance / Duty of Disclosure, Duty of Good Faith, Alteration of Risk and Warranties in the Civil Law countries", in *Scandinavian Yearbook of Maritime Law 2000*, Scandinavian Institute of Maritime Law, Yearbook 2000, 292, and especially at pages 270–271; Trine-Lise Wilhelmsen, "Issues of Marine Insurance, Duty of Disclosure, Duty of Good Faith, Alteration of Risk and Warranties", paper presented at the CMI Toledo conference, 15–19 September 2000; paper 1–84 and especially comments at p. 4, No. 4, "The duty of good faith"; Alexander von Ziegler, "The Utmost Good Faith", in "Marine Insurance Law on the Continent", in Marc A Huybrechts (ed.), *Marine Insurance at the Turn of the Millennium*, Volume II, 21–30.

36. BGB, para. 242 : "Leistung nach Treu und Glauben. Der Schuldner ist verpflichtet, die Leistung so zu bewerken, wie Treu und Glauben mit Rücksicht auf die Verkehrssite es erfordern."

37. JL Fagnard, "l'Exécution de Bonne Foi, des Conventions: Un Principe en Expansion", *Revue Critique de Jurisprudence Belge*, 1986, 287, nr. 5; W. Van Gerven, "Goede Trouw en Getrouw Beeld", in *Liber Amicorum, Jan Ronse*, 110.

contract, or can lead to a reduction of the contractual remedies granted, without "avoiding" the contract as such.

For Wilhelmsen, the concept of duty of good faith seems to overlap both the rules concerning the duty of disclosure and the rules concerning the alteration of risk.[38] It is, however, worth mentioning that von Ziegler, when discussing the principle of utmost good faith in continental legal systems, in fact deals with problems of disclosure and misrepresentation as emanations of the principle of good faith. In contrast, in most common law writings, the duty of utmost good faith is separately considered and dealt with in conjunction with the duty of full disclosure and the issue of misrepresentation, because the Marine Insurance Act of 1906 specifically deals with these two latter aspects, in addition to the general principle of utmost good faith, mentioned in s.17 of the MIA 1906.

Wilhelmsen concludes that the good faith requirement in continental systems is a more flexible tool, but as a drawback she quotes a total lack of predictability for the parties to the contract and especially for the assured.

Modern French law seems to provide more predictability.[39] Vialard is of the opinion that irrespective of the requirement of good faith in the French civil code, there is a higher obligation of good faith with reference to marine insurance: "Dire qu'un contrat est un contrat de bonne foi, ajoute de quelque chose à la prescription du Code civil: cela veut dire que l'on attend des contractants, et spécialement de l'assuré, une loyauté supérieure, une collaboration plus constante que celle que l'on attend d'un contractant ordinaire . . .".[40] 10.32

Strangely enough, the requirement of a higher degree of good faith in marine insurance contracts has been denied by Robert De Smet.[41] He is of the opinion that there is no distinction between contracts of good faith and other ordinary contracts. And Buisseret[42] is of the opinion that the insurance contract is a contract of good faith and that the good faith requirement is especially present with reference to marine insurance.

The author, like von Ziegler,[43] believes that the common law and civil systems can be reconciled. In the opinion of von Ziegler the differences in the common law rules in relation to the duty of utmost good faith can be reconciled with the continental concept "if the international community so wished". It would be a decided advantage to have one and the same concept in relation to good faith. The qualification "utmost good faith" or simply "good faith" is not that relevant. What is relevant is whether the 10.33

38. Trine-Lise Wilhelmsen, *Ibid.*, Toledo paper, 50.

39. Antoine Vialard, "Droit Maritime", *Ibid.*, 96, nr. 113: "La sanction de la fausse déclaration ou de la réticence est justement modulée en fonction de la bonne foi de l'assuré et de son impact sur l'appréciation du risque par l'assureur: nullité du contrat avec rétention de la prime en cas de mauvaise foi prouvée, nullité sans rétention de la prime, si la mauvaise foi n'est pas prouvée, simple réduction de l'indemnisation si l'assuré prouve sa bonne foi (dans la mesure où l'assureur, parfaitement informé, aurait tout de même contracté, mais à d'autres conditions); mais nullité malgré la bonne foi prouvée si l'assureur prouve que, parfaitement informé il n'aurait pas contracté. Bonne foi encore dans les déclarations de sinistre (article L.172–28 C.ass.) *et les diligences à exercer tant pour prévenir la réalisation du risque, que pour en limiter les effets.*" (article L.172–23 C.ass.; article 11 et 12 de la Police sur Corps . . .).

40. Antoine Vialard, *ibid.*, 96, No. 112.

41. Robert De Smet, *Traité Théorique et Pratiques des Assurances Maritimes*, Paris, 1959, 102, No. 86.

42. Buisseret, "Assurances Maritimes", in *Répertoire Pratique du Droit Belge*, No. 16.

43. Alexander von Ziegler, *ibid.*, 28.

law will impose a higher requirement of good faith with regard to certain transactions and whether there will be a recognition in law for that higher standard to be met by the parties.

The author takes the view that this is quite possible under the present rules, whereas Germany and France have statutory rules allowing for more flexible solutions. Belgian case law also follows in that direction. The continental system is perhaps preferable because it allows more flexibility, for certain defences by the assured, such as ignorance of the particular facts by the assured, or the absence of bad faith – as is the case in France – may be advanced, thereby avoiding radical consequences, e.g. avoidance of contract.

10C.4 Causation

10C.4(i) Common law countries

10.34 The issue of causation in marine insurance is another major divide between common law countries and countries of the continental legal culture. First, causation is specifically dealt with in the MIA 1906, whereas in continental statutes on marine insurance there are no specific provisions dealing with the issue of causation because it is dealt with in general contract law or in the general law of obligations.

Causation is dealt with in the MIA 1906, in s.55, which states that the insurer is liable for any loss proximately caused by a peril insured against, but, subject as aforesaid, he is not liable for any loss which is not proximately caused by peril insured against.

Section 55 contains certain exclusions to the effect that the insurer is not liable for:

(i) any loss attributable to the wilful misconduct of the assured;
(ii) loss caused by delay;
(iii) loss caused by ordinary wear and tear or inherent vice of the subject matter insured.

These rules on causation appear seductively simple, but that may be only a first impression. In the US courts the concept of proximate cause is the accepted norm. However, this does not mean that courts do not have a duty to refine the concept each time the proximate cause is to be selected from a series of concurrent causes. The issue of causation is particularly current with regard to the relationship between war risks and ordinary marine risks.[44]

10.35 The selection of the proximate cause can be a determination that often requires as complex an analysis as when "proximate cause" questions occur in tort. The position under English law has been explained by Bennett in the following terms:[45]

> "The proximate cause concept traces back its origins to a maxim of Bacon that 'it were infinite for the law to judge the cause of causes, and their impulsions one of another; therefore it contenteth itself with the immediate cause and judgeth of acts by that, without looking to any further degree' . . . ' "

44. Grant Gilmore and Charles L Black, Jr, *The Law of Admiralty*, 2nd edn. (New York 1975, 76); Thomas J Schönbaum, *Admiralty and Maritime Law* (Saint-Paul Minnesota, 1987) p.583.
45. Howard Bennett, *The Law of Marine Insurance* (Oxford, 1996) 115–135.

For that reason, remote causes are ignored and reference is made only to the immediate cause, leading to the damage.

Two other issues have to be specified: immediate doesn't mean "immediate in time" and proximate cause does not mean "last in time" but means dominant in effect. Bennett points out that "it is now settled beyond doubt that the proximate cause is identified by effect, not timing".

The seductive simplicity remains and the problems are not really solved. It is, of course, very much a question of fact to determine what is the proximate cause of an accident and this depends largely on the philosophical approach of the court dealing with the issue. That the proximate cause concept is not that easy has been demonstrated by the rather vague surrounding concepts that have been introduced in an effort to clarify the proximate cause. Reference is also made to "dominant cause" or, even better, the "*causa causans*" or the "real" cause.

For a long time causation has been projected as a chain of events, each event 10.36
causing another or the next event. But Lord Shaw rightly pointed out that causation is not a chain, but rather a net.[46] In English law the issue of causation is in many instances resolved by selecting one cause from many several concurrent causes. Of course, problems arise when some causes are specifically included in the list of insured risks and some are specifically excluded.

South Africa is one of the countries which adheres to the English law concept of 10.37
causation with great consistency.[47]

It seems beyond doubt that the common law concepts of causation in marine 10.38
insurance are not particularly satisfying. The general feeling is articulated by Sir Anthony Mason in the 1995 Ebsworth and Ebsworth Maritime Law lecture on the future of Marine Insurance, where he comments on the decision in *Scandia Insurance Company Ltd v. Skoljarev* and observed:[48] "When preparing my judgment in that case, I came to appreciate how complex were the relevant principles of marine insurance law. Nothing that happened since then has caused me to change my mind".

Indeed, the history of the litigation in the *Popi M*[49] demonstrates how complex 10.39
those principles are, though the ramifications of that decision in its application to proof of an occurrence and causation may well extend beyond marine insurance to other fields of liability. Further on in his lecture Sir Anthony Mason quotes Lord Mustill:[50] "One may venture the hope that one day a case will be brought before the Highest Tribunal on whether the relationship between 'debility', 'fortuity', 'burden of proof', s.39(1) and s.39(2) and causation can be worked out in a way which permits a rationalisation of the entire law in this field . . .".

The remarkable thing is that the selection of the proximate cause and the rejection 10.40
of remote causes is not the practice followed when it comes to enhancing safety in marine matters. Insurers, especially P & I Clubs, train their members and urge them

---

46. *Leyland Shipping Company Ltd v. Norwich Union Fire Insurance Society Ltd* [1918], A.C. 350, p.369.
47. John Hare, *Shipping Law and Admiralty Jurisdiction in South Africa*, Juta, Cape Town 1999, 714.
48. *Scandia Insurance Company Ltd v. Skoljarev* [1979] 142, C.L.R. 375, a case which dealt with the sinking of the ms Zadar.
49. *Popi M.* [1985] 2 Lloyd's Rep. I.
50. M Mustill, NJ, "Fault and Marine Losses" (1988), *LMCLQ*, 310, p.325.

to be aware of all remote causes that may ultimately lead to the occurrence of an accident. Experience of life is sufficient to show that accidents are avoided by going to the root of the matter and by trying to eradicate everything that can contribute to the occurrence of an accident. Perhaps lawyers should heed this, rather than merely "refer" to the commonsense of business people.[51]

10C.4(ii) Causation on the continent

10.41 Causation is one of those issues that characterise the divide between the common law and continental law countries. There are indeed a few significant differences.

10.42 First, there is the issue of causation, which is specifically dealt with in English marine insurance law, namely in the MIA 1906 itself (s.55 of the MIA 1906). In the civil law tradition, the issue of causation is much more the domain of the general law of torts, or contract law and even in the law on contracts or tort law; it is much more the domain of legal scholars (legal doctrine) or cases to define what one is to understand by "the causal link" or "causation".

Moreover, the continental countries seem divided as between themselves for they adopt two broad approaches to causation. A number of countries, such as Germany and France, adhere to the principle of the "adequate cause", whereas other countries, such as Belgium, adhere to the theory of "equivalent" causes.

John Hare has noted that "Civilian lawyers do not share the English common lawyers' predisposition with the complexities of causation. To many, including the Scandinavian systems, any happening which causes or contributes to an end result of loss, is a cause under the policy. The extent of that causative contribution can result in apportionment of liability (*cf.* the Norwegian Marine Insurance Plan, Version 1997, para. 2–11)".[52]

Ralph De Wit has also pointed out that there is no general theory of causation in "continental" law. He means that each legal system entertains its own view:[53] "In France, the theory generally applied is that of the '*causalité efficiente*' ('effective causation'), meaning that the event, which is deemed to have caused the damage, must have played a preponderant role in its occurrence, it must have been the *cause génératrice* ('generating cause')".

10.43 In the nineteenth century, the German author von Buri gave us an elaborate theory of "adequate cause and equivalent causes" (*Zur Kausalitätsfrage, Beitrage zur Theorie des Strafrechts, Ueber Kausalität under deren Verantwortung*). German law apparently took the English view on causation in the field of marine insurance with the result

51. Howard Bennett, "The Law of Marine Insurance", *Ibid.*, 115 : "In ascribing legal responsibility, the courts have eschewed philosophical refinements in favour of the commonplace test which the ordinary business man conversant with such matters would adopt".

52. John Hare, *Shipping Law and Admiralty Jurisdiction in South Africa*, Juta. 1999, 714, fn.223.

53. Ralph De Wit, "A Comparative Review of Recent Developments in the Concepts of inherent Vice and Latent Defect", in "Marine Insurance Policies", in Marc A Huybrechts (ed.), *Marine Insurance at the turn of the Millennium*, Vol. I, 58.

that German Transport Insurance, in accordance with the ADS Güter, 1973, is subject to the "*causa proxima* doctrine".[54]

The French theory, together with the German approach, resembles the English concept of causation, especially when one thinks of "the (English) proximate cause" as the cause proximate in efficiency. It is a theory which in continental countries is identified as the "adequate" cause. One looks to determine the adequate cause of a loss, i.e. the cause which according to the opinion of good commonsense effectively caused the damage. 10.44

Belgium, however, has another approach to the issue of causation, applying the theory of the "*equivalence des conditions*" or the theory of "equivalent" causes. This theory takes into account all relevant causes that may have contributed and without which the loss or damage would not have occurred, as it occurred specifically in the event, i.e. "any" condition *sine qua non*:[55] 10.45

"In Belgian Marine Insurance Law, the relevant statutory rule clearly states that exclusion applies to loss or damage, caused directly by the inherent vice of the goods. This has been held to mean that the inherent vice itself, without the intervention of any other cause which is an insured risk, must have caused the loss or damage. If the defect in the goods has been necessarily propitiated by an insured risk, the loss or damage will be covered, which is stating the obvious since in that case the vice was not inherently present in the goods."

The difficulty arises when damage has been caused by a number of circumstances, some of which are insured risks whilst others are not. The Belgian position in such cases is that each cause must contribute. The Belgian principle of equivalent conditions allows the apportionment of liability (see also van Huizen).[56]

The theory of the equivalent causes is explained by De Page.[57] According to this theory, the court will withhold, as a cause of the injury, each incident, without which the damage would not have occurred in the precise way it occurred. Each form of negligence which has been a necessary condition for the damage will result in liability, irrespective of the degree of relative importance or weight in the occurrence of the damage. The search for a fault or negligent act as the cause of damage or loss is done "*in concreto*", by applying the "*conditio sine qua non*" test.

This is the general Belgian theory with reference to causation. It has been said that Belgian marine insurance law does not deviate from the theory of equivalent causes in

54. Klaus Kostka, "Marine Transport Insurance in Germany, The general German cargo conditions in comparison to the institute cargo clauses and recent German Court decision", in Marc A. Huybrechts (ed.), *Marine Insurance at the Turn of the Millennium*, Vol. I, Antwerp, 1999, 370, states that: "Although the *causa proxima* rule is neither explicitly laid down in the ADS Güter 73, nor in the ADS, nor in any of the relevant German Insurance Laws, nonetheless the *causa proxima* standard is being applied". This shows the strong influence which the English Law of Marine Insurance has had on German Law in the area from the very beginning.

55. Ralph De Wit, *ibid.*, 58.

56. Philip van Huizen, "Some General Principles of Insurance Law: causality, retro-active/active coverage and uncertainty of the event covered", in Marc A Huybrechts (ed.), *Marine Insurance at the turn of the Millennium*, Antwerp, 1999, Vol. I, 41, states that the Netherlands have never adhered to the *causa proxima* doctrine theory of the UK. In the Netherlands, "*the causa remota*" doctrine has always been in force. "However, since under the doctrine of the *causa remota* we have also to find the most dominant cause, nowadays in my opinion there is no longer any difference between the doctrine of the *causa proxima* and the doctrine of the *causa remota*. . . ."

57. De Page, *Traité élémentaire de droit civil Belge*, Brussels, 3rd edn., Vol. II, 1962.

relation to causation. The Belgian marine insurance statute refers to losses and damages "caused by", whereas the wording of the Antwerp Marine Policy is different. The "all risk clause" of the Antwerp Marine Policy (version of 1 October 1986) uses the following phraseology: "losses which are 'immediately' caused by . . .".

However, one cannot conclude that in using the word "immediately", the Belgian marine underwriters wanted to depart from the traditional Belgian causation theory based on "equivalent" causes. The application of the theory of equivalent causes allows more freedom to the court to adjudicate the liability between insured and underwriter. A Belgian court can indeed take into account several concurrent causes which all contributed to the loss. The court can allocate a certain percentage to a given cause, so that the insured may collect at least a percentage from his underwriter when amongst the causes contributing to the loss, some are "named" perils, whereas other causes are not. Arguably, this result is more equitable for the insured, and it surely allows greater flexibility.

10.46 The common law theory of the proximate cause can lead to rather harsh results, i.e. "the winner takes all" principle and it leaves too much room for arbitrary decisions. What is to be considered as the "real cause of a loss" is very much a factual issue and a philosophical question. The continental theory of equivalent causes, on the other hand, allows more room for compromise.

10.47 At present, as has previously been observed, there is an ongoing debate in the circles of CMI, whilst at the same time IMO in its Assembly in November 1999 has issued guidelines on shipowners' responsibilities in respect of maritime claims. It was suggested that apart from encouraging uniformity between the different national laws on compulsory marine insurance, it is hoped that the guidelines will provide greater transparency regarding the insurance cover provided for ships and that they will improve the efficiency of enforcement efforts, since port state control could then be targeted on the minority of ships which do not have effective insurance.

Whether the shipping industry will operate under a uniform international instrument dealing with marine insurance or whether various States will enforce their national (future) compulsory marine insurance laws, the need for uniformity is clearly obvious in this international and global setting.

It is submitted that the world also needs a uniform approach on the issue of causation, because the result of a marine insurance claim introduced into a national court should not vary according to which theory of causation has been applied. Victims (in the case of direct actions) as well as insurers all have a genuine interest in being treated in the same way on the issue of causation.

10.48 If the shipping community has to decide on the issue of causation, a strong argument ought to be made for the theory of equivalent causes for two solid reasons. First, it reflects reality. Losses are caused most of the time by a number of causes (the image of a net, rather than of a chain); losses are fought in the marine industry by going to the root of the problem and not by trying to eliminate the last circumstance which may cause the incident. Second, the theory of equivalent causes allows the courts and arbitrators to apportion liability between various contributing causes, resulting in a more just compensation for the insured and avoiding the "winner takes all" approach offered by the "proximate cause" theory.

10D SPECIFIC ASPECTS OF GOOD FAITH

10D.1 Duty of disclosure

In common law countries, the duty of disclosure and representations is to be seen as an application of the duty of "utmost good faith". 10.49

The duty of disclosure is described in ss.18 and 19 of the MIA 1906, whereas representations are dealt with in s.20. These three sections immediately follow the provision stating that the marine insurance contract is based on the "utmost good faith". The duty to disclose is fairly well detailed in ss.18 and 19. However, this has not prevented substantial litigation on the issue with two important recent decisions, in *The Pine Top* and *The Star Sea*.[58]

Although common law countries are fairly harmonised on the issue of good faith, disclosure and representation, there are nonetheless some noteworthy differences.[59]

We are very much indebted to Professor Trine-Lise Wilhelmsen of the Scandinavian Institute of Maritime Law, who has examined the duty of disclosure and the duty of good faith in a leading article published within the framework of the ongoing work of the Comité Maritime International concerning the harmonisation of Marine Insurance clauses.[60] What strikes the reader is that the various continental countries, although imposing the duty to full disclosure, show, nonetheless, great variety in the way they have expressed that duty. 10.50

Professor Wilhelmsen has identified the issues that are dealt with in very different ways:

(i) the content of the duty of disclosure;
(ii) the sanctioning system;
(iii) the information to be disclosed and who is responsible for it;
(iv) the subjective approach to the question of materiality;
(v) the question is whether the approach is measured against the assured or against the insurer;
(vi) the question how material the information must be.

On the issue of how material the information must be, the divide is between the decisive influence test or decisive influence and the inducement for the actual insurer. A further dividing line is between the active and passive duty of disclosure (active disclosure on the basis of questionnaires to be filled out by the insurer).

Another cause of disparity is the consequence of either fraud or bad faith, negligence, and breach of disclosure but made in good faith.

Further, the time when the duty of disclosure applies is not answered in the same way in the various legal systems. Professor Wilhelmsen connects this with the sanctioning system, where various solutions are possible, such as the right to cancel

58. *Pan Atlantic Insurance Co. Ltd v. Pine Top Insurance Co. Ltd* [1994] 2 Lloyd's Rep. 427 and *Manifest Shipping Co. Ltd v. Uni Polaris Shipping Co. Ltd and others*, House of Lords (*The Star Sea*) [1997] 1 Lloyd's Rep. 389; [2001] 1 All E.R. 743 (HL).

59. K Schoenbaum, *Divergences between English and American Law of Marine Insurance* (Maryland, 1999) p.99.

60. Trine-Lise Wilhelmsen, "The Duty of Disclosure, Duty of Good Faith, Alteration of Risk and Warranties, An Analysis of the replies to the C.M.I. questionnaire", in *Yearbook 2000 CMI*, 232–411.

the contract, the right to claim additional premium, the right to claim freedom from liability for an incurred casualty and the right to a partial reduction in the liability and ultimately avoidance of the contract.

The issue of causation is also very important in dealing with nondisclosure and misrepresentation. In some countries causation is not required. But the position may be different in other countries in cases of unintentional breach of disclosure. For example, in France, a more favourable solution could be applied, namely the reduction of the indemnity.

Professor Wilhelmsen[61] considers all these topics as main issues identified for the purpose of future harmonisation. She submits a strong argument for a flexible sanctioning system depending on the degree of fault by the assured on the basis of economic efficiency and legal fairness. Therefore, she claims that the insurer will have a sufficient remedy if he has a right to cancel the contract and/or call for additional premium. This solution is followed in most civil law countries and also seems to get the support of some common law authors.[62]

10.51 As the Australian Law Reform Commission recognised in relation to general insurance contracts:

> "The nature and extent of the insurer's redress should depend on the nature and the extent of the loss which he has suffered as a result of the insured's contract. He should no longer be entitled to avoid the contract, and a heavy claim under the contract, merely because he has suffered a small, even insubstantial loss as a result of a non-disclosure or misrepresentation."

One alternative to this absolute approach is the proportionality approach, which has been adopted in some European countries, such as France.

10D.2 Sue and labour clause/duty to minimise losses

10.52 The sue and labour clause is dealt with in s.78 of the MIA 1906.

The first part of the section states:

> "Where the policy contains a suing and labouring clause, the engagement thereby entered into is deemed to be supplementary to the contract of insurance, and the assured may recover from the insurer any expenses properly incurred pursuant to the clause. . . ."

The last part of the section states:

> "It is the duty of the assured and his agents, in all cases to take such measures as may be reasonable for the purpose of averting or minimising a loss. . . ."

61. Trine-Lise Wilhelmsen, *ibid.*, 364:

"According to the discussion in item 36, some main issues may be identified for the purpose of harmonization. As a starting point, one will have to look into the relationship between disclosure and misrepresentation, and the need for separate regulation. The second main issue is what kind of information the regulation shall apply to (the questions concerning materiality and inducement and the difference between active and passive duty of disclosure). A third issue is the relevant point of time. The fourth issue is the very important question of the relevance of the assured's knowledge or the degree of fault. The fifth issue is the question of causation and the sixth issue the sanctions to be applied."

62. Sir Anthony Mason, 1995 Ebsworth and Ebsworth Maritime Law Lecture, 8 : "All or nothing approach precluded the Court from awarding damages to the insurer for the breach of the duty. Thus, the insurer may be entitled to a remedy which is impractical and which unduly exceeds his loss, to the unfair detriment of the insured".

In fact, one has to read s.78 together with the clauses on "sue and labour", contained in the Institute Time Clauses and Institute Cargo Clauses.

Professor Howard Bennett[63] has raised the following questions:

(i) Do the clauses impose genuine "duties"?

(ii) Does the duty to sue and labour depend on the existence of an express clause?

(iii) How can one reconcile the "duties" of the assured, his servants and agents to avert and minimise losses, recognised by s.78(4) of the MIA 1906 and the modern clauses, with the right granted to the assured by s.55(2)(a) of the 1906 Act to recover for losses caused by a covered peril, notwithstanding that the loss would not have happened, but for the misconduct or negligence of the master or crew?

Consideration is also given to the assured's reimbursement entitlement. Professor Bennett concludes that in return for exercising reasonable care in mitigating the consequences of a breach of contract, the innocent party benefits from an implied correlative right of reimbursement of reasonable expenses incurred.[64] This is described as an implied mitigation doctrine and it is claimed that s.78 (4) of the MIA 1906 may be viewed as merely spelling out this implied bargain. Bennett quotes an Australian decision[65] which held that "sue and labour" expenses can be recovered, even in the absence of a contractual sue and labour clause, apparently on the basis of s.78(4), which creates a genuine duty. However, what s.78(4) of the MIA 1906 creates is a genuine duty for the assured to take measures, but the section does not say that he is entitled to reimbursement, unless the policy contains a suing and labouring clause. For that reason the explicit statutory language is to be preferred.

In this respect, Art. 17 of the Belgian Statute on Insurance Contracts of 1874 is relevant.[66] Article 17 imposes an obligation on the insured to do whatever he can to prevent the damage from occurring and to mitigate its consequences. When the risk or damage occurs, the insured has an obligation to inform the insurer forthwith. The expenses which the insured had to incur in order to mitigate the damages can be claimed from the insurer, even if these go beyond the sum insured and even if these attempts were fruitless, notwithstanding the fact that the court can reduce these expenses if they were not reasonably made. This article is based on the general concept of good faith in general contract law and is viewed as an aspect of the duty of co-operation which exists between parties in implementing their contractual obligations.[67] 10.53

Modern French insurance law is similar.[68] Also, under French marine insurance 10.54

63. Howard Bennett, *The Law of Marine Insurance* (Oxford, 1996) pp.386–387.

64. Howard Bennett, *ibid.*, 390.

65. *Emperor Goldmining Company Ltd v. Switzerland General Insurance Company Ltd* (Sup.Ct. N.S.W.) [1964] 1 Lloyd's Rep. 348.

66. "*L'article 17 de la loi du 11 juin 1874 impose à l'assuré de faire toute diligence pour prévenir ou atténuer le dommage . . . La sanction de cette obligation n'est pas une nullité ou une déchéance mais bien, tout comme pour ce qui concerne l'avis du sinistre, le paiement de dommages-intérêts à l'assureur*" (Rép. Pratique de Droit Belge, verbo: Assurances Maritimes, nr. 307).

67. Hubert Libert, "Zeeverzekeringen", in *Zeerecht, Grondbeginselen van het Belgisch Privaatrechtelijk Zeerecht*, Volume I, Antwerp, 1998, p.350.

68. Antoine Vialard, *Droit Maritime* (Presse Universitaire de France, Paris, 1997) p.116.

law, there is an explicit duty to mitigate, with the correlative entitlement for reimbursement, and an obligation on the insured to provide all relevant information forthwith to the insurer.[69]

10.55 In German Law, the ADS also provides for a duty on the insured to take reasonable steps to mitigate damage and an entitlement to reimbursement.[70]

In the author's view there is a lot to be said for a clear statutory provision imposing an obligation on the assured to avoid or minimise loss, with the corresponding entitlement to reimbursement for all reasonable expenses that the insured had to lay out in taking these reasonable steps; and this irrespective of the existence of a "sue and labour" clause in the policy.

10E ABSENCE OF WARRANTIES IN THE CIVIL LAW TRADITION/WARRANTIES IN THE COMMON LAW

10.56 A very important and striking difference between common law and continental systems is the presence/absence of warranties in marine insurance law. In the MIA 1906, warranties are given the status of a "sacred cow", but judging from the very substantial criticism which is now being formulated in relation to "warranties", one can conclude, without exaggeration, that the "sacred cow" is affected by a very serious disease and is in need of treatment.

10E.1 United Kingdom

10.57 Warranties are dealt with in ss.33–39 of the MIA 1906. (It is not appropriate to explain here exactly how warranties work, as they are a well established part of the law, and well understood by marine insurance practitioners.[71])

10.58 Warranties may be seen as presumptions or conditions that have to be complied with as the basis for the marine insurance cover. These presumptions or conditions may either be imposed by the statute (implied warranties), or they may be the result of contractual consensus between parties (express warranties). The main feature of warranties is that they must be strictly complied with under penalty that the insured loses cover, even if there is no causal link between the breach of warranty and the risk. The insured automatically loses the benefit of his insurance in the event of breach of warranty, as was decided in the *Good Luck*,[72] but insurers may waive the

69. Loi, 92–665 of 16 July 1992, Art. 37, II, *Journal Officiel* of 17 July 1992: "*L'assuré doit contribuer au sauvetage des objets assurés et prendre toute mesure conservatoire de ses droits contre les tiers responsables. Il est responsable envers l'assureur du dommage causé par l'inexécution de cette obligation résultant de sa faute ou de sa négligence*".

70. Klaus Kostka, "Marine Transport Insurance in Germany : the General German Cargo Conditions in comparison to the Institute Cargo Clauses and recent German Court Decisions", in Marc A Huybrechts (ed.), *Marine Insurance at the turn of the Millennium* (Antwerp, 1999, Vol. I) p.366.

71. Howard Bennett, *The Law of Marine Insurance*, Oxford, 1996, pp.279–307; Chorley and Giles, NJJ Gaskell, C Debattista and RJ Swatton, *Shipping Law*, 8th edn. (London, 1987) pp.564–572. See also Chapters 5 (Soyer) and 6 (Hodges).

72. *Bank of Nova Scotia v. Hellenic Mutual War Risk Association (Bermuda)*, (*The Good Luck*) [1989] 2 Lloyd's Rep. 238 (CA).

breach of warranty, which they can do by anticipation in the so-called "held covered clauses" or on an ad hoc basis.

10.59 The English doctrine of warranties is followed in the various former colonies and dependencies of the UK that have adopted the MIA 1906, such as Australia, New Zealand, Canada and to a certain extent also the US and South Africa.[73]

10.60 The rule that warranties must strictly be complied with under penalty of loss of cover has met with severe criticism. Some common law jurisdictions have softened the consequence by introducing a condition of causation before the insurer is entitled to avoid the contract. The South African Short Term Insurance Act s.53 introduced the materiality test. In other words, if the breach of warranty is trivial and unimportant, cover will not be terminated.

10.61 Severe criticism of the warranty system, as applied in the MIA 1906, has also been formulated by Sir Anthony Mason.[74] He raised the following questions:

> "While respecting the need for the law to ensure that promises are upheld, in today's modern society, the approach taken in marine insurance law, unfairly distributes the rights and the obligations of the insured and insurer. It also appears to disregard the commercial needs of the parties involved .... Why should the insurer be absolved on liability where there is only minor or immaterial breach by the insured?"

And when Sir Anthony Mason is advancing a strong argument for a less radical sanction in cases of breach, such as compensation, he comes to the conclusion:

> "The unfairness created by these harsh penalties is associated with the unequal bargaining power which often exists between the insured and the insurer. (...) It seems inequitable then to allow the insurer to completely avoid the policy on the occurrence of a minor, inconsequential or none-causative breach."

Sir Anthony Mason is in very good company when he quotes Lord Mustill:[75]

> "The law seems woolly and erratic, lacking any clear relationship to the commercial realities, which it ought to reflect. The incidence of fault varies widely, for no apparent reason, from one stage of the enterprise to another. The links between unseaworthiness, disabling fault and causation are not skilfully forged. ... At all events ... there seems little prospect that even the most heroic efforts could ever assemble a synthesis from the existing fragments. The only recourse would be to start again. ..."

10.62 The comments of Lord Mustill and Sir Anthony Mason were recently reinforced in a leading article by Professor John Hare.[76] In this article, Professor Hare gives an overview of the common law jurisdictions where the harsh application of the English warranties theory has been mitigated or where amendments are being considered, such as the US, Australia, Canada and South Africa.

73. Trine-Lise Wilhelmsen, *ibid.*, *CMI Yearbook 2000*, 6.2–6.9, 386–411.
74. Sir Anthony Mason, "The Future of Marine Insurance", in the Ebsworth and Ebsworth Maritime Law Lecture 1995.
75. MJ Mustill, "Fault and Marine Insurance Losses" (1988), LMCLQ, 310, at pp.357–358.
76. John Hare, "The omnipotent warranty, England v. The World", in Marc A Huybrechts (ed.), *Marine Insurance at the turn of the Millennium*, Vol. II (Antwerp 2000) pp.37–55.

Professor Hare illustrates the shortfalls and the inequities in the current practices and he advances a strong argument for the adoption of basic and uniform international rules of marine insurance. After quoting Emerigon, he comes to the following conclusion: "Let natural reason again prevail. Let the same results again flow from the breach of an essential term (whatever its name may be in all countries alike). Let us consign the 'toxic' English warranty to the obscurity of history where it belongs . . .".

Quite radical and far-reaching words, but Professor Hare is certainly not alone in his severe criticism.

10E.2 The continental law tradition

10.63 Warranties such as described in the MIA 1906 do not exist in continental jurisdictions. The general continental contract law acknowledges a concept known as "La clause resolutoire expresse" or "the express resolutory condition". This is a clause agreed upon by the parties to a contract which allows a party to terminate the contract should the other party be in breach of its fundamental obligations. The contractual clause is normally written in such a way that termination is more or less automatic should one of the parties breach its specifically listed obligations. In the meantime, however, various legislators have introduced legislation to curtail the possibility for parties to rely on these types of clause in certain areas of the law, e.g. in relation to landlord and tenant or contracts and consumer sales.

In Belgium, express resolutory conditions are illegal in the field of lease contracts in relation to residential homes, and also under recent legislation they have been ruled out or strictly limited in a good number of consumer protection areas.[77] However, express resolutory conditions would certainly be permissible in marine insurance contracts as marine insurance is not subject to any of the protective consumer type legislation. Nonetheless, continental judges retain a certain judicial control over such clauses, which are subject to the "good faith" requirement and the public policy limitations of general contract law. But the continental marine insurance statutes, as such, do not provide a system of warranties as understood by the British MIA 1906.

10.64 Reference should be made to the article by Wilhelmsen[78] for further comment on warranties in continental countries. Wilhelmsen suggests that the concept of warranties "seems to be applied" in Portugal, Spain, Slovenia, Venezuela and China. With reference to China it is noteworthy that the Chinese Maritime Code mentions in art. 235 the word "warranties", but the concept is not defined in the statute and

77. (Belgian) Statute of 14 July 1991 on Commercial Practices and Aiming to Protect the Consumer, *Moniteur Belge*, 29 August, 1991; Art. 32, 9 c. Belgian Statute on Land-based Insurance, 25 June 1992, *Moniteur Belge*, 20 August, 1992, Art. 11.

78. Trine-Lise Wilhelmsen, "The Duty of Disclosure, the Duty of Good Faith, Alteration of Risk and Warranties, An analysis of the replies to the CMI questionnaire", in *CMI Yearbook 2000*, 385: "The concept of warranties is first and foremost a common law concept, but some civil law countries have adapted the principle as well. This concept will be discussed below under item 6.2. Most of the civil law countries in Europe do not have a concept of warranties in their insurance legislation. This is the situation in the Scandinavian Countries, Germany, Belgium, The Netherlands, France, Italy, Croatia, among the non-European countries, Japan has the same general attitude . . .".

Chinese courts treat the concept of warranties very much as a contractual clause. Hence, it seems that the conclusion that Chinese law recognises the concept of warranties is not entirely warranted.[79]

10.65 It may well be the case that continental courts apply English warranties, but then only on account of the ordinary application of the national rules on conflicts of law or the private international law rules. In that respect, one can refer to Belgian court decisions which have correctly recognised and applied English rules in relation to warranties in cases where English law governed the contract.[80]

10.66 In conclusion, it can be said that there is certainly at present no demand for the introduction of the English concept of warranties in marine insurance law generally, whereas at the same time it is noteworthy that the English warranty system is subject to some severe criticism from common law authors as well.

10F THE INSURED RISKS

10F.1 Are perils of the sea in the continental tradition more dangerous than in the common law?

10.67 One further noteworthy difference between England and the continent is the approach to marine risks or maritime perils. It must, however, be conceded that the difference is probably maybe more a difference of form than one of real substance.

10.68 The starting point is s.3 of the MIA 1906, where the statute gives us a definition of what is to be understood by maritime perils, or perils of the sea. These include perils consequent on or incidental to the navigation of the sea, that is to say, perils of the seas, fire, war perils, pirates, rovers, thieves, captures, seizures, restraints, and detainment of princes and peoples, jettisons, barratry and any other peril, either of the like kind or designated by the policy.

Section 3 of the MIA 1906 has to be read in conjunction with rule 7 of the Rules for Construction of the Policy, part of the First Schedule to the MIA 1906:

> "The term 'Perils of the Seas' refers only to fortuitous accidents or casualties of the seas. It does not include the ordinary action of the winds and the waves."

Rule 7 makes it clear that maritime perils must be in the nature of an accident. Bennett[81] goes on to say: "For a peril to be 'of the seas' it does not suffice that it occurs in fact or even customarily at sea. 'Of the seas' imports an exclusive connection with the sea".

79. Marc A Huybrechts, "A Belgian Look into Warranties in Marine Insurance both in Chinese and English Law", paper presented at the 4th International Conference of the Chinese Maritime Law Association.

80. Marc A Huybrechts, "A Belgian Contribution to Hull Underwriting", in *Marine Insurance at the turn of the Millennium* (Antwerp, 1999, Vol. I) 274.

81. Howard Bennett, *The Law of Marine Insurance* (Oxford 1996), p.139.

10.69 French marine insurance law basically shares the same approach: maritime risks mean risks which find their origin in the sea.[82]

10.70 In Belgium, however, all the authors on marine insurance have consistently and repeatedly stated that Belgian law offers better protection to the insured, because the approach to risks is not limited to risks caused by the sea, but risks caused whilst the insured interest is on the high seas.[83]

10.71 Sohr-van Doosselaere puts it this way: "Il ne faut donc pas que le sinistre soit directement causé par la mer ou par une cause maritime; il suffit que la mer soit le théâtre du sinistre, pour que l'assureur soit responsable envers l'assuré . . .". This approach has been followed by all the authors dealing with marine insurance law.[84] Buisseret stated: "A noter en particulier que l'expression 'perils of the sea' a un sens plus restreint que l'expression 'fortune de mer', usité en Belgique et en France. Les mots 'perils of the sea' visent uniquement l'action violente des flots et des vents, alors que les mots 'périls de la mer' visent tous les risques qui surviennent sur la mer".

So, Belgian legal doctrine is very firm in its position, with the consequence that Belgian marine insurance law offers better cover to the insured in comparison to English law, because the Belgian concept of perils of the sea encompasses all risks that take place on the sea, which is supposed to be more than the English perception of a peril of the seas. However, when one examines the Belgian Marine Insurance Statute, more precisely section 201 of the Belgian Maritime Code, the law refers to all losses caused by storm, shipwreck, stranding, collision, (forced) deviation, jettison, fire, explosion, robbery and in general any loss caused by any other peril of the sea. All the events listed by the statute are obviously fortuitous events, as are the "perils of the sea" listed in s.3 of the English MIA 1906. The question must then be raised what causes this difference in approach in Belgium *vis-à-vis* England.

The answer lies in the context in which the Belgian theory has been articulated. When one has a closer look at the statements of the various authors defending the "sea theatre theory", it is obvious that this theory has to be understood in the light of the wording of the Antwerp Marine Policy of 1859, and not so much in the light of the statute.

10.72 The authors do not comment on the risk clause of the Belgian statute as such, but on the risks covered by the Antwerp marine policy, a policy which is to a certain extent comparable to the famous and now obsolete S & G policy of the London market. The Belgian (Antwerp) policy, mainly used for cargo insurance, has its strong admirers and defenders,[85] and has been the Belgian export product on marine insurance, being a rival to the S & G policy of the London market.

---

82. Antoine Vialard, *Droit Maritime,* Paris, 1997: "L'assurance maritime couvre en principe, des dommages trouvant leur source dans un événement de mer: il s'agit de l'événement de mer lui-même, le péril, l'aléa de la navigation maritime ou de l'exploitation d'un navire contre lequel l'armateur cherche a protéger son navire . . .".

83. Sohr-van Doosselaere, *Les Assurances Transport*, Pandectes Belges, 1932, No. 547–548.

84. Robert Desmedt, *Traité Théorique et Pratique des Assurances Maritimes*, Vol. I, No. 230, 249; Pierre Wildiers et Marcel Caethoven, *Manuel Pratique des Assurances Maritimes*, Antwerp, 1964, 29; Buisseret, *Assurances Maritimes*, Répertoire Pratique du Droit Belge, No. 446; Dieryck Christian, "La Police Maritime d'Anvers (1859)", in *Tijdschrift Belgisch Handelsrecht*, 2000, No. 9, 533; Hubert Libert, "Zeeverzekeringen", in *Zeerecht, Grondbeginselen van het Belgisch Privaatrechtelijk Zeerecht*, Antwerpen, 1998, p.324.

85. P Hollenfeltz du Treux, "Portrait d'une très grande dame, restée jeune et séduisante malgré son age: La Police Maritime d'Anvers de 1859", in *Liber Amicorum Lionel Tricot*, Antwerp, 1988, p.293.

Because it was a commercial product, it needed promotion and good marketing and it is the author's suggestion that the "sea theatre theory" is more of a sales argument than anything else. Good reasons had to be given why the Antwerp marine policy was superior to the English S & G policy. Authors like Christian Dieryck[86] give us a good example of the "value for money" approach: "Ainsi, sous la couverture de la police, le dommage causé par la pluie ou la neige, au cours du voyage maritime, est une fortune de mer, parce qu'il est produit en mer par l'action des éléments. Tel ne serait pas le cas sous la couverture d'une police Anglaise qui requière les faits accidentels des flots . . .". The same is repeated by Hubert Libert, who also claims that damage caused by rain and snow during the sea voyage is covered according to Belgian case law, but will not be covered in England.[87] Whether that inference is correct is at least questionable.

The Belgian doctrine commenting on the risks covered in the framework of the Antwerp marine policy always refers to "*Les pleines conditions*" of the Antwerp marine policy, or even better "*les grandes conditions*". This amounts to the all risk policy of the English commercial practice. The author believes that under the English "all risk" conditions, damage caused by snow or rain would also be covered by ICL(A), 1982 cargo, at least according to the dictum of Lord Summer in *British and Foreign Marine Insurance Co. v. Gaunt*.[88]

In conclusion, it can be argued that the perceived difference between England and Belgium is in the first place attributable to a different interpretation and perception of the risk concept in the framework of existing policy conditions, rather than being based on the words of the respective statutes, which both seem to imply that risks are "fortuitous events" and nothing else. It is true that various English decisions have introduced a fairly restricted reading of the "peril of the sea" concept and insisted that the risk be connected with the sea, as the origin of it. These restricted views, of course, can always be corrected by the parties in spelling out the terms and conditions of the insured perils, as an insurance contract is very much a matter of agreement between parties. 10.73

Another example may be quoted to illustrate the difference between English marine insurance law and the civil law tradition: the problem of semantics. "Barratry" in English law differs from "*la baraterie du patron*" in Belgian and French law. 10.74

According to rule 11 of the Rules for Construction of Policy in the English MIA 1906, the term Barratry "includes every wrongful act wilfully committed by the master or crew to the prejudice of the owner, or as the case may be the charterer . . .". Under English law, barratry is wilfully committed by master or crew against the owner, and without the privity of the owner. A restrictive reading of the rule has lead to the conclusion that barratry can only be committed against an owner of the vessel (and in some circumstances against the charterer by demise).

In order to be protected against the risk of barratry, if barratry be an insured risk, the charterer needs to be a charterer by demise, i.e. he has to be an owner *pro hac*

86. Christian Dieryck, *ibid.*, 533.
87. Hubert Libert, "Zeeverzekeringen", in I. De Weerdt (ed.), *Zeerecht*, Antwerp, 1998, p.324.
88. *British and Foreign Marine Insurance Co. v. Gaunt* [1921] 2 A.C. 41; [1921] All E.R. 447.

vice. Therefore, barratry cannot be committed against cargo owners, which indeed is a fairly restricted view of barratry.

10.75 In Belgium, the vision is different. "Baraterie" indicates all the faults or negligent acts committed by the master or his crew. Here again we see a noteworthy difference between the common law and continental law.[89] A major difference from the English interpretation is that barratry under the continental-Belgian concept can also be committed to the detriment of the cargo owner.[90]

10.76 In France the concept of "baraterie" is no longer very popular.[91] French Law is much more concerned with the intentional or wilful misconduct of the master and crew and "*la faute inexcusable*". Modern French law in principle does not cover the intentional fault of the master, but allows for cover for "*la faute inexcusable*" of the master. "*La faute inexcusable*" can be described as gross negligence.[92]

10G CONCLUSION

10.77 An analysis of the common law and the civil law has revealed some important differences between the practice of marine insurance law on the continent and that in England. Some of the differences find their origin not in the law of marine insurance as such, but in the general law or general contract law, such as the issues of good faith and causation.

The differences with reference to the principle of good faith deal more with form than with real substance. Other differences, however, are fundamental, such as a very different approach to causation and the concept of warranties.

Other differences, such as the obligation of full disclosure, the sue and labour clause and the duty to minimise losses are differences of degree rather than of principle. And finally, with reference to marine risks, the differences between the common law and the continental law may also be more a question of form than content. With reference to the "theatre of the sea" approach, it has more the aura of a sales argument to promote a specific policy than a fundamental difference rooted in the respective statutory law.

The major differences in marine insurance law are undoubtedly to be found in the approach to causation and the warranties.

It is to be hoped that this analysis will help to clarify some issues, should an international convention on marine insurance ever be prepared and adopted. If such an international convention is ever to see the light of day, it will have to enjoy universal

89. Christian Dieryck, "La Police Maritime d'Anvers, 1859", *ibid.*, 535: "Le Droit Continental se distingue du droit Anglais ou la baraterie a conservé son sens primitif de fraude de tromperie. Les polices Anglaises couvrent la baraterie, mais par la différence entre ses deux notions, une telle couverture est nettement plus restreinte".

90. Buisseret, "Répertoire Pratique de Droit Belge", in *Les Assurances Maritimes*, No. 252, quoting: Brussels, 16 February 1949, Jurisprudence du Port d'Anvers, 1949, p.444.

91. Vialard, *ibid.*, No. 109bis, 93.

92. Vialard, *ibid.*, 94. For a good comparison between barratry on the continent and in England, see also Robert De Smet, *Traité Théorique et Pratiques des Assurances Maritimes*, Paris 1959, No. 264, 208.

acceptance in order to be successful. Acceptance can only come if the differences in the existing systems are acknowledged and if there is an awareness of the relative merits of these differences.

CHAPTER 11

AUSTRALIA: PERSPECTIVES AND PERMUTATIONS ON THE LAW OF MARINE INSURANCE

DR SARAH DERRINGTON

11A SOURCE OF AUSTRALIAN MARINE INSURANCE LAW AND IMPETUS FOR REFORM

Three years after the Parliament of the UK enacted the Marine Insurance Act 1906, the Parliament of the Commonwealth of Australia enacted the Marine Insurance Act 1909. In his second reading speech on the Marine Insurance Bill, the then Attorney-General said: *11.1*

"At the present time, in each of the states of Australia anyone who desires to ascertain what the law of marine insurance is, has to consult common law authorities and decisions. Of these there are no less than 2,000 in existence. Under these circumstances, of course the law is in some cases difficult to ascertain. In some instances, the authorities are uncertain; on some points where certainty is required, no certainty can be gathered; and some decisions rest upon old conditions which have now become obsolete. ... Marine insurance is a highly technical branch of the law. It requires for the complete mastery of it years of careful research and practice. At the same time it is a branch of the law which greatly affects the commerce of our people. It is, therefore, above all things highly desirable that this branch of the law should be made clear, definite and certain."[1]

Despite the expressed desire of the Attorney-General for the Marine Insurance Act

1. House of Representatives, Hansard, 6 October 1908.

1909 to create certainty in the Australian law of marine insurance, it is clear that, with the dawn of the new millennium, much uncertainty either remains or has emerged. Australian commentators have expressed similar sentiments to those expressed by commentators in the UK to the effect that the Marine Insurance Act, whether in its Australian or English form, is ripe for amendment.[2]

11.2 The emergence of any impetus for reform can be traced back to the Law Reform Commission Report on Insurance Contracts (ALRC 20) in 1982. That report dealt only with general insurance, marine insurance being expressly excluded from the terms of reference for the Law Reform Commission.[3] However, the legislation resulting from ALRC 20, the Insurance Contracts Act 1984 (Cwlth)(ICA) made significant changes to those areas of general insurance law which are also considered to be problematic by some commentators in marine insurance; the requirement of insurable interest, the concept of utmost good faith, the nature and extent of the duty of disclosure and the doctrine of warranties. In 1983 the New South Wales Law Reform Commission also undertook a review of insurance contracts and delivered a report on non-disclosure and misrepresentation.[4] Marine insurance was also excluded from the terms of reference for the New South Wales Law Reform Commission on the basis that marine insurance was subject to Commonwealth legislation which covers the field.[5] Despite this, the New South Wales Law Reform Commission expressed the opinion that the traditional principles of common law enshrined in the Marine Insurance Act 1909 were overdue for reform.[6]

11.3 In 1997, the Commonwealth Attorney-General's Department released an Issues Paper which identified warranties, disclosure and representation as the major areas for reform in the law of marine insurance.[7] After languishing somewhat over the next three years, the Commonwealth Attorney-General released a reference to the Australian Law Reform Commission (ALRC) on 21 January 2000 for review of the Marine Insurance Act 1909. In July 2000 the ALRC produced a Discussion Paper[8] and conducted extensive consultations within the industry. In May 2001, the ALRC released its report and recommendations to the Attorney-General.[9] If adopted by the federal government, the recommendations will result in significant changes to the requirement that an insured have an insurable interest, to the nature and extent of the duty of utmost good faith, to the doctrine of warranties and to the nature and extent of the remedies available for breach of those various obligations. The ambiguity which can arise in the Australian context as to the applicability of the Marine Insurance Act 1909 would also be alleviated to some extent.

---

2. Kirby, The Honourable Justice MD, "Marine Insurance: Is the Doctrine of 'Utmost Good Faith' Out of Date?" (1995) 13 *Australian Bar Review* 1; Mason, Sir Anthony, "The Future of Marine Insurance Law", the 1995 Ebsworth & Ebsworth Maritime Law Lecture; Derrington, SC "Does the Marine Insurance Act 1909 Still Serve the Needs of the Business Community?" (1995) 7 *Insurance Law Journal* 32.
3. RG Ellicott QC, Attorney-General, Terms of Reference to the Law Reform Commission, 9 September 1976.
4. New South Wales Law Reform Commission, Community Law Reform Program – First Report, Insurance Contracts – Non-Disclosure and Misrepresentation, 1983.
5. *Ibid.*, paragraph 7.39 and Appendix 2, para. 1.
6. *Ibid.*, Appendix 2, para. 2.
7. The Marine Insurance Act 1909, Issues Paper, 1997.
8. ALRC, DP 63, July 2000.
9. ALRC 91, April 2001.

11B SCOPE AND COVERAGE OF THE MARINE INSURANCE ACT 1909

Australia has a number of insurance law regimes. Contracts of marine insurance are governed by the Marine Insurance Act 1909 and may cover mixed sea and land risks. Most non-marine insurance is governed by the ICA. Contracts of insurance governed by the ICA include those covering risks in respect of commercial aircraft and all forms of land transport. Specific statutory regimes govern workers compensation, seaman's rehabilitation, motor vehicle accidents, health insurance and so on. Thus, the dichotomy which pertains between general and marine insurance is more acute in Australia than in the UK because of the variety of insurance regimes. Whether the Marine Insurance Act 1909 or the ICA applies to a particular contract of insurance is a threshold question which is crucial. The discrepancies between the Marine Insurance Act 1909 and the ICA relate not only to the substance of the law but also to the practice of writing insurance business in the market. 11.4

The provisions of the Marine Insurance Act 1909 apply to "contracts of marine insurance". Section 7 of the Marine Insurance Act 1909[10] defines a contract of marine insurance as follows: 11.5

> "A contract of marine insurance is a contract whereby the insurer undertakes to indemnify the insured, in manner and to the extent thereby agreed, against marine losses, that is to say, the losses incident to marine adventure."

Only losses incident to marine adventures are covered in marine insurance contracts. There is a marine adventure where loss, damage or liability may be incurred by reason of maritime perils and the definition of maritime perils in the Marine Insurance Act 1909 is identical to that contained in the Marine Insurance Act 1906. Section 9 of the Marine Insurance Act 1909[11] defines the subject-matter of marine insurance. 11.6

> "1. Subject to the provisions of this Act, every lawful marine adventure may be the subject of a contract of marine insurance.
> 2. In particular there is a marine adventure where:
> (a) any ship, goods, or other movables are exposed to maritime perils. Such property is in this Act referred to as "insurable property";
> (b) the earning or acquisition of any freight, passage money, commission, profit or other pecuniary benefit, or the security for any advances, loan, or disbursements is endangered by the exposure of insurable property to maritime perils;
> (c) any liability to a third party may be incurred by the owner of, or other person interested in or responsible for, insurable property, by reason of maritime perils."

The Marine Insurance Act 1909 requires the subject matter of a contract of marine insurance to be "designated in a marine policy with reasonable certainty".[12] Contracts of marine insurance may cover some non-marine risks and subject-matter and s.8 of the Act[13] provides for contracts of marine insurance to cover mixed sea and land risks. It is clear that the non-marine risks which s.8(1) permits to be covered by a 11.7

10. Marine Insurance Act 1906, s.1.
11. Marine Insurance Act 1906, s.3.
12. Section 32(1); Marine Insurance Act 1906, s.26(1).
13. Marine Insurance Act 1906, s.2.

policy of marine insurance are incidental to the sea voyage and that the maritime risks, therefore, remain the primary focus of the contract of marine insurance.

11.8 The ICA, which came into force in 1985, applies to all contracts of insurance and proposed contracts of insurance the proper law of which is the law of an Australian State or Territory, unless excluded by the Act. Section 9 provides a number of exceptions to the application of the Act, one of which is contracts to or in relation to which the Marine Insurance Act 1909 applies.[14]

In 1998, the ICA was amended by the Insurance Laws Amendment Act 1998 (Cwlth) to exclude pleasure craft insurance from the operation of the Marine Insurance Act 1909.[15] A "pleasure craft" is defined in the ICA to mean a ship which is owned by individuals and used wholly for recreational or sporting activities otherwise than for reward. For these purposes, any minor, infrequent or irregular use or other activities is ignored.[16]

The consequence of these competing insurance regimes is that situations may arise where one or both parties assume that an insurance contract is one of marine insurance, and, therefore, subject to the Marine Insurance Act 1909, when in fact the contract is governed by the ICA. As many of the provisions of the ICA extensively modify in favour of insured parties the common law principles on which the Marine Insurance Act 1909 is based, the legal and practical consequences of the application of the ICA are most likely to prejudice the insurer. Thus, where the ICA rather than the Marine Insurance Act 1909 covers a contract, the consequences for an insurer may include:

- (i) that the insurer may be unable to avoid liability under a contract where the insured has failed to disclose or has misrepresented a material circumstance unless the non-disclosure is fraudulent;
- (ii) that the insurer may be unable to rely on an insured's breach of a warranty to discharge it from all liability for subsequent loss unless the breach caused the loss;
- (iii) that the insurer may be liable under the contract where the insured has suffered economic loss notwithstanding that the insured did not have a strict insurable interest in the insured property.

11.9 Except where the contract provides for the application of foreign law (where this is permissible), it seems that either the Marine Insurance Act 1909 or the ICA must apply to the whole of any contract of general insurance not covered by another statutory scheme. Neither Act appears to contemplate the splitting of a contract or policy between them. The ICA was drafted with clear knowledge of the provisions of the Marine Insurance Act 1909 but there is no provision in the ICA which anticipates that one or other Act might apply to severable portions of the contract. Therefore, in some circumstances there may be uncertainty as to whether a contract of insurance is one to which the Marine Insurance Act 1909 applies. This uncertainty is most apparent in relation to contracts of insurance which cover both marine and

14. ICA s.9(1)(d). The ICA also excludes contracts of health insurance, insurance relating to workers compensation and third party injury motor vehicle insurance and reinsurance.

15. ICA, s.9A inserted by the Insurance Laws Amendment Act 1998 (Cwlth).

16. ICA s.9A.

non-marine activities, such as multi-modal transit and activities located on the foreshore.

An example of the difficulty raised by the two diverse Acts is the case of *Norsworthy & Encel v. SGIC*.[17] The plaintiffs in that case sustained personal injuries and property damage in a boating accident during a diving excursion operated by Glenelg Dive Charters Pty Ltd ("GDC"). GDC was insured by SGIC, the State Government Insurance Corporation, pursuant to a policy described as being one of "marine insurance". GDC went into liquidation and the insurer was sued directly by the plaintiffs. The issue as to which statute governed the policy then became important as s.51 of the ICA makes limited provision for a right of direct action by third parties against insurers.[18] There is no equivalent provision in the Marine Insurance Act 1909. The ICA expressly provides in s.9(1)(e) that it does not apply to contracts to which the Marine Insurance Act 1909 applies. Section 6 of the Marine Insurance Act 1909, however, is also expressed not to apply to "state marine insurance". There is, therefore, the potential for a significant hiatus in the law governing contracts of marine insurance written by state insurers. There was no doubt on the facts of this case that the policy covered a "marine adventure" and was, therefore, otherwise within the scope of the Marine Insurance Act 1909. The policy incorporated a specific provision in the following terms: *11.10*

> "Where applicable this insurance is subject to the provisions of the *Insurance Contracts Act* 1984 as amended and/or the *Marine Insurance Act* 1909."

It has become the almost invariable practice of state insurers to endorse their policies with such statements to voluntarily bring themselves within the provisions of one or the other of the relevant statutes. Were it not for this endorsement, the parties would have found themselves in the unusual situation of being party to a contract of insurance governed neither by the Marine Insurance Act 1909 nor the ICA. Were that indeed the case, it would seem that the applicable law would be the common law as it existed in Australia pre-1909; namely, before the enactment of the Marine Insurance Act 1909. Thus, being properly construed as a marine policy, the contract of insurance in this case was held to be governed by the Marine Insurance Act 1909 and thus there was no prospect of direct action by the third party plaintiff against the insurer. The plaintiff's remedy was to re-register the liquidated company for the *11.11*

17. Unreported, *per* Olsen J, Supreme Court of South Australia, November 30, 1999.
18. "Section 51 *Right of third party to recover against insurers.*
(1) Where:
(a) the insured under a contract of liability insurance is liable in damages to a person (in this section called the third party);
(b) the insured has died or cannot, after reasonable enquiry, be found;
(c) the third party may recover from the insurer an amount equal to the insurer's liability under the contract in respect of the insured's liability in damages.
(2) A payment under sub-section (1) is a discharge, to the extent of the payment, in respect of:
(a) the insurer's liability under the contract; and
(b) the liability of the insured or of the insured's legal personal representative to the third party.
(3) This section does not affect any right that the third party has in respect of the insured's liability, being a right under some other law of the commonwealth or under a law of a State or Territory."

purposes of the action against it and, having succeeded, then have the company proceed against the insurer.[19]

11.12 Another case in which the issue of the relevant statute fell to be decided was *Hansen Development Pty Ltd v. MMI Limited.*[20] The defendant was sued by the plaintiff for injuries received as a consequence of the defendant's negligence or breach of contract in operating a "wave sled ride". The insurer was joined as a third party and succeeded at first instance in maintaining that the policy did not cover the defendant. The New South Wales Appeal Court was asked to consider whether, although a public liability policy, the contract was also one governed by the Marine Insurance Act 1909 or whether the ICA was the relevant Act. Meagher JA said:

> "In the whole of Arnould's work I have not located a single example of a public liability risk being treated as a marine insurance risk, let alone a policy dealing with nothing but public liability being treated as marine policy. Particularly must this be so when no 'sea' is involved: Cugden Lake can hardly be said to be a sea."[21]

The Court of Appeal affirmed the trial judge's finding that the use of the wave sled did not fall within the scope of cover provided by the policy, as it would have been required to have been specifically endorsed on the policy. Aquaplaning was covered by the policy but not wave sled riding. In the result the plaintiff failed against the insurer.

11.13 Of course, public liability insurance can be marine insurance[22] and P & I insurance is liability insurance. In the Australian context, however, this case illustrates that for the liability insurance to be subject to the Marine Insurance Act 1909, the insured must be responsible for property that is insurable under the Marine Insurance Act 1909 or must be exposed to liability which arises due to a maritime peril.

11.14 The uncertainty as to the applicable law also arises in the context of cargo insurance where more than one form of carriage is often involved in the transit of goods. The High Court had occasion to consider the issue of mixed risks in *Con Stan Industries of Australia Pty Ltd v. Norwich Winterthur (Australia) Limited.*[23] The case involved the insurance of stock and trade from a variety of risks including "transit risk – road, rail, sea, air, parcel, post". However, the case is of limited assistance as no evidence was led to illustrate the importance of the carriage of goods by sea in the context of the whole policy and the terms of the policy indicated that it was but one part of one section of the cover afforded. The High Court held that it could not be held that the policy, viewed in its entirety, indemnified the insured against losses that were substantially incidental to a marine adventure. The case indicates that a policy covering various modes of transport will be governed by the ICA if there is no evidence that sea transport predominates.

11.15 Whilst the demarcation between marine and non-marine insurance in Australia contains uncertainty, the ALRC has concluded that no statutory reformulation of

19. Since 1 July 1998, s.601AG of the Corporations Law (Cwlth) has given a right of direct action against the insurer when the defendant company has been deregistered.
20. Unreported, New South Wales Court of Appeal, 23 June 1999.
21. *Ibid.* at para. 11.
22. Marine Insurance Act 1909, s.9(2)(c); Marine Insurance Act 1906, s.3(2)(c).
23. (1986) 160 CLR 226.

that demarcation will satisfactorily remove the uncertainty and accordingly recommended that the Marine Insurance Act 1909 remain unaltered in this respect.[24]

However, in relation to the more fundamental issue of coverage of the Marine Insurance Act 1909, the ALRC has recommended that the Marine Insurance Act 1909 be amended so that, subject to the terms of the contract, marine insurance covers risks on inland waters and that where appropriate the sea and the seas should be read as including inland waters. This recommendation arises out of the importance of the distinction between inland waters and the sea in determining the respective coverage of the Marine Insurance Act 1909 and the ICA. Whilst in practice the need to make this distinction is limited, there are instances in which commercial navigation may occur on inland waters whether incidental to a sea voyage or not. Of course, most inland waters in Australia are used for pleasure craft, the insurance of which is expressly covered by the ICA. 11.16

It has also been recommended that the insurance of the carriage of goods for non-commercial purposes be removed from the Marine Insurance Act 1909, that the Marine Insurance Act 1909 refer expressly to losses arising from any air risk incidental to a sea voyage and that the Act be amended to refer expressly to losses arising from the repair of the ship. 11.17

11C REQUIREMENT OF INSURABLE INTEREST

The principle of insurable interest is derived from the fundamental principle of indemnity, namely that the insurer is under an obligation to reimburse the insured for the actual loss from the covered risk and an insured is entitled to be restored, subject to the terms and conditions of the policy, to the financial position enjoyed immediately before the loss. To confirm that the insured suffered a loss, it must show that it had an insurable interest in the subject-matter insured. Section 10 of the Marine Insurance Act 1909[25] provides: 11.18

"(1) Every contract of marine insurance by way of gaming or wagering is void.
(2) A contract of marine insurance is deemed to be a gaming or wagering contract:
(a) where the insured has not an insurable interest as defined by this Act, and the contract is entered into with no expectation of acquiring such an interest; or
(b) where the policy is made 'interest or no interest', or 'without further proof of interest than the policy itself', or, 'without benefit of salvage to the insurer', or subject to any other like term.
Provided that, where there is no possibility of salvage, a policy may be effected without benefit of salvage to the insurer."

Section 11 of the Marine Insurance Act 1909[26] provides:

"(1) Subject to the provisions of this Act, every person has an insurable interest who is interested in the marine adventure.
(2) In particular, a person is interested in a marine adventure where he stands in any legal or equitable relation to the adventure, or to any insurable property at risk therein, in

24. ALRC 91, para. 8.72.
25. Marine Insurance Act 1906, s.4.
26. Marine Insurance Act 1906, s.5.

consequence of which he may benefit by the safety or due arrival of insurable property, or may be prejudiced by its loss, or by damage thereto, or by the detention thereof, or may incur liability in respect thereof."

The Marine Insurance Act 1909 does not provide an extensive definition of an insurable interest. However, it does provide that mortgagees[27] and lessees of insured property have an insurable interest and that an insurable interest may be partial[28] defeasible or contingent.[29] It also specifically refers to other interests as being insurable such as that of a lender of money on bottomry or *respondentia*,[30] the master or crew members in respect of their wages,[31] a person advancing freight[32] and an insured in costs of insurance which it effects[33]. In the general law of insurance in Australia, the ICA, in ss.16 and 17, modified the concept of insurable interest.

11.19 Section 16 of the ICA states that a "contract of general insurance is not void by reason only that the insured did not have, at the time when the contract was entered into, an interest in the subject matter of the contract". The ICA uses an economic loss test to determine whether the insured has a sufficient interest to claim under the policy. Section 17 states that where the insured has suffered a pecuniary or economic loss the insurer is not relieved of liability by reason only that, at the time of loss, the insured did not have an interest in law or in equity in the property.

Since the implementation of these provisions in the ICA some 15 years ago, there appear to have been only three cases dealing with s.16 or s.17. In *Pacific Dunlop Limited v. Maxifirm Boilers Pty Limited*,[34] Teaghe J in the Supreme Court of Victoria noted uncertainty as to whether s.17 could be relied upon by a non-party insured. In *Howard v. Australian Jet Charter Pty Limited*,[35] Hill J in the Federal Court held that, by virtue of ss.16 and 17 of the ICA, a company that had contracted to maintain and crew an aircraft could not be said to have an interest in a contract of insurance covering loss from damage to that aircraft. In *Advance (New South Wales) Insurance Agencies Pty Ltd v. Matthews*,[36] Samuels JA found that, under s.17, a husband had an economic, and, therefore, insurable interest in his wife's clothing and other personal effects.

11.20 The case which is of particular interest in the marine context and which has led to arguments for reform of the requirement for an insurable interest in marine insurance law is that of *New South Wales Leather Co. Pty Limited v. Vanguard Insurance Co. Limited*.[37] In that case, the insured had an insurance policy stated to insure "lost or not lost" certain consignments of leather that it had purchased FOB from various Brazilian suppliers. The insurance policy contained a "warehouse to warehouse" or "transit" clause in terms of the Institute Cargo Clauses (A) stating that:

"This insurance attaches from the time the goods leave the warehouse or place of storage at

27. Section 20; Marine Insurance Act 1906, s.14.
28. Section 14; Marine Insurance Act 1906, s.8.
29. Section 13(1); Marine Insurance Act 1906, s.7(1).
30. Section 16; Marine Insurance Act 1906, s.10.
31. Section 17; Marine Insurance Act 1906, s.9.
32. Section 18; Marine Insurance Act 1906, s.12.
33. Section 19; Marine Insurance Act 1906, s.13.
34. (1997) 9 ANZ Insurance Cases 61–357.
35. (1991) 6 ANZ Insurance Cases 61–054.
36. (1988) 12 NSWLR 250.
37. (1990) 103 FLR 70; [1991] NSWLR 699.

the place named in the policy for the commencement of transit, continues during the ordinary course of transit and terminates [on delivery]."

The goods were loaded in containers but most of them were stolen before the containers were loaded on board the ship. The insurers denied the claim on the grounds that the insured did not have an insurable interest at the time of the loss.

Under a standard FOB contract, the risk in respect of goods, whether or not loaded in a sealed container, does not pass to the buyer until the container has passed the ship's rail. In the Supreme Court of New South Wales, Justice Carruthers confirmed the rule that a purchaser FOB does not have an insurable interest in goods during transit from the seller's warehouse to the ship's rails. His Honour held that the transit clause could not operate to extend the cover to an earlier point in time in the absence of an insurable interest. On appeal, the New South Wales Court of Appeal agreed with the trial judge that the insured did not have an insurable interest in the goods at the time of loss, and therefore could derive no assistance from the transit clause. The pre-loading portion of the warehouse to warehouse clause is, viewed in isolation, worthless to a purchaser on FOB terms and does not in fact provide the cover as its name suggests. Of course, the position of an insured buyer FOB or C&F may be improved by the insertion of a "lost or not lost" clause in the policy and, ultimately, it was held in the Court of Appeal that the insured was able to recover relying on the "lost or not lost" clause in combination with warehouse to warehouse cover.

The operation of the requirement for insurable interest in this context has been extensively criticised.[38]

The inconsistency of understanding in this area of the law is illustrated by the differences in interpretation reached by Justice Carruthers at first instance and by the Court of Appeal. At first instance, Justice Carruthers stated that, consistently with the fundamental principle that a contract of insurance is a contract of indemnity, an insured cannot rely on a "lost or not lost" clause unless the loss falls on it. He held that the loss in question had clearly not fallen on the insured, even though it had already paid for the goods, who was entitled to recover the purchase price from the sellers. In contrast the Court of Appeal found that the insured had suffered a loss even though the insured was not at risk when the goods were stolen. It was sufficient that the insured suffered financial loss because of the prior loss of the goods. The fact that it had contractual remedies against its sellers was no barrier to a claim on the insurance.

Thus, in Australia, the only appellate decision that has recently considered the issue, namely *New South Wales Leather*, appears to be authority for the proposition that where an insured suffers a loss prior to obtaining the insurable interest in the goods (for example by paying cash against documents) and subsequently acquires an insurable interest in those goods, a combination of a "lost or not lost" clause and a warehouse to warehouse clause entitles the insured to indemnity.

As a consequence of the current law pertaining to the requirement of an insurable interest in marine insurance, the ALRC has recommended the abolition of the 11.21

38. D Galbraith, "An Unmeritorious Defence – The Requirement of An Insurable Interest in the Law of Marine Insurance and Related Matters" (1993) 5(3) *Insurance Law Journal* 177; Sir Anthony Mason, "The Future of Marine Insurance Law" 1995 *Ebsworth & Ebsworth Maritime Law Lecture*; M. Taylor "Is the Requirement of An Insurable Interest in the Marine Insurance Act Still Valid?" (2000) 11 *Insurance Law Journal* 147.

requirement for an insurable interest and the implementation of provisions in similar terms to ss.16 and 17 of the ICA. The Commission's purpose in doing this is stated to be simply to permit purchasers of insured goods to obtain insurance to cover their exposure to loss if they pay for the goods before they acquire an insurable interest in them under the contract of sale.[39] The sensitivity of the issue of insurable interest led the ALRC to make a number of alternative recommendations in the event that its primary recommendations in relation to insurable interest are not adopted. The effect of the alternative recommendations[40] would be that there would be no legal impediment in principle to the insurance of goods prior to loading aboard a ship or at any other early stage of the transit. A purchaser of goods would be able to seek cover for any loss of the value of the goods or any profit that it might earn from them with the risk attaching as soon as the goods are paid for. It is considered that this would avoid the need for the market to resort to "FOB or C&F Pre-shipment clauses" which, given the requirement of insurable interest in the Marine Insurance Act 1909, are probably unenforceable.[41]

11D DUTY OF UTMOST GOOD FAITH

11.22 The ALRC has recommended that the duty of utmost good faith be an implied term of a contract of marine insurance. This would be consistent with the position in general insurance law in Australia where s.13 of the ICA provides that there is an implied term in a contract of general insurance requiring each party to act towards the other party with utmost good faith.

11.23 The rationale for the inclusion of such a provision in an amended Marine Insurance Act 1909 arises out of the apparent inability of the mere reciprocal nature of the expression of the duty of utmost good faith in the Marine Insurance Act 1909 to afford any appropriate relief to an insured. Despite Lord Mansfield's statement in *Carter v. Boehm*[42] that, "The policy would be equally void, against the underwriter, if he concealed; as, if he insured a ship on her voyage which he privately knew to be arrived; and an action would lie to recover the premium". The next occasion on which such issues were considered at a judicial level did not arise until *Banque Keyser Ullman SA v. Skandia (UK) Insurance Co. Ltd & Others*.[43] The case involved an allegation that insurers had breached their duty of utmost good faith. The Court of Appeal held that there had in fact been a breach but that such a breach entitled the insured only to the

39. ALRC 91, para.11.92.

40. "Recommendation 30. If recommendation 28 is not adopted and the requirement for insurable interest is retained, a new provision should be inserted into the MIA providing that a purchaser of insurable property acquires an insurable interest in that property by no later than the time when it pays for the property or when it becomes bound to pay for the property provided that it subsequently pays for it.

Recommendation 31. If recommendation 28 is not adopted and the requirement for insurable interest is retained, MIA s.16 should be amended to cover secured loans over insurable property generally, not just bottomry and respondentia."

41. Taylor, M, "Is the Requirement of an Insurable Interest in the *Marine Insurance Act* still valid?" (2000) 11 *Insurance Law Journal* 147, 156–157.

42. (1766) 3 Burr.1905; 97 ER 1162.

43. [1990] 1 Q.B.D. 665 (Steyn J); [1990] 1 Q.B.D. 723 (CA); [1991] 2 A.C. 249 (HL).

return of the premium and not to damages, since it was neither a tort nor a breach of contract nor of fiduciary duty. In coming to this conclusion, the Court of Appeal was unable to cite any authority directly on point, other than Lord Mansfield in *Carter v. Boehm*. The Court said:[44]

> "By the very nature of insurance cases allegations of non-disclosure of material facts are more likely to be made by the insurers than by the insured, in the ordinary course insurers will know of no material facts of which the insured himself is ignorant. And in the ordinary course the right to avoid the policy will be an adequate remedy for the aggrieved insurer.
>
> In the rare case where there has been non-disclosure of a material fact *by the insurer* the position may be rather different. Avoidance of the policy and the return of the premium may well constitute entirely sufficient relief for the insured if he becomes aware of the non-disclosure before the occurrence of the contingency against which he has intended to insure. If, however, he becomes aware of it only after the occurrence of the contingency, relief of this nature may be quite inadequate."

The issue again came to be considered by the House of Lords in *The Star Sea*,[45] where Lord Hobhouse criticised the remedies available for breach of good faith: 11.24

> "An inevitable consequence in the post-contract situation is that the remedy of avoidance of the contract is in practical terms wholly one-sided. It is a remedy of value to the insurer and, if the defendants' argument is accepted, of disproportionate benefit to him; it enables him to escape retrospectively the liability to indemnify which he has previously and (on his hypothesis) validly undertaken."[46]

The consequence of making the duty of good faith an implied term of the contract is said to be to make a broad range of contractual remedies available to both insurer and insured for a breach of the duty of utmost good faith.[47] The proposal defines the scope of the duration of the duty of utmost good faith; it extends for the duration of the relationship between the parties as set out in the contract of marine insurance except in relation to any claim or other aspect of the relationship which becomes the subject of litigation between the parties. The requirement is said to cease when litigation is commenced but only in relation to the claim or other aspect the subject of the litigation.[48] It would seem that the lack of agreement amongst academic writers as to the remedy for breach of the implied duty[49] might, in the Australian context, continue for some time. The ALRC has not proposed any remedy for breach of the implied term and any amendment to the Marine Insurance Act 1909 would, therefore, be silent in this respect. Howard Bennett has suggested that; 11.25

> "... the juristic nature of the various duties generated by the pre-formation doctrine of utmost good faith is a contractual contingent condition precedent to the enforceability of the contract implied in law."[50]

Yvonne Baatz has stated that this analysis is appealing as it corresponds with the

44. [1990] 1 Q.B.D. 723, 775.
45. *Manifest Shipping Co. Ltd v. Uni-Polaris Insurance Co. Ltd (The Star Sea)* [2001] 1 All E.R. 743
46. *Ibid.*, at 762.
47. ALRC 91, para 10.150.
48. Recommendation 21.
49. Y. Baatz, "Utmost good faith in marine insurance contracts", in M. Huybrechts (ed.), *Marine Insurance at the Turn of the Millennium*, Vol 1 (1999, Intersentia) p.24.
50. HN Bennett, "Mapping the doctrine of utmost good faith in insurance contract law", [1999] *Lloyd's Maritime & Commercial Law Quarterly 165 at 183.*

remedy for breach of warranty where again there is no remedy of damages for breach.[51] If the proposals of the ALRC are adopted, there will, in Australia at least, be a remedy of damages for breach of warranty. Thus, the analogy which appears to work well in the English context may not be transposed to the Australian context if an Australian court takes the view that there was no intention to codify English law in relation to a common law implied duty of utmost good faith. It is, therefore, instructive to examine the position in general insurance law in Australia where there is, by virtue of s.13 of the ICA, an implied duty of utmost good faith.

11.26 Since the introduction of the implied duty of good faith into general insurance law in Australia, there appears to have been only one occasion where an insurer has been found to have breached the implied term and to have been found liable for damages in addition to the indemnity payable under the policy and interest.[52] In two other cases, courts have said, in *obiter dicta*, that the insurer was in breach of section 13 but, in both cases, the insured was entitled to indemnity under the policy on other grounds.[53]

11.27 In *Australian Associated Motor Insurers Ltd v. Ellis & Anor*,[54] a comprehensive policy of motor vehicle insurance contained a condition that the insured not make any modification to the car without the insurer's written consent. After the policy had been made and renewed, the insured modified the car by fitting it with "mag" wheels. The vehicle was damaged whilst being driven by the insured's 23-year-old daughter. The "mag" wheels played no part in causing the collision. Had the insurer been notified of the modification, it would have maintained the policy but declined cover whenever it was being driven by a person under 25 years of age. Thus, the particular collision would not have been covered by the policy.

Although it was not necessary to decide the case, Cox J in the Supreme Court of South Australia, held that the insurer was in breach of s.13 of the ICA, the implied duty of utmost good faith, because it had not notified the insured of the consequences of breaching the relevant clause in the policy. His Honour came to this conclusion by reasoning that, as s.22 of the ICA requires an insurer to give written notice of the nature and effect of the duty of disclosure, there seems to be "no good reason for not regarding the insurer's obligation under s.13 as including, at least in certain circumstances, an obligation to bring to an insured's notice the consequences of any breach by the insured of a condition of the policy that operates subsequently to the making of the contract".[55]

11.28 In *Beverley v. Tyndall Life Insurance Co. Ltd*,[56] the plaintiff was insured against total and permanent disability under a risk insurance policy with Tyndall Life. Following an accident in which the insured slipped and fell injuring her back, the insured claimed to be totally and permanently disabled within the meaning of the policy. The insurer rejected the claim on the basis that the insured had not provided proof that she

51. Y. Baatz, "Utmost good faith in marine insurance contracts", in M Huybrechts (ed.), *Marine Insurance at the Turn of the Millennium*, Vol 1 (1999, Intersentia) p.24.
52. *Moss & Anor v. Sun Alliance Australia Ltd* (1990) 6 ANZ Insurance Cases 60–967.
53. *Australian Associated Motor Insurers Ltd v. Ellis & Anor* (1990) 6 ANZ Insurance Cases 60–957; *Beverley v. Tyndall Life Insurance Co. Ltd* (1999) 10 ANZ Insurance Cases 61–453.
54. (1990) 6 ANZ Insurance Cases 60–957.
55. *Ibid.*, at 76,330.
56. (1999) 10 ANZ Insurance Cases 61–453.

was incapacitated to such an extent as to render her unlikely ever to resume work or attend to any gainful profession for which she was suited.

The Full Court of the Supreme Court of Western Australia held that the medical evidence demonstrated that the insured was totally and permanently disabled within the meaning of the policy and that the insurer should not have declined the claim. However, two members of the Court, in *obiter dicta*, commented on the scope of s.13 of the ICA. It had been argued by the insured that the insurer had acted unreasonably and unfairly in failing to disclose to the insured reports which it had obtained prior to rejecting the insured's claim. Chief Justice Malcolm and Justice Ipp considered that s.13 required the insurer to act towards the insured in the assessment and determination of the claim with the utmost good faith. This would require that the insured be given the opportunity of answering the medical reports which the insurer had obtained before the insurer made the final determination. Justice Anderson expressly declined to give an opinion on this aspect of the case.

In *Moss & Anor v. Sun Alliance Australia Ltd*,[57] the Supreme Court of South 11.29
Australia was concerned with a claim made following the destruction of business premises by fire. The insurer originally suspected arson but eventually admitted liability. The insureds had borrowed heavily to buy the property and the delay in receipt of the insurance monies had embarrassed them with their financiers. It was held that the insurer should have paid the indemnity amount by 15 July 1987, two months after the fire. As matters transpired, judgment was given by the court on 22 February 1990. Justice Bollen held that the delay in admitting liability to meet a sound claim and the delay in making prompt payment was a breach of the implied term to act in good faith. His Honour therefore allowed damages in addition to interest to compensate the insureds for late payment.

It is to be noted, however, that s.13 of the ICA does not provide for the duration of the implied duty of utmost good faith, unlike the proposal of the ALRC in relation to marine insurance. If this case were to be decided applying the ALRC's recommendation, it is possible that the "damages" award would be significantly reduced as, the time during which "interest" was calculated as damages would be curtailed; the duty being expressed to cease once litigation in relation to the claim is commenced.

By contrast, in *Kelly v. New Zealand Insurance Co. Ltd*,[58] the Supreme Court of 11.30
Western Australia held that it was not established that the insurer, who refused to pay a claim following a burglary, had failed to act with the utmost good faith notwithstanding that it renewed a house and contents policy and accepted increased premiums with full knowledge that the list of specific items of value had not been provided and with knowledge that the house contained many items of considerable value.

Justice Walsh accepted evidence that the insured was well aware of the provisions in the policy and the limitation on claims in relation to unspecified items. His Honour found that the insured had told the insurer he was reluctant to supply such a list because he was concerned about the "taxman". His Honour held that s.13 gives statutory recognition to the common law duty of utmost good faith so that "there is

57. (1990) 6 ANZ Insurance Cases 60–967.
58. (1993) 7 ANZ Insurance Cases 61–197.

implied into the Policy a provision to the effect that the parties act towards each other, in respect of any matter arising under or in relation to the Policy, with the utmost good faith".[59] In the circumstances of the case, his Honour was not prepared to hold that the insurer had failed to act with fairness and honesty.

11.31 A survey of those cases which have dealt with the application of s.13 of the ICA reveals a marked conservatism on the part of the judges who have considered the issue. It does not seem that, in the context of insurance law, the courts are inclined to impose the "broad range of contractual remedies" which might now be available. However, the existence of an equivalent provision to s.13 would, it is suggested, have overcome the difficulties which faced the Court of Appeal in *Banque Keyser Ullman SA v. Skandia (UK) Insurance Co. Ltd & Others*[60] and would have permitted an award of damages. An exact equivalent of s.13 is not, however, what has been proposed.

11E DUTY OF DISCLOSURE

11.32 For more than 200 years, it has been the case in English law that if an insured fails to disclose or misrepresents a "material circumstance" to the insurer, the insurer may avoid the contract of insurance.[61] Sir Mackenzie Chalmers'[62] legislative interpretation of the judgment in *Carter v. Boehm* is s.17 of the Marine Insurance Act 1906[63] and his subsequent extrapolation of specific manifestations of the duty of utmost good faith, namely the obligations relating to non-disclosure and misrepresentation, appear in ss.18 and 20 of the Marine Insurance Act 1906.[64] In 1995, in *Pan Atlantic Insurance Ltd v. Pine Top Ltd*[65] ("*the Pan Atlantic case*"), the House of Lords delivered the first extensive opinion on the interpretation of the obligations relating to non-disclosure and misrepresentation. The High Court of Australia has not yet had the opportunity to consider the interpretation of the equivalent Australian provisions and it seems that any such opportunity may be circumscribed by the legislature.

11E.1 Scope of the duty according to the House of Lords

11.33 In the *Pan Atlantic* case, Lord Mustill identified two questions of law which arose for decision on the facts:

> "1. where s.18(2) and s.20(2)[66] of the Marine Insurance Act 1906 relate the test of materiality to a circumstance 'which would influence the judgment of a prudent underwriter in fixing the premium, or determining whether he will take the risk', must it be shown that full and accurate disclosure would have led the prudent underwriter to a different decision on accepting or raising the risk; or is a lesser standard of impact on the mind of the prudent underwriter sufficient; and if so what is that lesser standard? (In the previous decision on this point by the Court of Appeal in *Container*

59. *Ibid.*, at 78,258.
60. [1990] 1 Q.B.D. 723.
61. *Carter v. Boehm* (1766) 3 Burr 1905; 97 E.R. 1162.
62. The draftsman of the Marine Insurance Act 1906 (UK).
63. Marine Insurance Act 1909, s.23.
64. Marine Insurance Act, 1909, ss.24 and 26.
65. [1995] 1 AC 501.
66. Marine Insurance Act 1909, ss.24 and 26.

Transport International Inc. v. Oceanus Mutual Underwriting Association (Bermuda) Limited[67] (the CTI case), it had been decided that a lesser standard of impact was sufficient; it was not necessary to show that the undisclosed fact would have had a *decisive* influence on the prudent underwriter).

2. is the establishment of the material representation on non-disclosure sufficient to enable the underwriter to avoid the policy; or is it also necessary that the misrepresentation or non-disclosure has induced the making of the policy, either at all or on the terms on which it was made?[68] (The CTI case had decided the effect on the actual insurer was irrelevant)."

In the result, His Lordship, with whom Lord Goff and Lord Slynn agreed, rejected the notion of "decisive influence" and held that under s.18 of the Marine Insurance Act 1906[69] a "material circumstance" was one that would have an effect on the mind of the prudent insurer in estimating the risk and it was not necessary that it should have a decisive effect on his acceptance of the risk or on the amount the premium demanded. A fact is material if a prudent insurer would have wished to be aware of it in reaching his decision. The minority, Lord Lloyd and Lord Templeman, preferred the "decisive influence" test. Thus, to that extent, the decision in the CTI case was upheld.

The second issue considered by the House was whether it must also be established that the non-disclosure induced the particular insurer to accept the risk. The Court of Appeal in the CTI case had said that the person who has to be considered is the hypothetical prudent insurer and no one else. The House of Lords appears to have unanimously adopted Kerr J's first thoughts in *Berger & Light Diffusers Pty Ltd v. Pollock*,[70] namely, that it was an absurd proposition that the defendant underwriter could avoid the policy if he would not have been influenced by the undisclosed fact but the hypothetical prudent underwriter would have been so influenced.[71] It must now be accepted as settled, at least in the UK, that the actual underwriter concerned will be required to testify as to the degree of influence the matters not disclosed would have had on his original decision.[72]

Their Lordships held, therefore, that before an underwriter could avoid a contract for the non-disclosure or the misrepresentation of a material circumstance, he had to show that he had actually been induced by the non-disclosure or the misrepresentation to enter into the policy on the relevant terms. This constituted a departure from the CTI case. Thus, the effect of the decision in the *Pan Atlantic* case is that it is not necessary to show that the matter not disclosed or misrepresented would have had a decisive influence on the mind of the prudent insurer, something less is sufficient. But an insurer cannot avoid the contract of insurance unless it can establish that it was nevertheless induced by the non-disclosure to enter into the contract on the terms on which it did.

67. [1984] 1 Lloyd's Rep 476.
68. [1995] 1 A.C. 501 at 521.
69. Marine Insurance Act 1909 (Cwlth) s.24.
70. [1973] 2 Lloyd's Rep 442 at 463.
71. This was a view from which Lord Justice Kerr (as he had then become) resiled in the CTI case; [1984] 1 Lloyd's Rep. 476 at 495.
72. Lord Lloyd of Berwick opined that Mr Justice Kerr's statement in *Berger & Light Diffusers Pty Ltd v. Pollock* was a correct statement of the law and that his second thoughts in the CTI case were erroneous; [1995] 1 A.C. 501 at 571.

11E.2 Australian views on the scope of the duty

11.34 Australian authority accords neither with the approach of the English Court of Appeal, nor the House of Lords. In New South Wales, the leading case is that of *Mayne Nickless Limited v. Pegler*,[73] where the court was concerned with the non-disclosure of a previous motor vehicle accident on a vehicle insurance application. Mr Justice Samuels J stated the test of materiality in the following terms:[74]

> "Accordingly, I do not think that it is generally open to examine what the insurer would in fact have done had he had the information not disclosed. The question is whether that information would have been relevant to the exercise of the insurer's option to accept or reject the insurance proposal. It seems to me that the test of materiality is this: a fact is material if it would have reasonably affected the mind of the prudent insurer in determining whether he will accept the insurance, and if so, at what premium and on what conditions."

The test postulated is unhelpful. All that can be said about it is that inducement is not required; it apparently rejects the decisive influence test but other than that does little more than restate the wording of the section with the additional requirement that the prudent insurer's mind be "reasonably affected". This is perhaps an attempt to place more objectivity into a test which is already objective.

11.35 The decision in *Mayne Nickless Limited v. Pegler* was cited with approval by Carruthers J in *Randall v. Atlantica Insurance Co. Limited*[75] and more recently has been followed by the New South Wales Court of Appeal in *Barclay Holdings v. British National Insurance Co. Limited.*[76] *Barclay Holdings v. British National Insurance Co. Limited* concerned a contract of general insurance effected prior to the enactment of the *Insurance Contracts Act* 1984 (Cwlth) and therefore the common law test of non-disclosure was relevant. The majority of the Court of Appeal, Priestly and Glass JJA, confirmed the correctness of the test postulated by Samuels J in *Mayne Nickless Ltd v. Pegler.*[77] Their Honours distinguished the CTI case and held that the CTI case involved a determination of materiality at the time when the underwriter investigates the risk, instead of the moment when the underwriter decides whether or not to accept the policy as was stated by Samuels J in *Mayne Nickless Ltd v. Pegler.*[78] This distinction is difficult to sustain. The President of the Court of Appeal, Kirby P (now a Justice of the High Court of Australia) wrote a dissenting judgment. His Honour criticised the test of Samuels J in *Mayne Nickless Ltd v. Pegler* as being ambiguous, as it could mean either: (a) that the insured must disclose anything of interest to the insurer; or (b) that the insured should only disclose those matters which would cause the insurer to decline the policy or to increase the premium.[79]

The President stated his interpretation of the test in *Mayne Nickless Ltd v. Pegler* in the following terms:[80]

---

73. [1974] 1 NSWLR 228.
74. at 239.
75. (1985) 80 FLR 253.
76. (1987) 8 NSWLR 514.
77. [1974] 1 NSWLR 228.
78. (1987) 8 NSWLR 514 at 523.
79. at 517.
80. at 517.

"The effect on the mind of the insurer, to which Samuels J was referring, should be something more than the effect produced by information which the insurer would have been generally interested to have. If, though interested to have it, such information would not, in the end, have determined for a reasonably prudent insurer the acceptance or rejection of insurance, the setting of the premium or the attachment of conditions, there is not such effect on the mind as requires disclosure by the insured. The information, although of interest, is not material."

This test accords neither with that postulated in the English Court of Appeal in the CTI case and later, post the Pan Atlantic case, in *St Paul Fire & Marine Insurance Co. (UK) Ltd v. McConnell Dowell Constructors Ltd*[81] (the McConnell Dowell case) nor with the narrower decisive influence test. It also omits any requirement for actual inducement now considered essential by the House of Lords.

The Full Court of the Supreme Court of Queensland in *Visscher Enterprises Pty Ltd* 11.36
v. Southern Pacific Insurance Co. Ltd[82] considered the duty of disclosure in a case in which a fishing trawler sank following the outbreak of fire in the engine room. The insured had failed to disclose that the vessel had four watertight bulkheads instead of five as represented to the underwriter. The court held that evidence as to the practice of the particular insurer may, in some cases, be relevant and admissible as to whether it would have been influenced had it known of the undisclosed circumstance. WB Campbell J (as he then was) said:[83]

"The authorities persuade me that evidence as to the practice of the particular insurer may in some cases be relevant and admissible, that at least in cases where the question of materiality is not obvious, evidence of experts as to insurance practice generally is admissible, and that in such doubtful cases it is desirable for the particular insurer to give evidence itself as to whether it would have been influenced had it known of the undisclosed circumstance."

The Court, therefore, drew a distinction between cases in which the undisclosed fact was "obviously" material, in which case the Court felt it appropriate to follow the test as stated by Samuels J in *Mayne Nickless Ltd v. Pegler*[84] and approved by the Privy Council in *Marene Knitting Mills Pty Ltd v. Greater Pacific General Insurance Ltd*,[85] and those cases in which the undisclosed fact was "not obviously material", in which case the Court preferred the view of Kerr J (as he then was) in *Berger & Light Diffusers Pty Ltd v. Pollock*.[86] Thus, the Full Court could apparently not quite make up its mind about the necessity for the actual insurer to be induced to enter the contract by the undisclosed or misrepresented fact. This requirement was apparently necessary if the undisclosed fact was not obviously material. The question which then necessarily arises is, to whom must it be not obviously material: the court, the seasoned underwriter, the insured, the man in the street? It seems a very loose test designed to overcome a situation where the Court evidently did not want to find against the insured; the evidence being that the vessel would have been insured on the same terms and conditions if the true state of affairs regarding the vessel's bulkheads had been revealed.

81. [1995] 2 Lloyd's Rep 116.
82. [1981] Qd R 561.
83. at 582–3.
84. [1974] 1 NSWLR 228 at 239.
85. [1976] 2 Lloyd's Rep. 63.
86. [1973] 2 Lloyd's Rep. 442.

11.37 In *Itobar Pty Ltd v. Mackinnon & Commercial Union Assurance Co. Plc*,[87] Macrossan J (as he then was) was concerned with a case in which His Honour found the vessel had been deliberately scuttled. It was, therefore, not strictly necessary for His Honour to consider allegations of non-disclosure relating to the appointment of receivers to the plaintiff, the existence of a prior mortgage and the plaintiff's director's convictions for various offences of dishonesty. Nonetheless, His Honour considered Kerr J's remarks in *Berger & Light Diffusers Pty Ltd v. Pollock*[88] and the Full Court's decision in *Visscher Enterprises v. Southern Pacific Insurance Co. Ltd*[89] and compared them with the decision in the CTI case which had, in the meantime, intervened. His Honour held that evidence as to whether matters were such that a prudent insurer would want to know about them was admissible from representatives of the general class of insurers and from the particular insurer concerned. His Honour then considered whether the final judgment of the particular insurer is relevant and whether we are concerned with the decisive influence test.

At this point it became clear that, as a result of the CTI case, the law in England was now different from the law in Australia and His Honour felt himself bound by the Full Court in *Visscher Enterprises Pty Ltd v. Southern Pacific Insurance Co. Ltd* to hold that:

> "1. for the purposes of s.24(2) of the Marine Insurance Act 1909, the question is, whether as an issue of fact, by applying the standard of the judgment of a prudent insurer, the insurer in question would have been influenced in fixing the premium or determining whether to take the risk; and
> 2. that the test of materiality is the capacity of the information to influence the decision of the insurer in the sense of having an effect upon the final decision to accept or decline the risk or to stipulate a higher premium."

11.38 The most recent relevant Australian decision is that of the Supreme Court of Victoria in *Akedian Co. Ltd v. Royal Insurance Australia Ltd.*[90] The plaintiff sued Royal Insurance under a policy of marine insurance insuring loss or damage to 15 packages of used pipe-rolling machinery which was damaged when, on 17 August 1992, the ship carrying the goods caught fire. The insurers denied liability, alleging that, on 17 September 1992, they had avoided it for the non-disclosure or misrepresentation of two material facts, namely:

(i) that the cost of the insured goods to Akedian when it purchased them was US$517,533 FOB and not A$3,750,000 CIF as represented; and
(ii) that the age of the goods was eight years and not five years as represented.

The plaintiff settled with the insurer but proceeded against the broker for negligently failing to disclose or misrepresenting the facts. The broker was informed that the machinery, which was some eight years old, was being purchased for A$650,000 by Akedian as part of a joint venture agreement; that in 1984 the machinery had been sold for $A1.5m and insured for A$1.7m, and that the cost of replacing the machinery with new was $US3 million in 1992. The broker obtained a quote from the insurer which, *inter alia*, stipulated that the cover was offered for a machine not exceeding five years of age and was subject to a pre-shipment report. The

87. [1985] 3 ANZ Ins Cas 60–610.
88. [1973] 2 Lloyd's Rep. 442.
89. [1981] Qd R 561.
90. [1999] 1 VR 80.

pre-shipment report was not available to the insurer before the ship sailed and so a different and less comprehensive cover was given to Akedian based on the ICC C Clauses.[91] The sum insured remained at A$3.75m but the excess of A$10,000 was removed and the premium was reduced from 0.35 per cent to 0.15 per cent.

The trial judge, Byrne J, was satisfied that the broker misrepresented the true age of the machinery and failed to disclose its purchase price. The issue was whether the misrepresentation and non-disclosure were material. Byrne J observed that, at least since the decision of the House of Lords in the Pan Atlantic case, the question of materiality must be addressed in two stages. The first stage requires an assessment of the impact of the non-disclosure or the misrepresentation on the mind of a hypothetical prudent insurer; the second requires the Court to determine whether the misrepresentation or the non-disclosure in fact induced the underwriter who assumed the risk to issue the policy which it did.

His Honour referred to the judgment of Evans LJ of the English Court of Appeal in the McConnell Dowell case where his Lordship concluded that a non-disclosed fact is material where, had it been disclosed, the prudent underwriter would have appreciated that it was a different risk. Byrne J noted that this definition imposes a less stringent test on the insured than Lord Mustill's words fairly bear. His Honour also observed that in New Zealand the test since the Pan Atlantic case has been expressed as "whether the relevant information would have had an effect on the mind of a prudent insurer in weighing up the risk".[92] His Honour then referred to the New South Wales decision of *Barclay Holdings v. British National Insurance Co. Ltd* and adopted the terminology of Samuels J as explained by the majority in that case.

The second stage of the inquiry requires that the underwriter should have actually been induced by the misrepresented fact or by the non-disclosure to undertake the risk and issue the policy. His Honour noted that, although this second requirement was said by Lord Goff[93] to mitigate the severity to the insured of the first stage test, cases such as the present show the difficulty for an insured where the underwriter, without fear of contradiction, is able to swear that it was so induced.

His Honour found that the difference of three years between the actual age of the machinery and its represented age would not have had an effect on the mind of a prudent insurer in assessing which, and on what terms, to take the risk. His Honour reached this conclusion by looking at all the surrounding facts, which included the evidence that the age of second-hand goods is relevant because of the expense and difficulty of repair but that the insurer had already been informed by the insured that repairs could be effected in Hong Kong.

His Honour dealt next with the non-disclosure of the cost price, which was about one-sixth of the insured sum, and found that the purchase price was a matter which would reasonably have affected the mind of a prudent insurer in determining whether to take the risk and on what terms. The first stage of the test for materiality was, therefore, satisfied. He further concluded that the insurers were in fact induced by the

91. Institute Cargo Clauses (Restricted Perils) Cover.

92. *Quinby Enterprises Limited (in liq.) v. General Accident Fire and Life Assurance Corporation Plc* (1994) 8 ANZ Ins Cas 61–292 at 76, 296; [1995] 1 NZLR 736 at 740 *per* Barker J; *Wayne Wilkinson Insurance Ltd v. Kaiana Douns Ltd* (1995) 8 ANZ Ins Cas 61–248 at 75, 785 *per* Tompkins J.

93. [1995] 1 A.C. 501 at 517.

non-disclosure to enter into the policy with Akedian. Therefore, on the basis of the non-disclosure, the insurers were entitled to avoid the policy as they did.

The approach taken by Byrne J was yet another variation on the possible approaches to the interpretation of the section of the Act. Before his elevation to the High Court of Australia, Kirby J, who delivered the minority judgment in *Barclay Holdings v. British National Insurance Co. Ltd*, expressed the opinion that an "Australian" Court would be likely to adopt the reasoning and process of interpretation outlined by the majority of the House of Lords.[94] His Honour's hopes for consistency have not been realised.

11E.3 The Australian and English views reconciled?

11.39 It is apparent that, in relation to the definition of a material circumstance and the definition of a material representation, there is no consensus as to the interpretation of that definition amongst any of the courts in the UK or Australia which have considered the definition in recent years. It is certainly not possible to reconcile the views expressed by the various judges. The materiality of a circumstance or representation is variously defined as something a prudent insurer would simply like to know about;[95] something which would reasonably affect a prudent insurer,[96] or at least which has the capacity to reasonably affect a prudent insurer;[97] something which is determinative of the acceptance or rejection of the risk by a prudent insurer,[98] and one case does not attempt a definition but merely refers to circumstances which are either "obviously material" or not.[99] Coupled with this situation is an equivalent degree of equivocation about whether or not the actual insurer must be induced by the matter not disclosed or the representation to enter into the contract. This results in uncertainty in the law.

11.40 What is needed is a precise definition of a material circumstance or representation and clarification of the necessity for the actual insurer to be induced by the non-disclosure or misrepresentation so that an insured can be as certain as possible about the scope of the duty of disclosure and thus the likelihood of recovering should the need to claim on the insurer arise. The question which faced the ALRC was whether or not the definition settled upon by the House of Lords in the Pan Atlantic case should be embraced in Australia. In its report, the ALRC has made a number of recommendations which go far beyond simply adopting the House of Lords' interpretation of the duty of disclosure.

11.41 The proposed reformulation of the duty of disclosure and the duty not to misrepresent material facts includes an element of materiality which accords with the

94. Justice M D Kirby, "Marine Insurance: Is the Doctrine of 'Utmost Good Faith' Out of Date?" (1995) 13 *Australian Bar Review* 1 at 9.

95. *CTI Transport International Inc v. Oceanus Mutual Underwriting Association (Bermuda) Ltd* [1984] 1 Lloyd's Rep 476; *Pan Atlantic Insurance Ltd v. Pine Top Ltd* [1995] 1 A.C. 501; *St Paul Fire & Marine Insurance Co. (UK) Limited v. McConnell Dowell Constructors Ltd* [1995] 2 Lloyd's Rep 116.

96. *St Paul Fire & Marine Insurance Co. (UK) Limited v. McConnell Dowell* [1995] 2 Lloyd's Rep 116; *Randall v. Atlantica Insurance Co. Ltd* (1985) 80 FLR 253; *Barclay Holdings v. British National Insurance Co. Ltd* (1987) 8 NSWLR 514; *Akedian Co. Ltd v. Royal Insurance Australia Ltd* [1999] 1 VR 80.

97. *Itobar Pty Ltd v. Mackinnon & Commercial Union Assurance Co. Plc* (1985) 3 ANZ Ins Cas 60–610.

98. *Barclay Holdings v. British National Insurance Co. Ltd* (1987) 8 NSWLR 514 (*per* Kirby J).

99. *Visscher Enterprises Pty Ltd v. Southern Pacific Insurance Co. Ltd* [1981] Qd R 561.

current interpretation of materiality by the courts of both Australia and England.[100] The duty is objective and does not incorporate any subjective element on the insured's behalf such as appears in the ICA.[101]

The proposed remedial scheme, which relates to both non-disclosure and misrepresentation, abolishes the "all or nothing" approach of Anglo/Australian marine insurance law.[102] An insurer will be entitled to avoid the policy and retain the premium only where the insurer proves that breach of the duty of disclosure (or the misrepresentation) was fraudulent. Where the breach is not fraudulent, there is a two-tiered approach: 11.42

(i) if the insurer can prove that it would not have entered into the contract had it known of the undisclosed circumstance or the truth of the misrepresented matter, the insurer may avoid the contract but must return the premium;
(ii) where the insurer would have entered into the contract, albeit on other terms, the insurer may not avoid the policy but:
 (a) is not liable for any loss proximately caused by the breach;
 (b) may vary its liability to reflect any additional premium, excess or deductible which it would have imposed; and
 (c) may cancel the policy pursuant to new cancellation provisions proposed in the recommendations; viz., on giving three business days' written notice to the insured.

Thus, the proposed remedial structure introduces an element of causation which is similar to that incorporated in the Norwegian Marine Insurance Plan,[103] but it avoids the difficulties of the application of the "proportionality principle" which exists in the ICA and also in marine insurance legislation of other jurisdictions such as France.[104]

100. "Recommendation 22: Marine Insurance Act s.24(1) and 26(1) should be amended to provide that an insured must disclose accurately all circumstances that it knows, or a reasonable person in its position would know, to be material"; *Pan Atlantic Insurance Ltd v. Pine Top Ltd* [1995] 1 A.C. 501; *Akedian Co. Ltd v. Royal Insurance Australia Ltd* [1999] 1 V.R. 80.

101. ICA s.21.

102. "Recommendation 25: The Marine Insurance Act should be amended to insert new provisions which provide that if the insured has breached its duties relating to non-disclosure and misrepresentation
(1) if the breach is fraudulent, the insurer is entitled to avoid the policy from its outset with no return of premium
(2) if the breach is not fraudulent
 (a) where the insurer would not have entered into the contract if it had known of the undisclosed circumstance or the truth of the misrepresented circumstance, the insurer is entitled to avoid the policy from its outset but with a return of premium
 (b) where the insurer would have entered into the contract but on other conditions, the insurer is not entitled to avoid the policy but
  (i) is not liable to indemnify the insured for a loss proximately caused by the undisclosed or misrepresented circumstance
  (ii) is entitled to vary its liability to the insured to reflect the amount of any variation in premium, deductible or excess that would have been imposed if it had known of the undisclosed circumstance or the truth of the misrepresented circumstance
 and
  (iii) is entitled to cancel the policy in accordance with the other provisions of the Marine Insurance Act on cancellation which are the subject of recommendation 18."

103. S Derrington, "Non-disclosure and misrepresentation in contracts of marine insurance; a comparative overview and some proposals for unification", [2001] *Lloyd's Maritime & Commercial Law Quarterly* 66, 76–84.

104. *Ibid.*, at 75.

11.43 Recommendation 26 provides that an insurer will not be permitted to impose greater duties, or provide for more favourable remedies, than those stipulated in the amended Marine Insurance Act. There is also a recommendation that the Marine Insurance Act 1909 provide that following underwriters are deemed to have been induced to enter into a contract if all leading underwriters were induced.[105]

11F DOCTRINE OF WARRANTIES

11F.1 Definition of a warranty

11.44 The Marine Insurance Act 1909 deals with delimitation and alteration of the risk insured by the use of a device unknown in civil law countries, namely the warranty. In this context we are concerned with promissory warranties. The promise which forms the subject-matter of a warranty consists of an undertaking by the insured that some particular thing shall be done or that some condition shall be fulfilled, or whereby the insured affirms or negatives the existence of a particular state of facts.[106] A warranty for the purposes of s.39(1)[107] is not confined to an undertaking that a particular thing shall or shall not be done. It also extends to an undertaking that some conditions be fulfilled. The word "particular" does not qualify the phrase "some conditions be fulfilled". In *Switzerland Insurance Australia Ltd v. Mowie Fisheries Pty Ltd*,[108] it was unsuccessfully argued that a warranty "That the vessel will be skippered, manned, crewed, operated and licensed in accordance with the regulations and by-laws and all other applicable laws of the appropriate governmental authorities of the State of Registration at all times during the currency of the policy", fell outside the terms of s.39(1) because it did not require a "particular thing to be done". A warranty must relate to the risk; it defines the essence of the risk. For example a promise by the insured to pay the premium by a particular date might be an undertaking to do a particular thing, but the obligation would be classified as a normal contractual undertaking and not as a promissory warranty.[109]

11.45 The nature of the warranty in insurance law differs from that in other areas of the law. In contract law, breach of a warranty gives rise to a right to damages but not to a right of discharge. Breach of a condition on the other hand gives rise to both damages and discharge, but the discharge occurs only on the election of the party not in breach. In insurance contracts in particular, a warranty can be distinguished from the exception, the effect of which is to exclude the insurer's undertaking to pay; and from the procedural condition, such as the duty to give notice of claims, which usually entitles the insurer to refuse to pay but does not discharge past or future liability.[110] The warranty in insurance law is a condition precedent, "the word 'condition' ...

105. Recommendation 27
106. Marine Insurance Act 1909 s.39(1); Marine Insurance Act 1906 s.33(1).
107. Marine Insurance Act 1906, s.33(1).
108. (1997) 144 ALR 234,274.
109. HN Bennett, *The Law of Marine Insurance* (Oxford, 1996), 280.
110. Malcolm A Clarke, *Breach of Warranty in the Law of Insurance*, (1991) *Lloyd's Maritime & Commercial Law Quarterly* 437, 441.

being used in its classical sense in English law, under which the coming into existence of (for example) an obligation, or the duty or further duty to perform an obligation, is dependent upon the fulfilment of the specified condition".[111] Non-fulfilment of the specified condition does not prevent the contract from coming into existence but compliance with the warranty is a condition precedent to the attaching of the risk.[112]

A warranty should also be distinguished from a representation. There are two important differences between express warranties and representations. An express warranty will always be written on the face of the policy, whilst a representation will seldom, if ever, be written in. The second difference is that, whilst substantial compliance is sufficient for a mere representation uttered in the negotiations leading up to the contract, express warranties require exact and literal performance of what has been promised. 11.46

There is, however, another sense in which the term warranty is used in marine insurance law, namely as a definition of the risk, as in "warranted free from capture and seizure", which defines the ambit of the policy as excluding risks of capture. 11.47

In English law, a warranty may be created in one of the following ways: 11.48

(i) by the use of the word "warranty"; for example, "the insured warrants...";
(ii) by an expression for strict compliance and the right to repudiate for breach;
(iii) by the use of a phrase, such as "condition precedent", from which the court can infer that the parties intended strict compliance and the right to repudiate for breach;
(iv) by the use of any other words such that the court concludes that, on the true construction of the whole document containing the term, the parties intended the term to possess the attributes of a warranty;
(v) by the use of a "basis of the contract clause".[113]

The Marine Insurance Act 1909 simplifies this classification by providing that a warranty may be "in any form of words from which the intention to warrant may be inferred".[114] Ultimately, whether or not a term constitutes a promissory warranty depends upon the intention of the parties as revealed by the contract as a whole. 11.49

No particular form of words is required to create a warranty and indeed the word "warranty" need not be used at all. The only protection provided for the insured is that the words must appear on the paper of the policy,[115] or if they are contained in some other document then they must be sufficiently incorporated by reference into the policy.[116]

A distinction must be drawn between promissory warranties and the duty of disclosure. The concept of materiality, which serves to delineate the scope of the duty of disclosure, has no role to play in the context of warranties: 11.50

111. *The Good Luck* [1992] 1 A.C. 233, 263 *per* Lord Goff.
112. Thomson v. Weems (1884) 9 App. Cas. 671, 684 *per* Lord Blackburn.
113. Gt Brit., Report of The Law Commission on Insurance Law – Non-Disclosure and Breach of Warranty, Cmnd. 104, (1980), para.6.3.
114. Marine Insurance Act 1909 s.41(1); Marine Insurance Act 1906 s.35(1).
115. Marine Insurance Act 1909 s.41(2); Marine Insurance Act 1906 s.35(2).
116. *Pawson v. Watson* [1778] Cowp. 785; 98 ER 1361; *De Hahn v. Hartley* [1786] 1 TR 343; 99 ER 1130.

"It is a first principle of the law of insurance, on all occasions, that where a representation is material it must be complied with – if immaterial, that immateriality may be inquired into and shown; but that if there is a warranty it is part of the contract and the matter is such as it is represented to be. Therefore the materiality or immateriality signifies nothing. The only question is as to the mere fact.[117]

In *De Hahn v. Hartley*[118] Lord Mansfield CJ said:

"A warranty must be strictly complied with. It is perfectly immaterial for what purpose a warranty is introduced; but, being inserted, the contract does not exist unless it be literally complied with."

In the same case Ashhurst J said:

"The very meaning of a warranty is to preclude all questions whether it has been substantially complied with; it must be literally so."

11.51 Causation is thus irrelevant. It makes no difference that the breach of warranty had nothing whatever to do with the loss which ultimately occurred. An example of the non-causative nature of a warranty is the case of *Azevedeo v. Australian & International Insurances Ltd*[119] in which the plaintiff brought an action under a marine policy which insured the plaintiff's fishing vessel for $20,000. The vessel had been destroyed by fire. The insurer denied liability on a number of grounds including breach of warranty. The alleged warranty was in the form of a basis clause which was at the foot of the proposal form and which stated that it was agreed: ". . . that the above shall form the basis of the contract and that all information has been disclosed which would influence the company's decision". One question on the proposal form was: "Will the vessel be let out on hire or charter or used for the carriage of paying passengers?" The answer given was "No". It appeared that during the term of the contract the vessel had in fact been let on informal hire to a friend of the insured. The loss of the vessel did not occur on one of those occasions but when the insured himself was in charge of the vessel. The Court held that it was an express warranty that the vessel would not be let out on hire and that the insured had broken the warranty. Consequently, the insured's claim failed although clearly the breach of warranty had nothing whatsoever to do with the loss.

11F.2 Statutory provisions

11.52 The Marine Insurance Act 1909 deals with the subject of warranties in a peculiar fashion, albeit in exactly the same fashion as the Marine Insurance Act 1906.

11.53 Section 39 of the Marine Insurance Act 1909[120] defines warranties and describes the consequences of breach. It provides:

"**39 Nature of warranty**

(1) A warranty, in the following sections relating to warranties, means a promissory warranty, that is to say a warranty by which the insured undertakes that some particular thing shall or shall not be done, or that some conditions shall be fulfilled, or whereby he affirms or negatives the existence of a particular state of facts.

117. *Newcastle Fire Insurance Co. v. Macmorran & Co.* (1815) 3 Dow 255, 262.
118. [1786] 1 TR 343.
119. Unreported, Supreme Court of the Northern Territory, Muirhead J, 18 August 1976.
120. Marine Insurance Act 1906 s.33.

(2) A warranty may be express or implied.
(3) A warranty, as above defined, is a condition which must be exactly complied with, whether it be material to the risk or not. If it be not so complied with, then, subject to any express provision in the policy, the insurer is discharged from liability as from the date of the breach of warranty, but without prejudice to any liability incurred by him before that date."

Section 40 then explains when a breach of warranty can be excused and importantly provides that it is no excuse to the breach that the breach has in fact been remedied before the occurrence of any loss. It provides:[121] 11.54

"**40 When breach of warranty excused**
(1) Non-compliance with a warranty is excused when, by reason of a change of circumstances, the warranty ceases to be applicable to the circumstances of the contract, or when compliance with the warranty is rendered unlawful by any subsequent law.
(2) Where a warranty is broken, the insured cannot avail himself of the defence that the breach has been remedied, and the warranty complied with, before loss.
(3) A breach of warranty may be waived by the insurer."

It appears that the draconian provision rendering remedy before breach of no avail was not always the common law position. In *Weir v. Aberdeen*,[122] in 1819, a vessel had sailed in an unseaworthy condition due to overloading. It encountered heavy weather and put back to a safe anchorage. She sailed later without having discharged any cargo. The vessel again encountered heavy weather and again the master put back. This time the master communicated to the underwriters that the vessel was too deeply laden and applied for permission to offload part of the cargo. This permission was given and a memorandum endorsed to the policy to this effect. The ship then sailed and was later lost by peril insured against.

The judges found for the insured and placed little or no weight on the action of the underwriters. Abbott CJ, commenting on the underwriters' plea that once the vessel was initially unseaworthy that put an end to their liability, despite the subsequent remedy before loss, said:[123]

"I confess that I was a little surprised at that proposition, because, if true in point of law, I fear we should find many cases indeed where it would turn out that the insured could have no claim upon the underwriters, because something was wanting, or something excessive, at the instant of the ship's departure, although the want had been supplied, or the excess removed before the loss happened. . . . These inconveniences, which would be continually occurring in practice would lead to dangerous consequences, by opening the doors to underwriters to break their engagements by means of trivial circumstances, the effect of which no one ever contemplated."

However, the whole possibility of remedying a breach before loss and not losing the policy was totally destroyed by a decision of the Privy Council in 1870. In *Quebec Marine Insurance Co. v. Commercial Bank of Canada*,[124] a vessel sailed in an unseaworthy state, put back to remedy the defect and then put out again to sea. She was later lost by reason of a peril insured against. Refusing to allow that a warranty might be mended, Lord Penzance said of the proposition set out in *Weir v. Aberdeen*:

"This is a proposition of perilous latitude. It is impossible not to see that such a doctrine would

121. Marine Insurance Act 1906 s.34.
122. (1819) 2 B. & Ald. 320; 106 ER 383.
123. *Ibid.*, 323–324; 385.
124. (1870) LR 3 PC 234.

tend, if carried to its legitimate consequences, to fritter away the value of this warranty altogether. It is all very well to talk of trivial and small things, but it is very difficult to define what should fall within the category of small or trivial things, and what should exceed it."

11.55 Section 41 prescribes the requirements for express warranties. It provides:[125]

> **"41 Express warranties**
> (1) An express warranty may be in any form of words from which the intention to warrant is to be inferred.
> (2) An express warranty must be included in, or written upon, the policy, or must be contained in some document incorporated by reference into the policy.
> (3) An express warranty does not exclude an implied warranty, unless it be inconsistent therewith."

11.56 The remainder of the division of the Marine Insurance Act 1909 dealing with warranties contains what appears to be a miscellaneous collection of provisions. The Act stipulates certain implied warranties. First, it provides that if a ship or goods are expressly warranted neutral there is an implied warranty that the property has such a character at the commencement of the risk and that, as far as the insured can control the matter, the neutral character of the property shall be preserved and that the ship shall be properly documented.[126] Second, it provides that, in a voyage policy, there is an implied warranty of seaworthiness at the commencement of the voyage[127] and, in a voyage policy on goods, that the ship is reasonably fit to carry the goods to the destination contemplated.[128] Third, the Act provides that there is an implied warranty that the adventure insured is lawful.[129]

11.57 The Act also provides that certain matters are not implied. There is no implied warranty as to the nationality of a ship.[130] There is no implied warranty of seaworthiness in a time policy[131] and, in a policy on goods or movables, there is no implied warranty that the goods or movables are seaworthy.[132]

11.58 Finally, the Act provides that, where the subject-matter insured is warranted "well" or "in good safety" on a particular day, it is sufficient if it be safe at any time during that day.[133] The Act, therefore, commences with the substantive law relating to warranties and continues with what are essentially procedural matters.

11.59 The operation of the doctrine of warranties in the Australian context has recently received attention in the case of *Switzerland Insurance Australia Ltd v. Mowie Fisheries Pty Ltd.*[134] Switzerland Insurance had denied liability to indemnify Mowie for the loss of a fishing vessel on the basis of alleged breaches of two express warranties and on the basis of the implied warranty that the adventure on which the vessel was to embark shall be carried out in a lawful manner.[135] The first express warranty required the vessel to be "in survey". A survey certificate had been issued for the vessel but was

125. Marine Insurance Act 1906 s.35.
126. Marine Insurance Act 1909 s.42; Marine Insurance Act 1906 s.36.
127. Marine Insurance Act 1909 s.45; Marine Insurance Act 1906 s.39.
128. Marine Insurance Act 1909 s.46(2); Marine Insurance Act 1906 s.40(2).
129. Marine Insurance Act 1909 s.47; Marine Insurance Act 1906 s.41.
130. Marine Insurance Act 1909 s.43; Marine Insurance Act 1906 s.37.
131. Marine Insurance Act 1909 s.45(5); Marine Insurance Act 1906 s.39(5).
132. Marine Insurance Act 1909 s.46(1); Marine Insurance Act 1906 s.40(1).
133. Marine Insurance Act 1909 s.44; Marine Insurance Act 1906 s.38.
134. (1997) 144 ALR 234.
135. Marine Insurance Act 1909 s.47.

subject to certain crewing requirements which were not fulfilled. By a majority, the Full Federal Court held that the failure to comply with the crewing requirements did not detract from the fact that a valid survey certificate had been issued and that the certificate had not been cancelled or suspended. The second express warranty required the vessel to be operated and crewed in accordance with the laws of the State of its registration. The vessel did not have on board a crew member who held the appropriate certificate for the length of the vessel (as required by the relevant regulation). Again by majority, the Full Federal Court held the regulation to be *ultra vires* the authorising legislation so there was no breach of warranty. Justice Beaumont, however, was clearly of the opinion that a breach of such a regulation constituted a breach of the implied warranty of legality.[136] The insured was ultimately found to be entitled to indemnity.

A similar conclusion was reached in *Doak v. Weekes*[137] in which case the owner had knowingly sent the vessel to sea with a crew which did not hold the certificate of competency required by the Queensland regulations. Ryan J held that there was a breach of the implied warranty of legality.[138] 11.60

11F.3 Difficulties of construction

The harshness of the rule relating to breach of warranty has resulted in judicial attempts to ameliorate its effects. Two approaches have been adopted: 11.61

(i) by interpreting the warranty restrictively;
(ii) by relegating the warranty to a lesser term, i.e. as a term delimiting the risk, which attracts less severe consequences.

An example of the former approach is the case of *In Re Morgan & Provincial Insurance Co.*[139] where in response to the question, "State the purposes in full for which the vehicles will be used; and the nature of the goods to be carried", the insured answered, "(a) delivery of coal; (b) coal". 11.62

At a time before the accident the subject of the claim, the relevant vehicle had in fact carried a load of timber and the insurer relied on the breach of warranty to refuse indemnity. The House of Lords applied a very narrow interpretation to the warranty which, if their Lordships had not decided the case on another point, would have deprived the warranty of all substance. Lord Buckmaster said:[140]

"To state in full the purposes for which the vehicle is to be used is not the same thing as to state in full the purposes for which the vehicle will be exclusively used, and as a general description of the use of the vehicle it is not suggested that the answer was inaccurate."

The analysis of the House of Lords show the absurdity of interpretation which is required to avoid the operation of the doctrine of warranties. Had the proposal form read "State the *purpose* for which the vehicle is to be used" one might forgive an interpretation which said the proposal asked only for the main or predominant

136. (1997) 144 ALR 234, 262.
137. (1986) 82 FLR 334.
138. *Ibid.*, at 338–339.
139. [1932] 2 K.B. 70.
140. *Ibid.*, at 247.

purpose. When, however, the proposal was couched in the plural to start with, it is suggested that the only reasonable interpretation of the provision is that the insurer wished to know all the purposes for which the vehicle might be used.

11.63 The second approach interprets warranties as clauses which define conditions precedent to cover being operative from time to time. Breach results in the cover being suspended for the duration thereof, but cover is automatically reinstated once the infringement ceases. The difficulty with this interpretation is that, in the cases in which it has been used, the requirements have been drafted as warranties but the courts have nevertheless been attracted by this interpretation of warranties, as a means of mitigating the harsh although logical effects of the promissory warranty doctrine. So, how does one come to the conclusion that a warranty is not a warranty?

11.64 In *Roberts v. Anglo Saxon Insurance*[141] a motor policy provided; "warranted used only for ... commercial traveling". It was held that this was to be construed as defining the risk so that the vehicle was not "on risk" during any period when it was used for other purposes but that it was again on risk once the vehicle was again used for commercial purposes.

11.65 Similarly, in *Dawson v. Mercantile Mutual Insurance Co. Ltd*,[142] the Full Court of the Supreme Court of Victoria declined to view as a warranty the plaintiff's answer in a proposal form (which incorporated a basis of the contract clause), that the vehicle would be used for "Business", in response to the question "state clearly the purpose for which the motor vehicle will be used" in view of:

"... the utter unreasonableness of a provision forfeiting the entire policy for an act which may or may not in any degree increase the risk of loss or accident and which may have no relation to the loss in fact claimed for. On the other hand, if the condition simply means to exclude liability for accidents not within the risk, it gives an intelligible meaning to the [policy] and is in itself a reasonable and natural safeguard."

The vehicle was stolen one evening whilst the plaintiff was at a Masonic Lodge meeting to which he had driven the vehicle. At first instance the trial judge had held that the plaintiff should be non-suited.

11.66 Likewise, in *Case Existological Laboratories Ltd v. Century Insurance Co. ("the Bamcell II")*,[143] it was regarded as significant that non-compliance with a "warranted" requirement had no bearing on the loss. The case involved a claim for loss under a policy which provided "warranted that a watchman is stationed on board" between stated hours. A watchman had not been so stationed but the casualty had not occurred during the hours referred to in the warranty. The Court held that the parties "cannot have intended that if a watchman was late one night or even missed a night, then the insurers should be discharged from liability for the remainder of the term of the policy". The Court decided that the term was a "suspensive condition".

11.67 In *Colledge v. Harty*,[144] however, a restriction upon the sailing of a vessel to or from certain ports was construed as a warranty despite argument that, on its true construction, it was an exception. The vessel having infringed the restriction, the court was influenced by, as it saw, the impossibility of the policy ever subsequently

141. (1927) 27 Lloyd's List Rep. 313.
142. [1932] VR 380.
143. (1982) 133 DLR 727.
144. (1851) 6 Ex. 205.

attaching despite the fact that, having sailed for a prohibited port, the vessel might thereafter have altered its destination in favour of a voyage to which the policy might attach.

In *Farr v. Motor Traders' Mutual Insurance Society*,[145] the insured/owner of two taxis filled in a proposal form which contained a basis of the contract clause. In response to the question asking for the number of shifts each taxi had to ply each day the insured answered, "Just one". This was correct at the time of applying for the insurance. There was in actual fact a short period when one taxi was driven for two shifts per day whilst the other underwent repairs but the two taxis resumed their one shift per day routine after the return of the repaired vehicle. The insurer in response to a claim in respect of one taxi pleaded the breach of warranty. 11.68

The Court of Appeal said that the question which had to be decided was whether the particular statement in the proposal form was a definition of the risk or a warranty. In reliance on the then current edition of *MacGillivray on Insurance Law*, the Court held, that if the description of the property is embodied in the policy then it has at least the force of a limitation of the risk to be run and so whilst the cab was driven in one shift per 24 hours the risk was covered, but if in any one day of 24 hours the cab was driven in more than one shift the risk would no longer be covered and would cease to attach until the owner resumed the practice of driving the cab in one shift only.

On that reasoning alone, the Court held that it was impossible to construe the answer to the question about the number of shifts as a warranty. The judgment demonstrates a certain sophistry in an effort to reach a "fair" result. It is evident from the reasons given that the real basis of the Court's decision was sympathy with the plaintiff. The cab had in fact been driven for two shifts for only a little over one day and to enable the other driver to earn "a few shillings".

The conclusion reached by the Court of Appeal in *Re Morgan and Provincial Insurance Co*,[146] referred to earlier, was that the user limitation was merely descriptive of the risk and the insurer was back on risk at the time of the loss since the lorry was no longer carrying timber but only coal at the time of the collision. 11.69

The Court reached this conclusion by posing the relevant question thus: did the answer in the proposal form that the lorries would be used only for carrying coal amount to an undertaking by the insured that, during the currency of the policy, the vehicles should be used only for the purpose of carrying coal or whether the questions and answers mean that the vehicle should only be insured when it is engaged in carrying or delivering coal?[147]

Posed in this way the answer was inevitable. It was reached in spite of the statement in the policy that the answers were promissory in nature. In the House of Lords,[148] the majority agreed with the judgment of the Court of Appeal but in reality found it unnecessary to do so. Even if the term were to be construed as a warranty, in their Lordships' opinion, the outcome would not have differed for the court would have construed it narrowly. On this view then it mattered not how the term was in fact categorised.

145. [1920] 3 K.B. 669.
146. [1932] 2 K.B. 70.
147. *Ibid.*, at 83 *per* Lawrence LJ.
148. [1933] AC 240.

11.70 In *de Maurier (Jewels) Ltd v. Bastion Insurance Co. Ltd*,[149] the insured claimed in respect of the theft of some jewellery pursuant to a policy which contained the following clause:

> "[warranted] road vehicles (whether owned by insured or otherwise) fitted with locks and alarm system (approved by underwriters) and in operation."

It transpired that the alarm to the boot from where the jewellery was taken was not in fact in operation and the insurer denied liability. Mr Justice Donaldson, as he then was, held that the warranty delimited the risk and was part of the description of the risk and was not a promissory warranty. No reasons were given for this conclusion apparently because counsel had conceded the point. The case then takes the matter no further in the quest for the principle behind this series of decisions.[150]

11.71 A similar line of reasoning appears in *CTN Cash & Carry v. General Accident, Fire and Life Assurance Corporation.*[151] In the CTN case the critical term was in the main policy (not the proposal) on the cash and carry warehouse of the plaintiff/insured. The policy was a general one consisting of 12 sections; two of the sections dealt with burglary and money insurance which were subject to a term that "warranted that the secure cash kiosk should be attended and locked at all times during business hours". Prior to the close of business one evening, robbers raided the warehouse soon after the cashier had left her place at the cash kiosk to collect the till key from the office upstairs.

Contending that the clause ought to be regarded as a term delimiting the risk, the insurer refused to indemnify the loss because the risk was suspended by reason of the non-compliance with the term at the time of the loss.

The argument put forward by the insurer was in this case accepted by the judge (MacPherson J) and the literal wording "warranty" was thus ignored. One basis for this decision can be traced to the judge's impression of the clause from an examination of its context. MacPherson J found that the clause was relevant only to two out of the 12 sections and hence it would be unrealistic to imagine a breach of this warranty bearing in any way upon the rest of the sections of the policy.[152]

These cases, in which the distinction between a warranty and a term delimiting the risk has been crucial to the outcome, contain very little, if any, reasoning behind the conclusions reached. It is suggested[153] that whether or not a particular clause should be regarded as a warranty depends upon whether or not its breach affects the nature or extent of the risks "falling outside the terms of the warranty". Professor Clarke has also said:

> "When an exception operates, the insurer is off risk, usually because the circumstance of the exception has increased the risk to a degree which he has not contracted to assume. When the exception ceases to operate, the risk returns to the contract level and the cover continues. When an insurer pleads a breach of warranty, the success of the plea not only defeats the particular

149. [1967] 2 Lloyd's Rep. 550.

150. See also *A Cohen & Co. Ltd v. Plaistow Transport Ltd* [1968] 2 Lloyd's Rep. 587 where the relevant policy provided, "Warranted vehicles locked in garage at night, except when employed on night journeys, but then never 'left unattended'". Mr Justice McKenna said that he need not decide whether it was a warranty but his strong inclination would be to hold that the words merely define the risk (at 592). No reasons were given for his Honour's views.

151. [1989] 1 Lloyd's Rep 299.

152. *Ibid.*, at 301.

153. *Maritime Review*, 1993, Volume 12, Clifford Chance, 11.

claim, but also entitles the insurer to terminate the insurance contract altogether. . . . This is because the breach of warranty has increased the risk insured, not just for the time being but for the rest of the contract period, to a level which the insurer has not contracted to assume, or raised that possibility so that the insurer wishes to reconsider his position."[154]

Professor Clarke has put a logical interpretation on the judgments but it is suggested that such an interpretation is not borne out by the cases which are illustrative of the point. In all cases, the relevant term was a warranty, either because the parties had used the term warranty or because of a basis of the contract clause. Causation is, therefore, irrelevant and it is not to the point to seek to argue in hindsight that a breach of what was termed a warranty only increased the risk for a particular time period and, therefore, does not operate as would a warranty ordinarily. An example of the flawed nature of such reasoning is *Farr's case*,[155] in which the Court held that the term requiring the cab to be driven in one shift per day only was a term delimiting the risk. The insurer, however, probably had a very good reason for making it a warranty. Driving the cab more often increased the wear and tear and exposed it to the risk of accidents for longer periods. Therefore, even on Professor Clarke's reasoning, it was a term which quite legitimately could be said to have increased the risk for the rest of the contract. Similarly in *Morgan's case*,[156] whilst the carrying of timber was innocuous, what if the truck had carried explosives in between its cargoes of coal. Would a different result have been reached? If so, the principle for such a distinction would have been difficult to discern. It is submitted that the decisions in these cases ignore the very point of warranties and that the courts have strained to come to results which, whilst *prima facie* just, are unsustainable in principle. They are, in reality, examples of the classic statement that hard cases make bad law and are probably the cases Anthony Diamond QC had in mind when he observed that "it is not unknown for courts to overcome the rule about warranties by misconstruing the contract".[157]

A recent example of judicial interpretation of what, *prima facie*, appeared to be a warranty can be found in the case of *L'Union des Assurances de Paris IARD v. HBZ International Exchange Co. (Singapore) Pte Ltd (the "HBZ Case")*.[158] HBZ was a foreign exchange dealer which traded in money and gold. It regularly withdrew substantial amounts in cash and gold bars from a nearby bank and so took out a policy with L'Union des Assurances de Paris IARD to cover loss of money or gold from any of the six causes itemised in sections A to F in the Schedule to the policy. Four of the causes dealt with losses incurred whilst the items were in transit whereas the remaining two causes covered non-transit losses for items kept in the locked safes. A number of items had been listed in the policy of which three are pertinent: 11.72

(i) Warranty No. 1 which "warranted that carryings exceeding S$100,000 be accompanied by at least two employees of the insured";

---

154. Clarke, MA, *The Law of Insurance Contracts,* (3rd edn., London: Lloyd's of London Press, 1997) para. 19–1B.
155. [1920] 3 K.B. 669.
156. [1932] 2 K.B. 70.
157. Diamond QC, A, "The Law of Marine Insurance – Has it a Future?" (1986) *Lloyd's Maritime & Commercial Law Quarterly* 25, 37.
158. [1993] 1 SLR 882, HC; [1993] 3 SLR 161, CA.

(ii) Condition 2 which required that "the insured shall take all reasonable precaution for the safety of the property insured";

(iii) Condition 9 which maintained that "the due observance and fulfilment of the terms, provisions, conditions and endorsements of this policy by the insured in so far as they relate to anything to be done or complied with by him and the truth of the statements and answers in the said proposal shall be conditions precedent to any liability of the company to make payment under this policy".

On 2 October 1989, HBZ instructed Talib (a general clerk) who was to be accompanied by Badron (a clerk cum driver) to cash a cheque for S$500,000 and purchase fourteen gold bars. After completing the transactions, they drove back from the bank to their regular carpark located one floor above the HBZ premises. Whilst walking down the flight of stairs leading from the carpark to their office they were overpowered by a group of assailants and robbed of all the cash and gold bars. L'Union denied liability on the grounds that there were breaches of certain terms in the policy, viz.;

(i) a breach of warranty in two respects:
   (a) Talib was only accompanied by one other person whereas it was contended that warranty No. 1 required at least two other persons;
   (b) There were three instances when the two men were not in the immediate vicinity of each other: when Talib went into a room in the bank to collect the cash and Badron was left to wait in the bank hall; when Badron went to drive the car to the bank entrance where Talib was waiting with the cash and gold; and when Talib stood near the staircase leading down to HBZ whilst waiting for Badron to park the car.

(ii) breach of condition precedent to liability in that reasonable precautions – such as the use of suitable personnel for such an assignment and variation of route from car park to HBZ premises – were not taken.

It was held at first instance, and not challenged on appeal, that there was no breach of conditions precedent to liability. The standard required in insurance law was generally expected to be lower.[159] At first instance, Rubin JC sought to ameliorate the effect of Warranty No. 1 by adopting a rather liberal construction to conclude that it had not been breached. His Honour looked to the "spirit" of the policy and said that as the separation of the two clerks was to enhance safety it could not be held against the plaintiffs.[160] In doing this, he appeared to have accepted at face value that this particular term did indeed function as a warranty. Proceeding similarly on the assumption that Warranty No. 1 was to be so regarded, counsel for the insurer argued in the appellate proceedings that L'Union should be discharged from all liabilities since a warranty once breached could not be cured even though there was no breach at the time of the loss. This point, however, was not addressed at all by the Court of Appeal since they chose to view the problem from another perspective.

159. Citing *Fraser v. B N Furman (Productions) Ltd* [1967] 1 W.L.R. 898.
160. [1993] 1 SLR 822, 834.

The court held that:

"Warranty No.1 is ... a risk delimiting clause under which the appellants would be off risk when the carryings were not accompanied by at least two employees but they would be back on risk the moment the carryings were so accompanied.[161]

In other words, Warranty No. 1 was not really a warranty.

The Court of Appeal reached this conclusion by adopting the reasoning of MacPherson J in *CTN Cash and Carry v. General Accident Fire and Life Assurance Corporation.*[162] Goh J (who delivered the judgment of the Court) noted that Warranty No. 1 bore no relevance to two of the six sections listed in the Schedule to the policy (since these two sections related only to non-transit losses). Adopting MacPherson J's line of reasoning, Goh J therefore ruled that the term was also not to be regarded as a warranty but merely as one that delimited the risk and the insurer was held to be on risk again since there was compliance with the warranty.

It could be inferred then that for a composite policy comprising different risks, terms relevant only to certain of the risks as well as terms not generally applicable to all the risk (regardless of the importance of such terms to specific risks) might in fact not be warranties at all but instead be construed as terms delimiting risks.[163]

His Honour went on to say that even if it were a warranty as contended by the defendant, then the defendant was obliged to repudiate the policy timeously. Not having done so, it was deemed to have waived the right to repudiate.[164] It appears from the report of the case that the Court of Appeal was not referred to the decision of the House of Lords in "*The Good Luck*", judgment in which had been delivered just over two years prior to the appeal. It is submitted, therefore, that the reasoning of the Court of Appeal is fundamentally flawed and cannot be relied on.

Thus, it can be seen that there is no guarantee that a term will be regarded by a court to be a warranty simply because it has been stated to be so in the contract. Courts appear to disregard usage of the term altogether if they feel that it is not what the parties intended. The approach adopted by the courts is unhelpful, uncertain and confusing. 11.73

Yeo Hwee Ying comments[165] that it is significant that an appellate court has striven to construe a term to be less than what is to be expected of a warranty as this suggests that judges do recognise, albeit tacitly, that the doctrine of warranty in insurance law is indeed unduly harsh. However, judges should not be put in the position of having to circumvent principle to reach a solution to this unsatisfactory situation.

161. [1993] 3 SLR 161, 169.

162. [1989] 1 Lloyd's Rep 299.

163. Yeo Hwee Ying, "Of Warranties and Terms Delimiting Risks in Insurance Contracts" (1994) *Singapore Journal of Legal Studies* 369, 378.

164. [1993] 3 SLR 161, 169.

165. Yeo Hwee Ying, "Of Warranties and Terms Delimiting Risks in Insurance Contracts" (1994) *Singapore Journal of Legal Studies* 369, 378.

11F.4 The consequences of breach of warranty in Anglo/Australian marine insurance law

11.74 The lengths to which courts have gone to avoid construing a term in a contract of insurance as a warranty are, of course, recognition of the consequences of a breach of warranty: viz., that upon any breach of a warranty, however trivial, the insurer is entitled to terminate the policy.[166] It follows that upon breach of a warranty, the insurer has the right to terminate the whole contract from the date of the breach regardless of the materiality of the term, the state of mind of the insured or of any connection between the breach and the loss.

11.75 The nature of warranties as determinative of the risk insured means that breach will automatically discharge the insurer from liability. Where the warranty relates in time to circumstances at the inception of the risk, breach will result in the insurer never coming on risk. In this sense a warranty may be said to be a condition precedent to attachment of the risk.[167] In such circumstances, there will have been a total failure of consideration which will entitle the insured to the return of the premium.[168] Where the risk attaches and the warranty is subsequently broken, the risk ceases to be that which the insurer agreed to cover and the insurer's liability will be automatically discharged prospectively. Causation is entirely irrelevant. In these circumstances the insurer must refund that proportion of the premium which relates to the unexpired component of the contract unless the insured's contract is tainted by fraud or illegality.[169]

11.76 The automatic nature of the discharge of the contract was challenged in *Bank of Nova Scotia v. Hellenic Mutual War Risks Association (Bermuda) Ltd ('The Good Luck')*.[170] The *Good Luck* was owned by the Good Faith group, mortgaged to the appellant bank and entered with the respondent P&I Club whose rules provided for the declaration of prohibited areas and contained an express warranty of compliance with such prohibitions. When the appellant bank advanced money to the owners on the primary security of mortgages of a number of vessels including the *Good Luck,* it obtained an undertaking from the association "to advise you promptly if the association ceases to insure" the vessel.

In November 1981 the association discovered the *Good Luck* was being operated in a prohibited area, breaking the warranty, but did not inform the bank. In 1982, while the owners were renegotiating and seeking to increase the bank loan, the vessel was rendered a constructive total loss while inside the prohibited area. The owners lodged a claim with the club, pretending ignorance of the prohibition.

In July 1982, the bank extended Good Faith's credit facilities, the maximum total indebtedness being limited to 67 per cent of the value of the security furnished. The valuation of the security included US$4.8 million attributed to the *Good Luck* and the insurance claim, the bank taking an assignment of the insurance proceeds. On 4

166. *Pawson v. Watson* [1778] 2 Cowp 785, 787; 98 ER 1361, 1362; *de Hahn v. Hartley* [1786] 1 TR 343; 99 ER 1130; Marine Insurance Act 1909 s.39(3); Marine Insurance Act 1906 s.33(3).
167. *Thomson v. Weems* (1884) App Cas 671, 684.
168. Marine Insurance Act 1909 s.90(1); Marine Insurance Act 1906 s.84(1).
169. Marine Insurance Act 1909 s.90(1); Marine Insurance Act 1906 s.84(1).
170. [1992] 1 A.C. 233.

August, the club rejected the claim and, when sued by the bank on its undertaking, responded that it was not until 4 August that the club had ceased to insure the vessel.

Were s.33(3) of the Marine Insurance Act 1906 to be read literally, the club would clearly be in breach of its undertaking, but it was argued that breach of an insurance warranty should be assimilated to the general contract law concept of a repudiatory breach which triggers no automatic discharge but merely affords the innocent party the right to accept the breach, such acceptance prospectively discharging the parties from future performance.

This argument found favour in the Court of Appeal[171] but was rejected by the House of Lords.[172] Lord Goff declined to depart from the plain meaning of section 33(3):

"If a promissory warranty is not complied with, the insurer is discharged from liability as from the date of the breach of warranty, for the simple reason that fulfilment of the warranty is a condition precedent to the liability of the insurer. This moreover reflects the fact that the rationale of warranties in insurance law is that the insurer only accepts the risk provided that the warranty is fulfilled. . . . In the case of conditions precedent, the word 'condition' is being used in its classical sense in English law, under which the coming into existence of (for example) an obligation, or the duty or further duty to perform an obligation, is dependent upon the fulfilment of the specified condition."[173]

From the time of the breach of warranty, the *Good Luck* had, therefore, ceased to be insured by the club which had consequently broken its undertaking to the bank. 11.77

One of the perceived difficulties with a literal reading of s.33(3) was the statement in s.34(3) that the insurer can waive a breach of warranty. If the remedy for breach is automatic discharge there would appear to be nothing to waive. According to Lord Goff, however, the effect of waiver as contemplated by s.34(3) is simply that, "to the extent of the waiver, the insurer cannot rely upon the breach as having discharged him from liability".[174]

The question must be, however, whether there is any liability to begin with given the automatic nature of the discharge of liability for breach. This issue was discussed by the Queensland Court of Appeal in *Freshmark Ltd v. Mercantile Mutual Insurance (Australia) Ltd.*[175] In that case, the appellant insured a trailer owned by the respondent. The trailer was damaged in circumstances not covered by the insurance policy as the driver at the time of the accident was under 25 years. The respondent lodged a claim under the policy and the insurer authorised repairs to be made. Five days later that authority was revoked when it was discovered the policy did not cover an under-age driver. 11.78

At first instance it was held that there was no detriment sufficient to found an estoppel but that the insurer had waived its right to rely upon the relevant policy endorsement. The insurer appealed successfully.

The majority (McPherson JA and Dowsett J) held that there was no independent doctrine of waiver separate from estoppel or election.[176] His Honour Dowsett J (with

171. [1990] 1 Q.B.D. 818 and see *CTN Cash & Carry* [1989] 1 Lloyd's Rep. 299, 303.
172. [1992] 1 AC 233.
173. *Ibid.*, at 262– 263.
174. *Ibid.*, at 263.
175. [1994] 2 Qd R 390.
176. *Ibid.*, at 404.

whom McPherson JA agreed) reviewed the concepts of estoppel, election and waiver as articulated by the High Court in *Verwayen v. The Commonwealth*[177] and observed[178] that, in the absence of an estoppel or a contractual variation, the respondent could only justify the plea of waiver if it constituted an election. On the facts of the case there was no scope for any election because the appellant was not confronted with choosing between two alternative and inconsistent rights, nor did it elect to pursue one of those rights to the exclusion of the other. There was no choice between a right to accept liability under the policy and a right to reject liability. That is so because there was never any liability under the policy.[179]

11.79 The position would appear to be the same in the UK where the issue was considered by the House of Lords in *Motor Oil Hellas (Corinth) Refineries SA v. Shipping Corporation of India ("The Kanchenjunga")*.[180] In *The Kanchenjunga* it was argued that the owners of the vessel had waived their right not to comply with the charterers' orders to proceed to Kharg Island in circumstances where, when the order to proceed to Kharg Island was given, it was clear that it was not a prospectively safe port and the owners were, therefore, entitled to reject the order. Instead, the master proceeded to Kharg Island, tendered notice of readiness and asserted that laytime had commenced to run before leaving the port on the commencement of air raids by Iraq and prior to loading the cargo.

Lord Goff said:[181]

"It is commonplace that the expression 'waiver' is one which may in law bear different meanings. . . . Here we are concerned with waiver in the sense of abandonment of a right which arises by virtue of a party making an election. . . . In the present case, we are concerned with an election which may arise in the context of a binding contract, when a state of affairs comes into existence in which one party becomes entitled, either under the terms of the contract or by the general law, to exercise a right, and he has to decide whether or not to do so. His decision, being a matter of choice for him, is called in law an election."

His Lordship contrasted election with equitable estoppel before stating:[182]

"His election has generally to be an informed choice, made with knowledge of the facts giving rise to the right. His election once made is final; it is not dependent upon reliance on it by the other party."

His Lordship held that the owners had elected to waive their right to reject the nomination. In other words there is no independent doctrine of waiver, it is either an aspect of election or estoppel, depending upon the circumstances.

11.80 The Full Court of the Federal Court of Australia considered the same issue in *Switzerland Insurance Australia Ltd v. Mowie Fisheries Pty Ltd*[183] where Justice Beaumont raised the question of the true meaning of the expression "waived" where used in the Marine Insurance Act 1909 in light of the observations of the High Court in *Verwayen v. The Commonwealth*.[184] Without expressing any opinion, His Honour

177. (1990) 170 CLR 394.
178. [1994] 2 Qd R 390, 398.
179. *Ibid.*, at 395.
180. [1990] 1 Lloyd's Rep. 391.
181. *Ibid.*, at 397.
182. *Ibid.*, at 399.
183. (1997) 144 ALR 234.
184. (1990) 170 CLR 394.

held that even if it be accepted that the notion of waiver as it is employed in s.34(3) should be interpreted in the light of modern developments in the law of estoppel and election, it was open to the primary judge to conclude on the facts that the plaintiff's plea of waiver, estoppel or election could not be made out. The case, therefore, does not advance the debate although importantly it acknowledges the existence of room for debate.

The insurer may, therefore, be held to the contract through either an election to waive his right to rely on the automatic discharge of the contract or an equitable estoppel barring him from so relying. In general, a failure positively to exercise a right of election can prejudice the continued existence of that right. Under certain circumstances, such passivity may be viewed as an election not to rescind the contract or as a representation that the contract will not be rescinded on which the other party may rely so as to found an estoppel. Inactivity favours no change and the existing contract will not be avoided. *11.81*

A breach of warranty, however, triggers an automatic discharge which is not required to be perfected by the insurer and inactivity can only favour preservation of that discharge. Waiver by silence, notably by delay, appears to be ruled out by *The Good Luck*[185] as the only reasonable inference from silence on the part of the insurer is that the contract does not continue.[186] Professor Clarke writes:[187] *11.82*

"Courts have spoken in the past of waiver of a breach of warranty as if the rules are broadly the same as those governing waiver of rescission (affirmation) in respect of misrepresentation or non-disclosure, waiver of claim conditions and waiver of forfeiture for non-payment of premiums. The similarity must now be considered, as it now appears that the nature of waiver of breach of warranty is that it is not waiver at all but estoppel . . . waiver concerns an election but if the contract has been terminated automatically the insurer has no election to make. One suggestion is that it is resurrection by reinstatement. However in terms of the law of today, and indeed of Lord Goff's own judgment in *The Kanchenjunga*, it is submitted that (what was once) waiver of breach of warranty should now be regarded as a case of estoppel whereby the insurer is estopped from pleading that the insurance has terminated by reason of the breach of warranty."

These cases demonstrate that, far from adopting a lenient construction of s.40(3) of the Marine Insurance Act 1909,[188] the courts in recent years have affirmed one of the most draconian aspects of Anglo/Australian marine insurance law. It has been seen as another example of the apparent inability of the common law to adapt to modern commercial needs. *11.83*

The ALRC has considered the criticisms which have been levelled at the doctrine of warranties over the years and has concluded that the concept of warranties, both express and implied, should be abolished.[189] The purpose of the recommendations *11.84*

185. [1992] 1 A.C. 233.

186. Clarke, MA, "Breach of Warranty in the Law of Insurance" (1991) *Lloyd's Maritime & Commercial Law Quarterly* 437, 439.

187. Clarke, M A, *The Law of Insurance Contracts*, 2nd edn. (London: LLP Limited, 1997) para. 20–7A.

188. Marine Insurance Act 1906 s.34(3)

189. "Recommendation 7: The concept of warranties, both express and implied, as used in the law of marine insurance should be abolished and replaced with a system permitting the subject matter currently covered by them to be the subject of express terms of the contract. Except as provided by the Act as amended and subject to the terms of the contract, a breach by the insured of an express term (including those replacing warranties) will entitle insurers to be relieved of liability to indemnify the insured for a loss where the breach is causative of that loss."

relating to warranties is twofold: the first is to ameliorate what has been perceived as the harsh and unfair consequences of the operation of the doctrine of warranties;[190] the second is to ensure that provisions in contracts of marine insurance which nevertheless might have the effect of operating as a warranty appear clearly in the policy or contract as express terms.[191]

11.85 One major question for the ALRC was whether or not it was appropriate to utilise, in the context of marine insurance, the provisions of the ICA which deal with the doctrine of warranties. The ICA provides that any "statement made in or in connection with a contract of insurance, being a statement made by or attributable to the insured" does not take effect as a warranty but only as a pre-contractual representation.[192] The insurer's remedies are also strictly circumscribed such that the insurer is only entitled to avoid liability if the insured has acted fraudulently.[193] In the absence of fraud, the insurer may only seek a remedy if the breach induced the insurer to enter the contract.[194] In such circumstances, however, the insurer is limited to the remedy of damages.[195] Thus the ICA essentially deals with what is not a warranty, rather than providing a definition of a warranty. At the heart of the reform relating to warranties in Australian general insurance law is s.54 of the ICA which denies the insurer a right to avoid liability simply by relying on a breach of warranty or some other condition of the contract of insurance. Instead, the section provides that the insurer is limited to a reduction in liability to the insured by an amount representing the extent to which the insurer's interests were prejudiced. The provision was included in the ICA in recognition of the fact that, to allow insurers the right to avoid liability where there is only a minor or immaterial breach of warranty by the insured cannot be justified by reference to the doctrine of utmost good faith.[196] Termination is available to the insurer but only where the breach could reasonably be regarded as being capable of causing or contributing to the loss. The insured has the opportunity of showing that the loss was either in part or wholly not caused by the act. In this way, if an act can reasonably be regarded as capable of causing or contributing to a loss the insurer may refuse to pay the claim. However, this presumption may be rebutted by the insured.

11.86 The ALRC concluded that ICA did not provided a suitable model for reform of the Marine Insurance Act. Apart from the fact that even the High Court has commented

190. O'May, D, "Some Current Controversies in Connection with Marine Insurance", Paper delivered at Marine Insurance Seminar, Lloyd's of London Press, 17–18 April 1978; Diamond QC, A, "The Law of Marine Insurance – Has it a Future?" (1986) *Lloyd's Maritime and Commercial Law Quarterly* 25; Derrington, SC, "Does the *Marine Insurance Act 1909* still serve the needs of the business community?" (1995) 7 *Insurance Law Journal* 32; Kirby, The Hon Justice MD, "Marine Insurance: Is the Doctrine of 'Utmost Good Faith' Out of Date?" (1995) 13 *Australian Bar Review* 1; Luxford, D, "The Marine Insurance Act: Chronologically Challenged Legislation?", Paper delivered at the Annual General Meeting of the Maritime Law Association of Australia and New Zealand, Wellington, November 1995; Mason, Sir Anthony, "The Future of Marine Insurance Law", The 1995 Ebsworth & Ebsworth Maritime Law Lecture.

191. ALRC 91, para. 1.17.

192. ICA s.24.

193. ICA s.28(2).

194. ICA s.28 (1).

195. ICA s.28(3).

196. ALRC 20, para. 194.

that the provisions are "not without difficulty"[197] and that they have generated a large amount of litigation in the years in which they have been operating, the ALRC considered that the ICA provisions are much broader than is required to address the deficiencies of the present law of marine insurance. In particular, the ALRC was not minded to adopt the element of proportionality which is inherent in the ICA provisions.[198]

The ALRC has recommended that terms which might have been included in a policy as express warranties, or alternatively, have been implied into a policy by virtue of the Marine Insurance Act must now be expressly included as terms of the contract insurance.[199] However, a distinction has been retained between express terms relating to seaworthiness and illegality, should an insurer choose to incorporate such terms into the policy, and other express terms. 11.87

The substance of the distinction relates to causation. In relation to express terms generally, an insurer will be entitled to be relieved of liability only where the breach is "proximately" causative of the loss.[200] In relation to contracts of marine insurance which contain express terms relating to seaworthiness or the adventure's being carried out in a lawful manner, an insurer will be relieved of liability for any loss "attributable to" a breach of the term.[201] An insurer is still entitled to be relieved of liability where an insured breaches an express term that the adventure shall have no unlawful purpose, regardless of whether or not the unlawful purpose had anything to do with the loss.[202] 11.88

---

197. *Ferrcom Pty Ltd v. Commercial Union Assurance Co. of Australia Ltd* (1993) 176 CLR 332 *per* Brennan, Deane, Dawson, Gaudron and McHugh JJ.

198. ALRC 91, para 9.123.

199. "Recommendation 8: Obligations currently covered by express warranties should be dealt with as express terms of the contract.

Recommendation 10: The Marine Insurance Act should be amended to repeal the implied warranties of seaworthiness. Obligations of seaworthiness should be dealt with as express terms of the contract.

Recommendation 13: The Marine Insurance Act should be amended to repeal the implied warranty of legality. Obligations of legality should be dealt with as express terms of the contract.

Recommendation 16: The provisions of the Marine Insurance Act s 48 and 51–55 relating to change of voyage, deviation and delay should be repealed, permitting these concepts to be dealt with as express terms of the contract. Marine Insurance Act s 49–50, which deal with the attachment of the risk, should be retained.

Recommendation 17: The provisions of the Marine Insurance Act dealing with the warranties of neutrality, nationality and good safety (Marine Insurance Act s 42–44) should be repealed as redundant because they are rarely used in practice and can be the subject of express terms."

200. "Recommendation 9: Subject to the contract, the Marine Insurance Act should be amended so that an insurer is entitled to be discharged from liability to indemnify the insured for any loss proximately caused by a breach by the insured of any express term of the contract."

201. "Recommendation 11: The Marine Insurance Act should be amended so that an insurer is discharged from liability to indemnify the insured for any loss attributable to a breach of an express term of the contract relating to the seaworthiness of a ship where the insured knew or ought to have known of the relevant circumstances and that they rendered the vessel unseaworthy and where the insured failed to take such remedial steps as were reasonably available to it.

Recommendation 15: The Marine Insurance Act should be amended so that where the insured is in breach of an express contractual term to the effect that, so far as the insured can control the matter, the insured adventure shall be carried out in a lawful manner, the insurer is discharged from liability to indemnify the insured in relation to any loss that is attributable to that breach."

202. "Recommendation 14: The Marine Insurance Act should be amended so that where the insured is in breach of an express contractual term to the effect that, so far as the insured can control the matter, the insured adventure shall have no unlawful purpose, the insurer is discharged from all liability under the contract."

11.89 The decision to differentiate between a loss "proximately caused by" and one "attributable to" a breach of a particular term of the contract was deliberate. Account was taken of Howard Bennett's view that the use of words "attributable to" in s.61 of the Marine Insurance Act 1909[203] reflect:

"the nineteenth century approach to causation according to which the loss of a vessel to a sea peril which a seaworthy vessel could have withstood would be regarded as proximately caused by the sea peril as the cause immediate in time. Consequently, a formula was required to permit the courts to consider an otherwise legally remote if factually significant cause. Thus, if the unseaworthiness necessarily increased the danger which led to the loss, the insurer would have a good defence even if, when the accident overtook the vessel, the accident was the cause of the loss most immediate in time. The position is the same today, except that the unseaworthiness should be classified as the or a proximate cause."[204]

11.90 However, the ALRC's view was that, despite the modern adoption of "proximate cause" as the link between cause and loss, the use of the words "attributable to unseaworthiness" in s.45(5) is critical in cases where the unseaworthiness is a more remote cause of loss. The Marine Insurance Act effectively dilutes the rule of proximate cause of loss where there is privity of the insured.[205] If unseaworthiness is an excluded peril and is the (or a) proximate cause of the loss, the insurer will be able to deny liability under Marine Insurance Act s.61(1). If unseaworthiness is not a proximate cause of loss but the loss can nonetheless be attributed to it, the insurer can still establish a defence under s.45(5) if it can prove the insured's privity.[206] The ALRC has proposed that an amended Marine Insurance Act specifically provide for the distribution of the onus of proof. It did not, however, consider that a general codification of the law of causation was warranted.

11.91 Where a contract of marine insurance is subject to the amended Marine Insurance Act, an insurer will not be permitted to include in the contract terms which are more favourable to the insurer than as provided for in the Marine Insurance Act.

11.92 As with the recommendations relating to disclosure and misrepresentation, the approach taken by the ALRC in relation to the doctrine of warranties is similar to that which appears in the Norwegian Marine Insurance Plan.

11G CONCLUSION

11.93 As with many other areas of Australian law, the original importation of English marine insurance law is gradually developing and mutating in ways which no longer depend upon developments in English law. Whether or not this is a desirable result in this particular area of international commercial law, in which English law remains pre-eminent, remains to be seen. The adoption of the recommendations made by the ALRC would have the effect of implementing a marine insurance regime which is significantly different from its English counterpart. It would result in a regime which

203. Marine Insurance Act 1906, s.55.
204. Bennett, H: *The Law of Marine Insurance* (Clarendon Press, Oxford, 1996), 318.
205. *George Cohen, Sons and Co. v. Standard Marine Insurance Co.* (1925) 21 LlL Rep. 30, 36.
206. ALRC 91, para 9.152.

is perhaps more familiar to those involved in the Norwegian marine insurance system. The extent to which the recommendations will result in any fundamental change occurring, however, will depend upon whether the recommendation relating to choice of law and jurisdiction is adopted.[207] If Australian law does not compulsorily apply to contracts of marine insurance, the proper law of which is in fact Australian, insurers will be able to continue to write policies subject to the familiar marine insurance law regime.

207. "Recommendation 35. The law of marine insurance in Australia should not restrict the right of parties to choose some other body of law as the governing law of the contract or to decide that disputes be resolved by a foreign court or other forum."

CHAPTER 12

A US PERSPECTIVE ON MARINE INSURANCE LAW

PROFESSOR MICHAEL F. STURLEY

12A INTRODUCTION

In this era of expanding globalisation, it has become increasingly common to see "comparative perspectives" in legal literature. Of course, scholarly discussion in the maritime field has long been filled with comparative perspective. It would be virtually impossible fully to understand the law governing the carriage of goods by sea, for example, without considering at least US and British perspectives on the subject. In marine insurance, the dominance of the London market long required other nations to pay attention to English law, but the broader comparative trend has nevertheless been somewhat less pronounced. The Comité Maritime International's recent venturing into this field,[1] however, illustrates the current heightened interest in the law and practice of marine insurance in other countries. Thus, it should not be surprising that this volume includes a comparative section, and that the editor has included a US perspective on the modern law of marine insurance. *12.1*

Although it may not be surprising to find a US perspective in this volume, it is surprisingly difficult to identify a US law of marine insurance. On some issues, there is almost certainly a uniform national rule that could be described as part of the country's marine insurance law. On other issues, there is clearly no national approach, with the result that marine insurance disputes must be resolved by reference to the law of one of the 50 states (if the court decides that US law governs). In these circumstances, therefore, varying state laws must be considered part of the US law of marine insurance. And between these two extremes, there is a wide gulf of even more uncertainty. The courts in some part of the country may look to a theoretically uniform national law of marine insurance, while courts in other parts of *12.2*

1. See, e.g., 2000 CMI Yearbook 325–411.

the country look to state law for answers to the same questions. The problem is exacerbated by the lack of any clear rules on when to apply federal law (the uniform, national solution) and when to apply state law, or even which state's law to apply when state law governs.

12.3 It has not always been so hard to find the US law of marine insurance. Indeed, there was a time when the US Supreme Court regularly decided marine insurance cases. It was universally assumed that marine insurance issues were governed by the general maritime law, which is largely the creation of the federal courts. Moreover, it was widely thought that the general maritime law governing marine insurance was largely the same as English law (subject to only minor[2] exceptions). In *Queen Insurance Co. of America v. Globe & Rutgers Fire Insurance Co.*, for example, Justice Holmes declared that "[t]here are special reasons for keeping in harmony with the marine insurance laws of England, the great field of this business".[3] The Supreme Court cited this language with approval just two years before its infamous *Wilburn Boat* decision, explaining that a House of Lords decision was "persuasive authority" because of these "special reasons".[4] One US commentator went so far as to cite *Queen Insurance* for "the extraordinary doctrine ... that English decisions could be cited as *binding* authority in US courts",[5] although this is certainly an overstatement.[6]

12.4 These times have passed. The parties in marine insurance cases today rarely seek Supreme Court review, and the Court declines to hear even these rare cases. Old assumptions about the broad scope of the general maritime law have proven false. And the deference once shown to English law has been replaced by a much stronger deference to state law. The turning point came almost half a century ago in the Supreme Court's last marine insurance decision: *Wilburn Boat Co. v. Fireman's Fund Insurance Co.*[7] It is this decision, more than anything else, that distinguishes marine insurance law in the US from the comparable laws in other countries (particularly common law countries). The *Wilburn Boat* decision will accordingly be the focus of this chapter.

12B THE *WILBURN BOAT* CASE

12.5 The *Wilburn Boat* case had its origin in some very mundane facts.[8] In May 1947, the Fireman's Fund Insurance Company issued a marine hull policy on the *Motor Yacht Wanderer*, a small houseboat. The company issued the policy in the state of Illinois

2. For example, compare s.60 of the Marine Insurance Act of 1906 (defining constructive total loss) with, e.g., *Bradlie v. Maryland Insurance Co.*, 37 US (12 Pet.) 378, 388 (1838) (recognising constructive total loss when the cost of recovery or repair would exceed half of the repaired value).

3. *Queen Insurance Co. of American v. Globe & Rutgers Fire Insurance Co.*, 263 US 487, 493, 1924 AMC 107, 109 (1924).

4. *Calmar SS Corp. v. Scott*, 345 US 427, 442–443, 1953 AMC 952, 964–965 (1953).

5. Thomas J Schoenbaum, *Marine Insurance*, 31 J Mar L & Com 281, 282 (2000) (emphasis added).

6. See generally, David W Robertson, Steven F Friedell & Michael F Sturley, *Admiralty and Maritime Law in the United States* 527 (2001).

7. 348 US 310, 1955 AMC 467 (1955).

8. The Supreme Court's opinion gives only a bare outline of the facts. A more detailed account of the case can be found in Joel K Goldstein, *The Life and Times of Wilburn Boat: A Critical Guide*, 28 J Mar L & Com 395, 400–401 (1997).

through an Illinois broker to assureds who resided in Iowa and Illinois. The policy provided, among other things, that the vessel could neither be sold nor pleged without the insurer's consent. Furthermore, the vessel could be used "solely for private pleasure purposes", and could not be "hired or chartered" without the insurer's permission.

In June 1948, three brothers from Texas – Glenn, Frank, and Henry Wilburn – purchased the *Wanderer*. The insurer endorsed the policy in favour of the new owners doing business as a partnership known as "Wilburn's Boat Company". They moved the vessel to Lake Texoma, an artificial lake on the Texas-Oklahoma border. A policy endorsement authorised the trip and provided that the *Wanderer* would thereafter be confined to Lake Texoma.

In September 1948 the brothers sold the *Wanderer* to the "Wilburn Boat Company", an Oklahoma corporation that they owned. On three occasions, they or their corporation pledged the vessel to secure promissory notes. Finally, the owners leased the vessel on several occasions and carried passengers for hire. The insurer did not consent to any of these transactions, all of which were admitted policy breaches.

On 25 February, 1949, a fire destroyed the *Wanderer* while it was moored near the Oklahoma shore of the lake. The origin of the fire remains unknown, but the insurer accepted that the policy breaches did not contribute to the loss. The Wilburn brothers thus made a claim under the policy, which by its terms covered loss due to fire. Fireman's Fund, however, declined to pay the claim. It argued that under the general maritime law governing marine insurance, an assured's breach of a policy warranty permits the insurer to avoid payment of a claim for a subsequent loss – even if the breach was unrelated to the loss.[9] The Wilburns replied that Texas law governed the policy. Under Texas law, the policy breaches relating to the sale and use of the vessel would not defeat coverage unless they had contributed to the loss, and the anti-encumbrance provision in the policy would be ineffective.

The Wilburn brothers and their company sued under the insurance contract. The district court ruled that federal maritime law governed and that – because of the "literal compliance" rule for warranties – the Wilburns were not entitled to any recovery. On appeal, the US Court of Appeals for the Fifth Circuit affirmed.[10]

On 28 February, 1955, six years after the fire, the Supreme Court reversed the Fifth Circuit's decision and remanded the case to the district court "for a trial under appropriate state law".[11] Justice Black wrote the Court's opinion. Justice Frankfurter concurred in the judgment, but rejected much of the Court's reasoning. Two justices dissented (in an opinion by Justice Reed). 12.6

Justice Black, having noted that there was no relevant federal legislation, began his 12.7

9. *Cf.* s.33(3) of the Marine Insurance Act of 1906.

10. *Wilburn Boat Co. v. Fireman's Fund Insurance Co.*, 201 F.2d 833, 1953 AMC 284 (5th Cir 1953), *rev'd*, 348 US 310, 1955 AMC 467 (1955).

11. 348 US at 321, 1955 AMC at 477. The Court did not discuss which state's law was "appropriate". See 348 US at 313 fn.6, 1955 AMC at 470 fn.6. On remand, the lower courts held that Texas law governed the effect of the breach of warranties, but despite this favourable ruling the Wilburns ultimately recovered nothing. The Fifth Circuit, in a two-to-one decision, found them guilty of eight material misrepresentations or nondisclosures, and held that these permitted Fireman's Fund to avoid the claim under either Texas law or federal maritime law. See *Wilburn Boat Co. v. Fireman's Fund Insurance Co.*, 330 F.2d 631, 640–647, 1962 AMC 1593, 1604–16 (5th Cir. 1962), *cert. denied*, 370 US 925 (1962).

analysis by posing two questions: "(1) Is there a judicially established federal admiralty rule governing these warranties? (2) If not, should we fashion one?"[12] In answering the first question, he distinguished or ignored several cases that appeared to establish the literal compliance rule. He thus concluded that the rule "has not been judicially established as part of the body of federal admiralty law in this country".[13] He did not offer any guidance on what is required for a rule to become "judicially established", or any justification for why the question was worth asking in the first place.

Turning to the second question, the Court declined to fashion a "new" admiralty rule for two principal reasons. First, the regulation of insurance has historically been a matter for the states (even if the federal government does have the power to regulate insurance if it chooses to do so), and Congress has recognised and acted upon this division of responsibility.[14] Second, even if the Court wished to fashion a new rule, doing so would be a complex and difficult task that courts are poorly equipped to undertake.[15] In the case before it, for example, Justice Black was clearly uncomfortable with the "harsh" literal compliance rule, but apparently felt uncomfortable in choosing a new rule to replace it.[16] Deferring the problem to Congress or the states, with their greater expertise and experience, was much easier.

12.8 Justice Frankfurter concurred in the result,[17] meaning that he accepted the Court's judgment (remanding the case for a decision under appropriate state law) but did not agree with the majority's reasoning. In essence, he argued for a middle ground under which cases requiring a uniform rule throughout the country would be governed by the general maritime law, while cases of essentially local interest could be governed by state law. Because he thought this case, arising on an inland lake, was of merely local interest, he had no objection to the application of state law.[18] But because he thought the majority's reasoning was unnecessarily broad, and could be "directed with equal force to oceangoing vessels in international maritime trade"[19] he refused to join – and, indeed, harshly criticised – the Court's opinion. But he was also critical of Justice Reed's dissent:

> "[T]he demand for uniformity is not inflexible and does not preclude the balancing of the competing claims of state, national and international interests. . . . In rejecting abdication of all responsibility by this Court for uniformities in marine insurance and its complete surrender to the States, one is not required to embrace another absolute, complete absorption by this Court of the field of marine insurance and entire exclusion of the States."[20]

12.9 Justice Reed, joined by Justice Burton, dissented.[21] He hinted that he would be prepared, as a matter of general maritime law, to modify the literal compliance rule "insofar as the breached warranty does not contribute to the loss".[22] Until Congress

12. 348 US at 314, 1955 AMC at 471.
13. 348 US at 316, 1955 AMC at 472–473.
14. 348 US at 316–319, 1955 AMC at 473–475.
15. 348 US at 319–320, 1955 AMC at 475–476.
16. 348 US at 320, 1955 AMC at 476.
17. 348 US at 321, 1955 AMC at 477 (Frankfurter J concurring in the result).
18. 348 US at 322, 1955 AMC at 477–478 (Frankfurter J concurring in the result).
19. 348 US at 323, 1955 AMC at 478 (Frankfurter J concurring in the result).
20. 348 US at 323–324, 1955 AMC at 479 (Frankfurter J concurring in the result).
21. 348 US at 324, 1955 AMC at 479 (Reed J dissenting).
22. 348 US at 326, 1955 AMC at 481 (Reed J dissenting).

or the Court modified the rule, however, he argued that it should be applied in all maritime cases to preserve uniformity.

It is always risky to speculate on exactly what motivates a particular decison, but Professor Goldstein has found considerable evidence in several of the Justices' private papers that the result in *Wilburn Boat* was largely driven by the equities of the case.[23] Justice Black, in particular, wished to avoid the "harsh" literal compliance rule. Requiring the application of state law appeared to be an easy way to accomplish this result. Formulating a new rule to replace the literal compliance rule would probably have been no more difficult than many of the other tasks that common law courts regularly undertake, but the *Wilburn Boat* court may have felt that it still was not worth the effort. "Hard cases", according to the maxim, "make bad law".[24] Whether or not Professor Goldstein is correct to suggest that *Wilburn Boat* was a hard case for several of the justices who decided it, almost everyone agrees that it made bad law. 12.10

12C THE DIFFICULTIES CREATED BY *WILBURN BOAT*

Wilburn Boat creates problems on many levels, most of which go to the need for predictability and uniformity in the law governing marine insurance contracts. In almost every case since *Wilburn Boat*, it has been an issue for debate whether state law or federal maritime law governs a particular question. With virtually no guidance from the Supreme Court, the lower courts are hopelessly divided in their approach to this "vertical" choice of law question. Even when a court decides that state law should apply, it is often a complicated and difficult exercise to decide *which* state's law should apply, thus raising "horizontal" choice of law questions. Finally, when a court has chosen a paticular state's law, there is yet a further problem in applying that state's insurance law in the marine insurance context. Each of these issues merits separate discussion here. 12.11

12C.1 The vertical choice-of-law problem

The Supreme Court began its vertical choice-of-law analysis by asking whether there was an established federal admiralty rule governing the issue. The Court concluded that there was no such rule in the case before it, but offered no further guidance on what would be required for a rule to become sufficiently established. Presumably the Court expected something more than two court of appeals decisions, for it argued that "only two circuits appear to have thought of the [literal compliance] rule as a part of the general admiralty law".[25] Would one Supreme Court decision have been enough? Professors Gilmore and Black argued that *Insurance Co. v. Thwing*[26] "seems squarely to have decided th[e] very point [at issue in *Wilburn Boat*], or at least inevitably to have rested on the assumption of the correctness of the strict 12.12

23. See Goldstein, *supra* fn.8, at 410–417.
24. *Cf. Winterbottom v. Wright*, 10 M. & W. 109, 116, 152 Eng. Rep. 402, 406 (1842) (Rolfe, B).
25. 348 US at 315, 1955 AMC at 472.
26. 80 US (13 Wall.) 672 (1872).

rule".[27] But the Court did not cite *Thwing*, so one can only speculate why it was not sufficient to "establish" the literal compliance rule.

12.13 On a deeper level, simply approaching the issue in this way creates problems. The approach can make the choice of law depend on the frequency with which a particular issue is litigated. But some of the most basic legal principles are never litigated; they are so basic that no one would waste the effort to challenge them. As a result, courts are unable to rule on these principles and it could then be argued that they are not sufficiently established. Similarly, legal principles that have truly become established are not likely to be challenged. The lack of any judicial reaffirmation of the principle, however, may lead a later court to assume that the principle is no longer established.[28] Finally, the approach makes it difficult for the law to respond to new situations. If a principle was not established before 1955, it is hard for it to pass the *Wilburn Boat* barrier, and thus it is unlikely ever to become established.

12.14 The court's lack of guidance in *Wilburn Boat* itself was compounded by its subsequent abandonment of the marine insurance field. Despite a steady diet of these cases before 1955, the court has not heard a single marine insurance case since *Wilburn Boat* (almost 50 years ago). This combination of factors has left lower courts and commentators to guess what kind of impact *Wilburn Boat* was intended to have. Soon after the decision was announced, Professors Gilmore and Black were among the first to speculate on the alternative possibilities:

> "Wilburn may mean merely that the States are to have a limited competency to regulate certain terms of marine policies. It could as a matter of cold logic be read to mean that there is no federal maritime law at all. It may very well turn out to mean anything between these extremes."[29]

In practice, the subsequent cases have occupied a broad range between these extremes.

12.15 *Kossick v. United Fruit Co.*,[30] which was not a marine insurance action, clarified that *Wilburn Boat* did not require state law to govern in every admiralty case. Applying general maritime law rather than a New York statute to a contract between a seaman and his employer, the Supreme Court distinguished its earlier decision with the observation, "needless to say, the situation presented here [in *Kossick*] has a more genuinely salty flavor than that [in *Wilburn Boat*]".[31] Some lower courts have picked up on this cue and attempted to limit *Wilburn Boat* to the maritime-but-local context,[32] as Justice Frankfurter had suggested in his concurring opinion.[33] Others, however, have applied *Wilburn Boat* more broadly, at least in the marine insurance context.

27. Grant Gilmore & Charles L Black, Jr., *The Law of Admiralty*, section 2–8, at 68 & fn.71a (2d edn 1975 Foundation Press, N.Y.).

28. See, e.g. *Albany Insurance Co. v. Anh Thi Kieu*, 927 F.2d 882, 890, 1991 AMC 2211, 2219 (5th Cir.), *cert. denied*, 502 US 901 (1991).

29. Grant Gilmore & Charles L Black, Jr, *The Law of Admiralty*, section 2–8, at 63 (1st edn 1957).

30. 365 US 731, 1961 AMC 833 (1961).

31. *Kossick*, 365 US at 742, 1961 AMC at 842. *Kossick* is particularly relevant to the interpretation of *Wilburn Boat* because four of the five members of the *Wilburn Boat* majority (including Justice Black, the author of the *Wilburn Boat* opinion) joined the *Kossick* opinion.

32. See, e.g., *Aasma v. American SS Owners Mutual Protection & Indemnity Association*, 95 F.3d 400, 404, 1997 AMC 1, 5 (6th Cir. 1996).

33. See 348 US at 322–323, 1955 AMC at 477–478 (Frankfurter, J, concurring in the result). See also *supra* fnn.17–18 and accompanying text.

Commentators and lower courts have suggested several other ways to limit *Wilburn Boat*. At one end of the spectrum, some have suggested that it requires the application of state law to the effect of warranties (which was the precise issue before the Court) but not to other aspects of marine insurance,[34] although this is a difficult distinction to defend. One district court recently read *Wilburn Boat* to say "that federal admiralty law should apply to issues that are maritime in nature and that state law should apply to issues that are common to all sorts of insurance contracts".[35] 12.16

Although *Wilburn Boat* has had little influence outside the marine insurance context, how broadly it should apply within that field still remains unclear. Despite widespread criticism of the decision, the judiciary has not uniformly or predictably limited or distinguished it. One good example of the lower courts' unwillingness forthrightly to limit *Wilburn Boat* can be found in the Second Circuit's two opinions in *Youell v. Exxon Corp.*[36] Although the court was willing essentially to disregard *Wilburn Boat* (without principled explanation), it did not take the simple step of declaring that the *Exxon Valdez* disaster "has a more genuinely salty flavor than" the *Wilburn Boat* fire on Lake Texoma. For every case that cuts back on the broad application of Justice Black's *dicta*, there seems to be another new case that extends the reach of the holding. If anything, the sporadic efforts to distinguish or limit the case have probably made the situation worse, as each of the distinctions becomes just one more variable for the parties to consider when predicting how a marine insurance suit will be resolved. 12.17

Even on questions of methodology, the lower courts are spread out along a spectrum. Courts continue to apply federal law in marine insurance cases, either because they find that there is an established federal admiralty rule[37] or they conclude that they should fashion one.[38] But not all courts dutifully proceed through Justice Black's two-question analysis. Indeed, the second question – should the court fashion a federal admiralty rule – is regularly ignored. A recent First Circuit decision at least explains why it is not giving careful consideration to Justice Black's second question: 12.18

"Under a well-established principle of federal law applicable to cases of this genre [i.e., marine insurance cases], if federal and state law collide, then the federal rule prevails. ... But in the absence of such a conflict, '*Wilburn Boat* has generally been interpreted, "in deference to state hegemony over insurance, to discourage the fashioning of new federal law and to favor the application of state law".' "[39]

34. See, e.g., Goldstein, *supra* fn.8, at 435–437; *ibid.* at 579 & fnn.424–425. Professor Goldstein finds some support for this reading in both *Kossick*, 365 US at 742, 1961 AMC at 842, and *Romero v. International Terminal Operating Co.*, 358 US 354, 373, 1959 AMC 832, 847 (1959). *See* Goldstein, *supra* fn.8, at 569 & fn.348.

35. *Home Insurance Co. v. Vernon Holdings*, 1995 AMC 369, 372 (S.D. Fla. 1994).

36. See 48 F.3d 105, 1995 AMC 1147 (2d Cir.), *vacated* 516 US 801 (1995); 74 F.3d 373, 1996 AMC 752 (2d Cir.) (*per curiam*), *cert. denied*, 517 US 1251 (1996).

37. See, e.g., *American Natural Fire Insurance Co. v. Kenealy*, 72 F.3d 64, 270–271, 1996 AMC 584, 593 (2d Cir. 1995) (finding that admiralty law now had a settled rule on the award of attorney's fees).

38. See, e.g., *Aasma v. American SS Owners Mutual Protection & Indemnity Association*, 95 F.3d 400, 1997 AMC 1 (6th Cir. 1996) (fashioning federal admiralty rule upholding the P & I Clubs' "pay-to-be-paid" clause in the face of a direct action by personal injury plaintiffs with judgments against a bankrupt member).

39. *Acadia Insurance Co. v. McNeil*, 116 F.3d 599, 603, 1997 AMC 2409, 2415 (1st Cir. 1997) (quoting *Windsor Mount Joy Mutual Insurance Co. v. Giragosian*, 57 F.3d 50, 54, 1995 AMC 2542, 2546–47 (1st Cir. 1995) (quoting *Albany Insurance Co. v. Wisniewski*, 579 F. Supp. 1004, 1013–14, 1985 AMC 689, 702 (D. R.I. 1984))).

12.19 Some courts ignore even the first question, apparently applying state law simply because the case before it involves marine insurance.[40]

12.20 Two recent cases – drawn from opposite ends of the spectrum – help to illustrate the range of views that exists in the federal courts. In *Aasma v. American Steamship Owners Mutual Protection & Indemnity Association*,[41] personal injury plaintiffs with default judgments against a bankrupt shipowner brought direct actions against the owner's former P & I Clubs, which had provided coverage during the period that the injuries arose. The clubs asserted defences under their "pay-to-be-paid" clauses. The Sixth Circuit concluded that no existing federal admiralty rule addressed the validity of such clauses, but that the need for a single, uniform rule in this "uniquely maritime" context justified the fashioning of a federal admiralty rule. The court thus recognised the validity of a "pay-to-be-paid" clause as a matter of federal maritime law.[42]

12.21 In *Albany Insurance Co. v. Anh Thi Kieu*,[43] the Fifth Circuit took a very different approach. The principal issue was whether the doctrine of utmost good faith was an established rule of federal admiralty law. Supreme Court decisions in the nineteenth century had recognised the doctrine. Fairly recent decisions in the Fifth Circuit – including the decision in *Wilburn Boat* on remand from the Supreme Court – had not only explicitly recognised the doctrine, but had declared that it was "solidly entrenched"[44] or "established"[45] in the federal law of marine insurance. The *Anh Thi Kieu* court distinguished all of these cases, however, and held that the "doctrine is entrenched no more".[46]

12C.2 The horizontal choice-of-law problem

12.22 The *Wilburn Boat* Court gave virtually no guidance on resolving the vertical choice-of-law problem, but it at least offered the illustration of its own analysis concerning the literal compliance rule. The majority opinion gave absolutely no guidance on how to decide which state's law should apply when federal law does not. It simply noted that the horizontal choice-of-law problem was not before the Court,[47] and remanded the case to permit the lower courts to resolve the issue.[48]

12.23 Justice Frankfurter's separate opinion might be read as implicitly suggesting a choice-of-law rule when he asked, "Is it to be assumed that were the *Queen Mary*, on a world pleasure cruise, to touch at New York City, New Orleans and Galveston, a Lloyd's policy covering the voyage would be subjected to the varying insurance laws of New York, Louisiana and Texas?"[49] But it seems unlikely that Justice Frankfurter

---

40. See, e.g., *Commercial Union Insurance Co. v. Flagship Marine Services Inc.*, 190 F.3d 26, 30, 2000 AMC 1, 4 (2d Cir. 1999).

41. 95 F.3d 400, 1997 AMC 1 (6th Cir. 1996).

42. 95 F.3d at 404, 1997 AMC at 6.

43. 927 F.2d 882, 1991 AMC 2211 (5th Cir., *cert. denied*, 502 US 901 (1991).

44. *Fireman's Fund Insurance Co. v. Wilburn Boat Co.*, 300 F.2d 631, 647 fn.12, 1962 AMC 1593, 1615 fn.12 (5th Cir. 1962), *cert. denied*, 370 US 925 (1962).

45. *Gulfstream Cargo Ltd v. Reliance Insurance Co.*, 409 F.2d 974, 980, 1969 AMC 781, 790 (5th Cir. 1969).

46. *Anh Thi Kieu*, 927 F.2d at 890, 1991 AMC at 2219.

47. See *Wilburn Boat*, 348 US at 313 fn.6, 1955 AMC at 470 fn.6.

48. *Ibid.*, 348 US at 321, 1955 AMC at 477.

49. 348 US at 323, 1955 AMC at 478 (Frankfurter, J, concurring in the result).

himself would have endorsed a location-of-the-loss rule for determining the law governing a marine insurance contract if he had actually been called upon to make that decision. His rhetorical point was clearly that the law governing the *Queen Mary*'s insurance policy should *not* vary as the vessel called at different ports. In any event, the lower courts have not been applying a location-of-the-loss rule in this context. On remand in *Wilburn Boat*, for example, it appears that neither party advocated the application of Oklahoma law.[50]

Justice Reed's dissent mentions three possible choice-of-law rules, suggesting that the case might be governed by the law "of the State where the insurance contract was issued, the State of the accident, or the State of the forum".[51] These rules would have pointed to Illinois, Oklahoma, and Texas, respectively. Once again, however, the rhetorical point is not to advocate a particular choice-of-law rule but to criticise the majority for requiring a choice to be made. 12.24

The complications and difficulties on this issue are well illustrated by a quartet of marine insurance decisions within a single circuit over just six years. In 1985, the Fifth Circuit held that "the law of the state where the marine insurance contract was issued and delivered is the governing law".[52] Two years later, the same court wrote, "the law of the state in which the [marine insurance] contract was formed" governs.[53] Another two years later the court announced a different rule: "In identifying the appropriate state law to apply, we look to the state having the greatest interest in the resolution of the issues."[54] Two years after that, the court reviewed the field and, in an attempt to reconcile the cases, declared that it would adopt a two-step process. In step one, the court identifies the states in which the policy was formed, issued, and delivered. In step two, it decides which of these states has the greatest interest in the application of its law.[55] None of these fairly recent statements, however, represents the Fifth Circuit's choice-of-law approach on remand in *Wilburn Boat* itself. At that time, the court chose to apply the law of Texas (where the Wilburn brothers resided) in preference to the law of Illinois (where the original policy appears to have been formed, issued, and delivered).[56] 12.25

12C.3 Applying state law in the marine insurance context

When a court has chosen a particular state's law, there is rarely a relevant judicial decision or statute in the maritime context.[57] Indeed, many states explicitly exclude 12.26

50. Not only was Oklahoma where the loss occurred, but the vessel owner was an Oklahoma corporation.

51. 348 US at 334, 1955 AMC at 487 (Reed J dissenting).

52. *Elevating Boats Inc. v. Gulf Coast Marine Inc.*, 766 F.2d 195, 198 (5th Cir. 1985). See also *Gulf Fleet Marine Operations Inc. v. Wartsila Power Inc.*, 797 F.2d 257, 261 (5th Cir. 1986).

53. *Graham v. Milky Way Barge Inc.*, 811 F.2d 881, 885 (5th Cir. 1987).

54. *Truehart v. Blandon*, 884 F.2d 223, 226 (5th Cir. 1989). See also *Transco Exploration Co. v. Pacific Employers Insurance Co.*, 869 F.2d 862, 863 (5th Cir. 1989).

55. *Albany Insurance Co. v. Anh Thi Kieu*, 927 F.2d 882, 890–891, 1991 AMC 2211, 2220–22 (5th Cir.), *cert. denied*, 502 US 901 (1991).

56. *Fireman's Fund Insurance Co. v. Wilburn Boat Co.*, 259 F.2d 662, 663–664, 1958 AMC 2337, 2338–40 (5th Cir. 1958), *cert. denied*, 359 US 925 (1959).

57. See, e.g., *Acadia Insurance Co. v. McNeil*, 116 F.3d 599, 600, 1997 AMC 2409, 2410 (1st Cir. 1997). ("This case involves an issue of New Hampshire law as to which we have found no decisive New Hampshire precedent.")

marine insurance from significant portions of their insurance legislation.[58] The court is, therefore, left to resolve a marine insurance dispute with reasoning designed for automobile or homeowners' insurance. In *5801 Associates Ltd. v. Continental Insurance Co.*,[59] for example, a decision involving the sinking of a barge in the open seas off the coast of South Carolina, the federal court felt compelled to look to the law of Missouri. Finding no marine insurance decision on point, it followed an automobile insurance decision.[60]

12.27 An even more striking example of this problem can be found in the litigation between Exxon and its underwriters to determine coverage under a global corporate excess policy for hundreds of millions of dollars of the clean-up expenses following the *Exxon Valdez* oil spill. One issue in the coverage dispute was whether the loss was fortuitous. The underwriters argued that the loss was not fortuitous because it was caused by Exxon's reckless conduct in permitting its vessel-owning subsidiary to employ a known alcoholic as the captain of the *Exxon Valdez*. Exxon not only denied that it had been reckless, it also argued that the loss in question would have been "fortuitous" even if the conduct had been reckless. Exxon contended that the fortuity rule was the same under any law (state or federal) that might be relevant, but it had filed suit in a Texas state court and taken the position that Texas law generally applied to the case as a whole. Thus Exxon needed authority in support of its contention that Texas law permits insurance coverage for the unforeseen consequences of reckless or even intentional acts. In the absence of any statute or decisions in the marine insurance context, its principal authority on this central issue was a decision of the Texas Supreme Court addressing whether a homeowner's policy covered liability for transmitting genital herpes to a sexual partner.[61]

12D THE PRACTICAL IMPACT OF *WILBURN BOAT*

12.28 *Wilburn Boat* is undoubedly a problem for US law, for it undermines – at least to some extent – the predictability and uniformity on which both underwriters and policyholders depend. At the most basic level, insurance is all about dealing with

58. See, e.g., Ala. code section 27–14–2(3) (1986) (excepting "[w]et marine and transportation insurance" from chapter governing the insurance contract); La. Rev. Stat. Ann. section 22:611(A) (West 1995) (excepting "ocean marine and foreign trade insurances" from part XIV of the Insurance Code, which governs the insurance contract); Va. Code Ann. section 38.2–300(1) (1994) (excepting "[o]cean marine insurance other than private pleasure vessels" from chapter governing insurance policies and contracts); Wash. Rev. Code Ann. section 48.18.010 (1984) (excepting "ocean marine and foreign trade insurances" from chapter governing the insurance contract). See generally Machale A Miller, "Scrapping Wilburn Boat—The Need For Uniformity in Marine Insurance Law Outweighs Local Interests", The [US] MLA Report, US MLA doc. no. 719, at 10319, 10326, 10333 (September 30, 1995). In *St Paul Insurance Co. v. Great Lakes Turnings Ltd*, 829 F. Supp. 982, 984–985, 1993 AMC 2539, 2541–43 (ND Ill 1993), the court relied in part on a statutory exclusion for marine insurance to decide that Illinois had no interest in the application of its law in general to the pending dispute.

59. 983 F.2d 662, 1993 AMC 1453 (5th Cir. 1993) (*per curiam*).

60. See 983 F.2d at 666 & fn.10, 1993 AMC at 1459 & fn.10 (following *Shelter Mutual Insurance Co. v. Brooks*, 693 S.W.2d 810 (Mo. 1985) (en banc) (automobile insurance decision)).

61. See, e.g., Petition for a Writ of Certiorari at 13 & fn.9, *Exxon Corp. v. Youell*, 516 US 801 (1995) (No. 94–1971) (citing *State Farm Fire & Casualty Co. v. SS*, 858 S.W.2d 374 (Tex. 1993)).

uncertainty. When the law leaves unclear the terms on which the parties are contracting, then a second layer of uncertainty must be added to the analysis. The costs of insurance increase (at least marginally), as underwriters must charge a higher premium in light of the additional uncertainty, but the value of the insurance is diminished, as assureds are less confident that they will recover in the event of a loss. Litigation is more often necessary to resolve disputes, once again increasing the costs. Ultimately, all of these costs are borne by the consumers who purchase goods that are transported by sea – goods that are insured under marine policies, carried on insured vessels, and handled by workers whose health and safety are covered by marine insurance.

Recognising these very real and serious problems, however, does not mean that they should be exaggerated. The *Wilburn Boat* problem undoubtedly affects insurers, but it does not appear to have driven significant numbers of them out of the US market. The American Institute of Marine Underwriters (AIMU), the industry's trade group in the US, can perhaps serve as a useful barometer of the magnitude of the problem. The AIMU recognises *Wilburn Boat* as a problem, as demonstrated by its requests to the Supreme Court to revisit the issue[62] and the effort that its representatives have exerted to seek a solution to the problem. But when the US Maritime Law Association (US MLA) suggested a comprehensive federal statute (on the model of the 1906 British Act) to overrule *Wilburn Boat*, AIMU representatives objected. They apparently feared that the proposal might call marine insurance matters to regulators' attention, and result not in a sensible federal statute but in greater regulatory oversight. Even though *Wilburn Boat* is a problem for the industry, underwriters would apparently prefer to live with that problem rather than risk more extensive government regulation. 12.29

When the US MLA began work on its project to draft a comprehensive federal statute on the British model, it started with a detailed study of the 1906 Act and the US decisions on issues that are covered by the Act.[63] The study demonstrated that, "[i]n most cases, the British law and United States law are in complete accord".[64] This should hardly be surprising. Marine insurance law is a specialised branch of insurance law, which is itself a specialised branch of contract law. Although there are some differences between English and US contract law, in most cases they are at least in substantial accord.[65] Furthermore, insurance law in general is broadly similar in most states, and differences among the states are often attributable to consumer protection decisions or regulatory actions that are less likely to apply in this context. Even if there had never been a general maritime law governing marine insurance, one would expect US and English marine insurance law to be very similar. 12.30

For the same reasons, there is frequently little or no difference between state and federal law on marine insurance issues. Many of the problems that arise in marine 12.31

62. See, e.g., the AIMU amicus brief in *Holmes v. Taylor*, 507 US 952 (1993) (No. 92–1107) (denying cert. to *Taylor v. Lloyd's Underwriters*, 972 F.2d 666, 1994 AMC 607 (5th Cir. 1992)).

63. See Robert Bocko, *et al*, *Marine Insurance Survey: A Comparison of United States Law to the Marine Insurance Act of 1906*, 20 Tul Mar LJ 5 (1995).

64. Edward C Cattell, Jr, "An American Marine Insurance Act: an Idea Whose Time Has Come", 209 Tul Mar LJ 1, 4 (1995) (Introduction to *Marine Insurance Survey*).

65. The third-party beneficiary doctrine is probably the most significant difference in the law of contracts between the two legal systems.

insurance also arise in other insurance contexts, and one would expect the solutions to be broadly similar. The "fortuity" rule in marine insurance, for example, addresses the same concerns as the "fortuity" rule in insurance law generally. The law imposes an "insurable interest" requirement in the marine insurance context for the same reason that it imposes the requirement more generally. Thus, it is not surprising to find courts avoiding the *Wilburn Boat* problem by finding that state law and general maritime law point to the same result, and thus there is no need to choose between them.[66]

12.32 Because there is widespread consistency in insurance law on many issues, the most troubling *Wilburn Boat* problems (at least in practical terms) are confined to a few topics. The most obvious of these is the effect of breaching a warranty in the policy, for this was the question before the Court in *Wilburn Boat* itself. As a result of the court's decision, it is clear that the consequences of at least some[67] warranty breaches must be determined under state law. While some major states approach warranty breaches in essentially the same way as the general maritime law,[68] enough states take a more "consumer-friendly" approach[69] that uniformity and predictability suffer on this question.

12.33 Perhaps the most controversial *Wilburn Boat* problem in recent years has involved the doctrine of utmost good faith. As noted above, in *Albany Insurance Co. v. Anh Thi Kieu*[70] the Fifth Circuit looked to a more generous state law because it held that the doctrine was no longer an established rule of federal admiralty law. Although the First Circuit has shown some sympathy to this approach,[71] most circuits continue to treat the doctrine as an established part of the general maritime law.[72] Of course, it is not surprising that the doctrine of utmost good faith is a controversial part of marine insurance law in the US. The doctrine is now controversial throughout the world, including in the nation that invented and codified it.

12.34 Similar issues that have created problems under *Wilburn Boat*, just as they have been problematic in insurance law generally, include the awarding of punitive

---

66. See, e.g., *Victrix Steamship Co. v. Salen Dry Cargo AB*, 825 F.2d 704, 713, 1987 AMC 2945, 2950 (2d Cir. 1987); FB *Walker & Sons Inc. v. Valentine*, 431 F.2d 1235, 1239, 1970 AMC 2261, 2266 (5th Cir. 1970).

67. Some courts have distinguished between general warranties and warranties that are particularly maritime in character, such as a warranty of seaworthiness. See, e.g., *DJ McDuffie, Inc. v. Old Reliable Fire Insurance Co.*, 608 F.2d 145, 147 & fn.1, 1980 MC 1886, 1888 & fn.1 (5th Cir. 1979) (applying general maritime law rather than Louisiana law to seaworthiness warranty). Other courts have applied state law even to maritime warranties. See, e.g., *Albany Insurance Co. v. Anh Thi Kieu*, 927 F.2d 882, 892, 1991 AMC 2211, 2224 (5th Cir.) (applying Texas law to owner-aboard and seaworthiness warranties), *cert. denied*, 502 US 901 (1991).

68. See, e.g., *Pacific Fisheries Corp. v. HIH Casualty & General Insurance Ltd*, 239 F.3d 1000, 1003, 2001 AMC 952 (9th Cir. 2001) (under California law, breach of an immaterial warranty can void the policy), *Newark Insurance Co. v. Blair*, 1994 AMC 1061, 1066 (SDNY 1994) (under New York law, breach of an immaterial warranty can void the policy).

69. In *Wilburn Boat*, for example, Texas law excused the breaches of warranty.

70. 927 F.2d 882, 1991 AMC 2211 (5th Cir.), *cert. denied*, 502 US 901 (1991).

71. See *Windsor Mount Joy Mutual Insurance Co. v. Giragosian*, 57 F.3d 50, 54–55, 1995 AMC 2542, 2547–48 (1st Cir. 1995) (*aff'g* 864 F. Supp. 239 (D. Mass. 1994) (following *Anh Thi Kieu*)).

72. See, e.g., *Ingersoll Milling Machine Co. v. M/V Bodena*, 829 F.2d 293, 308, 1988 AMC 223, 246 (2d Cir. 1987), *cert. denied*, 484 US 1042 (1988); *Kilpatrick Marine Piling v. Fireman's Fund Insurance Co.*, 795 F.2d 940, 942 (11th Cir. 1986).

damages for a bad faith denial of coverage[73] and the availability of direct actions against insurers.[74]

In sum, *Wilburn Boat* is not even implicated in most marine insurance cases. There is no need for a choice-of-law rule when the two choices point to the same result. In those cases in which *Wilburn Boat* is implicated (and thus controversial), there is a good chance that the case would have been controversial even if the general maritime law applied – simply because controversial issues are involved. If choice-of-law rules are being used to avoid results that are considered unduly harsh (as appears to have been the case in *Wilburn Boat* itself), taking away the choice of law does not take away the desire to avoid the harsh doctrine under the general maritime law. The focus simply shifts. Instead of arguing whether state law displaces maritime law, the argument becomes whether the general maritime law should be revised, or whether an exception should be recognised. 12.35

Quite apart from the evidence of the justices' private papers, there is strong reason to believe that the desire to avoid harsh, traditional doctrines under the general maritime law is a major factor in these cases. A very high proportion of the cases in which the courts strain to apply state law in order to avoid harsh federal doctrines involve recreational vessels,[75] small fishing boats,[76] and other vessels comparable to the *Wanderer*. *Youell v. Exxon Corp.*,[77] the insurance coverage dispute following the *Exxon Valdez* disaster, is a rare example of a *Wilburn Boat* case involving a significant commercial vessel – and it is perhaps noteworthy that the Second Circuit was quite adamant that federal law should apply. 12.36

Finally, even in the problematic areas, *Wilburn Boat* is rarely forced upon defenceless parties who are unable to protect themselves. Much of the uncertainty created by *Wilburn Boat* could be corrected with clear policy terms if the parties wished to address the specific issues at the time they entered into the insurance contract. More generally, the parties can usually override *Wilburn Boat*'s choice of state law with an explicit choice-of-law clause that called for the application of some other law.[78] The parties could even avoid litigation in a court that would apply *Wilburn Boat* if they were truly serious about avoiding its problems. As a general rule, forum selection clauses in marine insurance contracts will be enforced.[79] 12.37

None of the observations here contradict the basic fact that *Wilburn Boat* causes real problems for those in the marine insurance field. By undermining uniformity, certainty, and predictability, it has impacted every marine insurance policy subject to 12.38

73. See, e.g., *Pace v. Insurance Co. of North America*, 838 F.2d 572, 578–584 (1st Cir. 1988).

74. See, e.g., *Kiernan v. Zurich Cos.*, 150 F.3d 1120, 1998 AMC 2533 (9th Cir. 1998); *Morewitz v. West of England Ship Owners Mutual Protection & Indemnity Association*, 62 F.3d 1356, 1362–63, 1996 AMC 707, 714–717 (11th Cir. 1995).

75. See, e.g., *All Underwriters v. Weisberg*, 222 F.3d 1309, 2000 AMC 2926 (11th Cir. 2000); *Acadia Insurance Co. v. McNeil*, 116 F.3d 599, 1997 AMC 2409 (1st Cir. 1997).

76. See, e.g., *Albany Insurance Co. v. Anh Thi Kieu*, 927 F.2d 882, 1991 AMC 2211 (5th Cir.), *cert. denied*, 502 US 901 (1991).

77. See 48 F.3d 105, 1995 AMC 1147 (2d Cir.), *vacated* 516 US 801 (1995); 74 F.3d 373, 1996 AMC 752 (2d Cir.) (*per curiam*), *cert. denied*, 517 US 1251 (1996).

78. See, e.g., *Advani Enterprises, Inc. v. Underwriters at Lloyd's*, 140 F.3d 157, 162–163, 1998 AMC 2045, 2050–52 (2d Cir. 1998) (enforcing English choice-of-law clause).

79. See, e.g., *Montauk Oil Transp. Corp. v. Steamship Mutual Underwriting Association (Bermuda) Ltd*, 79 F.3d 295, 1996 AMC 1379 (2d Cir. 1996).

US jurisdiction. But it is appropriate to maintain some perspective. *Wilburn Boat* is not the worst problem that insurers face. In most litigated cases the doctrine will not explicitly arise, and in those cases in which it does arise the parties still have some ability to protect themselves from the Supreme Court's mistakes.

12E CONCLUSION

12.39 This chapter makes no attempt to summarise all of US marine insurance law. That task would require multiple volumes (and much of the substantive discussion would correspond closely to English law). The goal here has instead been to give an overview of US marine insurance law by focusing on the primary way in which the law in the US differs from the rest of the world. For almost half a century, *Wilburn Boat* has been a defining feature of US marine insurance law. This chapter has, therefore, explained the decision, noted the problems that have arisen under it, and attempted to put those problems in perspective.

APPENDICES

MARINE INSURANCE ACT 1906

(6 Edw 7 c 41)

An Act to codify the Law relating to Marine Insurance. [21 December 1906]

MARINE INSURANCE

Marine insurance defined

1. A contract of marine insurance is a contract whereby the insurer undertakes to indemnify the assured, in manner and to the extent thereby agreed, against marine losses, that is to say, the losses incident to marine adventure.

Mixed sea and land risks

2.—(1) A contract of marine insurance may, by its express terms, or by usage of trade, be extended so as to protect the assured against losses on inland waters or on any land risk which may be incidental to any sea voyage.

(2) Where a ship in course of building, or the launch of a ship, or any adventure analogous to a marine adventure, is covered by a policy in the form of a marine policy, the provisions of this Act, in so far as applicable, shall apply thereto; but, except as by this section provided, nothing in this Act shall alter or affect any rule of law applicable to any contract of insurance other than a contract of marine insurance as by this Act defined.

Marine adventure and maritime perils defined

3.—(1) Subject to the provisions of this Act, every lawful marine adventure may be the subject of a contract of marine insurance.

(2) In particular there is a marine adventure where—

(a) Any ship, goods or other moveables are exposed to maritime perils. Such property is in this Act referred to as "insurable property";

(b) The earning or acquisition of any freight, passage money, commission, profit, or other pecuniary benefit, or the security for any advances, loan, or disbursements, is endangered by the exposure of insurable property to maritime perils;

(c) Any liability to a third party may be incurred by the owner of, or other person interested in or responsible for, insurable property, by reason of maritime perils.

"Maritime perils" means the perils consequent on, or incidental to, the navigation of the sea, that is to say, perils of the sea, fire, war perils, pirates, rovers, thieves, captures, seizures, restraints, and detainments of princes and peoples, jettisons, barratry, and any other perils, either of the like kind or which may be designated by the policy.

INSURABLE INTEREST

Avoidance of wagering or gaming contracts

4.—(1) Every contract of marine insurance by way of gaming or wagering is void.

(2) A contract of marine insurance is deemed to be a gaming or wagering contract—

(a) Where the assured has not an insurable interest as defined by this Act, and the contract is entered into with no expectation of acquiring such an interest; or

(b) Where the policy is made "interest or no interest", or "without further proof of interest than the policy itself", or "without benefit of salvage to the insurer", or subject to any other like term:

Provided that, where there is no possibility of salvage, a policy may be effected without benefit of salvage to the insurer.

Insurable interest defined

5.—(1) Subject to the provisions of this Act, every person has an insurable interest who is interested in a marine adventure.

(2) In particular a person is interested in a marine adventure where he stands in any legal or equitable relation to the adventure or to any insurable property at risk therein, in consequence of which he may benefit by the safety or due arrival of insurable property, or may be prejudiced by its loss, or damage thereto, or by the detention thereof, or may incur liability in respect thereof.

When interest must attach

6.—(1) The assured must be interested in the subject-matter insured at the time of the loss though he need not be interested when the insurance is effected:

Provided that where the subject-matter is insured "lost or not lost," the assured may recover although he may not have acquired his interest until after the loss, unless at the time of effecting the contract of insurance the assured was aware of the loss, and the insurer was not.

(2) Where the assured has no interest at the time of the loss, he cannot acquire interest by any act or election after he is aware of the loss.

Defeasible or contingent interest

7.—(1) A defeasible interest is insurable, as also is a contingent interest.

(2) In particular, where the buyer of goods has insured them, he has an insurable interest, notwithstanding that he might, at his election, have rejected the goods, or have treated them as at the seller's risk, by reason of the latter's delay in making delivery or otherwise.

Partial interest

8. A partial interst of any nature is insurable.

Re-insurance

9.—(1) The insurer under a contract of marine insurance has an insurable interest in his risk, and may re-insure in respect of it.

(2) Unless the policy otherwise provides, the original assured has no right or interest in respect of such re-insurance.

Bottomry

10. The lender of money on bottomry or respondentia has an insurable interest in respect of the loan.

Master's and seamen's wages

11. The master or any member of the crew of a ship has an insurable interest in respect of his wages.

Advance freight

12. In the case of advance freight, the person advancing the freight has an insurable interest, in so far as such freight is not repayable in case of loss.

Charges of insurance

13. The assured has an insurable interest in the charges of any insurance which he may effect.

Quantum of interest

14.—(1) Where the subject-matter insured is mortgaged, the mortgagor has an insurable interest in the full value thereof, and the mortgagee has an insurable interest in respect of any sum due or to become due under the mortgage.

(2) A mortgagee, consignee, or other person having an interest in the subject-matter insured may insure on behalf and for the benefit of other persons interested as well as for his own benefit.

(3) The owner of insurable property has an insurable interest in respect of the full value thereof, notwithstanding that some third person may have agreed, or be liable, to indemnity him in case of loss.

Assignment of interest

15. Where the assured assigns or otherwise parts with his interest in the subject-matter insured, he does not thereby transfer to the assignee his rights under the contract of insurance, unless there be an express or implied agreement with the assignee to that effect.

But the provisions of this section do not affect a transmission of interest by operation of law.

INSURABLE VALUE

Measure of insurable value

16. Subject to any express provision or valuation in the policy, the insurable value of the subject-matter insured must be ascertained as follows:—

(1) In insurance on ship, the insurable value is the value, at the commencement of the risk, of the ship, including her outfit, provisions and stores for the officers and crew, money advanced for seamen's wages, and other disbursements (if any) incurred to make the ship fit for the voyage or adventure contemplated by the policy, plus the charges of insurance upon the whole:

The insurable value, in the case of a steamship, includes also the machinery, boilers, and coals and engine stores if owned by the assured, and, in the case of a ship engaged in a special trade, the ordinary fittings requisite for that trade:

(2) In insurance on freight, whether paid in advance or otherwise, the insurance value is the gross amount of the freight at the risk of the asured, plus the charges of insurance:

(3) In insurance on goods or merchandise, the insurable value is the prime cost of the property insured, plus the expenses of and incidental to shipping and the charges of insurance upon the whole:

(4) In insurance on any other subject-matter, the insurable value is the amount at the risk of the assured when the policy attaches, plus the charges of insurance.

DISCLOSURE AND REPRESENTATIONS

Insurance is *uberrimae fidei*

17. A contract of marine insurance is a contract based upon the utmost good faith, and, if the utmost good faith be not observed by either party, the contract may be avoided by the other party.

Disclosure by assured

18.—(1) Subject to the provisions of this section, the assured must disclose to the insurer, before the contract is concluded, every material circumstance which is known to the assured, and the assured is deemed to know every circumstance which, in the ordinary course of business, ought to be known by him. If the assured fails to make such disclosure, the insurer may avoid the contract.

(2) Every circumstance is material which would influence the judgment of a prudent insurer in fixing the premium, or determining whether he will take the risk.

(3) In the absence of inquiry the following circumstances need not be disclosed, namely:—

(a) Any circumstance which diminishes the risk;
(b) Any circumstance which is known or presumed to be known to the insurer. The insurer is presumed to know matters of common notoriety or knowledge, and matters which an insurer in the ordinary course of his business, as such, ought to know;
(c) Any circumstance as to which information is waived by the insurer;
(d) Any circumstance which it is superfluous to disclose by reason of any express or implied warranty.

(4) Whether any particular circumstance, which is not disclosed, be material or not is, in each case, a question of fact.

(5) The term "circumstance" includes any communication made to, or information received by, the assured.

Disclosure by agent effecting insurance

19. Subject to the provisions of the preceding section as to circumstances which need not be disclosed, where an insurance is effected for the assured by an agent, the agent must disclose to the insurer—

(a) Every material circumstance which is known to himself, and an agent to insure is deemed to know every circumstance which in the ordinary course of business ought to be known by, or to have been communicated to, him; and
(b) Every material circumstance which the assured is bound to disclose, unless it come to his knowledge too late to communicate it to the agent.

Representations pending negotiation of contract

20.—(1) Every material representation made by the assured or his agent to the insurer during the negotiations for the contract, and before the contract is concluded, must be true. If it be untrue the insurer may avoid the contract.

(2) A representation is material which would influence the judgment of a prudent insurer in fixing the premium, or determining whether he will take the risk.

(3) A representation may be either a representation as to a matter of fact, or as to a matter of expectation or belief.

(4) A representation as to matter of fact is true, if it be substantially correct, that is to say, if the difference between what is represented and what is actually correct would not be considered material by a prudent insurer.

(5) A representation as to a matter of expectation or belief is true if it be made in good faith.

(6) A representation may be withdrawn or corrected before the contract is concluded.

(7) Whether a particular representation be material or not is, in each case, a question of fact.

When contract is deemed to be concluded

21. A contract of marine insurance is deemed to be concluded when the proposal of the assured is accepted by the insurer, whether the policy be then issued or not; and, for the purpose of showing when the proposal was accepted, reference may be made to the slip or covering note or other customary memorandum of the contract, . . .

NOTE:

Amended by the Finance Act 1959, s.37(5), Sch. 8, Pt II.

THE POLICY

Contract must be embodied in policy

22. Subject to the provisions of any statute, a contract of marine insurance is inadmissible in evidence unless it is embodied in a marine policy in accordance with this Act. The policy may be executed and issued either at the time when the contract is concluded, or afterwards.

What policy must specify

23. A marine policy must specify—

(1) The name of the assured, or of some person who effects the insurance on his behalf:

(2)–(5) . . .

NOTE:

Subss.(2)–(5): repealed by the Finance Act 1959, ss.30(5), (7), 37(5), Sch. 8, Pt II.

Signature of insurer

24.—(1) A marine policy must be signed by or on behalf of the insurer, provided that in the case of a corporation the corporate seal may be sufficient, but nothing in this section shall be construed as requiring the subscription of a corporation to be under seal.

(2) Where a policy is subscribed by or on behalf of two or more insurers, each subscription, unless the contrary be expressed, constitutes a distinct contract with the assured.

Voyage and time policies

25.—(1) Where the contract is to insure the subject-matter "at and from", or from one place to another or others, the policy is called a "voyage policy", and where the contract is to insure the subject-matter for a definite period of time the policy is called a "time policy". A contract for both voyage and time may be included in the same policy.

(2) . . .

NOTE:

Subs.(2): repealed by the Finance Act 1959, ss.30(5), (7), 37(5), Sch. 8, Pt II.

Designation of subject-matter

26.—(1) The subject-matter insured must be designated in a marine policy with reasonable certainty.

(2) The nature and extent of the interest of the assured in the subject-matter insured need not be specified in the policy.

(3) Where the policy designates the subject-matter insured in general terms, it shall be construed to apply to the interest intended by the assured to be covered.

(4) In the application of this section regard shall be had to any usage regulating the designation of the subject-matter insured.

Valued policy

27.—(1) A policy may be either valued or unvalued.

(2) A valued policy is a policy which specifies the agreed value of the subject-matter insured.

(3) Subject to the provisions of this Act, and in the absence of fraud, the value fixed by the policy is, as between the insurer and assured, conclusive of the insurable value of the subject intended to be insured, whether the loss be total or partial.

(4) Unless the policy otherwise provides, the value fixed by the policy is not conclusive for the purpose of determining whether there has been a constructive total loss.

Unvalued policy

28. An unvalued policy is a policy which does not specify the value of the subject-matter insured, but, subject to the limit of the sum insured, leaves the insurable value to be subsequently ascertained, in the manner hereinbefore specified.

Floating policy by ship or ships

29.—(1) A floating policy is a policy which describes the insurance in general terms, and leaves the name of the ship or ships and other particulars to be defined by subsequent declaration.

(2) The subsequent declaration or declarations may be made by indorsement on the policy, or in other customary manner.

(3) Unless the policy otherwise provides, the declarations must be made in the order of dispatch or shipment. They must, in the case of goods, comprise all consignments within the terms of the policy, and the value of the goods or other property must be honestly stated, but an omission or erroneous declaration may be rectified even after loss or arrival, provided the omission or declaration was made in good faith.

(4) Unless the policy otherwise provides, where a declaration of value is not made until after notice of loss or arrival, the policy must be treated as an unvalued policy as regards the subject-matter of that declaration.

Construction of terms in policy

30.—(1) A policy may be in the form in the First Schedule of this Act.

(2) Subject to the provisions of this Act, and unless the context of the policy otherwise requires, the terms and expressions mentioned in the First Schedule to this Act shall be construed as having the scope and meaning in that schedule assigned to them.

Premium to be arranged

31.—(1) Where an insurance is effected at a premium to be arranged, and no arrangement is made, a reasonable premium is payable.

(2) Where an insurance is effected on the terms that an additional premium is to be arranged in a given event, and that event happens but no arrangement is made, then a reasonable additional premium is payable.

DOUBLE INSURANCE

Double insurance

32.—(1) Where two or more policies are effected by or on behalf of the assured on the same adventure and interest or any part thereof, and the sums insured exceed the indemnity allowed by this Act, the assured is said to be over-insured by double insurance.

(2) Where the assured is over-insured by double insurance—

(a) The assured, unless the policy otherwise provides, may claim payment from the insurers in such order as he may think fit, provided that he is not entitled to receive any sum in excess of the indemnity allowed by this Act;

(b) Where the policy under which the assured claims is a valued policy, the assured must give credit as against the valuation for any sum received by him under any other policy without regard to the actual value of the subject-matter insured;

(c) Where the policy under which the assured claims is an unvalued policy he must give credit, as against the full insurable value, for any sum received by him under any other policy;

(d) Where the assured receives any sum in excess of the indemnity allowed by this act, he is deemed to hold such sum in trust for the insurers, according to their right of contribution among themselves.

WARRANTIES, ETC

Nature of warranty

33.—(1) A warranty, in the following sections relating to warranties, means a promissory warranty, that is to say, a warranty by which the assured undertakes that some particular thing shall or shall not be done, or that some condition shall be fulfilled, or whereby he affirms or negatives the existence of a particular state of facts.

(2) A warranty may be express or implied.

(3) A warranty, as above defined, is a condition which must be exactly complied with, whether it be material to the risk or not. If it be not so complied with, then, subject to any express provision in the policy, the insurer is discharged from liability as from the date of the breach of warranty, but without prejudice to any liability incurred by him before that date.

When breach of warranty excused

34.—(1) Non-compliance with a warranty is excused when, by reason of a change of circumstances, the warranty ceases to be applicable to the circumstances of the contract, or when compliance with the warranty is rendered unlawful by any subsequent law.

(2) Where a warranty is broken, the assured cannot avail himself of the defence that the breach has been remedied, and the warranty complied with, before loss.

(3) A breach of warranty may be waived by the insurer.

Express warranties

35.—(1) An express warranty may be in any form of words from which the intention to warrant is to be inferred.

(2) An express warranty must be included in, or written upon, the policy, or must be contained in some document incorporated by reference into the policy.

(3) An express warranty does not exclude an implied warranty, unless it be inconsistent therewith.

Warranty of neutrality

36.—(1) Where insurable property, whether ship or goods, is expressly warranted neutral, there is an implied condition that the property shall have a neutral character at the commencement of the risk, and that, so far as the assured can control the matter, its neutral character shall be preserved during the risk.

(2) Where a ship is expressly warranted "neutral" there is also an implied condition that, so far as the assured can control the matter, she shall be properly documented, that is to say, that she shall carry the necessary papers to establish her neutrality, and that she shall not falsify or suppress her papers, or use simulated papers. If any loss occurs through breach of this condition, the insurer may avoid the contract.

No implied warranty of nationality

37. There is no implied warranty as to the nationality of a ship, or that her nationality shall not be changed during the risk.

Warranty of good safety

38. Where the subject-matter insured is warranted "well" or "in good safety" on a particular day, it is sufficient if it be safe at any time during that day.

Warranty of seaworthiness of ship

39.—(1) In a voyage policy there is an implied warranty that at the commencement of the voyage the ship shall be seaworthy for the purpose of the particular adventure insured.

(2) Where the policy attaches while the ship is in port, there is also an implied warranty that she shall, at the commencement of the risk, be reasonably fit to encounter the ordinary perils of the port.

(3) Where the policy relates to a voyage which is performed in different stages, during which the ship requires different kinds of or further preparation or equipment, there is an implied warranty that at the commencement of each stage the ship is seaworthy in respect of such preparation or equipment for the purposes of that stage.

(4) A ship is deemed to be seaworthy when she is reasonably fit in all respects to encounter the ordinary perils of the seas of the adventure insured.

(5) In a time policy there is no implied warranty that the ship shall be seaworthy at any stage of the adventure, but where, with the privity of the assured, the ship is sent to sea in an unseaworthy state, the insurer is not liable for any loss attributable to unseaworthiness.

No implied warranty that goods are seaworthy

40.—(1) In a policy on goods or other moveables there is no implied warranty that the goods or moveables are seaworthy.

(2) In a voyage policy on goods or other moveables there is an implied warranty that at the commencement of the voyage the ship is not only seaworthy as a ship, but also

that she is reasonably fit to carry the goods or other moveables to the destination contemplated by the policy.

Warranty of legality

41. There is an implied warranty that the adventure insured is a lawful one, and that, so far as the assured can control the matter, the adventure shall be carried out in a lawful maner.

THE VOYAGE

Implied condition as to commencement of risk

42.—(1) Where the subject-matter is insured by a voyage policy "at and from" or "from" a particular place, it is not necessary that the ship should be at that place when the contract is concluded, but there is an implied condition that the adventure shall be commenced within a reasonable time, and that if the adventure be not so commenced the insurer may avoid the contract.

(2) The implied condition may be negatived by showing that the delay was caused by circumstances known to the insurer before the contract was concluded, or by showing that he waived the condition.

Alteration of port of departure

43. Where the place of departure is specified by the policy, and the ship instead of sailing from that placd sails from any other place, the risk does not attach.

Sailing for different destination

44. Where the destination is specified in the policy, and the ship, instead of sailing for that destination sails for any other destination, the risk does not attach.

Change of voyage

45.—(1) Where, after the commencement of the risk, the destination of the ship is voluntarily changed from the destination contemplated by the policy, there is said to be a change of voyage.

(2) Unless the policy otherwise provides, where there is a change of voyage, the insurer is discharged from liability as from the time of change, that is to say, as from the time when the determination to change it is manifested; and it is immaterial that the ship may not in fact have left the course of voyage contemplated by the policy when the loss occurs.

Deviation

46.—(1) Where a ship, without lawful excuse, deviates from the voyage contemplated by the policy, the insurer is discharged from liability as from the time of deviation, and it is immaterial that the ship may have regained her route before any loss occurs.

(2) There is a deviation from the voyage contemplated by the policy—

(a) Where the course of the voyage is specifically designated by the policy, and that course is departed from; or

(b) Where the course of the voyage is not specifically designated by the policy, but the usual and customary course is departed from.

(3) The intention to deviate is immaterial; there must be a deviation in fact to discharge the insurer from his liability under the contract.

Several ports of discharge

47.—(1) Where several ports of discharge are specified by the policy, the ship may proceed to all or any of them, but, in the absence of any usage or sufficient cause to the contrary, she must proceed to them, or such of them as she goes to, in the order designated by the policy. If she does not there is a deviation.

(2) Where the policy is to "ports of discharge", within a given area, which are not named, the ship must, in the absence of any usage or sufficient cause to the contrary, proceed to them, or such of them as she goes to, in their geographical order. If she does not there is a deviation.

Delay in voyage

48. In the case of a voyage policy, the adventure insured must be prosecuted throughout its course with reasonable dispatch, and, if without lawful excuse it is not so prosecuted, the insurer is discharged from liability as from the time when the delay became unreasonable.

Excuses for deviation or delay

49.—(1) Deviation or delay in prosecuting the voyage contemplated by the policy is excused—

(a) Where authorised by any special term in the policy; or

(b) Where caused by circumstances beyond the control of the master and his employer; or

(c) Where reasonably necessary in order to comply with an express or implied warranty; or

(d) Where reasonably necessary for the safety of the ship or subject-matter insured; or

(e) For the purpose of saving human life, or aiding a ship in distress where human life may be in danger; or

(f) Where reasonably necessary for the purpose of obtaining medical or surgical aid for any person on board the ship; or

(g) Where caused by the barratrous conduct of the master or crew, if barratry by one of the perils insured against.

(2) When the cause excusing the deviation or delay ceases to operate, the ship must resume her course, and prosecute her voyage, with reasonable dispatch.

ASSIGNMENT OF POLICY

When and how policy is assignable

50.—(1) A marine policy is assignable unless it contains terms expressly prohibiting assignment. It may be assigned either before or after loss.

(2) Where a marine policy has been assigned so as to pass the beneficial interest in such policy, the assignee of the policy is entitled to sue thereon in his own name; and the defendant is entitled to make any defence arising out of the contract which he would have been entitled to make if the action had been brought in the name of the person by or on behalf of whom the policy was effected.

(3) A marine policy may be assigned by indorsement thereon or in other customary manner.

Assured who has no interest cannot assign

51. Where the assured has parted with or lost his interest in the subject-matter insured, and has not, before or at the time of so doing, expressly or impliedly agreed to assign the policy, any subsequent assignment of the policy is inoperative:

Provided that nothing in this section affects the assignment of a policy after loss.

THE PREMIUM

When premium payable

52. Unless otherwise agreed, the duty of the assured or his agent to pay the premium, and the duty of the insurer to issue the policy to the assured or his agent, are concurrent conditions, and the insurer is not bound to issue the policy until payment or tender of the premium.

Policy effected through broker

53.—(1) Unless otherwise agreed, where a marine policy is effected on behalf of the assured by a broker, the broker is directly responsible to the insurer for the premium, and the insurer is directly responsible to the assured for the amount which may be payable in respect of losses, or in respect of returnable premium.

(2) Unless otherwise agreed, the broker has, as against the assured, a lien upon the policy for the amount of the premium and his charges in respect of effecting the policy; and, where he has dealt with the person who employs him as a principal, he has also a lien on the policy in respect of any balance on any insurance account which may be due to him from such person, unless when the debt was incurred he had reason to believe that such person was only an agent.

Effect of receipt on policy

54. Where a marine policy effected on behalf of the assured by a broker acknowledges the receipt of the premium, such acknowledgment is, in the absence of fraud, conclusive as between the insurer and the assured, but not as between the insurer and broker.

LOSS AND ABANDONMENT

Included and excluded losses

55.—(1) Subject to the provisions of this Act, and unless the policy otherwise provides, the insurer is liable for any loss proximately caused by a peril insured against, but, subject as aforesaid, he is not liable for any loss which is not proximately caused by a peril insured against.

(2) In particular—

(a) The insurer is not liable for any loss attributable to the wilful misconduct of the assured, but, unless the policy otherwise provides, he is liable for any loss proximately caused by a peril insured against, even though the loss would not have happened but for the misconduct or negligence of the master or crew;

(b) Unless the policy otherwise provides, the insurer on ship or goods is not liable for any loss proximately caused by delay, although the delay be caused by a peril insured against;

(c) Unless the policy otherwise provides, the insurer is not liable for ordinary wear and tear, ordinary leakage and breakage, inherent vice or nature of the subject-matter insured, or for any loss proximately caused by rats or vermin, or for any injury to machinery not proximately caused by maritime perils.

Partial and total loss

56.—(1) A loss may be either total or partial. Any loss other than a total loss, as hereinafter defined, is a partial loss.

(2) A total loss may be either an actual total loss, or a constructive total loss.

(3) Unless a different intention appears from the terms of the policy, an insurance against total loss includes a constructive, as well as an actual, total loss.

(4) Where the assured brings an action for a total loss and the evidence proves only a partial loss, he may, unless the policy otherwise provides, recover for a partial loss.

(5) Where goods reach their destination in specie, but by reason of obliteration of marks, or otherwise, they are incapable of identification, the loss, if any, is partial, and not total.

Actual total loss

57.—(1) Where the subject-matter insured is destroyed, or so damaged as to cease to be a thing of the kind insured, or where the assured is irretrievably deprived thereof, there is an actual total loss.

(2) In the case of an actual total loss no notice of abandonment need be given.

Missing ship

58. Where the ship concerned in the adventure is missing, and after the lapse of a reasonable time no news of her has been received, an actual total loss may be presumed.

Effect of transhipment, etc.

59. Where, by a peril insured against, the voyage is interrupted at an intermediate port or place, under such circmstances as, apart from any special stipulation in the contract of affreightment, to justify the master in landing and re-shipping the goods or other moveables or in transhipping them, and sending them on to their destination, the liability of the insurer continues, notwithstanding the landing or transhipment.

Constructive total loss defined

60.—(1) Subject to any express provision in the policy, there is a constructive total loss where the subject-matter insured is reasonably abandoned on account of its actual total loss appearing to be unavoidable, or because it could not be preserved from actual total loss without an expenditure which would exceed its value when the expenditure had been incurred.

(2) In particular, there is a constructive total loss—

(i) Where the assured is deprived of the possession of his ship or goods by a peril insured against, and (a) it is unlikely that he can recover the ship or goods, as the case may be, or (b) the cost of recovering the ship or goods, as the case may be, would exceed their value when recovered; or

(ii) In the case of damage to a ship, where she is so damaged by a peril insured against that the cost of repairing the damage would exceed the value of the ship when repaired.

In estimating the cost of repairs, no deduction is to be made in respect of general average contributions to those repairs payable by other interests, but account is to be taken of the expense of future salvage operations and of any future general average contributions to which the ship would be liable if repaired; or

(iii) In the case of damage to goods, where the cost of repairing the damage and forwarding the goods to their destination would exceed their value on arrival.

Effect of constructive total loss

61. Where there is a constructive total loss the assured may either treat the loss as a partial loss, or abandon the subject-matter insured to the insurer and treat the loss as if it were an actual total loss.

Notice of abandonment

62.—(1) Subject to the provisions of this section, where the assured elects to abandon the subject-matter insured to the insurer, he must give notice of abandonment. If he fails to do so the loss can only be treated as a partial loss.

(2) Notice of abandonment may be given in writing, or by word of mouth, or partly in writing and partly by word of mouth, and may be given in terms which indicate the intention of the assured to abandon his insured interest in the subject-matter insured unconditionally to the insurer.

(3) Notice of abandonment must be given with reasonable diligence after the receipt of reliable information of the loss, but where the information is of a doubtful character the assured is entitled to a reasonable time to make inquiry.

(4) Where notice of abandonment is properly given, the rights of the assured are not prejudiced by the fact that the insurer refuses to accept the abandonment.

(5) The acceptance of an abandonment may be either express or implied from the conduct of the insurer. The mere silence of the insurer after notice is not an acceptance.

(6) Where a notice of abandonment is accepted the abandonment is irrevocable. The acceptance of the notice conclusively admits liability for the loss and the sufficiency of the notice.

(7) Notice of abandonment is unnecessary where, at the time when the assured receives information of the loss, there would be no possibility of benefit to the insurer if notice were given to him.

(8) Notice of abandonment may be waived by the insurer.

(9) Where an insurer has re-insured his risk, no notice of abandonment need to given by him.

Effect of abandonment

63.—(1) Where there is a valid abandonment the insurer is entitled to take over the interest of the assured in whatever may remain of the subject-matter insured, and all proprietary rights incidental thereto.

(2) Upon the abandonment of a ship, the insurer thereof is entitled to any freight in

course of being earned, and which is earned by her subsequent to the casualty causing the loss, less the expenses of earning it incurred after the casualty; and, where the ship is carrying the owner's goods, the insurer is entitled to a reasonable remuneration for the carriage of them subsequent to the casualty causing the loss.

PARTIAL LOSSES (INCLUDING SALVAGE AND GENERAL AVERAGE AND PARTICULAR CHARGES)

Particular average loss

64.—(1) A particular average loss is a partial loss of the subject-matter insured, caused by a peril insured against, and which is not a general average loss.

(2) Expenses incurred by or on behalf of the assured for the safety or preservation of the subject-matter insured, other than general average and salvage charges, are called particular charges. Particular charges are not included in particular average.

Salvage charges

65.—(1) Subject to any express provision in the policy, salvage charges incurred in preventing a loss by perils insured against may be recovered as a loss by those perils.

(2) "Salvage charges" means the charges recoverable under maritime law by a salvor independently of contract. They do not include the expenses of services in the nature of salvage rendered by the assured or his agents, or any person employed for hire by them, for the purpose of averting a peril insured against. Such expenses, where properly incurred, may be recovered as particular charges or as a general average loss, according to the circumstances under which they were incurred.

General average loss

66.—(1) A general average loss is a loss caused by or directly consequential on a general average act. It includes a general average expenditure as well as a general average sacrifice.

(2) There is a general average act where any extraordinary sacrifice or expenditure is voluntarily and reasonably made or incurred in time of peril for the purpose of preserving the property imperilled in the common adventure.

(3) Where there is a general average loss, the party on whom it falls is entitled, subject to the conditions imposed by maritime law, to a rateable contribution from the other parties interested, and such contribution is called a general average contribution.

(4) Subject to any express provision in the policy, where the assured has incurred a general average expenditure, he may recover from the insurer in respect of the proportion of the loss which falls upon him; and, in the case of a general sacrifice, he may recover from the insurer in respect of the whole loss without having enforced his right of contribution from the other parties liable to contribute.

(5) Subject to any express provision in the policy, where the assured has paid, or is liable to pay, a general average contribution in respect of the subject insured, he may recover therefor from the insurer.

(6) In the absence of express stipulation, the insurer is not liable for any general average loss or contribution where the loss was not incurred for the purpose of avoiding, or in connexion with the avoidance of, a peril insured against.

(7) Where ship, freight, and cargo, or any two of those interests, are owned by the same assured, the liability of the insurer in respect of general average losses or contributions is to be determined as if those subjects were owned by different persons.

MEASURE OF INDEMNITY

Extent of liability of insurer for loss

67.—(1) The sum which the assured can recover in respect of a loss on a policy by which he is insured, in the case of an unvalued policy to the full extent of the insurable value, or, in the case of a valued policy to the full extent of the value fixed by the policy, is called the measure of indemnity.

(2) Where there is a loss recoverable under the policy, the insurer, or each insurer if there be more than one, is liable for such proportion of the measure of indemnity as the amount of his subscription bears to the value fixed by the policy in the case of a valued policy, or to the insurable value in the case of an unvalued policy.

Total loss

68. Subject to the provisions of this Act and to any express provision in the policy, where there is a total loss of the subject-matter insured—

(1) If the policy be a valued policy, the measure of indemnity is the sum fixed by the policy:

(2) If the policy be an unvalued policy, the measure of indemnity is the insurable value of the subject-matter insured.

Partial loss of ship

69. Where a ship is damaged, but is not totally lost, the measure of indemnity, subject to any express provision in the policy, is as follows:—

(1) Where the ship has been repaired, the assured is entitled to the reasonable cost of the repairs, less the customary deductions, but not exceeding the sum insured in respect of any one casualty:

(2) Where the ship has been only partially repaired, the assured is entitled to the reasonable cost of such repairs, computed as above, and also to be indemnified for the reasonable depreciation, if any, arising from the unrepaired damage, provided that the aggregate amount shall not exceed the cost of repairing the whole damage, computed as above:

(3) Where the ship has not been repaired, and has not been sold in her damaged state during the risk, the assured is entitled to be indemnified for the reasonable

depreciation arising from the unrepaired damage, but not exceeding the reasonable cost of repairing such damage, computed as above.

Partial loss of freight

70. Subject to any express provision in the policy, where there is a partial loss of freight, the measure of indemnity is such proportion of the sum fixed by the policy in the case of a valued policy, or of the insurable value in the case of an unvalued policy, as the proportion of freight lost by the assured bears to the whole freight at the risk of the assured under the policy.

Partial loss of goods, merchandise, etc.

71. Where there is a partial loss of goods, merchandise, or other moveables the measure of indemnity, subject to any express provision in the policy, is as follows:—

(1) Where part of the goods, merchandise or other moveables insured by a valued policy is totally lost, the measure of indemnity is such proportion of the sum fixed by the policy as the insurable value of the part lost bears to the insurable value of the whole, ascertained as in the case of an unvalued policy:

(2) Where part of the goods, merchandise, or other moveable insured by an unvalued policy is totally lost, the measure of indemnity is the insurable value of the part lost, ascertained as in case of total loss:

(3) Where the whole or any part of the goods or merchandise insured has been delivered damaged at its destination, the measure of indemnity is such proportion of the sum fixed by the policy in the case of a valued policy, or of the insurable value in the case of an unvalued policy, as the difference between the gross sound and damaged values at the place of arrival bears to the gross sound value:

(4) "Gross value" means the wholesale price or, if there be no such price, the estimated value, with, in either case, freight, landing charges, and duty paid beforehand; provided that, in the case of goods or merchandise customarily sold in bond, the bonded price is deemed to be the gross value. "Gross proceeds" means the actual price obtained at a sale where all charges on sale are paid by the sellers.

Apportionment of valuation

72.—(1) Where different species of property are insured under a single valuation, the valuation must be apportioned over the different species in proportion to their respective insurable values, as in the case of an unvalued policy. The insured value of any part of a species is such proportion of the total insured value of the same as the insurable value of the part bears to the insurable value of the whole, ascertained in both cases as provided by this Act.

(2) Where a valuation has to be apportioned, and particulars of the prime cost of each separate species, quality, or description of goods cannot be ascertained, the division of the valuation may be made over the net arrived sound values of the different species, qualities, or descriptions of goods.

General average contributions and salvage charges

73.—(1) Subject to any express provisions in the policy, where the assured has paid, or is liable for, any general average contribution, the measure of indemnity is the full amount of such contribution, if the subject-matter liable to contribution is insured for its full contributory value; but, if such subject-matter be not insured for its full contributory value, or if only part of it be insured, the indemnity payable by the insurer must be reduced in proportion to the under insurance, and where there has been a particular average loss which constitutes a deduction from the contributory value, and for which the insurer is liable, that amount must be deducted from the insured value in order to ascertain what the insurer is liable to contribute.

(2) Where the insurer is liable for salvage charges the extent of his liability must be determined on the like principle.

Liabilities to third parties

74. Where the assured has effected an insurance in express terms against any liability to a third party, the measure of indemnity, subject to any express provision in the policy, is the amount paid or payable by him to such third party in respect of such liability.

General provisions as to measure of indemnity

75.—(1) Where there has been a loss in respect of any subject-matter not expressly provided for in the foregoing provisions of this Act, the measure of indemnity shall be ascertained, as nearly as may be, in accordance with those provisions, in so far as applicable to the particular case.

(2) Nothing in the provisions of this Act relating to the measure of indemnity shall affect the rules relating to double insurance, or prohibit the insurer from disproving interest wholly or in part, or from showing that at the time of the loss the whole or any part of the subject-matter insured was not at risk under the policy.

Particular average warranties

76.(1) Where the subject-matter insured is warranted free from particular average, the assured cannot recover for a loss of part, other than a loss incurred by a general average sacrifice, unless the contract contained in the policy be apportionable; but, if the contract be apportionable, the assured may recover for a total loss of any apportionable part.

(2) Where the subject-matter insured is warranted free from particular average, either wholly or under a certain percentage, the insurer is nevertheless liable for salvage charges, and for particular charges and other expenses properly incurred pursuant to the provisions of the suing and labouring clause in order to avert a loss insured against.

(3) Unless the policy otherwise provides, where the subject-matter insured is

warranted free from particular average under a specified percentage, a general average loss cannot be added to a particular average loss to make up the specified percentage.

(4) For the purpose of ascertaining whether the specified percentage has been reached, regard shall be had only to the actual loss suffered by the subject-matter insured. Particular charges and the expenses of and incidental to ascertaining and proving the loss must be excluded.

Successive losses

77.—(1) Unless the policy otherwise provides, and subject to the provisions of this Act, the insurer is liable for successive losses, even though the total amount of such losses may exceed the sum insured.

(2) Where, under the same policy, a partial loss, which has not been repaired or otherwise made good, is followed by a total loss, the assured can only recover in respect of the total loss:

Provided that nothing in this section shall affect the liability of the insurer under the suing and labouring clause.

Suing and labouring clause

78.—(1) Where the policy contains a suing and labouring clause, the engagement thereby entered into is deemed to be supplementary to the contract of insurance, and the assured may recover from the insurer any expenses properly incurred pursuant to the clause, notwithstanding that the insurer may have paid for a total loss, or that the subject-matter may have been warranted free from particular average, either wholly or under a certain percentage.

(2) General average losses and contributions and salvage charges, as defined by this Act, are not recoverable under the suing and labouring clause.

(3) Expenses incurred for the purpose of averting or diminishing any loss not covered by the policy are not recoverable under the suing and labouring clause.

(4) It is the duty of the assured and his agents, in all cases, to take such measures as may be reasonable for the purpose of averting or minimising a loss.

RIGHTS OF INSURER ON PAYMENT

Right of subrogation

79.—(1) Where the insurer pays for a total loss, either of the whole, or in the case of goods of any apportionable part, of the subject-matter insured, he thereupon becomes entitled to take over the interest of the assured in whatever may remain of the subject-matter so paid for, and he is thereby subrogated to all the rights and remedies of the assured in and in respect of that subject-matter as from the time of the casualty causing the loss.

(2) Subject to the foregoing provisions, where the insurer pays for a partial loss, he acquires no title to the subject-matter insured, or such part of it as may remain, but he

is thereupon subrogated to all rights and remedies of the assured in and in respect of the subject-matter insured as from the time of the casualty causing the loss, in so far as the assured has been indemnified, according to this Act, by such payment for the loss.

Right of contribution

80.—(1) Where the assured is over-insured by double insurance, each insurer is bound, as between himself and the other insurers, to contribute rateably to the loss in proportion to the amount for which he is liable under his contract.

(2) If any insurer pays more than his proportion of the loss, he is entitled to maintain an action for contribution against the other insurers, and is entitled to the like remedies as a surety who has paid more than his proportion of the debt.

Effect of under insurance

81. Where the assured is insured for an amount less than the insurable value or, in the case of a valued policy, for an amount less than the policy valuation, he is deemed to be his own insurer in respect of the uninsured balance.

RETURN OF PREMIUM

Enforcement of return

82. Where the premium or a proportionate part thereof is, by this Act, declared to be returnable,—

(a) If already paid, it may be recovered by the assured from the insurer; and
(b) If unpaid, it may be retained by the assured or his agent.

Return by agreement

83. Where the policy contains a stipulation for the return of the premium, or a proportionate part thereof, on the happening of a certain event, and that event happened, the premium, or, as the case may be, the proportionate part thereof, is thereupon returnable to the assured.

Return for failure of consideration

84.—(1) Where the consideration for the payment of the premium totally fails, and there has been no fraud or illegality on the part of the assured or his agents, the premium is thereupon returnable to the assured.

(2) Where the consideration for the payment of the premium is apportionable and

there is a total failure of any apportionable part of the consideration, a proportionate part of the premium is, under the like conditions, thereupon returnable to the assured.

(3) In particular—

(a) Where the policy is void, or is avoided by the insurer as from the commencement of the risk, the premium is returnable, provided that there has been no fraud or illegality on the part of the assured; but if the risk is not apportionable, and has once attached, the premium is not returnable;

(b) Where the subject-matter insured, or part thereof, has never been imperilled, the premium, or, as the case may be, a proportionate part thereof, is returnable:

Provided that where the subject-matter has been insured "lost or not lost" and has arrived in safety at the time when the contract is concluded, the premium is not returnable unless, at such time, the insurer knew of the safe arrival.

(c) Where the assured has no insurable interest throughout the currency of the risk, the premium is returnable, provided that this rule does not apply to a policy effected by way of gaming or wagering;

(d) Where the assured has a defeasible interest which is terminated during the currency of the risk, the premium is not returnable;

(e) Where the assured has over-insured under an unvalued policy, a proportionate part of the premium is returnable;

(f) Subject to the foregoing provisions, where the assured has over-insured by double insurance, a proportionate part of the several premiums is returnable:

Provided that, if the policies are effected at different times, and any earlier policy has at any time borne the entire risk, or if a claim has been paid on the policy in respect of the full sum insured thereby, no premium is returnable in respect of that policy, and when the double insurance is effected knowingly by the assured no premium is returnable.

MUTUAL INSURANCE

Modification of Act in case of mutual insurance

85.—(1) Where two or more persons mutually agree to insure each other against marine losses there is said to be a mutual insurance.

(2) The provisions of this Act relating to the premium do not apply to mutual insurance, but a guarantee, or such other arrangement as may be agreed upon, may be substituted for the premium.

(3) The provisions of this Act, in so far as they may be modified by the agreement of the parties, may in the case of mutual insurance be modified by the terms of the policies issued by the association, or by the rules and regulations of the association.

(4) Subject to the exceptions mentioned in this section, the provisions of this Act apply to a mutual insurance.

SUPPLEMENTAL

Ratification by assured

86. Where a contract of marine insurance is in good faith effected by one person on behalf of another, the person on whose behalf it is effected may ratify the contract even after he is aware of a loss.

Implied obligations varied by agreement or usage

87.—(1) Where any right, duty, or liability would arise under a contract of marine insurance by implication of law, it may be negatived or varied by express agreement, or by usage, if the usage be such as to bind both parties to the contract.

(2) The provisions of this section extend to any right, duty, or liability declared by this Act which may be lawfully modified by agreement.

Reasonable time, etc., a question of fact

88. Where by this Act any reference is made to reasonable time, reasonable premium, or reasonable diligence, the question what is reasonable is a question of fact.

Slip as evidence

89. Where there is a duly stamped policy, reference may be made, as heretofore, to the slip or covering note, in any legal proceeding.

Interpretation of terms

90. In this Act, unless the context or subject-matter otherwise requires,—

"Action" includes counter-claim and set off:

"Freight" includes the profit derivable by a shipowner from the employment of his ship to carry his own goods or moveables, as well as freight payable by a third party, but does not include passage money:

"Moveables" means any moveable tangible property, other than the ship, and includes money, valuable securities, and other documents:

"Policy" means a marine policy.

Savings

91.—(1) Nothing in this Act, or in any repeal effected thereby, shall affect—

(a) The provisions of the Stamp Act 1891, or any enactment for the time being in force relating to the revenue:

(b) The provisions of the Companies Act 1862, or any enactment amending or substituted for the same;

(c) The provisions of any statute not expressly repealed by this Act.

(2) The rules of the common law including the law merchant, save in so far as they are inconsistent with the express provisions of this Act, shall continue to apply to contracts of marine insurance.

92, 93. ...

NOTE:

Repealed by the Statute Law Revision Act 1927.

Short Title

94. This Act may be cited as the Marine Insurance Act 1906.

SCHEDULES

FIRST SCHEDULE (s.30)

Form of policy

BE IT KNOWN THAT ...... as well as ...... own name as for and in the name and names of all and every other person or persons to whom the same doth, may, or shall appertain, in part or in all doth make assurance and cause ...... and them, and every one of them, to be insured lost or not lost, at and from

......

Upon any kind of goods and merchandise, and also upon the body, tackle, apparal, ordnance, munition, artillery, boat, and other furniture, of and in the good ship or vessel called the ...... whereof is master under God, for this present voyage, ... or whosoever else shall to for master in the said ship, or by whatsoever other name or names the said ship, or the master thereof, is or shall be named or called; beginning the adventure upon the said goods and merchandises from the loading thereof aboard the said ship.

upon the said ship, etc.

and so shall continue and endure, during her abode there, upon the said ship, etc.

And further, until the said ship, with all her ordnance, tackle, apparel, etc., and goods and merchandises whatsoever shall be arrived at ......

upon the said ship, etc., until she hath moored at anchor twenty-four hours in good safety; and upon the goods and mercandises, until the same be there discharged and safely landed. And it shall be lawful for the said ship, etc., in this voyage to proceed and sail to and touch and stay at any ports or places whatsoever.

without prejudice to this insurance. The said ship, etc., goods and merchandises, etc., for so much as concerns the assured by agreement between the assured and assurers in this policy, are and shall be valued at ......

Touching the adventures and perils which we the assurers are contented to bear and do take upon us in this voyage: they are of the seas, men of war, fire, enemies, pirates, rovers, thieves, jettisons, letters of mart and countermart, surprisals, takings at sea, arrests, restraints, and detainments of all kings, princes, and people, of what nation, condition, or quality soever, barratry of the master and mariners, and of all other perils, losses, and misfortunes, that have or shall come to the hurt, detriment, or damage of the said goods and merchanidses, and ship, etc., or any part thereof. And in case of any loss or misfortune it shall be lawful to the assured, their factors, servants and assigns, to sue, labour, and travel for, in and about the defence, safeguards, and recovery of the said goods and mercandises, and ship, etc., or any part thereof, without prejudice to this insurance; to the charges whereof we, the assurers, will contribute each one according to the rate and quantity of his sum herein assured. And it is especially declared and agreed that no acts of the insurer or insured in recovering, saving, or preserving the property insured shall be considered as a waiver, or acceptance of abandonment. And it is agreed by us, the insurers, that this writing or policy of assurance shall be of as much force and effect as the surest writing or policy of assurance heretofore made in Lombard Street, or in the Royal Exchange, or elsewhere in London. And so we, the assurers, are contented, and do hereby promise and bind ourselves, each one for his own part, our heirs, executors, and goods to the assured, their executors, administrators, and assigns, for the true performance of the premises, confessing ourselves paid the consideration due unto us for this assurance by the assured, at and after the rate of ......

IN WITNESS whereof we, the assurers, have subscribed our names and sums assured in London.

N.B.—Corn, fish, salt, fruit, flour, and seed are warranted free from average, unless general, or the ship be stranded—sugar, tobacco, hemp, flax, hides and skins are warranted free from average, under five pounds per cent., and all other goods, also the ship and freight, are warranted free from average, under three pounds per cent. unless general, or the ship be stranded.

Rules for construction of policy

The following are the rules referred to by this Act for the construction of a policy in the above or other like form, where the context does not otherwise require:—

1. Where the subject-matter is insured "lost or not lost", and the loss has occurred before the contract is concluded, the risk attaches, unless at such time the assured was aware of the loss, and the insurer was not.

2. Where the subject-matter is insured "from" a particular place, the risk does not attach until the ship starts on the voyage insured.

3.—(a) Where a ship is insured "at and from" a particular place, and she is at that place in good safety when the contract is concluded, the risk attaches immediately.

(b) If she be not at that place when the contract is concluded, the risk attaches as soon as she arrives there in good safety, and, unless the policy otherwise provides, it is immaterial that she is covered by another policy for a specified time after arrival.

(c) Where chartered freight is insured "at and from" a particular place, and the ship is at that place in good safety when the contract is concluded the risk attaches immediately. If she be not there when the contract is concluded, the risk attaches as soon as she arrives there in good safety.

(d) Where freight, other than chartered freight, is payable without special conditions and is insured "at and from" a particular place, the risk attaches pro rata as the goods or merchandise are shipped; provided that if there be cargo in readiness which belongs to the shipowner, or which some other person has contracted with him to ship, the risk attaches as soon as the ship is ready to receive such cargo.

4. Where goods or other moveables are insured "from the loading thereof", the risk does not attach until such goods or moveables are actually on board, and the insurer is not liable for them while in transit from the shore to ship.

5. Where the risk on goods or other moveables continues until they are "safely landed," they must be landed in the customary manner and within a reasonable time after arrival at the port of discharge, and if they are not so landed the risk ceases.

6. In the absence of any further licence or usage, the liberty to touch and stay "at any part or place whatsoever" does not authorise the ship to depart from the course of her voyage from the port of departure to the port of destination.

7. The term "perils of the seas" refers only to fortuitous accidents or casualties of the seas. It does not include the ordinary action of the winds and waves.

8. The term "pirates" includes passengers who mutiny and rioters who attack the ship from the shore.

9. The term "thieves" does not cover clandestine theft or a theft committed by any of the ship's company, whether crew or passengers.

10. The term "arrests, etc., of kings, princes, and people" refers to political or executive acts, and does not include a loss caused by riot or by ordinary judicial process.

11. The term "barratry" includes every wrongful act wilfully committed by the master or crew to the prejudice of the owner, or, as the case may be, the charterer.

12. The term "all other perils" includes only perils similar in kind to the perils specifically mentioned in the policy.

13. The term "average unless general" means a partial loss of the subject-matter insured other than a general average loss, and does not include "particular charges".

14. Where the ship has stranded, the insurer is liable for the excepted losses, although the loss is not attributable to the stranding, provided that when the stranding takes place the risk has attached and, if the policy be on goods, that the damaged goods are on board.

15. The term "ship" includes the hull, materials and outfit, stores and provisions for the officers and crew, and, in the case of vessels engaged in a special trade, the ordinary fittings requisite for the trade, and also, in the case of a steamship, the machinery, boilers, and coals and engine stores, if owned by the assured.

16. The term "freight" includes the profit derivable by a shipowner from the employment of his ship to carry his own goods or moveables, as well as freight payable by a third party, but does not include passage money.

17. The term "goods" means goods in the nature of merchandise, and does not include personal effects or provisions and stores for use on board.

In the absence of any usage to the contrary, deck cargo and living animals must be insured specifically, and not under the general denomination of goods.

* * * *

SECOND SCHEDULE

. . .

NOTE:
Repealed by the Statute Law Revision Act 1927.

APPENDIX 2

IUA OF LONDON

INTERNATIONAL UNDERWRITING ASSOCIATION

IUA Marine Policy

We, the Insurers, hereby severally agree, in consideration of the payment to us by or on behalf of the Insured of the premium specified in the Schedule, to insure against loss, damage, liability or expense in the proportions and manner hereinafter provided. Each Insurer shall be liable only for its own respective proportion.

In witness whereof the name of the Chief Executive of the **International Underwriting Association of London** ("IUA") is subscribed on behalf of each of the IUA members and such entities not being members of the IUA who are participating in a qualifying consortium arrangement with the IUA members in accordance with the Memorandum and Articles of Association of the IUA.

____ Chief Executive

This policy is not valid unless it bears the embossment of the Policy Department of the International Underwriting Association of London.

Several Liability

The subscribing Insurers' obligations under this contract are several and not joint and are limited solely to the extent of their individual signed subscrpitions. The subscribing Insurers are not responsible for the subscription of any co-subscribing Insurer who for any reason does not satisfy all or part of its obligations.

Insurers' Proportions

For use by the Policy Department of the
International Underwriting Association of London

The International Underwriting Association of London.
London Underwriting Centre
3 Minster Court, Mincing Lane, London EC3R 7DD

IUA 1

APPENDIX 3

IUA Slip Policy (Direct)

IUA 5

We, the Insurers, hereby severally agree, in consideration of the payment to us by or on behalf of the Insured of the specified premium to insure against loss, damage, liability or expense in the proportions and manner provided in the slip. Each Insurer shall be liable only for its own respective proportion.

The subscribing Insurers' obligations under this contract are several and not joint and are limited to the extent of their individual signed subscriptions. The subscribing Insurers are not responsible for the subscription of any co-subscribing Insurer who for any reason does not satisfy all or part of its obligations.

This insurance shall be subject to the exclusive jurisdiction of the English Courts except as may be expresselу provided herein.

In witness whereof the name of the Chief Executive of the **International Underwriting Association of London** ("IUA") is subscribed on behalf of each of the IUA members and such entities not being members of the IUA who are participating in a qualifying consortium arrangement with the IUA members in accordance with the Memorandum and Articles of Association of the IUA.

________________________________ Chief Executive

This Slip Policy is not valid unless it bears the embossment of the Policy Department of the International Underwriting Association of London.

Note: A Formal Policy in substitution for this Slip Policy or any declaration hereunder may be issued at any time at the request of the Insured or any Insurer hereon.

INDEX

THE MODERN LAW OF MARINE INSURANCE